PALMER'S

COMPANY INSOLVENCY

IN SCOTLAND

PALMER'S

COMPANY INSOLVENCY

IN SCOTLAND

DAVID A. BENNETT, M.A., LL.B., W.S.,
Solicitor, Bennett & Robertson, Edinburgh

W. GREEN/Sweet & Maxwell
EDINBURGH
1993

First published in 1993 by W. Green,
The Scottish Law Publisher,
21 Alva Street, Edinburgh.

© 1993 W. Green & Son Ltd.

ISBN 0 414 01037 X

A catalogue record for this book
is available from the British Library.

Typeset by Mendip Communications Ltd., Frome, Somerset.
Printed in Great Britain by Hartnolls Ltd., Bodmin, Cornwall.

PREFACE

Palmer's Company Insolvency in Scotland is an edited reprint of relevant sections of *Palmer's Company Law* covering the Administration Procedure, Floating Charges and Receivers, Voluntary Arrangements and Winding Up. The text is that which appears in the current 25th Edition (looseleaf) of *Palmer* up to and including Release 48 (published in November 1992) but also incorporating material which will not be available until later Releases of the main work. The aim has been to state the law as it applies in Scotland as at September 30, 1992.

The text of the chapters on Floating Charges and Receivers and on Winding Up in Scotland, together with the Introduction which is unique to this publication, are the work of the Scottish Editor. The chapters on Administration Procedure and Voluntary Arrangements, as with the corresponding sections of *Palmer* itself, (Scottish material apart) are the work of Professor Ian Fletcher, Professor of Commercial Law, Queen Mary and Westfield College, University of London, whose permission to use this text is gratefully acknowledged. Scottish material for these chapters both in *Palmer* itself and this publication has been provided by the Scottish Editor who, of course, accepts responsibility for the present publication in its entirety. Careful readers will note a certain amount of duplication across the various chapters which has been retained for practical reasons and to avoid the risk of damaging the sense of the main text.

This publication is not intended to supplant the main publication but to provide Scottish users with the relevant material from *Palmer* in reasonably handy form. Accordingly, the opportunity has been taken to include in the Appendix reprints of the relevant statutes and subordinate regulations including the Insolvency Rules and the Rules of Court, which will also be found in Volume 5 of *Palmer* and in the *Parliament House Book*.

Cross-references to paragraphs in *Palmer* will be understood to refer to the current edition of the main publication.

References to the Companies Act 1985 (as amended) generally appear without reference to that Act, *e.g.* "s.410." References to the Insolvency Act may be abbreviated to "I.A." and refer to the Insolvency Act 1986 (as amended). References to the Insolvency (Scotland) Rules 1986 (as amended) are abbreviated to "1986 Rules," references to the Rules of the Court of Session are abbreviated to "R.C.S." and Sheriff Court Rules to "Sh.Ct.R."

David A. Bennett, W.S., Scottish Editor, *Palmer's Company Law*
Bennett & Robertson, Solicitors
16 Walker Street, Edinburgh EH3 7NN
November 1992

CONTENTS

TABLE OF CASES

xi

TABLE OF STATUTES

[References are to paragraph numbers.]

INTRODUCTION

THE CORK REPORT AND THE REFORM OF INSOLVENCY LAW

The Joint Stock Companies Act 1856, which introduced to Scotland the **001** modern procedure for company incorporation (available in England and Wales since the Joint Stock Companies Act 1844) included provisions for the winding up of companies either by the court or on a voluntary basis. These are clearly recognisable as the basis for today's law on liquidation contained in the Insolvency Act 1986. In the course of the next 125 years the law was strengthened and procedures refined in a number of respects. Until the Companies Act 1929, for example, a voluntary liquidation was under the effective control of the members, whether the company was solvent or insolvent, unless the court had made an order placing the proceedings under its supervision. The introduction by the 1929 Act of the "creditors' voluntary winding-up" for insolvent voluntary liquidations was a more effective procedure for the protection of creditors, and this rendered the supervision order redundant; winding up under the supervision of the court was formally abolished by the Insolvency Act 1985, s.88.

Insolvency law and procedure remained, however, open to **002** criticism, much of which was common to corporate insolvency and personal bankruptcy. In Scotland, the Scottish Law Commission commenced in November 1968 a review of insolvency, bankruptcy and liquidation and in 1971 it published a report on the proposals of its working party. The main thrust of the Scottish inquiry related to personal bankruptcy, although this would necessarily have an effect on corporate insolvency procedures since the legislation adapted many of the Bankruptcy Act provisions to the winding up of companies in Scotland. In 1977 the "Cork Committee" (chaired by Sir Kenneth Cork, a distinguished insolvency practitioner in England) was appointed to undertake a comprehensive review of the law and practice of insolvency and personal bankruptcy in England and Wales. The Cork Committee acknowledged that, in so far as its reports affected corporate insolvency, this was a matter of concern in Scotland as well, and the Committee took steps to ensure that its recommendations were prepared in consultation with the Scottish Law Commission. At the same time, the Scottish Law Commission proceeded with its examination of Scottish bankruptcy law and procedure, acknowledging that the Cork Committee would be making recommendations in the corporate field. The Scottish Law Commission report was published in February 1982[1] and the report of the Cork Committee in June of the same year.[2]

---

[1] *Report on Bankruptcy and Related Aspects of Insolvency and Liquidation* (Scot. Law Com. No. 68).
[2] *Insolvency Law and Practice* (Cmnd. 8558).

003   The recommendations of the Scottish Law Commission resulted in the Bankruptcy (Scotland) Act 1985 which effected major reforms in the law of personal bankruptcy and had some indirect impact on corporate insolvency as well. In particular, the law relating to the reduction of gratuitous alienations and fraudulent or unfair preferences, and the provisions for the equalisation of diligence, enacted for personal bankruptcies by the 1985 Act, were applied to corporate insolvencies from the same effective date (April 1, 1986) by Schedule 7, paragraphs 19 to 22 of that Act. The same Schedule also introduced consequential amendments on the ranking of claims and other matters where the Companies Act adopted Bankruptcy Act provisions.

004   The reports by the Cork Committee and the Scottish Law Commission were followed by a Government white paper "A Revised Framework for Insolvency Law" in February 1984.[3] This adopted many (but not all) of the recommendations of the Cork Committee. Thereafter, legislation was introduced which eventually became the Insolvency Act 1985. Some of the proposals which had been adopted in the white paper, and in the Bill, proved exceptionally controversial, particularly those relating to the automatic disqualification of directors who had been involved with insolvent companies. Other recommendations which had been put forward in the *Cork Report* were rejected by the Government and attempts to introduce them in the legislation were unsuccessful. Among the principal recommendations of the *Cork Report* which were subsequently adopted in the legislation (at least in substance) were:

   (i) the creation of administration and voluntary arrangement procedures for companies (Chapter 7, Part II);
   (ii) the requirement that all corporate insolvency proceedings and members' voluntary liquidations (as well as personal bankruptcies) should be placed in the hands of duly qualified "insolvency practitioners" (Chapter 15);
   (iii) procedural changes which were intended to result in the increased involvement of creditors through formally constituted committees in receiverships and administrations, as well as in liquidations (Chapter 19);
   (iv) that (to enable a business to continue) public utility creditors should not be able to withhold supplies from an insolvency practitioner until pre-existing debts had been paid (Chapter 33);
   (v) modifications of the law on challenging floating charges, particularly those in favour of persons connected with the company (paras. 1550 to 1586); and

---

[3] Cmnd. 9175.

(vi) disqualification of "delinquent" directors and personal liability of directors for "wrongful trading" leading to insolvency (Chapters 43 to 45).

The *Cork Report* made a number of more radical proposals which **005** were not adopted, such as:

(i) the concept of a court "protection order" which would create a moratorium on the pursuit of claims by creditors while the company had an opportunity to re-construct or to choose the appropriate form of insolvency process (Chapter 12);

(ii) curtailment of the categories or amounts of preferential debts, particularly for taxation (Chapter 32);

(iii) the protection, for a limited period, of a receiver against the realisation of assets which were subject to a fixed security (but such protection was granted to an administrator) (paras. 1500 to 1515);

(iv) the creation of a fund of 10 per cent. of the assets which were subject to a floating charge for the benefit of unsecured creditors (paras. 1538 to 1549);

(v) automatic personal liability for the debts of a company in insolvent liquidation which would attach to directors who had been directors of another company which had gone into insolvent liquidation within the previous two years (paras. 1826 to 1837); and

(vi) the reduction to the status of deferred claims of inter-company loans within a group which were considered to be part of the debtor company's long term finance (paras. 1958 to 1965).

There were, of course, numerous other detailed proposals in the **006** *Cork Report* and in the white paper which were enacted by the Insolvency Act 1985. One of the curious ironies of the changes under the legislation was that, although Scots law had borrowed by legislation the floating charge and the concept of receivership from English Chancery procedure, English law found it necessary to re-import many of the statutory provisions of Scots law to reform its own system on these matters.

While this comprehensive amendment of insolvency law was going through Parliament, companies' legislation since 1948 was consolidated as the Companies Act 1985. The Insolvency Act 1985 amended the Companies Act in many respects and eventually the legislation was detached and itself consolidated mostly in the Insolvency Act 1986, which is the main statute now in force. Provisions relating to the disqualification of company directors (which are referred to in the present work only in so far as they relate to insolvency) were separately consolidated as the Company Directors' Disqualification Act 1986. Most of these came into force on December 26, 1986.

COMPANY DIRECTORS' DISQUALIFICATION AND PERSONAL LIABILITY[4]

007 Disqualification of company directors by court order was provided for under the Companies Acts prior to the reforms of 1985 and 1986. Some of these provisions remain under the greatly extended provisions of the current legislation:

   (i) Conviction of an indictable offence (Company Directors' Disqualification Act 1986, s.2; formerly Companies Act 1985, s.296). Disqualification is at the discretion of the court and the maximum period is five years (sheriff court) or 15 years (Court of Session).

   (ii) Persistent default in the making of returns to the registrar of companies (Company Directors' Disqualification Act 1986, s.3; formerly Companies Act 1985, s.297). Disqualification is at the discretion of the court for a maximum period of five years.

   (iii) Fraudulent trading, fraud or breach of duty which is discovered in the course of the winding up of the company, whether the company is insolvent or otherwise (Company Directors' Disqualification Act 1986, s.4; formerly Companies Act 1985, s.298). Disqualification is at the discretion of the court and the maximum period is 15 years.

   (iv) On summary conviction for persistent default in the making of returns to the registrar (Company Directors' Disqualification Act 1986, s.5; formerly Companies Act 1985, s.299). Disqualification is discretionary and the maximum period is five years.

Grounds (ii) and (iv) are similar. The principal difference is that disqualification under (ii) is by separate application and disqualification under (iv) is normally by the court which convicts the individual for default on the latest occasion.

A further ground for disqualification under the previous legislation was for being a director of two companies which were the subject of insolvent liquidation within five years, coupled with a finding that the director was "unfit" to be concerned in the management of a company (Companies Act 1985, s.300). This ground has been repealed and replaced with much stronger provisions in the 1986 Act.

008 The Company Directors' Disqualification Act 1986 provides for three additional grounds for disqualification, of which the first replaces the previous "unfitness" ground:

   (v) Compulsory disqualification of a director if he is or has been the director of a company which has at any time become

---

[4] See further, on disqualification orders, *Palmer*, paras. 8.101 *et seq.*, and on directors' personal liability, paras. 522–526, *post*.

insolvent (whether while he was a director or subsequently) and if his conduct as a director (either taken alone or together with his conduct as a director of any other company) makes him unfit to be concerned in the management of a company (Company Directors' Disqualification Act 1986, s.6). For this purpose the company is regarded as "insolvent" if it goes into liquidation with insufficient assets to meet its debts and other liabilities and the expenses of the winding up, or if there is an administration order or the appointment of an administrative receiver. The relevant insolvency practitioner is required to submit reports to the Secretary of State on whether a disqualification order should be applied for[5] and it is the responsibility of the Secretary of State to apply for such an order either on the basis of such reports or on other information if satisfied that disqualification would be in the public interest. Whereas under the repealed section 300 of the Companies Act 1985 it was left to the discretion of the court to determine whether a director was "unfit" the 1986 Act attempts a definition which, nevertheless, requires the court to determine in its judgment the extent of the director's responsibility for the insolvency. If a finding of unfitness is made not only is disqualification mandatory, it must be for a minimum period of two years. The maximum period is 15 years.

(vi) If the report of official inspectors appointed under section 437 of the Companies Act 1985 (and certain other legislation) reveals that the conduct of a director makes it expedient in the public interest that a disqualification order should be made, the Secretary of State may apply for such an order on the ground that the person concerned is "unfit to be concerned in the management of a company" (Company Directors' Disqualification Act 1986, s.8). The company in question does not have to be insolvent, or in liquidation. The test of "unfitness" is the same as under (v). Disqualification is discretionary for a maximum period of 15 years.

(vii) If the court has made an order requiring a director, former director or "shadow director" to make a contribution to the assets of an insolvent company on the grounds of his responsibility for "fraudulent" or "wrongful" trading[6] the court may add a disqualification order against that person. Disqualification is at the discretion of the court for a maximum period of 15 years (Company Directors' Disqualification Act 1986, s.10).

Some concern has been expressed at the relatively few disqualifica-

---

[5] See further, para. 526, *post.*
[6] See further, paras. 522–526, *post.*

tion orders made under the new legislation. By June 1992 48 orders on the ground of "unfitness" had been granted and 58 cases were still undecided. Now that a significant body of case law (on both sides of the border) has developed, however, it is expected that the numbers will increase and the possibility of disqualification will become a real encouragement to directors to conform to acceptable standards of behaviour, as intended by the *Cork Report* and the white paper which preceded these reforms. A basic weakness is that if the company has no assets to pay an insolvency practitioner, the conduct of its directors is unlikely to be scrutinised.

009   It has for many years been an offence under the Companies Acts to act as a director while sequestrated (Company Directors' Disqualification Act 1986, s.11; formerly Companies Act 1985, s.302). While the 1985 legislation was being prepared, the particular problem of "Phoenix" companies, *i.e.* a new company deliberately formed to trade under the same or a similar name to an insolvent company, was identified as worthy of special attention. Accordingly, what is now the Insolvency Act 1986, s.216, makes it an offence for anyone who was a director of an insolvent company to be concerned in carrying on business (whether as a company or otherwise) within 12 months under a name which is the same as or similar to that of the insolvent company.[7]

010   The provisions for making directors personally liable to contribute to the debts of an insolvent company on the grounds of "wrongful" or "fraudulent" trading, referred to above, have also now begun to strike home to their intended targets, although again not without initial hesitation. Cases have now been reported showing the courts ready to make orders for the payment of substantial sums for the benefit of the creditors. In practice, of course, this tends to mean the preferential and secured creditors, mostly the Inland Revenue and the banks, and not the ordinary creditors where, arguably, the most commercial damage has occurred. Their hopes of some benefit from the Cork Committee's proposals for a "10 per cent. fund" from the floating charge holder and a reduction in the impact of preferential claims remain unfulfilled, and are likely to remain so.

011   There is no doubt that the "wrongful trading" provisions introduced by the 1986 Act, while having a salutary effect on the performance of directors, have also proved a handicap to more positive efforts of banks and others to rescue struggling companies. Any director they appoint to the board of such a company to attempt a rescue runs the risk of being found personally liable if his efforts are unsuccessful. The fact that he may have a good defence does not eliminate the risk or the

---

[7] See further para. 527, *post*.

pressure of having to confront a claim, however successfully. Furthermore, such liability extends to "shadow directors" and a bank or major creditor who intervenes to correct poor management for his own benefit and that of the company itself, runs the risk of being held liable as a shadow director if his intervention is unsuccessful. The "wrongful trading" legislation was not intended to target the "company doctor," and evidence is emerging that banks in particular are becoming uncomfortable about the risks they or their nominees may be running if they hold off the appointment of a receiver to give the company a chance of survival to the point where these risks become significant. Banks being cautious by nature, the fact that there is some risk however small is usually sufficient discouragement. The answer is not obvious but there is undoubtedly a case for reviewing the balance between the impact of the legislation and its effect in closing off legitimate attempts at corporate rescue.

ADMINISTRATION ORDERS AND VOLUNTARY ARRANGEMENTS

Administration orders and voluntary arrangements, which are **012** examined in detail in Chapters 1 and 3 of this work, were intended by the Cork Committee to enable an insolvent company to make a binding compromise with its creditors without the finality of liquidation or receivership and without the complexities of a scheme under the existing legislation, principally the Companies Act 1985, s.425. Although still available, section 425 has little application in practice to an insolvent company. It provides no effective moratorium on claims while the scheme is under consideration, does not bind secured creditors in any event and is subject to protracted and complex court procedures. A compromise could also be effected under section 601 of the Companies Act 1985, but this required the consent of three-quarters of all the creditors of the company, and the difficulty of attaining this meant that the section was not used. It was repealed by the Insolvency Act 1985.

The administration order procedure does establish an effective moratorium in respect of all claims, and prevents the enforcement of any security, fixed or floating, or other proceedings against the company without the leave of the court. In contrast to section 425, which is only effective when the court approves the scheme, the moratorium is in place from the moment a petition for an administration order has been presented, except to permit the company to be wound up or an administrative receiver to be appointed. Once the scheme has been approved, neither such step can be taken. The scheme under which the administrator is supposed to exercise his functions is drawn up by the petitioners (usually the directors) with, in practice, the active involvement of the insolvency practitioner who is intended to be the administrator. The court's function in scrutinising the proceedings and approving the report is largely formal.

The Act envisages an administration order being intended to achieve one of four specified purposes:

(a) the survival of the company and the whole or any part of its undertaking as a going concern;
(b) the approval of a voluntary arrangement;
(c) the sanction of a section 425 scheme; and
(d) a more advantageous realisation of the company's assets than would be effected on a winding up.

013   It was clearly the intention of the Cork Committee that (a), the possibility of at least partial survival of the business, should be the main reason for adopting administration order procedure. The statutory powers of the administrator (almost identical to those of an administrative receiver) are more than sufficient to achieve this end. In practice, however, the procedure has not proved as popular or as effective as the Cork Committee had hoped.

It seems that only about 15 administration orders have been granted in respect of Scottish companies in the six years since the 1986 Act became effective. In some cases it is suspected that administration order procedure was chosen, rather than receivership, because leases or other significant contracts by the company contained provisions which terminated on receivership but not (doubtless because it had not been invented at the time) on the making of an administration order. Furthermore, in most trading companies a bank holds a floating charge with the right to appoint an administrative receiver, and the legislation provides that no administration order may be granted without the holder of such a charge having the opportunity to pre-empt the making of the order by appointing a receiver. Most if not all administration orders have been granted with the consent of the holder of a floating charge in the expectation that the administrator will realise the security no less effectively than if the same insolvency practitioner had been appointed as receiver. In those circumstances, it is hardly surprising that the availability of administration order procedure has made little perceptible impact on the survival of companies, in whole or in part, as going concerns. In fairness it must be pointed out that many receiverships, before the 1986 Act and afterwards, did effect the survival of at least part of the undertaking in question. Partly this was for the obvious reason that the sale of a business as a going concern, if that is possible, is likely to be more advantageous than the sale of its separate assets. In addition, the management and staff are possible purchasers even if there is no other market.

014   The track record of such enterprises after the buy-out is not encouraging, statistically, although undoubtedly there have been successes. One possible reason is that a company which is insolvent was badly managed, or badly positioned in the market, before its insolvency and is likely to remain so after a buy-out. Another possibility is that, in desperation to save their jobs, the staff have become over-committed financially and sown the seeds of their own destruction in the terms of the contract and the borrowings made to finance it. The receiver, of course, has a duty to put pressure on the management to buy, in order to realise the asset for his creditor. It is clear that the alternative of administration procedure does not change this. The Cork Committee proposal for a protection order, initiated by the management, had the merit of allowing the terms of a buy-out along with other options to be considered under a less pressurised situation than the peremptory requirements of the insolvency practitioner, and those whose interests he represents, to push a deal through as quickly as possible at the highest possible price available on the day.

Voluntary arrangements as a means of effecting a compromise **015** between a company and its creditors were proposed by the Cork Committee as a logical extension of its proposals for voluntary arrangements in English bankruptcy law. The intention was to provide a simple scheme suitable for small companies to obtain the moratorium and binding compromise of an administration order but without its procedural complexities. A voluntary arrangement does not require to have any of the purposes specified for an administration order but must be for "a composition in satisfaction of its debts" or the "arrangement of its affairs" (Insolvency Act 1986, s.1(1)). The arrangement can be proposed by the directors (if the company is not in administration or liquidation), by the administrator or by the liquidator. Once approved by meetings of the company and the creditors it becomes binding on all parties. Unlike an administration order, however, the moratorium is not effective until the arrangement has been approved, and the rights of secured creditors may still be exercised. Because of its restricted suitability, the number of voluntary arrangements under the Act has been very small.

The members of the Cork Committee would no doubt regard the lack **016** of practical impact of administration order and voluntary arrangement procedures as disappointing. They were, after all, the only part of their radical proposals for reform of insolvency law which included the concept of the "protection order" designed to produce an immediate moratorium on claims while the directors considered, with appropriate advice, which of the insolvency procedures to invoke or if there were any alternative courses of action they should adopt. Similar devices exist in the United States of America, although it is not accepted without argument that they are successful or strictly comparable to the Cork Committee's proposals. It is hard to avoid the conclusion, therefore, that the introduction of administration orders and voluntary arrangements has done little to improve the chances of survival of viable elements in an insolvent company.

It is not clear whether it was lawyers' cynicism or a clear perception of reality which prompted a sheriff to comment recently: "This case was made no less unsatisfactory by the fact that the interim Administration Order was succeeded by a receivership which in turn has now been succeeded by a liquidation. I trust it is not a forlorn hope I express that there may be at least something left for the creditors at the end of the day."[8]

INSOLVENCY PRACTITIONERS AND INSOLVENCY RULES

017 In addition to complaints about the conduct of directors leading to insolvencies, the Cork Committee, and later the white paper, attached great importance to complaints about the conduct of liquidation proceedings themselves. Until the reforms of 1985 and 1986 no qualifications were required for appointment as liquidator (or receiver), although in practice the courts (and banks) would only appoint persons with appropriate professional qualifications, and the court rules also required a liquidator appointed by them to lodge a bond of caution for due performance of his duty to account. In voluntary liquidations, however, there was no such control. Even in creditors' voluntary liquidations, but more blatantly in liquidations which started as members' voluntary liquidations, the opportunity existed for unscrupulous persons to seize the appointment and exploit the situation to their own advantage. The case for removing this anomaly and requiring insolvency proceedings to be in the hands of suitably qualified personnel was unanswerable, and resulted in the creation of the "insolvency practitioner," licenced either directly by the Secretary of State or, more usually, by one of the established professional bodies of accountants or solicitors which were recognised by the Secretary of State as authorised to grant such certificates. The statutory basis for the new "sub-profession" of "insolvency practitioner" is in Part XIII (sections 388–398) of the Insolvency Act 1986 and in regulations made under section 419 of the Act.[9]

018 While there is no doubt that the introduction of the "insolvency practitioner" was long overdue, some aspects of the system which has developed are not beyond criticism:

(a) For reasons of expediency, but not logic, even in a members' voluntary liquidation which is undoubtedly wholly solvent and will never be anything else, the liquidator must be an "insolvency practitioner."

---

[8] Sheriff N. E. D. Thomson in *Sonido International Ltd., Petitioners*, 1991 S.C.L.R. 874, 877.
[9] See further, para. 440, *post*.

(b) There is no recognition in the system that insolvencies, personal and corporate, come in many different sizes. In theory at least an "insolvency practitioner" must be capable of handling everything from the winding up of a large international corporation down to the affairs of an individual bankrupt with no assets and a debt of £2,000 to local shopkeepers, including on the way a solvent company whose directors have sold all its assets and merely wish to distribute the cash proceeds to the members. This is already showing signs of developing the faults of elitism, high qualification standards leading to fewer practitioners and, therefore, restricted availability of practitioners, particularly outside the larger cities. The Bankruptcy (Scotland) Bill 1992 (completing its Parliamentary progress as this work goes to press) may be seen as, in some respects, the official response to the high costs inherent in such a system, if only in the limited field of personal bankruptcy in Scotland, in removing much of the work of administering personal bankruptcies from the control of insolvency practitioners.

It is clear that the Cork Committee did not envisage an insolvency **019** practitioner profession of this nature. Their recommendations for qualification (para. 758 of the *Cork Report*) include the observance of ethical standards, an obligation to account for funds (supported by a system of compulsory bonding), effective discipline through a professional body and certificates which require to be renewed regularly. While these qualifications are present in the system as it has been established, and are unexceptionable, the Cork Committee's recommendations do not contain two features of the present system which are responsible for the "elitist tendency" referred to:

(a) No requirement of practical experience was proposed by the *Cork Report*. The Secretary of State and, perforce, the professional bodies authorised by him, require practitioners to have significant practical experience, effectively restricting new entrants to those in existing practices;

(b) The *Cork Report* proposed that academic qualification should be simply a pass in a competitive examination including, if only as an optional item, a paper on "insolvency." Instead, an elaborate examination board, funded by the professions concerned, has had to be established, requiring candidates to present themselves successfully for two days of examination without being permitted to take in the substantial volume of insolvency legislation and regulations for reference (although the "open book" approach is now being introduced). Already, it is no surprise that the pass level even among apparently experienced accountants is extremely low and the subject of loud complaint.

It would seem that, before long, it will be necessary to refine the insolvency practitioner system so as to permit more candidates to obtain authorisation to do the simpler insolvencies, while reserving the highest qualification for the most elaborate cases. The alleged difficulties preventing such an arrangement do not strike this author as sufficiently substantial.

020   On a more practical level, the absence of detailed court rules for the regulation of insolvency proceedings was an acknowledged weakness of the system before 1985. Court rules did exist in England, of some elaboration, but in Scotland these were much less elaborate and had little application to voluntary liquidations. With the placing of the conduct of insolvency proceedings in the hands of a profession regulated directly or indirectly by the Secretary of State, the way was clear for detailed rules to be promulgated by statutory instrument, leaving the court to make rules for the presentation of petitions and other proceedings. Accordingly, as will be apparent from the text of this book, there are now detailed regulations for the conduct of all forms of insolvency process.

That is not to say, however, that the rules which have been provided are wholly satisfactory, particularly in the form in which they appear in Scotland. No real complaint can attach to the Scottish rules for covering in very much shorter terms precisely the same ground as the very long and often elaborate English insolvency rules. It is less satisfactory, however, that the Scottish rules adopt and adapt provisions from the Bankruptcy Act (now of course likely to be amended by the Bill referred to above) which require a tortuous process of cross-reference and "translation" which is difficult to achieve and leaves the reader with a residual sense of discomfort that he may not have followed the trail successfully. There is also the suspicion that the draughtsman may (on occasion) have lost his way as well.

Criticism can also be levied at some of the cost which the insolvency rules (and the Rules of Court) insist be incurred in the advertising of petitions and other matters. These, particularly advertisement in daily newspapers, often amount to a significant proportion of the expense in small bankruptcies or corporate insolvencies. Further, a casual glance at the advertisements which actually appear will show that the layout, typeface and information provided is unnecessarily elaborate and often serves to emphasise the unimportant at the expense of the significant. Perhaps in this field improvement lies in the hands of the practitioner, or his solicitor, but if he will not simplify the process there may be a case for a prescribed (and brief) form of advertising as well as other prescribed forms under the rules.

INSOLVENCY IN THE FINANCIAL MARKETS

021   It is a fundamental principle of insolvency law that all creditors be treated on the same basis (within the appropriate category provided by

the legislation) and that private persons cannot contract out of the statutory scheme for distribution of assets of the insolvent person.[10] For reasons of expediency, however, this principle has been departed from in relation to the financial markets. The Companies Act 1989, Part VII, which came into force on April 25, 1991,[11] is designed to create a separate insolvency regime with respect to the insolvency of a member of a recognised investment exchange and the investment contracts entered into by that person. Part VII includes (section 173 of the 1989 Act) special provisions relating to a "market charge" granted by such a member and intended to secure his liabilities arising in connection with contracts on the financial markets concerned. Further regulations made under the Act[12] make modifications to the general law with respect to the insolvency of members of such markets, and the ranking of charges granted by them, so as to preserve the integrity of the special insolvency regime introduced to protect the rights and liabilities of clients and other dealers, and to remove that regime from the impact of the general law of insolvency. The practical result is that the debit and credit obligations of an insolvent trader on a relevant financial market are set off before transfer of any surplus (or the submission of any claim) to the general insolvency procedure of that person. The purpose is to prevent those who have purchased shares or commodities through the trader having to submit a claim in its general insolvency process and at the same time to deny access to the sales which that trader has made on the market to his general creditors, on the view that the trader should be treated as effectively "transparent" so far as those dealing through him are concerned. The details of this regime are beyond the scope of this work.

---

[10] See para. 476, *post*.
[11] The Companies Act 1989 (Commencement No. 10 and Saving Provisions) Order 1991 (S.I. 1991 No. 873).
[12] The Financial Markets and Insolvency Regulations 1991 (S.I. 1991 No. 880).

CHAPTER 1

THE ADMINISTRATION ORDER PROCEDURE

INTRODUCTION

101 The administration order procedure made its first appearance in the law of company insolvency as Chapter III of Part II of the Insolvency Act 1985 (ss.27–44 inclusive), and was consolidated as Part II of the Insolvency Act 1986 (ss.8–27 inclusive) (hereinafter in this section referred to as "the Insolvency Act"). It is applicable exclusively to companies and is the result of proposals made in Chapter 9 of the Report of the Insolvency Law Review Committee (the *Cork Report*).[1] These proposals formed a part of the overall strategy advocated by the Committee for the provision of a variety of effective alternatives to the winding up of an insolvent, or near-insolvent, company where there are reasonable prospects of reviving the company as a going concern. One of the Committee's suggestions was for the introduction of improved provisions to enable an insolvent company to effect a voluntary arrangement with its creditors.[2] A further, and more radical, suggestion was that a completely new procedure should be introduced whereby a creative reconstruction of a failing company could be undertaken with a view either to procuring the rehabilitation and survival of a company as a going concern or, failing that, to securing a better realisation of the company's assets than would result from the winding up of a "going" concern.

102 The administration order procedure, though comparable to some extent with procedures available under foreign systems of insolvency law to effect the rehabilitation of a company under the protective shield of a moratorium against creditors,[3] is largely inspired by the example of what has sometimes been achieved under the developed law of receivership in Great Britain. In appropriate cases it has proved possible for a receiver of a company's entire undertaking,[4] making full

---

[1] Cmnd. 8558 (1982).

[2] See Cmnd. 8558, Chap. 7, paras. 400–430. I.A. 1986, Pt. I, discussed in paras. 301 *et seq.*, below.

[3] Chap. 11 of the U.S. Bankruptcy Reform Act 1978 is referred to as one possible model for the administration order procedure. There are however numerous differences of detail and of substance between the two procedures. One obvious example is that, under the Chap. 11 procedure, the board of directors remains in control of the company throughout.

[4] A receiver and manager of the entire undertaking is to be known in England and Wales as an administrative receiver: I.A. 1986, ss.29(2), 251. In Scotland an "administrative receiver" is one appointed under a floating charge which attaches the whole (or substantially the whole) of the company's property: I.A., s.251. The statutory powers

and imaginative use of the extensive powers conferred on him by a
well-drawn floating charge debenture, to initiate a corporate rescue
operation and thereby leave the company in a better economic
condition than that in which he found it, while at the same time
safeguarding the interests of the secured creditor by whom he was
appointed. The *Cork Report* advocated the creation of a rehabilitative
procedure that would be generally available, rather than being
dependent first on the existence of a floating charge, and secondly
upon the taking of appropriate initiatives by the receiver appointed
thereunder. The actual powers conferred upon the administrator,
when appointed, are in many cases identical to those enjoyed by an
administrative receiver by virtue of Chapter II of Part III of the
Insolvency Act.[5]

The proposals expressed in Chapter 9 of the *Cork Report* were
accorded a generally favourable and positive response in Chapters 6
and 14 of the Government White Paper *A Revised Framework for
Insolvency Law*,[6] although a number of points of divergence began to
emerge between the Committee's conception of the new procedure
and that of the Government. These indications were subsequently
confirmed in the original terms of the relevant clauses of the
Insolvency Bill when first presented to Parliament, and to an even
greater extent in the final version of Part II of the Insolvency Act itself.
Very substantial changes were made to the provisions within what is
now Part II during the course of its first enactment by Parliament.[7]
Some scepticism was also apparent with regard to the likelihood that
any appreciable amount of use would be made of the new procedure in
practice. During the first four years in which the administration order
procedure was in operation (from 1987 to 1990) the numbers of orders
were annually ranged between a minimum of 131 in 1987 and a
maximum of 198 in 1988. During those years, the numbers of
administrative receiverships were approximately 10 times the
numbers of administrations. It is submitted, however, that cogent
reasons arise under a separate provision in the Insolvency Act
(discussed in para. 103 below) to suggest that directors of an ailing
company should give serious and active thought to the use of the
administration order procedure.[8]

---

of a receiver in Scotland are capable of achieving the result indicated in these
comments (see paras. 218 *et seq., ante*).

[5] See I.A. 1986, ss.14, 15 and Sched. 1 (administrators); ss.55, 61 and Sched. 2
(administrative receivers in Scotland). An administrator in Scotland, unlike a receiver,
has explicit power to challenge gratuitous alienations and unfair preferences (see
below), and a number of further powers not enumerated in Sched. 1 which are not
available to a receiver (*e.g.* to remove directors or call meetings of members or
creditors, under the I.A., s.14(2)).

[6] Cmnd. 9175 (1984).

[7] The provisions were contained in Chap. II of Pt. II of the Insolvency Bill as first
published on December 10, 1984, and then comprised clauses 15–33.

[8] In Scotland there was at least one recorded use in the case of *Air Ecosse Ltd.*, 1987 S.L.T.
751 in January 1987, almost immediately the Act came into force. The figures quoted

DIRECTORS' PERSONAL LIABILITY AND THE ADMINISTRATION PROCEDURE

103 The considerations indicated in the previous paragraph of this section are reflected in Chapter X of Part IV of the Insolvency Act, and are concerned with directors' personal liability for wrongful trading, embodied in section 214 of the Act.[9] In order to avail himself of the statutory defence established by section 214(3), each director of a company which has gone into insolvent liquidation is required to satisfy the court that, from the moment when he had actual or constructive knowledge that there was no reasonable prospect that the company would avoid going into insolvent liquidation, he took every reasonable and practicable step with a view to minimising the potential loss to the company's creditors as, under the circumstances, he ought to have taken. It would seem to accord with the overall spirit and purpose of the Insolvency Act that in this context directors should be required to show that, during the critical period prior to the commencement of liquidation, they actively consider the possibility of recourse to the administration order procedure as one of the ways of minimising the ultimate loss to creditors. Thus, depending upon the extent to which courts are in future seen to lay emphasis upon the use of the pre-liquidation procedure as a factor which may help to save the individual directors from incurring personal liability for the company's debts, the practical importance to directors of the administration order procedure could in time prove to be considerable.

WHEN MAY AN ADMINISTRATION ORDER BE MADE?

104 Section 8(1) of the Insolvency Act lays down two main conditions which must be satisfied in order that the court may exercise the power to make an administration order in relation to a company.

Company's inability to pay its debts

105 The first condition, imposed by section 8(1)(*a*), is that the court must be satisfied that the company is, or is likely to become, unable to pay its debts. For this purpose, the subsection incorporates, by reference, the definition of inability to pay debts contained in section 123 of the Act. Thus, any of the alternative grounds described in section 123(1) of the Act, together with the ground added as section 123(2),[10] may furnish a basis upon which the court can find that the company is unable to pay its debts. These grounds include the demonstration that an attempt to enforce a decree against the company has been wholly or partially

---

include England and Wales. In the subsequent period there is no evidence of greater use of administration.

[9] I.A. 1986, s.214, discussed in para. 523, *post.*

[10] Formerly s.518 of the Companies Act, as amended, and subs. (1A) added thereto, by I.A. 1985, Sched. 6, para. 27. See para. 414, *post.*

unsuccessful,[11] or the adducing of any other evidence which persuades the court that the company is unable to pay its debts.[12] However, by far the most convenient means of establishing a company's inability to pay its debts is that provided for in section 123(1)(a) of the Act, namely a creditor's service upon the company of a statutory demand for payment of a debt for a sum in excess of £750, which sum the company fails to pay or compound for within the period of three weeks from the date of service.[13] Although the statutory demand has traditionally been employed for the purpose of preparing the ground for presentation of a creditor's petition for a compulsory winding up, it now has an alternative function in relation to an application for an administration order. It should be observed that by virtue of section 10(1) of the Insolvency Act the presentation of a petition for an administration order has the effect of precluding both the making of an order for the winding up of the company by the court and the passing of a resolution for winding up. Thus the possibility arises that, when a company has failed to satisfy a statutory demand within the time permitted, the creditor by whom the demand was originally served may encounter an interruption of his expected progress towards the obtaining of an order for winding up, by reason of the presentation of a petition for an administration order by any party qualified to take this step.[14] As will be seen, however, directors of a company would not be well advised to present such a petition merely as a device for postponing winding up since the appointment of an administrator divests the directors of their powers of management, although it does not absolve them from all responsibility for the manner in which the company's affairs either have been or are henceforth conducted.[15]

Finally, the additional ground now contained in section 123(2) of the Act provides that a company is deemed to be unable to pay its debts where there is shown to be a balance sheet deficiency, taking into account the company's contingent and prospective liabilities.[16] This means that a petition for an administration order can be presented where, despite the fact that the company may have sufficient funds presently available to meet debts as they fall due, the contingent and prospective liabilities are such that the company's assets will in due course be exhausted leaving some creditors unpaid. It is in such circumstances that timely recourse to the administration order procedure should offer a particularly suitable means of retrieving the enterprise while this is still technically possible.

---

[11] I.A. 1986, s.123(1)(c). See also paras. (b) and (d) of the same subs.
[12] I.A. 1986, s.123(1)(e).
[13] In Scotland the form of "statutory demand" is prescribed by the Insolvency (Scotland) Rules 1986, Form 4.1 (Scot) as amended 1987. See further para. 413, *post.*
[14] See I.A. 1986, s.9(1), discussed in para. 111, *post.*
[15] See I.A. 1986, ss.14 and 17, discussed in para. 128, *post.*
[16] See n. 10, *supra.*

Likelihood of attainment of an authorised purpose

106 The second condition, imposed by section 8(1)(*b*) of the Insolvency Act, is that the court must consider that the making of an administrative order would be likely to achieve one or more of the purposes mentioned in subsection (3). That subsection lists the following four purposes:

(a) the survival of the company, and the whole or any part of its undertaking, as a going concern;

(b) the approval of a voluntary arrangement under Part I of the Insolvency Act;

(c) the sanctioning under section 425 of the Companies Act 1985 of a compromise or arrangement between the company and any such persons as are mentioned in that section[17]; and

(d) a more advantageous realisation of the company's assets than would be realised on a winding up.

The foregoing list of authorised purposes for which an administration order may be made is an exhaustive one. Other possible purposes were suggested in the *Cork Report* as providing a suitable basis for use of the administration order procedure. These included: the reorganisation of the company with a view to restoring profitability or maintaining employment; the carrying on of a business in the public interest where the current management is unable to continue to function; and the undertaking of a feasibility study to explore the prospects for restoring the company to eventual profitability.[18] None of these purposes was expressly included in section 8(3) as finally enacted, although it may well be that some of them are effectively submitted, to a certain extent, under its terms. What is clear, however, is that none of the unenacted expressions of purpose is capable, standing on its own, of furnishing a valid basis for the making of an administration order: the purpose will need to be presented to the court as part of the incidental aspects of a proposal framed with reference to the actual terms in which section 8(3) is drafted.

The court's jurisdiction to make the order applied for hinges upon its own assessment of whether, in the terms of section 8(1)(*b*), the making of the order would be "likely to achieve" one or more of the specified purposes contained in subsection (3). The judicial attitude towards the concept of "likelihood" in this context is therefore of crucial importance. Initially, some divergence of approach was manifest as between different judges of the Chancery Division, sitting singly at

---

[17] The persons mentioned in s.425 of the Companies Act 1985 as potential parties to a compromise or arrangement under that section are: the creditors of the company, or any class of them; and the members of the company, or any class of them. See further *Palmer*, para. 12.002.

[18] Cmnd. 8558, para. 498. *Cf.* the White Paper, Cmnd. 9175, para. 150.

first instance, but the prevalent view which seems to have emerged is that expressed by Hoffmann J. in *Re Harris Simons Construction Ltd.*,[19] in which he stated:

> "For my part . . . I would hold that the requirements of s.8(1)(*b*) are satisfied if the court considers that there is a real prospect that one or more of the stated purposes may be achieved."

The learned judge considered that the alternative, more stringent formulations of the test using such expressions as "more likely than not," or "more probably than not"[20] were unduly exacting, and this view was endorsed by Vinelott J. in *Re Primlaks (U.K.) Ltd.*,[21] with the sobering observation that the use of too strict a test would "stultify the Act and achieve no useful purpose." Conversely, it appears that there is judicial consensus that it is not sufficient for the party applying for an administration order merely to show that it is "possible" that the requisite purpose may be achieved.

In deciding whether to appoint an administrator on the petition of a company's directors, the views of opposing creditors who also happen to be shareholders are likely to be disregarded, in so far as their objections are linked to their aspirations pursued in the latter capacity: since the company is at, or close to, a state of insolvency, the members lack sufficient interest to be heard in that capacity and must therefore pursue their proposals (for example, as to the refinancing of the company) with the administrator after his appointment.[22]

107   If the court decides to make an administration order, section 8(3) requires that the order must specify the intended purpose or purposes for which it is made. The drafting of the subsection imposes a clear requirement that the purpose or purposes to be specified must be selected from the list contained in section 8(3) itself. However, the drafting of the counterpart provisions in the 1985 Insolvency Act (s.27(1) and (3)) was somewhat looser, and appeared to leave the court with more freedom of action. The Insolvency Act 1986, as a consolidating measure, was technically not an appropriate or competent measure to employ for the purpose of altering the substance of the law. Nevertheless, it now seems to be outside the scope of the court's powers, by virtue of section 8(3) as enacted and currently in force, to make an administration order in which additional purposes are specified beyond those contained in the subsection itself,

---

[19] [1989] B.C.L.C. 202; (1989) 5 B.C.C. 11.
[20] See *Consumer and Industrial Press Ltd.* [1988] B.C.L.C. 177; (1988) 4 B.C.C. 68 (Peter Gibson J.); *Re Manlon Trading Ltd.* (1988) 4 B.C.C. 455 (Harman J.). Cf. *Re SCL Building Services Ltd.* [1990] B.C.L.C. 98; (1989) 5 B.C.C. 746 (Peter Gibson J.); *Re Rowbotham Baxter Ltd.* [1990] B.C.L.C. 397; [1990] B.C.C. 113 (Harman J.); *Re Land and Property Trust Co. plc.* [1991] B.C.C. 446 (Harman J.).
[21] [1989] B.C.L.C. 734; (1989) 5 B.C.C. 710.
[22] *Re Chelmsford City Football Club (1980) Ltd.* [1991] B.C.C. 133.

even though the court might consider them to be both worthwhile and capable of being achieved by means of an administration. However, it may be observed that under section 18(1) the administrator of a company may at any time apply to the court for the administration order to be varied so as to specify an additional purpose. Indeed, the administrator's proposals must in due course be presented, and must correspond to the purposes specified in the order of appointment; an administrator who pursues purposes falling outside the terms of his remit risks penalisation in terms of the grant of his release, and recovery of his fee and expenses.[23] No express reference is made in section 18(1) to the list of purposes contained in section 8(3), and hence it is just conceivable that the court may construe its power under section 18 as being free from the constraints of the earlier, and separate, provision of the Act.

THE EXERCISE OF THE COURT'S POWER IS DISCRETIONARY

108 If both conditions specified in paragraphs (*a*) and (*b*) of section 8(1) are met, the court enjoys the power to make an administration order. The language of subsection (1) in this respect is permissive, not mandatory, and hence it is left as a matter for the court in the exercise of its discretion to decide whether to make an administration order. Accordingly the court may take into account any factors which are capable of off-setting the advantages expected to accrue if the administration order succeeds in achieving the purposes which would serve as the basis for making it. Here, it is thought, the parties whose interests are likely to receive the closest consideration are those who would still receive something under a distribution of the company's assets if a liquidation were immediately to take place. In most cases such persons might well derive some advantage from the achievement of the purposes instanced in the administration order, but it is equally possible that they may consider that such advantage would be marginal at best, and may not outweigh the disadvantage of being kept out of their money for a further period while the administration is carried through.

Where a petition is presented by a creditor who already holds adequate real and collateral securities to enable him to recover payment without recourse to insolvency proceedings, the court may have regard to the interests of the management of the company, especially where the company's balance sheet shows a surplus, albeit without any money being presently available to pay the petitioner's debt.[24]

---

[23] See *Re St. Ives Windings Ltd.* (1987) 3 B.C.C. 634; *Re Sheridan Securities Ltd.* (1988) 4 B.C.C. 200.
[24] *Re Imperial Motors (U.K.) Ltd.* [1990] B.C.L.C. 29.

Administration order in relation to foreign company

It has been held that an English court has jurisdiction to make an administration order in relation to a company incorporated under the laws of a foreign country, where a request for judicial assistance is duly submitted by a court in a "relevant country or territory," within the meaning of section 426(11) of the Insolvency Act 1986. The provisions of section 426(5) empower the English court in such cases "to apply, in relation to any matters specified in the request, the insolvency law which is applicable by *either court* in relation to comparable matters falling within its jurisdiction" (emphasis added). Where the circumstances were such as to make an administration order the most appropriate procedure to be undertaken and where the conditions in section 8(1)(*a*) and (*b*) were satisfied with respect to the company in question, an administration order could be made.[25]

WHEN MAY AN ADMINISTRATION ORDER NOT BE MADE?

109 The provisions of section 8(1) regarding the circumstances in which the court may exercise the power to make an administration order are in all cases subject to the overriding force of section 8(4), which precludes the making of an administration order in relation to a company in two cases.[26]

These are:

(a) after the company has gone into liquidation; and
(b) where the company is an insurance company within the meaning of the Insurance Companies Act 1982.

While case (b) has the effect of excluding a certain category of company from the administration order procedure for the time being,[27] case (a) is of general application. In this context the key concept, namely that of the time at which a company goes into liquidation, is defined in section 247(2) of the Insolvency Act and means the date on which the company passes a resolution for voluntary winding up or alternatively, the date on which an order for its winding up is made by the court at a time when it has not already gone into liquidation by passing such a resolution.

A case in which an administration order may not be made is supplied by section 9(3) of the Insolvency Act. By this provision the court is required to dismiss a petition for an administration order upon being

---

[25] *Re Dallhold Estates (U.K.) Pty. Ltd.* [1992] B.C.C. 394. This would also apply to a Scottish court, since s.426(11) applies to Scotland.

[26] Formerly, the exclusionary provision of s.8(4) of the Insolvency Act also applied to banks and to authorised institutions under the Banking Act 1987 (formerly the Banking Act 1979). This exception was ended with effect from August 23, 1989 by virtue of the Banks (Administration Proceedings) Order 1989 (S.I. 1989 No. 1276).

[27] There is a possibility that the administration order procedure, or a closely analogous procedure, may be made available for insurance companies in due course following a full review of all the implications of such a development: *cf.* Cmnd. 9175, para. 35.

satisfied that there is an administrative receiver[28] of the company, unless the court is also satisfied either that the person by whom or on whose behalf the receiver was appointed has consented to the making of the order, or that if an administration order were made, any security by virtue of which the receiver was appointed would be liable to be released or discharged or avoided under sections 238 to 241 or section 245 of the Insolvency Act, or would be challengeable under section 242 or 243,[29] or under any rule of law in Scotland. Sections 238 to 241 of the Insolvency Act make provision for the avoidance of transactions at an undervalue entered into, and preferences given by, a company within the period of up to two years before the onset of insolvency, which here denotes the date of presentation of the petition on which an administration order is made.[30] Section 242 makes provision for the reduction of a gratuitous alienation made by the company in favour of any person within two years of the making of the administration order, or within five years if in favour of an "associate."[31] Section 243 makes provision for the reduction of preferences created within six months of the making of an administration order. Both sections apply, whether the transaction challenged took place before April 1, 1986 (when the original provisions which are now these sections came into force) or later, but can only be invoked by the administrator (or liquidator) (I.A., ss.242(1)(b) and 243(4)(b)). Common law grounds of challenge are preserved by the Insolvency Act, sections 242(7) and 243(8). In general, they apply to administration procedure as to liquidation.[32] Section 245 of the Insolvency Act is the provision under which a floating charge created by a company within a period of up to two years before the presentation of the petition for an administration order may be rendered invalid under certain circumstances.[33] The overall effect of the provisions in section 9(3) is therefore to furnish safeguards for the legitimate expectations of a secured creditor who has taken a valid floating charge over the whole of the company's property. If such a creditor, in the exercise of the rights conferred on him in Scots law by the terms of the Insolvency Act, section 51 or 54 or, in English law, by the terms of his debenture, has already appointed a receiver before the court hears the application for an administration order to be made,

---

[28] This term is defined in s.251 of the Insolvency Act 1986.
[29] ss.242 and 243 provide for the challenge of gratuitous alienations and unfair preferences in Scotland. They were originally added to the Companies Act 1985 as ss.615A and 615B by the Bankruptcy (Scotland) Act 1985, Sched. 7, para. 20. See paras. 505 to 511, *post*. Ss.238–241 of the Insolvency Act 1986 do not apply in Scotland, but s.245 does (see para. 513, *post*).
[30] I.A. 1986, s.240(3)(a).
[31] The Insolvency Act, s.242(3)(a) requires this term to be defined by reference to the Bankruptcy (Scotland) Act 1985, s.74, as applied to companies by the Bankruptcy (Scotland) Regs. 1985, and not to the Insolvency Act, s.435, but the two provisions are to almost the same effect. See further paras. 506 to 510, *post*.
[32] See paras. 506 to 509, *post*.
[33] I.A. 1986, s.245(3), (5)(a). See further para. 513, *post*.

the court may not entertain the application unless the floating charge or debenture holder has positively consented to the making of an order whose effect will be to oust the receiver.[34] However, where the status of the debenture holder as a secured creditor is capable of being impugned, section 9(3)(*b*) appropriately ensures that he is not enabled to forestall the making of the very order under which, in due course, steps may be taken to invalidate his security.

110   The specially protected position enjoyed by a debenture or floating charge holder under the provisions of section 9(3) is not accorded to other types of creditor, whether secured or unsecured. Nor does the subsection confer any power of veto upon a debenture or charge holder who, although entitled to appoint an administrative receiver, has not yet actually done so by the time that the application for an administration order is heard by the court. However, by section 9(2), where a petition for an administration order is presented to the court, notice of the petition must be given forthwith to any person who has appointed, or who is or may be entitled to appoint, an administrative receiver of the company. This requirement enables those with floating charges capable of leading to the appointment of an administrative receiver to be heard or represented at the hearing of the petition, when they may present arguments aimed at persuading the court as to the appropriate way in which to exercise its discretionary power.[35] One possibility is that the court may decide to refrain from making an administration order, subject to an undertaking by the charge holder to proceed to appoint an administrative receiver without further delay. It must be emphasised however that the charge holder who has not yet appointed a receiver enjoys no statutory right to prevent the making of an administration order. Accordingly, in many cases there may be strong arguments in favour of the charge holder taking appropriate steps to consolidate his legal position in advance of the hearing by

---

[34] See I.A. 1986, s.9(3)(*a*), where the words "has consented" are significant. *Semble* (in English law) it would not be enough for the petitioner to show merely that the debenture holder has not expressed *dissent* to the making of the order. The consent of the holder may be given in writing to the court. This interpretation does not appear to be valid in Scotland. Neither the Insolvency (Scotland) Rules 1986 nor the Rules of Court (Act of Sederunt (Rules of Court Amendment No. 11) (Companies)) 1986 (Court of Session); Act of Sederunt (Sheriff Court Company Insolvency Rules) 1986 require such a consent to be demonstrated before such a petition is presented, or indeed before it is granted. They merely provide for the petition to be intimated to any person who has appointed or may be entitled to appoint an administrative receiver, or to such a receiver. Such person's consent would therefore be inferred from his failure to object. The ouster of a receiver following the making of an administration order occurs by virtue of s.11(1)(*b*) of the Act.

[35] *Cf. Re A Company (No. 00175 of 1987)* [1987] B.C.L.C. 467 (on the need to ensure adequate opportunity for a secured creditor to exercise his power to appoint an administrative receiver, where the court exercises its power under r. 12.9 of the English Insolvency Rules to abridge the period of notice of hearing of the petition).

appointing an administrative receiver following service upon him of notice of the presentation of a petition for an administration order.[36]

The strategic importance, in commercial terms, of the special position enjoyed by the holder of a floating charge by virtue of the statutory provisions concerning administration orders has freshly enhanced the arguments in favour of taking this form of security, either on its own or, preferably, in combination with some kind of fixed security. The decision of Vinelott J. in *Re Croftbell*[37] furnishes confirmation that a so-called "lightweight" floating charge confers all these privileges in full measure, including the power to block the appointment of an administrator, despite the fact that, at the time the change was created, there were negligible assets, or even none at all, which could have been subject to it.

It has been held that the court would not normally appoint an administrator in a case where there has been a breakdown of trust and confidence between those managing the company, so that corporate affairs are deadlocked: a winding up would be the more appropriate course to adopt.[38] In Scots law, however, the appointment of a judicial factor would be, in many cases, preferable to either course.[39]

WHO MAY APPLY FOR AN ADMINISTRATION ORDER?

111 Section 9(1) of the Insolvency Act lists the persons who are eligible to present a petition for an administration order. These are: the company itself or the directors; or a creditor or creditors (including any contingent or prospective creditor or creditors); or all or any of those parties acting together or separately.

It is significant that the Act requires the directors to act collectively in presenting a petition for an administration order. The use in section 9(1) of the expression "the directors," and the omission of any alternative reference to "director" in the singular form, has the effect of denying to an individual director, or indeed to a group of directors forming a minority on the board,[40] the standing to present a petition for an administration order. On the other hand, where a decision of the board is duly passed by a majority of those present, any dissenting or absent members become bound by the resolution and a petition may

---

[36] See further para. 132, *post*, regarding the restraints upon the freedom of the secured creditor to realise his security during the period that an administration order is in force, and the rights of the administrator to dispose of secured property free from encumbrance (ss.11 and 15 of the I.A.).

[37] [1990] B.C.C. 781. This case was argued on the definition of "administrative receiver" in I.A., s.29, which applies only in England and Wales. The point which it illustrates, however, is equally valid in Scots law under s.251. See also *Oditah* [1991] J.B.L. 49.

[38] *Re Business Properties Ltd.* (1988) 4 B.C.C. 684.

[39] See *McGuinness* v. *Black (No. 2)*, 1990 S.L.T. 461; *Weir* v. *Rees*, 1991 S.L.T. 354 and *Palmer*, para. 8.910.

[40] Cf. *Re Instrumentation Electrical Services Ltd.* (1988) 4 B.C.C. 301 (decided under s.124 of the Act, in relation to a winding-up petition).

properly be presented.[41] However, any director or directors who happen also to be creditors of the company could properly present a petition in their latter capacity.

Where the board of directors acts collectively (including where the directors act on the basis of a majority of their number in accordance with the company's own articles) there is no requirement within the Insolvency Act that the directors must obtain the prior endorsement of a general meeting of the members before they may validly present a petition. On the other hand, the separate reference in section 9(1) to "the company" itself as an eligible petitioner indicates that it is open to the members, acting at a general meeting, to resolve that the company shall apply for an administration order. Where such a resolution is carried and put into effect in the face of opposition by the board of directors, it is unclear whether the directors can be heard or represented before the court in order to oppose the making of an order.[42] However, directors who show themselves to be firmly opposed to the company's application for an administration order should be mindful of the personal consequences for themselves under section 214 of the Insolvency Act and under the provisions of sections 6 and 7 of the Company Directors Disqualification Act 1986 in the event that the company subsequently goes into insolvent liquidation.[43] Conversely, the fact that any director is on record as having advocated the use of the administration order procedure could be instrumental in ensuring a favourable outcome of any subsequent proceedings concerning his possible disqualification from company management, or the imposition upon him of responsibility for wrongful trading.

In relation to a creditor's petition it is noteworthy that no figure has been included in the statutory provisions to impose a minimum sum of indebtedness which must be owed by the company to the petitioning creditor as a precondition to his being able to apply for an administration order. However, in the majority of cases a petitioning creditor will encounter the practical difficulty of obtaining sufficiently conclusive evidence of the company's inability to pay its debts. By far the most convenient means by which a creditor may establish the company's inability to pay its debts, and may thus satisfy the requirements of section 8(1)(a), is by the use of a statutory demand for payment in accordance with section 123(1)(a) of the Act.[44] In that event,

---

[41] *Re Equiticorp International Ltd.* (1989) 5 B.C.C. 599.

[42] There is no provision in the Scottish Insolvency Rules or the Rules of Court expressly giving directors the right to appear in such circumstances. Nevertheless, if a director can satisfy the court that it should not grant the members' petition on grounds of substance, he could be heard to assist the court in the exercise of its overall discretion under I.A., s.9(4).

[43] With regard to ss.6 and 7 of the Company Directors Disqualification Act 1986, see *Palmer*, para. 8.106, and para. 124, *post*. With regard to s.214 (responsibility for company's wrongful trading), see para. 523, *post*.

[44] s.123 of the I.A. 1986 is made applicable for the purpose of s.8 of the I.A. by virtue of s.8(1)(a). See further paras. 413 and 414, *post*.

it will be necessary for the company to owe the creditor a sum exceeding £750 which is currently due.

PROCEDURE ON APPLICATION FOR AN ADMINISTRATION ORDER

112 The procedural aspects of administration orders in Scotland are governed by the Insolvency (Scotland) Rules 1986[45] as amended by the Insolvency (Scotland) Amendment Rules 1987[46] (referred to in this chapter as "1986 Rules"), the Rules of Court contained in the Act of Sederunt (Rules of Court Amendment No. 11) (Companies) 1986 (for the Court of Session)[47] (referred to in this section as "R.C.S."), and the Act of Sederunt (Sheriff Court Company Insolvency Rules) 1986[48] (referred to in this section as "Sh.Ct.R."). All of these came into operation on December 29, 1986.[49]

"The Court" having jurisdiction to hear a petition for an administration order is the court having jurisdiction to wind up the company.[50]

The petitioner will normally commission a report by an "independent person," usually but not necessarily the intended administrator (but not an officer, manager, member or employee, of the company) to the effect that the appointment of an administrator is expedient. The report will identify which of the purposes specified in section 8(3) of the Insolvency Act may be achieved by the order (1986 Rule 2.1). The report is to be produced with the petition (R.C.S. 209(4); Sh.Ct.R. 10(2)) and if there is no such report, the petition must explain why not (R.C.S. 209(3)(*h*); Sh.Ct.R. 10(1)(*h*)).

In the Court of Session the petition is presented to the Outer House and is subject to the general rules for such petitions (R.C.S. 209(1) and (2)).

The petition must give details of the petitioner and his title to proceed, the grounds on which it is believed the company will be (or is likely to become) unable to pay its debts, its financial position including assets and liabilities (so far as known) and details of any secured creditors. It must state whether (so far as the petitioner is aware) there is any person entitled to appoint a receiver, whether one has been appointed and whether any steps have been taken to commence winding up. The petition must state which of the purposes specified in section 8(3) of the Insolvency Act is expected to be achieved

---

[45] S.I. 1986 No. 1915 (S.139).
[46] S.I. 1987 No. 1921 (S.132).
[47] S.I. 1986 No. 2298 (S.170).
[48] S.I. 1986 No. 2297 (S.169).
[49] The amendments to 1986 Rules made in 1987, although effective January 11, 1988, apply to all proceedings commenced on or after December 29, 1986 (see S.I. 1987 No. 1921).
[50] See I.A., s.251; Companies Act 1985, s. 744 and para. 408 *post*.

by the order, refer to the preliminary report and give any further information which may assist the court. The proposed administrator is to be identified and it must be stated whether he has the necessary qualification as an "insolvency practitioner." The report and other documents to be relied on are to be produced with the petition (R.C.S. 209(3) and (4); Sh.Ct.R. 10). The court must be satisfied that the administrator has found caution (1986 Rule 7.28(1)).

The petition has to be intimated to the persons specified in section 9(2) of the Insolvency Act and 1986 Rule 2.2, in the prescribed form (Form 2.1 (Scot)) and in the manner specified by R.C.S. 210 or Sh.Ct.R. 11 (or as the court directs). Those specified are any person who has appointed or who may be entitled to appoint an "administrative receiver" (see the Insolvency Act, s.251), any administrative receiver, any petitioner in a pending winding-up petition, any provisional liquidator, the proposed administrator, the registrar of companies, the company (if the petition is presented by the directors or by a creditor or creditors) and any other party directed by the court. It must also be intimated on Form 2.1 (Scot) to the Keeper of the Register of Inhibitions and Adjudications for recording in the personal register.

Thus, alone among company insolvency procedures, the fact that a petition for the appointment of an administrator has been presented will be published in the personal registers. This does not apply to Voluntary Arrangements under Part I of the Insolvency Act 1986, to petitions for the appointment of a receiver or to winding-up petitions.

As already observed, a petition for an administration order cannot be withdrawn without the leave of the court (I.A., s.9(2)(*b*)).

EFFECT OF AN APPLICATION FOR AN ADMINISTRATION ORDER

113 The presentation of a petition for an administration order marks the commencement of a statutory moratorium over the company's affairs. Under the terms of section 10(1) of the Insolvency Act the initial phase of the moratorium ends when the court, having heard the application, either makes the order sought or dismisses the petition. In the latter event the moratorium comes to an end, but if the court makes an administration order, section 11 of the Insolvency Act has the effect of extending the moratorium for the duration of the period for which the order is in force.

The following are the effects of the moratorium during the first phase, from the presentation of the petition until the conclusion of the hearing before the court (s.10(1) of the Act):

1. No resolution may be passed, or order made, for the winding up of the company. This does not however preclude the presentation of a petition for the winding up of the company, although the winding-up petition will not be disposed of unless and until the petition for an administration order is dismissed, or any such

order eventually discharged.[51] Advertisement of the winding-up petition may also be restrained by the court, lest the adverse publicity should so harm the company as to defeat the purpose of the administration petition before the latter can be heard and disposed of.[52]

2. No steps may be taken to enforce any charge on or security over the company's property, or to repossess goods in the company's possession under any hire purchase agreement, conditional sale agreement, chattel leasing agreement or retention of title agreement, except with the leave of the court and subject to such terms as the court may impose.[53]

3. No other proceedings, and no execution or other legal process, may be commenced or continued, and no distress may be levied, against the company or its property, except with the leave of the court and subject to such terms as the court may impose.[54] The reference to "other proceedings" has been construed *ejusdem generis* with the provisions of paragraphs (a) and (b), and so will not apply in relation to "proceedings" which are not similar to those which bring about the winding up of a company, the appointment of an administrative receiver, or the enforcement of a security.[55] In Scotland, diligence cannot be carried out or continued without leave of the court and subject to such conditions as the court may impose (I.A., s.10(5)).

Any creditor who applies to the court for leave to do anything which would constitute an exception to the moratorium whose effects are described above must serve prior notice of the application upon the company and the petitioner. However, section 10(2)(*b*) and (*c*) expressly excludes two important matters from the need to obtain leave of the court. These are the appointment of an administrative receiver of the company, or the carrying out by such a receiver (whenever appointed) of any of his functions. Thus, the first phase of the moratorium does not extend to the exercise by a floating charge holder of his right to appoint a receiver, nor does it extend to the proper actions of any receiver so appointed. Only if an administration order is actually made, thus marking the commencement of the second phase of the moratorium, does the charge holder's right to appoint a receiver

---

[51] I.A. 1986, s.10(1)(*a*), (2)(*a*).

[52] *Re A Company (No. 001992 of 1988)* [1989] B.C.L.C. 9.

[53] *Ibid.*, s.10(1)(*b*), (4). For the definitions of "hire purchase agreement" and "conditional sale agreement" see Consumer Credit Act 1974, s.189(1). For the definitions of "chattel leasing agreement" and "retention of title agreement" see I.A. 1986, s.251. For the modified form in which the terms of sections 10(1) and 11(3) apply to Scotland, see s.10(5).

[54] I.A. 1986, s.10(1)(*c*).

[55] *Air Ecosse Ltd.* v. *Civil Aviation Authority*, 1987 S.L.T. 751.

become suspended for the duration of the order, and any receiver who has previously been appointed become required to vacate office.[56]

In contrast to the position in English law,[57] the Scottish courts have seen no obstacle to the appointment of interim administrators to safeguard the company's assets.[58]

Postponed commencement of the moratorium

114 What has been said above with respect to the commencement of the moratorium over the company's affairs from the date of presentation of the petition admits of an importance exception in the case where there is already an administrative receiver of the company at the date in question. Section 10(3) of the Act provides that in such a case the moratorium imposed by subsection (1) of that section will not apply if the person by or on whose behalf the receiver was appointed has not consented to the making of the order, and will not begin to apply unless and until that person so consents. This provision is a further affirmation of the legislative policy of maintaining the basic legal position of such a charge holder, and is functionally complementary to the provision in section 9(3) whereby the court is required to dismiss the petition for an administration order if the charge holder's consent has not been given by the time of the hearing of the application.[59]

Concurrent petitions for winding up and for an administration order

115 In a case where the company's application for an administration order had been made virtually concurrently with the presentation by a creditor of a petition for the winding up of the company, the company's costs in the administration order petition, which was in due course dismissed, were allowable as costs in the winding up.[60] It was observed that, if this were not the case, directors, solicitors or accountants who had acted in good faith might have difficulty in recovering costs incurred in preparing and presenting the administration order petition which the legislature had introduced as a possible means of averting the winding up of an insolvent company.[61]

---

[56] *Ibid.*, s.11(1)(*b*), (3)(*b*).
[57] *Re A Company (No. 00175 of 1987)* [1987] B.C.L.C. 467.
[58] In *Air Ecosse Ltd.* v. *Civil Aviation Authority, supra* such an appointment was made and not questioned.
[59] See para. 109, *ante*.
[60] *Re Gosscot (Groundworks) Ltd.* (1988) 4 B.C.C. 372. Contrast *Re. W. F. Fearman Ltd. (No. 2)* (1988) 4 B.C.C. 142.
[61] In Scotland, 1986 Rule 4.67(3) would permit a similar approach to the expenses of an attempted administration order.

HEARING OF THE ADMINISTRATION ORDER PETITION AND MAKING OF THE ORDER

Procedure

116 The rules applicable in Scotland[62] contain no specific provisions relating to the hearing of a petition for an administration order. The matter is, therefore governed by the normal rules of procedure for petitions.

As noted above (see paragraph 112), intimation of the presentation of the petition has to be given to a number of parties with an actual or potential interest in its outcome. All of these will be entitled, if so advised, to lodge answers and be heard before the application is granted or refused. There is no requirement, however, to serve the petition on the person who prepared the preliminary report (if any) unless, of course, he is the intended administrator. Neither the reporter nor the intended administrator requires to be present or represented at the hearing.

The petitioner is not required by the rules to demonstrate that any person entitled to appoint an administrative receiver has consented to the petition. His consent will, therefore, be inferred from his failure to lodge answers or to appoint a receiver. If, however, (as required by the rules) the petition discloses that an administrative receiver has been appointed the court must dismiss the petition unless it is satisfied that the person who appointed him consents to the making of an order or the petitioner demonstrates that the floating charge under which he was appointed is invalid under the Insolvency Act, section 242, 243 or 245 or under any rule of law in Scotland[63] (I.A., s.9(3)). Invalidity for want of registration of the charge or some other flaw, *e.g.* in the appointment of the receiver, does not lead to this result, since these are capable of being rectified by the court. It appears, therefore, that in any case where a receiver has actually been appointed the court should require to be satisfied that the charge holder consents before making an order.

The court's power as to the disposal of the petition under section 9(4) and (5) are wide and fully discretionary.[64] There is no specific rule as to the form of an administration order, but in practice it will follow the established form in use in nominating and appointing liquidators. The Insolvency Act, section 8(2) indicates that the court's order must direct

---

[62] See para. 112 and notes 45–49, *ante.*
[63] See paras. 505 to 516, *post.* The omission of I.A., s.244 ("extortionate credit transactions") is presumably deliberate, but is not explicable. In Scotland it might be covered by "any rule of law" but this will not, obviously, serve to import s.244 into English law where s.9 also applies.
[64] In *Re Arrows Ltd. (No. 3)* [1992] B.C.C. 131 the court refused to grant an administration order which was opposed by creditors raising serious questions about the reasons for the company's insolvency, on the ground that compulsory liquidation was more appropriate.

that, while it is in force, the affairs, business and property of the company are to be managed by the administrator; the Insolvency Act, section 8(3) further requires the court to specify for which of the statutory purposes the order has been made.

If the court dismisses the petition the petitioner must forthwith send a copy of the court's order and Form 2.3 (Scot) to the Keeper of the Register of Inhibitions and Adjudications for recording, and within 14 days send a copy of the order certified by the court with Form 2.3 (Scot) to the registrar of companies. The court may make such further order with respect to such notice as it thinks fit (1986 Rule 2.3 (4) and (5)).

The administrator's role in the presentation of the petition

117   The administrator's appointment, status and powers, and duties will be considered in later paragraphs of this chapter but it is necessary to deal here with his role in the presentation of the administration petition.

The above-mentioned, almost incidental, reference to the administrator which is contained within the definition of "administration order" supplied by section 8(2) is the nearest that the Insolvency Act comes to supplying a formal definition of the term "administrator." However, it is to be understood from what has already been stated in this chapter, and from what follows hereafter, that the task of nominating a suitably qualified person to be appointed as administrator is one which falls to the petitioner to perform. From the time when the intention is formed to present a petition for an administration order, if not before then, the intending petitioner will be well advised to retain the services of a person capable of eventually acting as an administrator. Such a person must be qualified to act as an insolvency practitioner in relation to the company,[65] and as such could competently undertake the preparation of the report upon the company's affairs, and of the other supporting documents which are required (or, in Scotland, normally required) to accompany the petition itself.[66] Indeed, the administrator-elect, as a qualified insolvency practitioner, will be ideally placed to supervise the entire process of presentation of the petition on behalf of the petitioner, and in the latter's name, and should further be able to ensure that the petition itself is served, and requisite notice thereof is given, to all parties in accordance with the law's requirements.[67] In selecting an insolvency practitioner to nominate as administrator, the petitioner must bear in mind the need to avoid any transgression of the principles of ad hoc disqualification which may arise on account of a personal link or association between the insolvency practitioner and the company in relation to which he is to act. These principles will be found within the

---

[65] I.A. 1986, ss.388, 389.
[66] See para. 112, *ante*.
[67] On the giving of notice see para. 112, *ante*.

rules of professional conduct applicable to members of the professional body to which the administrator belongs, and by virtue of which he enjoys current authorisation to practise as an insolvency practitioner.[68] Alternatively if the insolvency practitioner does not belong to any professional body recognised for this purpose by the Secretary of State, analogous principles of professional conduct will have been made applicable to the person in question as part of the conditions attaching to his authorisation to practise as an insolvency practitioner and granted under the provisions of sections 392 to 398 of the Insolvency Act.[69]

Notification and advertisement of the order

118 If the court makes an administration order it must forthwith notify the person appointed as administrator (1986 Rule 2.3(1)). The administrator must forthwith advertise the order once in the *Edinburgh Gazette* and once in a newspaper circulating in the area of the company's principal place of business, or in such other newspaper as he thinks appropriate for bringing the order to the notice of creditors (s.21(1)(*a*); 1986 Rules 2.3(2)). He must also, within 14 days, send a copy of the order certified by the clerk of the court to the registrar of companies along with the prescribed form (Form 2.2 (Scot)) and within the same period send a copy (not a certified copy) to any person who has appointed an administrative receiver or may be entitled to do so (*i.e.* the holder of most forms of floating charge), any administrative receiver, any provisional liquidator and the Keeper of the Register of Inhibitions and Adjudications for recording in the personal register (I.A., s.21(2); 1986 Rule 2.3(3)). Within 28 days he must notify all creditors whose addresses are known to him that he has been appointed (s.21(1)(*b*)). Failure to comply may incur a fine under Insolvency Act 1986, section 21(3).

EFFECT OF THE ADMINISTRATION ORDER

119 The making of an administration order has the effect of maintaining in force the moratorium over the company's affairs whose first phase commenced with the presentation of the petition for the order. In its second phase, however, the moratorium is extended in certain vital respects. Section 11(3) of the Insolvency Act stipulates that during the period for which an administration order is in force no resolution may be passed or order made for the winding up of the company; no administrative receiver of the company may be appointed; no other steps may be taken to enforce any security over the company's property, or to repossess goods in the company's possession under

---

[68] I.A. 1986, ss.390(2)(*a*), 391.
[69] See also para. 440, *post.*

any hire purchase agreement, conditional sale agreement, chattel leasing agreement or retention of title agreement,[70] except with the consent of the administrator or the leave of the court and subject (where the court gives leave) to such terms as the court may impose. It has been held in England that assertion by a lien holder of a right to retain goods subject to a lien constitutes the taking of steps to enforce security, within the meaning of section 11(3)(c),[71] and that a landlord's right of re-entry for non-payment of rent is to be regarded as a species of security for the payment in question, and as such is within the meaning of section 11(3) and amounts to a "legal process" against the company whose exercise requires either the administrator's consent or the leave of the court.[72] These decisions, to the extent that they are based on English property law, are of limited relevance in Scotland. It is clear, however, from the judgments in *Air Ecosse Ltd.* v. *Civil Aviation Authority*[73] that the Scottish courts would take a broad view of what constituted "proceedings" (*cf.* I.A., s.11(3)(*d*)) by a creditor which are restrained by the Act provided that the *ejusdem generis* rule of construction was observed. It is possible, therefore, that steps to enforce a lien or hypothec, or to recover possession of leased heritage, could be restrained. In the case of a lease of heritage, however, there may be a contractual term providing for the lease to terminate *inter alia* on the appointment of an administrator to the tenant or in the event of rent not having been paid (or other breach of the tenant's obligations). There is no basis in Scots law for regarding the landlord's right to terminate the lease in such circumstances as a "security" (in the sense apparently relied on in *Exchange Travel Agency* v. *Triton Property Trust plc*[74]). It is no more than recognition of the contract in its terms. It must, therefore, remain an open question whether the Scottish courts would prevent the landlord from exercising his rights under the contract.

It was held in *Air Ecosse Ltd.* v. *Civil Aviation Authority*[75] that the moratorium imposed by section 11 only applies in relation to the actions of creditors of the company. Hence, competitors of the company are not debarred from taking steps aimed at enhancing their business position. In that case, it was held that a rival airline would not be restrained from making application to the licensing authority, aimed at bringing about the revocation of the operating licences of the company undergoing administration.

The principal addition to be found in the provisions of section 11(3), when compared to those of section 10(1),[76] is that it is rendered

---

[70] The four types of agreement are included by virtue of s.10(4). See para. 113, *ante*, at n. 53.
[71] *Re Paramount Airways Ltd.* [1990] B.C.C. 130; *Re Sabre International Products Ltd.* [1991] B.C.L.C. 470.
[72] *Exchange Travel Agency* v. *Triton Property Trust plc.* [1991] B.C.C. 341.
[73] 1987 S.L.T. 751; (1987) 3 B.C.C. 492 (Court of Session).
[74] *Supra*, n. 72.
[75] *Supra*, n. 73.
[76] Discussed above, para. 113.

impossible for an administrative receiver to be appointed during this second phase of the moratorium. Thus if a floating charge holder has not exercised his right to appoint a receiver before, at the latest, the date of hearing of the petition, he is thereafter denied the right to do so while the administration order remains in force. The other notable modification to the rules governing the moratorium during its second phase is that the administrator is authorised to give consent to the taking of steps to enforce security, or to repossess goods, or to commence or continue proceedings or execution or the levying of distress (in Scotland, to carry out or continue diligences (I.A., s.10(5)) against the company or its property. This authority is enjoyed by the administrator concurrently with the court, but is exercisable by him independently and of his own initiative.

120   There is a growing body of case law in England concerning the granting of leave under section 11(3)(c) to enable a secured creditor to enforce his security, or to enable an owner to repossess goods in the possession of the company, during the period when an administration order is in force. It has been emphasised that the court must balance the interests of the secured creditor as against those of the other creditors, and in the light of what the administrator's proposals and progress towards their implementation, seem destined to achieve.[77] On the other hand, it is not a precondition to the granting of leave to a secured creditor or an owner that the administrator's conduct should be capable of being criticised in some legitimate way.[78]

The process of balancing the competing interests as between a secured creditor or owner of goods on the one hand, and the general body of creditors on the other, arises both under section 11(3)(c) and also under section 15, when an administrator proposes to deal with secured property free from encumbrance.[79] Cases decided under either of these sections may therefore be instructive in relation to the operation of the other provision, although the two lines of authorities remain distinguishable from each other in the final analysis. The leading decision to date decided under section 11(3) is *Re Atlantic Computer Systems plc*. In that case,[80] the Court of Appeal made a number of important, general observations regarding cases where leave is sought to exercise existing proprietary rights, including security rights, against a company in administration. These may be summarised as follows[81]:

---

[77] *Re Meessan Investments Ltd.* (1988) 4 B.C.C. 788, also reported as *Royal Trust Bank* v. *Buchler* [1989] B.C.L.C. 130; *Re Paramount Airways Ltd.* [1990] B.C.C. 130, also reported as *Bristol Airport plc.* v. *Powdrill* [1990] B.C.L.C. 585.
[78] *Ibid.*
[79] See further, para. 132, *post.*
[80] [1990] B.C.C. 859.
[81] [1990] B.C.C. at 880.

121   1. In every case the onus is on the person who seeks leave to make out a case for this to be given.

2. If granting leave to a lessor of land or the hirer of goods (a "lessor") to exercise his proprietary rights and repossess his land or goods is unlikely to impede the purpose for which the administration order was made, leave should normally be given.

3. Where the giving of leave would impede the achievement of the purpose for which the order was made, the court has to carry out a balancing exercise, balancing the legitimate interests of the secured creditor lessor and the legitimate interests of the other creditors of the company. The exercise is not a mechanical one, but calls for the exercise of judicial judgment in the light of all the circumstances of the case, having regard to the overall objectives of the administration order, and the possible inequity of any refusal of leave.

4. In carrying out the balancing exercise great weight is to be given to the proprietary interests of the lessor or secured creditor. The Court of Appeal approved the *dicta* of Browne-Wilkinson V.C. in *Re Paramount Airways Ltd.*,[82] to the effect that: "... so far as possible, the administration procedure should not be used to prejudice those who were secured creditors when the administration order was made in lieu of a winding-up order." The same underlying principle is applicable in relation to the proprietary interests of the lessor; namely that an administration for the benefit of unsecured creditors should not be conducted at the expense of those who have proprietary rights, save to the extent that this may be unavoidable.

5. Therefore, leave will normally be granted if significant loss would be caused to a lessor or secured creditor by a refusal. For this purpose loss comprises any kind of financial loss, direct or indirect, including loss by reason of delay, and may extend to loss which is not financial. But if substantially greater loss would be caused to others by the grant of leave, or loss which is out of all proportion to the benefit which leave would confer on the lessor or secured creditor, that may outweigh the argument in favour of granting leave.

6. In assessing these respective losses, the court will have regard to matters such as: the financial position of the company; its ability to pay the rental arrears; the administrator's proposals; the period for which the administration order has already been in force and is expected to remain in force; the effect on the administration if leave were given, and the effect on the applicant if leave were refused; the end result sought to be

---

[82] *Supra*, n. 77.

achieved by the administration and the prospects of its attainment; and the history of the administration thus far.

7. The court will often have to take account of probabilities, assessing virtual certainties and remote possibilities in relation to the various factors under consideration.

8. The foregoing list is not exhaustive. The conduct of the parties may also be a material consideration. All of these factors may be relevant not only to the decision whether to grant or refuse leave, but also whether to impose terms if leave is granted, or indeed if it is refused.

122 A further point of considerable importance was ruled upon by the Court of Appeal in the *Atlantic Computers* case, namely the question of whether goods are to be treated as being "in the company's possession" for the purposes of section 11(3)(*c*) in a situation where, under the terms of the headleases with the founders of a commercial activity, the company is permitted to enter sub-leases under which the end-users of the goods will take them to their own sites for the purpose of utilisation. The Court declared that section 11(3)(*c*) contemplated the position as between the owner of the goods and the company in administration, and that as between these parties the location of the goods was irrelevant. Hence, the goods were still in the company's possession within the meaning of section 11(3)(*c*), so that the owner of the goods could not repossess them without obtaining either the consent of the administrator, or the leave of the court.[83]

Further important effects of the making of an administration order occur under section 11(1), which provides that any petition for the winding up of the company shall thereupon be dismissed, and that any administrative receiver of the company shall vacate office. No automatic requirement to vacate his office is imposed upon any receiver of part only of the company's property, but section 11(2) provides that such a receiver shall also vacate office on being required to do so by the administrator. The provisions of subsection (4) of section 11 further specify that where any administrative receiver or receiver of part of the company's property vacates office in accordance with the requirements of the section, his remuneration and any expenses properly incurred by him, and any indemnity to which he is entitled out of the assets of the company, shall be charged on and paid out of any property of the company which was in the custody or under the control of the administrative receiver or receiver at that time, in priority to any security held by the person by or on whose behalf he was appointed. This provision thus provides the displaced administrative receiver with a continuing indemnity out of the charged assets in respect of his own remuneration and costs. Vacation of office by an administrative receiver or receiver pursuant to the provisions of

[83] [1990] B.C.C. at 871.

section 11 of the Insolvency Act also has the effect of releasing the person concerned from any duty to pay preferential creditors under section 40 or 59 of the Act.[84]

Notification of order

123 In order that all parties dealing with the company at a time when an administration order is in force may have notice of this fact, section 12(1) of the Insolvency Act imposes the requirement that every invoice, order for goods or business letter, being a document on or in which the company's name appears[85] and which is issued by or on behalf of the company or the administrator during that period, must also contain the administrator's name and statement to the effect that he is for the time being managing the company's affairs, business and property. If default is made in complying with this requirement strict criminal liability is imposed upon the company, and in addition if the administrator or any officer of the company has without reasonable excuse authorised or permitted the default, that person also commits a criminal offence.[86]

Although evidently modelled upon what are now sections 39 and 64 of the Insolvency Act (formerly sections 493 and 480 respectively of the Companies Act 1985), which impose notification requirements where a receiver or a receiver or manager is appointed in relation to a company, the drafting of section 12(1) of the Insolvency Act is far from comprehensive or exhaustive in its coverage of the variety of means by which a company may have dealings with third parties. Thus the omission from the subsection of any reference to oral communications, or to those conveyed in the form of a telegram, telemessage or telex or by other electronic means, appears to give rise to important exceptions under which contact or dealings with outside parties may avoid violating the letter, if not the spirit, of section 12. Other significant means of business documentation, such as catalogues or brochures, receipts or even company cheques, may also be found to be outside the ambit of the phrase "invoice, order for goods or business letter," and so escape the requirement that they carry the special information that the company is in the hands of an administrator. Further problems may arise in practice concerning the precise meaning and effect of the word "issued" within the context of section 12(1). For an offence to be committed under this section, the document in question must be "issued" at a time when an administration order is in force. Although the Act supplies no definition of the term "issued," it is likely to be construed strictly in view of its function in relation to the imposition of

---

[84] I.A. 1986, s.11(5).
[85] Failure to include the company's name on or in any of the documents in question would constitute an offence by the company under s.349 of the Companies Act 1985.
[86] I.A. 1986, s.12(2). The maximum fine which may be imposed for each offence is expressed as one-fifth of the statutory maximum, and is therefore currently £400.

criminal liability under the section being considered. Thus, where documents are dispatched before the administration order enters into force (albeit possibly at a time when a petition has been presented and a hearing is pending) it would seem that no offence is committed under section 12, even though the administration order may have entered into force by the time the documents are received, read or acted upon by any third party for whom the administration order might well be a relevant factor for consideration. It may be expected however that an administrator would seek to ensure that the company's dealings with all parties are conducted with candour and integrity, even in cases apparently falling outside the limits of the notification requirement imposed by section 12. Indeed, as an office holder whose appointment arises under an order of the court, it would seem appropriate to regard the administrator as subject to a general and overriding duty to display exemplary standards of good faith in his dealings with all parties, just as is required of a liquidator in a winding up by the court, or of a trustee in bankruptcy. Hence, it is suggested, the rule in *Ex p. James*[87] should be applicable to an administrator.

General effects of the order; the position of directors

124 In addition to the matters described above, which constitute the principal effects resulting from the making of an administration order, several other effects ensue as a necessary consequence of the administrator's taking over management of the affairs, business and property of the company, and thereafter exercising his general and specific powers under sections 14 to 16 of the Insolvency Act, for the purpose of fulfilling the statutory duties imposed principally by sections 17 to 25 of the Act. These matters will be discussed in the ensuing paragraphs of this chapter, but one which deserves special mention here is the effect of the administration order upon the position of the directors of the company. Although the directors are not automatically dismissed from office as a consequence of the making of the order, the corollary to the transfer of all managerial power to the administrator is that the powers of the directors are suspended for the duration of the administration order. Despite being deprived of their powers however, the directors remain liable to perform their statutory duties in relation to the company's fulfilment of any requirements imposed upon it by law, such as the proper filing of annual returns by the company. However, the administrator has power under section 14(2)(*a*) to remove any director of the company and to appoint any person to be a director of the company, whether to fill any vacancy or otherwise. Thus, during the period of an administration order, the composition of the board of directors may be changed through

---

[87] (1874) 9 Ch.App. 609. See also *Re Wyvern Developments Ltd.* [1974] 2 All E.R. 535 (a case on compulsory winding up); contrast *Re John Bateson & Co.* [1985] B.C.L.C. 259 (a case on voluntary winding up).

the administrator's exercise of his personal judgment in relation to the company's needs, and the best way in which to achieve the purposes for which he himself was appointed.

A further consequence of the making of an administration order, from the directors' point of view, is that the provisions of sections 6 and 7 of the Company Directors Disqualification Act, under which persons may be disqualified from company management by order of the court, become applicable to all persons who are, or who have been, directors of the company.[88] The power of the court to make a disqualification order under section 6(1) arises where the person in question is or has been a director of a company "which has at any time become insolvent," an expression whose meaning includes, by virtue of subsection (2)(*b*), the case where an administration order is made in relation to the company. Moreover, a duty is cast upon the administrator by the terms of section 7(3)(*c*) of that Act to report to the Secretary of State forthwith if he becomes aware of matters which constitute a prima facie case for the making of a disqualification order under section 6(1).[89] Thus the possibility arises that proceedings may be initiated against one or more of the directors by means of an application for a disqualification order made by the Secretary of State under section 7(1)(*a*) of the Company Directors Disqualification Act 1986.[90] Although the further possibility of the imposition of responsibility for the company's wrongful trading under section 214 of the Insolvency Act will not arise unless the company subsequently goes into insolvent liquidation, the information gathered by the administrator, and submitted by him to the Secretary of State in fulfilment of the aforementioned reporting requirement, will inevitably be of considerable significance in any proceedings which may subsequently be brought by the liquidator under section 214 if the company is later wound up.[91]

---

[88] Under the Insolvent Companies (Report on Conduct of Directors) (No. 2) Rules 1986 (S.I. 1986 No. 2134), r. 4(2), the office holder is required to report upon the conduct of all persons who have been directors of the company at any time within the three years prior to the commencement of the insolvency proceedings. In Scotland, a similar duty arises under the Insolvent Companies (Reports on Conduct of Directors) (No. 2) (Scotland) Rules 1986 (S.I. 1986 No. 1916 (S.140), r. 3(2)).

[89] See also s.7(4) concerning the power of the Secretary of State to require the administrator to furnish information. More detailed requirements concerning the duties of an administrator, as an office holder within the meaning of the Insolvency Act, to report upon past and present directors of the company are contained in the Insolvent Companies (Reports on Conduct of Directors) Rules 1986 (S.I. 1986 No. 612). The rules for Scotland are to be found in the Insolvent Companies (Reports on Conduct of Directors) (No. 2) (Scotland) Rules 1986 (S.I. 1986 No. 1916 (S.140)).

[90] On directors' disqualification generally, and with regard to ss.6 and 7 of the Company Directors Disqualification Act 1986 in particular, see *Palmer*, paras. 8.101 *et seq.*

[91] Liability for wrongful trading is discussed in para. 523, *post.*

THE ADMINISTRATOR: HIS APPOINTMENT, REPLACEMENT, RESIGNATION AND REMOVAL

125 The holder of the office of administrator in relation to a company must be a person who is qualified to act as an insolvency practitioner in relation to the company.[92] The appointment of an administrator is made either by the administration order itself, in accordance with section 13(1) of the Insolvency Act, or subsequently, under section 13(2), by an order of the court to replace an administrator who has died, resigned or vacated office for any other reason. It is permissible for more than one person to be appointed or nominated to the office of administrator so that the position is held jointly, but in that event the appointment or nomination must declare whether any act required or authorised to be done by the office holder is to be done by all or any one or more of the persons for the time being holding the office.[93]

Where different nominations are submitted for the office of administrator—for example by the company and by a group of creditors respectively—the court must decide which of the nominees to appoint. Assuming that there is parity of professional experience and integrity, the court is unlikely to attach any particular weight to the fact that each of the nominating parties may be said to have a particular interest to serve. What is likely to influence the court in making its final choice is the extent to which one or other of the nominees is already thoroughly acquainted with the details of the company's affairs, so as to be able to act expeditiously upon appointment, and without there being a costly duplication of investigative work which has already been carried out by one of the nominees prior to the hearing.[94]

In the event that a vacancy occurs in the office of administrator, application to the court for an order under section 13(2) of the Insolvency Act to fill the vacancy may be made by any continuing administrator (if there has been a joint administratorship); or failing such by any committee of creditors established under section 26 of the Act,[95] or in the absence of both of the foregoing, by the company or the directors or by any creditor or creditors of the company.[96] Where a change occurs in the incumbent of the office of administrator the incoming administrator must advertise the fact and notify the registrar of companies of his appointment.[97]

An administrator of a company may at any time resign his office, in the prescribed circumstances, by giving notice of his resignation to the

---

[92] I.A. 1986, s.230(1). For the statutory requirements attaching to qualification to practise as an insolvency practitioner: see ss.388–398 of the Act.
[93] I.A. 1986, s.231(2).
[94] *Re Maxwell Communications Corporation plc* [1992] B.C.C. 372.
[95] See para. 142, *post.*
[96] I.A. 1986, s.13(3).
[97] See para. 127, *post.*

court.[98] The rules prescribe that an administrator may resign office in any of the following circumstances:[99]

1. ill health;
2. if there is some conflict of interest which precludes him from further discharging the duties of administrator;
3. in the case of a joint appointment, where it is no longer considered to be expedient that both or all should continue in office; or
4. if the court is satisfied that there are good reasons why the resignation should be permitted.

In addition to those cases where the administrator resigns for personal reasons, or for reasons of expediency falling within the circumstances prescribed in the rules, there is a statutory requirement in section 19(2) of the Insolvency Act that the administrator must vacate office if he ceases to be qualified to act as an insolvency practitioner in relation to the company, or if the administration order is discharged.[1]

126   Section 19(1) of the Insolvency Act provides that the administrator of a company may at any time be removed from office by the order of the court. Such an order may be made by the court in consequence of proceedings brought under section 27 of the Act, which provides that at any time when an administration order is in force a creditor or member of the company may apply to the court by petition alleging that the company's affairs, business and property are being or have been managed by the administrator in a way which is unfairly prejudicial to the interests of its creditors or members generally, or of some part of its creditors or members (including at least the petitioner himself). Alternatively a petition under section 27 may complain that any actual or proposed act or omission of the administrator is or would be prejudicial to the interests of the parties in question. The court is empowered by section 27(2) to make such order as it thinks fit for giving relief in respect of the matters complained of, and various particular matters are mentioned in subsection (4) in respect of which the order may make provision. These include the laying down of precise instructions to regulate the future management by the administrator of the company's affairs, business and property,[2] or the imposition of more particular requirements upon the administrator either to refrain from doing an act complained of or to do an act which the petitioner has complained he has omitted to do.[3] The court may also order the summoning of a meeting of creditors or members for the

[98] I.A. 1986, s.19(1).
[99] 1986 Rule 2.18(1) and (2).
[1] Discharge of an administration order is governed by s.18 of the I.A. See para. 144, *post*.
[2] I.A. 1986, s.27(4)(*a*).
[3] *Ibid.*, s.27(4)(*b*).

purposes of considering matters in accordance with the court's directions,[4] and in the face of the most extreme evidence of unsatisfactory circumstances, the court may discharge the administration order and make whatever consequential provision it thinks fit.[5] Where the evidence suggests that the personal shortcomings of the administrator are mainly the cause of the dissatisfaction expressed in a petition under section 27, the court may invoke its widely drawn powers to make "such order as it thinks fit," and make an order under section 19(1) removing the administrator from office. If no nomination of a suitable alternative administrator has been made in the petition itself, it may be expected that the court will take the necessary steps under section 13(2) to fill the vacancy before the conclusion of the hearing.[6]

Finally it should be noted that under section 17(3) of the Insolvency Act an administrator may be compelled to summon a meeting of the company's creditors in two specified cases. The first is when he is requested to do so by creditors representing at least one-tenth in value of the company's debts, and the second is when the administrator is directed to do so by the court. Therefore, if a sufficient number of creditors wish to oblige the administrator to explain his conduct before a general meeting, and to hear the creditors' views, this can be brought about in a direct manner. On the other hand, if the requisite one-tenth of the creditors cannot be gathered in support of any proceedings under section 17(3)(*a*), the aggrieved minority could petition the court under section 27, including in their petition the suggestion that the court should order the administrator to convene a meeting pursuant to the direction under section 17(3)(*b*).

Procedural aspects

127 On the death of an administrator it is the duty of his executors or his professional partners (if any) to notify the court, but any person may notify the court by producing a copy of the death certificate (1986 Rule 2.19). If an administrator intends to resign on ground of ill health, because he intends to cease practice as an insolvency practitioner, because there is a conflict of interest or change of personal circumstances which precludes or makes impracticable the further discharge by him of his duties, or on any other ground acceptable to the court he must give at least seven days of notice of intention to resign on Form 2.13 (Scot) to any continuing administrator or, if there is none, to the creditors' committee or, if there is neither a continuing administrator nor a committee, to the company and its creditors (1986 Rule 2.18(3)). Notice is thus to be given to those entitled to apply to the

---

[4] *Ibid.*, s.27(4)(*c*).
[5] *Ibid.*, s.27(4)(*d*).
[6] See para. 125, *supra*. On the administrator's release following his vacation of office, see para. 145, *post*.

court to fill the vacancy under the Insolvency Act, section 13(3). In the last situation the burden of notifying all creditors seems unnecessarily onerous. The rules do not expressly permit the administrator to do this by advertisement although he may be able to do so if so directed by the court under the general powers of the Insolvency Act, section 14(3). An application to remove an administrator or to fill a vacancy in the office of administration under the Insolvency Act, section 13(2) or 19(1) is to be made by way of note in the process (R.C.S. 211; Sh.Ct.R. 12). Where the court fills the vacancy the rules for notifying and advertising the appointment (1986 Rule 2.3(1)–(3), see paragraph 118) are to apply with respect to the new administrator (1986 Rule 2.20).

THE ADMINISTRATOR: HIS STATUS AND POWERS

128 It has been explained above[7] that the general conception of the administration order procedure was inspired by certain aspects of the beneficent operation of the procedure for appointing an administrative receiver under a floating charge. The status and powers of an administrator are therefore modelled closely upon those of an administrative receiver, but in certain respects the powers with which an administrator is invested are more extensive than those enjoyed by an administrative receiver. A principal aspect of the legal status of an administrator is that, by virtue of section 14(5) of the Insolvency Act, in exercising his powers he is deemed to be acting as an agent of the company. This places the administrator in a position identical to that of an administrative receiver,[8] and has the consequence that the company is both bound by, and liable in respect of, all acts validly performed by the administrator. Moreover, by virtue of section 232 of the Insolvency Act the acts of an individual as administrator are valid in law notwithstanding any defect in his appointment, nomination or qualifications.

It has been held that there is no analogy between an administrator and a receiver or an administrator and an administrative receiver, as far as concerns the right of the administrator not to fulfil the company's outstanding contracts.[9] On the other hand, in *Re Home Treat Ltd.*[10] an administrator was held to occupy a position analogous to that of a liquidator for the purpose of being entitled to apply for relief under section 727 of the Companies Act 1985 in respect of any potential allegation of negligence, default or breach of duty. It was held that an administrator is an "officer of the company" for this purpose, and may thus seek relief against possible liabilities resulting from a discovery

---

[7] See para. 101, *ante*.
[8] *Cf.* I.A. 1986, s.44(1). However, an administrator does not incur personal liability for his acts in the way that an administrative receiver does by virtue of s.44(1)(*b*). In Scotland, the same comments apply by reference to I.A., s.57(1) and (2).
[9] *Astor Chemical Ltd.* v. *Synthetic Technology Ltd.* [1990] B.C.C. 97.
[10] [1991] B.C.C. 165.

that the company's business was being run in contravention of the objects clause of the memorandum of association.

A further aspect of the legal provisions associated with the office of administrator arises under section 14(6) of the Act, whereby a person dealing with the administrator in good faith and for value need not be concerned to inquire whether the administrator is acting within his powers. This protection for third parties dealing with an administrator in the manner specified has the effect of precluding either the administrator or the company in relation to which he acts from raising the defence of *ultra vires* in relation to acts performed by the administrator. However, no presumption is imported into the drafting of section 14(6), and it is therefore incumbent upon the party who seeks to rely upon its provisions to prove that the conditions imposed therein were satisfied in the particular case.

A further statutory safeguard operates against any attempt by means of provisions in the company's memorandum or articles of association to create an obstacle to the administrator's ability to exercise to the full powers conferred upon him under the Insolvency Act. Section 14(4) of the Act provides that any power conferred on the company or its officers either by the Insolvency Act or by the Companies Act 1985, or by the company's own memorandum or articles, which could be exercised in such a way as to interfere with the exercise by the administrator of his powers, shall not be exercisable except with the consent of the administrator himself. Such consent may be given by the administrator in general terms or in relation to particular cases. The effect of this provision is thus to confirm the overriding nature of the status and legal powers of the administrator in relation to the company and its directors throughout the period for which the administration order is in force.

General powers

129 The general powers conferred upon an administrator are contained in section 14 of the Insolvency Act together with Schedule 1 thereto. The powers listed in the Schedule are made applicable also to an administrative receiver in England and Wales by section 42 of the Act and the powers of a Scottish receiver under Schedule 2 are virtually identical, thus underlining the close connection between those two kinds of office holder. Section 14(1)(a) is drafted in extremely wide terms, so that the administrator is expressly empowered to do "all such things as may be necessary for the management of the affairs, business and property of the company." Moreover in paragraph (b) of that subsection, whereby the powers specified in Schedule 1 are made applicable to an administrator, it is stated that the powers contained in the Schedule are enjoyed "without prejudice to the generality of paragraph (a)." Therefore the fact that any given matter has not been included within the powers conferred by the Schedule cannot of itself constitute a basis for denying that the administrator has and can exercise such a power. Provided, at any rate, that the thing which the administrator proposes to do can be reconciled with the broad language of section 14(1)(*a*), as quoted above, it follows that the administrator enjoys the power to do it.

130   By virtue of Schedule 1 to the Act, the administrator has the following powers:

> "1. Power to take possession of, collect and get in the property of the company and, for that purpose, to take such proceedings as may seem to him expedient.[11]
> 2. Power to sell or otherwise dispose of the property of the company by public auction or private contract or, in Scotland, to sell, feu, hire out or otherwise dispose of the property of the company by public roup or private bargain.
> 3. Power to raise or borrow money and grant security therefor over the property of the company.
> 4. Power to appoint a solicitor or accountant or other professionally qualified person to assist him in the performance of his functions.
> 5. Power to bring or defend any action or other legal proceedings in the name and on behalf of the company.[12]
> 6. Power to refer to arbitration any question affecting the company.
> 7. Power to effect and maintain insurances in respect of the business and property of the company.
> 8. Power to use the company's seal.
> 9. Power to do all acts and to execute in the name and on behalf of the company any deed, receipt or other document.
> 10. Power to draw, accept, make and endorse any bill of exchange or promissory note in the name and on behalf of the company.
> 11. Power to appoint any agent to do any business which he is unable to do himself or which can more conveniently be done by an agent and power to employ and dismiss employees.
> 12. Power to do all such things (including the carrying out of works) as may be necessary for the realisation of the property of the company.
> 13. Power to make any payment which is necessary or incidental to the performance of his functions.
> 14. Power to carry on the business of the company.
> 15. Power to establish subsidiaries of the company.
> 16. Power to transfer to subsidiaries of the company the whole or any part of the business and property of the company.
> 17. Power to grant or accept a surrender of a lease or tenancy of any

---

[11] See below for a note of problems which might arise from these powers (1) and (5).
[12] See n. 11, *supra*.

of the property of the company, and to take a lease or tenancy of any property required or convenient for the business of the company.

18. Power to make any arrangement or compromise on behalf of the company.

19. Power to call up any uncalled capital of the company.

20. Power to rank and claim in the bankruptcy, insolvency, sequestration or liquidation of any person indebted to the company and to receive dividends, and to accede to trust deeds for the creditors of any such person.

21. Power to present or defend a petition for the winding up of the company.

22. Power to change the situation of the company's registered office.

23. Power to do all other things incidental to the exercise of the foregoing powers."

131   Most of these powers have been enjoyed in statutory form by receivers in Scotland (s.472(1), originally the Companies (Floating Charges and Receivers) (Scotland) Act 1972, s.15(1)). Powers (1) and (5) in particular have been the subject of conflicting judicial opinion. In one case[13] it was held that the exercise of power (1) would permit the receiver (or presumably, administrator) to sue in his own name for recovery of sums due to the company, in which case a plea of compensation or set-off available against the company was not pleadable against him. In a later case[14] it was held that power (1) could not be used for such purposes, but power (5) was appropriate in which case compensation or set-off would be pleadable. The latter decision,[15] however, further held that the rules restricting pleas of compensation or set-off relevant to insolvency (*e.g.* by barring such a plea in respect of a debt acquired by the company's debtor after insolvency) did not apply to receiverships, a view since disapproved.[16] In the context of receivership and the statutory effect of an attached ("crystallised") charge the conflict among these decisions can be resolved by noting that crystallisation effectively completes a title to the debt in the receiver by way of security,[17] but this argument is not available in the context of an administration order. Nevertheless, since such an order proceeds on the basis that the company "is or is likely to become unable to pay its debts" (I.A., s.8(1)(*a*)), it is clear that the law with respect to compensation or set-off in administration should be that which applies

---

[13] *McPhail* v. *Lothian Regional Council*, 1981 S.L.T. 173; 1981 S.C. 109.

[14] *Taylor, Petr.*, 1982 S.L.T. 172. It appears to be settled that power (1) should be used to recover possession of an asset and power (5) for payment of a debt; *Myles J. Callaghan Ltd.* v. *City of Glasgow D.C.*, 1988 S.L.T. 227; 1987 S.C.L.R. 627.

[15] *Taylor, Petr., supra.*

[16] *William Loudon & Son Ltd.* v. *Cunninghame District Council*, 1985 S.L.T. 149; *Myles J. Callaghan Ltd.* v. *City of Glasgow D.C., supra.*

[17] *Forth & Clyde Construction Co. Ltd.* v. *Trinity Timber & Plywood Co. Ltd.*, 1983 S.L.T. 372; affmd. 1984 S.L.T. 94. See further para. 231, *post.*

in insolvency. It is regrettable, however, that when applying these powers to administrators (and administrative receivers in England and Wales), the opportunity was not taken to remove any uncertainty remaining as a result of these irreconcilable decisions.[18]

The following further powers of a general nature are conferred upon an administrator by section 14 of the Insolvency Act. By section 14(2)(*a*) he may remove any director of the company and appoint any person to be a director of the company, whether to fill any vacancy or otherwise. By means of this most sweeping power, the administrator may take appropriate action to rebuild the management team of the company with a view to leaving it in capable hands when the administration order expires or is discharged. Under section 14(2)(*b*) the administrator may at any time call a meeting of members of creditors of the company. This allows the administrator, at his discretion, to consult the relevant sectors of interest in a direct manner on matters of importance, and on which their assent or support is judged to be desirable. Such a step could be taken, for example, when the administrator concludes that the company is in a position to be handed back to its management, as reconstituted by means of the powers just referred to. If the meetings of the members and creditors were in effect to pass votes of confidence in the new board and in the administrator's achievements in office, this would help to ensure that the ending of the administratorship could take place under the most favourable conditions.

The right to make direct contact with creditors or members of the company via a general meeting is supplemented by the right conferred on the administrator by section 14(3), whereby he may at any time apply to the court for directions in relation to any particular matter arising in connection with the carrying out of his functions.

Power to deal with property subject to security rights

132 By virtue of section 15 of the Insolvency Act, important and specific powers are conferred upon the administrator in relation to property of the company which is subject to any floating charge or other security. The purpose of section 15 is to enable the administrator to deal with or dispose of encumbered property free from the encumbrance in question, subject to the provision that the rights of the secured creditor shall be transferred and attached to any property which is substituted for the charged asset, or to the net proceeds of any disposal thereof. The commercial advantages of the administrator's ability thus to deal with encumbered property are considerable and should in the majority of cases ensure that the rationalisation of the company's business is efficiently carried through, and that the disposal value of assets is duly maximised. The powers of disposal accorded to an administrator under section 125 are in some ways comparable to those accorded to a

---

[18] See further para. 231, *post*.

receiver under section 61 of the Insolvency Act,[19] but in certain respects are more extensive since an administrator is empowered to dispose of property encumbered by a floating charge without any need to obtain authorisation from the court.[20]

Under subsection (1) of section 15, where there is property of the company which is subject to a security which, as created, was a floating charge the administrator may dispose of or otherwise exercise his powers in relation to that property as though it were not subject to the security. Subsection (4) supplies the necessary protection for the holder of the security in question by providing that where property is disposed of under subsection (1) the charge holder shall have the same priority in respect of any property directly or indirectly representing the property disposed of as he would have had in respect of the property subject to the security in its original form. The greater freedom of the administrator to dispose of property which is subject to a floating charge, as opposed to a fixed charge, is a further instance of the vital importance of the essential distinction between these two forms of security. Since the test of the nature of a charge as created is ultimately a functional one, the mere use of the words "fixed charge" will not of itself be conclusive as to the nature of the security which is being created, but regard must be had to the substance of the arrangement between the debtor and the creditor in whose favour the security is being granted.[21]

133   Under subsection (2) of section 15 the administrator may apply to the court for an order authorising him to dispose of any property of the company which is subject to a security other than one which, as created, was a floating charge, or of any goods in the possession of the company under a hire purchase agreement, conditional sale agreement, chattel leasing agreement or retention of title agreement.[22] The court may authorise the disposal (either alone or in conjunction with other assets) of property or goods which are the subject of such application provided that the court is satisfied that the disposal would be likely to promote the purpose, or one or more of the purposes, specified in the administration order.[23] The order of the court authorises the administrator to dispose of secured property as if it were

---

[19] See further para. 245, *post.*
[20] I.A. 1986, s.15(1), (3). *Cf.* I.A. 1986, s.61, which applies to receivers in Scotland.
[21] *Cf. Re Keenan Bros.* [1985] I.R. 401 (a charge upon present and future book debts due to the debtor company was held to be a fixed charge as created, since the substance of the arrangement with the creditor was to deprive the company of the free use of the proceeds of the asset in question). See also *Barclays Bank plc* v. *Willowbrook International Ltd.* [1986] B.C.L.C. 45. Although the details of these decisions relate to English law, the comment in the text would be valid in Scotland, were the situation to arise.
[22] I.A. 1986, s.15(2), (3) and (9). For the statutory definitions of the various types of credit agreement referred to, see references in para. 113, *ante,* at n. 53.
[23] See para. 108, *ante* on the exercise of the court's discretion; see *Re ARV Aviation Ltd.* [1989] B.C.L.C. 664; (1988) 4 B.C.C. 708.

not subject to the security, or to dispose of goods which are subject to a credit agreement as if all the rights of the owner under the agreement were vested in the company.[24] Any order made by the court under subsection (2) is subject to the mandatory condition that the net proceeds of the disposal shall be applied towards discharging the sums secured by the security or payable under the credit agreement.[25] Where the proceeds, net of the costs and expenses incurred in making the sale, are less than the notional amount determined by the court to be that which would be realised on sale of the property or goods in the open market by a willing vendor, the amount actually realised must be augmented by such other sums derived from the company's funds as may be required to make good the deficiency below the notional minimum return on the disposal.[26] Where there are two or more securities attaching to the same item of property, the net proceeds of disposal, augmented where necessary under the requirements just described, are to be applied towards discharging the sums secured by the securities in the order of their respective priorities.[27] Where property is disposed of under these provisions in Scotland, the granting of the appropriate disposition, transfer, assignation, etc., and the completion of the purchaser's title has the effect of disencumbering the property of the security. The disposal under the Insolvency Act, section 15, of goods subject to hire-purchase agreements, etc., also extinguishes the rights of the owner as against the purchaser (I.A., s.16).

Where the court makes an order under section 15(2) authorising disposal of property or goods by the administrator, the latter must send a copy of the order to the registrar of companies within 14 days. Failure on his part to do so without reasonable excuse constitutes a criminal offence punishable by a fine of up to £400 plus, for a continued contravention, a daily default fine not exceeding £40.[28]

There is no express requirement in the Rules of Court in Scotland requiring notice to be given to any charge holder or other person affected. Rule of Court 211 and Sheriff Court Rule 12 require the application to be by way of note in the process. The court would, in the exercise of its discretion, require service on relevant parties. There is no Rule of Court specifying the contents of such a note, thus leaving it to the noter to aver the matters necessary to persuade the court to grant the order. It may be observed that, even where the administrator is empowered by section 15(1) to dispose of property without first having to seek the authorisation of the court, it will always be open to any interested and duly qualified parties to make an application under

---

[24] I.A. 1986, s.15(2).
[25] *Ibid.*, s.15(5).
[26] *Ibid.*
[27] *Ibid.*, s.15(6).
[28] *Ibid.*, ss.15(7), (8), 430, Sched. 10.

section 27 in respect of any matters affected by the operation of section 15.[29]

Avoidance of antecedent transactions, etc.

134 As an "office holder" within the meaning of Part VI of the Insolvency Act,[30] an administrator enjoys significant powers under that Chapter to bring about the avoidance of antecedent transactions to which the company is or has been a party, to assist him in carrying out the investigation of the company's affairs, and to obtain control or possession of property or records belonging to the company. These powers, being common to administrators and liquidators, are fully described elsewhere and it will suffice here to refer to other parts of this work where the relevant provisions are considered.[31]

Supplies by utilities

135 Where, as in most cases, the continuation of the company's business is dependent upon the continued availability of any of the following services supplied by public utilities, namely gas, electricity, water, or telecommunication services, the administrator may invoke the special protection conferred upon office holders by section 233 of the Insolvency Act. By this section, if a request is made by or with the concurrence of the administrator for the giving after the date on which the administration order was made of any of the supplies referred to,[32] the supplier may make it a condition of the giving of the supply that the administrator personally guarantees the payment of any charges in respect of the supply, but may not make it a condition of the giving of the supply, or do anything which has the effect of imposing such a condition, that any outstanding charges in respect of a supply given to the company before the date of the administration order are paid.[33] The purpose of this provision, whose enactment was recommended in the *Cork Report*,[34] is to ensure that the public utilities are not enabled to exploit the advantage resulting from the essential nature of the services which they are legally obliged to provide, so as to impose terms for the continuation or resumption of supplies which have the effect of enhancing the supplier's rights or status in relation to the outstanding charges in respect of previous supplies to the company. Thus the imposition of any specially increased tariff or surcharge for the reconnection or resumption of supplies, or in respect of the rate of

---

[29] Creditors' and members' rights of petition under s.27 are discussed in para. 126, *ante* and in para. 143, *post*.

[30] See I.A. 1986, ss.232, 233(1), 234(1), 235–237, 238(1), 239–243, 244(1), 245(1), 246(1).

[31] See paras. 505 to 517, *post* (challenge of antecedent transactions) and paras. 519 to 521, *post* (duty to assist, powers of investigation, etc.).

[32] The formal description of the supplies to which s.233 of the I.A. relates is given in subs. (3).

[33] I.A. 1986, s.233(2).

[34] Cmnd. 8558, Chap. 33, especially paras. 1451–1462.

charge for supplies, would contravene section 233 and be consequently invalid.

THE ADMINISTRATOR: GENERAL DUTIES

136 Section 17 of the Insolvency Act requires the administrator on his appointment to take into his custody or under his control all the property to which the company is or appears to be entitled. To assist him in accomplishing this task, the administrator not only may avail himself of the general powers invested in him as administrator by virtue of section 14 of the Act,[35] but also may invoke the assistance of the court by seeking an order under section 234 in respect of any person who has in his possession or control any property, books, papers or records to which the company appears to be entitled. The person in respect of whom the order is made may thereby be required to pay, deliver, convey, surrender or transfer the items in question to the administrator.

In his efforts to trace and take control of the company's property, and to investigate the company's affairs, the administrator may derive further assistance from section 235 of the Insolvency Act which imposes upon a wide circle of persons, presently or formerly connected with the company in a variety of capacities, the duty to co-operate with the administrator. This duty consists of an obligation to give the administrator such information concerning the company and its promotion, formation, business, dealings, affairs or property as the administrator may at any time reasonably require, and an obligation to attend on the administrator for private examination at any time when he may reasonably require it.[36] The administrator may further avail himself of the assistance of the court by making an application for an order under section 236 of the Insolvency Act, whereby persons may be summoned to appear before the court, or may be required to submit an affidavit, for the purpose of furnishing sworn evidence on any matter relating to the company's affairs.[37] The same statutory provision may be used by the administrator to obtain from such parties as the company's bankers the disclosure and production of books, documents and records relating to the company.[38] The Court of Appeal, in *Re British and Commonwealth Holdings plc. (No. 2)*,[39] has confirmed the principles which apply in relation to the exercise of the court's power to order discovery of

---

[35] See para. 129, *ante.*

[36] s.235 of the I.A. is further considered in para. 484, *post.*

[37] s.236 of the I.A. is further considered in paras. 519 and 520, *post.*

[38] *Re Cloverbay Ltd.* [1989] B.C.L.C. 724. See however *Re Cloverbay Ltd. (No. 2)* [1990] B.C.C. 299, where attempts to obtain still more information from the same bankers in the same case were disallowed by the court as superfluous, and oppressive to the party concerned.

[39] [1992] B.C.C. 172. See also the judgment of the same court in a linked appeal arising out of the same case: *Re British and Commonwealth Holdings plc (No. 1)* [1992] B.C.C. 165.

information under section 236, on the application of the office holder in insolvency proceedings. The court enjoys an unfettered and general discretion in the exercise of this extraordinary power, and must balance the requirements of the office holder against possible oppression to the person from whom information is sought. On the other hand, there is no rule of limitation to the effect that the office holder is confined to reconstituting that knowledge which the company once had and was entitled in law to possess[40]: the terms of section 236 itself, and the logical requirements of the office holder's function, admit of a broader approach to the exercise of the court's power, with a view to discovering relevant information with as little expense and as much ease as possible.[40a]

A further duty of the administrator, and one which is the very *raison d'être* of his administratorship, is to manage the affairs, business and property of the company.[41] This is to be done, in the first instance, in accordance with any directions given by the court, but after the administrator's proposals have been approved under section 24 of the Insolvency Act the administrator is required to carry out his managerial functions in accordance with those proposals, as from time to time revised by means of the procedures established for this purpose.[42]

Other duties which the administrator is required to perform without delay following the making of the administration order are concerned with the sending out of notice of the order,[43] the investigation of the company's affairs and the preparation of a statement of proposals to be submitted in due course to a meeting of the company's creditors in accordance with the requirements of sections 23 and 24 of the Insolvency Act.[44]

Statement of affairs

137 A central aspect of the administrator's duties at the outset of his tenure of office is the obtaining of a statement of the company's affairs, which is required by section 22 of the Insolvency Act. Under this section the administrator must require some or all of the persons mentioned in subsection (3) thereof to make out and submit to him a statement in the prescribed form as to the company's affairs. Although a considerable standardization has taken place with regard to the statutory provisions

---

[40] On this point, the Court of Appeal has ruled that a statement to the contrary contained in the judgment of Browne-Wilkinson V.C. in *Cloverbay Ltd.* v. *Bank of Credit and Commerce International* [1991] Ch. 90, at p. 102, was an *obiter dictum* and did not correctly state the law.

[40a] This view appears to have been supported by the House of Lords on appeal (*Re British and Commonwealth Holdings plc (Nos. 1 and 2)*, *The Times*, November 3, 1992.

[41] I.A. 1986, s.17(2). *Cf.* s.8(2).

[42] For approval of the administrator's proposals under s.24 of the I.A., and for revision or modification of the proposals under s.25, see para. 140, *post*.

[43] See I.A. 1986, s.21(1), (2), discussed in para. 118, *ante*.

[44] See para. 138, *post*.

under which, in various circumstances, a statement of a company's affairs is required to be prepared,[45] the mandatory terms in which section 22(1) is drafted are such as to deprive the administrator of any discretion as to whether a statement of affairs shall be required at all.[46] Subject to that qualification, however, the administrator does possess certain discretionary powers, both with regard to the extension of the period of 21 days within which the statement of affairs must be submitted by those persons on whom the requirement has been imposed by him,[47] and with regard to the releasing of any such person from the obligation to submit the statement within the prescribed time.[48]

The persons upon whom the obligation of submitting a statement of the company's affairs may be imposed by the administrator are:

(a) those who are or have been officers of the company;

(b) those who have taken part in the company's formation at any time within one year before the date of the administration order;

(c) those who are in the company's employment or have been in its employment within that year, and are in the administrator's opinion capable of giving the information required; and

(d) those who are or have been within that year officers of or in the employment of a company which is, or within that year was, an officer of the company.[49]

Any of the foregoing persons on whom the administrator elects to serve a requirement under section 22(1) of the Insolvency Act must submit a statement of the company's affairs in the prescribed form and verified by affidavit. Section 22(2) specifies that the statement must show:

(a) particulars of the company's assets, debts and liabilities;

(b) the names and addresses of its creditors;

(c) the securities held by the creditors respectively;

(d) the dates when the securities were respectively given; and

(e) such further or other information as may be prescribed.

In Scotland, the procedure relating to the statement of affairs is laid down in the 1986 Rules 2.4 to 2.6, 7.30 and Sched. 5 (Forms). The administrator must send to each person whom he requires to provide a statement a notice on Form 2.5 (Scot) with a copy of the prescribed

---

[45] *Cf.* I.A. 1986, s.66 (concerning receivership), discussed in para. 249, *post* and s.131 (concerning compulsory winding up), discussed in para. 484, *post*.

[46] *Cf.* I.A. 1986, s.131(1), where the material phrase reads: "the (liquidator or provisional liquidator—see s.131(8)) *may* require..." (emphasis added). On the other hand, s.66(1) of the Act is drafted in mandatory terms which are effectively identical to those of s.22(1).

[47] I.A. 1986, s.22(4), (5)(*b*).

[48] *Ibid.*, s.22(4), (5)(*a*).

[49] *Ibid.*, s.22(3). It is expressly provided that the term "employment" here includes employment under a contract for services.

form of statement (Form 2.6 (Scot)). The deponent is allowed to claim his reasonable expenses and can appeal any refusal to the court (1986 Rule 2.6). The statements are to be retained by the administrator in the sederunt book of the administration (1986 Rule 2.5(2)).

Failure without reasonable excuse by any person (including the administrator himself) to fulfil any obligation imposed by section 122 of the Insolvency Act constitutes a criminal offence punishable by fine.[50]

The administrator's proposals; meeting of creditors

138 The primary duty of the administrator upon entering office is to devise the most appropriate means of achieving the purpose or purposes which are specified in the administration order under which he was appointed, and whose attainment is the ultimate objective of the making of the order itself. To this end, section 23(1) of the Insolvency Act requires the administrator within three months after the making of the order to formulate his proposals for achieving the purpose or purposes specified therein. If it proves to be impracticable for the administrator to complete this task within the three-month period, the court is empowered by the subsection to grant an extension of time. In *Re Newport County Association Football Club*,[51] Harman J. held that it is preferable if the application for an extension of time is made by the administrator since he is the person on whom is laid the statutory obligation to report within three months, and who is liable to criminal proceedings should he fail to do so. He is actively interested in the company, and at the same time is able to adopt an independent and detached view of its affairs. The permission of the court is not needed for the administrator to enter a contract to sell a company asset prior to the creditors' meeting.[52] The administrator is required within the specified period to send a statement of his proposals to the registrar of companies and (so far as he is aware of their addresses) to all creditors. He must also lay a copy of the statement before a specially convened meeting of the company's creditors, summoned on not less than 14 days' notice.[53] The further requirements imposed upon the administrator by section 23(2) are that within the same time limit he must either send a copy of his statement of proposals to all members of the company of whose addresses he is aware, or alternatively publicise by advertisement a notice stating an address to which members of the company should write for copies of the statement to be sent to them free of charge. The administrator may well deem it expedient to postpone, as far as the rules will allow, the incurring of expenditure in

---

[50] I.A. 1986, s.22(6).
[51] [1987] B.C.L.C. 583. *Cf. Re Charnley Davies Business Services Ltd.* (1988) P.C.C. 1, 5–6, *per* Harman J.
[52] *Re N.S. Distribution Ltd.* [1990] B.C.L.C. 169, distinguishing *Re Consumer and Industrial Press (No. 2)* [1988] C.L.Y. 290.
[53] I.A. 1986, s.23(1)(*a*), (*b*).

relation to the giving of notice to members until he is assured of the support of the creditors for the proposals he has devised.

Where the implementation of the administrator's proposals will entail the dismissal of employees of the company, the proper consultation procedures under section 99 of the Employment Protection Act 1975 must be undertaken, just as in the case of redundancies which result from a company going into liquidation.[54]

The procedure in Scotland for submitting the administrator's proposals is laid down in 1986 Rules 2.7 and 2.8. The proposals submitted to the meeting of creditors must contain the detailed information as to the administrator's appointment and its purposes, the company (its officers and affairs), a copy of any statement of affairs and the administrator's comments thereon, a statement of how the company has been managed and financed since his appointment and his proposals for the further management and finance of the company and the reasons for approving the proposals. A copy of the proposals must be attached to the notice submitted to the registrar under the Insolvency Act, section 23 on Form 2.7 (Scot). If the administrator decides to publish a notice under the Insolvency Act, section 23(2)(*b*) instead of notifying creditors individually, he must insert it once in the *Edinburgh Gazette* and once in the newspaper in which his appointment was advertised.

If the administrator fails without reasonable excuse to comply with any of the requirements of section 23, he commits a criminal offence which is punishable by a fine in accordance with the provisions of section 23(3) of the Act.[55]

139   Section 24 of the Insolvency Act contains the statutory requirements pertaining to the consideration of the administrator's proposals by a creditor's meeting convened under section 23(1)(*b*).[56] For the purpose of voting on a resolution approving the proposals in accordance with section 24(1) of the Act, the rules provide that the resolution may be passed by a simple majority in value of those present or represented.[57] A creditor, such as a trustee for bondholders, who stands as the representative of a plurality of interested parties who may hold differing views as to the course to be adopted at the meeting, is allowed to split the electoral value of his vote, and thus give effect to those views, provided that he does not vote in total for more than the total in respect of which he is qualified to vote.[58]

Those creditors whose debts have arisen during the course of the administration may attend and speak at the meeting, but will normally

---

[54] *Cf. Re Hartlebury Printers Ltd.* [1992] B.C.C. 428.
[55] I.A. 1986, ss.23(3), 430; Sched. 10.
[56] The rules applicable in Scotland for the conduct of the meeting are contained in the 1986 Rules 2.9 to 2.14 and 7.1 to 7.13. See further para. 141 below.
[57] 1986 Rule 7.12.
[58] *Re Polly Peck International plc* [1991] B.C.C. 503.

be excluded from voting in respect of any part of the debt which has arisen after the administration order since, by virtue of section 19(5), this constitutes a secured debt enjoying first priority of entitlement to be paid out of any property of the company which is in the custody of the administrator when he vacates his office.[59] Apart from those whose secured status results from the operation of section 19(5), secured creditors are only permitted to vote at the meeting in respect of the unsecured balance (if any) of their debt, the amount of which must have been agreed in advance between the chairman and the creditor concerned.[60] Other creditors who are entirely debarred from voting are any who are, in relation to the company, associated companies or connected persons within the meaning of sections 249 and 435 combined of the Insolvency Act.

If the meeting is not prepared to approve the administrator's proposals in the form in which they are tabled, section 24(2) of the Act allows the proposals to be approved with modifications, provided that the administrator assents to each modification. If no majority can be obtained for the approval of the proposals either in their original or in modified form, the chairman may, and must if a resolution is passed to that effect, adjourn the meeting for not more than 14 days.[61]

When the meeting is concluded, the administrator must report the result of the meeting to the court within four days and give notice of the result to the registrar of companies. The report must set out the proposals in the form in which they have been approved (if such is the case).[62] If the report is to the effect that the meeting has declined to approve the administrator's proposals (even in modified form) the court may discharge the administration order, or may adjourn the proceedings or make an interim order, or otherwise dispose of the case in the exercise of its discretion.[63] These widely drawn powers enable the court to respond in a flexible way to the creditors' refusal to endorse the administrator's proposals. However, unless there is persuasive evidence to suggest that the purposes for which the administration order was made may yet be attained, possibly through the substitution of a new or additional administrator, the court is likely to deploy its discretionary powers in such a way as to ensure the smoothest possible transition to the next appropriate form of insolvency proceedings, such as a voluntary or compulsory winding up.[64]

---

[59] See para. 145, *post*. Creditors whose position is protected under s.19(4) or (5) of the I.A. may be permitted to vote when the administrator's proposals will directly affect them.
[60] Sched. 1, para. 5 of the Bankruptcy (Scotland) Act 1985, as applied by 1986 Rules 7.9 and Chap. 5 (see below).
[61] 1986 Rule 2.10(2).
[62] I.A. 1986, s.24(4); 1986 Rule 2.14(1) (see below).
[63] I.A. 1986, s.24(5).
[64] See s.140(1) of the I.A., which makes provision for the appointment of a liquidator by the court following the discharge of an administration order.

Revision of administrator's proposals

140 If the administrator's proposals are approved by the creditors he is thereafter required to manage the affairs, business and property of the company in accordance with the proposals as so approved, or as from time to time revised in accordance with the provisions of section 25 of the Insolvency Act.[65] The latter section operates upon the premise that the administrator enjoys a certain latitude in carrying out his duty to implement his proposals, and hence may of his own initiative validly effect such minor and incidental revisions as may prove to be expedient, in his judgment, in the interests of achieving the ultimate purpose for which the proposals were devised. Where, however, the administrator wishes to make revisions of his proposals which he perceives to be of a substantial nature, section 25 renders it obligatory for him to submit his fresh proposals to the same procedure as that whereby the original proposals were approved. He is therefore required to circulate all creditors with a statement in the prescribed form of his proposed revisions, and to lay a copy of the statement before a creditors' meeting summoned for that purpose on not less than 14 days' notice.[66] Only if the proposed revisions are approved by the meeting may the administrator make them and put them into effect. In a case of genuine urgency, where there is no suggestion of overriding the spirit and substance of the terms to which creditors originally gave approval, the court may exercise its residual jurisdiction under section 14(3) to authorise the administrator to implement a modified scheme without obtaining approval from a meeting of creditors.[67] In addition to submitting a statement of his fresh proposals to the creditors, the administrator must either send a copy of the statement to all members of the company of whose addresses he is aware, or publish by advertisement a notice of the fact that such a statement has been prepared, stating an address to which members of the company may write for copies of the statement to be sent to them free of charge.[68]

The conduct of a meeting of creditors convened under section 25 follows the same course as that of a meeting summoned under sections 14, 17 and 23.[69] The creditors, voting on the same basis as at the previous meeting, may by resolution approve the proposed revisions as submitted, or with modifications.[70] In the latter event, however, no modification may be approved unless the administrator assents to it. Once again, the administrator is required to report the outcome of the meeting to the court and to the registrar of companies.[71]

---

[65] I.A., 1986, s.17(2).
[66] *Ibid.*, s.25(1), (2).
[67] *Re Smallman Construction Ltd.* (1988) 4 B.C.C. 784.
[68] *Ibid.*, s.25(3).
[69] *Ibid.*, s.25(5); r. 2.19(1).
[70] *Ibid.*, s.25(4).
[71] *Ibid.*, s.25(6).

Procedure

141 The procedure for convening and conducting meetings of creditors under the Insolvency Act, sections 23 to 25 is laid down in the 1986 Rules. 1986 Rule 2.9 applies the general rules for meetings contained in Rules 7.1 to 7.13, subject to the necessary modifications. These provisions are, in general, subject to variation by the court. The rules are discussed in more detail in relation to winding up (paras. 454 to 458, *post*). What follows summarises the rules in relation to administration.

A creditors' meeting is called for a "business day"[72] between 10 a.m. and 4 p.m. At least 14 days' notice is to be given to creditors and to any directors or other officers (including past directors and officers) whose presence the administrator requires (1986 Rule 2.10(1)). Notice must also be published in the *Edinburgh Gazette* and at least one other suitable newspaper (1986 Rule 7.3(3)). The notice must state its purpose and refer to rights of attendance, voting and the appointment of proxies (including a form of appointment of proxies) (1986 Rule 7.3(4) and (5)). The appointment of proxies and company representatives is dealt with in 1986 Rules 7.14 to 7.20.

Voting is in accordance with the value of unsecured claims as accepted by the administrator as at the date of the administration order. The relevant rules applying in liquidations[73] also apply, with appropriate modifications, in administration procedure (1986 Rule 7.9). Special rules apply to the deduction of the value of rights arising under retention of title clauses and hire-purchase, etc., agreements (1986 Rules 2.11 and 2.12).

The chairman will be the administrator or his (qualified) nominee (1986 Rule 7.5) and the quorum is one creditor (1986 Rule 7.7). Where the quorum is constituted by the chairman alone, or one person in addition to the chairman, and other creditors may be expected to attend, the start of the meeting must be delayed at least 15 minutes (1986 Rule 7.7(3), added in 1987). If there is no quorum the meeting is adjourned one week, but the chairman can increase the period of adjournment up to 21 days or dissolve the meeting (1986 Rule 7.8). If, however, the meeting declines to approve the administrator's proposals (with modifications, if any) the chairman may (and shall if the meeting so resolves) adjourn for up to 14 days (1986 Rule 2.10(2)).

The administrator is required to maintain a sederunt book in which to record the proceedings at meetings, statements of affairs and other important information. This book and its contents must be available for inspection and will (in general) constitute sufficient evidence of the facts recorded (1986 Rule 7.33). The administrator's report of the

---

[72] Any day other than a Saturday, a Sunday, Christmas Day, Good Friday or a day which is a bank holiday in any part of Great Britain (1986 Rule 0.2(1)).
[73] See para. 470, *post*.

meeting to consider his proposals must be recorded in the sederunt book, with the details prescribed (1986 Rules 2.13 and 7.13).

Within 14 days after conclusion of the meeting the administrator must notify the result to creditors (1986 Rule 2.14(1)), to the court and to the registrar of companies (I.A., s.24(4); Form 2.8 (Scot)). If there are no approved proposals the court may discharge the order, or make any other order (including adjournment or interim order) as it thinks fit (I.A., s.24(5)). If the order is discharged, the administrator must forthwith send a certified copy of the court order to the Keeper of the Register of Inhibitions and Adjudications for recording,[74] and within 14 days lodge Form 2.4 (Scot) and a certified copy of the order with the registrar of companies (I.A., s.25(6); 1986 Rule 2.3(4)).

The procedure for approving and notifying "substantial revisions" of proposals already in force, under the Insolvency Act, section 25, is the same, *mutatis mutandis*, as for the approval of the original proposals. Such modifications require the administrator's consent (I.A., s.25(4)).

CREDITORS' COMMITTEE AND PROTECTION OF CREDITORS' AND MEMBERS' INTERESTS

142 The foregoing account of the procedures by which the administrators' proposals are to be approved and, if necessary, revised involves the active participation of the creditors, and the ultimate assent of a majority in value of the unsecured creditors. The close and active involvement of creditors in this, as in other forms of insolvency proceeding, and the maintenance of a steady supply of information about the administrator's conduct in office was seen by the Insolvency Law Review Committee as an important aspect of the revised basis for the operation of insolvency law.[75-76] Although the provisions of the Insolvency Act fall well short of the high ideals expressed in the *Cork Report*, section 26 of the Act makes provision for the creditors to take the initiative of establishing a committee of their number to maintain contact with the administrator and to keep themselves, and the body of the creditors on whose behalf they serve, informed of his progress and intentions. The creditors' decision to establish such a committee may be taken at the meeting convened under section 23 for the purpose of approving the administrator's proposals.[77] The committee may consist of between three and five members, elected by the general meeting on the basis of a vote by value of those present or represented at the meeting. The value of each creditor's vote is taken as the amount of the debt due from the company at the date of the administration order.[78]

---

[74] Form 2.4 (Scot) does not bear to be a form to be sent to the Keeper, although the side-note to 1986 Rule 2.3(4)(*a*) suggests it is to be used.

[75-76] Cmnd. 8558, Chap. 19, especially paras. 930–967.

[77] I.A. 1986, s.26(1).

[78] See para. 141, *supra*. 1986 Rule 2.15 applies to administrations the rules (Rules 3.4 to 3.8) applicable in receiverships with respect to the constitution of the creditors'

The names and addresses of the persons originally elected to serve must be notified by the administrator to the court and to the registrar of companies at the same time as he reports to them upon the result of the creditors' meeting.[79] Subsequent changes in the composition of the committee should be notified as and when they occur.[80] Committee members may resign at any time by notifying the administrator in writing, and may be replaced through co-option by the continuing members of the committee.[81] The minimum number of members with which the committee may continue in being is three.[82] The members of the committee may be paid travelling expenses as agreed by the administrator, such expenses being payable out of the assets of the company.[83]

A creditors' committee established pursuant to the Insolvency Act, section 23 is regulated by the 1986 Rule 2.14. This applies the rules pertaining to the committee of creditors in receivership, which are discussed at paragraph 254 below. The only significant difference in the creditors' committee in administrations from that in receiverships is the definition of its function (1986 Rule 2.15(4)):

> "The creditors' committee shall assist the administrator in discharging his functions and shall act in relation to him in such manner as may be agreed from time to time."

This is in addition to the power to require explanations under the Insolvency Act, section 26(2) and suggests that the administrator may ask for the committee's active assistance, as well as simply provide it with information.

Before an insolvency practitioner is appointed as administrator it is the court's duty to establish that he has the necessary caution, and the creditors' committee, if any, must keep its adequacy under review (1986 Rule 7.28).

143   The creditors' committee has no coercive or directory powers which may be exercised in relation to the administrator. The extent of the powers invested in the committee consists of the right to require the administrator to attend before it at any reasonable time, upon seven days' notice and to furnish it with such information relating to the

---

committee and r. 3.6 in turn applies to both procedures certain of the rules (Rules 4.40 to 4.59A) on the constitution and proceedings of the liquidation committee (in each case with appropriate modifications). These are discussed in more detail in paras. 451 to 458, *post*. The text summarises their application to administrations. On the principles governing the electoral procedure for constituting the committee, see *Re Polly Peck International plc* [1991] B.C.C. 503.

[79] A certificate of due constitution is required: (1986 Rule 4.42(1) to (5), as applied; Forms 4.20 (Scot) and 4.22 (Scot)).
[80] 1986 Rule 4.42(6) (as applied).
[81] 1986 Rules 4.49 and 4.52 (as applied). For termination of membership and removal see 1986 Rules 4.50 and 4.51 (as applied).
[82] 1986 Rule 4.47 (as applied).
[83] 1986 Rule 4.57 (as applied and as amended by r. 3.6(4)).

carrying out of his functions as it may reasonably require.[84] Although this appears to give the creditors' committee a somewhat negligible role, the regular supply of information which the committee should be capable of obtaining from the administrator should enable the general body of creditors to monitor the extent to which the administration order is fulfilling its intended purposes. On the basis of the information which is periodically revealed any creditor may at any time see fit to invoke the intervention of the court under section 27 of the Insolvency Act. This is equally the case if, in his relationship and dealings with the committee, the administrator falls under suspicion of being less than candid about his actions and intentions.

The provisions of section 27 of the Insolvency Act, which is expressed to be for the protection of the interests of creditors and members, are quite widely drawn. Under section 27(1) any creditor or member may at any time petition the court for an order on the ground that the company's affairs, business and property are being or have been managed by the administrator in a manner which is unfairly prejudicial to the interests of its creditors or members generally, or of some part of its creditors or members (including at least the petitioner personally), or that any actual or proposed act or omission of the administrator is or would be so prejudicial. As has been explained above,[85] the court's powers under section 27 are wide ranging, and include the ability by order to issue specific directions to the administrator and to regulate his exercise of his managerial powers for the future.[86] Additionally, the administrator may be required by the court to convene a meeting of creditors or members, and in an extreme case the court could discharge the administration order and make any consequential provisions it thinks fit.[87]

An alternative approach may be adopted by the creditors in a case where their dissatisfaction is attributable to the terms in which the administration order itself is expressed. This entails the use of the power established by section 17(3)(*a*) of the Insolvency Act whereby upon the request of one-tenth in value of the creditors the administrator can be compelled to convene a creditors' meeting. At the meeting a resolution may be moved to the effect that the administrator should apply to the court for an order varying the original administration order by specifying an additional purpose. If such a resolution is duly passed, the provisions of section 18(2)(*b*) oblige the administrator to apply to the court for the making of such an order. The same approach may be adopted where a majority of creditors conclude that the administration order is no longer serving a useful purpose and should be discharged: by means of a suitably worded resolution

---

[84] I.A. 1986, s.26(2) but see also 1986 Rule 2.15(4) discussed above.
[85] See para. 126, *ante.*
[86] I.A. 1986, s.27(4)(*a*), (*b*).
[87] *Ibid.*, s.27(4)(*c*), (*d*).

passed at a creditors' meeting, the administrator may be compelled (in accordance once again with s.18(2)(*b*)) to apply to the court for an order discharging the administration order, as described in the paragraph next following.

Discharge of administration order and release of administrator

144   The administrator may give notice of his intention to resign on Form 2.13 (Scot) on the grounds of ill health or because he intends to cease practice as an insolvency practitioner or because there is some conflict of interest or change of personal circumstances which precludes or makes impracticable the further discharge by him of his duties. The court can allow him to resign on other grounds at its discretion. The notice of resignation, or of his intention to apply to the court for leave to resign, must be given to any continuing joint administrator or, in the absence of a joint administrator continuing in office, to the creditors' committee or, if neither exists, to the company and its creditors (1986 Rule 2.18). In the latter situation, there is no specific provision in the rules for the administrator to avoid giving formal notice to all creditors, but he may be able to obtain the leave of the court under the Insolvency Act, section 14(3) to dispense with this requirement. In the event of the death of an administrator his executors or his professional partners (if any) require to give notice to the court, but any other person may give notice by producing a copy of the death certificate (1986 Rule 2.19). If the court makes an order filling the vacancy in the office of the administrator, the same provisions apply in respect of giving notice of and advertising the appointment as in the case of an original appointment (1986 Rule 2.20). If the administrator intends to apply for the administration order to be discharged under the Insolvency Act, section 18 before he has circulated his proposals to creditors (see para. 138 above) he must, at least 10 days before the application, circulate to creditors a report containing the information which would have been circulated, omitting reference to continuing management and the reasons for approving his proposals (1986 Rule 2.7(2), added in 1987).

Section 18(1) of the Insolvency Act permits the administrator at any time to apply to the court for the administration order to be discharged.[88] While the terms of section 18(1) have the effect of making the timing of such an application a matter for the administrator's personal judgment and discretion, section 18(2) renders it obligatory for him to make an application under the section if either of two alternative circumstances arises. The first of these is if it appears to the administrator that the purpose, or each of the purposes, specified in the order either has been achieved or is incapable of being achieved.[89]

---

[88] s.18(1) of the I.A. 1986 also permits the administrator to apply to the court for an order varying the administration order so as to specify an additional purpose: see para. 106, *ante* and also the concluding paragraph of para. 143, *ante*.
[89] I.A. 1986, s.18(2)(*a*). *Cf. Re Charnley Davies Business Services Ltd.* (1988) P.C.C. 1.

The second, alternative circumstance is if the administrator is required to make the application to the court by a meeting of the company's creditors summoned for the purpose in accordance with the Rules.[90]

The court's powers upon hearing an application under section 18 are as usual very widely drawn: it may by order discharge or vary the administration order and make such consequential provision as it thinks fit, or adjourn the hearing conditionally or unconditionally, or make an interim order or any other order it thinks fit.[91] If the administration order is discharged or varied, the administrator must within 14 days send a certified copy of the order to the registrar of companies. Failure on the part of the administrator to comply with the requirement of sending notice constitutes a criminal offence punishable by fine, unless a reasonable excuse can be shown.[92]

145   If the administration order is discharged the administrator must vacate office.[93] In that event section 19(3) to (5) of the Insolvency Act contains important provisions controlling the manner in which, and the assets from which, the administrator's own fees and expenses, and also any debts or liabilities incurred during the administration, are to be paid. With regard to the administrator's remuneration and his expenses properly incurred,[94] section 19(4) provides that these shall be paid out of, and shall enjoy a first charge against, any property of the company which is in his custody or under his control at the time he ceases to be administrator of the company. Subsection (4) is so drafted as to confer upon the charge thereby created a priority ahead of any security which, as created, was a floating charge. However, any other form of charge or security may still enjoy priority, if suitably expressed. With regard to any sums payable in respect of debts or liabilities incurred during the time when the administration order has been in force, section 19(5) provides that any sums thus incurred under contracts entered into or contracts of employment adopted by the administrator or a predecessor of his in the carrying out of his or the predecessor's functions shall be charged on and paid out of the same property as is available for meeting the administrator's own claim for remuneration and expenses, but in priority to these latter claims. Thus, persons dealing with an administrator during the period of his stewardship of the company's assets and affairs may do so with confidence in the fact that any debts which become due to them from the company enjoy priority ahead of both the administrator's own fees and expenses and the rights of any floating charge holders. In respect

---

[90] *Ibid.*, s.18(2)(*b*). On general provisions relating to the convening of creditors' meetings, and on voting thereat, see paras. 138 and 139, *ante*.
[91] I.A. 1986, s.18(3).
[92] *Ibid.*, s.18(4), (5). (For "certified copy" see s.251.)
[93] *Ibid.*, s.19(2)(*b*).
[94] On the fixing of the administrator's remuneration, and on the expenses properly allowable to him in the performance of his functions, see para. 146 below.

of claims arising under contracts of employment with the company, however, it should be noted that the concluding words of section 19(5) introduce the proviso that the administrator is not to be taken to have adopted a contract of employment by reason of anything done or omitted to be done within 14 days after his appointment.[95]

The release of the administrator following his vacation of office occurs pursuant to the provisions of section 20. Where the vacation of office occurs through the death of the incumbent, his release is effective from the time at which notice is given to the court in accordance with the rules that that person has ceased to hold office.[96] In all other cases, including the most usual case where the administration order itself is discharged, the administrator's release takes effect from such time as the court may determine.[97] This is one of the matters which the court will usually resolve in the course of settling the order discharging the administration order itself, although it could if necessary be held over to enable the administrator's conduct to be properly investigated before his release is made effective. In this context it may be noted that a person who has acted as administrator of a company remains liable, notwithstanding he has obtained his release, to proceedings brought under section 212 of the Insolvency Act to obtain a summary remedy against a person who has misapplied or retained or become accountable for any money or other property of the company, or been guilty of any misfeasance or breach of duty in relation to the company.[98] Apart from this continuing liability to proceedings under section 212, which is expressly preserved by section 20(3), the release of an administrator has the effect of discharging him from that time onwards from all liability in respect of acts or omissions of his in the administration of his duties, and otherwise in relation to his conduct, as administrator.[99]

The court has a discretion to fix a date upon which the administrator's release shall take effect. If there is any suggestion that the administrator has acted improperly in the administration of the company, his release may be postponed to enable the official receiver and the creditors to consider whether any claim may be pursued against him.[1]

The administrator: remuneration, accounting and records

146   The administrator's remuneration, payable from the assets of the company, is agreed with the committee, which failing the court, on the

---

[95] *Cf.* I.A. 1986, s.57(5) (receivers) discussed in para. 240, *post.*
[96] I.A. 1986, s.20(1). On the filling of a vacancy caused by the death of an administrator, see s.13(2) of the Act, discussed in para. 125, *ante.* On the giving of notice to the court following the death of an administrator, see para. 144, *ante.*
[97] I.A. 1986, s.20(1).
[98] On the further aspects of liability imposed by s.212 of the I.A., see para. 524, *post.*
[99] I.A. 1986, s.20(2).
[1] *Re Sheridan Securities Ltd.* (1988) 4 B.C.C. 200.

basis of the amount of work undertaken and the value of the company's assets. The rules applicable to the remuneration of a liquidator and payment of his outlays (1986 Rules 4.32 to 4.34) are applied to administrators, but without the right conferred by 1986 Rule 4.35 on 25 per cent. of the creditors to question the majority decision.[2] Application can be made to the court to resolve any dispute.[3]

The administrator is required to submit half-yearly accounts on Form 2.9 (Scot) to the court, the registrar of companies and the creditors' committee (if any), within two months of each period or such longer period as the court may allow (1986 Rule 2.17; R.C.S. 211(2); Sh.Ct.R. 12(2)).

The administrator must maintain a sederunt book and leave it open for inspection, recording meetings, statements of affairs, etc. (1986 Rule 7.33). He must (subject to any claim of confidentiality) make documents and particulars of creditors available for inspection (1986 Rules 7.26 and 7.27). There are presumptions in favour of the validity of proceedings and any defects may be cured by order of court (1986 Rules 7.23–7.25, 7.32 and 7.33(4)).

The rules relating to the issue of a certificate of insolvency for the purposes of VAT bad debt relief which apply to an administrative receiver also apply to administrators with the appropriate modifications (1986 Rules 3.12 to 3.14 as applied by Rule 2.21).[4]

---

[2] See further para. 448, *post*.
[3] *Sonido International Ltd.*, 1991 S.C.L.R. 874.
[4] See para. 260, *post*.

CHAPTER 2

FLOATING CHARGES AND RECEIVERS

INTRODUCTION

201 Until 1961 Scots law did not recognise any form of security right other than a "fixed security" which specified the property over which the creditor's security right subsisted. The creditor had to complete his real right to that property by the appropriate method, and the company was unable to deal with the property without the consent of the creditor. This put Scottish companies at a disadvantage as compared to companies in England, where the concept of the "floating charge" was well established. As noted below, the concept of the "floating charge" was introduced into Scots law in 1961. After a brief period during which the holder of such a charge could only enforce his security by petitioning for winding up the debtor company, in 1972 Scots law also borrowed from England the concept of a receiver appointed by the holder of a floating charge to realise his security. The powers and duties of a receiver in Scotland have, therefore, to be understood in the context of the floating charge and its legal effect, which are examined in the first part of this chapter.

Strictly speaking, the appointment of a receiver and the exercise by him of his powers to realise the assets of the company is the enforcement by a creditor of his security rights, and is not necessarily (if at all) the reconstruction, "rescue" or winding up of a company which has become insolvent. In practice, however, the possibility of a receiver being appointed in respect of a company which is solvent is theoretical and exceptional, and may never have actually occurred. As a rule, the company will be insolvent and for that reason the Insolvency Act 1986 requires that an "administrative receiver" must be an authorised "Insolvency Practitioner."[1] Also, the powers and duties of a receiver and the rules for conducting the receivership are closely based upon the rules applicable to winding up and administration. For practical reasons therefore it is appropriate to consider receivership as part of the law and practice of corporate insolvency.

THE FLOATING CHARGE

202 The practical limitations of fixed securities make them of limited value to commercial borrowers, who require to retain freedom to deal with their assets. In many companies the need for credit, and the capacity to raise finance, is greater than the security value of fixed tangible assets.

---

[1] The significance of these terms is discussed in paras. 219 and 440 respectively.

English law solved the problem by the concept of a "floating charge" which "crystallises" as a fixed charge only on the happening of a certain event, such as the commencement of winding up or the appointment of a receiver. Prior to such event the company is able to sell and acquire assets which are accordingly removed from or brought within the scope of the security right potentially arising on crystallisation. This flexible device was repugnant to Scots law and so not available to Scottish companies nor would the Scottish courts give effect to English (or other) floating charges over Scottish property.[2]

The Companies (Floating Charges) (Scotland) Act 1961[3] made two innovations vital to the development of Scottish commerce. It permitted Scottish companies to grant floating charges and it created a system (modelled on English law) for registration of fixed and floating charges in the public file kept by the registrar of companies. The 1961 Act had two major defects. It prescribed a form of floating charge which was difficult to apply in practice. More significantly, it failed to grant a satisfactory means for enforcement of the creditor's rights. The creditor could only enforce his security by petitioning for winding up, although in addition to the normal grounds he was given the right to petition on the basis that his security was "in jeopardy" (as defined). Such action would involve additional expense as well as actual prejudice to the creditor, since the value of the company as a going concern would be lost.

Both these defects were removed by the Companies (Floating Charges and Receivers) (Scotland) Act 1972.[4] The appointment of receivers is discussed below. The 1972 provisions (as subsequently amended) on the granting of floating charges now appear as sections 462 to 466 and those on registration of charges as sections 410 to 424. While criticism of the legislation continues, only minor amendments were made by the Insolvency Acts 1985 and 1986. The Scottish Law Commission has proposed reforms in the law relating to floating charges and receivers[5] and proposals for a wider review of the law of security over moveables in both Scotland and England have also been published by the DTI[6] but these have not resulted in legislation, except the provisions of Part IV of the Companies Act 1989 relating to the registration of charges (which as at December 31, 1992 are not yet in force[7] and, accordingly, are not referred to in this section).

---

[2] *Carse* v. *Coppin*, 1951 S.L.T. 145; *Re Anchor Line (Henderson Bros.) Ltd.* [1937] Ch. 483.
[3] Effective October 27, 1961.
[4] Effective November 17, 1972 and referred to in this section as "the 1972 Act." The 1972 Act repealed the 1961 Act except for s.7(*b*), (*c*) and (*d*); s.7(*d*) was repealed by the Companies Act 1980 and s.7(*b*) and (*c*) by the Companies Consolidation (Consequential Provisions) Act 1985.
[5] Consultative Memorandum No. 72 "Floating Charges and Receivers" (October 1986).
[6] Professor Aubrey Diamond, "A Review of Security Interest in Property" (HMSO, 1989).
[7] The estimated commencement date for Pt. IV is not before Spring 1993. Part IV is discussed in *Palmer*, paras. 13.401 *et seq.*

Recognition of floating charges

203 The 1961 Act (now s.462(1)) declared it to be competent under Scots law for an incorporated company (whether a company within the meaning of the Companies Act or not) to grant a floating charge. Effect will thus be given to floating charges by companies incorporated by private Act or royal charter, or under any of the older Companies Acts and their predecessors, and likewise such charges granted by companies incorporated in other parts of Great Britain and by foreign companies.

The recognition in Scotland of a floating charge by a foreign company does not depend on either the company itself or the charge in question being registrable here under section 691 or 424, both of which apply only if the company has a place of business in Great Britain (s.691) or Scotland (s.424). It is necessary only that the company is "incorporated," *i.e.* is accorded separate status as a legal person in its local legal system and that the charge is seen to be of the nature of a "floating charge." Neither condition is precisely defined.

The effect of the 1961 Act was to recognise a floating charge by a non-Scottish company over Scottish assets even if the charge had been created before the Act came into force (October 27, 1961), subject to any requirement with respect to registration.[8] So far as Scottish companies were concerned, however, the 1961 Act did not retrospectively validate "floating charges" granted before that date. The 1972 Act (s.30(2)) did grant retrospective validity to any purported floating charge subsisting on November 17, 1972 which would have been valid if created on or after that date. This was intended to cure defects of form in charges granted under the 1961 Act but could also be read as validating even pre-1961 Act Scottish floating charges, in the event of any being in existence.

Form of floating charge

204 A floating charge may secure any debt or other obligation including a cautionary obligation (guarantee), incurred or to be incurred by the company or any other person (s.462(1)). It may therefore be used to secure an obligation *ad factum praestandum* (*i.e.* to perform a specific non-monetary obligation).

The charge may "float" over all or any part of the property which may from time to time be comprised in the company's property and undertaking, including uncalled capital (s.462(1)); the reference to uncalled capital was added in 1972. Uncalled capital, which has been constituted a reserve liability under section 120 or 124, may not be capable of being charged.[9] Heritable property may be subject to a floating charge, notwithstanding that the instrument is not recorded in

---

[8] See *Palmer*, para. 13.415.
[9] See *Palmer*, para. 4.007.

the Register of Sasines or Land Register (s.462(5)). There is no restriction on the acquisition or disposal of property by the company while the charge floats, unless imposed by the terms of the loan agreement. The company could, for example, dispose of property by way of gift. Accordingly, a creditor taking a floating charge generally has to impose terms restraining the company from disposing of at least major parts of its undertaking or incurring substantial capital commitments without the creditor's consent and may also insist on board representation to protect the creditor's interests further.

The charge holder could seek to interdict a disposal in breach of his loan agreement, but neither he nor a receiver appointed by him has *locus* to reduce a gratuitous alienation until the commencement of winding up (I.A. 1986, s.242). Accordingly, if the charge holder finds that the company is acting to his prejudice, his only effective remedy may be to petition for its winding up.

The 1961 Act (s.2 and First Schedule) laid down a form of words for a floating charge which proved cumbersome in practice. The 1972 Act (s.2) (now s.462) abandoned the 1961 form and required merely the execution of an instrument or bond or other written acknowledgment of debt or obligation which purports to create a floating charge. This may be in the same instrument as the bond, or a separate document. The instrument will define the property comprised within the charge as circumstances require. Although it is possible to charge a restricted class of assets, in practice most floating charges are "all assets" charges, using the form of words in s.462(1).

The abandonment of a statutory form of floating charge raises the question of whether the particular words employed are sufficient to constitute a floating charge. In English law the words "floating charge" need not appear so long as there is a charge over a class of assets of the company which the company is free to release from or bring within the charge until crystallisation.[10] This interpretation is equally valid in Scotland, whether in relation to a floating charge by a Scottish company or one created in England or overseas.

205   In its original form, the Act (s.462(2)) required a floating charge to be executed under seal, *i.e.* sealed with the common seal of the company and signed by two directors or one director and the secretary, pursuant to section 36(3) (as it stood before amendment by the Companies Act 1989, s.130). The manner of execution of documents by companies under Scots law was, however, amended by the Companies Act 1989, s.130(3) (and Sched. 17), and later further amended by the Law Reform (Miscellaneous Provisions) (Scotland) Act 1990, s.72 (and Sched. 8).[11] These amendments affect the execution of a floating charge by a Scottish company on or after July 31, 1990 (when section 130(3) of the

---

[10] *Re Yorkshire Woolcombers Association Ltd.* [1903] 2 Ch. 284, 295. See *Palmer*, para. 13.122.
[11] See further *Palmer*, paras. 3.201 *et seq.*

1989 Act became effective). From that date until December 1, 1990 (when section 72 of the 1990 Act became effective) a floating charge had to be executed by signature at the end of the last page[12] by a director or by the secretary, or by a person bearing to have been authorised to sign the document on the company's behalf[13] and also bearing to have been signed by a person as witness[14] to that subscription or (if there is no witness) bearing to have been sealed with the common seal of the company.[15] The effect of the 1990 Act is, first, to abolish that method of execution as from and after December 1, 1990[16] and, secondly, to replace it with a revised code which took effect retrospectively in respect of any floating charge executed on or after July 31, 1990, but preserving the validity of a charge executed under the superseded provisions.[17] A charge which was deficient in form under the 1989 Act is, therefore, valid if it complies with the 1990 Act. The provisions now in force[18] make no reference to the manner of execution of a floating charge, nor do they contain an express requirement that it be in writing. Under Scots law, however, an obligation for payment of money must be "probative," and any floating charge which contains such an obligation must be executed accordingly, *i.e.* by two officers or two authorised persons under section 36B(3) of the 1985 Act (as amended) or by one authorised person before two witnesses.[19] Scots law also requires that an obligation granting security, or a cautionary obligation, be proved by writing, although probative writing is not required.[20] If the floating charge does not contain an obligation for payment, therefore, it may be executed by a single director, secretary or authorised person under section 36B(2), without witnesses.[21]

Crystallisation of floating charges

206 Until the commencement of winding up (s.463(1) and (2)) or the appointment of a receiver (Insolvency Act 1986, ss.53(7) and 54(6)) the company is free (unless the terms of its agreement with the charge holder provide otherwise) to dispose of property which is the subject of a floating charge, and to acquire property which may become subject to the charge. On the occurrence of such an event, however, the charge

---

[12] The problems created by these phrases are discussed in *Palmer*, paras. 3.201 *et seq.*
[13] *Ibid.*
[14] *Ibid.*
[15] Companies Act 1985, s.36B (inserted by the Companies Act 1989, s.130(3)) and s.464(2) and (3) of the 1985 Act as amended by Sched. 17, para. 8 to the 1989 Act.
[16] Law Reform (Miscellaneous Provisions) (Scotland) Act 1990, Sched. 9.
[17] Companies Act 1985, s.36B(1) (as inserted by the Law Reform (Miscellaneous Provisions) (Scotland) Act 1990, s.71(1)) and s.72(2) and (3) of the 1990 Act.
[18] Companies Act 1985, s.462 as amended by Sched. 8, para. 33(6) to the 1990 Act. The Companies Act 1985, s.462(3) was repealed by the 1989 Act, and s.462(2) as amended by the 1989 Act was repealed by the 1990 Act.
[19] See *Palmer*, paras. 3.201 *et seq.*, and Walker, *Principles of Scottish Private Law* (3rd ed.), Vol. II, Chap. 4.4.
[20] Walker, *op. cit.*, Vol. II, Chap. 4.4.
[21] See further *Palmer*, para. 3.202.

attaches to the charged property then comprised in the company's property and undertaking as if it were a fixed security for the debt or obligation to which it relates. This is referred to (though it is not a term defined or used by the Act) as "crystallisation." It is, of course, subject to the charge being duly registered (s.410) and not open to challenge (Insolvency Act 1986, s.245, replacing s.617). These conditions were explicitly mentioned in the 1961 and 1972 Acts, their omission from section 463 on consolidation implying that they are self-evident. Crystallisation cannot occur except on either of the events specified. Neither the approval of a voluntary arrangement nor the appointment of an administrator under the Insolvency Act 1986, Parts I and II causes crystallisation. Section 463(1) gives rise to a problem if a company (not already in voluntary liquidation) is the subject of a petition for winding up by the court. In that case, if the court grants a winding-up order, the winding up commences on the date the petition was presented.[22] If, however, the winding-up order is delayed neither the company nor the charge holder knows whether the charge will (retrospectively) be treated as having crystallised and uncertainty arises with respect to any transactions in the meantime.[23]

The commencement of winding up does not terminate the right of the holder to interest at the rate stipulated in the charge.[24]

In *Ross* v. *Taylor*[25] a receiver was appointed by the holder of a charge "over the whole of the property (including uncalled capital) which is or may be while this instrument is in force comprised in (the company's) property and undertaking." While in office he carried on the business of the company in a manner duly authorised by his powers and, in effect, repurchased on credit terms certain stock which the company had sold shortly before his appointment.[26] He then sold this stock, inmixed with other goods, for the benefit of the charge holder. Subsequently, a liquidator was appointed by the court, who challenged the actings of the receiver, in the event on two grounds (1) that the stock not having been part of the company's "property and undertaking" at the time of the receiver's appointment, it was not attached by crystallisation of the charge on that date, and (2) that the

---

[22] Insolvency Act 1986, s.129(2); see further para. 433, *post*.

[23] To cure this, the Companies Act 1989, s.140(1) (which is, as at December 31, 1992, not yet in force) will substitute "Where a company goes into liquidation within the meaning of s.247(2) of the Insolvency Act 1986," for "On the commencement of the winding up of a company." This has the effect of postponing crystallisation in these circumstances to the date of the winding-up order.

[24] s.463(4). This originally appeared as s.1(4) of the 1972 Act where it was prefaced by the words "for the avoidance of doubt," and confirms the decisions in *National Commercial Bank of Scotland Ltd.* v. *Liquidator of Telford Grier Mackay & Co. Ltd.*, 1969 S.C. 181; 1969 S.L.T. 306 and *Royal Bank of Scotland* v. *Williamsons*, 1972 S.L.T. (Sh.Ct.) 45.

[25] 1985 S.L.T. 387.

[26] He did so by persuading the seller, a loan creditor, that his title to the goods was potentially (*i.e.* on liquidation) challengeable as a "fraudulent preference." It was never determined that the receiver's argument was correct, and the reference to this aspect in the case before the court was, rightly, regarded as irrelevant.

holder of a charge who appoints a receiver loses the benefit of crystallisation on the later appointment of a liquidator in respect of any assets not already attached on the "first" crystallisation. Both arguments were rejected, but both the case stated and the court's opinion do nothing to clarify, and much to confuse, understanding of the effect of "crystallisation."

The court began by pointing out that what was attached on crystallisation depends on the terms of the charging instrument. Decisions (in practice English) which turn on the use of particular and different terminology in debenture deeds are of no assistance.[27] The difficulties which followed, however, arose from the court's analysis of the relationship between such terms and the statutory provisions of what are now section 463, and sections 53(7) and 54(6) of the Insolvency Act 1986.

The court held that the charge crystallised twice, once on the appointment of the receiver, and again on the appointment of the liquidator.

207 The concept of double crystallisation was introduced by the court to dispose of the liquidator's second argument. This was unnecessary for the decision, since the court had already held that the stock repurchased by the receiver fell within the scope of the charge, and there was no need to suggest that it, or the proceeds of sale, were "attached" for the benefit of the charge holder on the appointment of the liquidator. As has been pointed out[28] the effect of a double attachment might be to give preferential creditors under section 175(2) of the Insolvency Act 1986[29] an unintended additional ranking on the second attachment. The court's reason for holding that a second attachment occurs on liquidation derives from the wording of section 1(2) of the 1972 Act which provided that a floating charge "*shall*, on the commencement of the winding up ... *attach* to the property *then* comprised in the company's property and undertaking etc." On consolidation this terminology has been altered and section 463(1) provides that "On the commencement of the winding up of a company, a floating charge created by the company *attaches* to the property *then* comprised in the company's property and undertaking, etc."[30] The current statute is, therefore, less emphatic than its predecessor but it would seem that the change would not have deterred the court from holding that a second attachment could occur. This, however, ignores the effect of the Insolvency Act 1986, sections 53(7) and 54(6), both of which provide that on the appointment of a

---

[27] See also *National Commercial Bank of Scotland Ltd.* v. *Liquidator of Telford Grier Mackay & Co. Ltd.*, 1969 S.C. 1981, *per* Lord Fraser at p. 184; 1969 S.L.T. 306, 308.

[28] D. P. Sellar, "Future assets and double attachment," 1985 J.L.S. 242.

[29] Formerly s.614(2).

[30] The amendment to s.463(1) proposed by the 1989 Act (see n. 23, *supra*) does not affect this argument in principle.

receiver the charge "*attaches* to the property *then* subject to the charge." Again there is a change from the terminology of the 1972 Act which provided (ss.13(7) and 14(7)) that on the appointment the charge "*shall attach* to the property *then* subject to the charge," but this does not appear to alter the underlying sense. Section 463(3) (as amended by the Insolvency Act 1986)[31] provides, however, that nothing in section 463 "derogates from the provisions of sections 53(7) and 54(6) of the Insolvency Act 1986." This must mean that if either section has taken effect, attachment has occurred and does not recur.

The court's main reason for rejecting the liquidator's first contention, and finding that goods acquired by the company while the receiver was in office fell within the charge, was the terms of the charge (quoted above). As the charge was stated to subsist over any property of the company from time to time while the instrument of charge remained in force anything becoming part of such property during the receiver's appointment was "attached." A floating charge couched in the normal terms of the instrument under consideration would therefore charge "future assets" acquired at any time up to (at least in the court's view) commencement of liquidation. This approach was taken to avoid the apparent meaning of the statute (ss.13(7) or 14(7) of the 1972 Act, ss. 53(7) and 54(6) of the 1986 Act) that on the appointment of a receiver the charge shall attach to the property "then subject to the charge." At first sight, and as the liquidator argued, only property of the company in its hands at the time of appointment could be so attached. If, however, the property "then subject to the charge" included, by virtue of the charging instrument, property to be acquired later, such property had to be regarded as "then" attached. Since the charge in this case simply adopted the terminology of section 462(1) (and its predecessor), adding only the redundant "while this instrument is in force," the court's reasoning must be applicable to all floating charges.

The court's argument has, however, a strong air of artificiality. It would appear that even if the company acquired "future assets" by way of gift they would still be attached. It is difficult to see how, in the world of commercial reality for which floating charges are intended, the possibility of acquiring a future asset could be said to be part of the company's property and undertaking at the time a receiver is appointed, for there is no doubt that only such rights as the company then has can be "attached." All the relevant statutory provisions (ss.13(7) and 14(7) of the 1972 Act, ss.53(7) and 54(6) of the Insolvency Act 1986) clearly state that on that event there is deemed to be a fixed security over "the property to which (the charge) *has attached.*"

The court's approach creates a difficulty on the commencement of winding up. Evidently, on that event, the power of the charge to attach

---

[31] s.1(3) of the 1972 Act is in similar terms.

"future assets" ceases because the Act (s.463(1), s.1(2) of the 1972 Act) then provides for crystallisation of the charge on all property "then comprised in the company's property and undertaking." It seems to be implicit in the court's analysis that while crystallisation under sections 53(7) and 54(6) of the 1986 Act would permit "future assets" to be attached if the charge appeared to cover them, this would not be possible under section 463(1) since the latter makes no reference to the terms of the charging instrument. On the other hand, sections 53(7) and 54(6) of the 1986 Act are saved from the effect of section 463 by section 463(3) as amended by the 1986 Act.[32] If a floating charge crystallises on liquidation, the holder is not to be prejudiced by losing the possibility of applying "future assets" towards his debt. Not only can there be only one crystallisation, but it must have the same effect whether on the appointment of a receiver or on liquidation.

208   In *Ross* v. *Taylor* the court was confronted with a stated case for its opinion on issues which should not have arisen. The goods which the receiver acquired were the result of his exercising his powers under section 15(1) of the 1972 Act (now s.55 of and Sched. 2 to the Insolvency Act 1986) which include power to carry on the company's business. It was unnecessary and irrelevant to consider whether stock-in-trade bought in under such powers was "attached" by the charge. The purchase and subsequent sale of such stock by the receiver was simply a transaction in normal course of business which should not have been questioned on the grounds raised in the case. Admittedly, the receiver did not pay for the goods but succeeded in getting them on credit by threatening the seller with proceedings to impugn his title to them.[33] Whether he was justified in doing so, or alternatively had incurred personal liability for the price under section 17 of the 1972 Act (s.57 of the Insolvency Act 1986) was a question not before the court.

Property excluded from the charge

209 The security obtained on crystallisation of a floating charge is postponed to the rights of any person who:

(a) has effectually executed diligence[34] on the property, or
(b) holds a fixed security or floating charge having a prior ranking (s.463(1)). Rules for ranking of floating charges are contained in section 464 (see paras. 212 *et seq.*, below).

The right of a receiver to intromit with assets which are the subject of inchoate diligence is irrelevant if the assets have been removed from

---

[32] The equivalent sections of the 1972 Act are of like effect.
[33] See n. 26, *ante*.
[34] As to the meaning of this phrase see *Lord Advocate* v. *Royal Bank of Scotland*, 1976 S.L.T. 130; 1978 S.L.T. 38; 1977 S.C. 155; *Taymech Ltd.* v. *Rush & Tompkins Ltd.*, 1990 S.L.T. 681 and paras. 237, 238, 499 and 500, *post*.

the ambit of the charge prior to crystallisation. In *Hawking* v. *Hafton House Ltd.*,[35] prior to the receiver's appointment, when the charge crystallised, a sum had been consigned with the Clerk of Court to await settlement of an action, and arrestments on the dependence were recalled. It was held that the receiver had no claim on the funds, because consignation with the court effectively removed the assets from the property of the consignor (*i.e.* the company).

If, however, the inchoate diligence was executed before the creation of the floating charge, the rights of the charge holder and the receiver are subject to those of the person doing diligence.[36]

Identifiable goods which are subject to a clause reserving title to the seller until the price has been paid or other conditions for the transfer of title to the purchaser have been satisfied remain the property of the seller and are thus excluded from any floating charge granted by the purchaser.[37] Assets which are the subject of a validly constituted trust by the company are also excluded.[38]

Enforcement of a floating charge

210 Prior to the 1972 Act, the only method whereby the holder of a floating charge could enforce his security was to obtain a winding-up order. The 1972 Act provided the additional remedy of appointing a receiver (s.11 of 1972, now s.51 of the I.A. 1986). If the company goes into liquidation, however, the holder of a floating charge will enforce his rights by lodging a claim with the liquidator[39] unless a receiver is appointed by him or by the court on his application.

Extension of power to wind up

211 The circumstances in which the court has power to wind up a company are extended for the advantage of a creditor entitled to the benefit of a floating charge (I.A. 1986, ss.122(2) and 221(7) (unregistered companies)). The court must be satisfied that the creditor's security is in jeopardy. The security is deemed to be in jeopardy if the court is satisfied that events have occurred, or are about to occur, which render

---

[35] 1990 S.L.T. 497.
[36] *Iona Hotels Ltd.*, 1991 S.L.T. 11; 1990 S.C.L.R. 614. In *Iona Hotels* the Lord President seems to place emphasis on registration of the charge as the effective step; with respect, this must be incorrect. Diligence prohibits a subsequent voluntary act by the debtor, which is why it prevails against a subsequent floating charge. It is the granting of the charge which is relevant, so that an arrestment (or inhibition) laid after the creation of the charge but before its registration must be ineffective against the receiver.
[37] *Armour* v. *Thyssen Edelstahlwerke A.G.*, 1990 S.L.T. 891 (H.L.); [1990] 3 All E.R. 481 (H.L.). See further *Palmer*, para. 13.212 (13.403A in later editions).
[38] *Tay Valley Joinery Ltd.* v. *C.F. Financial Services Ltd.*, 1987 S.L.T. 207; *Allan's Trs.* v. *Lord Advocate*, 1971 S.C.(H.L.) 45; 1971 S.L.T. 62; *Clark Taylor & Co. Ltd.* v. *Quality Site Development (Edinburgh) Ltd.*, 1981 S.C. 111; 1981 S.L.T. 308.
[39] *National Commercial Bank of Scotland Ltd.* v. *Liquidator of Telford Grier Mackay & Co. Ltd.*, *supra*; *Libertas-Kommerz GmbH*, 1978 S.L.T. 222, 225.

it unreasonable in the interests of the creditor that the company should retain power to dispose of the property which is subject to the floating charge.[40] The holder of a floating charge may, of course, also rely on the grounds available generally in seeking a winding-up order.

Ranking of floating and other charges

212 The provisions of the 1961 Act (s.5) regulating the ranking of floating and other charges were substantially amended by the 1972 Act (s.5, now s.464). The rules are now as follows (subject always to the priorities preserved by section 463(1), above):

1. A fixed security arising by operation of law ranks in priority to a floating charge, and it is not competent to provide otherwise (s.464(1) and (2));
2. Subject to rule (1), the instrument creating the floating charge, or any instrument of alteration under section 466 (*infra*), but not, apparently, any collateral deed such as the bond or acknowledgment of the debt secured, may contain provisions—
    (a) restricting or prohibiting the creation of fixed or floating charges ranking prior to or *pari passu* with the charge or
    (b) regulating the order in which the floating charge shall rank with any other subsisting or future fixed or floating charges (s.464(1))[41]; and
3. In the absence of any conventional ranking clause under rule (2), a fixed security which has been constituted a real right before crystallisation of a floating charge has priority over the floating charge; floating charges rank *inter se* in order of registration with the registrar of companies, charges received by the same postal delivery ranking equally (s.464(4)).[42]

These rules also apply to an instrument of alteration (s.466(3)).

It is normal practice for a floating charge to prohibit the subsequent creation of prior or *pari passu* fixed securities, thus applying rule (2)(*a*) above. The presence of such a provision is one of the "prescribed particulars" which have to be supplied for registration under section 410. If, however, the registered particulars are incorrect the rules as to ranking are not affected. The holder of the floating charge has, therefore, an interest to ensure that the form presented for registration (and the particulars transferred to the official register of charges by the registrar's officials) correctly put any subsequent creditor on notice as

---

[40] See para. 418, *post*.
[41] The Companies Act 1989, s.140(2)–(5) which is not yet (December 31, 1992) in force proposes to amend these rules as follows: (i) to make it clear that a ranking agreement under rule 2(b) requires the consent of the holders of securities adversely affected by it; (ii) a provision such as described in rule 2(a) will be effective to grant priority to the floating charge; and (iii) to make it clear that the statutory rules apply except to the extent that they are effectively replaced by a valid ranking agreement.
[42] See n. 41, *supra*.

to the ranking rules. A creditor taking a subsequent security would also be unwise to rely solely on the absence of any reference on the register to a ranking clause under rule (2), but should inspect the instrument of charge to ascertain the correct position.

An agreement providing for the ranking of charges proceeds on the assumption that the charges are valid. If one ceases to be valid, *e.g.* by want of registration, its conventional ranking is also lost.[43]

Restriction of security

213 The holder of a floating charge having a postponed ranking may restrict the preference of a prior ranking floating charge by giving written intimation of the registration of his charge to the holder of the prior charge (s.464(5)). "Holder" is not defined, and this may create difficulty in the event of an assignation of the creditor's interests. In that event the register of charges maintained by the registrar of companies will show the "holder" to be the original creditor, but the register to be maintained by the company should disclose the true position.[44] Thus, a creditor giving notice under section 464(5) should inspect the company's own register of charges to ascertain the identity of the true "holder" of the existing charge. Nevertheless the Act makes no reference to assignation of floating charges and it is open to debate whether section 464(5) is intended to refer to the original holder or to the assignee. Logic suggests the latter, but prudence may suggest intimation to both.

On receipt of such intimation, the preference in ranking of the prior floating charge is restricted to present advances, future advances the holder is required to make in terms of the instrument creating the charge or any "ancillary document," interest due or to become due on all such advances and any expenses which the holder may reasonably incur (s.464(5)). It appears that this restriction applies generally, and not merely in a question with the holder of the postponed charge. "Ancillary document" is defined (s.486(1)) as a document relating to the floating charge executed by debtor or creditor therein prior to registration of the charge with the registrar of companies, or an instrument of alteration under section 466.

The Act makes no provision for charges granted to secure other forms of liability than an existing debt or future advances. An amendment in the Companies Act 1989, section 140(6), which is not yet (December 31, 1992) in force, will provide that, where the liability is contingent, other than a liability in respect of future advances, the full value of the contingent liability remains secured.

[43] *Bank of Scotland* v. *T.A. Neilson & Co.*, 1991 S.L.T. 8.
[44] See *Libertas-Kommerz GmbH*, 1978 S.L.T. 222, 224.

Alteration of charges

214 There was no express provision for the alteration of floating charges in the 1961 Act. The 1972 Act (s.7, now s.466) introduced provisions for the execution and registration of an "instrument of alteration."[45]

The instrument of alteration may alter "the instrument creating a floating charge under section 462" or any "ancillary document" (s.466(1)).[46] Reference in any enactment to a floating charge, unless the context otherwise requires, includes the charge as altered by instrument of alteration (s.466(6)).

The instrument of alteration must be executed by the company, the holder of the charge and the holder of any charge (fixed or floating) which would be adversely affected by the alteration (s.466(1)). As with floating charges themselves, the manner of execution of an instrument of alteration by the company has changed from the original provisions of the 1985 Act through two codes imposed successively by the Companies Act 1989 and the Law Reform (Miscellaneous Provisions) (Scotland) Act 1990.[47] Originally, section 466(2)(*a*) required the company to execute under seal (with two directors or one director and the secretary) or by its duly authorised attorney, but section 466(2)(*d*) also permitted execution by any manner provided for in the charge itself. These provisions ceased to have effect on July 31, 1990 by virtue of the Companies Act 1989[48] which also substituted the provisions for the execution of documents by companies enacted by section 130 of the 1989 Act. The signature of a single director, secretary or authorised person was effective, but if the instrument had to be "probative" it was intended that the addition of a single witness, or the company seal, would be effective. The Law Reform (Miscellaneous Provisions) (Scotland) Act 1990, section 72 repealed the 1989 Act rules with effect from December 1, 1990 and replaced them with a new code, although a single authorised signature remains sufficient if the instrument does not require to be probative. If it does, however, (and this will be normal, since a probative instrument of charge can, in principle, only be altered by an instrument which is also probative) the signature of two directors, one director and the secretary, or two authorised persons (without seal or witness) will be required, although it is competent for execution to be by a single authorised person with two witnesses. These 1990 provisions are retrospective to July 31, 1990.[49]

---

[45] For registration of instruments of alteration see *Palmer*, paras. 13.410 and 13.411. It appears that failure to register does not affect the validity of the instrument, unless it increases the sum secured.

[46] The 1972 Act, s.7 provided for instruments of alteration in relation to floating charges created under "section 2 of this Act," which created doubt over the competence of altering a charge created under the 1961 Act. This doubt does not arise under the wording of s.466.

[47] See para. 205, *ante.*

[48] Sched. 17, para. 9.

[49] See *Palmer*, paras. 3.201 *et seq.* for a full discussion of these matters.

The Act (s.466(2) as amended) also makes provision for the execution of the instrument by or on behalf of debenture holders. If trustees are acting for debenture holders the trustees execute the instrument. If no trustees are acting the instrument may be validly executed on behalf of a series of debenture holders by a specified proportion of them.

Floating charges as fraudulent preferences

215 At common law a preference would be challenged as fraudulent if the grantor was insolvent at the time it was created, no matter how great the interval between its creation and the challenge. Under section 322 of the 1948 Act a floating charge could only be challenged if created within 12 months prior to the commencement of the winding up. This provision only applied to England. The 1961 Act extended it to Scotland without making it clear that it was to supplant the common law rule. The 1972 Act (s.8) sought to remove all grounds for such a challenge other than section 322.

Section 245 of the Insolvency Act 1986 now provides that floating charges granted within 12 months (two years if in favour of a "connected person") before commencement of winding up or administration may be challenged or restricted on grounds of insolvency. In addition, a floating charge may be challenged as a gratuitous alienation (at common law or under the Insolvency Act 1986, s.242), as an unfair preference (under the Insolvency Act 1986, s.243), as a fraudulent preference at common law or as an extortionate credit transaction (under the Insolvency Act 1986, s.244).[50]

Validation of doubtful provisions in floating charges created prior to the 1972 Act

216 Section 465 retrospectively validates *ab initio* certain provisions in floating charges created prior to, and subsisting on, November 17, 1972, which might otherwise have been open to challenge. These are:

1. floating charges which might have been invalid because they were not in the form prescribed in the First Schedule to the 1961 Act (s.465(1)); and
2. ranking clauses contained in an instrument of charge or ancillary document (s.465(2)).

The document in question must have been executed prior to, and the charge must still be subsisting on, November 17, 1972. The floating charge or ranking clause must be such as would have been valid if created under the 1972 Act. These provisions do not in terms refer to charges created under the 1961 Act but to floating charges purporting to subsist at the commencement of the 1972 Act. *Quaere* whether this

---

[50] See further paras. 513 to 516, *post*.

might validate a purported floating charge created *before* the commencement of the 1961 Act.

Change of creditor

217 In Scots law it is always open to the creditor in a security right to assign his interest. Neither the 1961 Act nor the 1972 Act mentioned the assignation of the benefit of a floating charge, but it has been established that a floating charge is assignable by the creditor. The assignation must be intimated to the company in writing. The company must enter the change of creditor in its own register of charges, even though there is no provision for recording a change of creditor in the register of charges kept by the registrar of companies.[51]

It is not possible to assign the debtor's interest in a floating charge since by its nature it is a security created by a particular company and does not attach to any specific property until crystallisation.

RECEIVERS

Appointment

218 The Companies (Floating Charges and Receivers) (Scotland) Act 1972 introduced, as from November 17, 1972, the facility of appointing a receiver of property belonging to a Scottish company. The office of receiver in Scotland is, however, different in many respects from its English counterpart and precedents of English law on the subject must be treated with caution. The principal differences are as follows:

(a) only the "holder" of a floating charge may appoint or secure the appointment of a receiver;

(b) while it is possible for the instrument creating the floating charge to add to or limit his powers, the powers of a Scottish receiver under statute are extensive and will generally be sufficient[52];

(c) express power to appoint a receiver need not be taken in the instrument; and

(d) the law referring to receivers in Scotland is wholly statutory, with no origins in common law.

The original provisions introducing receivers in Scotland were in Part II of the 1972 Act which became Chapter II of Part XVIII (ss.467–485) of the 1985 Act. These were substantially amended by Chapter V of Part II (ss.56–65) of the Insolvency Act 1985. The Insolvency Act 1986 consolidated the provisions of both Acts (before the Insolvency Act 1985 amendments became effective) as Chapter II of Part III (ss.50–71). The Companies Act 1989 did not amend these

---

[51] *Libertas-Kommerz GmbH*, 1978 S.L.T. 222.
[52] Since the I.A. 1986, however, administrative receivers in England and Wales have been accorded statutory powers (see I.A. 1986, s.42 and Sched. 1).

provisions in any material respect. In this section references to the Insolvency Act 1986 are indicated by the abbreviation "I.A." A receiver appointed before the amending provisions of the 1985 and 1986 Insolvency Acts came into force is not subject thereto, but is subject to the (unamended) provisions of the Companies Act 1985 (I.A. 1985, Sched. 9, para. 8 (effective March 1, 1986) and Insolvency Act 1986, Sched. 11, para. 3). Further provisions are contained in the Insolvency (Scotland) Rules 1986[53] (referred to in this section as "1986 Rules") and the Receivers (Scotland) Regulations 1986[54] (referred to in this section as "1986 Regulations"), both of which also prescribe forms for use in receiverships. The 1986 Rules were amended by the Insolvency (Scotland) Amendment Rules 1987[55] (referred to in this section as "the 1987 Amendments") effective January 11, 1988, but applying to all receiverships under the 1986 Act and Rules. Unless otherwise stated, references to the 1986 Rules are to those rules as amended. Court proceedings are governed by Acts of Sederunt for the Court of Session[56] (referred to in this section as "R.C.S.") and Sheriff Court[57] (referred to in this section as "Sh.Ct.R."). All these subordinate legislative provisions came into force on December 29, 1986. The only exception to the foregoing is the Company Directors Disqualification Act 1986 (whose application to receivers is discussed at paragraph 257 below), which came into force on April 28, 1986.[58]

The introduction of receivership into Scots law removed a basic weakness in the remedies available to the holder of a floating charge. Under the Companies (Floating Charges) (Scotland) Act 1961, the holder of a floating charge could enforce his security only by obtaining a winding-up order, to the detriment of the value of the undertaking held as security, apart from being unnecessarily harmful to other interests. This remedy is still available where the appointment of a receiver would be or has proved to be inadequate, for example, to enable the liquidator to reduce a fraudulent preference or gratuitous alienation, which a receiver has no power to do.[59] If the company is already in liquidation, the holder of a floating charge may, instead of appointing a receiver, claim a preferential ranking in the liquidation.[60]

References to a floating charge include references to a charge as altered under section 466 (I.A., s.70(3)).

---

[53] S.I. 1986 No. 1915 (S.139).
[54] S.I. 1986 No. 1917 (S.141).
[55] S.I. 1987 No. 1921 (S.132).
[56] Act of Sederunt (Rules of Court Amendment No. 11) (Companies) 1986 (S.I. 1986 No. 2298 (S.170)).
[57] Act of Sederunt (Sheriff Court Company Insolvency Rules) 1986 (S.I. 1986 No. 2297 (S.169)).
[58] The old law is discussed in the 23rd ed. of *Palmer*, Chap. 48.
[59] See para. 418, *post*.
[60] *Libertas-Kommerz GmbH*, 1978 S.L.T. 222, 225.

Receivership and administration or voluntary arrangement

219 A petition for the appointment of an administrator under Part II of the Insolvency Act requires to be intimated (*inter alia*) to any person who has appointed or is or may be entitled to appoint an "administrative receiver."[61] In a Scottish context "administrative receiver" means a receiver appointed under the Insolvency Act, s.51 where "the whole (or substantially the whole) of the company's property is attached by the floating charge."[62] In view of the universal practice of taking a floating charge over the whole of a company's property and undertaking it is perhaps academic to speculate on the precise scope of this definition. Presumably a charge which excluded uncalled capital would still be within the definition, but a charge over part of the assets only would not be covered, unless the part was "substantially the whole." It is regrettable that this difficulty has not been avoided by the simple expedient of requiring intimation to the holder of any floating charge.

If there is an "administrative receiver" in office an administrator cannot be appointed without the consent of the holder of the charge.[63] If, however, the court is satisfied that any security constituted by the charge is liable to be released or discharged as invalid under one of the relevant statutory provisions[64] or "under any rule of law in Scotland" the administration order may still be made without the charge holder's consent.[65]

After an administration order has been granted an "administrative receiver" cannot be appointed, and any other proceedings to enforce a charge holder's security are prohibited.[66]

A voluntary arrangement between the company and its creditors under the Insolvency Act, sections 1 to 7 cannot prejudice the charge holder's right to appoint a receiver without his consent (I.A., s.4(3)).

Circumstances in which receivers may be appointed

220 The holder of a floating charge created by a company which the Court of Session has jurisdiction to wind up (whether a company within the meaning of the Act or not) has power to appoint a receiver (I.A., s.51(1)), or to apply to the court for such an appointment (I.A., s.51(2)).[67] Where applicable, the provisions with respect to registration

---

[61] I.A., s.9(2). For further discussion of administration orders see paras. 101 *et seq., ante.*
[62] I.A., s.251, definition (*b*).
[63] I.A., s.9(3)(*a*).
[64] *i.e.,* I.A., s.245 (applicable to floating charges generally), I.A., ss.238–240 (England) or I.A., ss.242 and 243 (Scotland) which apply to "gratuitous alienations" and "fraudulent" or "unfair" preferences and I.A., s.244 (extortionate credit transactions). See further paras. 505 to 516, *post.*
[65] I.A., s.9(3)(*b*).
[66] I.A., s.11.
[67] As the 1972 Act, s.11 made explicit, this includes the holder of a charge created under the 1961 Act.

of the charge must have been complied with.[68] As noted in paragraph 203 above, Scots law will recognise a floating charge granted by a company incorporated under Royal Charter or by Private Act, or by an oversea company, whether or not it is registered in Scotland under Part XXIII of the Act, provided that it has corporate status, and that the Scottish courts have jurisdiction to wind it up.[69] The Insolvency Act, section 51 extends to such a company and, therefore, provided the instrument satisfies the requirements of Scots law as to the form and substance of a "floating charge,"[70] a receiver may be appointed on the same basis as for a company incorporated and registered in Scotland under the Act. Such a receiver is subject to the Insolvency Act, and the Rules and Regulations made thereunder, as if he were appointed to a Scottish-registered company (I.A., s.70(1)). He will, therefore (if he is an "administrative receiver") have to be recognised as an "insolvency practitioner" in the United Kingdom.[71]

A European Economic Interest Group ("E.E.I.G.") is treated as a company subject to the jurisdiction of the Scottish courts if its registered "official address" is in Scotland. It may grant a floating charge, which must be registered under Part XII of the Act, and the Insolvency Act, Part III (which relates to the appointment of a receiver) also applies to it.[72]

The circumstances in which the holder may appoint a receiver (or apply to the court for such appointment) may be specified or restricted by the instrument of charge. Subject thereto, this appointment may be made by the holder on the occurrence of any of the following events:

(a) the expiry of 21 days after the making of a demand for payment of the whole or any part of the principal sum secured by the charge, without payment having been made;

(b) the expiry of a period of two months during the whole of which interest due and payable under the charge has been in arrears;

(c) the making of an order or the passing of a resolution to wind up the company; or

(d) the appointment of a receiver by virtue of any other floating charge created by the company.

The holder cannot apply to the court for an appointment under (d) but (again subject to any conditions in the charge) he can secure such appointment under (a) to (c) or if the court is satisfied that his position is likely to be prejudiced if a receiver is not appointed (I.A., s.52(2)). It

---

[68] Registration is required only if the company is incorporated under the Companies Acts or their predecessors (see s.735) in Scotland (s.410(5)) or if, being an oversea company, it has a place of business in Scotland (s.424) or if it is an E.E.I.G. whose official address is in Scotland (see below).

[69] s.462(1); see further para. 203 *ante*, and paras. 410 and 411 *post*.

[70] See para. 203, *ante*.

[71] See paras. 440, *et seq.*, *infra*.

[72] European Economic Interest Regulations 1989 (S.I. 638), paras. 18, 19 and Sched. 4; see further para. 411A, *post*.

is therefore unnecessary to stipulate for power to appoint a receiver in the floating charge unless it is desired to enlarge the holder's statutory powers. If the charge empowers the holder to appoint a receiver in circumstances which are more beneficial to him than the Insolvency Act, section 52(1) the procedure laid down in the deed must be strictly adhered to; where the holder was entitled to appoint a receiver immediately on the issue of a notice of indebtedness (without waiting 21 days as under the Insolvency Act, s.52(1)(*a*)) signed by one of a group of specified officials, a notice signed by or on behalf of another official (even one senior to those named), or on behalf of one of those named, was not a valid basis for appointing a receiver.[73] If the company wishes to oppose the appointment of a receiver by the holder, it may apply to the court for suspension and interdict.[74]

Qualification for appointment: joint receivers

221 Part I (ss.1–11) of the Insolvency Act 1985 (now Part XIII (ss.388–398) of the Insolvency Act 1986) introduced the concept of "insolvency practitioners," individuals duly recognised by an appropriate professional or authorised body or the Secretary of State. Only an insolvency practitioner may be appointed as an "administrative receiver," *i.e.* over the whole or substantially the whole of the company's property.[75] No such restriction applies to the appointment of a receiver over a part of its property which is less than "substantial." The appointment of undischarged bankrupts, firms or bodies corporate is prohibited by the Insolvency Act 1986, section 51(3) to (5). Also disqualified are persons disqualified from acting as directors[76] and patients under the Mental Health Acts.[77]

Joint receivers are competent (I.A., s.51(6)) and must act jointly unless otherwise provided in their instruments of appointment (I.A., s.56(3)).

One individual may be appointed receiver by virtue of several floating charges (I.A., s.56(7)).

The person appointing a receiver (the holder of the charge or the court) has to satisfy himself that the receiver has in force a satisfactory bond of caution for the proper performance of his functions. Thereafter, it is for the committee of creditors (see below) to review its adequacy from time to time (1986 Rule 7.28). If no committee of creditors is established, there is no machinery for reviewing the level of caution, except by application to the court under the Insolvency Act 1986, section 63.

---

[73] *Elwick Bay Shipping Co. Ltd.* v. *Royal Bank of Scotland Ltd.*, 1982 S.L.T. 62.
[74] *Toynar Ltd.* v. *Whitbread & Co. plc.*, 1988 S.L.T. 433.
[75] I.A., s.251; para. 219, *ante.*
[76] ss.296 to 299 and Insolvency Act 1985, ss.12 to 19 (now consolidated in the Company Directors Disqualification Act 1986).
[77] I.A., s.390(4).

Mode of appointment

By the holder of the charge

222 Where the holder of a floating charge may appoint a receiver directly by virtue of powers in the charge or under the Insolvency Act, section 52(1), the power is exercised by means of a validly executed instrument of appointment (I.A., s.53(1)). The instrument of appointment may be executed either by the holder or by any person duly authorised in writing to execute it on his behalf (I.A., s.53(4)(*a*)). If the appointment is by the holders of a series of secured debentures, a resolution of the debenture holders is required to authorise a person to execute the instrument on their behalf (I.A., s.53(4)(*b*)).

The manner of execution of an instrument of appointment by a company was not clearly specified in the legislation in force prior to July 31, 1990. The Insolvency Act 1986, section 53(3)(*a*), as it then stood, required that it be executed in accordance with the Companies Act 1985, section 36 "as if it were a contract," but section 36 provided alternative methods of executing a contract under Scots law, under seal or by the signature of a duly authorised person. In practice, an instrument of appointment was usually executed under seal with the signature of two directors (or director and secretary) as if it was a probative deed. The Companies Act 1989 (s.130(3)) amended section 36 of the 1985 Act, inserting *inter alia* a new section 36B which sought to provide that a document be executed for a company by a single director, the secretary or an authorised person, with, if it was to be probative, the addition of a single witness or the company seal. At the same time, the 1989 Act (Sched. 17, para. 10) amended the Insolvency Act 1986, section 53(3)(*a*) so as to provide that an instrument of appointment of a receiver was to be executed by a company "in accordance with section 36B." Thus, a single signature by one of those authorised, without witness or seal, would be sufficient. The 1989 amendments came into force on July 31, 1990 but, after criticism of the new section 36B, that section was replaced by the Law Reform (Miscellaneous Provisions) (Scotland) Act 1990, s.72, which enacted a replacement version of section 36B with effect retrospective to July 31, 1990.[78] At the same time, the 1990 Act (Sched. 8, para. 35) further amended the Insolvency Act 1986, section 53 by repealing section 53(3) *in toto*. The 1990 amendments came into force on December 1, 1990,[79] but the repeal of the Insolvency Act 1986, section 53(3) was not retrospective. The practical effect is, nevertheless, that an instrument of appointment of a receiver by a company dated on or after July 31, 1990 requires no greater formality than being executed by a single director, the secretary or a duly authorised person, in accordance with

---

[78] See further *Palmer*, paras.3.201 *et seq.*
[79] Law Reform (Miscellaneous Provisions) (Scotland) Act 1990 Commencement (No. 1) Order 1990 (S.I. 1990 No. 2328).

section 36B(2) (1990 version). There is no requirement that it should be a probative document.

In terms of the Insolvency Act 1986, section 53(3)(*b*), an instrument of appointment by any person other than a company had to be executed as an attested deed, which included the signature of two witnesses. The requirement of attestation ceased to have effect with the repeal of the Insolvency Act, section 53(3) on December 1, 1990, and for instruments executed on or after that date signature by or on behalf of the charge holder is therefore sufficient.

Acceptance of an appointment made by the charge holder

223 By provisions introduced in the Insolvency Act, section 53(6) the appointment is ineffectual unless accepted by the person appointed "before the end of the business day next following that on which the instrument is received by him or on his behalf" (I.A., s.53(6)(*a*)). "Business day" is defined (I.A., s.251) so as to exclude Saturdays, Sundays, Christmas Day, Good Friday or any day which is a bank holiday in any part of Great Britain. A purely local holiday is a "business day" for the purposes of the Insolvency Act, section 53.

The initial acceptance must, apparently, be by the receiver in person and not by an authorised representative. It need not be in writing (although a written acceptance must follow) and can be intimated to the holder of the charge or his agent (1986 Rule 3.1(1)). The receiver or someone acting on his behalf must then accept the appointment in writing (I.A., s.53(6)(*b*)) and the receiver or his agent must "also" endorse a docquet of acceptance on the instrument of appointment giving the date of its receipt, and deliver it as soon as possible to the holder of the charge or his agent (1986 Rule 3.1(2) and (3)). These provisions clearly envisage that, as a general rule, the receiver will intimate his acceptance in person verbally within the "business day" limit, confirm this in writing himself or from his firm or his solicitors and arrange for the acceptance docquet to be endorsed personally or by his firm or his solicitors. The appointment (if duly accepted) is deemed to be effective on the day the instrument is received by the person to be appointed (I.A., s.53(6)(*b*)).

In the case of joint receivers the same procedure applies to each of them. They can endorse their acceptance docquets on separate copies of the instrument of appointment, but if more than one docquets a single copy, the duty of sending it to the charge holder falls on the last to sign (1986 Rule 3.1(4)). They must separately intimate acceptance within the "business day" limit but the appointment of any of the joint receivers only takes effect when all have accepted, and on the date the instrument of appointment was received by the last of them, as evidenced by the docquets of acceptance (1986 Reg. 5).[80]

---

[80] The consequences of irregularity in the appointment are discussed in para. 232, *post.*

The appointment of a receiver must be notified to the registrar of companies and to the company (see paras. 225 to 228 and 245 below).

Appointment by the court

224 If the holder of a floating charge requires to apply to the court for the appointment of a receiver, the procedure is by petition, served on the company (I.A., s.54). The Court of Session is required to frame Rules of Court to include special provision for cases of urgency (I.A., s.54(7)); the rules[81] do not appear to contain any such "special provision." The requirement in the original provisions (s.470) as to finding caution has been superseded by the Insolvency Act and the necessity of appointing an "insolvency practitioner" to the office. Such practitioners will have to find caution or equivalent under the Insolvency Act regulations. Such appointment takes effect on the date of the court's interlocutor (I.A., s.54(5)). There is no requirement for the appointee to intimate acceptance.

Intimation of the appointment to the registrar and to the company is again necessary (see paras. 225 to 228 and 245 below).

Registration of appointments

225 The appointment of a receiver requires to be intimated to the registrar of companies, who enters the particulars in the register of charges (I.A., ss.53(5) and 54(4)). The registrar must, however, be satisfied that the appropriate formalities have been complied with. Both sections make provision for payment of a fee for registration of the appointment, but no such fee has been prescribed.

Registration of instrument of appointment

226 When the holder of a floating charge executes an instrument of appointment he must deliver to the registrar, within seven days of its date, a certified copy of the instrument, together with a notice (1986 Regulation 3 and Form 1 (Scot), s.53(1)) giving details of the appointment, including a statement of the circumstances justifying it. The form requires reference to the floating charge and the name of the person entitled to the benefit thereof (or the first-named of several). This may give rise to difficulties where the benefit has been assigned, since the registrar has no means of checking the assignee's identity, assignations not being recorded in the official register of charges.[82]

Registration of appointment by the court

227 A copy, certified by the clerk of court, of the interlocutor appointing the receiver must be delivered to the registrar within seven days of its date or such longer period as the court may allow, together with a

---

[81] R.C.S. 214/215; Sh.Ct.R. 15/16. See further McBryde and Dowie, *Petition Procedure in the Court of Session* (2nd ed.), Chap. 19.
[82] See para. 217, *ante*.

notice (Form 2 (Scot), s.54(3)) giving particulars (I.A., s.54(3)). The difficulty as to assignations may not arise, simply because the registrar is unlikely to question the correctness of the court's order.

Effect of non-registration

228 Non-registration of the appointment of a receiver carries no sanction other than a possible fine (I.A., ss.53(2) and 54(3)).[83] The failure of the Act to provide adequate sanctions against non-registration or delay is most unfortunate, since inspection of the official register of charges may not disclose the fact that a receiver has been appointed.

Effect of appointment of a receiver

229 The appointment is in respect of such part of the property of the company (including uncalled capital) as is subject to the floating charge (I.A., s.51). The directors' power to deal with the property comprised in the receivership is superseded but not extinguished.[84] Although they cannot interfere with the receiver's discretion in dealing with assets under his control, they retain a limited power to sue in name of the company if the receiver has decided not to do so, or has a conflict of interest, provided that the charge holder and the company are protected against prejudice, *e.g.* by an indemnity against an award of expenses.[85] They must keep accounting records under section 221.[86]

On appointment the charge crystallises and attaches to the property then subject to it as if it were a fixed security. Although the title to its assets remains with the company, the receiver is regarded as if he held a completed security (for behoof of the charge holder) at the date of crystallisation.[87]

It appears from the terms of the Insolvency Act, section 51(1) and (2) that the holder of the floating charge cannot restrict the scope of the appointment to a part only of the property subject to the charge.

Powers of receiver

230 The receiver's powers may be defined in the floating charge and, in addition, he has the following statutory powers in relation to the property attached by the charge in so far as they are not inconsistent with any provision in that instrument (I.A., s.55 and Sched. 2; amendments from the former law (s.471(1))[88] are indicated by italics):

---

[83] The references to a "daily default fine" in these sections were removed by the Companies Act 1989, Sched. 24.

[84] *Imperial Hotel (Aberdeen) Ltd.* v. *Vaux Breweries Ltd.*, 1978 S.L.T. 113.

[85] *Newhart Developments Ltd.* v. *Co-operative Commercial Bank Ltd.* [1978] Q.B. 814; [1978] 2 All E.R. 896 (C.A.); *Shanks* v. *Central Regional Council*, 1987 S.L.T. 410; *Tudor Grange Holdings Ltd.* v. *Citibank N.A.* [1991] 3 W.L.R. 750.

[86] *Smiths Ltd.* v. *Middleton* [1979] 3 All E.R. 842. See para. 257, *post*.

[87] See paras. 206 to 209, *ante*.

[88] An omitted power (s.471(1)(*f*)), to apply to the court for directions, duplicated I.A., s.63(1); see para 244, *post*.

1. to take possession of, collect and get in the property from the company or a liquidator thereof or any other person, and for that purpose, to take such proceedings as may seem to him expedient;
2. to sell, feu, hire out or otherwise dispose of the property by public roup or private bargain and with or without advertisement;
3. to *raise or* borrow money and grant security therefor over the property;
4. to appoint a solicitor or accountant or other professional qualified person to assist him in the performance of his functions;
5. to bring or defend any action or other legal proceedings in the name and on behalf of the company[89];
6. to refer to arbitration all questions affecting the company;
7. to effect and maintain insurances in respect of the business and property of the company;
8. to use the company's seal (if any)[90];
9. to do all acts and to execute in the name and on behalf of the company any deed,[91] receipt or other document;
10. to draw, accept, make and endorse any bill of exchange or promissory note in the name and on behalf of the company;
11. to appoint any agent to do any business which he is unable to do himself or which can more conveniently be done by an agent and to employ and *dismiss employees*[92];
12. *to do all such things (including the carrying out of works) as may be necessary for the realisation of the property*[93];
13. to make any payment which is necessary or incidental to the performance of his functions;
14. to carry on the business of the company *or any part of it*[94];
15. to grant *or accept a surrender of a lease or tenancy of any of the property,*

---

[89] This includes to oppose a winding-up petition (*Foxhill & Gyle (Nurseries) Ltd.*, 1978 S.L.T. (Notes) 29) and to petition for recall of diligence (*Iona Hotels Ltd.* v. *Craig*, 1991 S.L.T. 11; 1990 S.C.L.R. 614). See para. 237, *post*.

[90] Companies Act 1985, s.36B(5) (introduced by the Companies Act 1989, s.130(3) and substituted by the Law Reform (Miscellaneous Provisions) (Scotland) Act 1990, s.72(1)) abolished the requirement to have a seal and (in the form of s.36B in the 1990 Act) its practical function; see further *Palmer*, paras. 3.201, *et seq.*

[91] Deeds run in the name of the company and should narrate the appointment of the receiver. The receiver's signature will require two witnesses, in accordance with normal Scottish practice. See *Palmer*, paras. 3.201 *et seq.*

[92] The original words were "discharge servants"; the change has no legal significance.

[93] The original wording of this power was "to have carried out to the best advantage any work on the property of the company and in general to do all such other things as may be necessary for the realisation of the property." The change improves the wording and may remove a suggestion that if works were not done to "best advantage" the receiver was acting *ultra vires*.

[94] The original words were "so far as he thinks it desirable to do so," which appear to be of similar effect.

and to take a lease or tenancy[95] of any property required or convenient for the business of the company;

16. *to make any arrangement or compromise on behalf of the company;*
17. *to call up any uncalled capital of the company;*
18. *to establish subsidiaries of the company;*
19. *to transfer to subsidiaries of the company the business of the company or any part of it and any of the property*[96];
20. to rank and claim in the bankruptcy, insolvency, sequestration or liquidation of any person or company indebted to the company and to receive dividends, and to accede to trust deeds for creditors of any such person[97];
21. to present or defend a petition for the winding up of the company[98];
22. *to change the situation of the company's registered office*[99];
23. to do all other things incidental to the exercise of the powers mentioned in the Insolvency Act, section 55(1) or above.

231 The statutory powers of a receiver are extensive, and he is accorded wide discretion as to whether he should exercise them and in what manner. A notable omission, however, is express power to reduce fraudulent or unfair preferences, gratuitous alienations and extortionate credit transactions, which can only be challenged in a winding up or administration.[1] A receiver may, however, procure repayment by the threat of liquidation.

The detailed recitation of the powers of a receiver in the Insolvency Act, Schedule 2 has given rise to confusion, particularly in a series of conflicting decisions on powers (1) and (5), which appear to give a receiver a choice in the nature of the proceedings available to him in seeking to recover sums due to the company.

---

[95] The original version referred to power "to input and output tenants" and did not mention "tenancy."

[96] In powers (16) to (19) the I.A. added a specific power to make calls and removed doubts as to the validity of a compromise by a receiver, and the common practice of "hiving down" a viable part of the undertaking for sale as a going concern. This practice is (purportedly) assisted by para. 4 of the Transfer of Undertakings (Protection of Employment) Regulations 1981 (S.I. 1981 No. 1794) which exempts a receiver's "hive-down" from automatic transfer of the contracts of the company's employees to the subsidiary. The Regulations apply when the subsidiary, or its business, is disposed of and they cannot be avoided by artificial devices, such as dismissing the employees shortly before the sale, thereby largely nullifying any benefit from para. 4; *Litster* v. *Forth Dry Dock Engineering Co. Ltd.* [1990] 1 A.C. 546; [1989] 1 All E.R. 1136; 1989 S.L.T. 540 (H.L.). See further *Palmer*, para. 14.148.

[97] There is no specific reference to power to accede to a voluntary arrangement under the I.A., s.1 (see paras. 301 *et seq.*) but this must be competent under power (23).

[98] It is the person who has appointed the receiver, not the receiver himself, who is entitled to object to the appointment of an administrator (I.A., s.29(2)(*a*) and (3)(*a*)).

[99] An added power, of obvious practical advantage to the receiver. However, the transfer of the records and registered address to the receiver's premises may increase the difficulty of the directors in discharging their continuing responsibilities.

[1] See I.A., ss.242(1), 243(4) and 244(1).

The first of these cases, *McPhail*,[2] held that a receiver could choose between suing in his own name under (1) or in the name of the company under (5); if he sued in his own name the defender could not plead compensation (or "set-off") in respect of sums due to him by the company, but such a plea was available if the action was in the name of the company. It is now accepted that this decision was incorrect and, although it has not been formally overruled, it has been disapproved and disregarded in subsequent decisions.

In the first of these, *Taylor*,[3] it was held that power (1) could not be used to sue for a debt due to the company. Although an absolute bar to the use of power (1) in such circumstances seems to restrict the prima facie meaning of the Act, it is now accepted that power (1) is appropriate for recovery of physical possession or title to an asset, not the recovery of a debt.[4]

If the receiver sues in the name of the company, using power (5), there is no doubt that all the defences which were open to the defender against the company remain available against the receiver, with the exception of a claim to compensate a debt due by the company before crystallisation which the defender acquired from the original creditor after the crystallisation of the charge. If the receiver's position was the same in this respect as a liquidator, compensation in respect of such an after-acquired debt would not be permitted.[5] In one case[6] it was held that this was correct, and liquidation rules were applicable, but in two other decisions[7] it was held that there was no warrant for applying this common law rule of bankruptcy to a receivership. This must be correct in principle, for (in theory at least) a receiver may be appointed without the company being insolvent, provided the terms of the instrument of charge so permit and it is arguable that the appointment of a receiver is the enforcement of a security right, not an insolvency process. Nevertheless, compensation of an after-acquired debt should still be refused but on a different basis. Crystallisation puts the charge holder (by way of the so-called "statutory metaphor" of I.A., ss.53(7) and 54(6)) in the position of holding a fixed charge which, in the case of debts due to the company, means it is as if these had been assigned to him and that assignation had been duly intimated to the debtor.[8] Therefore, there would be no *concursus debiti et crediti*, and therefore no

---

[2] *McPhail* v. *Lothian R. C.*, 1981 S.L.T. 173; 1981 S.C. 109.
[3] *Taylor, Petr.*, 1982 S.L.T. 172.
[4] *Myles J. Callaghan Ltd.* v. *City of Glasgow D.C.*, 1988 S.L.T. 227; 1987 S.C.L.R. 627.
[5] See para. 475, *post.*
[6] *William Loudon & Son Ltd.* v. *Cunninghame D.C.*, 1985 S.L.T. 149. See also Patrick, "Set-off and Receivership," 1988 J.L.S. 357 and 392.
[7] *Taylor, supra; Myles J. Callaghan Ltd., supra.*
[8] *Forth & Clyde Construction Co. Ltd.* v. *Trinity Timber & Plywood Co. Ltd.*, 1983 S.L.T. 372, affrmd 1984 S.L.T. 94.

compensation, between the company and the subsequent assignee of any book debt attached by the charge.[9]

PROTECTION OF THIRD PARTIES

232 Under the Insolvency Act 1986, section 55(4) third parties dealing in good faith with a receiver are accorded protection against reduction on the grounds that the receiver has acted *ultra vires*. The amendments made by the Insolvency Act, section 55 to the preceding provisions (s.471(3)) are significant. The original wording[10] contained certain ambiguities. Did it matter whether the third party was acting in good faith? Was it necessary to establish that his appointment was valid? The amended wording confines the protection to a third party dealing in good faith and for value,[11] and further restricts it to the question of whether the receiver is acting *ultra vires*. Third parties, therefore, must still inquire whether the receiver has been validly appointed. It is clear from the Insolvency Act, section 63(2) and its predecessor (s.479(2) and (3)) that if the appointment is invalid, because of a defect in the instrument of appointment or the invalidity of the charge itself or for any other reason (including failure to accept office timeously under the Insolvency Act 1986, section 53(6)), the third party must look to the receiver personally for performance.[12] Third parties must, therefore, for their protection, examine at least the instrument of charge, its certificate of registration, the instrument of appointment and the docquet of acceptance of office endorsed thereon for any irregularity.

Receivers appointed furth of Scotland or in Scotland over assets elsewhere

233 A receiver or manager appointed under the law of any part of the United Kingdom in respect of a floating charge may exercise his powers (*i.e.* the powers given by the jurisdiction in which he has been appointed) in any other part of the United Kingdom so far as their exercise is not inconsistent with the law applicable there (I.A., s.72). This would apply to the receiver or manager of an English company with property in Scotland and vice versa. The appointment of a receiver or manager of an English company causes the charge to crystallise over its Scottish property in the same way as a charge by a Scottish company crystallises on the appointment of a receiver. Although under English law the floating charge may have been converted to a fixed charge at an earlier date, it remains a "floating

---

[9] See W. A. Wilson, "The Receiver and Book Debts," 1982 S.L.T. (News) 129; David P. Sellar, " 'Set Off' in Receivership," 1992 J.L.S. 262.
[10] "A person transacting with a receiver shall not be concerned to inquire whether any event has happened to authorise the receiver to act."
[11] "A person dealing with a receiver in good faith and for value shall not be concerned to inquire whether the receiver is acting within his powers."
[12] See para. 240 *post*.

charge" so far as Scots law is concerned until the appointment of a receiver (or liquidation). The earlier "conversion" to a fixed charge does not affect the validity of the receiver's subsequent appointment or his title to dispose of assets located in Scotland.[13] The precise effect of the provision that an English receiver may exercise his powers over property in Scotland "so far as their exercise is not inconsistent with" the law of Scotland has given rise to difficulty. It appears that it ought to mean that an English receiver only has the powers in relation to Scottish property of a Scottish receiver so far as he has those powers in England, but he has been accorded by extension the same "powers" to cut down diligence on crystallisation as a Scottish receiver would have.[14] This decision, however, has more to do with the question of what assets are "caught" by the charge on crystallisation than with the receiver's powers as such. It is suggested by the present author that the Insolvency Act, section 72 is in need of further clarification.

Foreign receivers

234   As noted above,[15] it is competent to appoint a receiver to administer assets in Scotland which are subject to a floating charge granted by a foreign corporation, provided that the Scottish courts have jurisdiction to wind up the foreign corporation, and such a person is treated as a receiver subject to Scots law in all respects. If a receiver is appointed in accordance with foreign law, however, his power to intromit with assets in Scotland is less certain. In principle, a foreign floating charge should be recognised (s.462) and given effect to, provided that the Scottish court can be satisfied that the person purporting to exercise the powers conferred by that charge has been duly appointed under the foreign law and is acting *intra vires*. Neither he nor any person dealing with him, however, will have the benefit of the statutory powers and protections afforded to a "receiver" appointed under the Act. The ranking of the charge holder's claim in a competition with secured or unsecured Scottish creditors will also depend on Scots law, but standing the terms of section 462 this must recognise the essential validity of the foreign charge and the security conferred thereby.[16]

Duties of a receiver

235   Although no statutory statement of the general duties of a receiver is provided, it is clear that his primary concern is to realise the assets of the company to satisfy the claims of the charge holder, and any claims

---

[13] *Norfolk House plc. (in receivership)* v. *Repsol Petroleum Ltd.*, 1992 S.L.T. 235.
[14] *Gordon Anderson (Plant) Ltd.* v. *Campsie Construction Ltd.*, 1977 S.L.T. 7. See W. A. Wilson [1977] J.B.L. 160. *Taymech Ltd.* v. *Rush & Tompkins Ltd.*, 1990 S.L.T. 681.
[15] Para. 220, *ante*.
[16] It is unfortunate that the Act provides no statutory basis for these propositions (apart from section 462), which have to be derived from basic principles of International Private Law.

which have a preference to them. In doing so, he has complete discretion with respect to the assets which he chooses to realise, regardless of the effect on other creditors or guarantors.[17] A receiver is, however, liable for negligence if he fails to exercise reasonable care in securing a reasonable price for company assets, or in the exercise of his powers in general.[18] In an extreme case of misconduct, a receiver may be liable for "misfeasance" under Insolvency Act, section 212.[19] The Act recognises that a receiver may find himself in conflict with the charge holder, by providing protection against his removal except by order of the court,[20] and also enables him to obtain directions from the court on any point of difficulty.[21]

Orders to recover property: examination of persons, etc.

236 An administrative receiver may apply to the court for an order to recover property or records of the company in the possession of a third party (I.A., s.234(1) and (2)). Directors and others have a duty to co-operate with him, and to meet him to provide information reasonably required (I.A., s.235). An administrative receiver may also obtain a court order for the examination of any officer or promoter of the company or any person having information or property of the company, and for delivery or payment of sums due to the company (I.A., ss.236, 237). These powers were not available to receivers prior to 1986, and are also applicable to administrators, liquidators and provisional liquidators.[22]

The receiver in competition with securities, diligence and liquidation

237 Under the Insolvency Act, section 55(3)(*b*) the powers of a receiver are subject to the rights of the holder of a fixed security or floating charge having a prior or *pari passu* ranking.

Under the Insolvency Act, section 55(3)(*a*) the receiver's powers are subject to the rights of "any person who has effectually executed diligence on all or any part of the property of the company prior to the appointment of the receiver." This provision, which has given rise to much discussion in the courts and academic circles,[23] parallels section

---

[17] *Forth & Clyde Construction Co. Ltd.* v. *Trinity Timber & Plywood Co. Ltd.*, 1984 S.L.T. 94; 1985 S.L.T. 169.
[18] *Standard Chartered Bank Ltd.* v. *Walker* [1982] 1 W.L.R. 410; [1982] 3 All E.R. 936; *Lord Advocate* v. *Maritime Fruit Carriers Co. Ltd.*, 1983 S.L.T. 357; *Macrae* v. *Henderson*, 1989 S.L.T. 423; *Larsen's Exrx.* v. *Henderson*, 1990 S.L.T. 498; see also para. 524, *post.*
[19] See further para. 524, *post.*
[20] I.A., s.62(3); see further para. 245, *post.*
[21] I.A., s.63(1); see further para. 247, *post.*
[22] See further paras. 483 (s.234); 484 (s.235); 519 to 521 (ss.236 and 237).
[23] J.A.D.H., "Inhibitions and Company Insolvencies," 1983 S.L.T. (News) 177; Simmons, "A Legal Black Hole," 1983 J.L.S. 352; Gretton, "Receivership and Sequestration for Rent," 1983 S.L.T. (News) 277 and "Receivers and Arresters," 1984

463, under which a floating charge crystallises on winding up subject to the rights of any person who has "effectually executed diligence" on any property of the company.

Since the phrase "effectually executed diligence" is not defined in the Act, nor is it a term of art in Scots law, the precise point in a particular process of diligence when it ceases to be challengeable is open to doubt. The commencement of diligence (other than arrestment to found jurisdiction, discussed below) renders the subjects affected "litigious," so that the company is prevented from alienating its rights therein by voluntary act. Where diligence has commenced before the creation of the floating charge, therefore, the subjects are incapable of being attached on crystallisation.[24] If the charge has already crystallised when diligence commences, the company's power to alienate the asset affected has already terminated, and diligence can have no effect.[25] The issues which arise concern diligence commenced after creation of the charge but not yet completed when the charge crystallises.

Moveable property of a company (corporeal or incorporeal) which is in the hands of a third party may be arrested on the dependence of an action, or in execution of a decree, including a duly registered warrant for summary diligence. If no further steps have been taken, the diligence remains inchoate and, for the purposes of Insolvency Act, section 55(3)(a) "ineffectual."[26] Arrestment is completed by action of furthcoming against the arrestee, decree having the effect of requiring the arrestee to account to the arrester for incorporeal moveable property arrested, or to deliver to him arrested corporeal moveables. In the leading case of *Lord Advocate* v. *Royal Bank of Scotland Ltd.*[27] it is suggested that only at the time when such decree is granted is an arrestment "effectual" for the purposes of the Act. It is also suggested in the *Royal Bank* case that decree granting warrant to sell arrested corporeal moveables is only "effectual" when the sale has occurred.

Arrestment may also be used *ad fundandam jurisdictionem*, but in this case the subjects are not rendered "litigious" or, if they are, only until the relevant proceedings commence, at which point the arrestment ceases to be effective.[28] Such diligence is, by its nature, incapable of

---

S.L.T. (News) 177; Sim, "The Receiver and Effectually Executed Diligence," 1984 S.L.T. (News) 25.

[24] *Iona Hotels Ltd.* v. *Craig*, 1991 S.L.T. 11; 1990 S.C.L.R. 614. In the leading judgment, the Lord President (Hope) states that *registration* of a floating charge "can be taken to be equivalent" to intimation of the assignation in security of a book debt. There is no statutory or other basis for this potentially confusing *obiter dictum*, which was unnecessary for the purpose of the decision. See also *Murray* v. *Long*, 1992 S.L.T. 292 (inhibition prior to crystallisation).

[25] *Forth & Clyde Construction Ltd.* v. *Trinity Timber & Plywood Ltd.*, 1984 S.L.T. 94.

[26] *Lord Advocate* v. *Royal Bank of Scotland*, 1976 S.L.T. 130; affirmed 1977 S.C. 155; 1978 S.L.T. 38; *Hawking* v. *Hafton House Ltd.*, 1990 S.L.T. 496; *Iona Hotels Ltd.* v. *Craig*, 1991 S.L.T. 11; 1990 S.C.L.R. 614.

[27] *Lord Advocate* v. *Royal Bank of Scotland Ltd.*, *supra*.

[28] *Fraser Johnston Engineering Co. Ltd.* v. *Jeffs*, 1920 S.C. 222.

being made effectual against a creditor of the company and, *a fortiori*, a charge holder.

Diligence may also be executed (after decree) by poinding corporeal moveables in the hands of the company, and this is enforced by warrant sale. Again, the opinions in the *Royal Bank* case suggest that until the sale has actually occurred, such diligence remains "ineffectual."

Inhibition, like arrestment, may be used either on the dependence of proceedings or in execution of a decree (but not to found jurisdiction). The effect is to prevent the company from alienating or burdening its heritable property in Scotland by voluntary act. It is completed by decree of adjudication, transferring title to the inhibiting creditor. The question of whether an inhibition is effective against a floating charge holder raises similar issues to an arrestment. It appears to be accepted that an inhibition laid after creation of the charge, which has not been followed by adjudication, is ineffectual on crystallisation.[29]

If (as appears to be the effect of the opinions in the decided cases) diligence commenced after the creation of a floating charge can only prevail against the charge holder if it has been completed when the charge crystallises, Insolvency Act, section 55(3)(*a*) seems to be devoid of any practical effect. Completed diligence results in the asset in question ceasing to be the property of the company, and *ipso facto* it is no longer capable of being attached on subsequent crystallisation of a floating charge. It is hard to avoid the somewhat ironic conclusion that section 55(3)(*a*) is, when its true effect has been understood, no more than a statement ("for the avoidance of doubt?") of the simple fact that crystallisation of a floating charge cannot attach assets which have ceased to be the property of the company as the result of diligence. Nevertheless, the Act does contain other provisions which imply that "effectually executed diligence" is not the same as diligence which has been completed, to the extent that the relevant asset has ceased to be property which can be attached on crystallisation. The Insolvency Act, section 60(1) provides for payment to the holder of "effectually executed diligence" in priority (*inter alia*) to the charge holder. Section 61(1) empowers the receiver to apply to the court for an order allowing him to dispose of "property or an interest in property affected or attached by effectual diligence." Neither of these provisions is consistent with the view that nothing less than completion of diligence is "effectual." It must, therefore, be regarded as still open to argument that at some stage in the process of diligence, later than the initial step but before completion, it is supposed to become "effectual" for the purposes of the Act. It is absurd that no statutory clarification has been supplied. The Insolvency Act, section 55(3)(*b*) is open to similar

---

[29] *Armour and Mycroft, Petrs.*, 1983 S.L.T. 453 (where the creditor conceded this point without argument); *Taymech Ltd.* v. *Rush & Tompkins Ltd.*, 1990 S.L.T. 681.

criticism, in that it must be trite law that a floating charge holder's rights are subject to those of prior or *pari passu* securities.

238   A receiver appointed in respect of a company incorporated in England or Wales is, in relation to diligence executed in Scotland, in the same position as a Scottish receiver.[30]

In contrast to the position on liquidation[31] a creditor whose diligence is cut down by crystallisation of a floating charge has no claim for his expenses. Section 61 of the Insolvency Act[32] does not provide an alternative basis for requiring a receiver to accord a preference to the holder of ineffectual diligence.[33]

If diligence has been made effectual, it is liable to be cut down if the company goes into liquidation within 60 days.[34] A receiver may, therefore, be able to persuade the creditor to relinquish his preference by agreement, on the threat of immediate liquidation.

Diligence which is ineffectual may, nevertheless, be an inconvenience to the receiver, and may be recalled subject to preserving any preference the creditor may have as against the company itself.[35] In practice, this is most likely to arise where heritable property is sold subject to the delivery of "clear searches," which requires the receiver, as a matter of contract, to arrange for the removal of an inhibition, whether or not it has legal effect.[36]

Where an arrestment or inhibition has been laid on the dependence of an action, it may be recalled on consignation of an appropriate sum with the Clerk of Court. The sum consigned ceases to be the property of the company and is, therefore, not attached on subsequent crystallisation of a floating charge.[37]

At common law, a landlord enjoys a right of hypothec over moveable property on the leased subjects in respect of unpaid rent. This right, however, is not protected by Insolvency Act, section 55(3) against a floating charge holder.[38]

A receiver with the normal statutory powers takes precedence over a liquidator and may recover property from him, even if the receiver is appointed after commencement of a winding up.[39]

Precedence of and among receivers: joint receivers

239 Since there may be several floating charges created by one company,

---

[30] I.A. 1986, s.72; *Taymech Ltd. v. Rush & Tompkins Ltd., supra.*
[31] See para. 499, *post.*
[32] See para. 242, *post.*
[33] *Armour and Mycroft, Petrs., supra.*
[34] See paras. 499 and 500, *post.*
[35] *Armour and Mycroft, Petrs., supra; Taymech Ltd. v. Rush & Tompkins Ltd., supra.*
[36] This was the position in the cases cited at n. 35, *supra.*
[37] *Hawking v. Hafton House Ltd., supra.*
[38] *Cumbernauld Development Corporation v. Mustone Ltd.,* 1983 S.L.T. (Sh.Ct.) 55.
[39] *Manley, Petr.,* 1985 S.L.T. 42.

the Act provides rules of precedence among the receivers who may be appointed by each holder (I.A., s.56).

As between the holders of floating charges, the receiver appointed in respect of the charge having prior ranking takes precedence and exercises his powers to the exclusion of any other receiver (I.A., s.56(1)). Receivers appointed in respect of charges having equal ranking are deemed to be joint receivers (I.A., s.56(2)). Joint receivers may also be appointed by the holder of a single charge (I.A., s.51(6)). Unless otherwise provided in the instrument or instruments of appointment, joint receivers must act jointly (I.A., s.56(3)). The same receiver can be appointed under more than one charge (I.A., s.56(7)).

The powers of a receiver are suspended as from the date of appointment of a receiver having precedence over him, to such extent as may be necessary to enable the receiver having precedence to exercise his powers (I.A., s.56(4)). The postponed receiver can, therefore, continue to exercise his powers in so far as they do not conflict with those of the prior receiver, for example over property excluded from the prior charge. If, for any reason (including failure by the prior receiver to act, by virtue of I.A., s.62(6)[40]), the prior charge ceases to attach to the property, and is either extinguished or re-floats, the suspended powers of the postponed receiver then revive. A suspended receiver is entitled to retain property and papers of the company under his control until he receives a valid indemnity from the prior receiver in respect of expenses, charges and liabilities incurred before suspension, limited to the value of that part of the company's property subject to the charge by virtue of which he was appointed (I.A., s.56(5)).

Suspension of the receiver's powers does not re-float the charge (I.A., s.56(6)).

Agency and liability of receivers

240 A receiver is deemed to be the agent of the company in relation to the property attached by the charge (I.A., s.57(1)). It has been suggested[41] that section 57(1) creates a rebuttable presumption of agency, which may be overturned if the receiver acts on his own account, improperly, rather than on behalf of the company or charge holder. Unlike an agent under the general law, however, a receiver is personally liable on any contract made by him in that capacity, unless the contract provides otherwise (I.A., s.57(2)).[42] Suspension of his powers does not relieve him of personal liability, if incurred (I.A., s.57(2)).

A receiver does not incur personal liability on any contract which continues in force by virtue only of his appointment (I.A., s.57(4)), but he may incur such liability if he adopts it after his appointment.

---

[40] See paras. 245 and 246, *post.*
[41] *Inverness D.C.* v. *Highland Universal Fabrication Ltd.*, 1986 S.L.T. 560.
[42] *Hill Samuel & Co. Ltd.* v. *Laing*, 1988 S.L.T. 452; affirmed 1989 S.L.T. 760.

These rules are subject to modification in the case of contracts of employment. As a result of amendment to the original provisions (s.473(2)) by the Insolvency Act, section 57(2) a receiver cannot avoid personal liability "on any contract of employment adopted by him in the carrying out of (his) functions." This appears to apply whether the employee is an existing employee of the company or has been recruited elsewhere. The Insolvency Act, section 57(5) (also a new provision), however, allows the receiver 14 days' grace after his appointment, during which any act or omission is not to be taken as signifying adoption of such a contract. The purpose of I.A., section 57(5) seems to be to protect a receiver from personal liability being incurred unintentionally as a result of action or inaction within the 14-day period,[43] but there is nothing in I.A., section 57(5) to restrict "anything done or omitted to be done" to acts which were not intended to be the "adoption" of a contract of employment. In practice, a receiver will usually dismiss employees or re-engage them on new contracts within the 14-day period, so as to avoid the risk of personal liability on the existing contracts if he does nothing, but it is arguable that the very short period available may not be enough to enable him to make a proper assessment of what the circumstances require.[44]

A receiver may incur personal liability both under the Insolvency Act, section 57 and as a result of acting on the basis of an invalid appointment, or a valid appointment on a charge which is itself invalid. He has limited protection against personal liability on contracts entered into or adopted by him in regard to which he can claim a right of indemnity from the property in his control under the Insolvency Act, section 57(3). If his powers are suspended by the appointment of a prior receiver he has rights of retention and lien against the supervening receiver in respect of his personal liabilities under the Insolvency Act, section 56(5). If the appointment is invalid he may obtain an indemnity from the court against the person who appointed him under the Insolvency Act, section 63(2). The statutory provisions, however, do not afford the receiver complete protection and, indeed, the Insolvency Act, section 57(6) preserves his personal responsibility for unauthorised actings. Accordingly, it is desirable for a receiver, before accepting his appointment, to secure a comprehensive indemnity from the person seeking to appoint him. The Insolvency Act, section 57(6) also preserves the effect of such an arrangement.

A receiver may be regarded as the occupier of company premises (jointly with the company) for the purposes of enforcing a statutory

---

[43] Cf. *Nicoll* v. *Coutts* [1985] B.C.L.C. 322, (C.A.).
[44] It is understood that amendments to these provisions will be proposed in an Employment Bill to be introduced in 1992/1993.

duty imposed on the occupier of premises[45] but not for the purpose of liability for rates.[46]

The Act (I.A., s.234(3) and (4)) provides that an administrative receiver[47] is not liable to a third party for loss arising if he seizes or disposes of property which does not belong to the company, provided he had reasonable grounds to believe he was acting correctly, unless the loss is caused by his negligence. The Act also gives him a lien over the property or the proceeds of its sale for his expenses, in accounting to the true owner for the assets or proceeds.

Effect of appointment or suspension on contracts

241 Unless otherwise provided in the contract, a contract entered into by the company before the appointment of a receiver, or a contract entered into by a receiver before suspension of his powers, continues in force thereafter (I.A., s.57(4) and (7)). An order of specific implement in respect of a contract entered into by the company before his appointment will only be granted if the receiver is in a position to comply; if not, the creditor has to claim damages.[48]

Remuneration and expenses of receivers

242 The receiver's remuneration is, in the first instance, for agreement between himself and the holder of the charge by virtue of which he was appointed (I.A., s.58(1)). Unless he has a contractual basis for recovery from the charge holder, he can only look to the assets of the company for payment.[49]

If agreement cannot be reached, or the amount is disputed, the auditor of the Court of Session may fix his remuneration. Application can be made by the receiver, the holder of any charge, the company or its liquidator (I.A., s.58(2)). The receiver must account for any excess if the auditor fixes his remuneration at less than the sum agreed or retained (I.A., s.58(3)).[50]

Rule 7.31 provides that "all fees, costs, charges and other expenses incurred" in the course of the receivership are to be regarded as expenses thereof. As well as this general statement the rules also refer to a number of specific items as expenses in the receivership (in some cases subject to the receiver's approval): the expenses of a deponent in completing a statement of affairs (1986 Rule 3.3); expenses incurred by

---

[45] *Lord Advocate, Petr.*, 1990 S.C.L.R. 794.
[46] *Ratford and Hayward* v. *North Avon D.C.* [1987] Q.B. 357.
[47] See para. 219 for the definition.
[48] *Macleod* v. *Alexander Sutherland Ltd.*, 1977 S.L.T. (Notes) 44; *Freevale Ltd.* v. *Metrostore Holdings Ltd.* [1984] 1 All E.R. 495; [1984] Ch. 199.
[49] *Hill Samuel & Co. Ltd.* v. *Laing*, 1988 S.L.T. 452; *affrmd.* 1989 S.L.T. 760.
[50] The original provisions (s.473(3)) required application to be made to the auditor within one month of receipt of the receiver's abstract accounts under the former s.481(2). The Insolvency Act 1985 repealed s.481(2), thus rendering s.473(3) meaningless. The I.A., s.58 omits the provisions of s.473(3).

members of the creditors' committee in attending meetings (1986 Rule 4.57 as adopted by Rule 3.6(4)) and the cost of the receiver's caution (1986 Rule 7.28(3)).

Payments and distributions

243 When a receiver is appointed and the company is not at the time of his appointment being wound up, he must pay out of any assets in his hands, in priority to the claims of the holder of the floating charge, claims which would have ranked as preferential debts in a winding up under the Insolvency Act, sections 175, 386 and Schedule 6 and the Social Security Pensions Act 1975, Schedule 3,[51] provided that they have come to his notice within six months after he has advertised for claims in the *Edinburgh Gazette* and a local newspaper (I.A., s.59(1) and (2)). It follows that the receiver will arrange for such advertisement early in his period of office, and cannot safely make payments to the holder of the floating charge for at least six months thereafter. The Insolvency Act does not make clear the status of a crystallised floating charge for the purpose of the Insolvency Act, section 175. If a liquidator is appointed while a receiver is in office, the liquidator can assert preferential claims by reference to the date of liquidation (I.A., s.386(3)). Under section 175(2)(*b*) these are said to have priority over the claims of the holder of any floating charge, which might be construed as including the charge under which the receiver has been appointed. The receiver, however, is obliged to calculate preferential claims by reference to the (earlier) date of his appointment (I.A., s.387(4)). This potential conflict can perhaps be resolved by construing the effect of the Insolvency Act, sections 53(7) and 54(6), which provide that on crystallisation the charge attaches "as if" it were a fixed charge, as meaning that the charge ceases to be a "floating charge" for all purposes, including the Insolvency Act, section 175(2)(*b*). This would be consistent with the Insolvency Act, section 62(6), which refers to a charge "re-floating," and the decision in *Forth & Clyde Construction Co. Ltd.* v. *Trinity Timber & Plywood Co. Ltd.*[52]

In construing the statutory provisions relating to preferential debts (I.A. (Sched. 6) and the Social Security Pensions Act 1975 (Sched. 3)), the date of appointment of the receiver is the "relevant date" (I.A., s.387(4)).

The receiver has a right of relief in respect of any payments made under the Insolvency Act, section 59 out of the assets available for payment of ordinary creditors (I.A., s.59(3)).

The Insolvency Act, section 60 lists the claims having priority to that of the charge holder. This sequence also regulates priorities among such claims, except so far as otherwise provided "in any instrument":

---

[51] See paras. 478 to 480, *post.*
[52] *Forth & Clyde Construction Co. Ltd.* v. *Trinity Timber & Plywood Co. Ltd.*, 1984 S.L.T. 94.

(a) Holders of prior or *pari passu* fixed securities over the property subject to the floating charge[53];
(b) Persons who have effectually executed diligence over such property[54];
(c) Creditors in respect of liabilities incurred by the receiver;
(d) The receiver in respect of his remuneration, expenses and liabilities (including his indemnity under I.A., s.62(4) or otherwise); and
(e) The preferential creditors under the Insolvency Act, section 59.

Subject to the foregoing, the receiver is to pay moneys received by him to the holder of the floating charge on account of the debt secured (I.A., s.60(1)). Any surplus is to be paid in accordance with their respective rights and interests to any other receiver, the holder of a fixed security over the property subject to the floating charge, or the company or its liquidator (I.A., s.60(2)). If any dispute arises, or if the receiver cannot get a proper receipt or discharge, he must consign the amount in question in a Scottish bank in the name of the accountant of court for behoof of the person or persons entitled thereto (I.A., s.60(3)).

The Insolvency Act, section 127 provides that, in a winding up by the court, any disposition of the company's property made after the commencement of the winding up is, unless the court otherwise directs, void. It has been held, however, that this does not apply to a disposition by a receiver.[55]

Disposal of burdened property

244 If the receiver wishes to dispose of property which is subject to any security, burden or other interest, or to effectual diligence, held by another creditor, he will normally require that creditor's consent. If consent cannot be obtained he may apply to the court for authority to sell free from such encumbrance or diligence (I.A., s.61(1); R.C.S. 216; Sh.Ct.R. 17). The court's power to grant authority is discretionary and it may impose conditions (I.A., s.61(2)). In its original form (s.477(2)) the court was prevented from giving consent where there was a fixed security having a prior ranking which had not been met or provided for in full. By amendments effected by the Insolvency Act the court can grant consent in such circumstances if satisfied that the sale or disposal is a more advantageous realisation of the asset than would otherwise be effected (I.A., s.61(3)). The court must make it a condition of consent that the net proceeds of disposal are applied towards discharging the prior security, and if the security holder can persuade the court that these are less than would have been secured in the open

---

[53] "Fixed security" is defined in I.A., s.70(1) as an effective security over property other than a floating charge or "a charge having the nature of a floating charge."
[54] See paras. 237 and 238, *ante*.
[55] *Sowman* v. *David Samuel Trust Ltd. (In Liquidation)* [1978] 1 All E.R. 616.

market the receiver can be ordered to make up the deficiency (I.A., s.61(4)). Further amendments require the order of priority of two or more fixed securities to be observed (I.A., s.61(5)). The receiver must file a certified copy of the court order with the registrar of companies within 14 days, on pain of a default fine (I.A., s.61(6) and (7)).

If the court authorises a sale under the Insolvency Act, section 61, the receiver will grant an appropriate document of transfer or conveyance and, on the purchaser completing his title in the appropriate way, the property is freed from the encumbrance or diligence in question (I.A., s.61(8)).

The procedure under section 61 for dispensing with his consent does not prejudice the creditor's right to rank for the debt in a winding up (I.A., s.61(9)).

At common law, the court may also discharge a diligence by motion in the action to which it relates, and may discharge a diligence or disburden property of a security by separate petition. Such steps are necessary, for example, where the diligence is ineffectual, and therefore section 61 does not apply, but the receiver is contractually bound to clear the record.[56]

Resignation and removal of a receiver: re-floating

245 A receiver may be removed from office by the court (I.A., s.62(3); R.C.S. 216; Sh.Ct.R. 17). He may resign by giving at least seven days' notice in writing to the holder of the charge by virtue of which he was appointed, the holder of any other floating charge, any other receiver, the members of the committee of creditors (if any) (see below), and the company or, if it is in liquidation, its liquidator. The notice must specify the date it is to take effect,[57] (I.A., s.62(1)).[58] He must also vacate office if he ceases to be qualified as an "insolvency practitioner" (I.A., s.62(2)). There is now no requirement for a receiver appointed by the court to obtain the approval of the court to his resignation.[59]

A receiver can only be removed by the court on cause shown, whether he was appointed by the court or directly by the holder of the charge. In terms of the Act (I.A., s.62(3)) only the holder of the charge by virtue of which he was appointed may apply to the court for his removal. It is suggested, however, that there may be circumstances in which the Court of Session might, in the exercise of its *nobile officium*, entertain a petition for removal by a party who can show an interest, such as the company or another creditor.

Under the Insolvency Act, section 62(4) a receiver who "vacates office" is entitled to be paid his remuneration, expenses properly

---

[56] *Armour and Mycroft, Petrs., supra; Taymech Ltd.* v. *Rush & Tompkins Ltd., supra; Iona Hotels Ltd.* v. *Craig, supra.*
[57] 1986 Regs., para. 6.
[58] Amending s.478(1).
[59] s.478(2) in its original form, omitted from the I.A. 1986, s.62.

incurred and any indemnity to which he is entitled out of the property of the company from the property subject to the charge as provided for in the Insolvency Act, section 60(1).[60] The fact that section 62(4) specifically applies only to a receiver who "vacates office" introduces a doubt, which was not present under the previous legislation,[61] whether the statutory priority applies in all circumstances where a receiver ceases to hold office. The section refers to a receiver "vacating office" only in the context of his ceasing to be a duly qualified insolvency practitioner (I.A., s.62(2)). In other cases the term "removed" or "resign(s)" is used (I.A. s.62(1) and (3)). The impression that this distinction is deliberate is reinforced by subsequent provisions in section 62(5) and (6) which refer to "cessation or removal." On the other hand, there is no suggestion in the relevant substantive sections that the receiver's statutory indemnity in respect of personal liability (I.A., s.57(3)) or priority for liabilities, expenses and remuneration (I.A., s.60(1)(*d*)) is liable to be lost by the circumstances in which he ceases to hold office. Also, the power of the court to remove a receiver on cause shown (I.A., s.62(3)) is expressly made subject to section 62(4), so that a receiver who has been removed is entitled to the same priority and indemnity as one who has "vacated office." A receiver who resigns ought not to be in a worse position than one who has been removed by the court. The reference to a receiver "vacating office" in section 62(4) should not, therefore, be interpreted as a conscious distinction between resignation under section 62(1) and vacation of office under section 62(2).

The Insolvency Act, s.62(5), the 1986 Rules and the 1986 Regulations contain unnecessarily complex provisions for giving notice to the registrar and others that a receiver has ceased to hold office. If he is removed by the court or dies the duty to give notice falls on the holder of the charge by virtue of which he was appointed, whether or not his removal was at the instance of that holder; in all other circumstances this duty falls on the receiver himself (see I.A., s.62(5); 1986 Rule 3.11, 1986 Regs. Form 3 (Scot)). If he resigns, his intention to do so will already have been notified to the relevant interested parties under 1986 Regulation 6 (see above), and on his resignation taking effect he must notify the registrar of companies on Form 3 (Scot) (1986 Regs.) within 14 days (I.A., s.62(5)).[62] If he is removed by the court, the relevant petition or note will have been intimated in accordance with the appropriate Rules of Court (see R.C.S. 216 and Sh.Ct.R. 17), and again the holder must notify the registrar on Form 3 (Scot) within 14 days of the order (I.A., s.62(5)).

If he ceases to be an insolvency practitioner or vacates office on completion of the receivership he must give notice to the registrar on

---

[60] Para. 244, *ante.*
[61] s.478(4) "Where a receiver ceases to act as such, etc."
[62] Amended from seven days by the I.A. 1986, s.62(5).

Form 3 (Scot) within 14 days (I.A., s.62(5); 1986 Rule 3.11) and also within 14 days notify other relevant interested parties (see below), but no form is prescribed for notice to parties other than the registrar (1986 Rule 3.11). If the receiver dies the notice by the holder of the charge to the registrar (to be given "forthwith on his becoming aware of the death") is on Form 3.3 (Scot) (1986 Rule 3.10).

246 The relevant interested parties for the purposes of receiving notice under 1986 Rules 3.10 and 3.11 are the members of the creditors' committee (if any), the company or, if it is in liquidation, its liquidator, the holder of any other floating charge and any receiver appointed by him. Where 1986 Rule 3.11 applies, the receiver must also notify the holder of the charge by virtue of which he was appointed.

1986 Rule 3.11 implies that, when he has completed the receivership, the receiver does not require to give notice of intention to resign, but will simply vacate office and give notice accordingly. If the receiver decides he cannot realise any more assets, but the charge holder has not been fully paid, the receiver can simply give notice that he has vacated office, and it will then be for the charge holder to appoint a successor, if he so wishes.

The notice given to the registrar under the foregoing provisions is entered in the company's register of charges. Failure to give such notice renders the party responsible liable to a default fine (I.A., s.62(5)).

If one month after the receiver has been removed or has ceased to act, no other receiver has been appointed by the holder of the same charge, the floating charge re-floats (I.A., s.62(6)). The time during which an administration order is in force is excluded from this period.[63] Re-floating is automatic on expiry of the time limit, and the property ceases to be attached by the charge.

Some of the events giving rise to a receiver ceasing to act (*e.g.* death, or loss of qualification) occur on a definite date which will trigger the operation of the Insolvency Act, section 62(6) without the charge holder necessarily being aware of the situation (although in practice this may be rare).

Since "re-floating" may prejudice the holder of the charge, a receiver who has failed to give proper notice to the holder that he intends to resign, or has vacated office, may be liable in damages.

General powers of the court

247 In addition to its powers as to the appointment and removal of receivers and various specific powers referred to *passim* in this chapter, the court is given further powers under section 63 of the Insolvency Act (see R.C.S. 216; Sh.Ct.R. 17):

---

[63] Amendment added in the I.A., s.62(6).

1. The holder of a floating charge by virtue of which a receiver has been appointed or the receiver may apply for directions on any matter connected with the receiver's functions.
2. Where the receiver's appointment is discovered to be invalid, whether by virtue of the invalidity of the instrument of appointment or otherwise (*e.g.* through want of registration or other defect in the charge) the court may order the holder of the charge to indemnify the person appointed against any liability which arises solely by reason of the invalidity. Although section 63(2) refers only to "the appointment," if the appointment is invalid because of a defect in the *acceptance* procedure which has been overlooked (see above), the section should still permit the court to make an order.

The 1986 Rules (Rule 7.32) also give the court the same power to cure procedural defects as it has in bankruptcy proceedings under the Bankruptcy (Scotland) Act 1985, section 63.[63a]

Publication and notification of appointment of a receiver

248 Where a receiver has been appointed, every invoice, order for goods or business letter issued by or on behalf of the company or the receiver or the company's liquidator, on which the company's name appears, must contain a statement that a receiver has been appointed (I.A., s.64(1)). Failure may incur a default fine (I.A., s.64(2)).

In addition to filing notice of his appointment with the registrar (I.A., ss.53(1) and 54(3)) the receiver must notify the company "forthwith" and publish notice of his appointment (I.A., s.65(1)(*a*)).[64] Unless the court otherwise directs he must also notify all creditors of whose addresses he is aware within 28 days of his appointment (I.A., s.65(1)(*b*)). These provisions do not apply if the receiver is appointed to act jointly with an existing receiver, or in place of a receiver who had died or ceased to act, except as may be necessary to complete the procedure (I.A., s.65(2)). These notices must still be given if the company is in liquidation, even if the liquidator and the receiver are the same person but then "with any necessary modifications" (I.A., s.65(3)). Failure to comply without reasonable excuse may incur a default fine (I.A., s.65(4)).

Statement of affairs

242 The Insolvency Act (ss.66, 67) substantially amended the previous provisions (sections 481 and 482) with respect to the preparation and circulation of information about the company in receivership. Like the earlier provisions, these apply to every receiver and are not restricted

---

[63a] See para. 539, *post.*
[64] The form of notice is prescribed by the 1986 Regs., Form 4 (Scot).

(as are the equivalent English provisions[65]) to "administrative receivers."

"Forthwith" after his appointment the receiver "shall" (see below) require some or all of the persons listed in the Insolvency Act, section 66(3) to submit a statement of the assets, debts and liabilities of the company, the names and addresses of its creditors, and the dates of creation and other particulars of any securities held by such creditors. The statement must be by affidavit in the prescribed form[66] and contain the information prescribed in this form (I.A., s.66(1) and (2)). The notice calling for a statement must itself be in the form prescribed by 1986 Rule 3.2(1) (Form 3.1 (Scot)) and be accompanied by a copy of Form 5 (Scot) for completion by the deponent. The statement must be retained in the receiver's sederunt book (1986 Rule 3.2(3)). The receiver can pay the reasonable expenses incurred by a deponent in making up the statement, as an expense in the receivership, subject to a right of appeal to the court (R.C.S. 216; Sh.Ct.R. 17), but this does not relieve the deponent of his duty to provide the receiver with a statement or other information (1986 Rule 3.3).

Those whom the receiver may choose to make the prescribed statement are (I.A., s.66(3)):

(a) those who are or have been officers of the company, *i.e.* any person who has been a director or secretary since its formation;

(b) those who have "taken part in the company's formation" at any time within one year before the date of the appointment of the receiver; this would extend to solicitors, accountants, formation agents and others, particularly the persons giving the "declaration of compliance" (Form 12) or the agent signing the statement of first directors, etc. (Form 10) as well as the initial subscribers or promoters;

(c) all current employees and any employees who left employment within a year before the receiver's appointment if such employees and ex-employees are in the opinion of the receiver capable of giving the required information (a condition which is meaningless since the receiver has discretion whom to call upon for a statement); and

(d) those who are or have been within the year before the receiver's appointment officers of or in the employment of a company which is or within that year was an officer of the company; it appears that this is in addition to the obligation of the company itself under (a).

For the purposes of the Insolvency Act, section 66(3) "employment" includes employment under a contract for services, thus bringing within the scope of the receiver's inquiry those who have provided

---

[65] I.A., ss.47, 48, replacing ss.495–497.
[66] Form 5 (Scot).

professional services to the company within the year before his appointment.

The statement must be supplied within 21 days but the receiver may extend this time. He may also excuse any person from supplying a statement, but the court may supersede this release by itself ordering a statement to be given. The peremptory wording of Insolvency Act, section 66(1) and the requirement that the contents of the statement be circulated (see below) suggests that even if the receiver believes no one can usefully be asked to supply a statement, he must, strictly speaking, still call for one and then exercise his discretion to excuse all those he has asked (subject to the court's power to overrule him). A default fine may be imposed for non-compliance with these provisions (I.A., s.66(4)–(6)).

These provisions are substantially identical to the provisions of the Insolvency Act, section 131 (as adapted for Scotland) relating to the statement of affairs to be provided to the liquidator in a winding up by the court.[67] As in that case, there is nothing to prevent the receiver making a series of calls upon the same, or different, persons for a statement of affairs, and several different statements may result.

The receiver must call for a statement of affairs "forthwith" on his appointment. (There is no like obligation on a liquidator). This term is not further specified but, by inference from the Insolvency Act, section 67 (see below), the receiver must call for statements within four to eight weeks of his appointment, so that he can submit his report within the three months normally required.

Report by receiver

250 Within three months of his appointment (or such longer period as the court may allow)[68] the receiver must circulate a report on the company (I.A., s.67). This must be sent to the registrar of companies, the holder of the charge under which he has been appointed, to any trustees for secured creditors and to all secured creditors (I.A., s.67(1)). "Secured creditors" is to be interpreted in the strict (and normal) sense of holding in respect of their debt a security over property of the company (I.A., s.67(9)).

The Act here introduces a gratuitous difficulty. The receiver need not send a report to any secured creditors of whose addresses he is unaware (by necessary inference he is presumably excused if he is also unaware of their identity). This qualification, however, does not apply to any *trustees* for secured creditors. The register of charges maintained by the company may give the necessary information, but if not or if the register is inaccurate the receiver appears to have no easy solution. It is surely absurd to require him to apply to the court for directions under

---

[67] See para. 484, *post.*
[68] R.C.S. 216(2); Sh.Ct.R. 17(2).

the Insolvency Act, section 63 for a routine circular which is, in any event, to appear on the public file.

The material content of the receiver's report, as specified in the Insolvency Act, section 67(1) is:

(a) "the events leading up to his appointment, so far as the receiver is aware of them." This may be as little as the execution of the instrument of appointment or the making of the court order (both self-evident) or a detailed history of the difficulties of the company. The Act provides no guidance, and this requirement achieves no practical benefit;

(b) "the disposal or proposed disposal" of the company's property and "the carrying on or proposed carrying on" of its business;

(c) the principal and interest payable to the floating charge holder and the amounts payable to preferential creditors; and

(d) the amount (if any) likely to be available for the payment of other creditors.

The report must include a summary of the statement of affairs submitted by the directors, etc. of the company under the Insolvency Act, section 66 and the receiver's comments (if any) thereon (I.A., s.67(5)). Presumably, if several statements have been provided to the receiver, he should refer to any material differences among them in the "summary," but he is under no obligation to make any comment. The report may omit any information "which would seriously prejudice the carrying out by the receiver of his functions" (I.A., s.67(6)). There is no suggestion that anyone but the receiver himself has the right to decide what information should be excluded on this ground, although he or the charge holder may of course apply to the court for directions under the Insolvency Act, section 63(1).

The period of three months includes the time taken to ingather statements from the directors and others under the Insolvency Act, section 66. In many cases it will be inadequate for a full report, although it is an improvement on the two months allowed under section 481 prior to amendment, and the receiver is likely, in many cases, to require to apply to the court for an extension of time. The degree of accuracy required of the report is, however, not specified, so the receiver is able to present the information "so far as he is able to ascertain the same" without infringing the Act.

UNSECURED CREDITORS

251 The Insolvency Act and the 1986 Rules introduced a number of further requirements for the protection of unsecured creditors.

Circulation of report

252 If the company is not in liquidation, the receiver must, within the same period of three months for circulating a report to secured creditors, etc., (above) (or longer if the court allows) send a copy of his report to all unsecured creditors (so far as he is aware of their addresses), or publish a notice giving an address to which such creditors can apply for a free copy. The notice is to be published in a newspaper circulating in the area where the company has its principal place of business or in such other newspaper as the receiver thinks most appropriate for bringing it to the notice of unsecured creditors.[69] He must also, (within the same period) lay a copy of his report before a meeting of the unsecured creditors (I.A., s.67(2)). The court may however excuse the receiver from convening this meeting if (a) the report states the receiver intends to apply for such a direction and (b) not less than 14 days before the court considers the application the receiver has complied with his obligation to circulate copies or notify unsecured creditors where they may obtain a copy (I.A., s.67(3)). If the company is in liquidation the receiver must send a copy of his report to the liquidator within seven days of sending it to the secured creditors, and he is then excused from further communication with unsecured creditors or holding a meeting under the Insolvency Act, section 67(2). If the liquidator is appointed after the receiver, he must submit his report to the liquidator within seven days of the report to secured creditors or the liquidator's appointment (whichever is later), and if he does so within the period for circulating his report to unsecured creditors he is excused compliance with the Insolvency Act, section 67(2) (I.A., s.67(4)). The provisions of the Insolvency Act, section 65(2) (*ante*) modifying the procedure where a joint or successor receiver is appointed, also apply to the procedure under the Insolvency Act, section 67 (I.A., s.67(7)). Default may be penalised (I.A., s.67(8)).

The requirement of the receiver to issue an abstract of receipts and payments annually (and on his ceasing to act) formerly imposed by section 481(2) has been removed by the Insolvency Act amendments.

Meeting of creditors

253 The procedure for the creditors' meeting is contained in the 1986 Rules, Part 7. These are similar to the rules for meetings of creditors in liquidations, which are discussed in detail in paragraphs 454 to 458 below. What follows is a summary of the rules as they apply in a receivership.

The receiver must convene the meeting for a "business day"[70] between 10 a.m. and 4 p.m. and he may also advertise it in a suitable newspaper. He must give at least 14 days' written notice, and the notice must specify the purpose of the meeting and those who are

---

[69] 1986 Regs., para. 7.
[70] "Business day" is defined (1986 Rule 0.2(1)) as any day other than a Saturday, a Sunday, Christmas Day, Good Friday or a day which is a bank holiday in any part of Great Britain. A meeting under I.A., s.67(2) in a *Scottish* receivership cannot, therefore, be held (*inter alia*) on a day which is an *English* bank holiday.

entitled to attend and vote. The notice must refer to the need to lodge claims to be entitled to vote, and to the right to appoint a proxy; proxy forms are to be provided (1986 Rules 7.1 to 7.3). For the details of giving notice by post, etc., see 1986 Rules 7.21 to 7.23.

Voting is in proportion to the value of claims submitted to and accepted for voting purposes by the receiver. The procedure for having claims adjudicated is the same as in liquidations under 1986 Rules 4.15 to 4.17 (discussed in paragraphs 470 to 473 below) with appropriate modifications (1986 Rule 7.9). Resolutions are passed by majority in value (1986 Rule 7.12). The chairman is the receiver or his nominee (being his employee or another insolvency practitioner) and he must retain a report of the proceedings in the sederunt book (1986 Rules 7.5 and 7.13). Proxy voting is dealt with in 1986 Rules 7.14 to 7.20. The 1987 Amendments supply a form of proxy (Form 4.29 (Scot)) which must be issued with every notice of meeting. A single creditor will constitute a quorum (1986 Rule 7.7) but adjournment by the chairman is possible if no creditor appears (1986 Rule 7.8). The 1987 Amendments require the chairman to wait 15 minutes before commencing business if the quorum is constituted by himself alone, or himself and one other, if he is aware of other persons who might attend and vote (1986 Rule 7.7(3)). There is a presumption that meetings which appear to have been regularly called, and whose proceedings are recorded, are valid (1986 Rules 7.24 and 7.25).

Committee of creditors

254 The Insolvency Act, section 68 introduced the possibility of a committee of unsecured creditors being set up in a receivership under statutory authority. It is understood that an informal creditors' committee was sometimes established to assist the receiver under the former law. This can, however, only be done at the meeting (if any) summoned to consider the receiver's report under the Insolvency Act, section 67 (I.A., s.68(1)). No such committee can exist, therefore, if the court has excused the receiver from holding such a meeting, or if a liquidator has been appointed before it was due to be held, nor can the creditors set one up later. A committee of creditors is unlikely to be established unless there is the possibility of a surplus of assets available for unsecured creditors of sufficient size to justify the additional expense involved.

The constitution and procedure of the committee are laid down in the 1986 Rules, which adopt and modify the rules for the liquidation committee, discussed in detail in paragraphs 449 to 453 below. The following paragraphs summarise these, as they apply in receiverships.

The committee is to consist of at least three and not more than five creditors elected at the meeting held under the Insolvency Act, section 67. Any creditor whose claim has not been rejected for voting purposes (see above) can be a member. Partnerships and bodies corporate can be represented on the committee (1986 Rule 3.4). The receiver has to issue a certificate of due constitution (Form 4.20 (Scot)) giving details of the membership before the committee can act, and the receiver must lodge with the registrar of companies the certificate and any amended certificate along with Form 4.22 (Scot) (1986 Rule 4.42 as adapted by Rule 3.6). The committee can, however, act before the forms are lodged with the registrar.

A committee member can appoint a representative to attend in his place (1986 Rule 4.48, as adapted by Rule 3.6). A committee member may resign by written notice to the receiver. He will cease to be a member automatically if he goes bankrupt, fails to attend at least three consecutive meetings without being excused at the last of these or ceases to be a creditor, and he can be removed by majority vote of the unsecured creditors (1986 Rules 4.49 to 4.51, as adapted by Rule 3.6). Vacancies are filled under 1986 Rule 4.52, as adapted. The first meeting of the committee is to be held within three months of its establishment, convened by the receiver, and thereafter as requested by the committee. The time and place are determined by the receiver, and there is no requirement that such meetings be held on a "business day." Not less than seven days notice is to be given (1986 Rule 4.45, as adapted). The chairman will be the receiver or his nominee (being his employee or another insolvency practitioner). The quorum is two and voting is by simple majority. Postal or circulated resolutions are permitted (1986 Rules 4.66, 4.47, 4.54 and 4.55, as adapted). 1986 Rule 4.57 is adapted to the effect that committee members are entitled, as of right, to recover as an expense of the receivership, the reasonable travelling expenses of attendance or otherwise in the business of the committee unless a meeting is called otherwise than by the receiver within three months of the previous meeting (1986 Rule 3.6(4)).

The committee's functions are to represent to the receiver the views of the unsecured creditors and to "act in relation to him in such manner as may be agreed from time to time" (1986 Rule 3.5). It is not clear who is to be involved in such an agreement, but prima facie the committee could agree on some function with the receiver, or agree among themselves without his consent. In the latter case, if the receiver objects to the cost of holding superfluous meetings, even if they are at longer intervals than three months, he could apply to the court under the Insolvency Act, section 63 to relieve the receivership of the unnecessary expense. In addition, the committee can summon the receiver to attend before it and give such information about his administration as it may reasonably require. The notice to the receiver must be in writing signed by a majority of the committee (or their representatives). It must give him at least seven days' notice. It must be for a "business day"[71] chosen by the committee, but the receiver

---

[71] See n. 70, para. 253, *supra*.

chooses the time and place. The committee can elect a temporary chairman for such a meeting in place of the receiver, who would normally be the chairman (I.A., s.68(2); 1986 Rule 3.7). It is also the duty of the committee to review the receiver's caution from time to time, to ascertain that it is adequate (1986 Rule 7.28).

Unlike the situation in a liquidation, where transactions between the company and members of the liquidation committee and their "associates" are strictly regulated by 1986 Rule 4.59, members of the creditors' committee in a receivership are prima facie entitled to enter into normal commercial contracts with the company, subject to the power of the court to set aside any transaction which is not on proper terms, and to order compensation (1986 Rule 3.8).

The acts of the committee are valid notwithstanding any defect in the appointment, election or qualification of any member or representative of a member, or in the formalities of its establishment (1986 Rule 4.59A, added by the 1987 Amendments).

Default by receiver

255 In addition to the default penalty for failure to publish his appointment (I.A., s.65(4)) or failure to issue his report (I.A., s.67(8)) (*ante*) (or any other default provision) the court may order a receiver to make good any omission under Insolvency Act, section 69(1) (R.C.S. 216; Sh.Ct.R. 17). If the default relates to the filing or issue of returns, reports, etc., the application can be at the instance of any creditor or member of the company or by the registrar of companies. If the receiver has failed to submit a proper accounting to the liquidator of the company the application for an appropriate order must be by the liquidator (I.A., s.69(2)). Expenses may be awarded against the receiver.[72] Although the Act no longer says so in terms[73] the receiver remains subject to the general law of accounting for his intromissions to any person properly entitled to require the same, such as the company itself. This is now supplemented by the duty to submit regular abstracts of receipts and payments under 1986 Rule 3.9 in the prescribed form (Form 3.2 (Scot)). Such accounts have to be made up by the receiver within two months after the end of each year in office, and within two months after he ceases to act, for the period since the last such accounts. Copies must be sent to the registrar of companies, the holder of the charge under which he was appointed, the members of the creditors' committee (if any) and the company or, if it is in liquidation, its liquidator. The court may grant the receiver an extension of the time limit (R.C.S. 216(2); Sh.Ct.R. 17(2)). Compliance with 1986 Rule 3.9 does not *per se* relieve the receiver of any general obligation to render proper accounts (1986 Rule 3.9(4)).

---

[72] Under the general principles of court procedure.
[73] s.481(6) is omitted from the I.A., s.67.

Appointment of a receiver and other acts on behalf of a series of debenture holders

256 A floating charge securing a debenture or series of debentures may have no one holder entitled to appoint a receiver and to perform other functions assigned to the holder. If the relevant document provides for a receiver to be appointed by a specified person or body, he or it is to be treated as the holder of the charge. In the absence of any such nomination and in the case of a series of debentures, the trustees are to be regarded as the holder. If there are no trustees, the holder is a specified majority of debenture holders (I.A., s.70(2)).

The receiver and the directors

257 Section 7 of the Company Directors Disqualification Act 1986[74] provides for the Secretary of State to apply to the court for a disqualification order under section 6 of that Act against a director of a company which has become insolvent[75] and whose conduct makes him unfit to be concerned in the management of a company.[76] The Act applies to any person who is or has been a director (or shadow director) of a company which has become insolvent while he was a director or subsequently. Regulations made under the Act[77] require an "administrative receiver"[78] to submit Form D2 (Scot) and appendices in respect of the company and every person who was a director or shadow director within three years prior to the commencement of the receivership indicating whether, in his opinion, any of them is "unfit" and giving reasons. Form D2 (Scot) is not required unless the receiver considers one at least of such persons is "unfit" (Disqualification Act 1986, s.7(3)). If Form D2 (Scot) is not submitted, however, the receiver must within six months of the commencement of the receivership furnish the Secretary of State with a return on Form D4 (Scot) indicating either that there is nothing requiring a report, or that he is still gathering the necessary information for it.[79]

The directors are not relieved of their duty to prepare statutory accounts in respect of the company under sections 226 *et seq.* of the Act, and the receiver must give them sufficient information to enable them

---

[74] Originally s.12(3)–(6) of the I.A. 1985 (effective April 28, 1986).

[75] "Insolvency" is defined in a technical sense for this purpose. The appointment of an administrative receiver is *per se* "insolvency" for the purposes of the reporting provisions (see s.6(2) of the Company Directors Disqualification Act 1986).

[76] See *Palmer*, paras. 8.101 *et seq.*

[77] The Insolvent Companies (Reports on Conduct of Directors) (Scotland) Rules 1986 (S.I. 1986 No. 626 (S.59)) replaced (from December 29, 1986) by the Insolvent Companies (Reports on Conduct of Directors) (No. 2) (Scotland) Rules 1986 (S.I. 1986 No. 1916 (S.140).

[78] See para. 219, *ante.*

[79] See further *Palmer*, paras. 8.101 *et seq.* The Department of Trade and Industry has published a guide on the completion of these reports, to which reference should be made.

to prepare the accounts.[80] If the directors genuinely propose to redeem the amount secured by the charge, the receiver must give them information reasonably required to enable them to redeem, and also about the assets remaining in his hands.[81] His common law duty of accounting has already been mentioned.[82]

PENSION SCHEMES

258 Assets held by trustees for an occupational pension scheme are, of course, not assets of the company which established the scheme and are, therefore, incapable of being attached by a floating charge unless and until they become repayable to the company, on the fund being wound up or in the event of its being over-funded (subject always to the terms of the trust deed constituting the scheme). By amendments made to the Social Security Act 1975 by the Social Security Act 1990 an "insolvency practitioner" (including an administrative receiver) appointed on or after November 12, 1990 is, however, required to ensure that there is at least one "independent trustee" (as defined) of the scheme and, if necessary, he is required to appoint such a trustee.[83] The Act does not, however, make it clear how a receiver is to effect such an appointment. Assuming, as will usually be the case, the company is empowered to appoint trustees, the receiver's general power to act in the name of the company[84] should suffice for this purpose.

A receiver's duty of care extends to the beneficiaries of a pension scheme, so that he may be liable in damages to them if he terminates it to their prejudice without giving adequate notice.[85]

Receiver's records

259 In addition to the accounting requirements referred to above the receiver must maintain a "sederunt book" in which are recorded the proceedings at meetings of the creditors and the creditors' committee, and the important documentary records of his administration. This must be open for inspection. An entry constitutes sufficient evidence of the facts stated therein "except where it is founded on by (the receiver) in his own interest" (1986 Rule 7.33). Right of access may be refused on grounds of confidentiality or the damage to the interests of

---

[80] *Cf. Smiths Ltd.* v. *Middleton* [1979] 3 All E.R. 842 (decided on the equivalent English provisions). The practicability of retaining this duty in the context of a receivership, without modification, has not been addressed in the legislation (including the Companies Act 1989).

[81] *Gomba Holdings UK Ltd.* v. *Minories Finance* [1986] 3 All E.R. 94; affrmd. [1989] 1 All E.R. 261 (C.A.).

[82] Para. 250, *supra*.

[83] Social Security Act 1990, Sched. 4, para. 1; Social Security Act 1990 (Commencement No. 2) Order 1990 (S.I. 1990 No. 1942); Occupational Services Schemes (Independent Trustee) Regulations 1990 (S.I. 1990 No. 2075).

[84] See paras. 230 and 231, *ante*.

[85] *Larson's Exrx.* v. *Henderson*, 1990 S.L.T. 498.

creditors which might follow disclosure, subject to right of appeal to the court against refusal (1986 Rule 7.27). If the company objects to the receiver releasing information which it regards as confidential application would require to be made to the courts for interdict under the general law.

Documents prepared by the receiver for his own use belong to him or the charge holder, not the company.[86]

Additions to the 1986 Rules made by the 1987 Amendments require the sederunt book to be capable of being reproduced in legible form, if it is maintained in non-documentary form, *e.g.* as a computer tape or disc. The sederunt book is to be retained for at least 10 years from the resignation of the receiver without a further receiver being appointed (1986 Rule 7.33(5)–(7)). The records of the receivership must be passed on to the insolvency practitioner responsible for any subsequent insolvency proceedings within 30 days of this being requested, or in any event within six months. If the receivership has terminated and no subsequent insolvency proceedings have commenced within six months, he may dispose of the books, records and papers of the company but only in accordance with directions obtained from the creditors' committee (if any), the members of the company by extraordinary resolution, or the court (1986 Rule 7.34(1) and (2)).

VALUE ADDED TAX

260 By regulation[87] every administrative receiver[88] must issue a certificate in the prescribed form if the company is insolvent within the meaning of section 22(3) of the Value Added Tax Act 1983. He must notify every known creditor or supplier that such a certificate has been issued, but the certificate itself is retained as part of the company's accounting records. Creditors cannot demand a copy of the certificate (1986 Rule 3.13(3)) but the fact of its issue enables them to claim a credit in respect of any VAT which has become irrecoverable.

The practical value of this certificate to creditors has largely disappeared with amendments allowing VAT to be reclaimed on unpaid accounts after one year.[89]

FIXED SECURITIES: POWER OF SALE

261 The holder of a fixed security over Scottish property has no power to appoint a receiver and, in the case of heritable property, will require to

---

[86] *Gomba Holdings U.K. Ltd.* v. *Minories Finance* [1989] 1 All E.R. 261 (C.A.).
[87] The Administrative Receivers (Value Added Tax Certificates) (Scotland) Rules 1986 (S.I. 1986 No. 304 (S.23)) (effective April 1, 1986). Superseded (from December 29, 1986) by the 1986 Rules 3.12–3.14.
[88] See para. 219, *ante.*
[89] Finance Act 1991, s.15; initially two years under Finance Act 1990, s.11.

reserve power in his security deed to sell or otherwise realise the property.[90]

In the case of a fixed security over heritable property, however, the remedies of the creditor are now governed by the Conveyancing and Feudal Reform (Scotland) Act 1970. This Act provides for a statutory power of sale in every such security and other remedies. The purchaser is protected against reduction of his title, any remedy being restricted to a claim for damages by the debtor against the seller.[91]

---

[90] *United Dominions Trust* v. *Site Preparations Ltd. (No. 1),* 1978 S.L.T. (Sh.Ct.) 14.
[91] *Imperial Hotel (Aberdeen) Ltd.* v. *Vaux Breweries Ltd.,* 1978 S.L.T. 113.

CHAPTER 3

VOLUNTARY ARRANGEMENTS

INTRODUCTION

301 Part I of the Insolvency Act 1986 contains provisions to enable a company, including one for which an administration order is in force or which is being wound up, to enter into a voluntary arrangement with its creditors.[1] The need for a suitably simple procedure whereby a company may conclude a legally effective arrangement with its creditors had long been recognised. In Part II of Chapter 7 of their Final Report, the Review Committee on Insolvency Law and Practice[2] surveyed the various procedures which were provided under the then-existing companies legislation,[3] and amply demonstrated that for a combination of technical and practical reasons each procedure proved to be cumbersome and unsuitable in the context of an attempt to rationalise the affairs of a company which is nearly or actually insolvent. In the opinion of the Committee, the complexity and expense of the requisite procedures was such as to preclude the majority of insolvent companies from effecting compositions with their creditors. Accordingly the Committee proposed, as a solution for this specific problem, a new form of voluntary arrangement which would be concluded without an order of the court but which would nevertheless constitute a formal and binding arrangement between the company and its creditors.[4] The procedure was envisaged as serving to complement the administration order procedure which, among numerous other points of distinction, notably involves the obtaining of a court order.[5] The successive Insolvency Acts of 1985 and 1986 duly made provision for both types of procedure, and in the case of the new form of voluntary arrangement for companies the Committee's recommendations, deliberately based upon their parallel proposals for cases of individual insolvency, have been closely followed and implemented. In accordance with those recommendations, it is made a principal feature of the procedure under Part I of the Insolvency Act 1986 that any voluntary arrangement proposed and, in due course,

---

[1] Pt. I of the I.A. 1986 (ss.1–7 inclusive) corresponds in substance to Chap. II of Pt. II of the I.A. 1985 (ss.20–26 inclusive). The provisions of the I.A. 1985 were repealed without ever having come into force (I.A. 1986, s.438 and Sched. 12).

[2] Cmnd. 8558 (1982), paras. 400–430 inclusive.

[3] The relevant provisions referred to were ss.206, 287 and 306 of the Companies Act 1948, subsequently contained in ss.425, 582 and 601 respectively of the Companies Act 1985. Ss.583 and 601 were repealed by Sched. 12 to the I.A. 1986.

[4] Cmnd. 8558, paras. 419–422, 428–430.

[5] For a description of the Administration Order procedure see paras. 101 *et seq., ante.*

concluded under that Part of the Act will be required first to be appraised and endorsed, and subsequently to be administered and implemented, by a qualified insolvency practitioner.[6]

THE PROPOSAL FOR A VOLUNTARY ARRANGEMENT[6a]

302 Section 1 of the Insolvency Act 1986 indicates that the procedure for the conclusion of a voluntary arrangement is commenced by the making of a proposal to the company and to its creditors for a composition in satisfaction of its debts or a scheme of arrangement of its affairs.[7] The proposal must provide for some person (known as "the nominee") to act in relation to the voluntary arrangement either as trustee or in some other capacity for the purpose of supervising its implementation.[8]

Who may make a proposal?

303 Important limitations are imposed by the provisions of section 1 both with regard to the persons who are eligible to make a proposal for a voluntary arrangement, and with regard to the persons who are eligible to serve as the nominee. As to the former, section 1(1) indicates that the directors of the company may make the proposal, but that they may do so only under the circumstances that no administration order is in force in respect of the company, and that it is not being wound up. The subsection requires the directors to act collectively in making the relevant proposal and it may be observed that, unlike the situation which obtains under an administration order proceeding, the directors are not deprived of their powers of management during the implementation of a voluntary arrangement, nor do the company's property and affairs gain the benefit of any general and automatic moratorium either prior to the formal conclusion of the voluntary arrangement, or subsequently, save in so far as a wide circle of parties, both assenting and non-assenting, become bound by the voluntary arrangement once it has been duly approved.[9] Where the company is already the subject of an administration order, or where it is being wound up, a proposal for a voluntary arrangement may only be made by the administrator or the liquidator respectively, as the case may be.[10] The question of eligibility to serve as nominee is considered below.

---

[6] *Cf.* Cmnd. 8558, paras. 350–399, 428–430. The meaning of the expression "qualified insolvency practitioner," as governed by Pt. XIII of the I.A. 1986, is explained in para. 440, *post.*

[6a] The procedural aspects are discussed further in para. 315, *post.*

[7] I.A. 1986, s.1(1).

[8] *Ibid.*, s.1(2). The procedural rules are contained in Pt. I of the Insolvency (Scotland) Rules 1986 (S.I. 1986 No. 1915) as amended by the Insolvency (Scotland) Amendment Rules 1987 (S.I. 1987 No. 1921) effective (including the 1987 amendments) December 29, 1986, the date that Pt. I of the Insolvency Act 1986 came into force. The rules are referred to in this chapter as "the 1986 Rules."

[9] *Ibid.* (discussed *infra*).

[10] *Ibid.*, s.1(3).

The terms of the proposal

304 Section 1 of the Insolvency Act 1986 prescribes only the barest essentials with regard to the required terms and substance of any proposal made for the purposes of Part I of the Act. The provisions of the section stipulate in effect that the proposal must embody the terms of a compact between the company and its creditors for a composition in satisfaction of the company's debts, or a scheme of arrangement of its affairs. In the absence of any statutory provisions regulating the permissible terms of such an arrangement, it becomes in effect a pure question of whether the terms themselves are capable of commanding the requisite measure of approval from the two respective sides so as to render the arrangement effective and binding. It is true that deliberate safeguards are contained in subsections (3) and (4) of section 4 to protect the positions of secured or preferential creditors, but even in this respect an overall policy of *laissez-faire* is adopted, and the rights of such creditors are permitted to be modified as part of the terms of the arrangement, provided that in each instance this is done with the concurrence of the individual creditors who are thereby affected.

305 The one express statutory requirement of a positive nature, with regard to the terms of the proposal, is that already referred to whereby section 1(2) requires provision to be made for a named person ("the nominee") to act in relation to the arrangement either as trustee or in some other way for the purpose of supervising its implementation. Section 1(2) imposes the further requirement that the nominee must be a person who is qualified to act as an insolvency practitioner in relation to the company. This is a further consequence of the implementation, via Part XIII of the Insolvency Act 1986, of one of the main recommendations of the Insolvency Law Review Committee with regard to the attainment of assured minimum standards of competence, integrity and experience with respect to every person, other than the official receiver himself, who is appointed to any of the key administrative positions in the various types of insolvency proceeding. The statutory provisions which determine those persons who are qualified to act as an insolvency practitioner in relation to a company are contained in sections 388 to 398 of the Insolvency Act 1986, together with Schedule 7 thereto.[11] It should be noted that, in addition to possessing the general qualifications prescribed by Part XIII of the Act, the nominee must ensure that he is not precluded on an ad hoc basis from accepting the appointment in question, for example by virtue of the guidelines and rules of conduct prescribed by any professional body to which he may belong, and by virtue of whose standing the nominee enjoys his own basic authority to act as an

---

[11] See also para. 440, *post*.

insolvency practitioner.[12] An exclusionary rule in point would be one which forbids or discourages members of the professional body in question from acting as insolvency practitioners in circumstances where an actual or potential conflict of interest may arise by reason of their personal association with a company or with any persons who are concerned in its management or who are creditors of the company.[13] No criminal sanction is prescribed in relation to any acts performed by a person in the capacity of nominee under a proposal for a voluntary arrangement, where it transpires that the nominee is not qualified to act as an insolvency practitioner in relation to the company. It should be borne in mind however that if such a person is in due course elevated to the position of supervisor of the arrangement[14] he will, by so acting at a time when he is unqualified to do so, commit a criminal offence of strict liability by reason of sections 388(1)(*b*) and 389(1) of the Insolvency Act 1986.

Functions of the nominee

306 Where the nominee is not the administrator or liquidator of the company, his first function is to prepare a report upon the basis of his personal assessment of the soundness and fairness of the proposed voluntary arrangement. Section 2 of the Insolvency Act 1986 requires that the nominee shall submit his report to the court within 28 days after he is given notice of the proposal for a voluntary arrangement, or within such longer period as the court may allow. Although the nominee is under a statutory obligation to furnish the court with a report stating whether, in his opinion, meetings of the company and its creditors should be summoned to consider the proposal (and if so, when and where this should take place),[15] the Act does not establish any positive role for the court to fulfil subsequently to having received the nominee's report. Although, by virtue of section 3(1) of the Insolvency Act, it is effectively made a precondition to the nominee's proceeding to convene the requisite meetings of the company and its creditors that he shall first have reported to the court in favour of this course of action, his ability to convene the meetings is not dependent upon the making of any order to that effect by the court in question. On the contrary, section 3(1) provides that the nominee is obliged, as a consequence of his own report in favour of so proceeding, to summon those meetings for the time, date and place proposed in the report, unless the court otherwise directs. The court can become involved in a more positive sense as a consequence of the provision contained in

---

[12] See I.A. 1986, ss.390(2)(*a*), 391(1), (2). See also the Insolvency Practitioners Regulations 1990 (S.I. 1990 No. 439) and the Insolvency Practitioners (Recognised Professional Bodies) Order 1986 (S.I. 1986 No. 1764).

[13] *Cf.* the concept of "associate," as defined in s.435 of the I.A. 1986.

[14] See I.A. 1986, s.7(2).

[15] *Ibid.*, s.2(2)(*a*), (*b*).

section 2(4) if the nominee altogether fails to submit the report required by section 2. To overcome the possibility of a stultifying delay, or stalemate, subsection (4) enables the person intending to make the proposal for a voluntary arrangement to apply to the court for the original nominee to be replaced by another suitably qualified person. When such an application is made the original nominee must be given at least seven days' notice thereto.[16] Rule 1.7(2) of the Insolvency (Scotland) Rules 1986 imposes the requirement that where the nominee's opinion is to the effect that meetings should not be summoned, he must in his report give reasons for that opinion.

The underlying purpose of the provisions contained in sections 1(2) and 3(1) is to ensure that no abortive or futile meetings are convened in an effort to conclude a voluntary arrangement. To this end the Insolvency Act imposes the requirement that every intended proposal for such an arrangement shall first be appraised and approved by an independent and properly qualified insolvency practitioner. In practice, it may be assumed that the directors of a company will prepare the draft proposal in consultation with the person who is to be named therein as the nominee. In cases where the company is either the subject of an administration order, or is being wound up, the office holder, who is the only party competent to make a proposal in the circumstances, will in either case be a qualified insolvency practitioner.[17] Hence, it may be assumed that the requisite degree of professional judgment and discernment will be brought to bear by the office holder in formulating the terms of his proposal, and on that premise the office holder, if he provides for himself to be nominee, is permitted to summon meetings of the company and its creditors to consider the proposal at such time and place as he thinks fit, without the need to submit a report to the court as a prerequisite to the taking of this step.[18] If however an administrator or liquidator, while wishing to formulate a proposal for a voluntary arrangement, does not intend to nominate himself to serve as the person responsible for its implementation he must select as nominee someone who is personally qualified to act as an insolvency practitioner in relation to the company, and it is then necessary for such a nominee to fulfil the requirements of section 2(2) of the Insolvency Act before proceeding to convene meetings pursuant to the provisions of section 3(1).[19]

Statement of affairs

307 Essentially, the nominee's report must be based upon an informed professional judgment. For the purpose of enabling the nominee to form the requisite judgment, and to prepare his report, section 2(3) of

[16] 1986 Rule 1.8.
[17] I.A. 1986, ss.388(1)(*a*), 389. *Cf.* ss.19(2)(*a*), 171(4), 172(5).
[18] *Ibid.*, s.3(2). See 1986 Rules, Pt. 1 Chap. 3.
[19] *Cf.* I.A. 1986, s.2(1), and see the 1986 Rules, Pt. 1, Chap. 4.

the Insolvency Act requires that the person intending to submit the proposal must submit to him: (a) a document setting out the terms of the proposed voluntary arrangement, and (b) a statement of the company's affairs, together with other information, in correspondence with the requirements imposed by the 1986 Rules. The latter contain detailed provisions concerning the information which is required to be comprised within the statement of affairs, which the directors are required to lodge with the nominee within seven days after their proposal is delivered to him.[20] The required contents of the statement of affairs are broadly identical to those of a statement of affairs which is to be prepared in the context of an administration or winding up of the company, or where an administrative receiver is appointed over a company.[21] Provision is made in the rules to enable the nominee to oblige the directors to provide him with further and better particulars relating to the company's insolvent circumstances, and such other relevant information with respect to the company's affairs which he thinks necessary for the purpose of enabling him properly to prepare his report.[22] In this connection the directors must give the nominee access to the company's accounts and records, and must supply him with information relating to the business connections and financial circumstances of any past or present director or officer of the company who has been concerned with any other company which has become insolvent, or who has himself been adjudged bankrupt or entered into an arrangement with creditors.[23]

Where the proposal for a voluntary arrangement is made in relation to a company which is subject to an administration order or which is being wound up, the maker of the proposal (the administrator or liquidator, as the case may be) will have obtained the necessary information as to the company's affairs and circumstances, on which to formulate the terms of the proposed arrangement, as a consequence of the filing of the company's statement of affairs pursuant to section 22, 99 or 131 of the Insolvency Act 1986.

MEETINGS OF THE COMPANY AND OF ITS CREDITORS

308 Meetings to consider the proposal are summoned either (where the nominee is not the liquidator or administrator of the company) by the nominee in accordance with section 3(1) of the Insolvency Act or (where he is) by the liquidator or administrator, in accordance with section 3(2). In the former case no step can be taken to summon meetings until the nominee has reported under section 2(2) stating that meetings should be summoned. Under section 3(2) the liquidator or

---

[20] See para. 315, *post*. The nominee may allow a longer period of time than seven days for the lodging of the statement: 1986 Rule 1.5(1).
[21] *Cf*. I.A. 1986, ss.22, 66 and 133, together with the relevant provisions of the 1986 Rules.
[22] 1986 Rule 1.6.
[23] 1986 Rule 1.6(2), (3).

administrator proceeds straight to the summoning of meetings with nothing having to be notified to the court. Under section 3(1) the date on which the meetings are held must be not less than 14 nor more than 28 days from the date on which the nominee's report is filed in court. Under section 3(2), where the nominee is the liquidator or administrator, he must summon meetings on at least 14 days' notice for such time, date and place as he thinks fit. The persons to be summoned to the creditors' meetings by means of notices sent at least 14 days in advance are every creditor of the company of whose claim and address the person summoning the meeting is aware, whether the nominee's knowledge of the creditor's identity results from the information included in the company's statement of affairs or from any other source.[24] Unlike the procedure for concluding a scheme of arrangement under section 425 of the Companies Act 1985, there is no requirement that separate meetings of different classes of creditor be held.[25]

In the case of the meeting of members of the company, notices calling the meeting must be sent, at least 14 days in advance, to all persons who are, to the best of the belief of the person summoning the meeting, members of it.[26]

The purpose of the meetings summoned under section 3 of the Insolvency Act is to decide whether to approve the proposed voluntary arrangement, either in its original form or with modifications.[27] The conduct of the respective meetings is governed by the Insolvency Rules,[28] which impose upon the person summoning the meetings ("the convener") a duty to have regard primarily to the convenience of the creditors when fixing the venue for the meetings.[29] The meetings must be held on the same day, and in the same place, but the creditors' meeting must be fixed for a time in advance of the company meeting.[30] Voting by proxy is permitted at both meetings, and forms of proxy must be sent together with every notice summoning either meeting.[31]

At both the creditors' meeting and the company meeting, and at any combined meeting, the convener acts as chairman, but if he is unable to attend he may nominate another person to act as chairman in his place provided that the person so nominated is either a person qualified to act as an insolvency practitioner in relation to the company, or is an employee of the convener or of his firm and is experienced in

---

[24] I.A. 1986, s.3(3); See para. 315, *post*. The same requirements are imposed where the proposal is made by an administrator or liquidator, and he is not himself the nominee: 1986 Rule 1.12(6).

[25] See *Palmer*, paras. 12.015 to 12.018.

[26] 1986 Rule 1.15. See para. 315, *post*.

[27] I.A. 1986, s.4(1).

[28] *Ibid.*, s.4(5). See para. 315, *post*.

[29] 1986 Rule 1.14(1).

[30] 1986 Rule 1.14(2).

[31] 1986 Rules 7.14 to 7.20 (as applied by Rules 1.13 and 7.3).

insolvency matters.[32] The convener must give to all directors of the company, and to any officers or any former directors or officers whose presence he thinks desirable, at least 14 days' notice to attend the meetings.[33] Conversely, the chairman of the meeting is empowered at his discretion to exclude any present or former officer from attendance at a meeting, regardless of whether notice to attend the meeting was sent to the person so excluded.[34]

Voting

309 Apart from the requirement that any resolution at a creditors' meeting approving the proposal or modification requires the approval of a majority in excess of three quarters in value of the creditors present in person or by proxy and voting thereon,[35] the general principles applicable to questions of voting rights, and the requisite majorities for any resolution to be validly passed at a meeting, correspond closely to those applicable to other kinds of insolvency procedure. With respect to the voting rights of creditors, the basic rules are that every creditor who was given notice of the creditors' meeting is entitled to vote thereat, and that each creditor's vote is calculated according to the amount of his debt as at the date of the meeting or, where the company is being wound up or is subject to an administration order, the date of its going into liquidation, or the date of the administration order, as the case may be. In the usual way the chairman of the meeting has the power to admit or reject a creditor's claim for the purpose of his entitlement to vote, and there is provision for appeal to the court against the chairman's decision.[36]

310 At the company meeting the members vote according to the rights attaching to their shares respectively in accordance with the articles.[37] Where no voting rights attach to a member's shares he is nevertheless entitled to vote either for or against the proposal or any modification of it.[38]

As mentioned above, the prescribed majority at the creditors' meeting for any resolution to pass approving any proposal or modification is a majority in excess of three quarters in value of the creditors present in person or by proxy and voting on the resolution.[39] In respect of any other resolution proposed at a creditors' meeting the

---

[32] *Ibid.*, Rule 7.5 (as applied).
[33] *Ibid.*, Rule 1.15(1).
[34] *Ibid.*, Rule 1.15(2).
[35] *Ibid.*, Rule 7.12(2).
[36] *Ibid.*, Rule 7.9, applying Rules 4.15 to 4.17. See further paras. 457, 470 and 471, *post*.
[37] *Ibid.*, Rule 7.10(1). See Rule 7.10(3) for companies without share capital.
[38] *Ibid.*, Rule 7.10(2). The Scottish rules do not have the (odd) proviso in the English Insolvency Rules 1986 (Rule 1.20(2)) that such a vote is not to be counted in determining whether a majority vote has been obtained.
[39] *Ibid.*, Rule 7.12(2).

requisite majority is reduced to one in excess of one half of the creditors present and voting.[40] There are additional provisions in the Insolvency Rules where in certain cases a creditor's vote may be left out of account, for the purpose of counting towards a majority.[41]

The requisite majority whereby any resolution at a company meeting is to be regarded as passed is if the resolution is voted for by more than one half of the members present in person or by proxy and voting on the resolution.[42] This is subject however to the overriding effect of any express provision made in the company's own articles,[43]

The rules[44] make provision for the meetings to be adjourned from time to time on the day on which they are held, and for the two meetings to be consolidated at the chairman's discretion for the purpose of obtaining simultaneous agreement to the proposal. If no requisite majority for approval of the proposal by both meetings is obtained on the day on which they are held the chairman may at his discretion adjourn them for not more than 14 days, and he must so adjourn them if a resolution to that effect is duly passed. The rules are silent as to whether it is sufficient if a resolution for adjournment is duly passed by only one of the meetings, or whether it is necessary that both meetings pass resolutions to the same effect. However, since it is forbidden to adjourn either meeting unless the other is also adjourned to the same business day it would seem reasonable to expect the chairman to exercise his power to adjourn the one meeting if the other had duly passed a resolution for adjournment. There may be further adjournments, provided that the final adjournment is to a day not later than 14 days after the date on which the meetings were originally held, and if at the final adjournment of the meeting the proposal, in its original or in a modified form, is not agreed in identical terms by both meetings it is deemed rejected.

Approval of the proposal

311 The meetings summoned under section 3 of the Insolvency Act must decide whether to reject the proposed voluntary arrangement, or to approve it as it stands or with modifications.[45] Any modification of the original proposal must be approved in identical form by both meetings, but no modification may be validly adopted whose effect is to take the substance of the proposal outside the ambit of section 1 of the Insolvency Act.[46] However, the modifications may include one substituting as eventual supervisor of the arrangement a person other

---

[40] *Ibid.*, Rule 7.12(1).
[41] *Ibid.*, Rule 7.12(4). This applies to a vote cast by the responsible insolvency practitioner where the resolution relates to his conduct or remuneration as supervisor.
[42] *Ibid.*, Rule 7.12(1).
[43] *Ibid.*, Rule 7.10(1).
[44] 1986 Rule 1.16.
[45] I.A. 1986, s.4(1).
[46] *Ibid.*, s.4(2) proviso. See also s.5(1).

than the nominee himself, provided always that the person substituted is qualified to act as an insolvency practitioner in relation to the company.[47]

Further limitations upon the extent to which it is competent for the meetings to approve proposals or modifications are imposed by subsections (3) and (4) of section 4 of the Insolvency Act. These limitations are designed to ensure that no alterations may be effected which disturb the legitimate expectations, and usual rights and remedies, of any secured or preferential creditor except with the concurrence of the creditor concerned. Thus, the right of any secured creditor of the company to enforce his security may not be affected except with his concurrence.[48] It is submitted that the statutory force of the word "concurrence" is such as to require the open and positive assent of the creditor concerned, rather than his merely tacit or passive acquiescence. Similarly, in the case of any preferential creditor no arrangement whereby any preferential debt is to lose its entitlement to be paid in priority to such of the company's debts as are non-preferential, or whereby a preferential creditor[49] is to be paid a smaller proportion *pro rata* than that which is to be paid to any other preferential creditor, may be approved without the concurrence of the creditor who is thus adversely affected. Once again, the significance of the term "concurrence" should be noted.

After the conclusion of each of the meetings the chairman is required within four days to report the result to the court, and immediately thereafter to give notice of the result to all those who were sent notice of the meeting in question.[50] If the voluntary arrangement has been approved by the meetings, the person who has thereby become supervisor of the arrangement must forthwith send a copy of the chairman's report to the registrar of companies.[51]

EFFECT OF APPROVAL

312 Where a voluntary arrangement is validly approved, whether with or without modifications, by each of the meetings summoned for the purpose of considering it, the approved arrangement takes effect as if made by the company at the creditors' meeting, and binds every person who in accordance with the rules had notice of, and was entitled to vote at, that meeting as if he were a party to the voluntary arrangement, regardless of whether or not he was present or represented at the meeting.[52] The requirements of natural justice are

---

[47] *Ibid.*, s.4(2).
[48] *Ibid.*, s.4(3).
[49] The terms "preferential debt" and "preferential creditor" are, by virtue of s.4(7), to be given the meaning conferred by s.386 of the Act. See further paras. 478 and 479, *post*.
[50] I.A. 1986, s.4(6); 1986 Rule 1.17.
[51] 1986 Rule 1.17(5); Form 1.1 (Scot).
[52] I.A. 1986, s.5(2).

thus satisfied since it is necessary that a person shall have been furnished with a reasonable opportunity to attend and to vote at the meeting whereby, on a majority basis, a decision was taken to adopt a voluntary arrangement which thereby became binding also upon the non-assenting minority. Nevertheless, section 6 of the Insolvency Act provides a right to challenge either the approved voluntary arrangement itself or the manner by which its approval was obtained. This right is exercisable only within the period of 28 days beginning with the first day on which each of the reports of the outcome of the meetings is made to the court[53] and is exercisable only by one of the persons mentioned in section 6(2) of the Insolvency Act. These are: (a) a person entitled, in accordance with the rules described above, to vote at either of the meetings; or (b) the nominee or any person who has replaced him under section 2(4) or section 4(2); or (c) if the company is being wound up or an administration order is in force, the liquidator or administrator. The grounds on which an application may be made to challenge a voluntary arrangement under section 6 are either: (a) that the voluntary arrangement as approved unfairly prejudices the interests of a creditor, member or contributory of the company; or (b) that there has been some material irregularity at or in relation to either of the meetings.[54] The court's powers on such an application include the power to revoke or suspend the approvals given by the meetings, or by the particular meeting at which any material irregularity is shown to have taken place, and to give directions for the holding of further meetings to consider any revised proposal, or to reconsider the original proposal.[55] The court may grant discovery of relevant documents, and may order individuals to attend for examination, if the party challenging the voluntary arrangement can establish that this is necessary in the interests of justice, to enable the full facts and circumstances to be ascertained.[56]

Unless an application to challenge a decision is successfully brought under section 6 within the limited time allowed for this purpose, the decisions taken at any meeting, and in particular any approval thereby given to a voluntary arrangement, are unimpeachable notwithstanding any irregularity which may have occurred at or in relation to the meeting in question.[57]

If the company is being wound up or an administration order is in force, section 5(3) of the Insolvency Act empowers the court to make an order staying all proceedings in the winding up or discharging the administration order, or alternatively to issue appropriate directions as to the further conduct of the winding up or administration. By section

---

[53] *Ibid.*, s.6(3).
[54] *Ibid.*, s.6(1)(*a*), (*b*).
[55] *Ibid.*, s.6(4). See also subs. (5) and (6).
[56] *Re Primlaks (U.K.) Ltd. (No. 2)* [1990] B.C.L.C. 234.
[57] *Ibid.*, s.6(7).

5(4) however the court is forbidden to make such an order until the expiry of the 28 day time limit for the bringing of a challenge under section 6, or until all proceedings and appeals in respect of any application under section 6 are finally completed.

IMPLEMENTATION OF THE PROPOSAL

313 Where a voluntary arrangement has taken effect by virtue of its having been duly approved by meetings convened under section 3, responsibility for its implementation resides with the person identified for this purpose by the terms of the arrangement as finally agreed. This will in most instances be the nominee but may be some other person who has been substituted for the nominee under section 2(4) or section 4(2). In any event, the person who is for the time being carrying out the function of implementing an approved voluntary arrangement is known as "the supervisor of the voluntary arrangement."[58] It will be recalled that under sections 388(1)(*b*) and 389 of the Insolvency Act it is a criminal offence for a person to act as a supervisor of a composition or scheme at a time when he is not qualified to do so.[59] Provision is also made by section 7 of the Insolvency Act for any interested party to apply to the court in the event that the supervisor's conduct in office proves unsatisfactory, and the court enjoys overriding powers in relation to anything the supervisor may have done, and can issue directions to him as to his future conduct in discharge of his responsibilities.[60] Correspondingly, the supervisor may take the initiative in seeking directions from the court by way of an application, and is clothed with the potent right to apply for the company to be wound up or for an administration order to be made.[61] Finally the court enjoys the right to replace any person as supervisor, and to appoint further persons to act in that capacity either instead of or in addition to any person who may previously have exercised the functions of supervisor, or to fill any vacancy.[62]

If the voluntary arrangement authorises or requires the supervisor to carry on the business of the company or to trade on its behalf or in its name, or to realise assets of the company, or otherwise to administer or dispose of any of its funds, he must keep accounts and records of his acts and dealings in discharging his allotted functions, including in particular records of all receipts and payments of money. Not less often than once in every 12 months beginning with the date of his appointment, the supervisor must prepare an abstract of his receipts and payments and send copies of it, together with his comments on the progress and efficacy of the arrangement, to the court, to the registrar

---

[58] *Ibid.*, s.7(2).
[59] See para. 305, *ante.*
[60] I.A. 1986, s.7(3).
[61] *Ibid.*, s.7(4).
[62] *Ibid.*, s.7(5).

of companies, to the company and to the company's auditors, to all creditors who are bound by the arrangement, and (unless the court in this particular dispenses with the need to do so) to the members of the company who are bound by the arrangement.[63]

COMPLETION OF THE ARRANGEMENT

314 After the voluntary arrangement has been finally and fully implemented the supervisor must within 28 days of the completion send notice to that effect to all creditors and members of the company who are bound by the arrangement. The notice must be accompanied by a copy of a report by the supervisor summarising all receipts and payments made by him in pursuance of the arrangement, and explaining any difference in the actual implementation of it as compared with the proposal which was approved by the creditors' and company meetings. The notice and report must likewise be sent within the same 28 day period to the registrar of companies and to the court.[64]

1986 Rule 4.66(1)(*aa*)[65] has the effect of making the expenses of the administration of a voluntary arrangement a first charge on the company's assets, where a winding-up order is made and there was a voluntary arrangement in force at the time when the winding-up petition was presented.

VOLUNTARY ARRANGEMENTS—PROCEDURAL ASPECTS

315 The rules for preparing a proposal, having it approved and implementing it are contained in Parts 1 and 7 of the Insolvency (Scotland) Rules 1986.[66] The Rules were amended by the Insolvency (Scotland) Amendment Rules 1987[67] with effect from January 11, 1988, but the amendments apply to voluntary arrangements which commenced before that date. These rules also prescribe the forms for reporting the approval of the arrangement to the registrar,[68] the revocation or suspension of the arrangement,[69] the supervisor's abstract accounts[70] and the notice of completion of the arrangement.[71] The rules allow the court to correct any procedural errors. The court aspects of the procedure are prescribed in two Acts of Sederunt.[72]

---

[63] 1986 Rule 1.21.
[64] 1986 Rule 1.23.
[65] Inserted by the 1987 Amendments (S.I. 1987 No. 1921).
[66] S.I. 1986 No. 1915.
[67] S.I. 1987 No. 1921.
[68] Form 1.1 (Scot).
[69] Form 1.2 (Scot).
[70] Form 1.3 (Scot).
[71] Form 1.4 (Scot).
[72] The Act of Sederunt (Rules of Court Amendment No. 11) (Companies) 1986 (S.I. 1986 No. 2298) (for the Court of Session) and the Act of Sederunt (Sheriff Court Company Insolvency Rules) 1986 (S.I. 1986 No. 2297).

Detailed information about the financial affairs of the company has to be included in the directors' proposal, with a "short explanation" of why a voluntary arrangement is desirable and why the creditors may be expected to concur. A copy has to be given to the insolvency practitioner who has agreed to be nominated as supervisor, and he must return a copy endorsed with the date of receipt. The period of 28 days for him to report to the court[73] commences with that date. The directors must, within seven days of sending the nominee their proposals, provide him with a statement of affairs supplementing (so far as necessary) the information in the proposal, and including any further information required by the nominee. The statement must be made up to a date not earlier than two weeks prior to the date of the proposal (but this may be extended by the nominee). The nominee can call on the directors and former directors to give further explanation of why the company is insolvent, and other matters. The proposal can be altered (with the nominee's consent) until it is lodged in court.

The nominee prepares a report on the proposal[74] and lodges it in court with a copy of them and the statement of affairs. It is lodged in the Petition Department (or placed before the sheriff). No "process" is required, but the nominee must provide a covering letter. The nominee states whether meetings of the company and creditors to consider the proposal should be convened.[75] Such meetings are to be held 14 to 28 days after the lodging of the report, under the general rules of Part 7 of the Insolvency (Scotland) Rules 1986.[76] Copies of the proposal, statement of affairs (or summary) and the nominee's comments must be sent with the notice. The Insolvency Act 1986, section 4 provides for the conditions which must be satisfied by a proposed arrangement before it may be approved. The result of the meetings is to be reported to the court within four days, and also sent to all who received notice of the meeting. If the meetings approve the voluntary arrangement Form 1.1 (Scot) must be lodged with the registrar of companies. The arrangement then binds all those who had notice of the meeting.[77]

If the nominee fails to submit a report within the 28 day period, an application to replace him[78] requires seven days' notice to the first nominee. It must be made by petition intimated and served as the court shall direct.

These procedures are modified if an administrator or liquidator is the proposer. In that case, if he is the intended nominee, the proposal and statement of affairs are prepared by him and he convenes the meetings required by giving at least 14 days' notice to the company and

[73] I.A., s.2(2).
[74] I.A., s.2.
[75] I.A., s.3.
[76] As modified by Chap. 5 of Pt. 1. Part 7 is discussed further in paras. 454 to 458, *post*.
[77] I.A., s.5.
[78] I.A., s.2(4).

creditors. If the intended nominee is another insolvency practitioner, the administrator or liquidator must give him notice of the proposals.

Before a nominee is appointed supervisor he must provide a written statement that he is an insolvency practitioner and consents to act. He must provide caution, and this is kept under review by any committee of creditors which may be established.[79]

The supervisor will take possession of the assets, and proceed to implement the arrangement. Accounts of his intromissions must be kept, and a sederunt book to record all proceedings.[80] An abstract of his accounts[81] is to be submitted annually to the court, the company, the creditors and the auditors (if the company is not in liquidation). It must also be sent to the members unless the court dispenses with this.

A voluntary arrangement may be suspended or revoked under the Insolvency Act 1986, section 6. Anyone applying for such an order must intimate to interested parties and give the proposers of the arrangement an opportunity to amend.[82] If the arrangement is revoked or suspended Form 1.2 (Scot) is to be filed with the registrar.

Not more than 28 days before the arrangement is completed the supervisor must send a final report and account to all creditors and members. This period may be extended by the court. A copy of the final report and accounts must be filed with the registrar.[83]

Amendments added in 1987 require the sederunt book to be retained by the supervisor for 10 years from the date of final completion of the arrangement (1986 Rule 7.33(5) and (7)). The 1987 amendments also provide for the delivery of the company's books, papers and records to the responsible insolvency practitioner if a voluntary arrangement is followed by other insolvency proceedings, and for the disposal of such records if there are no such subsequent proceedings (1986 Rule 7.34).

---

[79] 1986 Rule 7.28.
[80] 1986 Rule 7.33. If in non-legible form, it must be capable of being reproduced in legible form: 1986 Rule 7.33(6) (added in 1987).
[81] In Form 1.3 (Scot).
[82] 1986 Rule 1.20.
[83] On Form 1.4 (Scot).

CHAPTER 4

WINDING UP

INTRODUCTION

The role of winding up in company law

401 A company incorporated under the Companies Acts does not cease to exist until formally dissolved.[1] If it has ceased to carry on business, has neither assets nor liabilities and is not heritably vest in any property, the registrar of companies may be asked to exercise his powers to strike the company off the register under section 652 of the Act.[2] This is often used as an alternative to winding up. Apart from section 652, the machinery of winding up (also termed liquidation) is a necessary preliminary to dissolution.[3] It is not competent to sequestrate the estate of a company registered under the Companies Acts under the Bankruptcy Acts,[4] but its estate may be sequestrated and a judicial factor appointed at common law,[5] which merely transfers the powers of administration of its estate to the factor and does not have the same effect as the appointment of a trustee in bankruptcy.[6]

The Companies Act 1989, Part VII, which came into force on April 25, 1991[7-8] is designed to create a separate insolvency procedure for the financial markets, with respect to the insolvency of a member of a recognised investment exchange to which the Act applies and the investment contracts entered into by that person.

Legislative background

402 The statutory provisions relating to winding up were first consolidated as sections 501 to 674 of the Companies Act 1985. Certain provisions of the earlier Scottish Bankruptcy Acts were included in the statutory code, with adaptations for companies. The Insolvency Act 1985 and the Bankruptcy (Scotland) Act 1985 substantially amended the pre-existing law, although not all of the Insolvency Act 1985 was brought into effect before the consolidating Insolvency Act 1986. Sections 651 to 658 of the Companies Act 1985, relating to the restoration of dissolved

---

[1] Restoration to the register is possible for 20 years thereafter. (See paras. 536 to 538, *infra.*)
[2] As to which, see para. 564, *infra.*
[3] *Princess of Reuss* v. *Bos* (1871) L.R. 5 H.L. 176, 193.
[4] *Standard Property Investment Co. Ltd.* v. *Dunblane Hydropathic Co. Ltd.* (1884) 12 R. 328; Bankruptcy (Scotland) Act 1985, s.6(2).
[5] *Patrick Fraser, Petr.*, 1971 S.L.T. 146; *McGuinness* v. *Black (No. 2)*, 1990 S.L.T. 461; *Weir* v. *Rees*, 1991 S.L.T. 345.
[6] See further N. M. L. Walker, *Judicial Factors* (W. Green, 1974).
[7-8] See para. 406, *post.*

companies,[9] remain in force but the remainder of sections 501 to 674 have been repealed, and the statutory code relating to winding up is now contained in sections 73 to 251 (and related Schedules) of the Insolvency Act 1986 and (by reference) certain sections of the Bankruptcy (Scotland) Act 1985. The definitions in Part XXVI of the Companies Act apply to the Insolvency Act, unless the latter Act contains an alternative definition (I.A., s.251).

In addition, other sections of the Insolvency Act 1986 apply to all forms of company insolvency procedure (winding up, administrative receivership, administration and voluntary arrangements).[10] Detailed procedure in all forms of winding up is governed by the Insolvency (Scotland) Rules 1986[11] as amended by the Insolvency (Scotland) Amendment Rules 1987.[12] Although some parts of the Insolvency Act 1985 became effective earlier than the main body of the legislation (as noted at the appropriate point in the text), the 1986 Act and Rules were brought into force on December 29, 1986[13] and apply to all winding-up proceedings which commenced on or after that date.[14] The 1987 amendments to the Rules took effect on January 11, 1988 but apply to all liquidations under the 1986 Rules.[15] The Companies Act 1989 amended the Insolvency Act 1986 in some detailed respects, as noted in the text, but also contained substantial amendments to the law of insolvency in relation to the financial markets which became fully effective on April 25, 1991.[16]

References to the Insolvency Act 1986 in this chapter are shown as "I.A., s.73, etc." References to the Insolvency (Scotland) Rules 1986, as amended by the 1987 Amendment Rules, are shown as "1986 Rule 4.1, etc."

Forms of winding up

403 Winding up may take one of the following forms (I.A., ss.73, 90):

(1) Winding up by the court ("Compulsory"),
(2) (a) Members' voluntary winding up, or
   (b) Creditors' voluntary winding up.

The Insolvency Acts 1985 and 1986 repealed the provisions of sections 606 to 610 and thereby abolished the form of voluntary

---

[9] See paras. 535 to 538, *post.*
[10] Notably I.A., ss. 386 and 387 (preferential debts), 388–398 (insolvency practitioners), 411 (rules) and 416 and 417 (monetary limits).
[11] S.I. 1986 No. 1915.
[12] S.I. 1987 No. 1921.
[13] 1986 Rule 0.1.
[14] I.A., s.443; this section tied the commencement date of the Act to the commencement of Pt. III of the Insolvency Act 1985, which was effected by the Insolvency Act 1985 (Commencement No. 5) Order 1986 (S.I. 1986 No. 1924; see para. 3 thereof). 1986 Rules 0.1 to 0.3.
[15] S.I. 1987 No. 1921, para. 3(2).
[16] See further para. 406, *post.*

winding up subject to the supervision of the court. Voluntary winding up is initiated by the shareholders and is accordingly the commonest form. A members' voluntary winding up is one where the directors, at its commencement, have declared that the company will meet its liabilities within 12 months (I.A., ss.89, 90). If they do not the liquidation is a creditors' voluntary winding up. This normally, but not necessarily, implies insolvency. A members' voluntary winding up may become a creditors' voluntary winding up if the company cannot pay its debts (I.A., ss.95, 96).

Extended meaning of "member of a company"

404 Section 250 of the Insolvency Act provides that for the purposes of the insolvency legislation a person who is not a member of a company, *i.e.*, not on the register of members, but to whom shares have been transferred, or transferred by operation of law (executors, trustees in bankruptcy, *curators bonis*, etc.) is to be regarded as a member of the company and references to a member or members are to be read accordingly. This means (for example) that when the Act requires notice to be given to "members" persons within the extended definition are included.

The definition of "contributories" in the Insolvency Act, section 74 also includes "members" in this wider sense. Although the rights and obligations of "members" in liquidations are extended to transferees, etc., by the Insolvency Act, section 250, those which arise otherwise than from the Insolvency Act 1986, such as the voting and other rights of members as such, are unaffected.

Administration orders, voluntary arrangements and receivers

405 An administration order cannot be made if the company is already in liquidation (I.A., s.8(4)) but after a petition for such an order has been presented, no resolution or order for winding up can be passed or made (I.A., s.10(1)).

A proposal for a voluntary arrangement does not prevent the company being wound up, but once the arrangement has been duly approved the court will either sist the winding up or make some other order to allow the arrangement to proceed (I.A., s.5). A liquidator may act as the proposer of a voluntary arrangement (I.A., s.1(3)).

If a receiver is validly appointed he takes precedence over any liquidator and is empowered to take over the assets which are subject to the floating charge from him (I.A., s.55 and Sched. 2, para. 1). The appointment of a receiver does not prevent the company being wound up.

Financial markets and insolvency

406 The Companies Act 1989 (Part VII, ss.154–191) contains what is, in effect, a separate code for regulating the insolvency of a person operating in a recognised financial market. The purpose is to separate the rights and obligations of such a person in relation to "market contracts" (as defined) from the insolvency régime which would otherwise be applicable to them so that, for example, in the liquidation of a company to which these provisions apply, assets and liabilities relating to market contracts will be offset and only the net surplus (or deficit) will be transferred to the liquidation. This approach is not permitted in liquidations generally.[17] Those sections in Part VII which empowered the Secretary of State to make the necessary regulations came into force on March 25, 1991[18] and most of the substantive provisions on April 25, 1991.[19] The details of these are beyond the scope of this chapter.

WINDING UP BY THE COURT

The provisions applying to the winding up by the court

407 Chapter VI of Part IV (ss.117–162) of the Insolvency Act 1986 applies to winding up by the court, along with Chapters I, VII, VIII, IX and X of Part IV (ss.73–83 and 163–219) which apply to all forms of winding up. The conduct of the liquidation is also governed by the 1986 Rules.[20] Court proceedings relating to liquidation are governed by Acts of Sederunt. The Court of Session Rules[21] are referred to in this chapter as "R.C.S." and the Sheriff Court Rules[22] as "Sh.Ct.R." All these took effect on December 29, 1986 and apply to liquidation proceedings commenced on or after that date. Proceedings commenced before that date continue to be governed by the rules previously in force.[23]

Both sets of court rules contain a general provision requiring any application not specifically mentioned to be by way of note in the process (R.C.S. 218M; Sh.Ct.R. 30). Notes and appeals are to be

---

[17] *British Eagle International Air Lines Ltd.* v. *Compagnie Nationale Air France* [1975] 2 All E.R. 390.

[18] The Companies Act 1989 (Commencement No. 9 and Saving and Transitional Provisions) Order 1991 (S.I. 1991 No. 488).

[19] The Companies Act 1989 (Commencement No. 10 and Saving Provisions) Order 1991 (S.I. 1991 No. 878). See also the Financial Markets and Insolvency Regulations 1991 (S.I. 1991 No. 880, effective April 25, 1991) which contains amendments to the statutory code of insolvency (including the 1989 Act itself) in this field, and the Act of Sederunt (Applications under Pt. VII of the Companies Act 1989) 1991 (S.I. 1991 No. 145, made January 30, 1991 and effective February 25, 1991) which amends the Rules of Court in the Court of Session and sheriff court in relation to proceedings relating to financial market insolvencies and charges.

[20] S.I. 1986 No. 1915 (S.139), as amended by S.I. 1987 No. 1921.

[21] Act of Sederunt (Rules of Court Amendment No. 11) (Companies) 1986 (S.I. 1986 No. 2298 (S.170)).

[22] Act of Sederunt (Sheriff Court Company Insolvency Rules) 1986 (S.I. 1986 No. 2297 (S.169)).

[23] Rules of the Court of Session 1965, Chap. IV, s.3 (as amended) and Act of Sederunt (Sheriff Court Liquidations) 1930 (as amended) which are discussed in the 23rd edition of *Palmer*, Chap. 87.

intimated, served and, if necessary, advertised as the court shall direct (R.C.S. 218Q(1); Sh.Ct.R. 32). In the Court of Session matters pertaining to winding up (and voluntary arrangements, administration orders and receivers) are appointed to the insolvency judge (R.C.S. 218Q(2)). The court may accept affidavit evidence (R.C.S. 218R; Sh.Ct.R. 33). The Insolvency Rules Committee originally established under the Companies Act 1976, section 10 to advise on insolvency rules in England and Wales (see now I.A., s.413) has no equivalent in Scotland.

COURTS HAVING JURISDICTION TO WIND UP

408 Where the Companies Acts use the expression "the Court," this means "the court having jurisdiction to wind up the company in question" (s.744). The English courts have no jurisdiction to wind up a company registered in Scotland, and vice versa. Jurisdiction is conclusively determined by the registrar's certificate.[24]

The Court of Session has jurisdiction to wind up any company registered in Scotland (I.A., s.120(1)). During vacation this jurisdiction may be exercised by the vacation judge (I.A., s.120(2)). Where the paid-up share capital does not exceed £120,000, the sheriff court of the sheriffdom where its registered office is situated has concurrent jurisdiction (I.A., s.120(3)).[25] The Court of Session has power (having regard to the assets of the company) to remit a petition for the winding up of a company whose issued capital does not exceed the limit[26] to the sheriff court or to transfer the petition from one sheriff court to another (I.A., s.120(3)(a) and (b) (R.C.S. 218B)). The sheriff may also submit a stated case on any question of law for the opinion of the Court of Session (I.A., s.120(3)(c)). The sheriff court does not have jurisdiction to wind up a company not having a share capital, either limited by guarantee or an unlimited company.[27]

For the purpose of the Insolvency Act, section 120, "registered office" means the place which has been the company's registered office for the longest time during the six months preceding the presentation of the petition (I.A., s.120). A company could not, therefore, frustrate a petition in the sheriff court by moving its office outside its jurisdiction at the last moment. A person taking proceedings against a company is

---

[24] *Re Baby Moon (United Kingdom) Ltd.*, 1985 P.C.C. 103; [1985] 8 C.L. 36.
[25] Prior to December 20, 1976 the limit of sheriff court jurisdiction was £10,000. The Insolvency Act 1976, s.1 increased the limit to £120,000. This limit may be varied by statutory instrument (I.A., ss.120(5), 416).
[26] *Chayney & Bull Ltd., Petrs.*, 1930 S.C. 759; 1930 S.L.T. 623.
[27] *Pearce & Cannon, Petrs.*, 1991 S.C.L.R. 861 (Sh.Ct.). The sheriff's statement (*obiter*) that the sheriff court has no jurisdiction to wind up an unlimited company is too wide and ignores the fact that an unlimited company may (and in most cases will) have a share capital. (See ss.3(1)(f) and 737.) An unlimited company (or a company limited by guarantee and having a share capital) which has a share capital paid up or credited as paid up of £120,000 or less may be wound up in the sheriff court.

entitled to act on the basis of the registered office as disclosed on the registrar of companies' official file.[28]

A change of registered office does not take effect until the prescribed form intimating the change has been registered by the registrar of companies, and for 14 days thereafter documents may be validly served at the former address.[29]

Appeals

409 In general, appeals against court orders in Scotland in respect of liquidation matters follow the same lines as in court actions generally. A sheriff's order may be appealed to the sheriff principal and from him to the Court of Session (Inner House) or direct to the Inner House, and the interlocutor of an outer house judge of the Court of Session (Lord Ordinary) may be appealed to the Inner House (see I.A., s.162(1)). The Court of Session will not, however, entertain an appeal against the appointment of a particular person as liquidator by the sheriff unless the circumstances are exceptional.[30] For appeals in the sheriff court and to the Court of Session see Sheriff Court Rules 36. Special provision is made in respect of interlocutors pronounced by the vacation judge in liquidations (I.A., s.162(2) and Sched. 3). Those provisions also apply to orders pronounced by the Lord Ordinary within 14 days of the end of the court session if not reclaimed against during the session (I.A., s.162(4)). Under these provisions, certain orders by the vacation judge are to be final (I.A., Sched. 3, Pt. I) and others are to be treated as effective notwithstanding an appeal, until the appeal has been disposed of (I.A., Sched. 3, Pt. II). The list in Schedule 3 is not exhaustive, and orders not referred to therein are appealable.[31] The Insolvency Act, section 162(2)(*b*) and (4) requires appeals against an interlocutor of the Lord Ordinary or vacation judge to be appealed by reclaiming motion enrolled within 14 days from the date of the order. This limit is imperative and if no reclaiming motion is enrolled within the statutory period the order becomes final.[32] If a Lord Ordinary's order is timeously reclaimed but has not been heard by the end of the session, it is treated for the purposes of the Insolvency Act, section 162 as if it were an order by the vacation judge (I.A., s.162(4)). Section 162 does not affect decrees for payment of calls (I.A., s.162(5)).

Where the court had recalled the appointment of a provisional liquidator and this order was the subject of an appeal, it was held that the provisional liquidator remained in office until the reclaiming motion had been disposed of.[33]

---

[28] *Ross* v. *Invergordon Distillers Ltd.*, 1961 S.L.T. 358; 1961 S.C. 286.
[29] Companies Act 1985, s.287(4) (as inserted by 1989 C.A., s.136); see further, *Palmer* para. 2.504.
[30] *Steel Scaffolding Co.* v. *Buckleys Ltd.*, 1935 S.C. 617; 1935 S.L.T. 467.
[31] *Magistrates of Edinburgh* v. *Union Billposting Co. Ltd.*, 1912 S.C. 105; 1912 2 S.L.T. 336.
[32] *Cumpstie* v. *Waterston*, 1933 S.C. 1; 1933 S.L.T. 10; *Macarthur* v. *Mackay*, 1914 S.C. 547; 1914 S.L.T. 336; see also R.C.S. 264(*g*).
[33] *Levy*, 1963 S.C. 46.

COMPANIES WHICH MAY BE WOUND UP

410 The Scottish courts have jurisdiction to wind up any company registered in Scotland[34] (I.A., s.120). "Company" means a company formed and registered under the Act or an "existing company"; an "existing company" is one formed and registered under the various earlier Acts 1856–1983, other than a company registered in Ireland (s.735). The reference in the Insolvency Act, s.120(1) to companies "registered" in Scotland includes companies registered but not formed under the older Acts.[35]

Unregistered companies

411 Part V of the Insolvency Act 1986 contains special provisions for the winding up of unregistered companies.[36]

An "unregistered company" means "any association and any company"[37] except a railway company incorporated by Act of Parliament or a company registered under the Acts (I.A., s.220(1)). It includes a foreign company, whether or not it is an "oversea company" (as defined in s.744) or registered as such in Great Britain under Part XXIII, provided that the company has a "proper connection" with Scotland. This may take the form of assets in Scotland or a person within the jurisdiction who has an interest in their proper distribution. There must, however, be a reasonable possibility of benefit to creditors.[38] In winding up a foreign company, the court must have regard to the interests of its creditors world-wide and not just those within its jurisdiction.[39] A trustee savings bank is an unregistered company until an order is made under the Trustee Savings Bank Act 1985 to remove such banks from the scope of the Act (I.A., s.220(2)). An unregistered company with a principal place of business in Scotland (whether or not it has one elsewhere) may be wound up by the Scottish courts (I.A., s.221(1) and (2)). An oversea company[40] which has been carrying on business in Great Britain may be wound up by the British courts even though it has been "dissolved" under the laws of its country of incorporation (I.A., s.225).

In Scotland it has been held that a building society, not registered under the Building Societies Act 1874 or subsequent legislation, could

---

[34] *Re Baby Moon (United Kingdom) Ltd., supra.*
[35] *e.g. Liquidators of Western Bank v. Douglas, etc.* (1860) 22 D. 447; *Western Bank v. Ayrshire Bank* (1860) 22 D. 540. Ss.676, 677 and *In Re A Company (Okeanos Maritime Corporation)* [1987] 3 All E.R. 137.
[36] See further *Palmer*, paras. 15.204 and 15.222 to 15.224.
[37] *e.g. Aberdeen Provision Society* (1863) 2 M. 385.
[38] *Re Compania Marabello San Nicholas S.A.* [1973] Ch. 75; *I.R.C.v. Highland Engineering Ltd.*, 1975 S.L.T. 202; *Re Allobrogia Steamship Corporation* [1978] 3 All E.R. 423; *Re Eloc Electro-Optieck and Communicatie BV* [1982] Ch. 43; *International Westminster Bank v. Okeanos* [1987] 3 All E.R. 137; *Re Real Estate Development Co.* [1991] B.C.L.C. 210; *Re A Company (No. 003102 of 1991), ex p. Nyckeln Finance Co.* [1991] B.C.L.C. 539.
[39] *Re Bank of Credit & Commerce International S.A.* [1992] B.C.L. 83.
[40] See s.744 for formal definition.

be wound up as an unregistered company.[41] An order for winding up under the Companies Act was also granted where a friendly society could not comply with winding-up procedure under the Friendly Societies Act.[42] An association in which there are no mutual obligations or liabilities among the membership is not, however, capable of being wound up under the Companies Acts.[43]

The grounds for winding up of an unregistered company (I.A., s.221(5)) are:–

(a) If the company is dissolved, or has ceased to carry on business or is carrying on business for the purpose of winding up its affairs;

(b) If the company is unable to pay its debts;

(c) If the court is of opinion that it is just and equitable that the company should be wound up; and

(d) In Scotland (I.A., s.221(7)), if the court is satisfied that the security of the holder of a floating charge is in jeopardy.

These provisions are supplemented by further sections (I.A., ss.222–224) similar to I.A., ss.122(2) and 123 but they include a provision (s.223) allowing an unregistered company to be wound up for non-payment of a debt due by a member in his character as such. The procedure is that of Scots law, subject to Part VI.[44]

Further examples of the exercise of this jurisdiction in respect of unregistered companies have occurred in England and are detailed in *Palmer*, paragraph 15.204. An international organisation established by treaty to which the United Kingdom is a party is not subject to winding up by the court.[45]

EUROPEAN ECONOMIC INTEREST GROUPINGS (EEIGs)

411 A European Economic Interest Grouping[46] is an entity with corporate personality and unlimited liability created by Council regulation of the European Community[47] (the "Council Regulations") as implemented in the United Kingdom by the European Economic Interest Grouping Regulations 1989[48] (the "EEIG Regulations"). It consists of at least two persons located in more than one member state of the Community (Council Regulations, art. 4) and its purpose is "to facilitate or develop the economic activities of its members" and not to make a profit for itself (Council Regulations, art. 3).

---

[41] *Smith's Trs.* v. *Irvine and Fullarton Property and Investment Building Society* (1903) 6 F. 99; 11 L.T. 395.

[42] *Canavan and Others, Petrs.*, 1929 S.L.T. 636.

[43] *Caledonian Employees Benevolent Society*, 1928 S.C. 633; 1928 S.L.T. 412. See also *Munro* v. *Edinburgh & District Trades Council Social Club*, 1989 G.W.D. 6–240.

[44] I.A., s.229; *Re Suidair International Airways Ltd.* [1951] Ch. 156, 173.

[45] *Ibid.*

[46] *Re International Tin Council* [1987] 1 All E.R. 890.

[47] Council Regulation 2137/85.

[48] S.I. 1989 No. 638.

The winding up of an EEIG is governed by national law (Council Regulation 35.2) and under the EEIG Regulations it is to be treated as an unregistered company subject to Part V of the Insolvency Act 1986 together with the provisions of the Council Regulations (EEIG Regulations, reg. 8(1)). Every EEIG must register an "official address" where it has its central administration and this must be within a member state (Council Regulations, art. 12). If an EEIG has registered its official address within Great Britain, the courts of the country where that address is registered have jurisdiction to wind it up (EEIG Regulations, reg. 9(1)); the Council Regulations, and therefore the EEIG Regulations, allow for the transfer of the official address between England and Wales and Scotland (EEIG Regulations, reg. 9(9)). For the purpose of winding up an EEIG is to be treated as if it were a company having a paid-up share capital of less than £120,000, and therefore subject to the concurrent jursidiction of the sheriff court and the Court of Session (EEIG Regulations, reg. 19(2)).

An EEIG is required to register particulars of one or more "managers" (who must be natural persons) (Council Regulations, art. 19) and these persons are to be treated as directors (or former directors) for the purposes of the Insolvency Act and the Company Directors Disqualification Act 1986 (EEIG Regulations, regs. 8(1) and 20).

An EEIG is required to file particulars regarding its operation with the registrar pertaining to its official address (Council Regulations, art. 7) and the Regulations prescribe forms for this purpose including forms for the commencement of winding up, the appointment of liquidators and the completion of the winding up (EEIG Regulations, reg. 13).

Grounds for a petition for the winding up of an EEIG by the court (additional to those applicable to unregistered companies generally) are specified in Council Regulations, art. 32, and the petition may be presented either by "any person concerned" or by "a competent authority" which the EEIG Regulations identify as the Secretary of State (EEIG Regulations, reg. 7(1)). Article 32 provides for the winding up of an EEIG on the grounds of breach of certain articles in the Council Regulations, namely:–

(a) Article 3 which prohibits an EEIG (*inter alia*) from making a profit, interfering in the management of its members, holding shares in its members, employing more than 500 people, making unauthorised loans to directors or persons connected with them or being a member of another EEIG;

(b) Article 12 which requires the EEIG to have an official address at its place of central administration and within the European Community; and

(c) Article 31(3) which requires an EEIG to be wound up if it has less than two members in at least two member states.

The Regulations also allow an EEIG to be wound up by the court on a member's petition "on just and proper grounds" (art. 32.2) and by the "competent authority" on such "public interest" grounds as apply to companies generally (art. 32.3). In addition, an EEIG may be wound up voluntarily in terms of Council Regulations, article 31. The decision to wind up must be in accordance with the EEIG constitution, or unanimously if there is no such provision. It must be wound up if it has reached the expiry of any fixed period or in accordance with any other provision for winding up in the contract, or if the purpose of the EEIG has either been completed or has become impossible to achieve. If three months after any of these situations arises there has been no voluntary decision to wind up, any member may petition the court for a compulsory winding up.

GROUNDS FOR WINDING UP

412 The court may order a company to be wound up on any one or more of the following grounds:

(a) if the company has by special resolution resolved to be wound up by the court;

(b) if, having been incorporated as a public company, it has failed to obtain a certificate under section 117 that it satisfies the minimum share capital requirements within a year of its incorporation;

(c) if it is an "old public company" as defined in section 1 of the Companies Consolidation (Consequential Provisions) Act 1985, *i.e.* a company incorporated as a public company under the legislation in force prior to December 22, 1980 which has not subsequently re-registered as a public or private company;

(d) if the company does not commence its business within a year of incorporation, or suspends its business for a whole year;

(e) if (not being a private company limited by shares or by guarantee)[49] the number of its members falls below the statutory minimum of two;

(f) inability to pay its debts;

(g) if the court is of the opinion that it is just and equitable that the company should be wound up;

(h) if, on a petition by the Secretary of State under the Insolvency Act, section 124A,[50] the court is satisfied that it is in the public interest that the company be wound up; and

(i) if the court is satisfied that the security of the holder of a floating charge over some of the company's property is in jeopardy.

Of these, (a) to (h) apply equally to English companies (I.A., s.122(1)), but (i) applies only to Scottish companies, having been

---

[49] See the Companies (Single Member Private Limited Companies) Regulations 1992 (S.I. 1699), para. 8.

[50] I.A., s.124A was substituted for s.440, which was in similar terms, by C.A. 1989, s.60.

introduced by the Companies (Floating Charges) (Scotland) Act 1961, section 4, now the Insolvency Act, section 122(2).

A bank or institution licensed under the Banking Act may also be wound up on petition by the Bank of England.[51]

Inability to pay debts

413 The normal basis for a compulsory winding up is the company's inability to pay its debts, as defined in the Insolvency Act, section 123.

A company is deemed to be unable to pay its debts "if a creditor, by assignment or otherwise, to whom the company is indebted in a sum exceeding £750[52] then due has served on the company, by leaving it at the registered office of the company, a written demand (in the prescribed form)[53] requiring the company to pay the sum so due and the company has for three weeks thereafter neglected to pay the sum or to secure or compound for it to the reasonable satisfaction of the creditor."

Strict adherence to the statutory procedure is essential. The "statutory demand" cannot be served by post[54] and must be delivered personally by a person duly authorised by the creditor.[55] It does not require to be served by a messenger-at-arms or sheriff officer.[56]

If the creditor holds security which is marketable and of sufficient value to satisfy his claim, section 123(1)(*a*) is not appropriate.[57] It will be a sufficient answer to a petition founded on section 123(1)(*a*) if the company finds caution for the amount of the claim[58] or consigns the amount.[59] Section 123(1)(*a*) is not available to a creditor whose claim is contingent or prospective,[60] or disputed in good faith and on substantial grounds.[61] A company cannot be said to have "neglected" to pay where it admits (but had not paid) part of the sum claimed, the total amount due and claimed in the statutory demand being *bona fide* in dispute; section 123(1)(*a*) is available only where a creditor can specify a debt which cannot, without serious argument, be disputed as to its existence or quantum.[62] It is not available if the company admits

---

[51] Banking Act 1987, s.92.
[52] This figure may be varied by statutory instrument (I.A., s.123(3)).
[53] The form of demand is prescribed in Form 4.1 (Scot); see Insolvency (Scotland) Amendment Rules 1987 (S.I. 1921), para. 3(3).
[54] *Craig v. Iona Hotels Ltd.*, 1988 S.C.L.R. 130, 135 (Sh.Ct.)
[55] *Lord Advocate v. Blairwest Investments Ltd.*, 1989 S.L.T. (Sh.Ct.) 97 (which also discusses the documentary evidence to be lodged in support of a petition based on a statutory demand). *Lord Advocate v. Tulloch Castle Ltd.*, 1992 G.W.D. 24–1357.
[56] *Lord Advocate v. Traprain Ltd.*, 1989 S.L.T. (Sh.Ct.) 99.
[57] *Commercial Bank of Scotland Ltd. v. Lanark Oil Co. Ltd.* (1886) 14 R. 147.
[58] *W. & J. C. Pollock v. The Gaeta Pioneer Mining Co. Ltd.*, 1907 S.C. 182; 14 S.L.T. 526.
[59] *Cunninghame v. Walkinsaw Oil Co.* (1886) 14 R. 87.
[60] *Stonegate Securities Ltd. v. Gregory* [1980] 1 All E.R. 241.
[61] *Re Lympne Investments Ltd.* [1972] 1 W.L.R. 523; [1972] 2 All E.R. 385.
[62] *Re A Company (No. 003729 of 1982)* [1984] 3 All E.R. 78. See also *Blue Star Securities (Scotland) Ltd. v. Drake & Scull (Scotland) Ltd.*, 1992 S.L.T. (Sh.Ct.) 80.

the debt but is genuinely unsure whether it is owing to the petitioner or to a third party.[63]

It has been held in England that the expression "for three weeks thereafter" means a clear period of 21 days excluding the day of service of the demand.[64] In Scotland, however, the period may be held to have expired on the last day of that period.[65]

Section 123(1)(e) of the Insolvency Act 1986 provides that a company is deemed unable to pay its debts "if it is proved to the satisfaction of the court that the company is unable to pay its debts as they fall due." The requirement that the court *must* take into account contingent and prospective liabilities (see formerly s.518(1)(e)) no longer applies, but a company is also deemed to be unable to pay its debts if the court is satisfied that, taking account of contingent and prospective liabilities, the value of its liabilities exceeds that of its assets (I.A., s.123(2)). The petition may, therefore, be founded on either "practical" or "absolute" insolvency. Evidence of unsuccessful attempts to obtain payment is normally sufficient to satisfy the court.[66]

414   A winding-up petition is not the proper means of enforcing a debt which is disputed, and accordingly it is a good answer for the company to show that there is a *bona fide* defence to the debt claimed.[67]

Under the Insolvency Act, section 123(1)(c), a Scottish company is deemed to be unable to pay its debts if "the *induciae* of a charge for payment on an extract decree, or an extract registered bond, or an extract registered protest have expired without payment being made." This applies regardless of the amount of the debt.[68] A parallel provision referring to English companies is contained in the Insolvency Act, section 123(1)(b). These provisions enable a creditor who has obtained a decree against a company to petition for liquidation as an alternative to attempting diligence against its assets. In England, however, the courts have refused to grant a winding-up order where the debt is less than the relevant amount for the purposes of the Insolvency Act, section 123(1)(a) (£750 under current regulations) unless it is an unopposed petition or the debt is due on a court order, or if there are special circumstances such as the attitude of the company or the support of other creditors.[69] It is suggested that modern Scottish practice should be similar, since the contrary authority[70] dates from 1911.

---

[63] *Craig v. Iona Hotels Ltd., supra.*
[64] *Re Lympne Investments Ltd., supra.*
[65] *Neil McLeod & Sons, Petrs.,* 1967 S.L.T. 46; 1967 S.C. 16, following *Parish Council of Cavers v. Parish Council of Smailholm,* 1909 S.C. 195.
[66] *Gandy,* 1912, 2 S.L.T. 276; *Stephen v. Scottish Banking Co.* (1884) 21 S.L.R. 764; *Blue Star Securities (Scotland) Ltd. v. Drake and Scull (Scotland) Ltd., supra.*
[67] See paras. 422 and 423, *infra.*
[68] *Speirs & Co. v. Central Building Co. Ltd.,* 1911 S.C. 330; 1911, 1 S.L.T. 14.
[69] See *Palmer,* para. 15.213.
[70] *Speirs & Co. v. Central Building Co. Ltd., supra.*

If the petitioning creditor has been paid in full he cannot persist with his petition but if there is proof that the Insolvency Act, section 123(1)(*a*) had been satisfied (before payment) it has been suggested *obiter* that the court is obliged to find that the company is unable to pay its debts for the purposes of the Insolvency Act, section 122(*f*). This was held to be the effect of the opening phrase of the Insolvency Act, section 123(1): "a company is *deemed* unable to pay its debts" if any of the succeeding circumstances apply.[71] The practical effect of this sheriff court opinion is obscure, since if the petition fails for want of continuing interest in the petitioner it would seem academic to issue such a finding. Presumably, however, the fact that section 123(1)(*a*) had once been satisfied might assist the petitioner if other grounds existed, or assist a substituted petitioner with an unpaid debt.

Insurance and investment business companies

415 Special provision for the winding up of insurance companies is made by the Insurance Companies Act 1982, sections 53 to 59 (as amended by I.A., Sched. 14). A petition may be presented by 10 or more policy holders having policies of an aggregate value of not less than £10,000, subject to satisfying the court that there are prima facie grounds, and the petitioners may be required to find caution for expenses (1982, s.53).[71a] In addition, the Secretary of State may petition for winding up on the grounds of inability to pay debts, or failure in statutory duties imposed by the Insurance Companies legislation, or in the public interest (1982, s.54). If someone other than the Secretary of State petitions for the winding up of an insurance company, a copy of the petition is to be served on the Secretary of State, who may appear in the process (1982, s.54(5)). Unincorporated insurance companies carrying on "long-term business" cannot be sequestrated, nor can any insurance company carrying on such business be wound up voluntarily (1982, s.55(1) and (2)). There is provision for separating assets and liabilities relating to "long-term business" from those of other business, and separate treatment of each such class of creditor (1982, s.55(3)–(6)). There are further provisions requiring the liquidator to continue "long-term business" (1982, s.56), and providing for the winding up of an insurance company to extend to its subsidiaries (1982, s.57). The court may, instead of winding up an insurance company, abate the value of its contracts (1982, s.58).

The winding up of insurance companies (from December 29, 1986) is governed by the Insurance Companies (Winding Up) (Scotland) Rules 1986 (S.I. 1986 No. 1918 (S.142)) which apply (with modifications) the 1986 Rules, and supersede the Act of Sederunt (Winding Up of Insurance Companies Rules) 1986 (S.I. 1986 No. 341).

---

[71] *Frumston, Petr.*, 1987 S.L.T. (Sh.Ct.) 10.
[71a] A creditor may petition (under I.A., s.122) without requiring the sanction of the court; *Re A Company (No. 0010382 of 1982), The Independent*, November 9, 1992.

The Secretary of State may petition for the winding up of a company authorised to carry on investment business under the Financial Services Act 1986, section 72 on the grounds of inability to pay its debts or that it is just and equitable to wind such a company up. A company which defaults in any obligation to pay a sum due and payable under any "investment agreement" (as defined in that Act) is deemed to be unable to pay its debts. If the company is not directly authorised by the Secretary of State, but is entitled to carry on such business by virtue of membership of a self-regulating organisation, or by certification by a recognised professional body (as provided for in the Financial Services Act) the consent of such body is required before the Secretary of State can present the petition.

Failure to commence business, or suspension of business for a whole year

416 This is a most unusual ground for winding up.[72] A company which has ceased to operate directly in its field but has become a company holding shares in others so engaged has not suspended business within the meaning of this provision.[73]

Failure to obtain a trading certificate: "old public companies"

417 The Companies Act 1980 introduced the requirement (now in s.117) that a public company (registered as such) must, before commencing business or borrowing, obtain a certificate that it has issued the "authorised minimum" share capital and met the other requirements of the Act.[74] Alternatively, it may apply for re-registration as a private company (s.117(1)).[75] If it fails to take either course within a year of its incorporation, it may be wound up under the Insolvency Act, section 122(1)(*b*). Companies which were "public" before the 1980 Act were described as "old public companies" and were given 15 months (to March 22, 1981) to comply with the new rules as to minimum authorised capital, etc., or re-register as private companies. The provisions applicable to "old public companies" are now contained in sections 1 to 9 of the Companies Consolidation (Consequential Provisions) Act 1985. The transitional period having expired, such a company may be wound up under the Insolvency Act, section 123(1)(*c*) although it is open to the court, at its discretion, to grant the company time to comply with the re-registration provisions. Although a petition on such grounds will normally be presented by the Secretary of State,[76] they are theoretically available to other petitioners.

---

[72] See, *e.g. Re Middlesbrough Assembly Rooms* (1880) 14 Ch.D. 104; an unsuccessful attempt to invoke this provision.
[73] *Re Eastern Telegraph Co.* [1947] 2 All E.R. 104.
[74] See *Palmer*, paras. 2.1602 and 2.1603.
[75] See *Palmer*, paras. 2.210 to 2.212.
[76] See para. 426, *infra*.

Floating charge in jeopardy

418 As noted above, this ground applies only to a Scottish company which
has granted a floating charge, which subsists over property comprised
in its property and undertaking and the court is satisfied the security of
the creditor entitled to the benefit of the charge is in jeopardy (I.A.,
s.122(2)). Although it is unlikely that anyone other than the holder of
the charge (if he can show an interest to petition) would petition on this
ground, the Act does not in terms restrict its use to such a creditor.

The creditor's security is to be deemed to be in jeopardy "if the court
is satisfied that events have occurred or are about to occur which
render it unreasonable in the interests of the creditor that the company
should retain power to dispose of the property which is subject to the
floating charge." This is not an exhaustive definition of "jeopardy,"
and the court is left with complete discretion as to the events which it
may accept as sufficient to entitle the creditor to an order. An order
could be granted without the company being insolvent or unable to
pay its debts.

This section originally appeared in the Companies (Floating
Charges) (Scotland) Act 1961, section 4. That Act did not enable the
holder of a floating charge to appoint a receiver, and accordingly
liquidation was his only recourse if his security was endangered. Since
the Companies (Floating Charges and Receivers) (Scotland) Act 1972
the holder of a floating charge by a Scottish company (including one
granted under the 1961 Act) has been able to appoint a receiver, and
this facility may make it unnecessary to resort to the Insolvency Act,
section 122(2) as the main grounds for a petition.

THE "JUST AND EQUITABLE" GROUND

419 Until the passing of the Companies Act 1980 the courts had to consider
the question of whether it would be "just and equitable" to wind up a
company in two situations; first, in the context of a winding-up
petition under what is now the Insolvency Act, section 122(1)(g), and,
second, as an element in determining whether a remedy is available to
a member complaining of oppression in the conduct of the company's
affairs under provisions first enacted as section 210 of the 1948 Act.
Section 210 of the 1948 Act, was replaced by section 75 of the
Companies Act 1980 now (with amendments) sections 459 to 461,
which do not require the court to be satisfied that it would be "just and
equitable" to wind the company up.[77] Cases decided in the context of
section 210 (1948) still have relevance in connection with the
Insolvency Act, section 122(1)(g).

There is no justification for restricting the circumstances which may
be regarded as affording "just and equitable" grounds for winding up,

---

[77] See *Palmer*, para. 8.1101 *et seq*.

whether by confining the application of this phrase to cases similar to the earlier parts of section 122 or by restricting it to rigid categories such as "loss of substratum" or "deadlock."[78] The courts are at liberty to adopt a liberal approach and previous decisions on whether a winding-up order should be granted on this ground should be treated as illustrations only.[79] The court must nevertheless exercise its discretion judicially on grounds which can be examined and justified.[80] It must proceed on the facts as they are at the date of the hearing, not when the petition was presented.[81] Cases of the application of this rule in England, valid as illustrations for Scotland, are discussed in *Palmer*, paragraphs 15.219 to 15.221. In Scotland, a winding-up order on this ground has been granted in the following situations:

"Where the business of the company was unsuccessful and a majority of the shareholders, but not sufficient to pass a special resolution for voluntary liquidation, wished it to be wound up.[82]

Where there was a serious failure to comply with the rules of administration of a company laid down by the Companies Acts, such as to deprive the shareholders of the guarantee of commercial probity and efficiency afforded thereby.[83]

Where, in a 'quasi-partnership' family company, the petitioner had been treated in a high-handed manner and the company's assets diverted to the directors and their family."[84]

There is no reported case in Scotland of a company being wound up on the sole ground that its substratum had been lost but it features as a supporting justification.[85] The leading English authority,[86] which has been quoted with approval in Scotland,[87] lays down that before it could be said that the substratum of the company's business has gone and a winding-up order might therefore be justified it is necessary to show that business within its objects had become in a practical sense impossible. A mere discontinuance of business activities, even for a lengthy period, is not enough, so long as this does not show a final and conclusive abandonment of the business, and provided also that the company's resources are being conserved so as to make a resumption of business possible.[88] It may of course be possible to bring such a case within the scope of the Insolvency Act, section 122(1)(*d*) (suspension of

---

[78] *Baird* v. *Lees*, 1924 S.C. 83, 90; 1923 S.L.T. 749.
[79] *Ebrahimi* v. *Westbourne Galleries Ltd.*, *per* Lord Wilberforce [1973] A.C. 360, 374; [1972] 2 All E.R. 292, 296; *Re St. Piran Ltd.* [1981] 3 All E.R. 270; see also *Palmer*, paras. 15.219 to 15.221.
[80] *Baird* v. *Lees*, 1924 S.C. 83, 90; 1923 S.L.T. 749.
[81] *Re Fildes Bros. Ltd.* [1970] 1 W.L.R. 592; [1970] 1 All E.R. 923.
[82] *Pirie* v. *Stewart* (1904) 6 F.847; 12 S.L.T. 129.
[83] *Baird* v. *Lees, supra.*
[84] *Hyndman* v. *R. C. Hyndman Ltd.*, 1989 S.C.L.R. 294 (Sh.Ct.).
[85] *e.g.* in *Hyndman* v. *R. C. Hyndman Ltd., supra.*
[86] *Re Suburban Hotel Co.* (1987) 2 Ch.App. 737.
[87] *Galbraith* v. *Merito Shipping Co.*, 1947 S.C. 446, 456.
[88] *Galbraith* v. *Merito Shipping Co., supra.*

business for a whole year).[89] A petition for winding up was held to be premature where the trading business of the company had come to an end and would not be resumed, but the directors were still engaged in negotiations to bring its affairs to a conclusion.[90]

This ground for winding up has most frequently been invoked by shareholders complaining that the management of the company was being conducted in a manner harmful to their interests. It is not, however, a legitimate means of securing a personal advantage by the premature liquidation of a solvent company.[91]

420   In approaching the question of whether the complaining shareholders had made out their case, the courts have emphasised the need for the minority to show good cause for the courts to override the wishes of the majority where the question in issue has been simply that of whether to grant a winding-up order on the "just and equitable" ground.[92] The company itself is the proper forum for resolving domestic differences among shareholders, but if these cannot be resolved and a deadlock results a winding-up order will be granted.[93] It is apparent, however, that a strict adherence to the principles of "majority rule" will not always achieve a just and equitable result. Where the holder of the vast majority of the shares was running the company for his personal benefit and with no regard for the interests of the company as a whole, the court granted an order. The case was, however, decided to a large extent on the particular circumstances.[94] If the majority is abusing its position in disregard of statutory obligations, an order may be granted.[95] Cases decided under section 210 of the 1948 Act reflect this trend.[96]

A common reason for invoking the "just and equitable" ground for winding up in modern cases is that the company is a "quasi-partnership," and that the mutual trust and confidence which should obtain among the members considered as "partners" has broken down.[97] The court is entitled to examine the total relationship of the parties, including agreements outwith the memorandum and articles

---

[89] *Galbraith* v. *Merito Shipping Co., supra, per* Lord Mackay, p. 459.
[90] *Cox* v. *"Gosford" Ship Co.* (1894) 21 R. 334.
[91] *Anglo-American Brush Electric Light Corp. Ltd.* v. *Scottish Brush Electric Light and Power Co. Ltd.* (1882) 9 R. 972.
[92] *Martin* v. *Scottish Savings Investment Society* (1897) 7 R. 352; *Black* v. *United Collieries Ltd.* (1904) 7 F. 18; 12 S.L.T. 373; *Scobie* v. *Atlas Steel Works Ltd.* (1906) 8 F. 1052; 14 S.L.T. 212.
[93] *Symington* v. *Symington Quarries Ltd.* (1905) 8 F. 121; 13 S.L.T. 509.
[94] *Thomson* v. *Drysdale*, 1925 S.C. 311; 1925 S.L.T. 174; see also *Zolkwer* v. *Reid, Carr & Co.*, 1946 S.N. 141 and *Hyndman* v. *R. C. Hyndman Ltd., supra.*
[95] *Baird* v. *Lees, supra.*
[96] *Elder* v. *Elder & Watson*, 1952 S.C. 49; 1952 S.L.T. 112; *Meyer* v. *S.C.W.S.*, 1954 S.C. 381; 1954 S.L.T. 273; *Meyer* v. *S.C.W.S.*, 1958 S.C. (H.L.) 40; 1958 S.L.T. 241.
[97] *Ebrahimi* v. *Westbourne Galleries Ltd.* [1973] A.C. 360; [1972] 2 All E.R. 292; *Re Jermyn Street Turkish Baths Ltd.* [1971] 3 All E.R. 184; [1971] 1 W.L.R. 1042; *Re Zinotty Properties Ltd.* [1984] 3 All E.R. 754; *Teague, Petr.*, 1985 S.L.T. 469. *Hyndman* v. *R. C. Hyndman Ltd., supra; Jesner* v. *Jarrad Properties Ltd.*, 1992 G.W.D. 31–1797. See also *Palmer*, paras. 15.219 to 15.221.

of the company, in order to determine whether the company exhibits the characteristics of a partnership.[98] An arrangement for all shareholders to participate in management, broken by the dismissal of the petitioner as a director or employee, would prima facie justify the winding up of such a company.[98a] It is necessary, however, to demonstrate a specific agreement entitling the petitioner to participation in management.[99] Mere refusal to allow a member to sell his shares at a fair price is not a sufficient ground for a winding-up order,[1] but the petitioner may succeed if the reason for his refusal is the company's failure to produce accounts.[2] Allegations of prejudicial conduct must be averred with precision in the petition, and any answers fully dealt with.[3] It is not, however, necessary to aver fraud.[4]

A contributory may rely on a report by inspectors appointed by the Secretary of State in support of his petition.[5]

The decisions have to be considered in the context of the statutory provisions of the time. In particular, prior to 1948, there was no "alternative remedy" for an oppressed minority shareholder[6] and if the petitioners had some other remedy, they might be required to exhaust it before proceeding to a winding up.[7] The latter obstacle was removed, or at least substantially reduced, by section 225(2) of the 1948 Act (now I.A., s.125(2)) under which the existence of another remedy is not to be a reason for refusing to grant a winding-up order on the "just and equitable" ground unless the court is satisfied that the petitioners are acting unreasonably in seeking a winding-up order instead of the alternative remedy. If the petitioner has refused to accept a reasonable offer to settle the matter, *e.g.* by the purchase of his shares on fair terms, the petition will be dismissed.[8] The replacement of section 210 (1948) by section 75 of the 1980 Act (now ss.459–461) has increased the likelihood of the court holding that a winding-up petition was unreasonable since sections 459 to 461 now provide a wider range of alternative remedies.[9] There is, however, a distinction between seeking a winding-up order and merely the appointment of a provisional liquidator to preserve the assets of the company, and the existence of an "alternative remedy" such as sections 459 to 461 is not necessarily a ground for dismissing a winding-up petition where only

---

[98] *Ebrahimi* v. *Westbourne Galleries Ltd., supra; Re A Company (No. 00477 of 1986)* (1986) P.C.C. 372.
[98a] *Ebrahimi* v. *Westbourne Galleries Ltd., supra; Re A Company (No. 00477 of 1986), supra.*
[99] *Gammack, Petr.,* 1983 S.L.T. 250.
[1] *Ibid.,* n. 90.
[2] *Re Wessex Computer Stationers Ltd.* [1992] B.C.L.C. 366.
[3] *Gammack, Petr., supra.*
[4] *Hyndman* v. *R. C. Hyndman Ltd., supra.*
[5] *Re St. Piran Ltd.* [1981] 3 All E.R. 270.
[6] Companies Act 1948, s.210. See *Palmer,* para. 8.1101 *et seq.*
[7] See *Palmer,* para. 15.221.
[8] *Re A Company* [1983] 2 All E.R. 854.
[9] *Gammack, Petr., supra.*

the appointment of a provisional liquidator is sought.[10] The court will order a winding up if satisfied that sections 459 to 461 will not provide an effective remedy.[11] The appointment of a judicial factor may, however, be more appropriate.[11a]

A creditor (including a contingent creditor) may petition for winding up on the "just and equitable" ground, but not if he is simultaneously pursuing his claim by ordinary action.[12]

PETITION FOR COMPULSORY WINDING UP

421 Application to the court is by way of petition (I.A., s.124(1)), which may be presented by any or all of:

    (a) the company;
    (b) the directors;
    (c) any creditor;
    (d) any contributory;
    (e) a receiver[13];
    (f) the Secretary of State.[14]

In addition, the Bank of England has power to petition in certain circumstances for the winding up of a bank or an institution licensed to take deposits[15] and the Department of Trade may petition for the winding up of an insurance company.[16] Insurance companies may also be wound up, in certain circumstances, on a petition by policyholders.[17] The Chief Registrar of Friendly Societies also has power to present a petition for the winding up of a building society in the case of certain defaults by it.[18] For unregistered companies see paragraph 411, above.

A company may commence winding up by resolution under the Insolvency Act, section 84, but this requires either 21 days' notice or the necessary consents to short notice. Accordingly, if there is urgency, *e.g.* to cut down diligence or restrain other proceedings against the company, the directors may think it expedient for the company to petition for its own winding up, thereby establishing an earlier date for the commencement of liquidation. Until the Insolvency Acts of 1985/1986 there was no specific authority for the directors to

---

[10] *Teague, Petr., supra.* For the appointment of a provisional liquidator, see paras. 434 and 435, *infra.*
[11] *Hyndman v. R. C. Hyndman Ltd., supra. Jesner v. Jarrad Properties Ltd., supra.*
[11a] *McGuinness v. Black (No. 2),* 1990 S.L.T. 461; see *Palmer,* para. 8.910.
[12] *Re A Company (No. 003028 of 1987)* (1987) 3 B.C.C. 575.
[13] I.A., s.55 and Sched. 2, item 21 "in relation to such part of the property of the company as is attached by the floating charge" (s.55(1)).
[14] But only under I.A., s.122(1)(*b*) or (*c*) or I.A., s.124A, (I.A., s.124(4)); see para. 15.626, *infra.* For Insurance Companies see para. 415, *ante.*
[15] See *Palmer,* para. 15.231. Banking Act 1987, ss.92, 106(1).
[16] See para. 415, *ante.*
[17] Insurance Companies Act 1982, s.53.
[18] Building Societies Act 1962, ss.22, 50, 55 and Sched. 1, para. 5.

petition, as distinct from the directors instructing a petition in name of the company. Giving the directors such authority by statute removes any doubt whether instituting winding-up proceedings would be *ultra vires*, but the directors must still act in accordance with the articles in taking their decision. A single director acting on his own authority cannot petition for winding up (assuming there is more than one director in office) but a majority decision of the board will suffice.[19] The list of potential petitioners in the Insolvency Act, section 124(1) appears to be exhaustive (apart from the statutory additions indicated above).[20] The majority of petitions are presented by creditors.

Because of the effect of a winding-up order (or even a pending petition) on the value of the company as a going concern, it is often preferable to appoint a judicial factor *ad interim* to enable the assets and business of the company to be protected while a solution to the dispute is sought.[21]

Creditor's petition

Who is a creditor?

422 "Creditor" has its ordinary meaning of any person to whom the company is owing money, and by the Insolvency Act, section 124(1) this extends to contingent and prospective creditors. A person to whom a debt has been assigned is as much a "creditor" as the assignor even if the debt was assigned after the petition was presented.[22] It appears that the holder of a floating charge may petition for winding up notwithstanding his appointment of a receiver.[23]

The court's power to require a contingent or prospective creditor to find caution for expenses (s.519(5)) was repealed by the Insolvency Acts 1985/1986 along with the formal requirement (also in s.519(5)) that such a creditor establish a prima facie case for winding up. It remains the case, however, that a contingent or prospective creditor has to satisfy the court that his claim exists and that the winding-up order should be granted, *e.g.* on the ground that the company is unable to pay its debts.

"Contingent creditor" means a creditor in respect of a debt which will only become due in an event which may or may not occur; "prospective creditor" means a creditor in respect of a debt which will certainly become due in the future, either on some date which has already been determined or on some date determinable by reference to

---

[19] *Re Regent Insulation* [1981] C.L.Y. 250. *In Re Instrumentation Electrical Services Ltd.* (1988) 4 B.C.C. 301; *Re Equiticorp International* (1989) 5 B.C.C. 599.
[20] *Re William Hockley Ltd.* [1962] 1 W.L.R. 555, 558; 2 All E.R. 111; *Re H. L. Bolton Engineering Co. Ltd.* [1956] Ch. 577.
[21] See *Palmer*, para. 8.910; *McGuinness* v. *Black (No. 2)*, 1990 S.L.T. 461.
[22] *Perak Pioneer Ltd. etc.* v. *Petroliam Nasional Bhd.* [1986] A.C. 849.
[23] See para. 201, *ante*.

future events.[24] A member may be a creditor in respect of sums due to him by way of dividend, profits or the like even though his ranking is postponed to other creditors (I.A., s.74(2)(f)).

A winding-up petition is not the appropriate process for recovery of a debt which is disputed, and a petition presented in such circumstances may be dismissed with expenses.[25] Although caution was found by the company in both the Scottish cases cited, the court did not regard this as a necessary condition for dismissing the petition. A dispute over part only of a liquid claim is not a ground for refusing to grant an order.[26] The court has, however, the power to sist the petition to enable the petitioner to constitute (by separate court action) a debt which is disputed *in toto*.[27]

A creditor who has failed to establish the basis on which he petitioned cannot oppose an unconditional restraint on further such proceedings on the same basis, nor can the liquidation process be used to resolve a *bona fide* dispute as to whether a claim is presently due, contingent or prospective.[28]

Creditor's right to a winding-up order

423 Subject to the discretion of the court to dismiss, adjourn or make any other order in relation to the petition which it thinks fit (I.A., s.125(1)) a creditor who has established that his debt is due and that the company is unable to pay its debt is prima facie entitled to a winding-up order.[29] Such a petition will not in any event be summarily dismissed in the absence of very cogent reasons.[30] An order cannot be refused merely because there are securities equal to or greater than the value of the assets, or because there are no assets available to the liquidator,[31] or because the company is already in voluntary, liquidation[32] but the petitioning creditor must demonstrate the likelihood of some advantage accruing to him.[33] However, a creditor has no inherent right

---

[24] *Stonegate Securities Ltd.* v. *Gregory* [1980] 1 All E.R. 241, 243; *Walter L. Jacob Ltd.* v. *FIMBRA*, 1988 S.C.L.R. 184 (Sh.Ct.).

[25] *Cunninghame, etc.* v. *Walkinshaw Oil Co.* (1886) 14 R. 87; *W. & J. C. Pollok* v. *Gaeta Pioneer Mining Co.*, 1907 S.C. 182; 14 S.L.T. 526; see also *Re Lympne Investments Ltd.* [1972] 1 W.L.R. 523; [1972] 2 All E.R. 385; *Re A Company (No. 0010656 of 1990)* [1991] B.C.L.C. 464; *Re A Company (No. 001259 of 1991) ex p. Medialite* [1991] B.C.L.C. 594; *Re A Company (No. 0013925 of 1991), ex p. Roussell* [1992] B.C.L.C. 562.

[26] *Cowan* v. *Scottish Publishing Co.* (1892) 19 R. 437; *Re Tweeds Garages* [1962] Ch. 406; [1962] 1 All E.R. 121. *Re A Company (No. 008122 of 1989), ex p. Transcontinental Insurance Services* [1990] B.C.L.C. 697; *Blue Star Security Services (Scotland) Ltd.* v. *Drake & Scull (Scotland) Ltd.*, 1992 S.L.T. (Sh.Ct.) 80.

[27] *Landauer & Co.* v. *W. H. Alexander & Co. Ltd.*, 1919 S.C. 492; 1919 2 S.L.T. 2.

[28] *Stonegate Securities Ltd.* v. *Gregory, supra.*

[29] *Smyth & Co.* v. *Salem Flour Mills Co. Ltd.* (1887) 14 R. 441; *Gardner & Co.* v. *Link* (1894) 21 R. 967. *Re Tweeds Garages Ltd.* [1962] Ch. 406, 414; *Foxhall & Gyle (Nurseries) Ltd. (Ptnrs.)*, 1978 S.L.T. (Notes) 29; *Re Wessex Computer Stationers* [1992] B.C.L.C. 366.

[30] *Foxhall & Gyle (Nurseries) Ltd. (Petrs.), supra.*

[31] I.A., s.125(1).

[32] I.A., s.116.

[33] *In re Eloc Electro-Optieck* [1982] Ch. 43; [1981] 2 All E.R. 1111.

to information about the assets of the company and cannot obtain such information indirectly, *e.g.* by seeking that such disclosure or a Declaration of Solvency be made as a condition of the court restraining further procedure on a winding-up petition whose grounds have not been established.[34]

Section 195 of the Insolvency Act 1986 provides that the court may have regard to the wishes of the creditors (having regard to the value of their debts) or contributories (having regard to their voting rights), and may convene meetings to ascertain their wishes.[35] In a creditor's petition, apart from cases where there is doubt as to the existence of the creditor's claim, opposition by the company or its members will not result in the petition being refused.[36] Other creditors may, however, oppose the granting of a winding-up order. In such cases the court will normally have regard to the wishes of the majority in value of the creditors.[37] This is not, however, an inflexible rule, and if the court considers there are circumstances justifying its intervention, an order for winding up by the court will be granted notwithstanding the views of the majority of creditors.[38] It may also refuse to grant an order against the wishes of the majority of creditors if satisfied that it would be more appropriate to allow the wishes of the minority to prevail.[39]

An attempt to suggest some general principles was made in *Re J. D. Swain Ltd.*[40] If the creditors are agreed that the company should be wound up, but a minority (in value) seek a compulsory order, the court will be disposed to refuse the petition since all will in any event receive the class remedy in the voluntary liquidation. On the other hand, if the majority are opposed to winding up in any form, the wishes of the minority should normally prevail and the order be granted, since only thus will the petitioner receive the remedy to which he is prima facie entitled. These general considerations (persuasive only in Scotland) must, of course, be subject to any special factors which may be present in the particular case.[41] Objections by outside creditors will carry more weight than the views of creditors who are also directors or contributories.[42] Creditors who desire the fully independent status of a

---

[34] *Stonegate Securities Ltd.* v. *Gregory* [1980] 1 All E.R. 241.

[35] *Wilson* v. *Hadley* (1897) 7 R. 178. See para. 454, *infra.*

[36] See para. 422, *supra; Macdonnell's Trs.* v. *Oregonian Railway Co.* (1884) 11 R. 912 (bondholder with arrears of interest paid since the petition was presented); *Wotherspoons* v. *Brescia Mining and Metallurgical Co. Ltd.* (1896) 24 R. 207; 4 S.L.T. 184.

[37] *Elsmie & Son* v. *The Tomatin Spey District Distillery* (1906) 8 F. 434; 13 S.L.T. 722; *Pattisons Ltd.* v. *Kinnear* (1899) 1 F. 551; 6 S.L.T. 304; *Bell's Trs.* v. *The Holmes Oil Co.* (1900) 3 F. 23; *Drysdale & Gilmour* v. *Liquidator of International Exhibition of Electrical Engineering and Inventions* (1890) 18 R. 98. *Re R. J. Falcon Developments* [1987] B.C.L.C. 437.

[38] *Bouboulis* v. *Mann Macneal & Co.*, 1926 S.C. 637; 1926 S.L.T. 417. *Re MCH Services* [1987] B.C.L.C. 535.

[39] *Re Southard & Co. Ltd.* [1979] 1 All E.R. 582. (The minority wished the voluntary liquidation to continue.)

[40] [1965] 1 W.L.R. 909; [1965] 2 All E.R. 761.

[41] See also *Floors of Bristol (Builders) Ltd.* [1982] 7 C.L. 51a.

[42] *Re Holiday Stamps* [1985] 7 C.L. 472; *The Times*, July 11, 1985.

compulsory liquidator are, if there appears to be any substance in their misgivings, entitled to a compulsory liquidation.[43] Public interest, as expressed by a regulatory authority to whose jurisdiction the company had summitted, may be decisive.[43a]

Contributory's petition

424 The right of a contributory to petition for winding up cannot be excluded by the articles of the company,[44] but a shareholder's petition must overcome a number of obstacles:

First, unless the Insolvency Act, section 124(3) applies and the petitioner is a contributory by virtue of the Insolvency Act, section 76, which arises only when the company has purchased or redeemed its own shares out of capital, (see paragraph 459, below), the petitioner must be qualified under the Insolvency Act, section 124(2). This is designed to prevent persons buying shares merely to wreck the company. Unless the petition is on the ground that the number of members has been reduced below the statutory minimum,[45] some at least of his shares must have been originally allotted to him, or have been registered in his name for at least six of the 18 months before commencement of the winding up, or have devolved on him through the death of a former holder. Strict compliance with these requirements is necessary, unless perhaps the company is in default in allotting shares or registering a transfer.[46] If there is a genuine dispute whether the petitioner is an allottee he cannot proceed until he has established his rights.[47] Cross-petitions raising disputes as to ownership of shares have been allowed to proceed, in a case where both petitioners were registered holders of some shares, and relief under sections 459 to 461 was also sought.[48] Prior to the Bankruptcy (Scotland) Act 1985 it was accepted that the trustee upon the sequestrated estates of a bankrupt shareholder could not petition for the winding up of the company in his own name, but that he could present a petition in the name of the bankrupt.[49] Under the Bankruptcy (Scotland) Act 1985, section 31(1)(a), however, the bankrupt's estate automatically vests in the permanent trustee by virtue of the Act and warrant in the sequestration. Accordingly, the trustee is entitled to petition for winding up in his own name.[50] The Bankruptcy Act does not, however, clarify the position upon the discharge of the bankrupt

---

[43] *In re Palmer Marine Surveys Ltd.* [1986] 1 W.L.R. 573.
[43a] *S.I.B.* v. *Lancashire and Yorkshire Portfolio Management* [1992] B.C.L.C. 281.
[44] *Re Peveril Gold Mines* [1898] 1 Ch. 122.
[45] Now two in all cases: s.24.
[46] *Re Gattopardo Ltd.* [1969] 1 W.L.R. 619, C.A.; [1969] 2 All E.R. 344.
[47] *Re JN 2* [1977] 3 All E.R. 1104.
[48] *Re Garage Door Ltd.* [1984] 1 W.L.R. 35; [1984] 1 All E.R. 434.
[49] I.A., s.82(2); *Re K/9 Meat Supplies (Guildford) Ltd.* [1966] 1 W.L.R. 1112; [1966] 3 All E.R. 320; *Re H. L. Bolton Engineering Co. Ltd.* [1956] Ch. 577; [1956] 1 All E.R. 799.
[50] *Taylor, Petr.*, November 20, 1992, unreported.

or of the trustee. Upon the discharge of the bankrupt, all debts and obligations at the date of sequestration are extinguished (s.55) and upon the discharge of the permanent trustee, the trustee is discharged from all liability to the creditors or to the debtor arising from his actings (s.57(5)) but neither section provides for the re-vesting in the bankrupt of any estate still vested by virtue of section 31 in the trustee. In the case of shares in a company, however, if the bankrupt is still the registered member he remains a "contributory" within the meaning of the Insolvency Act 1986, section 74, and the Insolvency Act, section 82(2), which provides that the contributory's trustee in bankruptcy represents him for all purposes, can no longer apply after the trustee has been discharged. It would appear, therefore, that after the discharge of the trustee (but not before) the bankrupt as registered member of the company may petition for its winding up as a "contributory". If, however, the shares have been registered in the name of the trustee, the trustee himself is the "contributory" in respect of those shares by virtue of section 74 until such time as the shares have been transferred or transmitted to another party.[51] The personal representatives of a deceased shareholder may petition as contributories.[52]

Second, the petitioner must satisfy the court that constitutional methods of achieving a winding up within the company, such as a resolution for its voluntary liquidation, have been attempted without success or are impossible or inappropriate.[53] In *Galbraith* v. *Merito Shipping Co.*,[54] it is suggested that such preliminary steps would not be required if the grounds for the petition were "loss of substratum." Normally, this requirement will restrict contributories' petitions to the "just and equitable" clause.[55] There are, however, other circumstances where a shareholder's petition is appropriate, such as an aborted reconstruction scheme.[56]

Third, the petitioner must have a pecuniary interest in the outcome of the winding-up proceedings. Normally, this means that he must show a prima facie probability that a surplus will emerge for distribution to himself and other members.[57] Consequently, a contributory cannot petition on the ground of inability to pay debts. This rule, however, does not apply where the contributory's shares are

---

[51] *Cf. Re Wolverhampton Steel & Iron Co. Ltd.* [1977] 1 All E.R. 417 affd. [1977] 3 All E.R. 467.

[52] I.A., s.81; *Re Bayswater Trading Co. Ltd.* [1970] 1 W.L.R. 343 [1970] 1 All E.R. 608.

[53] *Symington* v. *Symington Quarries Ltd.* (1905) 8 F. 121; 13 S.L.T. 509; *Pirie* v. *Stewart* (1904) 6 F. 847; 12 S.L.T. 179, *Cox* v. *"Gosford" Shipping Co.* (1894) 21 R. 334; 1 S.L.T. 431; *Baird* v. *Lees*, 1924 S.C. 83; 1923 S.L.T. 749; *Scobie* v. *Atlas Steel Works* (1906) 8 F. 1052; 14 S.L.T. 212.

[54] 1947 S.C. 446; 1947 S.L.T. 265.

[55] See paras. 419 and 420, *ante*.

[56] *Re Gutta Percha Corporation* [1900] 2 Ch. 655.

[57] *Ptn. Walker* (1894) 2 S.L.T. 230 and 397; *Re W. R. Willcocks & Co. Ltd.* [1974] Ch. 163; *Re Chesterfield Catering Co. Ltd.* [1977] Ch. 373. *Munro* v. *Edinburgh & District Trades Council Social Club*, 1989 G.W.D. 6–240.

partly paid, since his interest then may be to minimise his loss which would result from having to contribute in an insolvent liquidation. Where the petitioner bases his application on the "just and equitable" clause (I.A., s.122(1)(g)) he may meet this requirement by alleging that information supplied by the company is inadequate to determine whether a surplus will emerge, or that its affairs require investigation which is likely to reveal a surplus.[58] A contributory cannot, however, succeed if the result of investigation would benefit only the creditors,[59] nor if he merely avers that the company is in substance a partnership.[60]

A shareholder who is in arrears with calls must make out an exceptional case to justify his petition, and may be required to pay the arrears into court or give an undertaking in respect of them.[61]

The existence of a voluntary winding up will normally leave no room for a shareholder to justify a compulsory order, but it is not an absolute bar. The court must, however, be satisfied that the rights of contributories would be prejudiced by a voluntary winding up.[62]

Petition by receiver

425 Section 55 and Schedule 2 of the Insolvency Act 1986 accord to a receiver wide powers of administration, which include a power to present a winding-up petition, but which will normally make such a petition unnecessary. If, however, the assets under his control do not suffice to satisfy the claims of the holder of the floating charge, and the prior claims which the receiver is required to satisfy, winding up may be the appropriate step. It may also be necessary to cut down diligence.[63]

Petition by Secretary of State

426 The Secretary of State has power to present a petition for the winding up of a company under the Insolvency Act, section 122(1)(b) (failure to obtain a trading certificate) or (c) (being an old public company) (I.A., s.124(4)(a)). He may also petition for the winding up of a company under the Insolvency Act, sections 124(4)(b) and 124A[64] on the basis of information received from a report under Part XIV of the Act or sections 94 and 177 of the Financial Services Act 1986, or information received under section 105 of the Financial Services Act, the Criminal Justice Act 1987, section 2, the Criminal Justice (Scotland) Act 1987,

---

[58] *Re Newman and Howard Ltd.* [1962] Ch. 257.
[59] *Re Othery Construction Ltd.* [1966] 1 W.L.R. 69; [1966] 1 All E.R. 145.
[60] *Re Expanded Plugs Ltd.* [1966] 1 W.L.R. 514; [1966] 1 All E.R. 877.
[61] *Re Diamond Fuel Co.* (1879) 13 Ch.D. 400; *Re Crystal Reef Co.* [1892] 1 Ch. 408.
[62] I.A., s.116. *Green & Sons* v. *Frasers (Aberdeen) Ltd.* (1939) 55 Sh.Ct.Rep. 133; *Re National Company for Distribution of Electricity* [1902] 2 Ch. 34; *Re Zinotty Properties Ltd.* [1984] 3 All E.R. 754.
[63] See paras. 221 and 222, *ante* and 499 and 500, *post*.
[64] I.A., s.124(4)(b) was amended, and I.A., s.124A was substituted for the similar provisions of s.440 by the Companies Act 1989, s.60.

section 52 or the Companies Act 1989, section 83. The Secretary of State cannot petition under section 124A if the company is already being wound up by the court.[65] The court must be satisfied that it would be "expedient in the public interest" and "just and equitable" to grant the order.[66] There has to be prejudice to the public interest, or fraud.[67]

The court should exercise that discretion in the light of the facts as they appear before it, not as they were when the Secretary of State decided to present the petition. Even where a company has ceased trading and there are no grounds for a winding-up order other than the public interest based on its past misconduct, it would be just and equitable to grant the order.[68] The Secretary of State may petition for the winding up of an insurance company under the Insurance Companies Act 1982.[69] A provisional liquidator may be appointed.[70] The Secretary of State may also apply for an order under section 460 in addition to or as an alternative to winding up.[71]

FORM OF PETITION[72]

427 Court of Session Rules 217 and Sheriff Court Rules 18 require the petition to design the petitioner, and to give the name of the company, its registered office (and any change of address in the last six months known to the petitioner), its nature and objects, details of nominal and issued capital and the amount of its assets so far as known to the petitioner. The facts on which the petitioner relies to establish his prima facie case, and particulars required to instruct his title to petition, must be set out. Any documents founded on as supporting the petitioner's title and the facts averred must be lodged with the petition. The petition must give the name and address of the proposed interim liquidator[73] and state that he is qualified to act as an insolvency practitioner in relation to the company. The petition must include details of the orders sought including intimation and advertisement and any appointment of an interim liquidator.

Presentation

428 Petitions in the Court of Session are presented in the Outer House and

---

[65] I.A., s.124A(2).

[66] I.A., s.124A(1).

[67] *Re Secure and Provide Ltd.* [1992] B.C.C. 405.

[68] In *Re Walter L. Jacob & Co. Ltd.* [1989] B.C.L.C. 345.

[69] *Re Lubin, Rosen and Associates Ltd.* [1975] 1 All E.R. 577; see para. 415, *ante*.

[70] I.A., s.135; paras. 434 and 435, *infra*; *Re Highfield Commodities Ltd.* [1984] 3 All E.R. 884. (The court's criticisms of the English Court Rules on this point are, of course, not applicable in Scotland.)

[71] See *Palmer*, para. 8.1102.

[72] For a discussion of procedural aspects see "Liquidation Procedure in the Court of Session" by William W. McBryde, 1977 S.L.T. (News) 237 and McBryde and Dowie, *Petition Procedures in the Court of Session* (2nd ed.), Chap. 16.

[73] See para. 436, *post*.

are dealt with by the liquidation judge (I.A., s.121 and R.C.S. 217(1)), unless in vacation, when the vacation judge deals with them under the Insolvency Act, section 120(2).

The company, any debenture holder, holder of a floating charge, receiver, shareholder or any person claiming an interest may lodge a *caveat* in the court offices, which has the effect of preventing any order being granted until that party has been given an opportunity to be heard. A *caveat* is effective for 12 months, after which it may be renewed (R.C.S. 218A; Sh.Ct.R. 20). Petitions are heard by the judge as soon as practicable after presentation. The court has complete discretion on how to dispose of a petition (I.A., s.125(1)), but the normal first order is for intimation, service and advertisement. In many cases a provisional liquidator is appointed (see below).

Advertisement of petition

429 The normal order is for the petition to be advertised once in the *Edinburgh Gazette* and in one or more newspapers selected to bring the matter to the notice of creditors. The advertisement must state the date the petition was presented, particulars of the petitioner and his solicitor, the precise order applied for, particulars of any provisional liquidator appointed and the *induciae* within which answers may be lodged (R.C.S. 218(6) and (7); Sh.Ct.R. 19(6) and (7)). Advertisement will often be dispensed with where a contributory is seeking to wind up a solvent company, *e.g.* on the "just and equitable" basis.

Service of petition

430 The petition is to be intimated on the walls of the court and (in the Court of Session) in the minute book of the court.[74] It is to be served on the company (if the company is not the petitioner)[75] and any voluntary liquidator or receiver who has been appointed. There is no specific requirement to serve on any administrator or supervisor of a voluntary arrangement, although the court may direct such service. If the company is a recognised bank or institution to which the Banking Act 1987 applies, service is to be effected on the Bank of England (if it is not itself the petitioner). These rules are subject to modification and any further directions by the court (R.C.S. 218(1) and (2); Sh.Ct.R. 19(1) and (2)). Service is normally by registered or recorded delivery post at the registered office or, if this is not possible, a place of business in Scotland or by messenger-at-arms or sheriff officer (R.S.C. 218(3)–(5); Sh.Ct.R. 19(3)–(5)). The *induciae* is normally eight days (R.C.S. 218(8); Sh.Ct.R. 19(8)).

---

[74] Intimation in the minute book is attended to by the court officials. Walling is effected by the petitioner's solicitor (Practice Note November 16, 1961).

[75] Service on the company will therefore be required (unless dispensed with) even if the petition is presented by the directors.

Hearing of petition

431 Under the Insolvency Act, section 125(1) the court may, on hearing the petition, dismiss it, adjourn the hearing conditionally or unconditionally, or make any interim or other order as it thinks fit. It may have regard to the wishes of creditors and contributories, and order meetings to be held to ascertain them (I.A., s.195). If the company is solvent the wishes of the contributories carry more weight than those of the creditors, but the reverse applies in insolvency.[76] A winding-up petition presented by the Secretary of State after an investigation must be given appropriate weight, even if unsupported by any creditor and opposed by many creditors with large claims and in face of a resolution for voluntary winding up.[77]

Substitute petitioner

432 When the original petitioner consents to dismissal or does not press for an order, a substitute petitioner may be sisted at the discretion of the court (R.C.S. 218C; Sh.Ct.R. 21). The substitute petitioner must lodge a note before the original petitioner has withdrawn or the petition is refused or dismissed; lodging of a minute of withdrawal by the petitioner is not itself withdrawal, and a note presented afterwards may still be timeous.[78] Where the Secretary of State's petition was withdrawn, contributories were not allowed to become substitute petitioners (under English procedure) because that would transfer a "public interest" petition into a contributories petition.[78a]

COMMENCEMENT OF WINDING UP

433 A winding up by the court commences on the date the petition is presented to the court (I.A., s.129(2)), unless a resolution for voluntary winding up has already been passed, when it commences on the date of the resolution (I.A., s.129(1)). Unless the court, on proof of fraud or error, directs otherwise, all proceedings in such a voluntary winding up are deemed valid (I.A., s.129(1)). Where a petition was first presented founding on a repealed statute (the Companies (Consolidation) Act 1908) and later re-served with amendments showing that it was founded on the current Act (of 1929), the date of commencement of the winding up was held to be the date of the order for re-service.[79] For the purpose of cutting down diligence, however, a different date of "commencement" applies.[80]

---

[76] See para. 423, *ante.*
[77] *Re Lubin, Rosen and Associates* [1975] 1 W.L.R. 122; [1975] 1 All E.R. 577.
[78] *Hepburn & Ross* v. *Tritonia Ltd.*, 1951 S.L.T. (Sh.Ct.) 6. See also *The Tudor Accumulator Co. Ltd.* v. *Scott Stirling & Co. Ltd.*, 1908 S.C. 331.
[78a] *Re Xyllyx (No. 1)* [1992] B.C.L.C. 376.
[79] *Ballantyne* v. *Train*, 1935 S.N. 111.
[80] See paras. 499 and 500, *post.*

Provisional liquidator

434 The court may appoint a provisional liquidator at any time after the presentation of the petition until an interim liquidator is appointed[81] (I.A., s.135(1) and (3)). Application may be made in the petition itself or by way of note in the process at the instance of the petitioner or any other party entitled to petition (1986 Rule 4.1; R.C.S. 218E(1); Sh.Ct.R. 23(1)). The application must state the grounds for seeking the appointment, give details of the proposed provisional liquidator and state that he is an insolvency practitioner[82] duly qualified to act in relation to the company. Details of any existing appointment of a voluntary liquidator or receiver known to the applicant must be given (R.S.C. 218E(2); Sh.Ct.R. 23(2)). It is almost invariable practice to apply for the appointment of a provisional liquidator on presentation of the petition and (assuming the petition is prima facie justified) to grant the application unless the petition is opposed on grounds which appear substantial. In considering whether to make an appointment the court is concerned to maintain the status quo in the affairs of the company and will attempt to avoid prejudice to either party.[83] Where the petition is at the instance of the Secretary of State under the Insolvency Act, section 124A the public interest may justify the appointment of a provisional liquidator even if the company is solvent.[84]

The court will expect the petitioner to have ascertained that the liquidator is willing to act before presenting the application. If there is dispute as to the proper person to be appointed, the court may nominate an independent person. The appointment may be recalled, but if the interlocutor recalling the appointment is the subject of an appeal the provisional liquidator remains in office until the reclaiming motion has been disposed of.[85]

The Insolvency Act 1986, section 135(5) provides that the court may limit the provisional liquidator's powers in the order appointing him. This reproduces section 532(4) (repealed). The orders of the Scottish courts under section 532(4), while conferring express powers, were ambiguous in not limiting the provisional liquidator to such powers as were mentioned, which might suggest that a provisional liquidator could exceed his express powers, contrary to section 532(4).[86] This view is at variance with cases suggesting that express powers were necessary.[87] The Insolvency Act, section 135(4) together with Court of

---

[81] I.A., s.138 requires the court to appoint an interim liquidator when granting a winding-up order; see para. 436, *infra*.

[82] *i.e.* an individual licensed as such by the Secretary of State or a recognised professional body under I.A., ss.388–398. See further para. 440, *post*.

[83] *Levy* v. *Napier*, 1962 S.L.T. 264; *Teague, Petr.*, 1985 S.L.T. 469.

[84] *Re Highfield Commodities Ltd.* [1984] 3 All E.R. 884.

[85] *Levy*, 1968 S.C. 46.

[86] Discussed in McBryde, "The Powers of Provisional Liquidators," 1977 S.L.T. (News) 145, based on *Drummond Wood Ltd.* (December 7, 1971; unreported).

[87] *Lochore and Capledrae Cannel Coal Co. Ltd.* (1889) 16 R. 556; *Wilsons (Glasgow & Trinidad) Ltd.*, 1912 2 S.L.T. 330.

Session Rules 218E(3) and Sheriff Court Rules 23(3) has removed the difficulty by providing for the court to specify the functions to be carried out by the provisional liquidator. Accordingly, the court has discretion to grant powers to the provisional liquidator as it thinks fit, but it must do so expressly. Before the Insolvency Act 1986, the court in appointing a provisional liquidator granted him power to bring or defend proceedings, to carry on the business of the company and to employ solicitors. The employment of solicitors is no longer an express power, but is clearly an implied power (I.A., s.167(2)(*b*)). The court's order appointing a provisional liquidator under the 1986 Act will doubtless refer to the remaining "traditional" powers. If the appointment is made to conserve the assets, it may be appropriate to substitute a power to this effect for the power to carry on business.[88] In addition, the Act empowers a provisional liquidator to require a "statement of affairs" from directors and others.[89]

435   The Insolvency Act, s.390(4) requires every insolvency practitioner to have in force caution for the proper performance of his functions, which meets the prescribed requirements.[90] 1986 Rule 7.28 imposes a general requirement to satisfy himself that adequate caution has been found on the person whose duty it is to appoint the practitioner to the relevant office. In the case of a provisional liquidator the Insolvency Act, section 135(1) implies that this duty lies with the court and (as noted above) the applicant seeking such an appointment must make appropriate averments as to his qualifications. 1986 Rule 4.1, as amended, provides that a statement in the petition (or lodged separately) that the proposed provisional liquidator is an insolvency practitioner, is duly qualified and consents to act will satisfy this requirement. Of necessity, the practitioner can only have in force at this stage the general bond lodged with his authorising body, not the "certificate of specific penalty" for the particular insolvency. The cost of caution is recoverable as an expense in the liquidation, or from the company if no winding-up order is made (1986 Rule 4.3). If the provisional liquidator fails to find or keep up his caution the court may remove him and give directions as to expenses and what steps (if any) should be taken to replace him (1986 Rule 4.4).

The successful applicant must send a certified copy of the interlocutor to the person appointed provisional liquidator, and the liquidator must advertise his appointment once in the *Edinburgh Gazette* and once in one or more newspapers as directed by the court to bring the matter to the notice of creditors (R.C.S. 218E (4) and (5); Sh.Ct.R. 23(4) and (5)). He must also give notice forthwith to the

---

[88] *Teague, Petr.*, 1985 S.L.T. 469.
[89] I.A., s.131(1) and (8); see para. 484, *post*.
[90] See the Insolvency Practitioners Regulations 1986 (S.I. 1986 No. 1995) as amended by S.I. 1986 No. 2247, regs. 9–13; reg. 13 requires the certificate issued in relation to the company to be kept in the sederunt book of the liquidation. See further para. 440, *post*.

registrar of companies, the company and any receiver (1986 Rule 4.2; Form 4.9 (Scot)).[91]

The remuneration of the provisional liquidator is to be fixed by the court. It may be on a commission basis calculated by reference to the value of the assets of the company, but in any event shall take into account the work reasonably undertaken having regard to that value and the extent of his responsibilities. His remuneration and expenses will be an expense of the liquidation or, if no winding-up order is made, recoverable from the company (1986 Rule 4.5, applying also s.53(4) of Bankruptcy (Scotland) Act 1985).

The court, on application by the provisional liquidator himself, or any of those entitled to apply for his appointment, may terminate his appointment (R.C.S. 218E(6); Sh.Ct.R. 23(6)).[91a] If the petition on which he was appointed is dismissed, his appointment falls and if it terminates for that or any other reason the court may (at its complete discretion) issue directions with respect to his accounts, remuneration, expenses or other matters (which are not automatically included in an order with respect to the expenses of the petition).[92] Unless the court directs otherwise, where there is no winding-up order, he may retain sufficient property of the company to meet his remuneration and expenses (1986 Rule 4.5(4)).

Even if a winding-up order has not been made, the appointment of a provisional liquidator has the effect of restraining proceedings against the company or its property without leave of the court (I.A., s.130(2)).[93]

THE WINDING-UP ORDER: INTERIM LIQUIDATOR'S APPOINTMENT

436 If no answers to the petition are lodged, or after answers have been disposed of, the court will order that the company be wound up under the provisions of the Act. The court must appoint an "interim liquidator" to hold office until the liquidator is formally appointed under subsequent procedure (I.A., s.138(1) and (2)).[94] The office of "interim liquidator" was introduced by the Insolvency Acts 1985/1986.

Before an interim liquidator is appointed there must be lodged with the court a statement to the effect that he is a duly qualified "insolvency practitioner" and that he consents to act (1986 Rule 4.18(2) R.C.S. 217(3)(*d*); Sh.Ct.R. 18(1)(*d*)). The interim liquidator must find caution (I.A., s.390(2)) and it is the court's responsibility to ascertain that he has done so (1986 Rule 7.28).[95]

---

[91] The form was amended by the 1987 Amendments (S.I. 1987 No. 1921).

[91a] *In Re Bank of Credit and Commerce International S.A. (No. 2)* [1992] B.C.L.C. 579 the court refused to replace provisional liquidators in order to protect delicate negotiations for the "rescue" of the company.

[92] 1986 Rules 4.5 and 4.6. *Graham* v. *John Tullis & Son (Plastics) Ltd.*, 1991 S.C.L.R. 823; 1992 S.L.T. 514.

[93] See further paras. 497 and 498, *post*.

[94] These sections imply that the interim liquidator has the same powers as the liquidator (if any) appointed to succeed him.

[95] See para. 440, *post*.

The court sends a copy of the winding-up order to the interim liquidator, whose appointment takes effect on the date of the order (1986 Rule 4.18(3)). Intimation of the winding-up order and of the appointment has to be given under the Insolvency Act, section 130(1) and 1986 Rule 4.18.[96]

Since the court's appointment is of an interim nature only and restricted to qualified insolvency practitioners, objection to the individual proposed as interim liquidator is likely to be very rare. The most likely basis is that he is not qualified to act in relation to the company by reason of an association with it (not necessarily an association which disqualifies him under the Act or the Rules).[97] The court has, however, full discretion as to the appointment among duly qualified practitioners.[98] Any objection should be stated at the bar, not by way of answers, and must be "of a tangible and definite nature."[99] The court will assume, in the absence of contrary proof, that the liquidator will properly discharge his statutory duty, mere allegations that he will not be independent being insufficient to sustain objections.[1] The court's decision on such an issue will not readily be disturbed on appeal.[2]

These decisions will also be relevant if the court is asked to order the removal of a liquidator.[3]

Expenses

437 The normal practice in Scotland is for the successful petitioner to be awarded his expenses against the company, and for any unsuccessful objector to be found liable in the expenses occasioned by his intervention.[4] The court may, however, award expenses or refuse them at its discretion if circumstances warrant this,[5] for example, if the court considers that the expense of a petition was not justified where a company with few assets was already in voluntary liquidation,[6] or if

---

[96] See para. 441, *post.*
[97] See I.A., ss.172 and 390; 1986 Rule 4.28(3); see para. 442, *post.*
[98] *Brightwen & Co.* v. *City of Glasgow Bank* (1878) 6 R. 244.
[99] *Anderson & Sons* v. *Broughty Ferry Picture House*, 1917 S.C. 622; 1917 2 S.L.T. 44; see also *Hume* v. *Directors of Highland Peat Fuel Co.* (1876) 3 R. 881; *Gilmour's Trs.* v. *Kilmarnock Heritable Property Investment Co.* (1883) 10 R. 1221; *Sanderson & Muirhead Ltd.* (1884) 21 S.L.R. 766.
[1] *Anderson & Sons* v. *Broughty Ferry Picture House, supra; Ecuadorian Association* v. *Stanmore*, 1904, 12 S.L.T. 92.
[2] *Steel Scaffolding Co.* v. *Buckleys Ltd.*, 1935 S.C. 617; 1935 S.L.T. 467.
[3] See paras. 443 and 444, *post.*
[4] *McGregor* v. *Ballachulish Slate Quarries Ltd.*, 1908 S.C. 1; 15 S.L.T. 397.
[5] For examples see *Pattullo* v. *Caithness Flagstone Co.*, 1908 S.C. 25; 15 S.L.T. 398; *The Seafield Preserve Co.*, 1911 S.C. 3; 1910 2 S.L.T. 199; *Liquidator of the Property Investment Co. of Scotland* v. *Blaik* (1873) 20 R. 1044. *Graham* v. *John Tullis & Son (Plastics) Ltd., supra.* In *Re Xyllyx plc* (No. 2) [1992] B.C.L.C. 378 expenses (partial) were awarded against the Secretary of State where he persisted in a petition after it had become clear that it was no longer justified.
[6] *Matthew Wishart, Petr.*, 1908 S.C. 690; 15 S.L.T. 953.

the petitioner had no title to bring the petition.[7] An award of the expenses of the petition does not dispose of the expenses of any provisional liquidator which may, however, be made payable by the unsuccessful petitioner under a further order.[8] The expenses of two petitions will not normally be allowed,[9] nor will the expenses of lodging answers merely objecting to the appointment of a particular person as liquidator, the appropriate procedure being to raise such objections at the bar.[10] The courts have used their discretion on expenses to discourage petitioners and objectors from increasing the cost of liquidation by procedures which have no practical value, however justifiable in theory.

The power of the court to require a petitioning contingent or prospective creditor to find caution for expenses (s.519(5)) was repealed by the Insolvency Act 1985. An appellant company may, however, be required to find caution under section 726.[11]

Publication of winding-up order

438 On the making of a winding-up order the company or the liquidator must notify the registrar of companies "forthwith" in the prescribed form (I.A., s.130(1); Form 4.2 (Scot)). There is no specific time limit for lodging this form with the registrar. A copy of the court order is to be attached to the form.

The order also requires official notification by the registrar of companies in the *Edinburgh Gazette* under sections 42 and 711.[12] Only 15 days after such notification is the order fully effective; if it is not notified the company (*i.e.* the liquidator) cannot rely on it against a third party who did not have actual notice of it. The company cannot rely on publication as constructive notice of the fact of liquidation to the prejudice of third parties not otherwise on notice of such event.[13] If it has been notified but the 15-day period has not expired the order may be relied upon unless a third party shows that he was unavoidably prevented from knowing of it. It is therefore prudent for the liquidator to ascertain whether such notification has in fact been given by the registrar.

Every invoice, order for goods or business letter issued by or on behalf of the company or the liquidator after the winding up order must contain a statement that the company is in liquidation (I.A., s.188).

---

[7] *Graham* v. *John Tullis & Son (Plastics) Ltd.*, *supra.*
[8] See para. 435, *ante.*
[9] *Graham, etc.* v. *Edinburgh Theatre Co.* (1877) 4 R. 1140.
[10] *Hume* v. *Directors of Highland Peat Fuel Co.* (1876) 3 R. 881; *Anderson & Sons* v. *Broughty Ferry Picture House*, 1917 S.C. 622; 1917 2 S.L.T. 44.
[11] *Cf. Pearson* v. *Naydler* [1977] 3 All E.R. 531.
[12] See *Palmer*, paras. 2.1401 *et seq.*
[13] *Official Custodian* v. *Parway Estates* [1984] 3 All E.R. 679; [1985] Ch. 151.

Meetings to choose a liquidator: the first meetings in the liquidation

439 On appointment the interim liquidator is required to convene separate meetings of the creditors and the contributories to decide who is to be the liquidator in place of himself. The liquidator must be an insolvency practitioner (I.A., s.230(3)). The interim liquidator is eligible for appointment (and in normal circumstances will be the liquidator). Such meetings are to be convened as soon as practicable after the interim liquidator's appointment, in any event within 42 days or such longer period as the court may allow (I.A., s.138(3)). If the company is being wound up on grounds that include inability to pay its debts, the interim liquidator may dispense with a meeting of the contributories for this purpose (1986 Rule 4.12(2A)).[14] These meetings are termed "the first meetings of creditors" and "the first meeting of contributories" respectively and are together referred to as "the first meetings in the liquidation" (1986 Rule 4.12(1) and (2)).

The rules for the convening and conduct of the first meetings are the same as those for meetings in the liquidation generally.[15] The chairman is the interim liquidator, although the meeting may (but is not obliged to) elect another chairman to consider a resolution to nominate the interim liquidator as liquidator (1986 Rule 7.5(4)). At the first meetings the only competent business is (1986 Rule 4.12(3)):

(a) to appoint a named liquidator or joint liquidators[16];
(b) whether to establish a liquidation committee[17];
(c) if a liquidation committee is not to be established, to determine how the liquidator's remuneration is to be fixed or (as will be more usual) to defer consideration thereof; (such a resolution is not necessarily the final determination of the liquidator's remuneration but if he dislikes the terms proposed the difficulty of securing an increase would make it prudent for him to decline the appointment[18]);
(d) a resolution to adjourn for not more than three weeks; and
(e) any other business admitted by the chairman.

The competent business at the meetings of creditors and of contributories is the same, except that contributories are debarred from discussing item (c), the liquidator's remuneration (1986 Rule 4.12(4)).

If there are first meetings of both creditors and contributories, the creditors' nominee is to be the liquidator (I.A., s.139(1)–(3)). The contributories' nominee will only be appointed if there is no creditors'

---

[14] I.A., s.138(4) stipulated 28 days, but this was altered to 42 by the 1987 Amendments to the Rules.
[15] See paras. 454 to 458, *post.*
[16] See para. 440, *infra.*
[17] See paras. 449 and 450, *infra.*
[18] See para. 448, *infra.*

nominee (I.A., s.139(3)), or on the basis of an application to the court within seven days by any creditor or contributory for an alternative or joint appointment (I.A., s.139(4); R.C.S. 218H(1); Sh.Ct.R. 26(1)).

If the first meetings do not nominate a liquidator, the interim liquidator must report this to the court which shall appoint either him or some other person to be the liquidator (I.A., s.138(5)). The court order is intimated to the appointee (R.C.S. 218H(2); Sh.Ct.R. 26(2)). If someone other than the interim liquidator is appointed by the first meetings he must notify the court of this event (I.A., s.138(6)).

The nominee must provide the chairman of the meeting at which he is elected with a written statement that he is an insolvency practitioner duly qualified under the Act and consents to be appointed liquidator. The chairman of the meeting, when satisfied that the statement is in order, will certify the appointment and state the date of the resolution for his appointment, on which the appointment takes effect, in the prescribed form (Form 4.8 (Scot)). This certificate is to be provided by the chairman of the creditors' meeting, unless that meeting makes no nomination, in which case it is the chairman of the meeting of contributories who certifies the appointment, if any (1986 Rule 4.19). There is no provision for the certificate to be lodged with the court or filed with the registrar of companies, but it will be retained by the liquidator among his official papers.

The court may also appoint as liquidator the person who is the administrator under an immediately preceding administration order, or the supervisor of a subsisting voluntary arrangement under Part I of the Insolvency Act 1986 (I.A., s.140). Section 140 cannot be used to appoint any other person as liquidator.[18a] Being "the liquidator" he has no duty to summon meetings under the Insolvency Act, sections 138 and 139, which apply only to the "interim liquidator."

THE LIQUIDATOR

440 The liquidator appointed to succeed the interim liquidator is referred to as "the liquidator" (I.A., s.163(a)). His acts are valid notwithstanding any defect in his appointment, nomination or qualifications (I.A., s.232).

In contrast to the position of interim and permanent trustees in bankruptcy, who must be resident within the jurisdiction of the Court of Session,[19] there is no statutory requirement that a liquidator should be resident in Scotland. Even before the Insolvency Act 1986 created the "insolvency practitioner" eligible to accept appointments throughout the United Kingdom, "foreign" liquidators were

---

[18a] *Re Exchange Travel (Holdings) Ltd.*, *The Independent*, November 16, 1992.
[19] Bankruptcy (Scotland) Act 1985, ss.2(2) and 24(2).

appointed,[20] even as sole liquidator.[21] The liquidator of a Scottish company, wherever he is resident and whether the company has been dissolved or not, remains subject to the jurisdiction of the Scottish courts.[22]

It is an offence to seek to influence the appointment of a liquidator by corrupt inducement (I.A., s.164). A liquidator who improperly solicits proxies or votes for his appointment may be penalised by loss of remuneration (1986 Rule 4.39).

The Insolvency Act, section 390 requires every liquidator (including a voluntary liquidator) to be an "insolvency practitioner" duly authorised by a recognised professional body[23] or by the Secretary of State. The Act requires every practitioner to find caution, as detailed in the Insolvency Practitioners Regulations 1990.[24]

The practitioner must enter into a general bond in the prescribed form for £250,000, which is held by his authorising body. On accepting each office, he must find caution for the value of the estimated assets available for unsecured creditors (including preferential creditors) subject to a minimum of £5,000 and a maximum of £5,000,000. He must increase the original amount (subject to the maximum) if the value of assets increases. The liquidation committee (if any) has to keep the sufficiency of his caution under review (1986 Rule 7.28). The certificate of specific penalty (and any supplementary certificate) evidencing the finding of caution is to be kept in the sederunt book, and a copy is lodged with the registrar of companies within 14 days. The cost is part of the expenses of liquidation.

A copy of the court order, certified by the clerk of court, or a copy of the certificate of appointment certified by the chairman of the meeting at which he was appointed under 1986 Rule 4.19(2), is sufficient evidence for all purposes and in any proceedings that the liquidator has been duly appointed (1986 Rule 4.20). Since, in the case of a liquidator appointed by one of the first meetings, it is only the chairman of the meeting who can supply the certificate which is conclusive evidence of his appointment, the liquidator would be well advised to obtain several copies at the time of his appointment. Other admissible evidence of his appointment may prove difficult to obtain at a later date.

Intimation and advertisement of appointment of liquidator

441 1986 Rules 4.18 and 4.19 provide for intimation of the appointment of a

---

[20] *Baberton Development Syndicate Ltd.* (1898) 25 R. 654; *Liquidators of Bruce Peebles & Co.* v. *Shiells*, 1908 S.C. 692; 15 S.L.T. 999.
[21] *Steel Scaffolding Co.* v. *Buckleys Ltd.*, 1935 S.C. 617; 1935 S.L.T. 467.
[22] *Lamey* v. *Winram*, 1987 S.L.T. 635.
[23] These include the Law Societies of Scotland and of England and Wales, the accountancy bodies of both countries and the Insolvency Practitioners' Association.
[24] S.I. 1990 No. 439 (which replaced the original Regulations S.I. 1986 No. 1995). The text summarises Part III of the Regulations as it applies to Scotland.

liquidator by the court (other than a provisional liquidator)[25] or by the first meetings.

Where the court appoints a liquidator it must send a copy of its order to the liquidator (1986 Rule 4.18(3); R.C.S. 218H(2); Sh.Ct.R. 26(2)).

The liquidator appointed by the court or the first meetings must notify the registrar of companies (and the court if he was appointed by the meetings) in the prescribed form (Form 4.9 (Scot))[26] within seven days of his appointment (1986 Rules 4.18(4)(*a*) and 4.19(4)(*a*)). If he is appointed by the court he must within 28 days of his appointment either notify all creditors and contributories or, if the court allows, advertise his appointment as the court directs (1986 Rule 4.18(4)(*b*)). If appointed at the first meetings he must within 28 days give notice of his appointment in a newspaper circulating in the area where the company has its principal place of business (not necessarily its registered office) or in such other newspaper as he thinks most appropriate for bringing it to the notice of creditors and contributories (1986 Rule 4.19(4)(*b*)). No official form is prescribed for such notice or advertisement. There is now no need for the liquidator to advertise his appointment in the *Edinburgh Gazette* and the notice of appointment of a liquidator in a winding up by the court does not require "official notification" under sections 42 and 711, but the court may order newspaper advertisement to bring the matter to the notice of creditors (R.C.S. 218D; Sh.Ct.R. 22).

The notice (and advertisement) to creditors and contributories must include a statement by the liquidator whether a liquidation committee has been established and, if not, whether he intends to convene meetings of creditors and contributories to establish a "liquidation committee," or whether he intends to summon a meeting of creditors only for this purpose. If he intends not to summon any such meeting his notice (and advertisement) must set out the powers of the creditors under the Insolvency Act, section 142(3) to require him to summon a meeting (1986 Rules 4.18(5) and 4.19(5)). As noted above,[27] the first meetings may already have decided this matter, but if no committee has been established, the Insolvency Act, section 142 provides for one to be established later.[28] The rules requiring notice to the registrar, creditors and contributories do not apply to a "liquidator" nominated by the first meeting of contributories but supplanted by the first meeting of creditors, provided this occurs on the same day (1986 Rule 4.19(6)).

The form prescribed for giving notice to the court and the registrar (Form 4.9 (Scot))[29] makes no provision for a statement as to the meetings to establish a liquidation committee which it should do in

---

[25] See rule 4.2; paras. 434 and 435, *ante*.
[26] This form was amended by the 1987 Amendments to the Rules.
[27] Para. 439, *ante*.
[28] See further para. 449, *post*.
[29] This form was amended by the 1987 Amendments to the Rules.

terms of Rule 4.18(5). It is understood that the registrar will require such a statement to be endorsed on the form or attached in a separate note by the liquidator.

The rules for intimation of the appointment also apply where a new liquidator is appointed by the court or a meeting of creditors,[30] with certain modifications. If the court makes the order, the procedure is the same as under 1986 Rule 4.18 (1986 Rule 4.26(5)(*c*)). If the creditors appoint the new liquidator 1986 Rule 4.19 applies except that the notice to the court registrar, creditors and contributories must also state that his predecessor has been removed, or has resigned and whether he has also been released (1986 Rules 4.27 and 4.29(5); Form 4.9 (Scot)).

RESIGNATION, REMOVAL AND RELEASE OF LIQUIDATOR

Resignation

442 A liquidator may resign office (I.A., s.172(6)) but only on the grounds and by the procedure prescribed in the 1986 Rules. If he is sole liquidator he may only resign on the grounds of ill health, or his intention to cease practice as an insolvency practitioner, or that a conflict of interest or a change of personal circumstances would inhibit the discharge of his duties (1986 Rule 4.28(3)). He cannot resign merely because he has difficulty in the administration of the liquidation, or considers his remuneration to be inadequate. A joint liquidator may also resign on the ground that continuation of a joint appointment is no longer expedient, in the opinion of himself and at least one other person (1986 Rule 4.28(4)). This implies that he will have consulted the other joint liquidator or liquidators, whose appointment continues.

The liquidator has to convene a meeting of creditors to receive his resignation (1986 Rule 4.28(1)). The notice of the meeting must refer to the power of the creditors to grant or withhold the liquidator's release, and be accompanied by an account of his administration and a summary of receipts and payments (1986 Rule 4.28(2)). The creditors may refuse or accept the resignation and will determine its effective date (1986 Rule 4.29(2)). They will also decide whether or not to grant the liquidator's release and determine its effective date (1986 Rule 4.29(4)). A liquidator whose resignation is accepted (whether or not he is also granted release) must forthwith (no time limit being prescribed) notify the court in the prescribed manner (I.A., s.172(6); 1986 Rule 4.29(3); Form 4.15 (Scot)) and also send a copy of his resignation to the registrar of companies (1986 Rule 4.29(3); Form 4.16 (Scot)). If the creditors resolve not to accept his resignation, the liquidator may apply to the court for leave to resign. The court's order should specify the notice to be given to the registrar and creditors "and shall determine the date from which the liquidator's release is effective" (1986 Rule

---

[30] See paras. 443 and 444, *post.*

4.30). It appears that a court order under 1986 Rule 4.30 could grant the liquidator his release without requiring him to apply to the Accountant of Court or suspend release until the Accountant has reported.

If no quorum is present at the meeting, the liquidator's resignation is deemed to have been accepted and the creditors are deemed not to have resolved against his release. The date for which the meeting was called is deemed to be the date of resignation and release (1986 Rule 4.29(6) and (7), added by the 1987 Amendments).

Removal

443 A provisional liquidator may only be removed from office by the court; a liquidator in a winding up by the court may only be removed by the court or by a meeting of creditors summoned specially for that purpose in accordance with the 1986 Rules (I.A., s.172(1) and (2)). A liquidator appointed by the Secretary of State may also be removed by the Secretary of State (I.A., s.172(4)). A meeting of creditors to replace a liquidator appointed by the court, or by the Secretary of State, can only be summoned if the liquidator agrees, or the court so directs, or if the meeting is requisitioned in accordance with the 1986 Rules by not less than one-quarter in value of the creditors. This restriction does not, however, apply to a meeting to replace a liquidator appointed by the court under the Insolvency Act, section 139(4)(*a*) or 140(1); these refer to the appointment of the contributories' nominee instead of or jointly with that of the creditors, and the appointment of a preceding administrator as liquidator (I.A., s.172(3)).

The Rules of Court[31] refer only to applications for removal of a liquidator by a creditor (by way of note in the process), but there can be no objection to the *locus* of a contributory presenting such an application if he can show sufficient cause and interest. The court will require cause to be shown even if the majority of creditors wish the liquidator's removal.[32] Misconduct does not require to be established, but removal of a liquidator will only be allowed if it is shown to be in the best interests of the liquidation[33] such as the existence of a conflict of interest.[34] The court removed a liquidator (in a voluntary liquidation) who was resident in England and supported a scheme of reconstruction of the company which the shareholders claimed was disadvantageous and unfair.[35]

444 A meeting of creditors to consider the removal of a liquidator shall be convened by him if so requested by not less than one-quarter in value

---

[31] R.C.S. 218J; Sh.Ct.R. 27.
[32] *Ker*, 1897 5 S.L.T. 126. See also *Brown, Petr.*, 1992 G.W.D. 27–1525.
[33] *Gaunt's Exrs.* v. *Liquidators of La Mancha Syndicate Ltd.*, 1907 14 S.L.T. 675; *McKnight & Co.* v. *Montgomerie* (1892) 19 R. 501. *Keypak Homecare* [1987] B.C.L.C. 409.
[34] *Monkland Iron Co.* v. *Dun* (1886) 14 R. 242; *Lysons* v. *Liquidator of the Miraflores Gold Syndicate* (1895) 22 R. 605; 3 S.L.T. 5.
[35] *Hannan's Development & Finance Corp.* (1899) 6 S.L.T. 388.

of the creditors, but "without prejudice to any other method of summoning the meeting" (1986 Rule 4.23(1)). The creditors or any of them could, therefore, themselves convene the meeting, subject always to the Insolvency Act, section 172(3), if applicable. The notice of the meeting must refer to Insolvency Act, section 174(4)(*a*) or (*b*) with respect to the liquidator's release. The general rules for convening, requisitioning and conducting meetings[36] will apply with certain modifications. The liquidator or his nominee may chair the meeting, or another person may be elected to do so. If the liquidator or his nominee is chairman, and a resolution for his removal is proposed, he may only adjourn the meeting with the consent of at least one-half (in value) of the creditors present (in person or by proxy) and entitled to vote (1986 Rule 4.23(3)). The court may also, on the application of any creditor, give directions on any matter relating to such a meeting (1986 Rule 4.23(4)).

If the meeting resolves that the liquidator be removed the chairman of the meeting issues a certificate in the prescribed form (Form 4.10 (Scot)), giving the date of removal (1986 Rule 4.24(2)). The certificate also states whether a new liquidator was appointed, and the chairman must deliver it "forthwith" (no time limit being prescribed) to the new liquidator who must, in turn, lodge a certified copy of the certificate and prescribed form with the registrar of companies, and also with the court (1986 Rule 4.24(1)(*b*); (Form 4.10 (Scot)). If no new liquidator is appointed the certificate (Form 4.10 (Scot)) is adapted to this effect, and a certified copy is sent to the court and the registrar (Form 4.11 (Scot); 1986 Rule 4.24(1)(*a*)).

If application is made to the court for the removal of a liquidator, or for an order directing the liquidator to summon a creditors' meeting to consider his removal, the applicant must give the liquidator at least 14 days' notice of the court hearing. He must also provide a copy of the application and of any evidence he intends to adduce in support of it (1986 Rule 4.26(1) and (3)). The applicant may be required to deposit a sum or find caution for the liquidator's expenses (1986 Rule 4.26(2)). Unless the court directs otherwise, the expenses of such an application are not to be payable as expenses of the liquidation (1986 Rule 4.26(4)).

If the court orders a liquidator's removal it must send him two copies of the order, one of which the former liquidator must send to the registrar of companies along with the prescribed form (Form 4.11 (Scot)). The court can include further orders arising from the removal, and appoint a new liquidator (1986 Rule 4.26(5)). 1986 Rules 4.18–4.21[37] apply if a new liquidator is appointed by the court, except that the prescribed form (Form 4.9 (Scot))[38] giving notice to the registrar of his appointment must refer to the removal and (if applicable) the release of the preceding liquidator (1986 Rules 4.26(5)(*c*) and 4.27).

---

[36] See paras. 454 to 458, *post*.
[37] See paras. 441, *ante* and 483, *post* (for rule 4.21).
[38] This form was amended by the 1987 Amendments to the Rules.

Release

445 Scots law and procedure before the Insolvency Act 1986 made no specific provision for the "release" (or discharge) of a liquidator at any stage of winding-up proceedings. Such provisions did exist in England, but only as the final step in a winding up by the court (s.545). The Insolvency Act, section 174 now provides for release of a provisional liquidator or a liquidator who has resigned or been removed, and on completion of the winding up.[39] Release has the effect of discharging him from all liability in respect of his acts or omissions in the winding up, and otherwise in relation to his conduct as liquidator or provisional liquidator. This, however, is without prejudice to any liability for misconduct or breach of duty arising under the Insolvency Act, section 212.[40] A former provisional liquidator's release operates from the time determined by the court on his application (I.A., s.174(5); R.C.S. 218E(6); Sh.Ct.R. 23(6)). In the case of other former liquidators the Insolvency Act, section 174(4) and (7) provides for the time of release as follows:

    (a) death, or

        removal by a creditors' meeting which did not resolve against release:

from the date the court is notified;

    (b) removal by a creditors' meeting which resolved against release, or removal by the Secretary of State, or

        ceasing to be an insolvency practitioner qualified to act in relation to the company (I.A., s.172(5)), or

        in Scotland only, following an order under the Insolvency Act, section 204 for early dissolution of the company[41]:

from such time as the Accountant of Court may, on the former liquidator's application, determine (under 1986 Rule 4.25, see below);

    (c) after resignation:

if the creditors' meeting which accepted his resignation resolved to grant his release, from the date the creditors determine, or

if there was no quorum present at that meeting, from the date for which the meeting was called, or

if the meeting resolved against release, from the date determined by the Accountant of Court (1986 Rules 4.25 and 4.29(4), (6) and (7));

    (d) after the final meeting in the liquidation[42]:

---

[39] I.A., s.173 makes the provision for voluntary winding up; see para. 550, *post*.
[40] See para. 524, *post*.
[41] See para. 535, *post*.
[42] See para. 534, *post*.

if that meeting resolved against his release, from the time determined on his application by the Accountant of Court, or

if that meeting did not resolve against release, from the time he gave due notice of the proceedings to the court and the registrar (see I.A., s.172(8)).

It is clear from 1986 Rules 4.25(1) and 4.29(4) that the question of whether or not to allow release is an essential item of business at the meeting of creditors summoned to receive a liquidator's resignation, or to consider his removal. If this business is not conducted it will be necessary for the liquidator to apply to the court for an order to rectify the procedure under the Bankruptcy (Scotland) Act 1985, section 63 as adapted by 1986 Rule 7.32.

The details of the procedure at the final meeting in the winding up are discussed below.[43] That meeting may resolve against the liquidator's release, in which case he must apply to the Accountant of Court (1986 Rule 4.31(3) and (6)). If the meeting does not resolve against his release, his release operates from the date of his notice of the final procedure to the court and the registrar (1986 Rule 4.31(6)). If no quorum was present at the meeting, the creditors are deemed not to have resolved against release (1986 Rule 4.31(5)), which therefore takes effect as from the date of the final return.

Where a liquidator has been removed or has resigned, and release has not been refused, the date of release is to be stated in the relevant return to the court and the registrar (1986 Rules 4.25(1) and 4.29(2); Form 4.10 (Scot) and Forms 4.15 (Scot) and 4.16 (Scot)).

Application to the Accountant of Court for release is under 1986 Rule 25 and on the prescribed form (Form 4.12 (Scot)). His decision is an administrative matter, not governed by the Act or the 1986 Rules. On being satisfied that release ought to be granted the Accountant of Court issues a certificate of release (Form 4.13 (Scot)) which takes effect as from its date. A copy is to be sent to the former liquidator, and the certificate itself is sent to the new liquidator who must issue copies to the court and to the registrar with the prescribed form (1986 Rule 4.25(3); Form 4.14 (Scot)). Where the Accountant of Court is granting release after the final meeting has resolved against release 1986 Rule 31(6) applies Rule 4.25(2) and (3) with the modification that the Accountant's certificate is to be sent to the former liquidator, who is responsible for lodging it with the court and the registrar. As noted above, if the court is overruling the decision of a creditors' meeting not to accept a liquidator's resignation, the court will also grant release (1986 Rule 4.30(2)), and the court's powers to make ancillary orders when removing a liquidator (1986 Rule 4.26(5)) would also include the question of his release. It may be assumed, however, that the court will remit the liquidator's account of intromissions to the Accountant of Court to report on whether release be granted.

[43] See para. 534, *post.*

Death of liquidator; loss of qualification

446 On the death of a liquidator intimation must be given to the court and to the registrar of companies. This may be done by production of a copy of the death certificate or on the prescribed form (Form 4.18 (Scot)), which should be lodged with the court and the registrar by the liquidator's executors or (if applicable) one of his business partners (1986 Rule 4.36).

If a liquidator ceases to be qualified in relation to the company he vacates office[44] and must give notice to the court and the registrar (Form 4.19 (Scot)). He will obtain his release from the Accountant of Court (1986 Rule 4.37).

In neither case (death or loss of qualification) is there any requirement to give formal notice to the company, its creditors or any joint liquidator. The Rules assume that these parties will be aware of the situation and take the necessary action to appoint a successor, if they have any interest in so doing. A liquidator who ceases to hold an insolvency practitioner's certificate vacates office but has sufficient *locus* to apply to the court for the appointment of a successor.[45]

Joint liquidators

447 It is competent at any stage to appoint or nominate more than one person to act as joint liquidators, or to appoint or nominate any person to act jointly with an existing office-holder (I.A., s.231(1)). The appointment or nomination must declare whether any act has to be done or authorised by all joint liquidators or by one or more of them (I.A., s.231(2)). Objection may be taken to a joint appointment on the ground of unnecessary expense.[46] Intimation to one joint liquidator is intimation to all (1986 Rule 7.21(4)). One may resign without prejudice to the appointment of the remainder (1986 Rule 4.28(4)).

Liquidator's remuneration and outlays

448 The provisions for a liquidator (other than a provisional liquidator)[47] to submit claims for his remuneration and outlays, and for the determination of any dispute relating to them, are contained in 1986 Rules 4.32 to 4.35, which also apply (with appropriate modifications contained in 1986 Rules 4.16 and 4.68) the provisions of the Bankruptcy (Scotland) Act 1985, section 53.

At their first meeting[48] the creditors may, if they dispense with a liquidation committee, resolve on the basis of the liquidator's remuneration (1986 Rule 4.12(3)(c)). A further meeting of creditors

---

[44] I.A., s.172(5).
[45] *Re A. J. Adams (Builders) Ltd.* [1991] B.C.C. 62.
[46] *Wishart*, 1908 S.C. 690; 15 S.L.T. 953.
[47] See para. 435, *ante*.
[48] See para. 439, *ante*.

convened under 1986 Rule 4.13[49] could modify the initial decision on the basis of the liquidator's remuneration. It is not competent for the first meeting of contributories to pass a resolution determining the basis of the liquidator's remuneration (1986 Rule 4.12(4)). In the absence of such determination, the remuneration may be a commission on the amount of estate realised but shall in any event take into account the work which, having regard to that value, was reasonably undertaken by him and the extent of his responsibilities in administering the assets.[50] If application is made to the court for a determination, it is appropriate for the court to remit the matter to a reporter.[51]

If a creditor is dissatisfied with the decision of the first meeting or any subsequent meeting with respect to the liquidator's remuneration, he could requisition a meeting under 1986 Rule 7.6 to review the decision. The court also has power to convene meetings to ascertain the wishes of creditors or contributories which would include such matters.[52] If the liquidator is dissatisfied he may apply to the court under 1986 Rule 4.34 (discussed below).

The liquidator will claim payment of his remuneration and outlays in the periodic accounts which he is required to submit to the liquidation committee or, if there is no committee, to the court.[53] He may also submit an interim claim for remuneration and outlays during an accounting period to the liquidation committee (if any) (1986 Rule 4.32(2)). If, however, there is no liquidation committee application for interim payment must be made to the court (I.A., s.142(5)).

The liquidation committee (if any) or the court is required to issue a determination on the liquidator's claim for remuneration and outlays within six weeks after the end of each accounting period taking account (in respect of the final period) of any previous award.[54] There is no obligation to determine a claim for interim payment within a particular time. If the liquidator considers that an award of remuneration by the committee is inadequate he may call a meeting of creditors to request that it be increased (1986 Rule 4.33) but this does not apply if the award is by the court (for which the usual appeal procedure is available). Alternatively, he may apply to the court (1986 Rule 4.34; R.C.S. 218K; Sh.Ct.R. 28). If he applies to the court he must give at least 14 days' notice to the members of the liquidation committee who may nominate a representative or representatives to appear or be represented and be heard on the application (1986 Rule

---

[49] See para. 454, *post*.
[50] Bankruptcy (Scotland) Act 1985, s.53(4) as applied.
[51] *Cf. Sonido International Ltd.*, 1991 S.C.L.R. 874 (Sh.Ct.).
[52] I.A., s.195; see para. 454, *post*.
[53] Bankruptcy (Scotland) Act 1985, s.53(1) as applied.
[54] Bankruptcy (Scotland) Act 1985, s.53(3) and (5) as applied; for accounting period see para. 492, *post*; however, the Bankruptcy (Scotland) Bill 1992 proposes to amend s.53(2) so that taxation is at the option of the office-holder.

4.34(2)); if there is no committee the court directs intimation of the application to one or more creditors who may then appear or be represented (1986 Rule 4.34(3)). The wording of the Rules would permit a creditor to appear in person. The court may direct the expenses of any of the parties to such proceedings to be expenses of the liquidation (1986 Rule 4.34(4)). A creditor or creditors holding at least 25 per cent. in value of the creditors may also appeal to the court for a reduction in the liquidator's remuneration by way of note (1986 Rule 4.35(1); R.C.S. 218K; Sh.Ct.R. 28). Notice of such an application must be given to the liquidator (R.C.S. 218K(3); Sh.Ct.R. 28(3)). The 1986 Rules 4.33 to 4.35 and relative Rules of Court apply only to claims for remuneration, not outlays.

The Bankruptcy (Scotland) Act 1985, section 53(6) is also applied to liquidations by the 1986 Rules. Under section 53(6) as applied, no later than eight weeks after the end of an accounting period[55] the liquidator, the company or any creditor may appeal to the court against a determination of the liquidation committee or (strangely) the court itself with respect to the liquidator's remuneration or outlays including a decision on an interim claim for payment. There is no reference in the relevant Rules of Court (R.C.S. 218K; Sh.Ct.R. 28) to appeals under section 53(6). Section 53(6) appears to offer an alternative and partly superfluous avenue for appealing determinations of the liquidation committee or the court with respect to remuneration to those provided by the 1986 Rules 4.33 to 4.35, but there is no doubt that the application of section 53(6) to liquidations is deliberate (1986 Rule 4.32(3)). Section 53(6) is, however, the only avenue for disputing outlays and it is the only avenue available to the company or to a creditor who is unable to get the support of 25 per cent. of creditors for contesting a decision with respect to remuneration.

All accounts for legal services incurred by a liquidator must be taxed by the auditor of the court before which the liquidation is pending before payment, unless the court authorises payment without taxation.[56]

In a case where joint liquidators were appointed, the court reserved power to overrule an agreement between them as to the apportionment of their remuneration.[57]

LIQUIDATION COMMITTEE

Constitution

449 The first meetings in the liquidation[58] may decide to establish a

---

[55] See para. 492, *post*.
[56] Bankruptcy (Scotland) Act 1985, s.53(2), as applied.
[57] *City of Glasgow Bank Liquidators* (1880) 7 R. 1196.
[58] See para. 439, *ante*.

liquidation committee, or subsequent meetings of creditors and contributories may so determine (I.A., s.142(1) and (2)). Meetings for this purpose must be convened by a liquidator who has been appointed by the court, unless he was appointed under the Insolvency Act, section 139(4)(*a*),[59] if requisitioned in accordance with the Rules by one-tenth in value of the creditors (I.A., s.142(3)). The 1986 Rules on the requisitioning of meetings under, *inter alia*, the Insolvency Act, section 142(3) (1986 Rule 7.6) appear to assume that the creditors will only requisition a meeting of creditors (see 1986 Rule 7.6(1)), but the Act specifically refers to meetings of both creditors and contributories. Accordingly, although only creditors may requisition such meetings, the liquidator must convene meetings of both groups to consider separately whether to establish a liquidation committee.[60]

If either the creditors or the contributories decide to have a liquidation committee, it is to be established in accordance with the rules unless the court orders otherwise. (I.A., s.142(4)). If the creditors do not seek to establish a committee the contributories may appoint one of their number to apply to the court for an order requiring the liquidator to convene a further meeting of creditors to reconsider the matter (1986 Rule 4.43(1) and (2)). If that further meeting of creditors does not establish a committee, a meeting of the contributories may establish a committee consisting of not less than three nor more than five contributories elected by them (1986 Rule 4.43(3) and (4)).

Where the creditors decide to establish a committee it will consist of at least three but not more than five creditors elected by them. If the winding up is "solvent"[61] the contributories may elect up to three further members (1986 Rule 4.41(1)). If the company is being wound up by reference to the Banking Act 1987, the Deposit Protection Board may appoint an additional creditor member (1986 Rule 4.41(6)). No person can be both a creditor member and a contributory member (1986 Rule 4.41(3)). A body corporate or partnership may be a member but must act through a duly appointed representative (1986 Rules 4.41(4) and 4.48). Secured creditors are only eligible if they are (at least in part) unsecured and have lodged their claim, and it has not been wholly rejected; if fully secured they must surrender their security (1986 Rule 4.41(2)).

The liquidator will normally be chairman of the meeting which establishes the committee. If not, the chairman must inform the liquidator of the names and addresses of its members. The liquidator must be satisfied that at least the minimum number for the committee have agreed to act, whereupon he must issue a certificate (Form 4.20 (Scot)) of its due constitution, and the committee is empowered to act

---

[59] *i.e.* where he is a contributories' nominee who has been appointed to act instead of or jointly with the creditors' nominee; see para. 439, *ante.*
[60] For details of the procedure relating to meetings see paras. 454 to 458, *infra.*
[61] *i.e.* the grounds do *not* include inability to pay debts (1986 Rule 4.40).

from the date of that certificate (1986 Rule 4.42(1) and (3)). The creditor's agreement to serve may be given in person or (subject to the terms of the authority) by his proxy or representatives (1986 Rule 4.42(3), as amended). The liquidator must issue a further certificate (Form 4.20 (Scot)) if any other members agree to act at a later date. The certificates (and any change in committee membership) must be lodged by the liquidator with the registrar of companies (1986 Rule 4.42(4)–(6); Form 4.22 (Scot)).

A member of the committee may resign by notice in writing to the liquidator (1986 Rule 4.49). A member vacates office in the event of bankruptcy, or if he is absent and not represented at three consecutive meetings (unless at the third this rule is disapplied). A creditor member ceases to be a member if he is no longer a creditor (1986 Rule 4.50). A meeting of creditors or contributories may remove a creditor or a contributory member, respectively (1986 Rule 4.51).

A vacancy among the creditor members need not be filled if the liquidator and a majority of remaining creditor members of the committee so agree, unless the number of members is below the minimum of three. The liquidator, with the consent of a majority of the remaining creditor members, may fill the vacancy, or it may be filled by a meeting of creditors called on at least 14 days' notice. The nominee must consent to act (1986 Rule 4.52).

A vacancy among the contributory members (if any) need not be filled if the liquidator and a majority of the remaining contributory members so agree. If the committee consists of contributory members only, however, the vacancy must be filled if their number is below the minimum of three (or two if creditors have been paid in full). The liquidator, with the consent of a majority of the remaining contributory members, may fill the vacancy, or it may be filled by a meeting of contributories called on at least 14 days' notice. The nominee must consent to act (1986 Rule 4.53).

450   Once creditors have been paid in full with interest under the Insolvency Act, section 189[62] the liquidator may certify accordingly.[63] A copy of that certificate is lodged by him with the registrar of companies (Form 4.24 (Scot)) and the creditor members vacate office on the committee. The committee may continue if there are at least two contributory members unless it is abolished by a meeting of contributories. It ceases to exist 28 days after the certificate if there are less than two members, and is in suspense if numbers are reduced below two at a later stage. Contributories may be co-opted by the liquidator or added by a meeting of contributories, up to a maximum of five. The Rules relating to the liquidation committee apply to a committee constituted in these circumstances as if all its members were "creditor members" (1986 Rule 4.59).

[62] See para. 482, *post*.
[63] Form 4.23 (Scot). There is no obligation to issue such a certificate.

On any change in membership of the committee the liquidator must issue an amended certificate of constitution and lodge it with the registrar of companies (1986 Rule 4.42; Forms 4.20 (Scot) and 4.22 (Scot)).

If winding up follows immediately upon discharge of an administration order, and the administrator is appointed as the liquidator, the creditors' committee in the administration will continue as the liquidation committee, provided that it has at least three members.[64] A fully secured creditor, who can be a member of the committee under an administration order, ceases to hold office unless he surrenders his security. The number of creditor members (and contributory members if the winding up is "solvent"[65]) is the same as if there had been no preceding administration, (*i.e.* three to five creditors and up to three contributories, if allowed). The members required to bring the size of the committee up to the requisite number are elected by meetings of creditors (and contributories, if appropriate). The nominees must consent to act. The liquidator must issue a certificate of continuance when the requisite minimum membership has agreed to act. (Form 4.21 (Scot)) and lodge it with the registrar of companies (Form 4.22 (Scot)). Pending the issue of that certificate the committee is suspended. Additional members and changes require an amended certificate lodged with the registrar (Forms 4.21 (Scot) and 4.22 (Scot)). The rules for filling vacancies, procedure, etc., then follow as if the committee had been established in the normal way (1986 Rules 4.60–4.65).

If there are insufficient creditors (or contributories) willing to act, such that the minimum number of members cannot be elected or appointed, there can be no liquidation committee (unless the court otherwise directs under its *nobile officium*). If there is no committee, its functions are vested in the court unless the rules provide otherwise (I.A., s.142(5)). The 1986 Rules do not, in fact, contain any provision which derogates from the powers of the court in the absence of a committee.

Powers and duties of the liquidation committee

451 Certain of the powers of the liquidator can only be exercised with the sanction of the court or the liquidation committee. These relate to the payment of debts, compromise of claims, legal proceedings and carrying on the business (I.A., s.167(1)).[66] The liquidator must also notify the committee if he disposes of property to a person connected with the company[67] or employs a solicitor (I.A., s.167(2)). The

---

[64] Administrator procedure is discussed in paras. 101 *et seq., ante.*
[65] See para. 449, n. 61, *supra.*
[66] See para. 486, *post.*
[67] "Connected person" is defined in I.A., s.249; see para. 515, *post.*

committee must also satisfy itself that the liquidator has found caution to a sufficient level (1986 Rule 7.28).[68]

The liquidator must report to the committee all matters which he considers should be of concern to them. He must also report on any matter at the request of the committee, unless it is frivolous or unreasonable, or the expense cannot be met, or is out of proportion. If the liquidator has been in office more than 28 days before the committee came into being he must provide and explain a summary of his actions to date. New members of the committee can require a summary of matters prior to their appointment. The restrictions on access to information or requiring explanation are not, however, applicable to the liquidator's cash book and sederunt book,[69] or matters within the committee's responsibility (1986 Rule 4.44).

Where a liquidation committee succeeds the committee of creditors in an administration, the liquidator must report to the reconstituted committee on his actions since the commencement of liquidation. The provisions as to further reports and information then apply as to a committee constituted in normal circumstances (1986 Rule 4.64).

The liquidator must give a written report on the conduct of the winding up at least every six months. The committee can require more frequent reports, but not more often than once in any period of two months (1986 Rule 4.56).

The Act (I.A., s.142(6)) provides that the liquidation committee is also to have such of the powers and duties of commissioners in a sequestration as may be conferred or imposed on it by the rules. The Rules (4.68) apply sections 52, 53 and 58 of the Bankruptcy (Scotland) Act 1985, which relate to the making up of 26-weekly accounts by the liquidator and their submission to the committee for audit, and the approval of certain payments.[70]

Meetings of liquidation committee

452   The liquidator must call a meeting of the liquidation committee within three months of his appointment or the committee's establishment, whichever is later. Thereafter he must call a meeting in accordance with any resolution of the committee or within 21 days of a request to do so by a creditor member. Other meetings may be called at the liquidator's discretion. At least seven days' written notice of a meeting is to be given to every committee member who has not waived this requirement (1986 Rule 4.45).

The meeting is chaired by the liquidator or his nominee (being either another duly qualified insolvency practitioner or an experienced employee of the liquidator or his firm) (1986 Rule 4.46). The quorum for a duly convened meeting is two creditor members (or two contributory

---

[68] See para. 440, *ante*.
[69] See para. 530, *post*.
[70] See para. 492, *post*.

members if the committee is of contributory members only) present or represented (1986 Rule 4.47).

Committee members may appoint representatives by mandate signed by the member. A body corporate, partnership or undischarged bankrupt cannot be a representative. One person cannot represent more than one member, or be both a member and another's representative. If a representative signs any document on behalf of the member his capacity must be stated below his signature. Mandates have to be available for inspection and verification by the chairman of the meeting (1986 Rule 4.48).

Any proxy or authorisation of a representative under section 375 in relation to any meeting of creditors (or contributories) is, unless it contains a statement to the contrary, deemed to be a mandate to act generally on behalf of the committee member (1986 Rule 4.48(2), as amended).

Every committee member or representative has one vote, and resolutions are determined by simple majority. Unless the committee consists solely of contributories, however, the votes of contributory members are to be recorded but not counted. The record of proceedings is to be signed by the chairman and retained in the sederunt book (1986 Rule 4.54). The liquidator may secure the passing of a resolution by circular by sending to each member or representative a copy of the proposed resolution. If there are several resolutions, the statement must be set out in such a way as to permit voting on each one separately. Any creditor member may within seven business days[71] require a meeting to discuss the matter, but otherwise the resolution is deemed to be passed when the liquidator has received a majority of creditor member consents to it. The resolution is to be recorded in the sederunt book (1986 Rule 4.55).

The acts of the committee are valid notwithstanding any defect in the appointment, election or qualification of any member or his representative or in the formalities of its establishment (1986 Rule 4.59A, added by the 1987 Amendments).

The reasonable travelling expenses incurred in attending meetings (or otherwise in connection with the liquidation) are to be met by the liquidator as part of the expenses of the liquidation, but this does not apply to any meeting held within three months of a previous meeting (1986 Rule 4.57).

Transactions between the company and committee members

453 The members of the "committee of inspection" under the procedure before the Insolvency Act 1986 were prohibited from purchasing assets from the company or deriving any profit from a transaction with it,

---

[71] *i.e.* excluding Saturdays, Sundays, Christmas Day, Good Friday or a day which is a bank holiday in any part of Great Britain (1986 Rule 0.2(1)).

except with the prior consent of the court.[72] The same principles apply to members of the liquidation committee, including a member's representative, an associate[73] of a member or representative or anyone who has been a member of the committee within the 12 months preceding the transaction in question (1986 Rule 4.58(1)).

Such a person is prohibited (subject to the exceptions provided for in the Rules) from receiving payment from the assets of the company for services or goods supplied in connection with the liquidation, obtaining any profit from the liquidation or purchasing any assets of the company (1986 Rule 4.58(2)). The exceptions to this rule (1986 Rule 4.58(3)) are:

1. Where the court gives prior approval;
2. In cases of urgency;
3. If the transaction is by way of performance of a pre-liquidation contract and the person concerned has applied for court sanction without undue delay, and
4. If the liquidation committee, on the basis of a full disclosure of the circumstances, has approved the transaction as being on normal commercial terms. No person concerned with the transaction may vote on the matter in the committee (1986 Rule 4.58(4)).

The expenses of seeking the sanction of the court for a transaction of this nature are not, unless the court directs otherwise, to be expenses in the liquidation (1986 Rule 4.58(7)).

The court may reduce a transaction which is in breach of these rules, and make an order for compensation or restitution, but an "associate" may defend such an order on the basis that he had no reason to suppose that he acted in breach of the rules (1986 Rule 4.58(5) and (6)).

In consequence of these rules, no partner or other "associate" of the liquidator can be a member of the liquidation committee.

MEETINGS OF CREDITORS AND CONTRIBUTORIES[74]

454 General meetings of creditors or contributories are to be held for a number of purposes under the 1986 Rules. These include the first meetings to elect a liquidator and a liquidation committee, and other meetings in connection with the liquidator's removal, resignation, release and remuneration, and meetings relating to the liquidation committee, discussed above. In addition to meetings for such specific purposes the liquidator is required to convene a general meeting of creditors in each year while the liquidation continues (1986 Rule

---

[72] *Dowling* v. *Lord Advocate*, 1963 S.L.T. 146; *Re Gallard* (1896) 1 Q.B. 68.
[73] I.A., s.435; See para. 517, *post*.
[74] For adaptation of these provisions in a creditors' voluntary winding up see para. 544, *post* and for an insolvent members' voluntary winding up see para. 545, *post*.

4.13(1)). The liquidator may also convene meetings of the creditors or of the contributories at any time to ascertain their wishes in all matters relating to the liquidation (1986 Rule 4.13(2)). The court may also convene meetings for such purpose (I.A., s.195(1)(*b*)). The 1986 Rules govern the proceedings at any such meetings, subject to any direction by the court (1986 Rule 7.1; I.A., s.195(1)(*b*)).

The meeting is to be held between 10 a.m. and 4 p.m. on a business day[75] at a place and date reasonably convenient for those due to attend (1986 Rule 7.2). At least 21 days' notice is to be given specifying the date, time and place to every person known to the liquidator as being entitled to attend (1986 Rule 7.3(1)).

In the case of the first meetings in the liquidation (I.A., s.138(3) or (4)), however, the period of notice is 14 days (1986 Rule 7.3(2)(*d*), added by the 1987 Amendments). The notice must also be published in a local newspaper (as described in 1986 Rule 7.3) at least 21 (or 14) days ahead of the meeting (1986 Rule 7.3(3A) also added by the 1987 Amendments). Rule 7.3 does not apply to meetings under the Insolvency Act, section 95 or 98, which have their own provisions (1986 Rule 7.3(7)); see paragraph 545, below.

The notice is also to state and refer to (1986 Rule 7.3(4)):

1. the purpose of the meeting;
2. those entitled to attend and vote;
3. the relevant provisions of the rules on voting and resolutions;
4. the right to lodge proxies at or before the meeting, and where they may be lodged, and
5. for a meeting of creditors, the right to lodge claims not already lodged at or before the meeting, and where they may be lodged.

In addition, notice of a creditors' meeting to remove a liquidator or to receive his resignation must, as required by 1986 Rules 4.23(2) and 4.28(2), refer to the power of the meeting to consider the liquidator's release under the Insolvency Act, section 174(4).[76]

Proxy forms must be issued with the notice (1986 Rule 7.3(5)). The liquidator may (but is not obliged to) publish notice of the date, time and place of the meeting in a newspaper circulating in the area of the company's principal place of business, or otherwise calculated to bring the matter to the notice of those entitled to attend (1986 Rule 7.3(3)). The court may, having regard to the cost of public advertisement in relation to the assets available and the interests of those concerned, order public advertisement of the notice instead of postal intimation (1986 Rule 7.3(6)). Additional requirements to give notice to the Bank of England and Deposit Protection Board arise if the company is a recognised bank or licensed institution, or one to which the Banking Act 1987 applies (1986 Rule 7.4).

---

[75] See para. 452, n. 71, *ante*.
[76] See para. 445, *ante*.

The liquidator or a person nominated by him in writing acts as chairman (whether the meeting is of creditors or contributories). The nominee must be either a duly qualified insolvency practitioner or an experienced employee of the liquidator or his firm. At the first meetings the interim liquidator is chairman, except that if he is to be nominated as liquidator the meeting may elect another ad hoc chairman. A person other than the liquidator may be elected as chairman if the meeting is to consider his removal (1986 Rule 7.5).

The quorum for a creditors' meeting is at least one creditor entitled to vote. For a contributories' meeting it is at least two contributories entitled to vote, or all contributories if their number does not exceed two. Persons represented by proxy by any person, including the chairman, are reckoned as present for this purpose (1986 Rule 7.7). There is, therefore, no rule against a "meeting" of one person in liquidation proceedings under the 1986 Act.

If, however, the quorum is constituted by the chairman alone, or by him and one other, and the chairman is aware that at least one other is entitled to attend and vote, he cannot commence business for at least 15 minutes (1986 Rule 7.7(3)).

455   A meeting of creditors or contributories is to be adjourned (unless the chairman decides otherwise) to the same time and place a week later (or to the following business day if that is not a business day),[77] if no quorum is present within 30 minutes of the appointed time. The chairman may also at his discretion adjourn a meeting at any time during its course, and shall do so if the meeting so resolves. If, however, the liquidator or his nominee is in the chair at a creditors' meeting to consider a resolution that he be removed, he is not allowed to adjourn the meeting without the consent of at least one-half (in value) of those creditors present in person or by proxy and entitled to vote (1986 Rule 4.23(3)). Adjournment at the chairman's discretion is not to be for a period in excess of 21 days. Proxies remain valid at the adjourned meeting (1986 Rule 7.8). The chairman may (but is not obliged to) give notice of the adjourned meeting (1986 Rule 7.8(5), as amended).

A meeting of creditors may be requisitioned at any time by a creditor sending a request to the liquidator. The request must specify the purpose of the proposed meeting and be accompanied by a list of those creditors who concur, stating the amount of the claims of those requesting the meeting, and written confirmation of his concurrence by each such creditor (1986 Rule 7.6(1) and (2)). A meeting to remove a liquidator can only be requisitioned by at least one-quarter in value of the creditors (I.A., s.172(3)). A meeting requisitioned for any other purpose must be requested by at least one-tenth in value of the creditors (I.A., s.142(3)). If the requisition is valid, the liquidator must

---

[77] See para. 452, n. 71, *ante*.

convene the meeting within 35 days of receiving the request (1986 Rule 7.6(3)). The creditors requesting the meeting must deposit or find caution in a sum determined by the liquidator to cover the cost of holding the meeting, and that cost is not to be an expense of the liquidation unless the meeting so decides; any unused balance of the deposit is repayable to the requisitioning creditors (1986 Rule 7.6(4)–(7)). While there is no express limitation on the liquidator's power to fix the amount of the deposit or caution, it must be assumed that he cannot fix an unreasonable sum. The same rules as apply to the requisition of a creditors' meeting also apply to the requisition of a contributories' meeting by a contributory with the substitution of voting rights for the value of claims in the list of those concurring (1986 Rule 7.6(8)).

Proxies and representatives at meetings of creditors and contributories

456 There is a general right to appoint a proxy to attend, speak and vote at meetings of creditors and contributories, either generally or for a specific meeting or class of meetings. The proxy must be an individual over 18, but alternate nominations can be made. The chairman of the meeting can be appointed a proxy and he cannot decline to act. The principal can direct how his vote is to be used, and he can instruct the proposal of a resolution in his name (1986 Rule 7.14). Every notice convening a meeting of creditors and contributories must be accompanied by a proxy form, but this cannot include the name or description of any proposed appointee. The form of proxy is prescribed (Form 4.29 (Scot)) by the 1987 Amendments, and must be sent with the notice and completed by the creditor or contributory (in place of such form as may be contained in the Articles of the company). The nomination must be signed by or on behalf of the principal, stating the agent's authority where it is not signed by the principal (1986 Rule 7.15). An instruction to vote for or against the appointment of a particular person as liquidator, unless it states otherwise, gives authority for the proxy-holder to vote at his discretion for or against his appointment as a joint liquidator (1986 Rule 7.16(4)). A proxy-holder has general authority to propose any resolution which he has authority to support (1986 Rule 7.16(5)). Unless the proxy provides otherwise, specific directions as to voting do not preclude the proxy-holder from voting at his discretion on any matter not dealt with in the proxy (1986 Rule 7.16(6)).[78] The proxy is to be lodged at or before the meeting where it is to be used (1986 Rule 7.16(2)) and the notice of the meeting must refer to this (1986 Rule 7.4(*d*)). Proxies are to be retained by the liquidator after the meeting (1986 Rule 7.17). They are to be available for inspection during the meeting and, afterwards, by interested

---

[78] 1986 Rule 7.16(4) to (6) was added by the 1987 Amendments.

parties; creditors whose claims are not fully paid (or rejected) can inspect creditors' proxies, members or contributories can inspect those of contributories, and if the company is in insolvent liquidation the directors can inspect all proxies. This includes claims and other documents relevant to determine the right to vote at the meeting (1986 Rule 7.18).

A person duly appointed to represent a company as a creditor or contributory under section 375 is required to produce to the chairman of the meeting a copy of the resolutions authorising him to act. That copy must either be certified by a duly authorised officer of the appointor, or be executed by it under seal in terms of section 36(3)[79] but the Rules do not require the execution of a proxy to be authorised by resolution of the company (1986 Rule 7.20).

If the proxy-holder or his associate[80] (including the chairman) could receive directly or indirectly any remuneration from the assets of the company as a result of any resolution he is not entitled to vote in favour of it, unless he has been specifically instructed to do so (1986 Rule 7.19) and in such a case he must produce to the chairman written evidence of his authority to vote in favour of the resolution (1986 Rule 7.19(1A), added by the 1987 Amendments). The Rules also prohibit the liquidator or his firm, partner or employee from voting on any resolution affecting his remuneration or conduct (1986 Rule 7.12(4)).

In the case of meetings of contributories, these Rules supersede the provisions of the Articles of the company.

Voting and resolutions at meetings of creditors and contributories

457 A creditor is entitled to vote if his claim has been lodged and accepted by the liquidator[81] (1986 Rule 7.9(1) and (2)). The Deposit Protection Board has special voting rights, in respect of creditors whose interests it represents, in meetings relating to the winding up of a bank or other institution subject to the Banking Act 1979 (1986 Rules 7.9(6), 7.4(6) and Schedule 3). Votes are calculated in accordance with the amount of the creditor's claim at the date of the commencement of the winding up, less any payment on account (1986 Rule 4.15(5)), and this may include a revised claim submitted under 1986 Rule 4.15(4), assuming it is a recalculation of the debt as at the commencement of winding up (which it ought, in principle, to be). A secured creditor must deduct the value of his security, or surrender it to the liquidator, if he is to vote in respect of his claim. He can then vote in respect of the balance unsecured (Bankruptcy (Scotland) Act 1985, Sched. 1, para. 5, as applied by 1986 Rule 4.16). A creditor is not, however, allowed to vote

---

[79] The Rules have not been amended to reflect the repeal of s.36(3) by the Companies Act 1989. "Execution under seal" now means signatures by two directors, one director and the secretary, or two authorised persons; see further *Palmer*, paras. 3.201 *et seq.*

[80] Defined in I.A., s.435; see para. 517, *post.*

[81] As to the lodging of claims, see paras. 470 and 471, *post.*

in respect of a debt acquired after commencement of liquidation, or in respect of any "postponed debt"[82] (Bankruptcy (Scotland) Act 1985, s.50(a) as applied by 1986 Rule 4.16.)[83] A creditor may "split" his vote on a resolution so as to cast it in respect of part of its value for, in part against or in part abstain, so long as the total voted does not exceed the total of his debt.[84]

Contributories vote in accordance with their rights under the Articles of the company (1986 Rule 7.10).

Resolutions may be proposed by any person, proxy or representative present at a meeting (1986 Rule 7.14(5)). A proxy-holder may propose any resolution which he is authorised to support, and vote at his discretion unless specifically instructed otherwise (1986 Rule 7.16(4) to (6); see paragraph 456, above). The chairman, if mandated to vote in favour of a resolution may, in the absence of any other proposer, and at his discretion, himself propose that resolution. If he does not he must explain his failure to do so to the person who granted that proxy (1986 Rule 7.11).

Resolutions are passed by simple majority in value of those voting in person or by proxy, unless otherwise provided in the Act or the Rules (1986 Rule 7.12(1)). At a meeting to nominate a liquidator, if there are more than two candidates, the election proceeds by single transferable vote unless the meeting resolves to appoint the remaining candidates jointly (1986 Rule 7.12(3)). If the resolution relates to a person's conduct or remuneration as liquidator, the vote of that person, or his firm, partner or employee, is to be disregarded (1986 Rule 7.12(4)). On the election of creditors to the liquidation committee (where there can be from three to five creditor members)[85] the members to be elected are those who receive the most votes (in value) on a single ballot.[86]

The chairman of the meeting is to record in the sederunt book[87] and sign a report of the proceedings containing a list of those present, a copy of every resolution passed and, if the meeting established a liquidation committee, the names and addresses of those elected (1986 Rule 7.13). That report, duly signed by a person purporting to be chairman of that meeting (not any subsequent meeting) is presumed to be sufficient evidence of the matters contained therein (1986 Rule 7.25), unless founded on by a liquidator in his own interest (1986 Rule 7.33(4)). This later provision limits the value of the book to the liquidator as a record of resolutions relating to his release,

---

[82] See para. 476, *post*, for the definition.
[83] By a tortuous series of cross-references these provisions import the prohibitions against voting contained in s.24(3) of the Bankruptcy (Scotland) Act 1985, described in the text.
[84] *Re Polly Peck International plc* [1991] B.C.C. 503; this case was decided on the English Insolvency Rules (which are to the same effect as the Scottish Rules in regard to voting rights) where the creditor was the trustee and nominee for a body of bondholders.
[85] See paras. 459 and 460, *ante*.
[86] *Re Polly Peck International plc*, *supra*.
[87] See para. 530, *post*.

remuneration, etc., which may be favourable to him. It remains evidence, but loses the presumption that it is sufficient.

Notices of meetings of creditors, contributories and committee

458 Notices of meetings of creditors or contributories, and of the liquidation committee, must be in writing unless the court allows otherwise or the Act or the Rules provide for notice to be given by any other means. Postal service is normal, but personal service is permitted. It may be given by or on behalf of the person who is required to send the notice, to the recipient or his duly authorised agent. Notice to or by one joint liquidator is effective notice to or by all (1986 Rule 7.21). Where first-class post is used, the notice is deemed to be received on the second business day,[88] and if by second-class post on the fourth business day after posting, unless otherwise proved (1986 Rule 7.22). A certificate of posting must be prepared under 1986 Rule 7.23. Proceedings are presumed to be valid notwithstanding that all those due to be given notice may not have received it (1986 Rule 7.24).

Since "clear days" are not required by the Rules, the period of notice is to be calculated by excluding the date of service or receipt (established as above) but not the date of the meeting itself.[89]

CONTRIBUTORIES

459 In the winding up of the company a "contributory" is every person who is liable (or alleged to be liable) to contribute to its assets for the purposes of meeting its liabilities, the expenses of the liquidation, or for the adjustment of the rights of contributories among themselves (I.A., ss.74(1) and 79). The term "contributory" does not, however, include persons whose liability arises by virtue of a court order under the Insolvency Act, section 213 (fraudulent trading)[90] or 214 (wrongful trading),[91] nor whose liability arises only by virtue of the Insolvency Act, section 76,[92] (I.A., s.79(2) and (3)). It therefore appears that the term is confined to those liable to contribute by virtue of the Insolvency Act, sections 74 and 75. It would not include a person liable to the company as an ordinary debtor, since his liability arises otherwise than by virtue of the winding up. For the purposes of the Insolvency Act, section 74 the contributories include persons to whom shares have been transferred, or transferred by operation of law, although not registered as members (I.A., s.250). If the court has ordered rectification of the register on finding that the petitioner never was a

---

[88] See para. 452, n. 53, *ante*.
[89] *Neil McLeod & Sons Ltd.*, 1987 S.L.T. 46.
[90] See para. 522, *infra*.
[91] See para. 523, *infra*.
[92] See para. 465, *infra*.

member, the liquidator cannot seek to reinstate the "member" as a contributory (list B) on the basis that he was in fact on the register up to the date of the court's order.[93] If the liquidator considers that the rectification order was improperly obtained, *e.g.* by the company failing to put forward a proper defence, it is suggested that his remedy would be to seek reduction of the interlocutor and damages from those who procured the order.

Under the Insolvency Act, sections 74 and 75 contributories consist of:

1. all[94] members of the company at the date of the commencement of the winding up;
2. certain past members[95]; and
3. a present or former director or manager of a limited company who has incurred unlimited liability under the terms of the Companies Act (I.A., s.75). (This refers to sections 306 and 307 of the Companies Act, under which a limited company may impose unlimited liability on such officers in terms of its memorandum of association. This situation is unlikely to arise in practice. If there are persons in this position, Insolvency Act, s.75(2) imposes restrictions on their potential liability.)

A contributory (including a past member) is entitled to attend meetings of contributories in the winding up, and to challenge the validity of relevant company proceedings, such as a resolution purporting to place the company in voluntary liquidation.[96] One of the first duties of the liquidator is to settle the list of contributories (I.A., s.148), but in many cases this will be unnecessary, and he will instead apply to the court to dispense with this requirement, under the Insolvency Act, section 148(2), on the ground that he will not need to make calls on or adjust the rights of contributories. The court will dispense with settling the list if the shares are fully paid and there is no likelihood of a surplus, or for any other reason.[97] If the shares of a limited company are all fully paid[98] and it is insolvent (*i.e.* in the majority of liquidations by the court), an early application to dispense with the list is appropriate.

The Act requires the liquidator to make up the list of contributories (or, presumably, apply for dispensation) "as soon as may be" after his appointment but does not impose any specific time limit. Failure to do either may prejudice his eventual discharge, but the comment in a

---

[93] *Barbor* v. *Middleton*, 1988 S.L.T. 288.
[94] Including holders of fully paid shares, even if no contribution will actually be required from them (*Re Phoenix Oil & Transport Co. Ltd.* [1958] Ch. 560).
[95] See para. 460, *infra*.
[96] *Howling's* v. *Smith* (1905) 7 F. 390; 12 S.L.T. 628.
[97] R.C.S. 211(*a*) (Sh.Ct.R. 37).
[98] Holders of such shares are still technically "contributories"; see *Re Phoenix Oil & Transport Co. Ltd.* [1958] Ch. 560.

Scottish case[99] that after five years it was "too late" to apply to the court is without authority. Circumstances can be conceived in which the liquidator would be justified in delaying this procedure, and in the leading English case a delay of seven years was accepted.[1]

Settling the list of contributories

460 If the liquidator requires to settle a list of contributories there are no specific rules of court now applicable. The list is in two parts, by convention referred to as list A and list B.

List A consists of those persons who are members at the commencement of the winding up. List B consists of past members, restricted in a limited company to those who ceased to be members within one year of the commencement of the winding up, but extended to certain other past members of a limited company which was previously registered as unlimited.[2]

On the death of a contributory his personal representatives take his place (I.A., s.81). The heirs of his heritable estate and legatees of heritage are also liable to be placed on the list, but this is unnecessary if his personal representatives are already listed; they may, however, be added as and when the court thinks fit (I.A., s.81(1) and (2)). If a contributory becomes bankrupt, his trustee in bankruptcy replaces him (I.A., s.82). The discharge of the bankrupt does not reinstate him as a "contributory" so as to entitle him to interfere in the liquidation in that capacity.[3]

The list of contributories must contain their full names and addresses, the number of shares and the interest to be attributed to each, the amount called and paid on each share, and it is divided into the two lists required; so far as practicable, the liquidator must distinguish between those who are contributories in their own name and those listed in a representative capacity (I.A., s.148(3)). The list prepared in accordance with the foregoing provisions is submitted by the liquidator to the court by way of note in the petition. The court will normally order intimation to all persons on the list allowing time (usually seven days) for answers to be lodged. The list is settled by the court after disposing of such objections as may be lodged. It is competent to settle "A" and "B" lists separately.[4]

Settlement of the list of contributories, even if the court's interlocutor has become final, will not bar a member's right to petition for his removal under section 359 (rectification of the register of

---

[99] *Lovat Mantle Manufacturers Ltd.,* 1960 S.L.T. (Sh.Ct.) 52.
[1] *Re Phoenix Oil & Transport Co. Ltd., supra.*
[2] See para. 462, *infra.*
[3] *Re Wolverhampton Steel & Iron Co. Ltd.* [1977] 1 All E.R. 417 affd.; [1977] 3 All E.R. 467.
[4] *Liquidator of Caledonian Heritable Security Co. Ltd.* (1882) 9 R. 1130. The details in this paragraph are based on practice under the Rules of Court in force before those of 1986; the current rules of court contain no specific requirements in regard to settling the list of contributories.

members).[5] It may also be possible to reclaim against or seek suspension of the subsequent decree for calls.[6]

Liability of contributories

461 The question of whether a person is a member of a company is considered fully in *Palmer*.[7] Prima facie membership is determined by the register of members, and a member is not entitled to insist on registration of a transfer presented on the eve of liquidation,[8] but he may escape if it is shown that he never agreed to be a member.[9]

The liability of a contributory in a company limited by shares cannot in any event exceed the amount (if any) unpaid in respect of his shares (I.A., s.74(*d*)).[10] The amount unpaid on a share is a question of fact and the liquidator may be personally barred from calling capital where the contributory (being a transferee for value and in good faith) holds a certificate bearing to show that it has been paid up.[11] If the company is limited by guarantee, his liability is limited to the amount which he has undertaken to contribute in its Memorandum of Association (I.A., s.74(3)). Where the company is limited by guarantee and has a share capital (a form of company which ceased to be competent after December 22, 1980 under the Companies Act 1980, now s.1(4)) every member is liable to contribute to the extent of any sums unpaid on his shares "in addition to" the amount of his guarantee (I.A., s.74(3)). This does not make it clear whether, if calls may be required in respect of both the guarantee and the share capital, the guarantees have to be called up before the unpaid capital, or on what basis the rights of contributories *inter se* are to be adjusted if it is not necessary to call up every liability. The inference from the words of the Insolvency Act, section 74(3) seems to be that the guarantees are to be exhausted first, although the nature of the obligations concerned would suggest the opposite.

The liability of B list contributories is further limited by the following:

1. they are not liable unless the list A contributories are unable to satisfy the amount required of them (I.A., s.74(2)(*c*));
2. a past member is not liable in respect of any debt or obligation contracted after he has ceased to be a member (I.A., s.74(2)(*b*));
3. a past member's liability is limited to the amount, if any, unpaid on the shares in respect of which he is liable (*i.e.* after crediting any sums paid by the list A contributory in respect of such

---

[5] *Stocker* v. *Liquidator of the Coustonholme Paper Mills Co. Ltd.* (1891) 19 R. 17; *Jackson* v. *Liquidator of Star Fire & Burglary Insurance Co.* (1902) 10 S.L.T. 279.
[6] *Cumpstie* v. *Waterston*, 1933 S.C. 1.
[7] Paras. 7.001 *et seq.* and 7.101 *et seq.*
[8] *Dodds* v. *Cosmopolitan Insurance Corp. Ltd.*, 1915 S.C. 992; 1915 2 S.L.T. 106.
[9] *Liquidator of Florida Mortgage and Investment Co. Ltd.* v. *Bayley* (1890) 17 R. 525.
[10] *Waterhouse* v. *Jamieson* (1870) 8 M. (H.L.) 88.
[11] *Palmer*, paras. 6.309 to 6.311; *Liquidator of Scottish Heritages Co. Ltd.* (1898) 5 S.L.T. 336.

shares) (I.A., s.74(2)(*d*)). In the case of a company limited by guarantee and having a share capital, it appears that a past member cannot be liable in respect of any unpaid share capital. In contrast to the position in a company limited by shares, where the Insolvency Act, section 74(2)(*d*) specifically refers to "shares in respect of which he is liable as a past or present member," the relevant provision (I.A., s.74(3)) imposes liability only "to the extent of sums unpaid on shares held" by the member, which necessarily excludes shares he has ceased to hold. There is, however, no exclusion of the potential liability of a past member in respect of his guarantee.[12]

Where a scheme of arrangement provides for partial payment of creditors and releases present members from a portion of liability it would appear to be impossible to place anyone on the B list.[13]

The Insolvency Act, section 74(2)(*e*) saves the validity of contracts which limit the liability of individual members, but this does not of course affect their liability on the "contract" between themselves and the company constituted by its Memorandum and Articles, etc., by virtue of which they become "contributories." The Insolvency Act, section 74(2)(*f*) debars a member from ranking in competition with other creditors in respect of dividends, profits or the like due to him in that character of a member, but he can rank in respect of such sums for the purposes of adjusting the rights of contributories *inter se*. Since this applies only to profits due to a member as such, it does not apply to sums due to a director or employee under a profit-sharing scheme, even if he is also a member.[14]

Companies re-registered as unlimited or limited

462 Special rules apply to an unlimited company which has been re-registered as limited under section 43 or 51,[15] and which commences its winding up within three years of re-registration. In this case the B list is extended so as to include as contributories all past members who were members at the time of re-registration, and they are liable to contribute without limit as to amount in respect of debts and liabilities contracted before re-registration (I.A., s.77(2) and (4)). If there are no persons on the A list of such a company who were members at the time of re-registration, the B list is further extended so as to include persons who ceased to be members within a year before re-registration, and

---

[12] See I.A., s.74(2)(*a*) and forms of Memorandum of Association in The Companies (Tables A to F) Regulations 1985 (as amended) Tables C and D.

[13] *Re Belgrave Mills*, October 13, 1927 unreported, see *Palmer*, para. 15.403.

[14] See also para. 469, *infra*.

[15] I.A., s.77(1): s.43 was originally part of s.5 of the 1980 Act and provides for re-registration of a private company having a share capital (including an unlimited company) as a public limited company. S.51 was originally part of s.44 of the 1967 Act and provides for re-registration of an unlimited company as a (private) limited company.

such past members and all members at the time of registration are liable to contribute without limit as to the amount in respect of debts and liabilities incurred before the re-registration, even if all those on the A list have paid in full (I.A., s.77(3) and (4)). Where a limited company is re-registered as unlimited (under s.49, formerly s.43 of the 1967 Act) a person who was not then a member may still be on the B list if the company is wound up within a year of his ceasing to be a member. Unless he again became a member at a later date, however, his liability is no greater than it would have been had the company not been re-registered (I.A., s.78). The liability of those on the extended B list is still limited by the Insolvency Act, section 74(2)(*b*) under which they are not liable for debts contracted after they ceased to be members.

Calls

463 The liability of a contributory is a debt due as from "the time when his liability commenced," but payable only when a call is made. Prescription (if not interrupted) can therefore operate to extinguish liability, five years after the date of the call.[16] It follows that, if a call made by the directors has prescribed, the liquidator cannot call up the same money.

Liability does not arise until a call in proper form has been made, and accordingly a B list contributory may effectively reduce his potential liability by procuring the extinction of debts in respect of which he may be liable between the commencement of the winding up and the making of the call and perhaps even later.[17]

Where shares have been forfeited their former holder is not liable as a contributory (unless under list B) but he may be liable to the company on some other grounds, *e.g.* by virtue of the terms of its articles in regard to forfeiture.[18]

In Scotland calls are issued by the court (I.A., s.150).[19] There is no provision, as in England (I.A., s.160), for calls to be made by the liquidator. The liquidator applies to the court by way of note, stating the proposed amount of call and the reasons for making it. The court may order intimation and service and, after consideration of any answers, may order the call to be made in a lump sum or by instalments.[20] The order may take account of the likelihood of some contributories not being able to pay in full (I.A., s.150(2)). Such an

---

[16] Prescription and Limitation (Scotland) Act 1973, s.6 and Sched. 1.
[17] *Apex Film Distributors Ltd.* [1960] Ch. 378.
[18] *Liquidators of Mount Morgan (West) Gold Mine* v. *McMahon* (1891) 18 R. 772; *Ladies' Dress Assoc.* v. *Pulbrook* [1900] 2 Q.B. 376.
[19] The details of procedure (so far as not prescribed by the Insolvency Act) are based on the rules of court in force before December 29, 1986; the 1986 Rules make no specific provision in regard to calls, and it is suggested that the former practices would be followed.
[20] *Re Law Guarantee Society* (1910) 26 T.L.R. 565.

order is conclusive evidence that the amount stated is due, and is also conclusive in all other respects except that it is only prima facie evidence for the purpose of charging the heritable estate of a deceased contributory unless his heirs or legatees of heritage were on the list when the call was made (I.A., s.152). The liquidator can obtain an order which may be enforced by summary diligence by lodging in court a certified list of contributories and particulars of calls due (I.A., s.161).[21]

It is not necessary, before a call is made, that the company's debts and liabilities be fixed; they need only be estimated for the purpose of the Insolvency Act, section 150.[22]

The Insolvency Act, section 149(1) allows the liquidator to recover from a contributory sums other than calls made "in pursuance of" the Acts (*i.e.* the Companies Act 1985 and the Insolvency Act 1986) by court order. Since the Acts refer only to calls made in a winding up this section can be invoked by the liquidator to sue for calls made by the directors prior to the commencement of the winding up as well as other debts notwithstanding that he has obtained an order under the Insolvency Act, section 150 for payment of the same sum.[23] If proceeding under the Insolvency Act, section 149 in respect of calls made by the directors the liquidator will be expected to give intimation (not necessarily formal service) to the contributory.[24]

The Insolvency Act, section 161 provides for recovery of calls by the liquidator by summary decree with interest at 5 per cent. If, however, the liquidator is seeking recovery of calls previously made by the directors he is entitled to demand payment of such higher rate as may be provided for in the articles.[24a] The wording of the Insolvency Act, section 149(1) appears to preclude the liquidator from seeking to recover calls made in the winding up by ordinary action with a view to obtaining interest at a rate higher than is provided for in the Insolvency Act, section 161. If he is proceeding under section 161, however, no notice need be given to the contributories, nor does it appear that a contributory can appear to contest the granting of summary decree for payment.[25] He may, however, proceed by way of suspension subject to finding caution, consignation of the sum due, or with leave of the court (I.A., s.161(2)).[26]

Compromises with contributories

464 The making of compromises with contributories is one of the powers of

---

[21] See *Cumpstie* v. *Waterston*, 1933 S.C. 1.
[22] *Re Contract Corporation* (1866) L.R. 2 Ch.App. 95.
[23] *Westmoreland Green, etc., Slate Co.* v. *Feilden* [1891] 3 Ch. 15.
[24] *Liquidators of Benhar Coal Co. Ltd.* (1882) 9 R. 763.
[24a] *Liquidators of Benhar Coal Co. Ltd., supra.*
[25] *Liquidators of Benhar Coal Co. Ltd., supra.*
[26] *Cumpstie* v. *Waterston*, 1933 S.C. 1. See also *Anderston* v. *Liquidators of City of Glasgow Bank* (1880) 8 R. 44.

the liquidator for which he requires the sanction of the court or the liquidation committee (if any).[27] The liquidator cannot be compelled to accept a compromise with a contributory.[28] A discharge obtained by fraud or concealment of assets may be reduced.[29] If the liquidator decides to disregard a discharge on the basis that it was obtained by concealment of assets and seeks to enforce a decree for payment of a call by summary process under the Insolvency Act, section 161, the contributory may apply for suspension without being required to find caution.[30]

Liability following redemption or purchase of a company's own shares

465 If winding up commences within one year of the date of payment of a sum out of capital by a company (necessarily a private company) for the redemption or purchase of its own shares under Chapter VII of Part V of the Act, the shareholders from whom the shares were redeemed or purchased, and the directors responsible for the transaction may incur liability under the Insolvency Act, section 76. Under section 76(1)(b) this liability only arises if there is a deficiency after taking account of all the assets of the company and "the amounts paid by way of contribution to its assets (apart from this section)." Clearly liability under the Insolvency Act, section 76 arises only if contributions from the A and B lists are insufficient. It may arise even if such contributions have proved irrecoverable, since section 76(1)(b) refers to actual payments by way of contribution. The contributions to be taken into account before applying the Insolvency Act, section 76 will, however, also include those arising from the Insolvency Act, section 75 (directors with unlimited liability), the Insolvency Act, section 213 (fraudulent trading) and the Insolvency Act, section 214 (wrongful trading) as well as all debts due to the company, which are of course part of its assets. Liability is restricted to the amount of the relevant payment which the former holder received for his shares, but is not related to the amount he would have been liable to contribute had he still been a member and contributory (I.A., s.76(3)). The former shareholder and the directors who signed the declaration of solvency under section 173 (which is an essential prerequisite of a payment out of capital for these purposes)[31] are jointly and severally liable (I.A., s.76(2) and (3)). A director who can show that he had reasonable grounds for forming the favourable opinion of the company's solvency set out in the declaration may escape liability (I.A., s.76(2)(b)). A person who has paid under the

[27] I.A., s.167(1), Sched. 4 para. 3.
[28] *Tennent* v. *City of Glasgow Bank* (1879) 6 R. 972.
[29] *Liquidators of City of Glasgow Bank* v. *Assets Co.* (1883) 10 R. 676; *Assets Co.* v. *Tosh's Trs.* (1898) 6 S.L.T. 96; *Assets Co.* v. *Shirre's Trs.* (1897) 24 R. 418; 4 S.L.T. 224; *Bain* v. *Assets Co.* (1905) 7 F. (H.L.) 104; [1905] A.C. 317; 13 S.L.T. 147.
[30] *Anderson* v. *Liquidators of City of Glasgow Bank* (1880) 8 R. 44.
[31] See *Palmer*, paras. 6.021 and 6.410.

Insolvency Act, section 76 may obtain an order for relief against any other party liable with him (I.A., s.76(4)). The provisions of the Act relating to "contributories" do not apply to persons liable only by virtue of this section (I.A., ss.76(5) and 79(3)). There is power to make regulations for the purposes of this section (I.A., s.76(6)).[32]

The Insolvency Act, section 76 deals only with the case where a company has made a redemption or purchase out of capital, with the appropriate statutory declaration and other requirements of sections 171 to 175. A payment out of capital which does not satisfy those requirements is "unlawful," as also is any payment for (or relating to) redemption or purchase (other than sanctioned by ss.171–175) which is not out of "distributable profits" or the proceeds of a fresh issue of shares made for the purpose.[33] Such unlawful payments will be recoverable by the liquidator in the normal way, as debts due to the company.

CREDITORS

466 It is fundamental to the concept of corporate personality that a creditor's remedy is solely against the company. This holds equally for a company whose members have unlimited liability.[34] If, however, a creditor has lost his claim against the company owing to the negligence of the liquidator, he may have a claim for damages against the liquidator personally.[35]

Retention of Title

467 There has never been any doubt that, if the seller of specific or ascertained goods reserves title until the price for them has been paid, the property therein remains with the seller until payment.[36] A series of cases[37] suggested that any attempt to reserve title for further debts or obligations was ineffective, as being an attempt to create security over corporeal moveables in a form not recognised by Scots law. The House of Lords has, however, now held[38] that this approach is misconceived, and that clauses retaining title have to be given effect in their terms so that goods to which they apply (at least so long as the goods remain identifiable) never become the property of the buyer until the relevant conditions have been satisfied, and are therefore not part of the assets of the company falling under the control of its liquidator.

---

[32] No such regulations have yet (December 31, 1992) been made.
[33] See further *Palmer*, paras. 6.410 *et seq.*
[34] See *Palmer*, para. 2.016.
[35] *Pulsford* v. *Devenish* [1903] 2 Ch. 625; *Argyll's Ltd.* v. *Coxeter* (1913) 29 T.L.R. 355.
[36] Sale of Goods Act 1979, ss.17 and 19(1); *Cowan* v. *Spence* (1824) 3 S. 42.
[37] *Emerald Stainless Steel Ltd.* v. *Southside Distribution Ltd.*, 1983 S.L.T. 162; *Deutz Engines Ltd.* v. *Terex Ltd.*, 1984 S.L.T. 273; *Armour* v. *Thyssen Edelstahlwerke A.G.*, 1986 S.L.T. 94, 452;. 1989 S.L.T. 182.
[38] *Armour* v. *Thyssen Edelstahlwerke A.G.* [1990] 3 All E.R. 481 (H.L.); 1990 S.L.T. 891 (H.L.)

Assets held in trust

468 If it is found that cash or assets held by the company are subject to a trust in favour of another party and can be identified, they may be recovered from the liquidator (in full) on that basis and not as a ranking in the liquidation.[39] Conditions in contracts for the sale of goods may, if couched in appropriate terms, create a trust in respect of the proceeds of sale of the goods in question.[40] It is, however, possible in Scots law for a company to constitute itself a trustee for its creditor in respect of incorporeal moveable assets in existence or to come into existence (*e.g.* book debts) by an appropriate declaration of trust in respect of such assets embodied in a contract with or deed delivered to the creditor. Intimation to the company's debtors is not necessary. The claim of the creditor beneficiary will prevail over a liquidator.[41]

Members as creditors

469 If the creditor is also a member of the company his claim is subject to the Insolvency Act, section 74(2)(*f*), under which it cannot be advanced in competition with other creditors (although it can be brought into account for adjustment of his rights with the contributories) if it is due to him in the character of a member and by way of "dividends, profits or otherwise." It has been held[42] that dividends declared but unpaid are capable of being "transmuted" into loans by express or implied agreement so as to escape the restriction of the Insolvency Act, section 74(2)(*f*), but in a recent English case[43] the court, while examining various authorities in which this argument appeared to have succeeded, reserved judgment on its validity. Unless the unpaid dividends are lent back to the company on a proper commercial basis, duly documented, it is difficult to see how they can become sums due to the member as lender/creditor rather than "in the character of a member"; also, the words "or otherwise" must refer to something other than "dividends or profits," although whether the *ejusdem generis* rule of construction would apply and, if so, to what effect, remains unclear.[44] It would seem, however, that if the member is due a share of profits as an employee enjoying a bonus scheme, the Insolvency Act, section 74(2)(*f*) can have no application. Under section 178, any unpaid liability of a company arising out of the redemption or purchase of its own shares is enforceable only after satisfaction of all

---

[39] *Turnbull* v. *Liquidator of Scottish County Investment Co. Ltd.*, 1939 S.C. 5; *Smith, etc.* v. *Liquidator of James Birrell Ltd.*, 1968 S.L.T. 174.

[40] *Clark Taylor & Co. Ltd.* v. *Quality Site Development (Edinburgh) Ltd.*, 1981 S.L.T. 308. See also *Export Credits Guarantee Dept.* v. *Turner*, 1981 S.L.T. 286.

[41] *Tay Valley Joinery Ltd.* v. *C. F. Financial Services Ltd.*, 1987 S.L.T. 207; see also Reid "Trusts and Floating Charges," 1987 S.L.T. (News) 113.

[42] *Liquidators of Wilson's (Glasgow and Trinidad) Ltd.* v. *Wilson's Trs.*, 1915 1 S.L.T. 424. *Re L. B. Holliday & Co. Ltd.* [1986] 2 All E.R. 367.

[43] *Re L. B. Holliday & Co. Ltd.*, *supra*.

[44] *Re L. B. Holliday & Co. Ltd.*, *supra*.

other debts and liabilities (excluding any due to the members in their character as such) (s.178(6)).[45]

Proof of claims

470 A creditor's right to vote or draw a dividend depends on him lodging a statement of claim with the liquidator in the prescribed form[46] together with an account or voucher constituting prima facie evidence of the debt. The liquidator may accept a less formal claim. To vote, the claim must be lodged at or before the relevant meeting. For dividend, it must be lodged no later than eight weeks before the end of the accounting period in which it is to rank for payment.[47] Once submitted and accepted, the claim remains valid for subsequent meetings and dividends. Claims can be recalculated, but a secured creditor is not entitled to adjust his claim by revaluing his security after the liquidator has offered payment of the earlier valuation in full[48] (1986 Rule 4.15). Claims may be stated in a currency other than sterling if the creditor holds a court order for payment in the foreign currency, or if the claim arises from a contractual obligation which may require the company to pay in foreign currency. Such a claim is to be converted into sterling at the London spot rate prevailing at the close of business on the date of commencement of winding up (1986 Rule 4.17).

The 1986 Rules (Rule 4.16) adopt, with modifications, certain provisions of the Bankruptcy (Scotland) Act 1985 in relation to claims. In the remainder of this section references to the Bankruptcy Act are to those provisions, as modified.

It is a criminal offence for the creditor to submit a false claim or evidence, and for the company to fail to report it to the liquidator as soon as practicable after becoming aware of such a false claim (Bankruptcy Act, s.22(5) and (10)).

The liquidator may require the creditor or any other person to produce further evidence relating to the claim. This may include a private examination on oath before the court (Bankruptcy Act, ss.48(5), (6) and (8), 44(2) and (3) and 47(1) as applied by s.48).

At the commencement of every meeting of creditors and not later than four weeks before the end of each accounting period in which a dividend is to be paid[49] the liquidator must adjudicate on claims so far as outstanding, including the value of any security accepted by him. Reasons for rejection must be given. The adjudication is to be recorded in the sederunt book, including the reasons for any rejection of claims. The company or any creditor may appeal to the court within two weeks

---

[45] See further *Palmer*, para. 6.027.
[46] Form 4.7 (Scot) in the revised form specified in the 1987 amendments; see 1986 Rule 7.30.
[47] See para. 492, *post*.
[48] See further para. 481, *post*.
[49] See para. 492, *post*.

of the decision, if it relates to voting, and not later than two weeks before the end of the accounting period, if it relates to dividend (Bankruptcy Act, s.49; R.C.S. 218G; Sh.Ct.R. 25). The court may prorogate these time limits.

The rules for determining the amount of claims are the same as those in Bankruptcy, so far as relevant. References here are to paragraphs in Schedule 1 of the Bankruptcy Act (as modified).

A debt due at the commencement of winding up may be claimed in full, together with interest so far as due to that date. A debt payable after commencement of winding up, so long as it is prospective and not contingent, may be claimed subject to deduction of interest at the rate prescribed in section 51(7) of the Bankruptcy Act for the period from date of commencement of winding up to the date for payment. Section 51(7) provides that the relevant rate of interest is either the prescribed rate[50] at the date of commencement of winding up or the rate otherwise due, whichever is higher. Normally, only the prescribed rate will be relevant for this purpose. Any discount allowable by contract, course of dealing or trade usage is to be deducted, other than a discount for cash payment (para. 1). Contingent claims are to be valued by the liquidator subject to a right of appeal to the court (para. 2). A secured creditor must deduct the value of his security as estimated by him, or he may surrender it to the liquidator. If he has realised the security, the amount realised, less expenses, is to be deducted. The liquidator may within 12 weeks of the commencement of winding up require the creditor to surrender his security on payment of value put upon it by the creditor (para. 5).[51]

471 The principle of converting claims in foreign currency into sterling at the rate applicable at commencement of the winding up, on the basis that all liquidation procedure theoretically occurs at that one moment, also applies where provable debts have been paid in full and a ranking arises on a surplus in respect of post-liquidation claims, such as interest.[52]

The Insolvency Act, section 153 retains the power of the court (on the liquidator's application) to fix a time for creditors to prove their claims or risk exclusion from any distribution made before their claims are proved. The time limit is normally six weeks after the order.[53] The 1986 Act and Rules, however, now provide for payment of claims by reference to 26-week accounting periods,[54] so recourse to the Insolvency Act, section 153 is no longer a routing procedure in winding up, and is likely to be required only in exceptional circumstances. If an

---

[50] The rate is 15 per cent. as from April 1, 1986 (Bankruptcy (Scotland) Regulations 1985 (S.I. 1985 No. 1925) para. 8).
[51] See para. 481, *post*.
[52] *Re Lines Bros. Ltd.* (No. 2) [1984] 2 W.L.R. 905; [1984] Ch. 438.
[53] McBryde, "Liquidation Procedure in the Court of Session," 1977 S.L.T. (News) 239.
[54] See para. 492, *post*.

order under the Insolvency Act, s.153 is granted, it will provide that claims lodged after the prescribed date are to be excluded from any distribution made before these debts have been proved. In this context "distribution" includes a distribution to contributories; if the company has been dissolved the Insolvency Act, section 149 ceases to apply and there is no room for the creditor to argue that he is subrogated to any rights the company might have against the contributories under that section.[55] Late lodgement of a claim precludes participation in distributions made before it was lodged even if the liquidator was aware of its existence before making a distribution, but it will be admitted to a ranking in subsequent dividends.[56] The context in which the Insolvency Act, section 153 now applies makes it clear that it is procedural, and does not preclude a late claimant from obtaining an equalising dividend under a later distribution under the general principle of *pari passu* treatment of all creditors (subject to preferential rights) enshrined in the Insolvency Act, section 107 for voluntary liquidations. A late claimant, unless his delay is "grotesque" and inexcusable, is entitled to protection against loss of effective recourse resulting from a proposed distribution, especially if the distribution is to members rather than creditors.[57] The court may prorogate the time for lodging claims under the Insolvency Act, section 153.[58]

Value added tax

472 Where the liquidator has issued a certificate of insolvency, as a result of which a creditor has recovered VAT from the Customs and Excise Commissioners and the company unexpectedly becomes solvent, the Commissioners are not subrogated to the creditor's claim and cannot, therefore, claim on the surplus, which the liquidator is at liberty to distribute among the contributories.[59]

Effect of claim on prescription and limitation of actions

473 Prescription extinguishes the creditor's rights. Rules as to the limitation of actions merely prevent their enforcement, but the rights remain.[60] Under the law in force prior to April 1, 1986 the presentation of, or the concurring in, a petition for the winding up of a company, or the lodging of a claim in the liquidation interrupted the running of prescription on the debt.[61] After April 1, 1986 only the lodging of a claim (not the presentation of or concurrence in a petition) had this

---

[55] *Butter* v. *Broadhead* [1975] Ch. 97.
[56] *Dickey* v. *Ballantine*, 1939 S.C. 783.
[57] *Re R-R Realisations Ltd.* [1980] 1 All E.R. 1019.
[58] *Silvela* v. *Ker*, 1900 8 S.L.T. 194.
[59] In *Re T. H. Knitwear Ltd.* [1987] 1 W.L.R. 371; 1988 P.C.C. 281.
[60] See further Walker *The Law of Prescription and Limitation of Actions in Scotland* (3rd ed.), Chap. 1.
[61] Prescription and Limitation (Scotland) Act 1973, s.9(1)(*b*).

effect. This was done by reference to the provisions of the Bankruptcy (Scotland) Act 1985 as applied to companies by section 613 of the Companies Act 1985.[62] The Insolvency Act 1986, Schedule 12, repealed section 613, but no consequential amendment to the Prescription and Limitation Act was made. Under the law in force from December 29, 1976, therefore, liquidation proceedings would not interrupt the running of prescription. This was acknowledged to have been a mistake in the drafting of the legislation.[63] If the law had been left in this condition, a creditor whose claim was in danger of prescribing would have required either to obtain an express admission of his debt from the liquidator (which, as a "relevant acknowledgement" would interrupt prescription)[64] or else initiate court proceedings to preserve his claim.[65] To rectify this, however, the Prescription (Scotland) Act 1987 amends the Prescription and Limitation (Scotland) Act 1973 by adding to section 9(1) a provision (*d*) to the effect that the running of prescription is to be interrupted by the presentation of or the concurring in a petition for winding up or the submission of a claim in a liquidation in accordance with the 1986 Rules. This is to have effect in any winding up which commenced on or after December 29, 1986, even if the claim was submitted before the 1987 Act came into force (May 1, 1987). A debt which prescribed under the unamended law because only a claim had been lodged has been re-validated by the retrospective effect of this amendment. The reference to a claim submitted "in accordance with" the rules is to one submitted on Form 4.7 (Scot) with supporting vouchers but would also include any debt in respect of which the liquidator has accepted a less formal claim.[66] The presentation of or the concurring in, a petition for winding up, or the lodging of a claim will bar the effect of any enactment or rule of law relating to the limitation of actions in any part of the United Kingdom, except where an enactment gives effect to an international agreement or obligation.[67]

Disputed claims

474 The liquidator is entitled to reject any claim which has not been properly formulated or vouched and until such a claim has been presented and rejected the court will not entertain an appeal.[68] In general, a claim for damages should be constituted by ordinary action

---

[62] Amendment of the Prescription and Limitation (Scotland) Act 1973, s.9(1)(*b*) by the Bankruptcy (Scotland) Act 1985, Sched. 7, paras. 11 and 19.

[63] 1987 J.L.S. 5.

[64] See the Prescription and Limitation (Scotland) Act 1973, ss.6(1)(*b*), 7(1)(*b*) and 10.

[65] Prescription and Limitation (Scotland) Act 1973, ss.6 and 7.

[66] See para. 470, *ante*.

[67] 1986 Rule 4.76, applying with modifications the Bankruptcy (Scotland) Act 1985, s.8(5), 22(8) and 73(5).

[68] *Knoll Spinning Co. Ltd.* v. *Brown*, 1977 S.C. 291 (following *Crawford* v. *McCulloch*, 1909 S.C. 1063 and distinguishing *Re Kentwood Constructions Ltd.* [1960] 2 All E.R. 655 and *Re Trepca Mines Ltd.* [1960] 1 All E.R. 304).

and the claimant should not seek to have the merits discussed in the liquidation process.[69] Similar principles should apply to any illiquid claim in respect of which there is a substantial dispute. Claims for damages should be determined as at the date of the winding-up order.[70] Facts relating to a dispute which are within the knowledge of the company must be taken to be within the knowledge of the liquidator also.[71]

Compensation: Set-off

475 In contrast to the position in England, the rules governing the question of whether claims due to a person by the company may be compensated by or set-off against a claim due by him to it are common law and not statutory. The right of compensation, in respect of pre-liquidation accounts, arises if both parties are debtor and creditor in the same capacity and (in a liquidation) applies equally to liquid and illiquid claims.[72] It is immaterial whether the liquidation is solvent or insolvent.[73] The illiquid claim must, however, be capable of ascertainment "almost immediately" and arise out of the same contract.[74] A claim arising after liquidation has commenced cannot be compensated against a pre-liquidation debt,[75] but if a debt and claim both arose after commencement of the winding up compensation is allowed.[76] A debtor cannot after winding up has commenced, acquire a claim against the company in order to plead compensation.[77] A contributory is in a special position. He cannot plead compensation against a call made in a liquidation[78] whether the call was made by the liquidator or by the directors (prior to the commencement of winding up),[79] even where the company had agreed in writing to hold money deposited with it against calls,[80] unless and until all creditors have been paid in full, (with interest) when he may claim compensation against subsequent calls (I.A., s.149(1) and (3)). In the case of an unlimited company, however, the court may allow him to compensate against

---

[69] *Crawford* v. *McCulloch, supra.*
[70] *Re Dynamics Corporation of America* [1976] 2 All E.R. 699.
[71] M. *Publications (Scotland) Ltd.* v. *Meiland*, 1981 S.L.T. (Notes) 72. But the liquidator's over-riding duty is to admit only *bona fide* claims, not an "unreal" claim which the company itself might be personally barred from rejecting: *Re Exchange Securities and Commodities Ltd., etc.* [1987] 2 All E.R. 272.
[72] *Booth and Anr.* v. *Thomson and Ors.*, 1972 S.L.T. 141.
[73] *G. & A. (Hotels) Ltd.* v. *T. H. B. Marketing Services*, 1983 S.L.T. 497; *Re A Company* [1983] 2 All E.R. 854.
[74] *Niven* v. *Clyde Fasteners Ltd.*, 1986 S.L.T. 344.
[75] See further Walker, *Scottish Private Law*, Vol. II, p. 166.
[76] *Booth & Anr.* v. *Thomson & Ors. supra*; *Smith* v. *Lord Advocate*, 1979 S.L.T. 233.
[77] *Smith* v. *Lord Advocate (No. 2)*, 1981 S.L.T. 19.
[78] *Liquidators of Coustonholme Paper Mills Co. Ltd.* v. *Law* (1891) 18 R. 1076, 1093; see also *Scottish Fishermen's Organisation Ltd.* v. *McLean*, 1980 S.L.T. (Sh.Ct.) 76.
[79] *Cowan* v. *Gowans* (1878) 5 R. 581.
[80] *Liquidators of the Property Investment Co. of Scotland* v. *Aikman* (1891) 28 S.L.R. 955; see also *Liquidators of the Property Investment Co. of Scotland* v. *National Bank of Scotland* (1891) 28 S.L.R. 884.

his liability sums due to him by the company as a result of any "independent dealing or contract," but not money due to him as a member in respect of dividend or profit. The directors of a limited company who have unlimited liability[81] can obtain like relief (I.A., s.149(2)).

Strictly speaking, a counter-claim against a company in compulsory liquidation constitutes action which cannot proceed without leave of the court under the Insolvency Act, section 130(2).[82] If, however, the counter-claim is restricted to such sum as would extinguish the liquidator's claim, it is unnecessary to obtain leave under that subsection.[83]

At common law the Crown is treated as an indivisible entity, and debts due to one department of government can be set off against sums due by another department (and vice versa). The Crown Proceedings Act 1947, section 35(2), as amended for Scotland by section 50, provides that; (1) compensation cannot be pled against a claim for taxes, duties or penalties, nor can a claim for repayment of such items be used to compensate a Crown claim of a different nature, and (2) in any other case compensation in respect of claims relating to different government departments is only allowed (to the Crown or to the company) with the leave of the court. This applies whether the company is solvent or insolvent. The requirement to seek leave of the court does not, however, derogate from the common law principle which would allow compensation to apply, but is essentially procedural. Leave will normally be granted (particularly in a liquidation) unless one of the claims is illiquid and would require extensive proceedings to establish.[84]

An English decision, that a surety cannot set off his contingent liability unless the principal creditor has waived his right of proof,[85] appears to be consistent with Scottish principles.

Where a bank held money borrowed by the company for a specific purpose, known to the bank, the bank was not entitled to set off that sum against the company's other indebtedness, but had to return it to the lender when it ceased to be available for that purpose because of the liquidation of the company.[86]

Where two companies were indebted to one another and were both insolvent and in liquidation, the liquidator of each was given liberty to distribute its assets among the other creditors without regard to the claim of the other company.[87]

[81] See para. 459, *ante*.
[82] See para. 476, *post*, for the definition.
[83] *G. & A. (Hotels) Ltd.* v. *T. H. B. Marketing Services Ltd., supra.*
[84] *Smith* v. *Lord Advocate (No. 2)*, 1981 S.L.T. 21; *Laing* v. *Lord Advocate*, 1973 S.L.T. (Notes) 81; *Atlantic Engine Co. (1920) Ltd.* v. *Lord Advocate*, 1955 S.L.T. 17.
[85] *Re Fenton* [1931] 1 Ch. 85.
[86] *Quistclose Investments* v. *Rolls Razor Ltd.* [1968] Ch. 540; affirmed, *sub nom. Barclays Bank Ltd.* v. *Quistclose Investments Ltd.* [1970] A.C. 567; [1968] 3 All E.R. 651; see also *Smith* v. *Liquidator of James Birrell Ltd.*, 1968 S.L.T. 174.
[87] *Re National Live Stock Co.* [1917] 1 Ch. 628.

Application of assets

476 The Insolvency Act, section 148(1) provides that "the court ... shall cause the assets of the company to be collected and applied in discharge of its liabilities." The assets in question will be those which remain after satisfying any secured claim.[88] The order of distribution is now prescribed in Chapter 9 of the 1986 Rules (Rules 4.66–4.68), together with the Insolvency Act, section 386 and Schedule 6, which define "preferential debts." Rule 4.66 provides that the order of ranking is:

(a) the expenses of the liquidation[89];
(b) where the court makes a winding-up order, the expenses of any voluntary arrangement in force when the petition for winding up was presented[90];
(c) any preferential debts[91] but excluding interest after commencement of the winding up;
(d) ordinary debts, not secured or otherwise mentioned in the Rule;
(e) interest at the "official rate"[92] on (i) preferential debts and (ii) ordinary debts after commencement of the winding up; and
(f) any postponed debt.

Debts in each of the categories (c) to (f) rank *pari passu* (Rule 4.66(4)), and claims to interest under (e) have the same ranking whether arising on a preferential or an ordinary debt (I.A., s.189(3)). The definition of "postponed debt" in Rule 4.66(2) is "a creditor's right to any alienation which has been reduced or restored to the company's assets under the Insolvency Act, s.242 or to the proceeds of sale of such an alienation" (the reference is to the reduction of gratuitous alienations).[93] It therefore appears that any other claim will be allocated to category (d) as an ordinary debt not being "mentioned in any other sub-paragraph" of the Rule. A foreign currency creditor is required to convert his claim into sterling as at the date of commencement of the winding up[94] and this preserves the fiction that the liquidation and the distribution of assets are deemed to occur simultaneously, notwithstanding the interval between these events occupied by the process of winding up.[95] Under the legislation in force prior to the Insolvency Act 1986 a foreign currency creditor who had suffered loss as a result of exchange rate changes during the liquidation had a claim postponed to all other creditors, *i.e.* after the fiction of simultaneous liquidation and

---

[88] 1986 Rule 4.66(6); see para. 481, *infra*.
[89] See para. 477, *infra*.
[90] Added by the 1987 Amendments.
[91] See paras. 478 to 480, *infra*.
[92] See para. 482, *infra*.
[93] See paras. 506 to 508, *infra*.
[94] 1986 Rule 4.17. See para. 508, *ante*.
[95] *Re Dynamics Corp. of America* [1976] 2 All E.R. 669.

distribution had been exhausted,[96] but such a claim does not fall within the definition of a "postponed debt" under the 1986 Rules. To accord it an "ordinary" ranking would be inconsistent with the underlying "fiction" and the apparent principles of Rule 4.66, so it would seem that such losses have ceased to be recoverable.

In *British Eagle International Airlines Ltd.* v. *Compagnie Nationale Air France*[97] it was held that the rule of *pari passu* distribution (as embodied in the English equivalent of Rule 4.66 for winding up by the court and in Insolvency Act, s.107 for voluntary liquidations) could not, on grounds of public policy, be avoided by contract, even one entered into for good commercial reason and not in contemplation of liquidation. This has led to doubts whether it is competent for a creditor to agree that his claim is to be postponed to the other ordinary debts of the company. In *British Eagle* the agreement in question was for the company and its creditors to operate a "clearing house" setting off their debits and credits *inter se*. It was held that this amounted to a "mini-liquidation" under which the assets and liabilities were to be dealt with otherwise than prescribed in the statutory scheme for liquidations. Clearly, such an arrangement could operate to the disadvantage of the ordinary creditors and was rightly struck down on that basis. This, however, is not a criticism which can be levelled at an arrangement which simply defers one claim to others; the general creditors benefit from that creditor's agreement to postpone. It is suggested, therefore, that the decision in *British Eagle* ought not to be extended to such an arrangement.

Claims by a contributory in the character of a member rank after all claims by creditors, including "postponed debts" (I.A., s.74(2)(*f*)).[98] So also does any claim for payment of the sum due by the company in respect of the redemption or purchase of its own shares (s.178(6)).[99] Any surplus remaining after paying of the expenses and debts is to be distributed in accordance with the articles or among the members (Rule 4.66(5)).[1]

Expenses

477 The expenses of liquidation are to be paid in priority to all preferential and unsecured debts (1986 Rule 4.66(1)). The 1986 Rules now regulate the order of payment of liquidation expenses as follows (Rule 4.67(1)):

1. Outlays properly incurred by the liquidator or provisional liquidator other than those specified below;

---

[96] *Re Lines Bros. Ltd.* [1982] 2 All E.R. 669.
[97] [1975] 2 All E.R. 390 (H.L.). See also *Carreras Rothmans Ltd.* v. *Freeman Mathews Treasure Ltd.* [1985] 1 All E.R. 155 (H.L.).
[98] See para. 469, *supra*.
[99] See Palmer para. 6.027.
[1] See further para. 532, *infra*.

2. the cost (or proportionate cost) of any caution provided by the liquidator, provisional liquidator or special manager[2];
3. remuneration of any provisional liquidator;
4. the petitioner's judicial expenses, and those of any party appearing, as allowed by the court;
5. remuneration of any special manager[3];
6. any expenses of preparation of a statement of affairs which are allowed by the liquidator[4];
7. remuneration of any person employed by the liquidator;
8. liquidator's remuneration, and
9. any corporation tax on chargeable gains on realisation of assets.[5] Such tax is a disbursement in the liquidation, not part of the cost of realisation.[6]

The outlays and remuneration of an immediately preceding voluntary liquidator may be accorded priority (1), the same as outlays in the compulsory liquidation, if the court so allows (1986 Rule 4.67(2)). The court's overriding powers to make orders with respect to judicial expenses are preserved (1986 Rule 4.67(3)).

The Insolvency Act, section 156 provides that, if the assets do not cover all liabilities, the court may make such order for the payment of "the expenses incurred in the winding up in such order of priority as the court thinks just." Since, in Scotland, a floating charge crystallises automatically on the commencement of winding up (s.463) assets subject to the charge are never "assets of the company" under the control of the liquidator. The position is different in English law, where the assets charged by an uncrystallised floating charge are subject to the liquidation process.[7] In Scotland, therefore, the bizarre circumstances of *Re M.C. Bacon Ltd.*[8] (where a liquidator sought to recover the costs incurred by him and awarded against him in an unsuccessful action to set aside a floating charge from the very assets subject to the charge) could not arise. Where the only assets available have been obtained by *ultra vires* activities, the court may authorise these to be used to pay the expenses of liquidation.[9]

The Insolvency Act 1986 includes provisions specifically designed to encourage the directors to seek an alternative solution to winding up, namely a voluntary arrangement or an administration order.[10] If the directors, acting in good faith, incur the expense of seeking such a

---

[2] See paras. 488 and 489, *post*.
[3] *Ibid.*, n. 79.
[4] See para. 484, *post*.
[5] The 1987 Amendments corrected the original reference which was to "capital gains tax" (which does not apply to companies).
[6] *Re Mesco Properties Ltd.* [1980] 1 All E.R. 117.
[7] *Re Barleycorn Enterprises Ltd.* [1970] Ch. 465.
[8] [1990] 3 W.L.R. 646.
[9] *Re Introductions Ltd. (No. 2)* [1969] 1 W.L.R. 1359; [1969] 3 All E.R. 697.
[10] See paras. 101 *et seq.* (Administration Orders) and 301 *et seq.* (Voluntary Arrangements), *ante*.

solution but in the event the company is wound up by the court it would be proper for the court, in the exercise of its discretion under Rule 4.67(3), to order that the expenses of such abortive proceedings be treated as expenses in the liquidation.[11]

If there are no assets the liquidator is not entitled to receive any remuneration and he is personally liable for legal expenses incurred in the liquidation; the legal expenses of the petition are the responsibility of those who instructed it. It is not competent to charge the expense of one liquidation against the assets ingathered in another liquidation, even where the first liquidation was undertaken with a view to securing a benefit for the creditors in the second one.[12]

Preferential payments

478 Both the *Cork Report*[13] and the Scottish Law Commission[14] recommended substantial reform of the list of unsecured debts which are to be paid in priority to other unsecured claims. In the event, while significant changes were made, the revised list of preferential debts does not adopt these proposals fully, and in particular still includes local rates and taxation. In relation to the liquidation of companies, the preferential debts are specified in the Insolvency Act, section 386 and Schedule 6:

1. PAYE deductions (less repayments) for the preceding 12 months;
2. Sums due under Finance (No. 2) Act 1975, section 69 (sub-contractors in the construction industry);
3. VAT referable to the preceding six months;
4. Car tax and various betting duties which became due in the preceding 12 months;
5. Social security contributions which became due in the preceding 12 months, and Class 4 (self-employed) contributions for any one year provided they have been assessed on the company up to the previous April 5;
6. Contributions to a revenue-approved occupational pension scheme, or the state pension scheme (without limit);
7. Unpaid remuneration to any employee subject to a maximum of four months' pay and up to a prescribed maximum amount. The prescribed maximum as from December 29, 1986 is £800[15];
8. Accrued holiday pay due to employees or former employees (without limit);
9. Any sum lent to meet payments which would fall within (7) or (8); and

---

[11] *Cf.* In *Re Gosscot (Groundworks) Ltd.* (1988) P.C.C. 297; 4 B.C.C. 372.
[12] *Taylor (Liquidator of Neil Middleton & Co. Ltd.), Petr.*, 1977 S.L.T. (Sh.Ct.) 82.
[13] "Insolvency Law and Practice" June 1982 (Cmnd. 8558).
[14] Report on Bankruptcy, February 1982 (Scottish Law Commission No. 68).
[15] Insolvency Proceedings (Monetary Limits) Order 1986 (S.I. 1996), reg. 14.

10. Any sum due to be paid under the Reserve Forces (Safeguard of Employment) Act 1985 subject to the prescribed maximum (£800[16]);

11. Levies on coal and steel production imposed pursuant to the European Coal and Steel Community requirements.[17]

The "relevant date," with respect to which all these preferential payments are calculated is defined (for the purposes of winding up) by the Insolvency Act, section 387(3). If the winding-up order immediately succeeds the discharge of an administration order,[18] it is the date of the administration order. If it is a winding up by the court with no previous voluntary liquidation, it is the date of appointment of a provisional liquidator, or of the winding-up order, whichever first occurs. In any other case it is the date of the resolution for voluntary winding up. This is not, of course, the same as the "commencement of the winding up."[19]

Preferential payments rank *pari passu* (I.A., s.175; 1986 Rule 4.66(1) (*b*) and (4)).[20] They must also be paid in priority to any debt secured by a floating charge (I.A., s.175(2)(*b*)).[21] Claims by the Crown enjoy no preference except to the extent allowed by the Act.[22] Where a liquidator paid a dividend to unsecured creditors in the mistaken belief that certain debts would be recovered to pay preferential claims he was held entitled to recover the dividends under the *condictio indebiti*.[23] Contrast the inability of a liquidator to recover payments made in error to contributories.[24]

A cautioner (or other party) who meets any preferential claim is entitled to a corresponding preferential ranking.[25]

Employees

479 The Insolvency Act 1986 has removed the archaic limitation which restricted the preference for remuneration, etc., to a person who was either a "clerk or servant" or a "workman or labourer" (Companies Act 1985, Sched. 19, paras. 9–12). The preference for remuneration, holiday pay, etc., (7)–(10) above now applies to all payments due as wages or salary (including time or piece work and commission) for

---

[16] *Ibid.*, n. 91.

[17] Added by the Insolvency (E.S.C. Levy Debts) Regulations 1987 (S.I. 1987 No. 2093) which came into effect January 1, 1988 but apply to liquidations whenever commenced. There are savings in respect of distributions made prior to January 1, 1988.

[18] See paras. 101 *et seq.*, *ante*.

[19] See para. 433, *ante*.

[20] See para. 476, *ante*.

[21] See also *Manley, Petr.*, 1985 S.L.T. 42.

[22] *Admiralty* v. *Blair's Trs.*, 1916 S.C. 247; *Food Controller* v. *Cork* [1923] A.C. 647.

[23] *Purvis Industries Ltd.* v. *J. & W. Henderson Ltd.* (1959) 75 Sh.Ct.Rep. 143.

[24] *Taylor* v. *Wilson's Trs.*, 1974 S.L.T. 298, affd. 1979 S.L.T. 105.

[25] *Ewart* v. *Latta* (1865) 3 M. (H.L.) 36; *Harvie's Trs.* v. *Bank Scotland* (1885) 12 R. 1141; *Veitch* v. *National Bank of Scotland*, 1907 S.C. 554.

services rendered to the company (I.A., Sched. 6, para. 13(1)(*a*)). This also extends to "Guarantee payments," "protective awards" and various other payments due under the employment protection legislation (I.A., Sched. 6, para. 13(1)(*b*) and (2)). It is no bar to a claim for accrued holiday pay that the employment terminated by virtue of the liquidation before the employee had worked a sufficient period to earn his right to a holiday (I.A., Sched. 6, para. 14). "Remuneration" includes sick pay, holiday pay or any other sums payable during absence from work for good cause (I.A., Sched. 6, para. 15).

A director will be entitled to a preference under the 1986 rules in respect of his remuneration but not for directors' fees. "Labour only" subcontractors cannot benefit from section 319.[26]

Advances for payment of wages

480 A person who has advanced money for the purpose of paying wages or salary or accrued holiday money of any employee of the company is entitled to the same priority in respect thereof as the employee would have had (I.A., Sched. 6, para. 11). A bank may obtain maximum benefit from this, on being asked to advance money for such payments, by operating a separate "wages account," requiring the company to make regular transfers from their current account to discharge the earliest advances. If the bank holds security for its advances, it is entitled to apply the proceeds thereof first against its non-preferential advances.[27]

Secured creditors

481 In Scots law a secured creditor is one who holds a valid fixed security over property, a floating charge, a lien, or a hypothec (a limited and exceptional class of security right over corporeal moveables arising without possession). Secured creditors will normally have rights over the property in question preferable to the liquidator (1986 Rule 4.66(6)(a)), but if such creditors wish to submit a claim for any unsecured balance, their securities must be valued and deducted from any claim in the liquidation, and the creditor cannot claim more than the balance. As a deterrent against undervaluing any such security, the creditor may be compelled to sell his security to the liquidator at his valuation (Bankruptcy (Scotland) Act 1985, Sched. 1, para. 5, as applied by 1986 Rule 4.16). The valuation may be adjusted provided the liquidator has not required the creditor to sell his security at the previous valuation (1986 Rule 4.15(4)). A security which is a registrable charge is void against the liquidator unless duly presented for

---

[26] *Re C. W. & A. L. Hughes Ltd.* [1966] 2 All E.R. 702.
[27] *Re William Hall (Contractors) Ltd.* [1967] 1 W.L.R. 948; 2 All E.R. 1150; and see further, *Palmer*, para. 15.427.

registration under the Companies Act 1985, sections 410 to 424.[28] If a right of lien arises it may be exercised against the liquidator to the effect of obtaining for the holder a preference for his claim in exchange for release of the subjects of lien.[29] The lien will be lost if the holder parts with the goods without reserving his rights.[30] A company secretary has no right of lien over its books by virtue of his office.[31] The liquidator can recover documents without prejudice to the lien, if necessary, but may prefer not to do so since that would force him to concede a preferential ranking.[32] The Insolvency Act, section 246 which invalidates liens over books, etc. does not apply to Scotland (I.A., s.440(2)) but if the liquidator obtains an order (under I.A., s.236) the lien is ineffective.[33]

While in England a landlord is in a special position,[34] in Scotland he is in the same position as any unsecured creditor except in so far as he is able to claim landlord's hypothec which is a limited security for one year's rent over certain moveables (not necessarily belonging to the tenant) brought onto the leased premises.[35]

The position of creditors who have executed diligence against the company's property is noted below (paras. 499 and 500).

A secured creditor may take one of the following courses:

1. rely on his security and not prove in the liquidation;
2. realise his security and prove for any deficiency;
3. value and deduct his security and prove for the balance;
4. surrender his security and prove for the whole debt.

The holder of a floating charge may, instead of pursuing his rights under the charge, be admitted to an appropriate ranking as a secured creditor in the liquidation.[36]

The Insolvency Act, section 185 and 1986 Rule 4.22(5) apply to liquidations the provisions of the Bankruptcy (Scotland) Act 1985, section 39(3), (4), (7) and (8) with respect to the sale of heritable property which is burdened with a prior heritable security. The sale may be by public sale or private bargain. The secured creditor will be

---

[28] See *Palmer*, paras. 13.401 *et seq.*
[29] 1986 Rule 4.66(6)(b) (as amended by the 1987 Amendments). *Train & McIntyre Ltd.* v. *Forbes*, 1925 S.L.T. 286; *Liquidator of Donaldson & Co.* v. *White & Park*, 1908 S.C. 309; 15 S.L.T. 578; *Rorie* v. *Stevenson*, 1908 S.C. 559; 15 S.L.T. 870; *Liquidator of Bar & Co.* v. *Stevenson & Brownlie* (1901) 10 S.L.T. 456; *Liquidator of Scottish Workmen's Assurance Co.* v. *Waddell*, 1910 S.C. 670; 10 S.L.T. 315.
[30] *London Scottish Transport Ltd.* v. *Tyres (Scotland) Ltd.*, 1957 S.L.T. (Sh.Ct.) 48.
[31] *Gladstone* v. *McCallum* (1893) 23 R. 783; 4 S.L.T. 41; *Barnton Hotel Co.* v. *Cook* (1899) 1 F. 1190; 7 S.L.T. 131.
[32] 1986 Rule 4.22(1) to (4) contained in the 1987 Amendments; see para. 483, *infra*; *Liquidator of Scottish Workmen's Assurance Co.* v. *Waddell*, *supra*; *Adam & Winchester* v. *White's Trs.* (1884) 11 R. 863; *Miln's J.F.* v. *Spencer's Trs.*, 1927 S.L.T. 425.
[33] See paras. 519 and 520, *infra* and *In re Aveling Barford Ltd.* [1988] 3 All E.R. 1019.
[34] See *Palmer*, paras. 15.429 to 15.433.
[35] *Cumbernauld Dev. Corpn.* v. *Mustone*, 1983 S.L.T. (Sh.Ct.) 55.
[36] *National Commercial Bank of Scotland Ltd.* v. *Liquidators of Telford Grier Mackay & Co. Ltd.*, 1969 S.C. 181; S.L.T. 306; *Libertas-Kommerz* v. *Johnson*, 1977 S.C. 191; 1978 S.L.T. 222.

barred from exercising his rights to enforce his security if the liquidator has intimated to him that he intends to sell the property; the liquidator cannot, however, take this step if the creditor has intimated to him that he intends to commence sale procedure. If there is undue delay in following up such intimation, the court may allow the other party to proceed. The liquidator can only sell the burdened property, however, if he has the consent of every prior secured creditor or if he obtains a sufficient price to discharge all such securities. A purchaser's title cannot be challenged on the basis of an alleged failure to comply with these requirements; it appears that this applies even if the purchaser acted in bad faith. The liquidator himself (or his associate)[37] cannot purchase any of the company's property under these provisions.

Interest

482 If there are sufficient funds remaining after payment of the expenses of the liquidation and the preferential and ordinary debts, interest at the "official rate" from the date of commencement of the winding up is payable on such debts (I.A., s.189(1) and (2); 1986 Rule 4.66(1)). Claims to such interest rank *pari passu* regardless of whether the debt is preferential or ordinary (I.A., s.189(3); 1986 Rule 4.66(4)). The "official rate" is 15 per cent. or such higher rate as may otherwise be due on the debt (I.A., s.189(4) and (5) as applied by 1986 Rule 4.66(2)(*b*)). Interest running on a secured debt continues to accrue after winding up until the security is exhausted. Any interest after the date of winding up not covered by the security is irrecoverable if the company is insolvent.[38] Interest due on a debt secured by a floating charge which has crystallised accrues until payment of the sum due under the charge (s.463(4)).

DUTIES AND POWERS OF LIQUIDATOR[39]

Custody of property; Vesting orders

483 In general terms the duties of the liquidator are to take control of the assets of the company, to make out lists of creditors and contributories, to resolve disputes, to realise the assets and to apply the proceeds in payment of the company's debts and liabilities in due course of administration; if there is any surplus he will adjust the rights of contributories and distribute the surplus in accordance with them. In a winding up by the court the liquidator can obtain a vesting order from the court under the Insolvency Act, section 145(1). The effect is to vest

---

[37] See para. 517, *post*.
[38] *National Commercial Bank of Scotland Ltd.* v. *Liquidators of Telford Grier Mackay & Co. Ltd.*, 1969 S.L.T. 306.
[39] It is clear from the wording of I.A., s.138(1)(2) that the interim liquidator has the same powers as the liquidator (if any) appointed to succeed him.

the property in the liquidator by his official name. After having obtained such an order and also subject to finding caution if the court so directs, the liquidator can bring or defend in his official name any action or other legal proceedings relating to that property (I.A., s.145(2)). In practice it is seldom necessary to make use of the Insolvency Act, section 145 since proceedings may be taken by the liquidator in the name of the company under his general powers.[40] It has also been suggested that, independently of the Insolvency Act, section 145(1), the liquidator can complete title to heritable property under the Titles to Land Consolidation (Scotland) Act 1868, section 25.[41]

Where a winding-up order has been granted, or a provisional liquidator has been appointed, the liquidator or provisional liquidator is to assume custody and control of all the assets of the company. If no liquidator is in office, the assets are in the custody of the court (I.A., s.144). Legal proceedings will normally be taken in name of the company.[42] If he sues in his own name, thereby accepting responsibility for expenses, he should not be required to find caution under section 726(2).[43] These provisions are supplemented by the Insolvency Act, sections 133, 198, 234 and 236, and by the 1986 Rules (as amended by the 1987 Amendments). As soon as possible after his appointment, the liquidator is to take possession of all assets, property, books, records, etc., in the possession or control of the company, or to which it appears to be entitled.[44] He is to make up an inventory and valuation of the assets to be retained in the sederunt book. Copies (not originals) of documents issued by the company may be recovered from a third party, by court order if necessary.[45] This extends to documents given by the company to a third party on a confidential basis, since the liquidator inherits the company's rights therein. A right of lien over books, papers, etc., can be asserted against him but documents may be recovered without prejudice to any preference conferred by the lien.[46] A previous liquidator must hand over all assets and papers to his successor, and give him all assistance and information reasonably required (1986 Rule 4.21).

Sections 133, 198 and 236 of the Insolvency Act are part of a number of overlapping or alternative provisions under which the court may order persons to appear for examination and/or to produce records.

---

[40] See para. 486, *infra*; *Munro* v. *Hutchison* (1896) 3 S.L.T. 268.
[41] Gretton and Reid, "Insolvency and Title: A Reply," 1985 J.L.S. 109.
[42] See para. 486, *post*; *Munro* v. *Hutchison, supra*.
[43] *Stewart* v. *Steen*, 1987 S.C.L.R. (Sh.Ct.) 34; S.L.T. 60; *Arch Joinery Contracts Ltd.* v. *Arcade Building Services Ltd.*, 1992 S.L.T. 755.
[44] 1986 Rule 4.22(1); see also 1986 Rule 4.66(6)(b) (as amended). I.A., s.234 enables him to seize property, etc. by court order. An application for an order under s.234 should normally be intimated to the person against whom this order is sought, *Re First Express* [1991] B.C.C. 782.
[45] 1986 Rule 4.22(2) and (3).
[46] 1986 Rule 4.22(4).

These are examined below.[47] If the property of the company includes licensed premises he is entitled to delivery of the licence certificate.[48] The liquidator represents the creditors because he represents the company, and the rights and obligations of the company are enforceable only through him.[49] There is no provision for disclaiming onerous property (as in England under I.A., ss.178–182).

Investigation of affairs and liabilities

484 The liquidator is assisted in his investigations by the provisions of the Insolvency Act, section 131 and 1986 Rules 4.7 to 4.9. The provisional liquidator or liquidator may by notice in the prescribed form (Form 4.3 (Scot)) require some or all of the persons mentioned in section 131(3) to provide a sworn statement as to the affairs of the company in the prescribed form (Form 4.4 (Scot)). The notice by the liquidator must have a copy of the form of statement attached. The statement covers assets, debts and liabilities, names and addresses of creditors, and if any creditors are secured, the dates of their securities. The notice may specify further matters on which information is to be provided (I.A., s.131(2)). The time limit for providing the statement is 21 days from receipt of the notice, but this may be extended by the liquidator, or by the court, if he refuses (I.A., s.131(5); R.C.S. 218F; Sh.Ct.R. 24). The statement of affairs is to be retained in the sederunt book (1986 Rule 4.8(2)). If the person required to provide a statement requires professional assistance, he must provide an estimate of cost, and the liquidator may reimburse the cost as an expense in the liquidation. The liquidator may impose conditions on the access to be granted to books and papers for the purpose of preparing a statement. Any refusal to grant assistance may be appealed to the court within 14 days (1986 Rule 4.9).

The persons who may be required to provide a statement of affairs are (I.A., s.131(3)):

(a) Current or previous officers[50] of the company;
(b) Anyone who took part in the formation of the company within a year before the winding-up order or a provisional liquidator's appointment;
(c) Employees, including any person who was employed by the company within the past year; and
(d) Officers or employees (or former officers or employees) of a company which is or was an officer of the company, within the past year.

The liquidator or provisional liquidator has full discretion as to which

---

[47] See paras. 519 to 521, *post*.
[48] *William Forbes Ltd.* v. *Robertson*, 1926 S.L.T. 654; see Licensing (Scotland) Act 1976, s.25.
[49] *Waterhouse* v. *Jamieson* (1870) 8 M. (H.L.) 88.
[50] *i.e.* "director, manager or secretary" (s.744).

(if any) of the relevant persons shall be required to provide a statement subject to appeal to the court (I.A., s.131(5); R.C.S. 218F; Sh.Ct.R. 24). "Employees" include persons providing services as well as those on the payroll of the company (I.A., s.131(6)). The persons listed in the Insolvency Act, section 131(3), together with (in the case of a company being wound up by the court) any former administrator, administrative receiver or liquidator are to give the liquidator assistance if required (I.A., s.235). The court may order such persons to provide information.[51] Information provided in confidence should not be voluntarily disclosed to a third party.[52]

It remains the duty of the liquidator to take all reasonable steps to investigate and discover the company's debts and liabilities. This includes advertising for claims and writing to all known creditors asking for confirmation of their claim[53]: advertising alone is not enough where claims are known to exist but have not been formally made.[54] The liquidator must make due provision for tax, including tax arising during his administration, and if he distributes the surplus without retaining sufficient for this purpose he will be personally liable without right of recovery from the shareholders.[55] A liquidator who has knowledge of a claim but does not deal with it, owing to a mistake by his solicitor, cannot evade responsibility.[56] In a situation where the liquidator has doubt whether he has ascertained all claims, he can ask the court to fix a time limit on claims which are to be considered (I.A., s.153).[57] Although creditors are (under the 1986 legislation) to be paid, in principle, on the basis of 26-week accounting periods,[58] these include the requirement to provide for "contingencies,"[59] which preserves the foregoing principles.

Powers of liquidator

485 Where the company is being wound up by the court, the liquidator has certain powers which require no sanction, and others which require the sanction of the court or the liquidation committee (if any) (I.A., s.167(1)). The powers requiring no sanction (I.A., Sched. 4, Part III) are:

    (a) to sell any assets by public auction or private contract in whole or

---

[51] See paras. 519 and 520, *post.*
[52] *Re Barlow Clowes Gilt Managers Ltd.* [1991] 4 All E.R. 385 (Ch.D.).
[53] *Pulsford* v. *Devenish* [1903] 2 Ch. 803.
[54] *Re Armstrong Whitworth Securities Ltd.* [1947] Ch. 673.
[55] *Taylor* v. *Wilson's Trs.,* 1974 S.L.T. 298, affd. 1979 S.L.T. 105.
[56] *Austin Securities Ltd.* v. *Northgate and English Stores Ltd.* [1969] 1 W.L.R. 529; 2 All E.R. 753.
[57] See para. 471, *ante.*
[58] See para. 492, *post.*
[59] Bankruptcy (Scotland) Act 1985, s.52(3), as adapted.

in parcels.[60] A disposition of heritage runs in the name of the company with the consent of the liquidator. The company grants absolute warrandice and the liquidator grants warrandice from his own facts and deeds only, although it has been doubted whether the liquidator requires to grant warrandice in any form[61];

(b) to do all acts and to execute deeds and other documents in the name of the company, using its seal where necessary[62];

(c) to prove, rank, claim and receive dividends from the estate of an insolvent contributory;

(d) to draw, accept make and indorse bills of exchange and promissory notes in name and on behalf of the company;

(e) to borrow on the security of the company's assets;

(f) to apply for confirmation as executor on the estate of a deceased contributory and to do all acts necessary to obtain sums due from a contributory or his estate;

(g) to appoint an agent to act on his behalf[63]; and

(h) to do all such other things as may be necessary for winding up the company's affairs and distributing its assets (see below).

If the liquidator disposes of any property to a person "connected with the company," *i.e.* a director or shadow director or an "associate" of such a person or of the company,[64] or if he employs a solicitor, he must notify the liquidation committee, if any (I.A., s.167(2)). The appointment of a solicitor does not relieve the liquidator of personal responsibility for the discharge of his duties.[65]

Powers requiring sanction

486 Certain other specific powers are, under the Insolvency Act, section 167(1) and Schedule 4, Parts I and II, to be exercised with the sanction

---

[60] A liquidator, unlike a trustee in bankruptcy, needs no further consent to exercise such powers; *Liquidators of Style & Mantle Ltd.* v. *Price's Tailors Ltd.*, 1934 S.C. 548; *Galbraith*, 1964 S.L.T. (Sh.Ct.) 75. *Cf.* The Bankruptcy (Scotland) Act 1985, s.39.

[61] *Liquidators of Style & Mantle Ltd.*, *supra*. This assumes that the liquidator has not completed his title in his own name, *via* I.A., s.145 (para. 483, *supra*).

[62] Section 36B (as enacted with effect from July 31, 1990 by the Law Reform (Miscellaneous Provisions) (Scotland) Act 1990, s.72(1)) provides that a company need not have a common seal (s.36B(5)) and envisages the execution of probative deeds in the name of a company by two directors, a director and a secretary or by two duly authorised persons (s.36B(4)). This, however, is without prejudice to any other method of execution permitted by rule of law (s.36B(8)(*a*)). Accordingly, a liquidator may execute a deed on behalf of a company as empowered by I.A., Sched. 4 before two witnesses (as under the practice before the 1990 Act) with or without the seal.

[63] Under the former law (s.539(1)(*c*)) the sanction of the court (or committee) was required for the appointment of a solicitor. This is now taken to be part of the general power to appoint an agent, requiring no sanction, but has to be reported to the liquidation committee (if any) (I.A., s.167(2)).

[64] I.A., s.249; "associate" is defined in I.A., s.435; see para. 517, *post*.

[65] *Austin Securities Ltd.* v. *Northgate and English Stores Ltd.* [1969] 2 All E.R. 753.

of the court or the liquidation committee (if any). Sanction may be granted retrospectively.[66]

These powers are:

(a) to pay classes of creditors in full.

(b) (i) to make compromises or arrangements with creditors including prospective, contingent or disputed creditors. An arrangement under which a creditor is to receive an agreed sum instead of a ranking is a "compromise" requiring the appropriate sanction.[67] Each proposed compromise with creditors should be sanctioned either individually or in batches, not by unspecific prior authority, but the court may consider a comprehensive or general compromise.[68] If shareholders object they may be permitted to proceed with the claims on granting appropriate indemnities to the liquidator.[69] It is not incompetent to use the power to make compromises so as to conjoin the administration of a liquidation and the sequestration of a bankrupt where the affairs of the company and the individual are so intermingled that the creditors of each cannot readily be disentangled, to the effect that a joint scheme of distribution to such creditors would be operated by the liquidator and trustee in bankruptcy.[70]

(ii) to compromise calls, debts and related liabilities and claims of all kinds between the company and any (alleged) contributory or other debtor, or any other question affecting the assets or winding up. He may also accept security for and discharge any such debt, liability or claim. In relation to compromises with creditors or members, the liquidator may also avail himself of the procedure for obtaining sanction to a scheme of arrangement binding on all parties under the Companies Act, section 425[71] especially where it is proposed to depart from the strict rights of creditors.[72] A compromise which has been sanctioned may be recalled, if matters are still entire, on the emergence of new facts.[73]

---

[66] *Re Associated Travel Leisure and Services Ltd.* [1978] 2 All E.R. 753.

[67] *Liquidator of R. D. Simpson Ltd.* v. *Beare* (1908) 15 S.L.T. 875.

[68] *Pattisons Ltd.* (1899) 6 S.L.T. 372; *T. H. Bennett & Co.* (1905) 13 S.L.T. 718; *Ecuadorian Assoc. Ltd.* v. *Fox* (1907) 14 S.L.T. 699.

[69] *Ecuadorian Assoc. Ltd.* v. *Fox* (1907) 14 S.L.T. 699.

[70] *Peter C. Taylor, Noter,* 1991 S.C.L.R. 877, affmd, 1992 G.W.D. 19–1084. Although this case was decided on the provisions of the Companies Act 1948, s.245(1)(f) and the Bankruptcy (Scotland) Act 1913, s.172, the equivalent provisions of the current legislation (I.A. Sched. 4, para. 3 and Bankruptcy (Scotland) Act 1985, s.65) with respect to the making of compromises in respect of claims are to the same effect. See also *Re Bank of Credit and Commerce International (No. 2), The Independent,* October 1, 1992 (C.A.).

[71] See *Palmer,* paras. 12.008 *et seq.*

[72] *Re Trix Ltd.* [1970] 3 All E.R. 397.

[73] *D. & W. Henderson & Co.* v. *Stewart* (1894) 22 R. 154; 2 S.L.T. 367.

(c) To bring or defend proceedings in name of the company. The action should not be in the name of the liquidator[74] (unless jointly with the company) although this seems on occasion to have been allowed without objection.[75] Failure to obtain the necessary sanction does not affect the competency of the action.[76] An official liquidator, as an officer of the court, is entitled to be master of the process.[77]

(d) To carry on the business of the company so far as may be necessary for the beneficial winding up thereof. This emphasis on the completion of the winding up as the objective of carrying on the business is not affected by the introduction of powers to make provision for employees under section 74 of the 1980 Act (now I.A., s.187 and s.719 of C.A. 1985). The liquidator may obtain sanction for carrying on the business for a limited period in order to seek a sale on a "going concern" basis.[78] It is the company which is carrying on business, not the liquidator, and employees retain continuity of employment for claims for redundancy and related matters.[79] If he makes it clear that the company is in liquidation he does not incur personal liability.[80]

If there is no liquidation committee, the court may by order in general terms allow the liquidator to bring or defend proceedings or carry on the business without further sanction (I.A., s.169(1)).

487   In addition to these particular powers, the liquidator has further powers of a general nature:

(a) Without the sanction of the court or committee of inspection, to do all things other than the powers enumerated above which may be necessary for winding up the company and distributing its assets (I.A., s.167(1) and Sched. 4, para. 13).

(b) "Subject to the rules," the same powers as a trustee on a bankrupt estate (I.A., s.169(2)). The reference to "the rules" is to the Insolvency (Scotland) Rules 1986,[81] replacing the previous ambiguous reference to "general rules" of law and bankruptcy (s.539(5)). The 1986 Rules apply, with modifications, various provisions of the Bankruptcy (Scotland) Act 1985 including

---

[74] *Munro* v. *Hutchison* (1896) 3 S.L.T. 268.
[75] *e.g. Stewart* v. *Steen*, 1987 S.C.L.R. 34; S.L.T. 60 (where a liquidator pursuing personally was not required to find caution under s.726(6)).
[76] *Stewart* v. *Gardner*, 1933 S.L.T. (Sh.Ct.) 11; *Dublin City Distilling Ltd.* v. *Doherty* [1914] A.C. 823.
[77] *Millar* (1890) 18 R. 179.
[78] *Liquidator of Burntisland Oil Co. Ltd.* v. *Dawson* (1892) 20 R. 180 (six months refused, six weeks allowed); *Liquidator of Victoria Public Buildings Co.* (1893) 30 S.L.R. 386 (one year sanctioned).
[79] *Smith* v. *Lord Advocate*, 1979 S.L.T. 233.
[80] *Stead Hazel and Co.* v. *Cooper* [1933] 1 K.B. 840.
[81] S.I. 1986 No. 1915 (S.139) as amended by the 1987 Amendments (S.I. 1987 No. 1921 (S.132)).

powers of the trustee. These are considered at the appropriate points in this chapter.

(c) The liquidator is entitled to apply to the court by note in the liquidation petition (see R.C.S. 218M; Sh.Ct.R. 30) if he is in doubt on any matter. Although there is no specific provision in the Act equivalent to the Insolvency Act, section 112 (which applies only in voluntary winding up) the liquidator is an officer of the court and has a recognised right to apply to the court for directions. The Insolvency Act, section 167(3), which places him under the general control of the court, supports this view. Such an application must be for approval of a specific act or clarification of a specific point and the court will apply the same test as it would under the Insolvency Act, section 112, *i.e.* whether the direction sought would be "just and beneficial."[82] The court may order meetings of creditors or contributories to be held to ascertain their wishes (I.A., s.195).

SPECIAL MANAGERS

488 The Insolvency Act, section 177 provides that if a company has gone into liquidation (including voluntary liquidation) or a provisional liquidator has been appointed, the court may appoint another person to be the "special Manager" of the business or property of the company. Previously this only applied in England and Wales, and only in a winding up by the court where the official receiver had become liquidator or provisional liquidator (s.556, now repealed). The person appointed to be special manager does not require to be an "insolvency practitioner" (see I.A., ss.230 and 388(1)). His powers will be defined by the court and may include any of the powers vested in a liquidator or provisional liquidator under the Act (I.A., s.177(3) and (4)). If appointed he will therefore derive his authority directly from the court and will not be an agent of the liquidator. Supplementary provisions are contained in 1986 Rules 4.69 to 4.73 and the Rules of Court (R.C.S. 218L; Sh.Ct.R. 29).

Application for the appointment of a special manager is appropriate in any case where the liquidator considers it would be advantageous having regard to the nature of the business or property of the company, *e.g.* because the management or realisation of the business or property demands the exercise of special skills or responsibilities not possessed by the liquidator himself, or his actual presence on the company's premises. Since the liquidator has the alternative of appointing an agent having the necessary attributes, without any sanction from the court or the creditors' committee, under the Insolvency Act, Schedule 4, paragraph 12, the occasion for making use

---

[82] *Liquidator of Upper Clyde Shipbuilders Ltd.*, 1975 S.L.T. 39; *Ross* v. *Smith*, 1986 S.L.T. (Sh.Ct.) 59.

of this power in Scotland must be rare. In England, where the official receiver may still be appointed as liquidator, the power will continue to be of practical advantage.

A report giving reasons for the application, and the value of the assets to be entrusted to the special manager must be prepared (Rule 4.69(2)) and lodged in process (R.C.S. 218S; Sh.Ct.R. 34)). Application is by way of note in the process (R.C.S. 218L(1); Sh.Ct.R. 29(1)) and the person to be appointed has to find caution for at least the value of the assets entrusted to him within a specified period (1986 Rule 4.70; R.C.S. 218L (2)–(5); Sh.Ct.R.(2)–(5)). If he fails to do so, the time may be extended or he may be discharged and another person may be appointed (1986 Rule 4.71). The court's order will indicate the duration of the appointment (which may be indefinite) and the appointment may be renewed (1986 Rule 4.69(3) and (4)). His remuneration, payable as an expense in the liquidation, is to be fixed from time to time by the court; he can be paid a salary or be remunerated on some other basis (1986 Rule 4.69(5)). His appointment will terminate if the petition for winding up is dismissed, or if a provisional liquidator is discharged without a winding-up order having been made. The liquidator can apply to the court to have the appointment terminated if he is satisfied it is no longer necessary or profitable, and he must make such an application if a resolution of creditors is passed, asking for its termination (1986 Rule 4.73).The special manager, while in office, must produce quarterly accounts for approval by the liquidator (1986 Rule 4.72).

489   The acts of a special manager are valid "notwithstanding any defect in his appointment or qualifications" (1986 Rule 4.69(6)). It is not clear how far the protection afforded by this provision extends. Clearly it must protect a third party in respect of any formal defect in the procedure for appointment, but the court's order is presumably sufficient in any event. No "qualifications" are in fact called for by the Act or subordinate legislation. It does not protect third parties against a special manager's *ultra vires* acts, *i.e.* beyond the powers conferred in the order of court. There is, however, no provision for lodging a copy of the court order with the registrar of companies or otherwise bringing its existence or terms to the notice of third parties. Except in the clearest of circumstances, therefore, third parties should exercise considerable caution in dealing with a "special manager," at least to the extent of examining the court order, and in any important transaction the express approval of the liquidator, and his execution of any deed or other document, should be required. The appointment does not, of course, derogate from the powers of the liquidator himself, but if the special manager exceeds his powers or acts to the detriment of the company or its creditors it is not clear whether the liquidator has any liability. The Insolvency Act, section 177(2) refers to the appointment by the court of "another person (than the liquidator) to manage the company's business or property" which suggests that the liquidator is not responsible, legally, for his actings. On the other hand, the 1986 Rule 4.70 refers to the special manager finding caution "to the person applying for his appointment," (*i.e.* the liquidator), not the court, and this suggests that the liquidator is ultimately responsible. It is suggested that the special manager is liable for his own actings and that the liquidator is not personally responsible for them once he has secured the appointment and duly satisfied the court (under 1986 Rule 4.70) that proper caution has been found. If there is a need to enforce the bond of caution, however, this will be done by the liquidator as the party to whom it is issued. 1986 Rule 4.69(6) will, however, protect the special manager from any liability on the ground that his appointment was defective.

CONTROL OF LIQUIDATORS

490 The liquidator acts under the general control of the court, and in a winding up by the court any creditor or contributory who is aggrieved may apply to it for an appropriate order on him (I.A., s.167(3)). Decisions in England to the effect that the court will only intervene if the liquidator has acted in bad faith or against all reason[83] must be regarded as unsound, in Scotland at least, where an application alleging merely a difference of opinion with the liquidator was heard and granted.[84] If a liquidator is in default with respect to the delivery of returns, accounts, etc., or the giving of notice, and refuses to comply within 14 days of being required to do so, the court may order compliance on the application of any creditor, contributory or the registrar of companies (I.A., s.170). If there is a liquidation committee, the liquidator must report regularly to it, and answer its reasonable requests for information.[85] The court's power to control remains even if the company has been dissolved and the liquidator does not reside in Scotland. If the liquidator is in breach of his duties to a creditor of the company he can be sued directly, without the necessity of first restoring the company to the register or declaring the dissolution void.[86]

Reduction of transactions

491 A transaction between the liquidator and an "associate"[87] may be reduced by the court under 1986 Rule 4.38. The court has discretion to refuse to grant an order. Application may be made by any interested

---

[83] See *Palmer*, para. 15.324; *cf. Leon* v. *York-o-Matic Ltd.* [1966] 1 W.L.R. 1450; 3 All E.R. 277. See also *Re Wyvern Developments Ltd.* [1974] 2 All E.R. 535.
[84] *Liquidator of Upper Clyde Shipbuilders Ltd.*, 1975 S.L.T. 39; *Ross* v. *Smith*, 1986 S.L.T. (Sh.Ct.) 59, 62; *Macrae* v. *Henderson*, 1989 S.L.T. 523.
[85] See para. 451, *ante.*
[86] *Lamey* v. *Winram*, 1987 S.L.T. 635.
[87] For the definition of this term see para. 517, *post.*

person, and the liquidator may be ordered to compensate the company for any loss. A transaction previously sanctioned by the court cannot be challenged. It is a defence to show that the transaction was for value and that the liquidator did not know, and had no reason to suppose, that the person concerned was an associate. This rule is without prejudice to other rules of law with respect to the liquidator's fiduciary duty.

Accounting obligations

492 The liquidator is to report to the creditors known to him and, unless he considers it inappropriate, the contributories, with respect to his proceedings within six weeks after the end of each "accounting period" or, alternatively, submit a report to meetings of creditors (and/or contributories) within that period. He may summarise and comment on any statement of affairs submitted to him[88] (1986 Rule 4.10). If he was previously the administrator of the company, he must send a copy of the statement circulated under 1986 Rule 2.7[89] to any creditor of whom he was not aware when acting as administrator (1986 Rule 4.10(4), added by the 1987 Amendments). The "accounting period" is each period of 26 weeks commencing with the date of commencement of winding up. The liquidator may shorten an accounting period (other than the first) if he wishes to accelerate payment of a dividend, with the consent of the liquidation committee (if any) and the next accounting period of 26 weeks will run from the end of the shortened period. The revised date must be recorded in the sederunt book.[90] Since the 1986 Rules do not disapply the Insolvency Act, section 142(5), if there is no liquidation committee, the shortening of an accounting period will require the consent of the court.

If the winding up is not concluded within a year, the liquidator must within 30 days of the expiration of that year, and thereafter at six-monthly intervals until the winding up is concluded, file a return (including a statement of receipts and payments, summarised balance sheet and progress report) with the registrar of companies on Forms 4.5 (Scot) and 4.6 (Scot) (I.A., s.192; 1986 Rule 4.11).

LEGAL EFFECT OF A WINDING-UP ORDER

493 A winding-up order operates for the benefit of all creditors and contributories (I.A., s.130(4)) and is deemed to be equivalent to completed diligence.[91] The property of the company is in the control of

---

[88] See para. 484, *ante*.
[89] See para. 138, *ante*.
[90] Bankruptcy (Scotland) Act 1985, s.52(1) and (6), as adopted with modifications by 1986 Rules 0.2(1), 4.16(2) and 4.68. The Bankruptcy (Scotland) Bill 1992 proposes to substitute "six months" for the period of 26 weeks specified in s.52.
[91] Bankruptcy (Scotland) Act 1985, s.37(1) as applied by I.A., s.185.

the liquidator (or the court if there is no liquidator) (I.A., s.144). Share transfers and dispositions, transfers, etc., of property after the commencement of a winding up by the court are void unless sanctioned by the court (I.A., s.127).[92] If the company has assets in England any attachment, sequestration, distress or execution against such assets after the commencement of the winding up is void (I.A., s.128). After a petition for winding up has been presented the court may sist proceedings against the company (I.A., s.126) and once a winding-up order has been made or a provisional liquidator appointed such proceedings are automatically sisted and cannot be continued except by leave of the court (I.A., s.130). These provisions are considered in detail below.

The directors' powers in relation to the assets and business of the company (and those of any other agent or servant having authority to act in its name) cease on the granting of a winding up order,[93] but only to the extent that such powers have passed to the liquidator. The powers to act in name of the company which do not pass to the liquidator and remain vested in the directors include the power to appeal against the winding up order itself, or to seek recall of the liquidator's appointment.[94]

Company pension schemes normally contain discretionary powers vested in the employer with respect to the provision of certain benefits and the disposal of any surplus in the fund. If these are fiduciary in character they cannot be exercised by the liquidator or receiver of the employer, but they may be exercised by the court.[95] If such powers are vested in the directors of the employer, the directors may continue to exercise them notwithstanding the liquidation.[96] Under the Social Security Pensions Act 1975, sections 57C and 57D (as inserted by the Social Security Act 1990) it is the duty of any insolvency practitioner (including a liquidator) appointed on or after November 12, 1990 to be satisfied that there is at least one "independent trustee" (as defined) of the scheme. Neither the Act nor the regulations,[97] however, indicate how this is to be achieved where there is no power of appointment granted by the trust deed which is available to the insolvency practitioner.[98]

The appointment of a liquidator does not affect the power of a

[92] See paras. 502 to 504, *post*.
[93] *Re Mawcon Ltd.* [1969] 1 All E.R. 188. This includes the power to pursue a claim which a shareholder would otherwise be entitled to maintain in name of the company (a "derivative action"); *Fargo Ltd.* v. *Godfray and others* [1986] 3 All E.R. 279.
[94] *Re Union Accident Insurance Co. Ltd.* [1972] 1 All E.R. 1105.
[95] *Mettoy Pension Trs. Ltd.* v. *Evans* [1990] 1 W.L.R. 1587.
[96] *Smith and Another, Petrs.*, 1969 S.L.T. (Notes) 94 (the court sanctioned an amendment of the scheme providing for the continued exercise of such powers after completion of the winding up and dissolution of the company).
[97] Occupational Pension Schemes (Independent Trustees) Regulations 1990 (S.I. 1990 No. 2075).
[98] See Talman, "Social Security Act 1990," 1991 J.L.S. 132.

receiver to enter into contracts in respect of that part of the property and undertaking of the company comprised in the charge by virtue of which he was appointed.[99]

Effect of liquidation on contracts

(a) Contracts other than contracts of employment

494 There is no power vested in a Scottish liquidator to disclaim onerous property, as in England under the Insolvency Act, sections 178 to 180. Contracts other than contracts of employment are not automatically terminated by liquidation, in the absence of a specific term to that effect. The liquidator has the option to take over any contract with future prestations in favour of the company independently of his decision in respect of any other contract, or to terminate it and concede a ranking for damages.[1] The liquidator must intimate his decision within a reasonable time, having regard to the nature of the contract, failing which he will be deemed to have abandoned the intention to proceed with it.[2] Any party who has a contract with the company may apply to the court to have the contract rescinded, subject to any claim for damages (as a debt in the liquidation) which the court thinks just (I.A., s.186). A provision in a lease which purports to exclude liquidators except with the landlord's prior consent does not have the effect of terminating the lease *ipso facto* on the liquidator's appointment, but entitles the landlord to determine it if the liquidator proposes to adopt the lease, or delays unreasonably in intimating his decision.[3]

A pre-liquidation contract to grant security is incapable of being adopted since this would amount to an illegal preference, and likewise the liquidator cannot adopt a contract whose unfulfilled provisions carry no advantage to the company.[4]

The liquidator cannot adopt contracts which, prior to the liquidation, existed as obligations binding in honour only and not legally enforceable (such as may arise from insurance brokerage practice) however much they formed part of the custom of the trade in which the company was engaged. There is no inherent power in the Scottish courts to overrule legal rights on equitable considerations, as claimed by the English courts.[5] In the event of the liquidator being duly authorised to carry on the business of the company, however, it may be proper to regard the discharge of such obligations as a legitimate

---

[99] I.A., s.55 and Sched. 2; see also para. 504, *post.*
[1] *Gray's Trs.* v. *Benhar Coal Co.* (1881) 9 R. 225; *Asphaltic Limestone Concrete Co. Ltd.* v. *Glasgow Corporation,* 1907 S.C. 463; 14 S.L.T. 706; *Clyde Marine Insurance Co.* v. *Renwick,* 1924 S.C. 113; S.L.T. 41; *Turnbull* v. *Liquidator of Scottish County Investment Co.,* 1939 S.C. 5; 1938 S.L.T. 584.
[2] *Crown Estate Commissioners* v. *Liquidators of Highland Engineering Ltd.,* 1975 S.L.T. 58.
[3] *Ibid.,* n. 71.
[4] *Turnbull* v. *Liquidator of Scottish County Investment Co., supra.*
[5] *e.g., Clark* v. *Texaco Ltd.* [1975] 1 All E.R. 453.

aspect of the carrying on of the business.[6] The liquidator may ratify on behalf of the company acts, in themselves invalid, which the company in general meeting could have ratified.[7]

(b) Contracts of employment

495 A winding-up order or a resolution for voluntary winding up is presumed to constitute constructive notice of termination of all contracts of employment with the company. If the winding up is on the grounds of insolvency, an employee is entitled to leave the services of the company immediately and claim damages. If he continues in the services of the company a separate contract may arise expressly or by implication between the liquidator and the employee.[8]

Prior to the Companies Act 1980, section 74 (now I.A., s.187 and s.719 of the 1985 Act), a gratuitous payment to employees (or former employees) of a company going into liquidation might be challenged as *ultra vires* on the grounds that it was contrary to the best interests of the company, which no longer had any interest in maintaining good relations with its employees since it had no continuing goodwill to protect, unless there was power to make such payments within the objects of its memorandum.[9] Section 719(1) provides that the powers of a company shall, if they would not otherwise do so, be deemed to include power to make provision for the benefit of persons employed or formerly employed by the company or any of its subsidiaries in connection with the cessation or the transfer of all or part of its undertaking or that of its subsidiary. The power conferred by this subsection may be exercised (s.719(2)) "notwithstanding that its exercise is not in the best interests of the company." Section 719(3) provides for the manner in which such payments must be sanctioned by the company.

Section 719(4) provides that any payment under section 719 must be provided, in the case of a payment before the commencement of winding up, out of profits available for distribution as dividend. The Insolvency Act, section 187(3) provides that if the company is in liquidation a payment under section 719 may be made out of assets available for distribution to the members. The Insolvency Act, section 187(1) provides that the liquidator may (but cannot be compelled to) implement any gratuitous provision for employees, etc., which has been validly sanctioned by the company prior to the commencement of winding up. In the case of a winding up by the court a creditor or contributory may apply to the court for an order under the Insolvency Act, section 187(4) to control the liquidator's exercise of this power.

---

[6] *Clyde Marine Insurance Co.* v. *Renwick, supra.*
[7] *Alexander Ward & Co. Ltd.* v. *Samyang Navigation Co. Ltd.*, 1975 S.C. (H.L.) 27; S.L.T. 126.
[8] *Day* v. *Tait* (1900) 8 S.L.T. 40. See further *Palmer*, para. 8.2015; Miller, *Industrial Law in Scotland*, p. 391.
[9] *Gibson's Exr.* v. *Gibson*, 1980 S.L.T. 2; *Parke* v. *Daily News Ltd.* [1962] Ch. 927.

The Insolvency Act, section 187(2) authorises a liquidator to make such provision, even if it has not been previously sanctioned by the company, provided that all liabilities, expenses, etc., have been met and he obtains the sanction of an ordinary resolution of the company or (if the memorandum or articles so require) a resolution passed by more than a simple majority. While a resolution of the directors may sanction such a payment prior to the winding up (assuming that it is authorised in the memorandum or articles), in a winding up the sanction of the directors would not be sufficient to fulfill the requirements of the Insolvency Act, section 187(2). The Insolvency Act, section 187(5) provides that the common law and statutory rules providing for the distribution of the property of the company to its members after satisfaction of all liabilities, etc., shall be modified to accommodate any payment validly made under these provisions.

The effect of these provisions is to confer upon a gratuitous payment for employees, etc., what is in effect a deferred ranking in the liquidation after ordinary creditors but prior to the claims of members. Section 719(2) does not prevent a challenge by the liquidator of any such payment which is made by a company prior to the commencement of winding up. In principle, such a payment should be open to challenge as a gratuitous alienation or unfair preference, but the liquidator would probably be able to challenge it more readily on the grounds that it had not been made out of profits available for dividend (s.719(4)). There appears to be no protection afforded to an employee against such a challenge, even if he received it in good faith and without knowledge of the financial position of the company. If, on the other hand, the payment is not made under section 719 but in terms of powers contained in the memorandum or articles, it may be argued that the requirements of section 719(4) as to the provision of funds from profits available for dividend do not apply.

PERSONAL LIABILITY OF LIQUIDATORS

496 A liquidator is not personally liable for the obligations of the company, but he is liable to the creditors or contributories for negligence in the performance of his duties. Such a claim cannot be maintained (in the absence of fraud or concealment of material facts) where the court (or liquidation committee) has sanctioned the act complained of.[10] If, having reasonable grounds for believing he was entitled to do so, he seizes or disposes of property which does not belong to the company, he is not liable for loss or damage (unless caused by his own negligence). Also, he has a lien in respect of his expenses over the property or its proceeds (I.A., s.234(3) and (4)). The protection afforded by the Insolvency Act, section 234 extends only to tangible property and not to incorporeal moveables.[11]

---

[10] *Highland Engineering Ltd.* v. *Anderson*, 1979 S.L.T. 122.
[11] *Welsh Development Agency* v. *Export Finance Co. Ltd.*, *The Times*, November 28, 1991.

If a liquidator has failed to obtain the proper sanction for the exercise of his powers he incurs personal liability but may be relieved of this by the court on cause shown.[12]

A liquidator who enters appearance and defends an action warrants the sufficiency of the company's assets to meet any expenses to which the pursuer may be found entitled, and accordingly incurs personal liability if the assets are insufficient.[13] If the court considers the conduct of the liquidator to be blameworthy, to the extent that he should be deprived of his right of relief against the assets of the company, the decree for expenses must state in terms that the liquidator is found "personally" liable.[14]

A liquidator in a members' voluntary liquidation is not entitled to recover from a liquidator subsequently appointed by the court, from funds required to meet creditors' claims, expenses incurred by him in endeavouring to implement a scheme for reconstruction under the Insolvency Act, sections 110 to 111.[15]

Proceedings against the company

497 When a winding-up order has been made or a provisional liquidator appointed actions or other proceedings[16] cannot be commenced or continued against the company except by leave of the court and subject to such conditions as the court may impose (I.A., s.130(2) and (3)). The expenses of a successful unopposed application for leave are, unless the court otherwise directs, to be added to the applicant's claim (I.A., s.199). The leave of the court is not required for a counter-claim in proceedings brought by the company, if it is pleaded by way of compensation, but leave is required to counter-claim for an amount in excess of the company's claim.[17]

The main purpose of section 130 is to prevent an accumulation of actions against an insolvent company, and the question of whether to grant or refuse sanction is one of expediency having regard to the interests of creditors generally.[18] Accordingly, while proceedings for which sanction has not been obtained are incompetent,[19] the pursuer

---

[12] *Re Associated Travel Leisure & Services Ltd.* [1978] 2 All E.R. 273.
[13] *Sinclair* v. *The Thurso Pavement Syndicate Ltd.* (1903) 11 S.L.T. 364; *Liquidator of the Consolidated Coal Co. of Canada* v. *Peddie* (1877) 5. R. 393, 413; *Anderson's Trs.* v. *Donaldson & Co.,* 1908 S.C. 385; 15 S.L.T. 702.
[14] *Kilmarnock Theatre Co.* v. *Buchanan,* 1911 S.C. 607; S.L.T. 225; *Cleghorn* v. *Fairgreave,* 1982 S.L.T. (Sh.Ct.) 17.
[15] *Liquidator of Scottish Assurance Corp.* v. *Miller* (1881) 18 R. 494; I.A., ss.110–111 are discussed in *Palmer,* paras. 12.101 *et seq.*.
[16] "Proceedings" should be construed widely: *Langley Constructions (Brixham) Ltd.* v. *Wells, infra; Re J. Burrows (Leeds) Ltd.* [1982] 2 All E.R. 882; and may include distress proceedings (*i.e.* diligence): *Re Memco Engineering Ltd.* [1985] 3 All E.R. 267.
[17] *Langley Constructions (Brixham) Ltd.* v. *Wells* [1969] 1 W.L.R. 503; 2 All E.R. 46.
[18] *Cf. Re Aro Co. Ltd.* [1980] 1 All E.R. 1067.
[19] *Grieve* v. *International Exhibition Assoc.* (1890) 29 S.L.R. 20; *Radford & Bright Ltd.* v. *Stevenson,* (1904) 6 F. 429; 11 S.L.T. 695.

should have an opportunity to apply for leave to proceed.[20] If the liquidator does not invoke the Insolvency Act, section 130(2) and (3) it is not for the court to apply it *ex proprio motu*.[21]

The Insolvency Act, section 130(2) and (3) cannot be invoked so as to validate diligence cut down by the Insolvency Act, section 185.[22]

An order by the court having jurisdiction to wind up the company is applicable to proceedings in any court in the United Kingdom (I.A., s.426(1) and (2)).[23] The Scottish court will not question the *ex facie* competent order of the court of jurisdiction in granting or refusing leave.[24] Questions touching on the internal conduct of the liquidation should, as a general rule, be disposed of in the court supervising the liquidation.[25]

Where the proceedings are in a foreign court, outwith Great Britain and Northern Ireland, there appears to be a divergence of opinion between the Scottish and English courts. It has been held in Scotland that, in principle, the Insolvency Act, section 130(2) and (3) is applicable and if the pursuers are subject to the jurisdiction an order restraining the foreign proceedings can be granted.[26] If the order could not be enforced because of want of jurisdiction, however, the court will not grant a restraining order.[27] In England it has been held that the Insolvency Act, section 130(2) and (3) does not apply to proceedings furth of the United Kingdom, although alternative equitable grounds for granting a restraining order exist provided that it can be made effective by virtue of the plaintiff being subject to the jurisdiction.[28] The Insolvency Act, section 426(4), (5) and (11) now provides that courts in the Channel Islands, Isle of Man or any other jurisdiction to which the section is extended by statutory instrument may require the assistance of United Kingdom courts in enforcing orders in insolvency proceedings.

498   Since the question of whether leave to proceed should be granted is one of expediency, precedents drawn from English practice[29] should be treated with caution. The court has to determine whether, in the particular circumstances, the balance of convenience lies with allowing

---

[20] *D. M. Stevenson & Co.* v. *Radford & Bright* (1902) 10 S.L.T. 82; *Martin* v. *Port of Manchester Insurance Co. Ltd.*, 1934 S.C. 143.
[21] *Hill* v. *Black*, 1914 S.C. 913; 2 S.L.T. 123; *Sinclair* v. *Thurso Pavement Syndicate Ltd.* (1903) 11 S.L.T. 364.
[22] *Allan* v. *Cowan* (1892) 20 R. 36; *Radford & Bright* v. *Stevenson*, *supra*.
[23] *Re Dynamics Corp. of America* [1972] 3 All E.R. 1046; *Martin* v. *Port of Manchester Insurance Co. Ltd.*, *supra*.
[24] *Queensland Mercantile & Agency Co. Ltd.* v. *Australasian Investment Co. Ltd.* (1888) 15 R. 935.
[25] *Carbon (New) Syndicate Ltd.* v. *Seton* (1904) 12 S.L.T. 191.
[26] *California Redwood Co. Ltd.* v. *Walker* (1886) 13 R. 816; *Redwood Co. Ltd.* v. *Merchant Banking Co. of London* (1886) 13 R. 1202.
[27] *California Redwood Co. Ltd.* v. *Walker*, *supra*.
[28] *Re Vocalion (Foreign) Ltd.* [1932] 2 Ch. 196.
[29] See examples at *Palmer*, para. 15.443.

an action to proceed in order to establish whether a claim exists against the company or to restrain proceedings at least until the liquidator has adjudicated on the claim. Leave to proceed should normally be granted where the interests of third parties are involved.[30] Leave will be refused if the action seeks to constitute a claim of debt or damages which can be resolved in the liquidation.[31] If the action is to reduce an allotment of shares, leave to proceed may (in the exercise of the court's discretion) be granted if the proceedings are well advanced or an issue is raised which can more readily be determined by a court other than the court of liquidation.[32] A counter-claim restricted to such sum as will extinguish the liquidator's claim by set-off does not require leave to proceed under the Insolvency Act, section 130(2) and (3).[33]

Security holders cannot, of course, be deprived of their legitimate rights, and may take such proceedings against the company as may be required to enforce them without leave of the court.[34]

The Insolvency Act, section 126 governs the position after a winding-up petition has been presented but before the Insolvency Act, section 130(2) and (3) takes effect. The company, any creditor or contributory may apply to the court having jurisdiction to wind up the company for an order restraining further proceedings in any action or proceedings against the company (I.A., s.126(1) (b)); if, however, the action or proceedings are pending in the High Court or Court of Appeal in England or Northern Ireland the application must be made in the court where the action is pending (I.A., s.126(1)(a)). The court may make a conditional order. An order under the Insolvency Act, section 126(1)(b) is effective throughout the United Kingdom.[35]

The Insolvency Act, section 126 will not be applied to prevent a creditor from proceeding with his claim to the point of decree[36] but it is appropriate to restrain diligence either by a particular creditor,[37] or, after a meeting of creditors directed by the court has expressed its agreement, by creditors generally.[38]

Any attachment, sequestration, distress or execution against the assets of a Scottish company situated in England after the commencement of compulsory winding up is void (I.A., s.128(2)), but

---

[30] *Coclas* v. *Bruce Peebles* (1908) 16 S.L.T. 7.

[31] *Coclas* v. *Bruce Peebles, supra; Main* v. *Azotine Ltd.*, 1916 2 S.L.T. 252.

[32] *London & Scottish Banking & Discount Corp.* (1895) 3 S.L.T. 21; *James Young & Sons Ltd.* (1900) 7 S.L.T. 301.

[33] *G. & A. (Hotels) Ltd.* v. *T. H. B. Marketing Services Ltd.*, 1983 S.L.T. 497.

[34] *Atholl Hydropathic Co. Ltd.* v. *Scottish Provincial Assurance Co. Ltd.* (1886) 13 R. 818; *Anderson's Trs.* v. *Donaldson & Co. Ltd.*, 1908 S.C. 38; 15 S.L.T. 409. In these cases a heritable creditor and a feudal superior were allowed to proceed with actions of poinding of the ground, which would now be subject to the limitations expressed in the Bankruptcy (Scotland) Act 1985, s.37(6), as applied by I.A., s.185 (see *infra*, para. 500). See also *Bell's Trs.* v. *The Holmes Oil Co.* (1901) 8 S.L.T. 360.

[35] *Re Dynamics Corporation of America* [1972] 3 All E.R. 1046.

[36] *Benhar Coal Co. Ltd.* v. *Sime* (1878) 6 R. 316.

[37] *New Glenduffhill Coal Co. Ltd.* v. *Muir* (1882) 10 R. 372.

[38] *Benhar Coal Co. Ltd.* (1879) 6 R. 706.

the English court may validate it under the Insolvency Act, section 130(2) and (3).[39]

Effect of liquidation on diligence

499 Rules for cutting down diligence executed within 60 days prior to the commencement of a winding up were introduced into Scots law by the Companies Act 1886, section 3. This followed criticism of the absence of such rules in a case where creditors who had not executed diligence applied unsuccessfully for the appointment of a trustee in bankruptcy on the assets of a company.[40] Originally consolidated as section 623 of the 1985 Act, these rules were amended by the Bankruptcy (Scotland) Act 1985, Schedule 7, paragraph 21, which came into force on April 1, 1986 and apply to any winding up which commenced on or after that date. These provisions are now found as the Insolvency Act, section 185, but are inconveniently expressed in the form of adaptations for companies of the rules in personal bankruptcies contained in the Bankruptcy (Scotland) Act 1985, section 37. It is to be hoped that, on the next occasion for consolidation or amendment, the need for cross-reference of this kind will be eliminated. References in the remainder of paragraphs 499 and 500 to "section 37" are to the Bankruptcy (Scotland) Act 1985, section 37 as adapted by the Insolvency Act, section 185.

In the case of a winding up by the court, section 37 takes effect as from the date of the court's winding-up order, not the date of commencement of the winding up (s.37(1); the Insolvency Act, s.185(3)).[41] As from that date the order has effect in relation to all forms of diligence done before or after its date in respect of any part of the property of the company as if it were a duly recorded decree of adjudication, an arrestment in execution and decree of furthcoming, an arrestment in execution and warrant of sale, and a completed poinding, in favour of the company's creditors generally (s.37(1)). The winding-up order is thus made equivalent to completed diligence in respect of heritage, incorporeal and corporeal moveables. It is, however, subject to such security rights as would prevail over the holder of completed diligence in the forms described in section 37(1), which include the right of a landlord entitled (by virtue of his common

---

[39] *Re Aro Co. Ltd.* [1980] 1 All E.R. 1067.
[40] *Standard Property Investment Co. Ltd.* v. *Dunblane Hydropathic Co. Ltd.* (1884) 12 R. 328, 334.
[41] *Morrison* v. *Integer Systems Control Ltd.*, 1989 S.C.L.R. 495 (Sh.Ct.) In a voluntary winding up s.37 takes effect from the date of commencement, since I.A., s.185(3) does not apply. Under the former law (s.623) the equivalent provisions applied with respect to the commencement of winding up in all cases. This has the unfortunate effect that diligence done 60 days before or even after a resolution for voluntary winding up will not necessarily be cut down if there is a subsequent order for winding up by the court although it would be if the voluntary winding up continued. This is subject, however, to I.A., s.127 (see paras. 502 to 504, *post*).

law hypothec) to sequestrate moveables for rent.[42] No arrestment or poinding executed within 60 days prior to the winding-up order (or later) is effectual, and any assets arrested or poinded (or the proceeds of their sale) must be delivered to the liquidator (s.37(4)).[43] A creditor whose arrestment or poinding has been cut down is entitled to a preference payable out of the assets or funds concerned, or the proceeds of sale, in respect of the expense incurred in carrying out such diligence, but this only applies to diligence executed prior to the winding-up order which is cut down under the 60-day rule (s.37(5)). The liquidator has the right to have an ineffectual arrestment or poinding recalled.[44]

Where an arrestment is made within the 60-day period, and the company satisfies the claim, the diligence thereby lapses and the liquidator cannot reclaim the money paid simply on the basis of section 37; he may, however, be able to claim on the grounds of fraudulent or unfair preference.[45] Unlike the position in receiverships,[46] an arrestment prior to the 60-day period creates a valid preference.[47] Section 37 also applies to the property of an English company (in liquidation) which is situated in Scotland (I.A., s.185(4)). This means that the liquidator of an English company can cut down diligences executed in Scotland under the Scottish law of bankruptcy (as adapted). It appears, however, that the liquidator of a Scottish company cannot avoid executions put in force against its assets in England before the commencement of winding up; the Insolvency Act, sections 185 and 37 do not extend to England, and the Insolvency Act, sections 183 and 184, which invalidate such executions, do not apply to a Scottish company. Executions in England after commencement of winding up are subject to the restraint of the Insolvency Act, section 128.[48]

500   An inhibition is only a personal diligence, which creates no *nexus* over the heritable property of the company,[49] although it may be an effectual preference over the debtor's reversionary interest in a competition with other creditors and in the absence of liquidation.[50] Since section 37(1)(*a*) puts the liquidator in the position of the holder of

---

[42] *Scottish Metropolitan Property Co.* v. *Sutherland Ltd.*, 1934 S.L.T. (Sh.Ct.) 62; *Cumbernauld Development Corpn.* v. *Mustone Ltd.*, 1983 S.L.T. 497; *cf.* Bankruptcy (Scotland) Act 1985, s.33(2) and (3)).

[43] *Allan* v. *Cowan* (1892), 20 R. 36.

[44] *Taymech Ltd.* v. *Rush and Tompkins Ltd.*, 1990 S.L.T. 681.

[45] *Johnston* v. *Cluny Trustees*, 1957 S.C. 184; S.L.T. 293 (for fraudulent and unfair preferences see *infra*, paras. 509 to 511).

[46] *Lord Advocate* v. *Royal Bank of Scotland*, 1977 S.C. 155; 1978 S.L.T. 38. See para. 221, *ante*.

[47] *Commercial Aluminium Windows Ltd.* v. *Cumbernauld Development Corp.*, 1987 S.L.T. (Sh.Ct.) 91, *Morrison* v. *Integer Systems Control Ltd.*, *supra*.

[48] See para. 498, *ante*.

[49] *McGowan* v. *A. Middlemas & Sons Ltd.*, 1977 S.L.T. (Sh.Ct.) 41.

[50] *Abbey National Building Society* v. *Shaik Azij*, 1981 S.L.T. (Sh.Ct.) 29; *Armour and Mycroft, Petrs.*, 1983 S.L.T. 453.

a duly recorded decree of adjudication he has a priority over any creditor whose diligence is not complete, such as the holder of an inhibition or even an unrecorded decree of adjudication. The liquidator can therefore proceed with a sale notwithstanding the existence of an inhibition.[51] He will, however, be forced to discharge the inhibition (or seek to have it recalled) if he has bound himself expressly or by implication to provide "clear searches."[52] He has the right to have an ineffectual inhibition recalled[53] Section 37(2) and (3) introduced for the first time an express provision invalidating inhibitions in similar terms to the cutting down of other forms of diligence. No inhibition taking effect within 60 days prior to the winding-up order can create an effectual preference. Any payment for discharge of the inhibition after the order is to be made to the liquidator. The liquidator is to enjoy the same rights to challenge the voluntary acts of the debtor company as would be vested in the holder of the ineffectual inhibition. This means that any voluntary alienation (gratuitous or onerous) by the inhibited company (which is barred by the inhibition) can be challenged on these grounds in addition to any right of challenge as a gratuitous alienation or unfair preference. Involuntary alienations, such as a disposition in implement of missives completed prior to the inhibition, are not open to challenge on this basis. If the company has paid the inhibitor for a discharge prior to the winding-up order the transaction cannot be challenged under section 37, although it is likely to be open to attack as an unfair preference (see below). If the inhibition was effected prior to the 60-day period the liquidator has to rely on his position under section 37(1), as discussed above.

A creditor holding a *debitum fundi*, such as a feudal superior, the creditor in a contract of ground annual or a heritable creditor (if not *ex facie* the owner) has a limited security over moveables on the ground over which his debt subsists, which he exercises by "poinding of the ground." Such procedure is not "diligence," nor does it require leave of the court, as it is strictly speaking the enforcement of a security.[54] The position of the holder of such a security has (with a limited exception in favour of a heritable creditor, but not others, entitled to poind the ground) been assimilated to that of a creditor doing diligence. A heritable creditor may obtain security by this process even after liquidation, but only to the extent of the interest due for the current half-year and one year's arrears. Subject to this no poinding of the ground which has not been completed by sale of the effects within 60 days of the liquidation is effective (s.37(6)).

---

[51] It is, however, competent for the inhibitor to seek interdict against such a disposal; *Murray* v. *Long*, 1992 S.L.T. 292.

[52] *Dryburgh* v. *Gordon* (1896) 24 R. 1; *Armour and Mycroft, Petrs, supra*. But this would not apply if the inhibition was, *ex facie* the records, no longer effective (*Newcastle Building Society* v. *White*, 1987 S.L.T. (Sh.Ct.) 81, 85).

[53] *Taymech Ltd.* v. *Rush and Tompkins Ltd.*, 1990 S.L.T. 681.

[54] See para. 498 and n. 86, *ante*.

If diligence has been recalled on consignation of a sum, the consigned fund is not available to the liquidator.[55]

Third party insurance

501 When a company which is being wound up is insured against liabilities to third parties, and a liability is incurred by the company to such a third party, the company's rights against the insurer are transferred to the third party.[56] Until the company's liability has been established, however, the creditor will require to maintain his claim against the liquidator.[57] The insurer cannot plead set-off in respect of unpaid premiums.[58] If the insured company has been dissolved before its liability has been established, the injured third party cannot assert the rights of the defunct company against its insurers until it has been restored to the register under section 651.[59] The Companies Act 1989, section 141 extended the period within which restoration is permitted, which is normally two years after dissolution, if this is for the purpose of pursuing a claim for personal injuries.[60]

DISPOSITIONS AND TRANSFERS AFTER A WINDING-UP ORDER

502 In a winding up by the court, any disposition of the property of the company, including incorporeal moveables, and any transfer of shares or alteration of the status of members after the commencement of winding up is void unless the court orders otherwise (I.A., s.127).[61] The validating order may be made even before winding up commences.[62] After commencement of the winding up a shareholder retains enough locus to apply for or to oppose an order under the Insolvency Act, section 127, even if the application relates to dispositions of property and not to share transfers.[63] For the purposes of the Insolvency Act, section 127 the property of the company is the sum total of its rights and assets, and it is immaterial whether the "disposition" under attack is granted by the company or by a third party, so long as it relates to company property.[64] The granting of a floating charge is a "disposition" for the purposes of the Insolvency

---

[55] *Hawking* v. *Hafton House Ltd.*, 1990 S.L.T. 496.
[56] Third Party (Rights Against Insurers) Act 1930, s.1; see also Road Traffic Act 1988, ss.151, 152.
[57] *Vickers Oceanic Ltd.* v. *Ross (Liquidator of Speedcranes Ltd.)*, 1985 J.L.S. 85.
[58] *Murray* v. *Legal and General Assurance Society* [1970] 2 Q.B. 495.
[59] *Bradley* v. *Eagle Star Insurance Ltd.* [1989] B.C.L.C. 469 (H.L.).
[60] See further para. 537, *post*.
[61] *Nelson & Mitchell* v. *City of Glasgow Bank* (1879) 6 R. (H.L.) 66; *Dodds* v. *Cosmopolitan Insurance Co. Ltd.*, 1915 S.C. 992; 2 S.L.T. 106.
[62] *A. I. Levy (Holdings) Ltd.* [1964] Ch. 19; *Operator Control Cabs Ltd.* [1970] 3 All E.R. 657.
[63] *Argentum Reductions (U.K.) Ltd.* [1975] 1 All E.R. 608; *Burton & Deacon Ltd.* [1977] 1 All E.R. 631.
[64] *J. Leslie Engineers Co. Ltd.* [1976] 2 All E.R. 85.

Act, section 127.[65] Although retrospective sanction is competent,[66] a transaction to which the section applies but which has not been sanctioned is void *ab initio* and not merely voidable at the instance of, *e.g.* the liquidator. Accordingly, third parties can obtain no valid right or title as a result of an unapproved disposition.

Credits paid into the company's bank account and payments to third parties debited against that account are, in principle, "dispositions of property" whether the account is in credit or debit at the time. Such payments are invalid under the Insolvency Act, section 127 unless sanctioned by the court.[67]

In the case of a solvent company, if the court is satisfied that the directors believe a disposition is necessary or expedient in the interest of the company, and that their reasons are tenable, a contributory's opposition will not prevent the disposition being sanctioned unless he adduces compelling evidence to show that it is injurious to the company.[68]

In the case of an insolvent company the applicant for a validation order under the Insolvency Act, section 127 must satisfy the court that the exercise of its discretion in favour of granting the order, whether in respect of transactions that have already taken place or for proposed transactions, would be just and fair in all the circumstances.[69] The creditors are entitled to assume that the court will sanction only such dispositions as are shown to be beneficial to the company.[70] The considerations which should guide the court have been subjected to exhaustive review by the Court of Appeal in England, in a case[71] which concerned the retrospective validation under the Insolvency Act, section 127 of operations on a company's bank account which the bank allowed to continue in the interval between presentation of the petition and the granting of the winding-up order.

503   The duty of the court under the Insolvency Act, section 127 is to protect the unsecured creditors. It should not allow particular transactions, or a series of transactions such as the carrying on of the business of the company, under which one or more pre-liquidation creditors are paid in full at the expense of other such creditors, unless there are special circumstances. If a bank (or a party in a like position) transacts with the company without first obtaining a validation order it

---

[65] *Site Preparations Ltd.* v. *Buchan Development Co. Ltd.*, 1983 S.L.T. 317.
[66] *Gray's Inn Construction Co. Ltd.* [1980] 1 All E.R. 814.
[67] *Gray's Inn Construction Co. Ltd.* [1980] 1 All E.R. 814; *Re McGuinness Bros. (U.K.) Ltd* (1987) 3 B.C.C. 571; see *Palmer*, para. 15.442.
[68] *Burton & Deacon Ltd., supra.*
[69] *Burton & Deacon Ltd., supra; A. I. Levy (Holdings) Ltd., supra; In re Tramway Building & Construction Co. Ltd.* [1988] 2 W.L.R. 640.
[70] *Steane's (Bournemouth) Ltd.* [1950] 1 All E.R. 21; *Clifton Place Garage Ltd.* [1970] Ch. 477; *Re Fairway Graphics Ltd.* [1991] B.C.L.C. 468.
[71] *Gray's Inn Construction Co. Ltd.* [1980] 1 All E.R. 814. But equitable considerations are paramount (*In re Tramway Building and Construction Co. Ltd., supra*).

does so at the risk of its transactions being invalidated. In exercising its discretion the court will be guided principally by the concern to validate such transactions as would be beneficial for the company and its creditors, which the court suggested would be capable of being placed in one of the following categories:

1. provided that there is no intention to confer a preference on the creditor, transactions carried out in the ordinary course of business and in ignorance of the presentation of the petition would normally be validated;
2. transactions which are entirely post-liquidation would normally be validated;
3. transactions which increase or preserve the value of the assets would normally be validated, even if this meant the payment in full of a pre-liquidation debt, such as the payment of suppliers to permit the company to continue in business.[72]

If the question is whether to allow the company to continue in business, by permitting the bank to maintain its account, the court would expect the bank to freeze the existing account of the company and any subsequent dealings should be carried out on a separate account. The bank should obtain assurances from the directors and such other precautions as it can adopt to ensure that no pre-liquidation debts would be paid out of the fresh account and that all transactions on that account would be in the normal course of business. If the bank chose to allow the company to continue to operate its account without a validation order it exposed itself to the risk of being liable (in addition) for trading losses incurred during that period. The bank should exercise diligence in obtaining adequate information about the affairs of the company and take suitable precautions to ensure that a trading loss is not incurred during that period.

If an order is sought after the disposition, the court will consider whether authority would have been granted if it had been sought before the disposition. It will not, however, necessarily approve a disposition retrospectively, merely on the grounds that it would have done so prospectively. The court will inquire into all the relevant facts and will not necessarily refuse authorisation for a disposition which was granted negligently or deliberately; there might have been legitimate reasons for not applying in advance.[73] Completion after liquidation of an unconditional enforceable contract entered into before winding up commenced will normally be sanctioned.[74]

504   A transfer of fully paid shares in a limited company will be permitted subject to the consent of the liquidator, since the creditors have no

---

[72] See *Denning v. John Hudson & Co., Financial Times*, May 8, 1992, (C.A.).
[73] *In re Tramway and Building Construction Co. Ltd., supra.*
[74] *Re French's Wine Bar* [1987] B.C.L.C. 499.

interest in the matter.[75] An assignation of the shareholder's interest in the company does not require sanction under the Insolvency Act, section 127 since the assignor remains a contributory.[76] Where preference shareholders had a right to convert their shares into ordinary shares, a notice given before the commencement of winding up could take effect afterwards.[77]

As a result of powers granted to him by the Conveyancing and Feudal Reform (Scotland) Act 1970, the holder of a standard security is, however, able to grant a valid disposition notwithstanding the Insolvency Act, section 127.[78] In *United Dominions Trust Ltd.*,[79] a creditor had obtained a warrant under section 24 of the 1970 Act from the sheriff court (which was not the court having jurisdiction in the winding up, *i.e.* for the purposes of the Insolvency Act, s.127) authorising him to sell the heritable property of a company in liquidation. The Court of Session, in the winding-up process, held that no further action was required and to that extent the Insolvency Act, section 127 had by necessary inference from the 1970 Act been amended. The opinion was also expressed that, even without a warrant under section 24, the provisions of the 1970 Act, in particular section 20, authorise the holder of a standard security to sell and grant a disposition of the property subject thereto, without any approval under the Insolvency Act, section 127. The holder of any other form of heritable security, it was suggested, is, however, still subject to the Insolvency Act, section 127.

It has also been suggested that *intra vires* dispositions by a duly appointed receiver while a winding-up order is in force might be open to attack, on a strict interpretation of section 127. Such a view appears to be at variance with the statutory powers of a receiver[80] and also ignores the general proposition that the exercise of a security holder's rights is external to the liquidation (and I.A., s.127 only applies "*In a winding up by the court*"). Nevertheless, it has been proposed that as some doubt remains, the disposal of property by a receiver should be expressly excluded from the Insolvency Act, section 127.[81] If section 127 applies, however, the requirement to obtain sanction from the court is essential for the validity of the transaction.

TRANSACTIONS BY INSOLVENT COMPANIES

505 Many of the amendments to the Companies Act 1985 which were

---

[75] *Benhar Coal Co. Ltd.* (1987) 6 R. 707; *Surma Valley Saw Mills Ltd.*, 1917 S.C. 105; 1916 2 S.L.T. 302.

[76] *Jackson* v. *Elphick* (1902) 10 S.L.T. 146.

[77] *Re Blaina Colliery* [1926] W.N. 30.

[78] Then s.227 of the 1948 Act.

[79] 1977 S.L.T. (Notes) 56.

[80] I.A., s.55 and Sched. 2; see paras. 214 and 215, *ante*.

[81] Scot. Law Com. Memorandum No. 72, "Floating Charges and Receivers" (1986), paras. 3.95 and 3.96.

effected by the Bankruptcy (Scotland) Act 1985 and the Insolvency Act 1985 concern the position of a company which has continued trading or disposed of its property while insolvent. In principle, an insolvent company is entitled to continue trading provided that it does not alienate its property gratuitously or without adequate consideration (contrary to common law or I.A., s.242), grant an unfair preference to a particular creditor (contrary to common law or I.A., s.243) or enter into a transaction whereby it obtains credit on extortionate terms (contrary to I.A., s.244).[82] The first two of these (I.A., ss.242 and 243) reflect, with substantial amendments, the former law on the reduction of "gratuitous alienations" and "fraudulent preferences." The third prohibition (I.A., s.244) is new, although perhaps implied by the principles of the old law. In addition, floating charges by the company may be invalidated under the Insolvency Act, section 245 (substantially amending the previous law under s.617). These provisions are considered further below, in paragraphs 506 to 517. The directors (and others) may incur criminal or civil liability, or be subject to disqualification if the company carries on business with intent to defraud creditors (contrary to I.A., s.213) or "wrongfully" (contrary to I.A., s.214), both of which require the company to be insolvent at some point. These latter provisions are considered elsewhere.[83]

The reforms relating to gratuitous alienations and unfair preferences are largely as recommended by the Scottish Law Commission in 1982.[84] A company is not permitted to grant a trust deed for behoof of its creditors[85] or a floating charge in favour of its creditors generally.[86]

Apart from the specific time limits applicable to the Insolvency Act, sections 242 to 245, a transaction may be challenged at any time short of the relevant prescriptive period, although delay may affect the burden of proof of insolvency.[87] Claims for repayment, restitution or repetition prescribe after five years[88] but actions concluding only for reduction may be brought for up to 10 years in the case of deeds recorded in the property register[89] or 20 years in other cases.[90] Claims based on fraud (which would appear to include the reduction of fraudulent preferences at common law) are subject to the long negative prescription of 20 years.[91]

Gratuitous alienations

506 At common law, any alienation of property is reducible if the

---

[82] *Nordic Travel Ltd.* v. *Scotprint Ltd.*, 1980 S.L.T. 189; S.C. 1.
[83] See paras. 522 and 523, *infra*.
[84] Scot. Law Com. "Report on Bankruptcy and Related Aspects of Insolvency and Liquidation" No. 68, 1982, Chap. 12.
[85] s.320(2).
[86] *London Joint City and Midland Bank* v. *Herbert Dickinson* [1922] W.N. 13.
[87] Goudy on *Bankruptcy* (4th ed.), p. 50.
[88] Prescription and Limitation (Scotland) Act 1973, s.6 and Sched. 1.
[89] 1973 Act, s.1 (as extended by the Land Registration (Scotland) Act 1979, Sched. 3).
[90] 1973 Act, s.7.
[91] 1973 Act, s.8, see further Walker, *The Law of Prescription and Limitation of Actions in Scotland* (4th ed.).

challenger can show that the consideration was gratuitous or inadequate and that the company was insolvent at the time, or became insolvent as a result.[92] Insolvency in this context means "absolute" insolvency, *i.e.* an excess of liabilities over assets.[93] Such alienations are classed as "gratuitous" even if not strictly for no consideration. Any creditor may challenge a gratuitous alienation at common law prior to liquidation regardless of the date of his debt,[94] and liquidation is no bar to such action.[95] A liquidator, who represents the creditors generally, or an administrator, who has similar powers, is also in a position to challenge a gratuitous alienation at common law.[96] The common law is expressly preserved and made available to liquidators and administrators by the Insolvency Act, section 242(7).[97]

At common law the onus lies with the challenger to establish that the alienation was "gratuitous" and that the company was (or became) insolvent at the time of the alienation. A liquidator and creditors whose debts preceded the alienation, however, had the benefit of rebuttable presumptions under the Bankruptcy Act 1621, c. 18 of the Scottish Parliament (now repealed) that it had been "gratuitous" and that the company was insolvent at the time, if they could show that the alienation was to a "conjunct and confident person" and that the company was insolvent at the time of challenge.[98]

Although the common law remains (I.A., s.242(7)), a challenge to a "gratuitous alienation" is now likely to be on the basis of the Insolvency Act, section 242, which effectively shifts the burden of proof from the challenger to the person seeking to uphold the transaction, unless the time limit for challenge under the Act has expired. The law now in force results from an amendment to the Companies Act 1985 in the Bankruptcy (Scotland) Act 1985, Schedule 7, paragraph 20, now consolidated in the Insolvency Act, section 242. These provisions mirror those applicable to personal bankruptcies (s.34 of the Bankruptcy (Scotland) Act 1985) and were brought into force on the same day, April 1, 1986. On that day also the 1621 Act was repealed.[99]

An alienation is challengeable under the Insolvency Act, section 242

---

[92] *Abram Steamship Co. Ltd. (in liquidation), etc.* v. *Abram*, 1925 S.L.T. 243. See further Goudy, *op. cit.*, Chap. III; Scot. Law Com. Report, *supra*, paras. 12.1–12.12.

[93] Goudy, *op. cit.*, p. 18.

[94] Goudy, *op. cit.*, pp. 33 and 51.

[95] *Brown and Co.* v. *McCallum* (1890), 18 R. 311.

[96] See para. 134 (administrators), *ante.*

[97] *Bank of Scotland, Petr.*, 1988 S.L.T. 282; (on appeal) 1988 S.L.T. 690. See also *Stuart Eves Ltd. (in Liquidation)* v. *Smiths Gore*, 1991 G.W.D. 32–1888.

[98] See further *Palmer*, paras. 87–67; the applicability of the 1621 Act to companies was confirmed in *Johnstone (Liquidator of Kelvin Development Co. Ltd.)* v. *Peter H. Irvine Ltd.*, 1984 S.L.T. 209.

[99] Bankruptcy (Scotland) Act 1985, Sched. 8 and the Bankruptcy (Scotland) Act 1985 (Commencement) Order 1985 (S.I. 1985 No. 1924). The 1621 Act had, therefore, achieved the remarkable and perhaps unique record of 365 years' useful life without amendment.

only where winding up has commenced, by the liquidator or a creditor, whether his debt arose before or after the commencement of winding up (or by the administrator, only, if an administration order is in force[1]) (I.A., s.242(1)). This applies to any transfer of property or the discharge or renunciation of any claim or right, whether before or after April 1, 1986, provided it became completely effectual on a "relevant day." The expression "completely effectual" is not further defined (nor is it defined by the Bankruptcy (Scotland) Act 1985, where it appears in s.34) but should be taken to mean the completion of the donee's real right to the property by, *e.g.* recording or registration of his title to land.[2] The expression "relevant day" is defined as a day not earlier than two years before the date on which the winding up commenced (or the administration order was made) unless the person who benefited is an "associate" of the company (see paras. 508 and 517, below) when the period is extended to five years (I.A., s.242(2) and (3)). In determining whether a transaction is an alienation by the company, the court will only consider it in the form in which it took place, not what might have been done to achieve the same effect without involving the company.[3]

507 The Insolvency Act, section 242 expressly applies to alienations which occurred before April 1, 1986, *i.e.* at a time when the old law (in so far as based on statute, *i.e.* the Companies Act 1948, s.320, latterly s.615) might not have procured their reduction. This retrospective effect is, presumably, justified on the basis that gratuitous alienations were always challengeable at common law and the Act simply amends the procedure for so doing. Such an argument is not wholly convincing, since one of the principal changes is to replace the former concept of "conjunct and confident persons" with the new definition of "associates," and there might be individuals (or companies) involved in pre-April 1986 transactions who are brought within the scope of challenge for the first time by the 1986 legislation. Although the Insolvency Act, section 242 bears to have this retrospective effect in regard to the alienation under attack, it is not clear whether it applies only in liquidations which commenced on or after April 1, 1986 or to those which commenced earlier and, if so, to what effect. In the transitional provisions of the Insolvency Act, Schedule 11, paragraph 4 states that "the new law" is to have effect only in liquidations which commenced on or before the "appointed day," and "the former law" is to continue to apply to those which commenced before that day. For the purpose of this provision, however, "the new law" means any provision in the Insolvency Act, sections 1 to 251 which replaces sections 66 to 87 and 89 to 105 of the Insolvency Act 1985 and "the former law" means sections 501 to 674 of the Companies Act 1985

---

[1] See paras. 101 *et seq., ante.*
[2] *Cf. Gibson* v. *Hunter Home Designs,* 1976 S.C. 23.
[3] *Stuart Eves Ltd. (in liquidation)* v. *Smiths Gore,* 1991 G.W.D. 32–1888.

without the amendments in the Insolvency Act 1985, Schedule 6, paragraphs 23 to 52 and the associated repeals made by that Act. The Insolvency Act, section 242 is not, on this definition, part of "the new law" because it does not originate from any of the sections of the Insolvency Act 1985 which are referred to. It is in fact part of "the former law" since it appears (as s.615A)[4] within sections 501 to 674 of the Companies Act 1985. The Insolvency Act, Schedule 11, paragraph 9, however, makes further provisions with respect to Part VI of the Act (I.A., ss.230–251) to the effect that "a preference given, floating charge created or other transaction entered into before the appointed day shall not be set aside under that provision except to the extent that it could have been set aside under the law in force immediately before that day." (For this purpose an administration order is equiperated to a winding up order, and "setting aside" includes any lesser remedy.) "Other transaction" must, of course, include a gratuitous alienation. "The appointed day" for the Insolvency Act, section 242 was December 29, 1986. The Insolvency Act, Schedule 11, paragraph 9 is, of course, to some extent inconsistent with the Insolvency Act, section 242 since the Schedule suggests that although section 242(2) makes an alienation prior to April 1, 1986 challengeable under the Act, if it took place before December 29, 1986 the Insolvency Act, section 242 does *not* apply. The express provisions of the Insolvency Act, section 242 must take precedence but, of course, an alienation prior to December 29, 1986 was already challengeable under the similar provisions of section 615A so the apparent conflict within the Act is academic. It follows however that neither of the relevant transitional provisions of the Insolvency Act, Schedule 11, paragraphs 4 and 9, resolve the question of the effect of the Insolvency Act, section 242 on "old" liquidations. If the liquidation commenced on or after April 1, 1986, but before December 29, 1986, the position is governed by section 615A. In all material respects section 615A is to the same effect as the Insolvency Act, section 242. Like section 242, it applies whether the alienation took place before or after the section took effect (April 1, 1986), provided it was on a "relevant day," which is defined as the period beginning with the day two (or five) years before the winding up commenced. There is no indication in section 615A that it applies only to liquidations which commenced on or after April 1, 1986. In the Bankruptcy (Scotland) Act 1985, section 75(3), however, it is provided that nothing in that Act is to affect "any of the enactments repealed or amended by this Act in their operation in relation to a *sequestration* as regards which the award was made before (April 1, 1986)." It is clear, therefore, that the new law in relation to gratuitous alienations in bankruptcy (similar to s.615A) does not apply to sequestrations commencing before April 1, 1986. Unfortunately, however, there is no adaption of section 75 of the Bankruptcy Act for *companies* affected by section 615A so it appears

---

[4] See the Bankruptcy (Scotland) Act 1985, Sched. 7, para. 20.

that, notwithstanding the attempt to secure a different result, the Insolvency Act, section 242 applies to any liquidation, whenever it commenced, and even if it has been concluded. The calculation of the period of "relevant days" is not limited by the antiquity of the commencement date, nor is there any provision restricting it to liquidations which are or were still continuing when section 615A or the Insolvency Act, section 242 came into force, so a transaction entered into before April 1, 1986 (provided it was within two (or five) years of liquidation) has now, perhaps for the first time, become open to attack. This unintentional and inconvenient (possibly unconstitutional) result must be ripe for amending legislation. In *Stuart Eves Ltd.* v. *Smiths Gore*[5] liquidators sought reduction of a gratuitous alienation made on May 15, 1985. The winding up commenced on November 15, 1985. The pursuers averred that the company had been absolutely insolvent from at least February 28, 1985 until the commencement of liquidation, and it was accepted that the pursuers had averred sufficient material to constitute a relevant case to challenge the transaction at common law. The defenders, however, sought to have the action dismissed on the basis that the pursuers' pleadings disclosed that the challenge was based on section 242, as applied by the transitional provisions of Schedule 11. Although the difficulty of interpreting those provisions was canvassed, the court was able to avoid addressing these arguments by holding that the pursuers' pleadings were enough to allow a proof on the common law case.

508   On a successful challenge, the court is to grant decree of reduction, or for such restoration of property or other redress as may be appropriate. On the identical provisions of the Bankruptcy (Scotland) Act 1985, section 34(4), it was held that the court's discretion to provide an alternative remedy arises only if reduction or restoration is not available.[6] The defences available are:

(a) that immediately, or at any other time, after the alienation the company's assets were greater than its liabilities; or
(b) that adequate consideration was given; or
(c) that it was "a birthday, Christmas or other conventional gift" (to anyone) or a gift for charitable purposes to a person who is not an associate of the company (see below), which it was reasonable in all the circumstances for the company to make (I.A., s.242(4)).

A defence that the consideration was adequate will not necessarily fail if, after the event, it emerges that the price might have been

---

[5] August 16, 1991 (O.H., Lord Coulsfield). Reported briefly at 1991 G.W.D. 32–1888; these comments are based on the written opinion.
[6] *Short's Tr.* v. *Chung*, 1991 S.L.T. 472.

bettered.[7] A disposition was reduced, however, when the price appeared to be prima facie inadequate, the parties were "associated" and the sale had been concluded privately, without advertisement or any competing offer.[8] The receipt of gifts from the transferee prior to the alienation under challenge is not "adequate consideration".[8a]

"Charitable purposes" is widely defined and not restricted to charitable purposes as defined by other rules of law (I.A., s.242(5)). Defence (a) above makes it possible to argue even if the company was insolvent when the gift was made (or as a result), the Insolvency Act, section 242 does not apply if it became solvent later, even if it yet again became insolvent thereafter. This curious result might, however, be defeated by showing that, in that case, the transaction was reducible at common law. Indeed, none of the defences to a challenge under the Insolvency Act, section 242(4) (other than (b) above) is available to resist a common law challenge (I.A., s.242(7)).

An alienation which is in implement of a prior obligation is reducible under the Act if the consideration for that obligation was inadequate (I.A., s.242(6)).

A curious feature of the Insolvency Act, section 242 is that it contains two definitions of "associate." For the purpose of section 242(3) (*i.e.* whether the two- or five-year limit applies) "associate" is defined expressly by reference to the Bankruptcy (Scotland) Act 1985. For the purpose of section 242(4)(*c*) (charitable gifts to non-associates) there is no such reference, so the definition in the Insolvency Act, section 435 must apply.[9] The definition in the Bankruptcy (Scotland) Act 1985 is contained in section 74 as extended to companies by the Bankruptcy (Scotland) Regulations 1985,[10] paragraph 11. There are no significant differences between the two definitions as they apply to relatives, British companies and the persons controlling them and employers/ employees or directors (*i.e.* I.A., s.435(1), (2), (4) and (6)–(10)). The Bankruptcy Act definition, however, exhibits the following deviations from the Insolvency Act, section 435:

(a) Whereas both the Insolvency Act, section 435(3) and the Bankruptcy (Scotland) Act 1985, section 74(3) state that "a person is an associate of any person with whom he is in partnership, and of the husband and wife or a relative (as defined) of any individual with whom he is in partnership" the Bankruptcy (Scotland) Regulations 1985, paragraph 11(2) expressly amend this, in respect of companies, to read "a person is an associate of any person with whom he is in partnership, and of any person who is an associate of any person with whom he is in

---

[7] *Short's Tr.* v. *Chung, supra.*
[8] *McLuckie Brothers Ltd.* v. *Newhouse Contracts Ltd.*, 1992 G.W.D. 25–1407.
[8a] *Matheson's Tr.* v. *Matheson*, 1992 S.L.T. 685.
[9] See para. 517, *post.*
[10] S.I. 1985 No. 1925 (s.147), effective (so far as relevant) April 1, 1986.

partnership." The effect is to add to the list of "associates" of a company (but only for the purposes of I.A., s.242) persons who have no connection with it other than being partners of or otherwise "associated" with a person with whom the company is in partnership.

While the husband, wife and other relatives (as defined) of an individual with whom a company is in partnership are in any event "associates" under other provisions of the Insolvency Act, section 435 and under the Bankruptcy (Scotland) Act 1985, section 74 (as applied), the employees (or the employer) of a person who is a partner of the company alleged to have made the alienation, who would not be its "associates" for any other purpose, appear to be regarded as such for the purposes of section 242, yet they would not be "associates" in the personal bankruptcy of the donor. Consequently, an alienation to someone who stands in the same relationship to the donor might be challengeable if the donor was a company but not if he was an individual. This strange result is, presumably, not intentional.

(b) The Insolvency Act, section 435(5) provides that a person can be an "associate" of another person if he is a trustee (with certain exceptions) and the other person is a beneficiary or, in certain cases, a potential beneficiary. This is not applied either to personal bankruptcies in Scotland nor to Scottish companies, since there is no equivalent provision in the Bankruptcy (Scotland) Act 1985, section 74 or in that section as extended by the Bankruptcy (Scotland) Regulations 1985. Consequently, an alienation by a company to a person who is "associated" with it only in the relationship of trustee and beneficiary (or vice versa) is challengable within the two-year period and not the five-year period.

(c) In the subsection which applies these provisions to "companies" so as to include any body corporate whether incorporated in Great Britain or elsewhere, the Bankruptcy (Scotland) Act definition (s.74(6) as extended by paragraph 11(4) of the Regulations) omits the phrase which appears in the Insolvency Act, section 435(11) "and references to directors and other officers of a company and to voting power at any general meeting of the company have effect with any necessary modifications." This appears to have no significant practical consequences. Presumably the draftsman of the Bankruptcy (Scotland) Regulations 1985 considered the definition to be sufficiently clear without it.

In so far as these definitions depart from section 435, there is the further difficulty that section 435(1) states that its definition of "associate" is to apply for the purposes of the Act, without qualification. There is no "saving" for the Insolvency Act, section 242(3)(*a*), which employs a different definition. Presumably the conflict has to be resolved by reading section 435 as subject to the express terms of section 242. It is desirable that these anomalies are rectified, perhaps by amending the 1985 Regulations.

Third parties acquiring property from the grantee in good faith and for onerous consideration are protected, without prejudice to the liability of the grantee to make restitution both under the Act (I.A., s.242(4)) and at common law.[11]

Fraudulent preferences

509 At common law, a "fraudulent preference" is any voluntary transaction by the company under which a creditor obtains a preference over other creditors either directly from the company or indirectly, as when a cheque received by the company from a debtor is endorsed to the creditor.[12] An instruction to a third party to remit to a creditor sums due to the company under a factoring agreement (in the absence of valid diligence) is a voluntary act and can be reduced.[13] It is reducible provided that the challenger can show that the preference was voluntary and that the company was insolvent (*i.e.* "absolutely insolvent") and aware of its insolvency. There is no time limit for challenge short of the long negative prescription (20 years).[14]

In practice, before the 1986 legislation, because of the difficulty of proving knowledge of absolute insolvency a fraudulent preference was normally challenged on the statutory basis of the Bankruptcy Act 1696, c. 5 of the Scottish Parliament, as amended and as applied to companies. This removed the burden of proving insolvency if the preference occurred within a certain period (originally 60 days) before notour bankruptcy, which in the context of companies became six months before the commencement of winding up (s.615). The 1696 Act and related legislation was repealed with effect from April 1, 1986 by the Bankruptcy (Scotland) Act 1985 which enacted replacement provisions for the reduction of "unfair preferences" both for personal bankruptcies and companies (s.615B, inserted into the Companies Act 1985 by Sched. 7, para. 20 to the Bankruptcy Act). These provisions were consolidated as the Insolvency Act, section 243. Although the new statutory provisions will be the normal basis for challenging a preference, the common law rules are preserved for the benefit of creditors, liquidators and administrators (I.A., s.243(6)).[15] The new

---

[11] Goudy, *op. cit.*, p. 54.
[12] *Liquidator of Walkraft Paint Co. Ltd.* v. *James H. Kinsey Ltd.*, 1964 S.L.T. 104; *Nicoll* v. *Steelpress (Supplies) Ltd.*, 1992 S.C.L.R. 332.
[13] *Bob Gray (Access) Ltd.* v. *T. M. Standard Scaffolding Ltd.*, 1987 S.C.L.R. 720.
[14] See para. 505, *ante.*
[15] See generally, Goudy, *op. cit.*, Chaps. IV and X and Scot. Law Com. Report, *supra*, (para. 505, n. 51) paras. 12.33–12.35.

statutory code is discussed below (paragraph 510), but it is still necessary to consider the former rules, in so far as they may be relevant to a challenge at common law.

A transaction which is involuntary cannot be challenged as a fraudulent preference. An undertaking to grant a security which was entered into in a legally enforceable form at a time of solvency can validly be completed at any time[16] but not if it is still incomplete when winding up has commenced.[17] Payment by the arrestee to the arresting creditor of sums arrested on the dependence of an action is voluntary and reducible unless and until the creditor has obtained decree in the principal action, after which it becomes involuntary whether decree of furthcoming has been obtained or merely a mandate by the company.[18]

The payment in cash (or by cheque on the company's own account)[19] of debts actually due, *i.e.* not anticipatory payments, and transactions in the ordinary course of business are not fraudulent preferences unless it can be shown that there was collusion between the company and the creditor receiving payment in a scheme to defraud other creditors.[20] A company which knows it is "practically" insolvent is not to be regarded as holding its assets in trust for its creditors, and the mere fact that a creditor receives payment in the knowledge that the company is insolvent, even irretrievably, does not demonstrate the existence of an intention to defraud other creditors.[21] The mere intention to prefer a creditor or to obtain a preference is not fraudulent.[22]

A transaction under which the company grants security in respect of some fair and present consideration (*i.e.* a *novum debitum*) is not a preference and thus remains valid.[23] This protects both securities for new advances[24] and substituted securities for existing loans.[25] The provision of the consideration and the granting of the security need not be simultaneous, provided that they are *unico contextu*.[26]

A fraudulent preference may be reduced at the instance of any

---

[16] *T.* v. *L.*, 1970 S.L.T. 243; *Bank of Scotland, Petr.*, 1988 S.L.T. 282; (on appeal) 1988 S.L.T. 690.

[17] *Turnbull* v. *Liquidator of Scottish County Investment Co. Ltd.*, 1939 S.C. 5.

[18] *Liquidator of Walkraft Paint Co. Ltd.* v. *Lovelock (No. 1)*, 1963 S.L.T. (Notes) 6; *Liquidator of Walkraft Paint Co. Ltd.* v. *Lovelock (No. 2)*, 1964 S.L.T. 103; *High-Flex (Scotland) Ltd.* v. *Kentallan Mechanical Services*, 1977 S.L.T. (Sh.Ct.) 91.

[19] *Liquidator of Walkraft Paint Co. Ltd.* v. *James H. Kinsey Ltd.*, 1964 S.L.T. 104 (endorsement of a cheque is a preference).

[20] *Whatmough's Trs.* v. *British Linen Bank*, 1932 S.C. 525; 1934 S.C. (H.L.) 51; 1932 S.L.T. 386; 1934 S.L.T. 392; *Nordic Travel Ltd.* v. *Scotprint Ltd.*, 1980 S.L.T. 189; S.C. 1.

[21] *Nordic Travel Ltd.* v. *Scotprint Ltd.*, *supra.* The position in England appears to be the opposite: *Re F. P. & C. H. Matthews Ltd.* [1982] 1 All E.R. 38.

[22] *Re Sarflax Ltd.* [1979] 1 All E.R. 529.

[23] Goudy, *op. cit.*, p. 90. See also *Thomas Montgomery & Sons* v. *Gallacher*, 1982 S.L.T. 138.

[24] *Renton and Gray's Trs.* v. *Dickison* (1880) 7 R. 951.

[25] *Roy's Trs.* v. *Colville and Drysdale* (1903) 5 F. 769.

[26] Goudy, *op. cit.*, pp. 91–98; *T.* v. *L.*, *supra.*

creditor who can show prejudice, or the liquidator or administrator.[27] It is an equitable remedy for the benefit of creditors and therefore cannot be used by a debtor of the company to seek recovery of a sum paid to one of its creditors.[28]

Unfair preferences

510 The Insolvency Act, section 243 provides for the reduction, in the case of any company being wound up in Scotland, of a preference which prejudices the general body of creditors which was created not earlier than six months before the commencement of the winding up (I.A., s.243(1)). The transaction can be challenged by the liquidator or any creditor by virtue of a debt incurred on or before the commencement of winding up (I.A., s.243(4)). An assignee of a pre-liquidation debt thus has the right to invoke the Act. The Act also extends to administrators by reference to the date of the administration order, but in that case only the administrator can take action (I.A., s.243(1) and (4)).[29] The court, if satisfied that the preference is reducible, is to grant decree of reduction or an order restoring the property to the company, or such other redress as it thinks appropriate, but a third party acquiring a right or interest in good faith and for value from the preferred creditor is protected (I.A., s.243(5)). Since the wording is identical to the Insolvency Act, section 242(4), as under that section the court's power to grant a remedy other than reduction and restitution arises only if that remedy is not available.[30]

The Act applies to any transaction, whether entered into before April 1, 1986 (the effective date of the amendments made by the Bankruptcy (Scotland) Act 1985) or otherwise. While this clearly applies in any liquidation which commenced on or after that date, for the same reasons as arise in the case of gratuitous alienations under the Insolvency Act, section 242, it is suggested that the Insolvency Act, section 243 also applies to liquidations which commenced before that date.[31] Again, this has inconvenient and unintended effects, and should be amended by legislation in early course.

For the purpose of the Act, the day on which a preference is created is the day on which it became "completely effectual" (I.A., s.243(3)). As in the case of gratuitous alienations, where the same phrase is used (I.A., s.242(3)), no definition is provided. There, it was suggested that a "completely effectual" alienation arises on the completion of the donee's title.[32]

511 The granting of a security within six months of liquidation would not

---

[27] See Goudy, *op. cit.*, pp. 42 and 99; I.A., s.243(6).
[28] *Thompson* v. *J. Barke & Co. (Caterers) Ltd.*, 1975 S.L.T. 67.
[29] See paras. 101 *et seq.*, *ante.*
[30] *Short's Tr.* v. *Chung*, 1991 S.L.T. 472; see para. 508, *ante.*
[31] See para. 507, *ante.*
[32] *Ibid.*, n. 89.

have been reducible under section 615 as a "fraudulent preference" if it was in implement of an obligation entered into before that period.[33] The effect of the Insolvency Act, section 243(3), however, is to remove this possible line of defence. Further, since no security is "completely effectual" until the creditor has completed title, mere delivery of the security document cannot be sufficient, and any security right made real within the six-month period is challengeable under the Insolvency Act, section 243. In the case of preferences effected otherwise than by the constitution of a right in security, the position is less clear. Delivery will normally be sufficient. In the case of a payment by cheque or similar method, however, the date when the cheque is presented and paid is when the transaction has become "completely effectual." The following are exempt from challenge under the Insolvency Act, section 243(2):

(a) a transaction in the ordinary course of trade or business (I.A., s.243(2)(*a*)). Although, in contrast to the position under the law prior to April 1, 1986, there is no exception for a transaction which was tainted by collusion between the company and the creditor to "defraud" other creditors[34] it is possible that such a transaction would not be regarded as being "in the ordinary course of trade or business."

(b) a payment in cash for a debt presently payable, unless the transaction was collusive with the purpose of prejudicing the general body of creditors (I.A., s.243(2)(*b*)). Under the law prior to April 1, 1986 "payment in cash" included a payment by cheque drawn on the company's own bank account,[35] and it is suggested that this would still apply to the Insolvency Act, section 243(2)(*b*).

(c) a transaction whereby the parties to it undertake reciprocal obligations (whether performance is to be at the same time or different times) unless it was collusive, with intent to prejudice the general body of creditors (I.A., s.243(2)(*c*)). This restates the former law protecting *nova debita*, but with an explicit provision allowing performance of the reciprocal obligations to be at different times. The obligations must still arise *unico contextu* and the company must receive new value to the same extent at least as the value of the assets which it has disposed of under the allegedly fraudulent preference. The extinction of a pre-existing debt does not qualify for protection.[36] Where there is no new advance, but the company substitutes new security subjects for those formerly held, it is suggested that no preference can arise,

---

[33] *T. v. L.*, 1970 S.L.T. 243; *Turnbull* v. *Liquidator of Scottish County Investment Co. Ltd.*, 1935 S.C. 5.

[34] See para. 509, n. 79, *ante*.

[35] *Liquidator of Walkraft Paint Co. Ltd.* v. *James H. Kinsey Ltd.*, 1964 S.L.T. 104.

[36] *Nicoll* v. *Steelpress (Supplies) Ltd.*, 1992 S.C.L.R. 332; see para. 509, *ante*.

except to such extent as the value of the new security subjects exceeds the former.

(d) the granting of a mandate by a company authorising an arrestee to pay all or part of the funds arrested to the arresting creditor, provided that the arrester holds a decree for payment or a warrant for summary diligence and this has been preceded by an arrestment on the dependence or followed by an arrestment in execution (I.A., s.243(2)(*d*)). It is suggested that this provision enacts the law as it stood prior to April 1, 1986.[37] Payment by an arrestee on a mandate in other circumstances, or on the basis of arrestment to found jurisdiction or other diligence, is not protected and would, accordingly, be a preference.

"Extortionate credit transactions"

512 Where a company "is, or has been, a party to a transaction for, or involving, the provision of credit to the company" on "extortionate" terms, the transaction may be challenged under the Insolvency Act, section 244. The words quoted (from I.A., s.244(1)) indicate that the Act will apply regardless of the precise nature of the company's involvement (so long as it obtains credit) and even if the company has ceased to be involved in the arrangement, *e.g.* as a result of repayment of the sums advanced. The Insolvency Act, section 244 is in addition to any basis for challenging the transaction as a gratuitous alienation under the Insolvency Act, section 242 which, by virtue of the Insolvency Act, section 242(7), includes a challenge at common law (I.A., s.244(5)).

The Insolvency Act, section 244 is stated as applying "as does (I.A.) s.238" which does not apply in Scotland. The Insolvency Act, section 244 does, however, apply in Scotland. These words refer to the Insolvency Act, section 238(1) and mean that the Insolvency Act, section 244 applies where a company has gone into liquidation (or where an administration order has been made). Only the liquidator (or administrator) can resort to section 244. The section applies to any transaction entered into within the period of three years ending with the commencement of winding up (or the date of the administration order) (I.A., s.244(2)). In regard to any such transaction there is a rebuttable presumption that it was "extortionate," which is defined as (having regard to the risk to the provider of credit) involving "grossly exorbitant" terms with respect to payments or "grossly" contravening "ordinary principles of fair dealing." No guidance is provided on how the courts are to interpret these tests, and the issue will, presumably, be a matter for expert opinion evidence. Persons advancing credit to companies should, for their own protection, endeavour to preserve evidence such as quotations from competing credit sources and any

---

[37] See para. 509, n. 77, *ante.*

evidence of special risks involved, against the possibility of a challenge under the Insolvency Act, section 244.

The court's powers under the Insolvency Act, section 244 are extensive but they are, nevertheless, limited to those specified in section 244(4). It can reduce in whole or in part any obligation created by the transaction, vary its terms or those of any security, order payment to the liquidator (or administrator) by any party of sums received (which includes such payments as fees or commission as well as payments relating to the credit fund itself), the surrender of any property held as security, or an order for an accounting.

The Insolvency Act, section 244 does not apply to any transaction entered into prior to December 29, 1986 (I.A., Sched. 11, para. 9).

Floating charges

513 A floating charge, is of course, capable of being a "gratuitous alienation," a "fraudulent preference" an "unfair preference" or part of an "extortionate credit transaction." When introduced to Scotland by the Companies (Floating Charges) (Scotland) Act 1961 what became section 617 was extended to Scotland, permitting a floating charge granted within 12 months of winding up to be challenged as (in effect) a "fraudulent preference." A challenge at common law, to which no such time limit applies, was not excluded until the Companies (Floating Charges and Receivers) (Scotland) Act 1972, section 8 added an express provision to section 617 excluding any challenge to a floating charge as a fraudulent preference or gratuitous alienation at common law or by statute, except under section 617 itself. The Insolvency Act, section 245 replaces section 617 but without re-enacting these restrictions, so that a floating charge is challengeable as a gratuitous alienation (at common law or under the Insolvency Act, s.242), a fraudulent preference (at common law), an unfair preference (under I.A., s.243) or as being part of an "extortionate credit transaction" (under I.A., s.244). It can also be challenged for want of registration.[38] All of these grounds are in addition to a challenge under the Insolvency Act, section 245.

Section 245 provides, in place of section 617, a revised code for challenging floating charges created within 12 months (or, if the charge is in favour of a "connected person," two years) prior to the commencement of winding up.[39] A "floating charge" is defined as "including" a floating charge in Scotland within the meaning of section 462 (I.A., s.251). The date of creation is the date of execution of the charge by the company (s.410(5)). A charge created after the commencement of winding up by the court is void under the Insolvency Act, section 127, unless the court orders otherwise.[40]

---

[38] See *Palmer*, paras. 13.401 *et seq.* and s.410.
[39] These provisions also apply in the case of an administration order; see paras. 101 *et seq.*, *ante*.
[40] *Site Preparations Ltd.* v. *Buchan Development Co. Ltd.*, 1983 S.L.T. 317.

A floating charge created within the 12-month period, and which is not in favour of a "connected person," will be sustained unless it is shown that, when the charge was created, the company was "unable to pay its debts" within the meaning of the Insolvency Act, section 123,[41] or became unable to pay its debts as a result of the transaction under which the charge was created (I.A., s.245(4)). "Inability to pay debts" in terms of section 123 is, in effect, insolvency in the "practical" sense rather than "absolute insolvency." This subsection means that, except where the charge was created in favour of a "connected person," the liquidator or other challenger has to prove inability to pay debts in order to overcome the presumption of validity. If the charge was granted within six months of liquidation, however, his challenge would be made under the Insolvency Act, section 243, as an "unfair preference," where this problem does not arise. The Insolvency Act, section 245(4) has reversed the burden of proof applicable under the former law; under section 617 the charge was presumed invalid unless the holder could prove that the company was solvent immediately after it was created.

Section 245(3) applies to the charge as it was *created*. Thus, a charge created in favour of a person not "connected" with the company remains challengeable only within one year even if subsequently assigned to a person who is "connected", and conversely a charge created in favour of a "connected" person can be challenged within two years even if assigned to a person who is not "connected."

514　If the Insolvency Act, section 245 applies, in terms of section 245(2) the charge will be invalid

> "except to the extent of the aggregate of:
> (a) the value of so much of the consideration for the creation of the charge as consists of money paid, or goods or services supplied, to the company at the same time as, or after, the creation of the charge;
> (b) the value of so much of that consideration as consists of the discharge or reduction, at the same time as, or after, the creation of the charge, of any debt of the company; and
> (c) the amount of such interest (if any) as is payable on the amount falling within paragraph (a) or (b) in pursuance of any agreement under which the money was so paid, the goods or services were so supplied or the debt was so discharged or reduced."

There are important differences in the Insolvency Act, section 245(2), as compared to the equivalent provisions of section 617. Interest is at the contractual rate (if any) and not (as under s.617(2)) the prescribed rate of 5 per cent. A charge in respect of the value of goods

---

[41] See paras. 413 and 414, *ante.*

or services, as well as money, is valid; section 617 applied only to "cash." For this purpose the value of goods or services is the market price in the ordinary course of business, but taking due account of any special terms of supply in the relevant transaction (I.A., s.245(6)). The Insolvency Act, section 245(2)(*b*) is clearly intended to cover a charge where a payment is made not to the company but to one of its creditors, which was not protected by section 617. Whether in respect of money, goods, services or the discharge of a debt, however, the Act does not protect the charge unless these are provided "at the same time as, or after" the creation of the charge. Cases decided under the superseded wording of section 617,[42] suggesting that a delay of some weeks between the making of the advance and the subsequent execution of the charge was not necessarily fatal, are no longer directly in point, having regard to the change of wording in the current legislation. In *Re Shoe Lace Ltd.*[43] it was suggested that these earlier decisions were unsound, even on the wording of the statute at that time, but in any event they confirm that it is a question of fact in each case whether the delay is sufficient to prevent "a businessman having knowledge of the kind of time limits imposed by the Insolvency and Companies Acts and using ordinary language (from saying) that the payments have been made at the same time as the execution of (the Floating Charge)." The Act makes no distinction between excusable and inexcusable delay. In the *Shoe Lace* case the advances were made at various dates from about 14 weeks to eight days prior to the execution of the charge, and it was held that none of them was effectively secured.

In relation to both (a) and (b), the charge is protected only to the extent of "the value of so much of the consideration for the creation of the charge." When faced with the equivalent phrase in section 617 ("cash paid . . . in consideration for the charge") the courts in England (to which country alone it applied until 1961) decided that this was not a reference to the English doctrine of "consideration" in the law of contract, but referred to payments made "in reliance upon and because of the existence . . . of the charge."[44] Although the wording of the Insolvency Act, section 245(2) differs, it is reasonable to assume that the same non-technical construction will be placed on the reference to "consideration," especially as the section applies to Scotland, where the word has no special meaning. It is unfortunate, however, that the point was not put beyond doubt by using different wording.

515   In the common case of a bank having advanced money to a company by way of overdraft on trading account, if it takes a floating charge and subsequently makes further advances (which includes the honouring of cheques), it is entitled to apply (on the basis of the rule in *Clayton's*

---

[42] *Columbian Fireproofing Co. Ltd.* [1910] 2 Ch. 120; *F. & E. Stanton Ltd.* [1929] 1 Ch. 180.
[43] [1992] B.C.C. 307 Ch.D.
[44] *Yeovil Glove Co. Ltd.* [1965] Ch. 148, 178.

Case) sums paid in by the company against the older debts first. The advances made subsequent to the charge will be secured in terms of the Insolvency Act, section 245(2)(*a*).[45] The *Cork Report*[46] recommended abolition of this rule, but without success.

A "connected person" suffers a double disadvantage under the Insolvency Act, section 245. A floating charge created in his favour is exposed to challenge for two years instead of 12 months (I.A., s.245(3)(*a*)), and he does not enjoy the benefit of the Insolvency Act, section 245(4). This means that not only does he lose the advantage of the company being presumed solvent when the charge was created, he cannot defeat a challenge even if he proves the company was fully solvent and able to pay its debts when the charge was created. The Insolvency Act, section 245(2) renders the charge invalid automatically, except to the extent provided for. In practice, of course, a charge in favour of a connected person (like any other) will still be valid in respect of new advances, goods or services supplied or debts discharged on or after the date of the charge, and interest (I.A., s.245(2)). If the person is not "connected" with the company at the time of creation it is irrelevant if he acquires such a connection later, and if he is "connected" at the outset the disadvantages continue to apply even if the link is severed later.

A person is "connected with" a company for these purposes if he is a director or shadow director[47] or an "associate" of such director or shadow director, or an "associate"[48] of the company (I.A., s.249).

516   The practical effect of the Insolvency Act, section 245, together with the Insolvency Act, sections 242, 243 and 244 and the common law is as follows:

1. A floating charge created more than three years before commencement of winding up (or administration) is free from challenge under the Act;
2. A floating charge created within three years can be challenged under the Insolvency Act, section 244 if it forms part of an "extortionate credit" transaction;
3. A floating charge created within two years in favour of a "connected person" is invalid, whether the company is solvent or not, except for new money, etc., under the Insolvency Act, section 245(2);

---

[45] *Yeovil Glove Co. Ltd., supra.*
[46] *Report on Insolvency Law and Practice* (1982: Cmnd. 8558), paras. 1560–1562.
[47] "Director" is defined as "any person occupying the position of director, by whatever name called"; "shadow director" is "a person in accordance with whose directions or instructions the directors of the company are accustomed to act" (excluding professional advisers) (I.A., s.251); these definitions are identical to those in the Companies Act (s.741).
[48] Defined in I.A., s.435; see para. 517, *post.*

4. A floating charge created in favour of a person who is not connected with the company more than 12 months before liquidation (or administration) is free from challenge under the Insolvency Act, section 245; if within that period, it is valid unless the challenger proves that the company was "practically insolvent" at the time of creation, and even then it remains valid for "new" money, etc.;

5. A charge created within six months is theoretically open to challenge as an "unfair preference" under the Insolvency Act, section 243, but the holder is likely to be able to defend it as a transaction involving mutual obligations (I.A., s.243(2)(c)) unless it is in respect of debts, etc., already in existence when the charge was created;

6. A floating charge is also challengeable under the Insolvency Act, section 242 as a "gratuitous alienation"; since the giving of a fair consideration is a valid defence the only situation in which section 242 might be of value against a floating charge is where it was created in respect of an "extortionate credit" transaction with an "associate" more than three years but less than five years prior to liquidation (or administration), which would take it beyond the Insolvency Act, section 244, but still within the Insolvency Act, section 242(3)(a);

7. A floating charge no matter when granted is challengeable at common law as a fraudulent preference (or gratuitous alienation) if the challenger can show that the company was absolutely insolvent at the time, or as a result of the charge (and, in the case of a preference, was aware of its insolvency).

The Insolvency Act, section 245 applies only to floating charges created on or after December 29, 1986 (I.A., Sched. 11, para. 9). A charge granted before that date will continue to be subject to the old law (s.617), and will therefore cease to be challengeable on any ground (including common law) 12 months after its creation.[49]

The Insolvency Act, section 245 (if applicable) provides only that the floating charge is invalid, and it applies only on liquidation (or on an administration order being granted). Section 617 was in similar terms. The debt secured remains a debt due by the company. Accordingly, if the company pays off the debt prior to liquidation (or administration) the Insolvency Act, section 245 is irrelevant and cannot be used as a basis for the liquidator claiming repayment as a fraudulent or unfair preference, if the conditions for this are present.[50] If the charge holder has appointed a receiver, who realises assets and repays the sum secured, the same principles apply, and the liquidator cannot claim repayment under the Insolvency Act, section 245 even where the

---

[49] For a discussion of s.617, see *Palmer*, (23rd ed.), para. 87–67.
[50] *Re Parkes Garage (Swadlincote) Ltd.* [1929] 1 Ch. 139.

charge was created within the relevant period. The appointment and acts of the receiver remain valid until liquidation (or administration) supervenes.[51]

"ASSOCIATES"

517 For most purposes[52] the question of whether a person is an "associate" of another person is determined by the Insolvency Act, section 435. An "associate" of a company (or its directors) is subject to a number of disabilities under the Insolvency Act, discussed elsewhere. Some examples are the extended periods for challenge of an alienation to him under the Insolvency Act, section 242, or a floating charge created in his favour under the Insolvency Act, section 245. Under the 1986 Rules, "associates" of the liquidator may have to justify any transaction with him (1986 Rule 4.38).[53]

The list of individuals who are to be treated as "associates" is very extensive and includes all close relatives (husband, wife, lineal ancestors and descendants, brothers, sisters, uncles, aunts, nephews and nieces and their respective husbands or wives). Half-blood, step and adoptive relationships are included. Illegitimate children are treated as the children of their mother and "reputed father." Former and "reputed" husbands or wives are included. Partners and their husbands and wives, and the close relatives (as indicated) of partners are "associates." A trustee is an associate of the beneficiaries (unless he is a trustee in bankruptcy or in an employees' share scheme). Employer and employee are associates of one another, and this includes directors and other officers and their company. A company and the person who controls it (or who, with his associates, controls it) are "associated," and companies are "associated" if they fall under the control of another company, or companies, or such control is held by an individual and persons associated with him.

---

[51] *Mace Builders (Glasgow) Ltd.* v. *Lunn* [1985] 3 W.L.R. 465; affmd [1986] 3 W.L.R. (C.A.). This case exhibits some curious features, of which the most significant in the long term is that it was a Scots Law case, involving a Scottish liquidation and receiver, argued by English counsel and decided by English judges of the Chancery Division and Court of Appeal, and based on the questionable proposition, accepted by all concerned, that there was "no relevant difference between the law of Scotland and the law of England" in the matters under dispute ([1985] 3 W.L.R. at p. 467), all of which casts doubt on its status as an authority in the law of either country. Accordingly, it is not surprising that no reference is made to the possibility of a claim for repayment of the amount in issue at common law, although the courts accepted that (if more than six months had not elapsed before liquidation) a claim under the statute as a "fraudulent preference" (s.615) would have been possible. A common law claim might well succeed on the facts in *Mace Builders* since it was admitted that the company had been insolvent when the charge was granted and the chargee was the managing director and beneficial owner of its issued capital, so that all the relevant criteria for attacking both the charge and subsequent payment as a fraudulent preference and gratuitous alienation at common law appear to have been present. Since the liquidator was reserving his position, however, on all matters except s.617, these issues were not before the court.

[52] An exception is I.A., s.242(3); see para. 508, *ante*.

[53] These examples are not intended to be exhaustive.

These provisions are complex and, in many respects, extremely difficult to apply, (*e.g.* the references to "reputed husband and wife" and "reputed father"). It would be an impossible task to make up a complete list of all individuals or companies with which a person is "associated," let alone expect him to be aware of the relationship in all but the clearest of situations. The statutory consequences, however, mostly flow from the fact of the relationship and not knowledge thereof. If the relationship of "association" is asserted, however, as the basis of challenge of a transaction, the challenger will require to establish that it exists.

PUBLIC UTILITY SUPPLIES

518 The monopoly enjoyed by the suppliers of public utility services (electricity, gas, water, telecommunications) enabled them to create a *de facto* preference for any unpaid accounts, by threatening to cut off supplies unless the liquidator (or similar office-holder) agreed to meet their account in full.[54] This effectively prevented the company being sold as a going concern or carrying on business. Under the Insolvency Act, section 233, however, the liquidator can request continuation of these services and the supplier cannot insist on payment of the outstanding account. The liquidator can, however, be required to guarantee personally payment for future supplies. The Insolvency Act does not prevent the supplier from refusing the service on other grounds available to it under the relevant constituting statute such as the Gas Act 1986, etc.

PRIVATE EXAMINATION OF BOOKS AND PERSONS

519 At any time after the making of a winding-up order the court may order that books and papers of the company be made available for inspection by creditors or contributories (I.A., s.155). After commencement of a winding up other sections giving the right to obtain an order for inspecting the books of the company, such as sections 356 and 383, cease to be available; accordingly, since the Insolvency Act, section 155 does not apply to persons other than creditors and contributories, a stranger to the company cannot obtain an order to inspect the register of members after commencement of the winding up (whether voluntary or compulsory).[55] The power granted by the Insolvency Act, section 155 should be exercised for the benefit of the liquidation, and not to assist actions by individual shareholders against the directors,[56] nor to assist creditors in obtaining information to pursue a scheme to

---

[54] *Cork Report* (1982; Cmnd. 8558), paras. 1451–1463.
[55] *Re Kent Coalfields Syndicate Ltd.* [1898] 1 Q.B. 754.
[56] *Re North Brazilian Sugar Factories* (1887) 37 Ch.D. 84; *Re Embassy Art Products* [1987] B.C.C. 389.

terminate the liquidation and reconstruct the company.[57] Although section 155 applies only in winding up by the court, the Insolvency Act, section 112 allows it to be used in voluntary liquidations.

If a company is being wound up, or if a provisional liquidator has been appointed, on the application of the liquidator or provisional liquidator the court may summon before it any officer of the company, any person known or suspected to have possession of property of the company or to be indebted to it, or whom the court thinks capable of giving information about the company (I.A., s.236(1) and (2)). The court may require such a person to submit an affidavit concerning his dealings with the company or to produce documents relating to the inquiry (I.A., s.236(3)). The court has powers of arrest and detention and seizure of papers where a person refuses compliance without reasonable excuse or is believed to be about to abscond (I.A., s.236(4)–(6)).

If satisfied, on the evidence submitted to it, that such orders would be appropriate, the court may order delivery of property or payment of sums due to the liquidator (I.A., s.237(1) and (2)). Persons can be examined on oath in other jurisdictions within the United Kingdom (I.A., s.237(3) and (4)).

520　The Insolvency Act, section 236 has been described as "an extraordinary and secret mode of obtaining information required for the proper conduct of the winding up"[58] and, that its purpose is to enable the liquidator "to get sufficient information to reconstitute the state of knowledge that the company should possess . . . not to put the company in a better position than it would have enjoyed if liquidation (or administration) had not supervened."[59] This should not, however, be interpreted as a restriction on the court's overall discretion.[60] Since two differently constituted Courts of Appeal in England[61] have arrived (by majority) at different views on how far section 236 allows the office holder to inquire, the matter cannot be regarded as finally resolved.[61a] Because of the potentially oppressive nature of this power it must be exercised with caution especially against persons who are not former officers of the company, so as to ensure that the information obtained by means of section 236 is used only for the purpose of the

---

[57] *Halden* v. *Liquidator of Scottish Heritable Security Co. Ltd.*, (1887) 14 R. 633.

[58] *Re Barlow Clowes Gilt Managers Ltd.* [1991] 4 All E.R. 385, 395 (Ch.D.).

[59] *Cloverbay Ltd. (Joint Administrators)* v. *Bank of Credit & Commerce International S.A.* [1991] 1 All E.R. 894, 900 (C.A.).

[60] *Re British and Commonwealth Holdings plc (No. 2)* [1992] B.C.C. 172.

[61] *Cloverbay Ltd. (Joint Administrators)* v. *Bank of Credit & Commerce International S.A.*, *supra*; *Re British and Commonwealth Holdings plc (No. 2)*, *supra*.

[61a] The House of Lords has now ruled that the court's discretion is not limited to the "reconstitution" of knowledge the company should possess, but the order should provide what was reasonably required by the office holder to carry out his function without imposing an unnecessary or unreasonable burden on those required to produce it; *Re British and Commonwealth Holdings (Nos. 1 and 2)*, *The Times*, November 3, 1992 (H.L.).

liquidation (or administration).[62] Although the Insolvency Act, section 236 is in different terms, it is clearly based on the former law in section 561. Accordingly, it is legitimate to refer to decisions on section 561 in relation to the circumstances in which it is proper to invoke section 236.[63]

The court has discretion whether to grant an order and the appeal court will not readily interfere, especially where an order has been refused.[64] The section should be used to enable the liquidator to obtain access to material which may assist him in the effective and economic discharge of his duties including Department of Trade inspectors' proceedings.[65] It is legitimate to resort to the Insolvency Act, section 236 to establish whether grounds for proceedings exist, even though the section does give the liquidator an advantage not available to ordinary potential litigants,[66] but it should not be used to enable the liquidator to gain an advantage not available to ordinary litigants in court proceedings which are already under way,[67] nor should it be exercised in a vexatious or offensive manner.[68] The authorities have recently been reviewed by the Court of Appeal in England.[69] In this case the court held that the appropriate test on whether to order an examination under section 236 was to balance the office holder's reasonable requirement to obtain information against the possible oppression of the person sought to be examined and the degree of oppression that he would suffer. This would necessarily be determined on the facts of each particular case. The court expressed the view that the case for making an order under section 236 for the examination of an officer or former officer of the company would usually be stronger than it would be against a third party, because of the fiduciary duty of the officer to the company, and that an order for oral examination is more likely to be considered oppressive than an order for the production of documents, but these were not firm rules. Among the factors which the court has to consider is the conflict between Insolvency Act, section 236 and the principle that a party to legal proceedings should not be able to subject his opponent to examination except as a witness at the trial or proof. There is, however, no rule that section 236 is not available if the office holder has

---

[62] *Re Barlow Clowes Gilts Managers Ltd.*, *supra*, p. 395.
[63] *Re Barlow Clowes Gilt Managers Ltd.*, *supra*, p. 395; *Cloverbay Ltd. (Joint Administrators)* v. *Bank of Credit & Commerce International S.A.*, *supra*.
[64] *Re Joseph Hargreaves Ltd.* [1900] 1 Ch. 347.
[65] *Re Rolls Razor Ltd.* [1963] 3 All E.R. 698.
[66] *Re Spiraflite Ltd.* [1979] 2 All E.R. 766; *Re Castle New Homes Ltd.* [1979] 2 All E.R. 775; *Re John T. Rhodes Ltd.* [1986] P.C.C. 366.
[67] *Re Bletchley Boat Co. Ltd.* [1974] 1 All E.R. 1255; *Re Malville Hose Ltd.* [1929] Ch. 32.
[68] *Re Rolls Razor Ltd. (No. 2)* [1970] Ch. 576, 592.
[69] *Cloverbay Ltd. (Joint Administrators)* v. *Bank of Credit and Commerce International S.A.*, *supra*. Significantly, although there was unanimity on the principles to be applied, the decision to refuse the application was by a majority. See also *Re British and Commonwealth Holdings plc*, *supra*.

commenced or decided to commence proceedings.[70] The views of the office holder ought to be taken into account but the court must decide whether the evidence he seeks is truly necessary to enable him to decide whether to commence proceedings. An order authorising messengers-at-arms to search for and recover books, and if necessary to open lockfast places, is competent.[71] The question of whether a lien may be claimed, to the effect of requiring the liquidator to concede a preference as a condition of obtaining the books, has already been considered.[72]

Section 236(4) allows only two excuses for non-attendance, the lack of an offer of reasonable expenses or the existence of a lawful impediment accepted by the court. The existence of civil proceedings between the parties is no excuse for non-attendance, but may justify a postponement.[73] The procedure adopted in Scotland in the event of an examination being called for includes the citation of the individual concerned to appear for examination on oath before the liquidation judge.[74] He may be represented by counsel and re-examined by him to explain his evidence but his counsel is not entitled to be present when other witnesses are examined.[75] An examinee may refuse to answer questions on the grounds that they might incriminate him, but the possibility of such questions being put is no excuse for refusing to attend.[76]

It is consistent with public policy in encouraging the proper and efficient functioning of the process of liquidation (or administration) that persons with information or other material which would be of assistance are able to volunteer it to the liquidator, whether or not under express threat of resorting to Insolvency Act, section 236, on a confidential basis, and the court will therefore restrain the liquidator from disclosing that information voluntarily to a third party, even if it is for use in the defence of criminal charges.[77] It remains to be determined upon what basis the court will hold that the public interest in the proper conduct of the other proceedings, for which disclosure is

---

[70] Based on comments of Slade J. in *Re Castle New Homes Ltd.*, *supra* and disapproved in *Cloverbay Ltd.*, *supra*.

[71] *Ker* v. *Hughes*, 1907 S.C. 380.

[72] See para. 481, *supra*.

[73] *Re Reliance Taxi-cab Co.* (1912) 28 T.L.R. 529; *Re London and Northern Bank, ex p. Archer* (1901) 85 L.T. 698; *Re North Australian Territory Co.* (1890) 45 Ch.D. 87.

[74] *Ker* v. *Hughes*, 1907 S.C. 380; *Welch*, 1930 S.N. 112. Procedure which may be used if the witness resides in England and is unwilling to attend is illustrated in *Liquidator of the Vegetable Oils Products Co. Ltd.*, 1923 S.L.T. 114.

[75] *Liquidator of Larkhall Collieries* (1905) 13 S.L.T. 752 (where there is a comprehensive form of interlocutor for such an examination).

[76] *Re Repetition Engineering Service Ltd.* (1945) 173 L.T. 75.

[77] *Re Barlow Clowes Gilt Managers Ltd.*, *supra*, p. 396. In *Re Esal (Commodities) Ltd. (No. 2)* [1990] B.C.C. 708, a creditor was allowed to use information obtained from a bank under the predecessor of I.A., s.236 to pursue a claim against it on the grounds of "fraudulent trading" under the Companies Act 1948, s.332 (later s.630). This decision, on unusual facts, is probably no longer valid since the right to pursue such a claim is now vested solely in the liquidator (I.A., s.213; see para. 522, *post*).

sought, overrides the public interest in protecting the ready availability of information to office holders under section 236. In the *Barlow Clowes* case[78] it was suggested that this might be analogous to the test applicable when considering whether disclosure should be ordered against a government minister's certificate that disclosure would not be in the public interest.[79] While the precise form of the test in the context of Insolvency Act, section 236 is unsettled, "fishing applications" would clearly be excluded, and the applicant would have to satisfy the court that the evidence which he sought to make available to it would constitute material evidence.[80]

A person subject to examination under the Insolvency Act, section 236 is not entitled to refuse to answer questions that might incriminate him; this applies also to Insolvency Act, sections 112, 133 and 235 but it applies only where the company is in liquidation, administration or administrative receivership.[81] Since the person under examination (or volunteering the information) cannot avoid self-incriminating answers and public policy requires the encouragement of voluntary information to the office holder in question, it is legitimate to order that information obtained by this means should not be disclosed to the prosecuting authorities to enable them to mount a prosecution.[82] It is no bar to granting an order under section 236 that criminal proceedings against the person to be examined have already begun.[83] If an order under section 236 is implemented, it is too late to seek to prevent documents disclosed from being used on the grounds that they were confidential.[84]

In addition to the Insolvency Act, sections 236 and 237, the Insolvency Act, section 198 also provides that the court may order the examination before the sheriff of any person concerning the winding up of a company, not necessarily a Scottish company, on cause shown, and the sheriff has appropriate powers of examination and report. The court may also order the arrest of a contributory who appears to be about to abscond or conceal property or evidence (I.A., s.158).

PUBLIC EXAMINATION OF OFFICERS

521 The liquidator may apply to the court at any time before the company is

---

[78] *Re Barlow Clowes Gilt Managers Ltd., supra.*
[79] By analogy from *Air Canada* v. *Secretary of State for Trade (No. 2)* [1983] 1 All E.R. 910, 916–917.
[80] *Re Barlow Clowes Gilt Managers Ltd., supra*, p. 397.
[81] *Re Jeffrey S. Levitt* [1992] 2 All E.R. 509; *Bishopsgate Investment Management (in provisional liquidation)* v. *Maxwell* [1992] 2 All E.R. 856, C.A.; *Re A. E. Farr* [1992] B.C.C. 150.
[82] *Re Arrows Ltd. (No. 2)* [1992] B.C.C. 125, affmd [1992] B.C.C. 446.
[83] *Re Arrows Ltd. (No. 2), supra.*
[84] *Re Polly Peck International plc* (Hoffman J., April 10, 1992), *The Independent*, May 18, 1992.

dissolved[85] for an order for the public examination of any person[86] who is or has been an officer of the company, or who has acted as liquidator, administrator or receiver, or who has taken part in or been concerned with the company's promotion, formation or management (I.A., s.133(1)). Unless the court orders otherwise the liquidator must make such an application if this is requested by one-half (in value) of the creditors or three-quarters (in value) of the contributories (I.A., s.133(2)). Creditors or contributories who wish to call upon the liquidator to apply for such an order must submit the request in writing, may be required to pay a deposit as caution for expenses and may have expenses awarded against them. If the request is in order, the liquidator must apply to the court within 28 days (1986 Rule 4.75, which prescribes further as to this procedure). Unless the court orders otherwise notice of the examination must be given to any special manager,[87] any creditor who has submitted a claim and any contributory. The liquidator may also advertise the hearing (1986 Rule 4.74). The examination is to be in public on any matter relating to the company (I.A., s.133(3)). Questions may be put by the liquidator, any special manager, creditor or contributory (I.A., s.133(4)). The court has power to enforce attendance (I.A., s.134). Unlike the English Insolvency Rules,[88] the Scottish Rules (and the Rules of Court) make no specific provision for the procedure at a public examination. A witness cannot refuse to answer questions on the ground that his answers might incriminate him.[89]

In a winding up by the court in Scotland, the court is also empowered to order the attendance of any officer of the company at any meeting of creditors or contributories or of the liquidation committee for the purpose of giving information as to the business or property of the company (I.A., s.157). The court may control the questions to be put at such a public examination.[90] Because of the powers existing under the Insolvency Act, sections 133 and 236 (above) it should not normally be necessary to resort to the Insolvency Act, section 157.

FRAUDULENT TRADING

522 If in the course of a winding up it appears that any of its business has been carried on with intent to defraud creditors of the company or of any other person or for any fraudulent purpose the court may on the application of the liquidator declare that any persons who were

---

[85] See para. 535, *post*.
[86] Including a person resident abroad or outwith the court's jurisdiction; *Re Seagull Manufacturing Co. Ltd.* [1991] 4 All E.R. 257.
[87] See paras. 488 and 489, *ante*.
[88] Insolvency Rules 1986 (S.I. 1986 No. 1925), rules 4.211 to 4.217.
[89] *Bishopsgate Investment Management Ltd.* v. *Maxwell* [1992] B.C.C. 214.
[90] See *Re London and Globe Finance Co.* (1902) 18 T.L.R. 661.

knowingly parties to the carrying on of business in such manner are to
be personally liable, without limit, for all or any debts or other liabilities
of the company (I.A., s.213). Such persons are also criminally liable
under section 458 (which applies whether or not the company is in
liquidation).[91] The court should order payment of the amount creditors
have lost in consequence of the fraudulent trading, and can include a
punitive element.[92]

For a successful application under the Insolvency Act, section 213
there must be evidence of actual dishonesty.[93] If the company carries
on trading and incurs debts when there is, to the knowledge of the
directors, no reasonable prospect of the creditors being paid, it is in
general a proper inference that the company is carrying on business
with intent to defraud.[94] "Defraud" is used in the criminal sense (a
view reinforced by the fact that the I.A., s.213 and s.458 were once a
single section, s.332 of the 1948 Act) and there must be actual
knowledge of a fraudulent scheme, not merely "lack of good faith."[95]
To be "knowingly a party to" fraudulent trading requires a positive
step, and mere failure by the secretary and financial adviser to draw
the directors' attention to the position of the company and its
consequences is not enough.[96] There must be intent to defraud, not
merely intent to prefer, so that the mere granting of a preference does
not give grounds for a claim under the Insolvency Act, section 213.[97] If,
however, the creditor was aware that the funds which have been used
to pay him were obtained from a third party with fraudulent intent, the
preferred creditor may be liable to repay the liquidator under section
213.[98] A single transaction may amount to "carrying on business."[99]
Where the defrauded creditor is "involuntary", such as the Inland
Revenue or Customs and Excise, the mere act of carrying on incurring
liabilities to such creditors with no honest belief that they will be paid
may be enough to establish intent to defraud.[1] Persons who participate
in fraudulent acts may be liable, even if they did not participate in the
business of the company; there must, however, be acts of fraud in the
business of the company itself, and an external party (even a parent
company) acting "fraudulently" is not liable under the section if there
has been no fraudulent trading by the company in liquidation.[2]

Before an application can be made under the Insolvency Act, section
213 the company must actually be in liquidation.

[91] See para. 525, *post.*
[92] *Re A Company (No. 001418 of 1988)* [1990] B.C.C. 526.
[93] *Re Patrick and Lyon Ltd.* [1933] Ch. 786.
[94] *Re William C. Leitch Bros. Ltd.* [1932] 2 Ch. 71; *R. v. Grantham* [1984] 2 W.L.R. 815; *Re Peake and Hall* [1985] B.C.C. 87.
[95] *Rossleigh Ltd. v. Carlaw,* 1986 S.L.T. 204.
[96] *Re Maidstone Buildings Ltd.* [1971] 1 W.L.R. 1085; 3 All E.R. 363.
[97] *Re Sarflax Ltd.* [1979] 1 All E.R. 529; *Rossleigh Ltd. v. Carlaw, supra.*
[98] *Re Gerald Cooper Chemicals Ltd.* [1978] Ch. 262; 2 All E.R. 49.
[99] *Ibid.,* n. 36.
[1] *Re A Company (No. 001418 of 1988), supra.*
[2] *R. v. Augustus Barnett & Son* [1986] B.C.C. 167.

The liquidator is bound to disclose to the general body of creditors a report he has obtained on the possibility of an application under the section.[3] Any order where the application was made by the liquidator, will enure to the benefit of the creditors in general.[4] Under section 630 a creditor or contributory could apply for a declaration under these provisions, for his own benefit,[5] but this aspect of the section was repealed by the Insolvency Act 1985, Schedule 6, paragraph 6, effective April 28, 1986.

Wrongful trading[6]

523 The Insolvency Act, sections 214 and 215 (originally section 15 of the Insolvency Act 1985, which came into force on April 28, 1986), allows a liquidator to apply to the court for an order requiring a director (including a shadow director and persons formerly directors or shadow directors) to contribute, without limit, to the assets of the company. This is in addition to any liability under the Insolvency Act, section 213 (I.A., s.214(8)). The company must be in insolvent liquidation, (*i.e.* its assets were, at the time winding up commenced, insufficient to meet its liabilities and the cost of winding up (I.A., s.214(6)) and the person against whom the order is sought must have been a director (or shadow director) at a time before liquidation commenced who knew or ought to have concluded that "there was no reasonable prospect that the company would avoid going into insolvent liquidation." The section does not, however, apply to events prior to April 28, 1986 (I.A., s.214(2)). The order is for the benefit of all creditors, without distinction between those whose debts were incurred before or after the "wrongful trading" commenced.[7] If a director is liable to make payment under the Insolvency Act, section 214 and other provisions, such as section 213, care should be taken to avoid requiring him to compensate twice for the same loss.[8]

A director can escape liability if he shows that he took every step to minimise the potential loss to creditors which (on the assumption that he knew insolvent liquidation was threatened) he ought to have taken. The tests to be applied are both objective and subjective. The director must measure up to the general standards reasonably to be expected of a director entrusted with the functions he bore, and also his own knowledge, skill and experience (I.A., s.214(4) and (5)).[9] The duty to take steps to minimise loss is positive, and is unlikely to be satisfied by his resignation unless that is the last step after unsuccessful efforts to persuade the board to act in accordance with duty. Proposing

---

[3] *Liquidator of Upper Clyde Shipbuilders*, 1975 S.L.T. 39.
[4] *Re William C. Leitch Bros. Ltd.* [1932] 2 Ch. 71, *ante*; and the same (*No. 2*) [1933] Ch. 261.
[5] *Re Cyona Distributors Ltd.* [1967] Ch. 889, C.A.; but see Russell L.J. at p. 908.
[6] See further, *Palmer*, paras. 15.459 to 15.461.
[7] *Re Purpoint Ltd.* [1991] B.C.C. 121.
[8] *Re Purpoint Ltd., supra.*
[9] *Re D.K.G. Contractors Ltd.* [1990] B.C.C. 903.

immediate liquidation will not necessarily be sufficient either, if a reasonable director (or that director from his special knowledge) could have seen a realistic alternative such as a sale of the undertaking.

Proceedings on an application under the Insolvency Act, section 214 are governed by the Insolvency Act, section 215. The liquidator may give evidence and call witnesses. The court may order the liability to be secured on the assets of the person liable. Liability may also attach to any person to whom a debt or obligation of the company has been assigned on the instructions of the person liable (other than in good faith and for value, without notice). If the person concerned is a creditor of the company, the court may impose a postponed ranking on his claim (I.A., s.215(4)).

A director may also incur personal liability if he participates in an incorrect declaration of solvency as a result of which the company redeemed or purchased its own shares without sufficient finance (I.A., s.76).[10]

Breach of trust

524 If in the course of a winding up, it appears that any person who has taken part in the formation, promotion or management of the company, or any past or present director, liquidator, administrator or administrative receiver or any officer of the company has misapplied company assets or been guilty of breach of trust in relation to the company, the court may order an investigation into his conduct and may order restoration of the property or other payment to the company by way of compensation (I.A., s.212). An application to the court under the Insolvency Act, section 212 may be made by the liquidator, or any creditor or contributory. A contributory requires the leave of the court, but need not have a financial interest in the outcome (I.A., s.212(5)).

The debate in England as to the nature of "misfeasance proceedings" under the predecessor of the Insolvency Act, section 212 (s.631) is of only indirect interest in Scotland. It appears that English law has reached the conclusion that the section refers to breach of fiduciary duty involving a misapplication or wrongful retention of the company's assets.[11] This, it is suggested, is equally true of Scotland where common law principles of breach of trust would apply. This section is procedural, designed to deal with claims based on "breach of trust" in a wide sense. It is intended to permit proceedings incidental to a pending liquidation, and strict rules of pleading do not apply.[12]

---

[10] See para. 465, *ante*.
[11] *Selangor United Rubber Estates Ltd.* v. *Cradock* [1967] 1 W.L.R. 1168, 1173, 1174; 2 All E.R. 1255; *Re Horsley & Wright Ltd.* [1982] 2 W.L.R. 431; and see *Palmer*, paras. 8.544 *et seq.*, and 15.466 to 15.471.
[12] *Liquidators of City of Glasgow Bank* v. *Mackinnon* (1892) 9 R. 535; *Blin* v. *Johnstone*, 1988 S.L.T. 335.

Nevertheless, the application must aver the facts upon which it is based, and section 212 is not the appropriate procedure for investigating the facts which might found a claim under this section, for which other sections provide.[13] An order under section 631 was granted where, after a winding-up petition had been presented before the order had been made, directors procured the payment of certain claims of their own against the company.[14] Illustrations of the application of section 631 in England include directors using funds for objects not sanctioned by the memorandum, paying dividends out of capital, making secret profits and selling their own property to the company.[15] An order has been refused where directors sold the company's business as a going concern, thus preserving employment for themselves and others, when (it was alleged) a higher price could have been secured by selling its assets.[16] If the company has received back the benefit of the funds misapplied, and has therefore suffered no loss, the director is not liable.[17] If an order is made, it cannot be compensated by the amount of any claim the person liable may have as a creditor.[18]

The Insolvency Act, section 212 is of wider scope than the former law (s.631) and extends to any person concerned in the management, etc., of the company. Previously, the Act only applied to persons holding the specified posts of director, manager, liquidator or officer, but section 212 includes persons employed by the company or providing services to it. The Act still applies only "in the course of" a winding up, so that dissolution of the company (even if that is later declared void) terminates any proceedings under the Insolvency Act, section 212, as under section 631.[19]

524A   Section 212 provides a remedy to the liquidator based upon facts which he is in a position to aver. It is not to be used as a method of obtaining information in order to establish such facts, for which other provisions in the Insolvency Act (such as sections 236 and 237) provide the appropriate procedure.[19a]

Criminal liability

525 It is a criminal offence to carry on the business of a company with intent to defraud creditors, whether or not the company is being wound up (s.458). This offence is historically linked to what is now the Insolvency

---

[13] *Gray* v. *Davidson*, 1991 S.L.T.(Sh.Ct.) 61; S.C.L.R. 38.
[14] *Liquidator of the Bankers and General Insurance Co. Ltd.* v. *Lithauer*, 1924 S.L.T. 775.
[15] See *Palmer*, para. 14.469.
[16] *Re Welfab Engineers Ltd.* [1990] B.C.C. 600.
[17] *Re Derek Randall Enterprises Ltd.* [1990] B.C.C. 749 (C.A.).
[18] *Re Anglo French Co-operative Society* (1882) 21 Ch.D. 492; *Re Derek Randall Enterprises Ltd.*, *supra*.
[19] *Re Lewis and Smart Ltd.* [1954] 1 W.L.R. 755; 2 All E.R. 19.
[19a] *Gray* v. *Davidson*, 1991 S.L.T. (Sh.Ct.) 61; S.C.L.R. 38.

Act, section 213, civil liability for "fraudulent trading,"[20] but the association with liquidation was severed by the Companies Act 1981, section 96, which removed the requirement that the company be in liquidation at the time of the prosecution.[21] The decisions on the former law, as to what constitutes an offence under section 458 and the basis of civil liability under the Insolvency Act, section 213 remain valid.[22]

Other criminal offences in connection with liquidation arise under the Insolvency Act, sections 206 to 211. These relate to concealment of property and falsification of records in advance of winding up, failure to co-operate with the liquidator and false statements to him, and fraudulent misrepresentations to creditors to procure their consent to any arrangement relating to the company. Corrupt inducement to procure the nomination of a particular person as liquidator is an offence under the Insolvency Act, section 164. If it appears that any past or present officer, or any member, of a company being wound up by the court has been guilty of an offence, the court may direct the liquidator to report the matter to the Lord Advocate. The liquidator has a duty to report any suspected offence, and to assist in any prosecution (I.A., ss.218, 219).

DISQUALIFICATION OF DIRECTORS[23]

526 If a person is found liable to contribute to the assets of a company under the Insolvency Act, section 213 or 214 the court may also disqualify him from acting as a director, etc., for up to 15 years (Company Directors Disqualification Act 1986: hereafter referred to as the "Disqualification Act," s.10).

Where a company has gone into liquidation and appears to be insolvent, (*i.e.* its assets will not meet its liabilities and the liquidation expenses) the liquidator must submit a return to the Secretary of State giving details of every director or shadow director whom he considers to be "unfit to be concerned in the management of companies" (Disqualification Act, s.6). A return (or a return stating there is no such person) is normally required within six months of the commencement of liquidation, in the prescribed form.[24] The Secretary of State may proceed to apply to the court for a disqualification order for a minimum of two years and a maximum of 15 years (Disqualification Act, ss.6 and 7).

PROHIBITED NAMES

527 It was considered particularly offensive and misleading to the public

---

[20] See *Palmer*, 23rd ed., para. 87–72; n. 19ᵃ, *Gray* v. *Davidson*, *supra*.

[21] It is immaterial whether the alleged offence occurred before or after December 22, 1981, when the 1981 amendment became effective; *R.* v. *Redmond and Redmond* [1984] 6 C.L. 44.

[22] See para. 522, *ante*.

[23] See further, *Palmer*, paras. 8.101 *et seq*.

[24] See the Insolvent Companies (Reports on Conduct of Directors) (No. 2) (Scotland) Rules 1986 (S.I. 1986 No. 1916 (s.140)).

that directors of insolvent companies could form a new business under the old name and resume trading free from the liabilities of the former company. The Insolvency Act, section 216 makes it an offence for a person who was a director or shadow director of a company at any time within 12 months before its insolvent liquidation to be concerned in carrying on business (as a company or otherwise) under a name which is the same as, or similar to, that of the insolvent company. The court may grant leave to use such a name, and the 1986 Rules (Rules 4.78–4.82) regulate the application procedure and allow the "prohibited" name to be used without leave in certain circumstances. The court's leave is not required if there is a "hive-down" or transfer of the company's business arranged by the liquidator and notice has been duly given to the creditors (1986 Rule 4.80). A director or shadow director may obtain a general exemption from the Insolvency Act, section 216 if he applies to the court within seven days of liquidation (1986 Rule 4.81). If there is a second company which is not in liquidation but has had a "prohibited" name (*i.e.* a similar name) for 12 months before the second company went into liquidation, and which has not been "dormant"[25] at any point during that time, leave of the court is not required for a director of the insolvent company to be associated with the company that is still active (1986 Rule 4.82).

RECIPROCAL ENFORCEMENT OF COURT ORDERS

528 The Insolvency Act, section 426 provides for the reciprocal enforcement of orders of the courts in the various parts of the United Kingdom in relation to insolvency matters.[26] It is similar to the superseded section 570, but applies to all "insolvency proceedings" (I.A., s.426(4) and (5)). Regulations[27] extend the obligation of mutual assistance to any "relevant territory." Orders relating to property are not automatically enforceable in another jurisdiction (I.A., s.426(2)), but the courts are under a general duty to provide mutual assistance. The Civil Jurisdiction and Judgments Act 1982 does not apply to insolvency proceedings.[28] The Insolvency Act, section 426 applies to any order made after the presentation of the petition, even if a winding-up order has not yet been granted.[29] The application for an enforcement order must be made to that court which would have had jurisdiction over the company if it was registered in the country concerned (I.A., s.426(5)).[30] The section should be confined to matters arising in course of the administration of the liquidation and the court

---

[25] ss.252, 253; see *Palmer*, para. 2.127.
[26] *e.g., Vegetable Oils Products Co. Ltd.*, 1923 S.L.T. 114.
[27] Operation of Insolvency Courts (Designation of Relevant Countries and Territories) Order 1986 (S.I. 1986 No. 2123).
[28] Civil Jurisdiction and Judgments Act 1982, s.17 and Sched. 5.
[29] *Re Dynamics Corp. of America* [1972] 3 All E.R. 1046.
[30] *Johnstone's Trs.* v. *Roose* (1884) 12 R. 1.

should not make an order which would require to be enforced by a court furth of Scotland if it cannot be made effectual.[31]

SISTING WINDING-UP PROCEEDINGS: RECALL OF WINDING-UP ORDER

529 The court has discretion on the application of the liquidator or any creditor or contributory to stay winding-up proceedings at any time either for a limited period or altogether and on such conditions as it thinks fit (I.A., s.147(1)). A copy of any such order must be sent by the company, or otherwise as the court may prescribe, to the registrar of companies (I.A., s.147(3)). In exercising its discretion under this section, the court will consider the interests of commercial morality and not merely the wishes of creditors, *e.g.* if there appear to be irregularities requiring investigation to continue.[32]

BOOKS AND PAPERS

530 All books and papers of the company and the liquidator are prima facie evidence of the matters recorded therein, in questions between the contributories and the company (I.A., s.191). The liquidator must maintain a sederunt book to record minutes of meetings, statements of affairs, accounts and other matters arising during the winding up. It is to be available for inspection at all reasonable hours by any interested person. Entries are sufficient evidence of the matters recorded, except where founded on by the liquidator in his own interest (1986 Rule 7.33). Statements of affairs and other statements made pursuant to the Insolvency Act and 1986 Rules are admissible in evidence against the person making or concurring in them (I.A., s.433).[33]

The sederunt book, if in non-documentary form, must be capable of reproduction in legible form. It is to be retained for at least 10 years after the date of dissolution of the company (1986 Rule 7.35(5) to (7), added by the 1987 Amendments).[34]

The Insolvency Act 1986 repealed the provisions (s.640) for retention and disposal of the books and papers of the company. Under section 222 as amended by the Insolvency Acts 1985 and 1986 accounting records are to be kept for at least three years (private companies) or six years (public companies) from the date they were made, subject to any provision contained in the Insolvency Rules. 1986 Rule 7.34 (added by the 1987 Amendments) contains an obligation to transmit the company's books and papers to any practitioner appointed to

---

[31] *Liquidators of the California Redwood Co. Ltd.* v. *Walker* (1886) 13 R. 810.
[32] *Re Telescriptor Syndicate Ltd.* [1903] 2 Ch. 174.
[33] The Insolvency Practitioners Regulations 1990 (S.I. 1990 No. 439) prescribe (in Part IV) the records to be maintained by an insolvency practitioner and provide for access thereto.
[34] See also the Insolvency Practitioners Regulations 1990, Pt. IV (n. 61.1, *supra*).

succeeding insolvency proceedings. If no such proceedings follow the liquidator may dispose of the records of the company as authorised by the appropriate body (as specified in the Rule) or, if no directions have been given within 12 months of dissolution of the company, at his discretion.

STAMP DUTIES

531 In a winding up by the court, or a creditors' voluntary winding up, every conveyance is exempt from stamp duty, provided that the subjects remain the property of the company for the benefit of its creditors and every other instrument which relates solely to the company's property is also exempt from duty (I.A., s.190).

ADJUSTING RIGHTS OF CONTRIBUTORIES: DISTRIBUTION OF SURPLUS

532 Subject to the payment of creditors and the expenses of liquidators, and to the adjustment of the rights of contributories *inter se*, any surplus is distributable among the persons entitled thereto by order of the court (I.A., s.154; 1986 Rule 4.66(5)). The same procedure for making up accounts every 26 weeks showing a scheme of division which applies to creditors' claims applies to the distribution of any surplus (1986 Rule 4.68, applying ss.52 and 53 of the Bankruptcy (Scotland) Act 1985).[35]

Uncalled capital is part of the assets of the company.[36] Where shares are unequally paid up, an adjustment must be made between the contributories by way of call (I.A., s.150),[37] unless the articles provide otherwise.[38] Where articles provided that losses were to be borne in proportion to capital paid up, no call could be made on partly paid shares for the benefit of those fully paid up.[39] If shares are issued at a discount the amount credited by way of discount is to be treated as so much uncalled capital and the rights adjusted accordingly.[40]

"Surplus assets" has no technical meaning, but must be determined by the context in which the phrase is used.[41] It may mean the fund in the hands of the liquidator after meeting all claims of outside creditors

---

[35] See para. 492, *ante*. The Bankruptcy (Scotland) Bill 1992 proposes to substitute "6 months" for "26 weeks".
[36] *Re Bridgewater Navigation Co.* (1889) 14 App.Cas. 525.
[37] *Paterson* v. *McFarlane* (1875) 2 R. 490; *Stewart* v. *Liquidator of Scottish American Sugar Syndicate Ltd.* (1901) 3 F. 585; 8 S.L.T. 786; *Re Phoenix Oil and Transport Co. Ltd.* [1958] Ch. 560.
[38] *Ex p. Maude* (1870) L.R. 6 Ch.App. 51.
[39] *Re Kinaton (Borneo) Rubber Ltd.* [1923] 1 Ch. 124.
[40] *Whelton* v. *Saffrey* [1897] A.C. 299.
[41] *Re Bridgewater Navigation Co.* [1891] 2 Ch. 317; *Re New Transvaal Co.* [1896] 2 Ch. 750; *Re Madame Tussaud & Sons Ltd.* [1927] 1 Ch. 657.

and expenses,[42] or it may mean what remains after payment also of the capital paid up on all classes of shares.[43] Surplus assets distributed are treated as capital for tax purposes, even if they consist to some extent of undistributed profits.[44]

The provisions of the Insolvency Act, sections 81 and 82 entitle the representatives of a deceased contributory and the trustee of a bankrupt one to participate in any distribution of capital in place of the contributory. Where the liquidator proves for calls in the estate of a bankrupt member, that does not *per se* make the shares paid up for the purpose of participating in surplus assets.[45]

Under the Bankruptcy (Scotland) Act 1985, section 32(6) and (1), discharge reinvests the bankrupt in any shares which still form part of his estate, and (in contrast to the position under the former law) he will therefore be entitled to any subsequent dividend or distribution.

Capital paid up in advance of calls and interest thereon must, as a rule, be repaid before distribution of capital paid up under calls.[46]

Surplus assets are distributable notwithstanding a provision in the memorandum to the effect that no part of the assets is to be transferred to the members.[47] Where, however, the memorandum not only prohibits distribution of surplus assets to the members but expressly provides for their distribution otherwise (*e.g.* to a charity carrying out similar objects) the court will give effect to these provisions, notwithstanding the absence of parallel provisions in the articles.[48] All shareholders are entitled to equal treatment unless and to the extent that their rights are modified by the contract (as found in the memorandum, articles or terms of issue) under which they hold their shares.[49] Allegations that fraud induced some shareholders to subscribe, but not others, are not grounds for departing from the principle of equal treatment.[50] Prima facie, the distribution of surplus assets is to be in proportion to nominal capital (or, in the case of a company limited by guarantee not having a share capital, equally), and any deficiency must be borne on the same basis.[51] Sums due to a member as such (dividends, distribution of profits, etc.), which are not

[42] *Re Crichton's Oil Co.* [1902] 2 Ch. 86; *Dimbula Valley (Ceylon) Tea Co. Ltd.* v. *Laurie* [1961] Ch. 353.

[43] *Re Ramel Syndicate Ltd.* [1911] 1 Ch. 749; *Re Dunstable Portland Cement Co.* (1932) 48 T.L.R. 223.

[44] *Staffordshire Coal and Iron Co. Ltd.* v. *Brogan* [1963] 1 W.L.R. 905 (H.L.); 3 All E.R. 277.

[45] *Re West Coast Goldfields* [1906] 1 Ch. 1.

[46] *Re Wakefield Rolling Stock Co.* [1892] 3 Ch. 165.

[47] *Re Merchant Navy Supply Association Ltd.* (1947) 177 L.T. 386.

[48] *Liverpool and District Hospital for Diseases of the Heart* v. *Att.-Gen.* [1981] 1 All E.R. 994.

[49] *Liquidators of Williamson* v. *Buchanan Steamers Ltd.*, 1936 S.L.T. 106. See also *Town and Gown Assoc. Ltd.*, 1948 S.L.T. (Notes) 71; *Scottish Acid and Alkali Co. Ltd.*, 1950 S.L.T. (Notes) 53; *Liquidator of the Humboldt Redwood Co. Ltd.* v. *Coats*, 1908 S.C. 751; 15 S.L.T. 1028; *Monkland Iron and Coal Co.* v. *Henderson* (1883) 10 R. 494.

[50] *Edinburgh Employers' Liability and General Insurance Co. Ltd.* (1893) 1 S.L.T. 321.

[51] *Re London India Rubber Co.* (1868) L.R. 5 Eq. 519; *Whelton* v. *Saffrey* [1897] A.C. 299.

to be treated as claims in the liquidation, are to be taken into account when adjusting the rights of contributories (I.A., s.74(2)(*f*)).

If a contract for the redemption or purchase of the company's own shares has not been implemented when winding up commences it may be enforced so long as the contract did not provide for a date of redemption subsequent to commencement of liquidation, and provided also the company has continued to satisfy the financial conditions for redemption or purchase. Subject to these conditions (and the prior rights, if any, of any other shares) the redemption or purchase price has priority over other payments to members (I.A., s.178(4)–(6)).

Unclaimed dividends and undistributed assets

533 Under the Insolvency Act, section 193 unclaimed dividends and other undistributed balances are to be deposited in an "appropriate bank or institution" as defined in the Bankruptcy (Scotland) Act, section 73(1) (as amended by the Banking Act 1987[52]) in name of the Accountant of Court. Claims for payment may be submitted to the Accountant of Court within seven years. Any unclaimed sums are thereafter forfeited to the Secretary of State.[53]

FINAL MEETINGS AND RETURN BY LIQUIDATOR

534 When the liquidation has been completed, apart from the final return and (possibly) the final distribution, the liquidator must summon a final meeting of creditors under the Insolvency Act, section 146. At least 28 days' notice must be given to all admitted creditors, including those whose claims have been settled (1986 Rule 4.31(1)). An account of his administration is to be submitted, and the creditors may question him on his final report (1986 Rule 4.31(2) and (3)). The meeting has to decide whether to grant the liquidator his release, and if it is refused he can seek release from the Accountant of Court (I.A., s.146(1)(*b*); 1986 Rule 4.31(3) and (6)). If no quorum is present at a duly convened final meeting the liquidator reports this to the court and the final meeting is deemed to have taken place, and not to have refused his release (1986 Rule 4.31(5)). When the meeting is held (or deemed to have been held) the liquidator must report the proceedings to the court and to the registrar of companies within seven days on the prescribed form (Form 4.17 (Scot)) along with a copy of his report, stating whether or not he has been released (1986 Rule 4.31(4)). The final meeting may be

---

[52] The Bank of England, an institution authorised under the Banking Act 1987 or a person for the time being specified in Sched. 2 to that Act (Banking Act, Sched. 6, para. 20).

[53] Bankruptcy (Scotland) Act 1985, s.58, as applied by I.A., s.193(3) and 1986 Rule 4.68. The Secretary of State has power to make a discretionary payment not exceeding £20 (plus interest) (Law Reform (Miscellaneous Provisions) (Scotland) Act 1940, s.6(2) as amended by S.I. 1974 No. 1274). The Banking Act 1979 (referred to in the Rules) was superseded by the Banking Act 1987.

convened before the final distribution but cannot be held until this has taken place (I.A., s.146(2)). The liquidator must retain sufficient funds to meet the cost of the final meeting (I.A., s.146(3)).

There is no provision in the Insolvency Act or the 1986 Rules for any "final meeting" of contributories in a winding up by the court (even if there is a surplus available for distribution to members). The liquidator can resign only in the circumstances prescribed in the Rules (I.A., s.172(6)), which do not include completion of the distribution of any surplus to contributories (1986 Rule 4.28(3)). It is a strange omission in the Act and the Rules that, although the liquidator's statutory duties include adjustment of the rights of contributories (I.A., s.154; 1986 Rule 4.66(5)) the liquidator in a winding up by the court is, apparently, to make his final report and obtain his release from the creditors alone, without considering whether (if at all) he has fulfilled his responsibilities to the members.

A liquidator who finds that the assets will not cover the liquidation expenses can proceed to obtain "early dissolution" and his own release under the Insolvency Act, section 204 (see below), but even a small balance available for creditors will require the full procedure, unless the court will consider that its general powers enable it to "simplify" the procedure on the ground of unreasonable cost (see paragraphs 535 and 539, below).

DISSOLUTION OF THE COMPANY

535 If, in the case of winding up by the court after the first meetings in the liquidation (I.A., s.138; 1986 Rule 4.12), the liquidator considers that the realisable assets of the company will not cover the liquidation expenses he may apply to the court for the immediate dissolution of the company (I.A., s.204). In the Court of Session, application is by letter to the deputy principal clerk who obtains a report from the Auditor of Court on whether in the Auditor's opinion the company may be dissolved and the liquidator "exonerated and discharged," and whether the liquidator should be allowed to retain any remaining funds as his remuneration.[53a] A copy of the order must be forwarded to the registrar of companies within 14 days along with the prescribed Form 4.28 (Scot) (I.A., s.204(4); 1986 Rule 4.77). The court may defer the effective date of dissolution on the application of any interested person, and a copy of any such order must also be forwarded to the registrar within seven days (there is no prescribed form) (I.A., s.204(5) and (6)). In the absence of any deferral, the company is dissolved three months after registration of the court's order (I.A., s.204(4)).

[53a] Court of Session Practice Note No. 4 of 1992 (December 3, 1992), 1992 S.L.T. (News) 393. It is assumed that by "exonerated and discharged" the practice note means "released" (which is the term used in the Insolvency Act and the Scottish Rules). While the practice note bears to refer to the Court of Session only, the procedure in the sheriff court will, presumably, be similar.

If the Insolvency Act, section 204 is inapplicable, and the winding up is completed in due course, dissolution follows automatically three months after the registrar of companies has registered the final return (Form 4.17 (Scot)) under the Insolvency Act, section 172(8) and 1986 Rule 4.31 (I.A., s.205(1) and (2)). There is power for the court to defer the date of dissolution on the application of any interested party, who must deliver a copy of any such order to the registrar within seven days (I.A., s.205(5) and (6)).

If the registrar has reasonable cause to believe either that no liquidator is acting, or that the affairs of the company are fully wound up and the returns which are required to be made by the liquidator have not been made for six consecutive months, the registrar may take steps under section 652 to have the company struck off. The formal warning notice to the company under section 652(2) does not apply, and the registrar publishes a notice in the *Edinburgh Gazette* (and sends it to the company and any liquidator) to the effect that the company will be struck off and dissolved on the expiry of three months, unless cause is shown to the contrary (s.652(4)). When the registrar in due course strikes the company off he publishes a notice of this in the *Gazette*, and on the date of publication the company is dissolved (s.652(5)). The liability of directors, etc., and members continues, as does the court's power to wind the company up (s.652(6)). A liquidator can still "request" the registrar to invoke section 652, but the simplified procedure for automatic dissolution under sections 204 and 205 should make this unnecessary.

Dissolution orders and final returns require to be notified in the *Gazette* by the registrar under sections 42 and 711.

Upon dissolution, all the property of the company vests in the Crown as *bona vacatia* subject to the power of the Crown to disclaim (ss.654, 656, 657). This does not affect property held by the company on trust, in respect of which a vesting order may be made, even where the property in question has vested in the Crown.[54] Property vested in the Crown may be disposed of by it notwithstanding any subsequent order declaring the dissolution void or restoring the company to the register, but if such an order is made the Crown is liable to account to the company for the proceeds (s.655) provided the disposal was on or after December 22, 1981, when the relevant section of the Companies Act 1981 took effect (s.655(5)). A dissolved company is not liable to sequestration as a "deceased debtor" under the Bankruptcy (Scotland) Act 1985, section 5.[55] A dissolved company does not exist and, therefore, an insurer to whom its right of action has not been assigned has no *locus* (by way of subrogation) to maintain an action in the dissolved company's name.[56]

---

[54] *Re Strathblaine Estates Ltd.* [1948] Ch. 228; see also *Smith & Another, Petrs.*, 1969 S.L.T. (Notes) 94 and cases cited at *Palmer*, para. 15.483.

[55] *Steward & McDonald* v. *Brown* (1898) 225 R. 1042; 6 S.L.T. 85.

[56] *M. H. Smith (Plant Hire) Ltd.* v. *Mainwaring* [1986] B.C.L.C. 342.

Power to declare dissolution void

536 Where a company has been dissolved the court may within two years declare the dissolution to have been void.[57] The order must be notified to the registrar of companies (s.651(3)). If the application is made timeously the order of the court may be made after expiry of the statutory period.[58]

The Court of Session has granted an order under this section 10 years after dissolution, when the time limit was two years, to authorise the liquidator to execute a conveyance of foreign property, in the exercise of its *nobile officium*,[59] but this decision has been distinguished as applicable to its peculiar facts only and is now of little practical importance. In general, with the exception created in respect of personal injury claims by the 1989 Act (noted below), no application under section 651 after the two-year period is competent and application for a grant of title must be made to the Crown.[60] The application under section 651 should not seek further orders authorising the liquidator to take certain steps, since the section itself provides (s.651(2)) that, on the dissolution being declared void, such proceedings may be taken as if the company had not been dissolved.[61]

An application under section 651 may be made by the liquidator or any person who appears to the court to be interested (s.651(1)). "Person" includes a legal person such as a company.[62] A person who has acted as liquidator without being appointed is sufficiently "interested" by virtue of a possible claim for remuneration *quantum meruit* or liability for unauthorised dealing with Crown property.[63] A solicitor acting for a client who would be "a person interested" is not himself so qualified.[64]

The purpose of an order under section 651 (apart from the issues raised by personal injury claims, discussed below) is to make possible the distribution of assets which belonged to the company before dissolution and which had for some reason been overlooked; accordingly the court refused to make a declaration in favour of a company to enable it to receive a legacy which had never belonged to it.[65] If the Crown has disposed of property vested in it as *bona vacantia*

---

[57] s.651, as amended by the Companies Act 1989, s.141 (effective November 16, 1989); Companies Act 1989, s.215(1)(*a*). The Insolvency Act 1985, Sched. 6, para. 45 would have extended the period to 12 years, but this provision was never brought into force, and is repealed by the Companies Act 1989, Sched. 24. *McCall & Stephen Ltd.*, 1920 2 S.L.T. 26.

[58] *Dowling, Petr.*, 1960 S.L.T. (Notes) 76; *Re Scad Ltd.* [1941] Ch. 386.

[59] *Collins Brothers & Co. Ltd.*, 1916 S.C. 620; 1 S.L.T. 309.

[60] *Lord Macdonald's Curator*, 1924 S.C. 163; S.L.T. 64; *Forth Shipbreaking Co. Ltd.*, 1924 S.C. 489; S.L.T. 381.

[61] *Champdany Jute Co. Ltd.*, 1924 S.C. 209; S.L.T. 143.

[62] *Re Spottiswoode, Dixon and Hunting Ltd.* [1912] 1 Ch. 410.

[63] *Re Wood and Martin (Brick Laying Contractors) Ltd.* [1971] 1 W.L.R. 293; 1 All E.R. 732.

[64] *Re Roehampton Swimming Pool Ltd.* [1968] 1 W.L.R. 1963; 3 All E.R. 661.

[65] *Re Servers of the Blind League* [1960] 1 W.L.R. 564; 2 All E.R. 298.

(on or after December 22, 1981) it must account to the company for the proceeds after the dissolution has been declared void (s.655).

The granting of an order declaring the dissolution to have been void does not render valid proceedings taken against the company after dissolution but before the date of the order.[66] It has been held in England that a summons under the Insolvency Act, section 213 which had been issued but had not been served prior to dissolution was not revived by an order under section 651.[67]

An application may be made under section 651 in all cases where a company has been "dissolved," including section 652. This is without prejudice to the further power of the court to restore to the register a company which has been struck off under section 652 (s.653). The conditions necessary to succeed under section 653 are more onerous than those required by section 651, which may therefore be chosen for preference if both are available.[68] Relief under sections 651 or 653 should be sought as soon as reasonably practicable after discovery of the dissolution.[69]

Personal injury claims

537 An individual who has a claim for damages in respect of personal injuries against his employer (if that is a company) cannot recover if the company employer has been dissolved. The injured party must first obtain an order under section 651 restoring the company to the register.[70] To enable such claims to proceed (and, in practice, to be recoverable from the employer's insurers under the Third Parties (Rights Against Insurers) Act 1930)[71] the Companies Act 1989, section 141 amended section 651 so as to remove the two-year time limit, but only in respect of claims for damages for personal injuries. "Personal injuries" means "any disease and any impairment of a person's physical or mental condition" (s.651(7)) and includes claims under the Law Reform (Miscellaneous Provisions) Act 1934, section 1(2)(c) (funeral expenses), the Fatal Accidents Act 1976 or the Damages (Scotland) Act 1976 (s.651(5)). Restoration may be refused if the court considers that the proceedings would be time-barred, but this is at the court's discretion.[72] Section 141 of the 1989 Act came into force on the

---

[66] *Morris* v. *Morris* [1927] A.C. 252.
[67] *Re Lewis & Smart Ltd.* [1954] 1 W.L.R. 755; 2 All E.R. 19.
[68] *Re M. Belmont & Co. Ltd.* [1952] Ch. 10; *Re Wood and Martin (Brick Laying Contractors) Ltd.*, *ante*, *per* Megarry J. who may be read as impliedly withdrawing his criticisms of this proposition expressed in *Re Test Holdings (Clifton) Ltd.* [1970] Ch. 285, 392; see *Palmer*, para. 15.487.
[69] *Re Thompson & Riches Ltd.* [1981] 1 W.L.R. 682; 2 All E.R. 477.
[70] *Bradley* v. *Eagle Star Insurance Co. Ltd.* [1989] A.C. 957.
[71] See para. 501, *ante*; s.141 was passed to reverse the specific injustice identified in *Bradley* v. *Eagle Star*, *supra*.
[72] *Re Workvale Ltd.* [1991] 1 W.L.R. 294; upheld on appeal [1992] B.C.C. 349; 1 W.L.R. 416; *Percy* v. *Garwyn Ltd.*, 1991 G.W.D. 2–80.

passing of the Act (November 16, 1989; s.215(1)(*a*)) but it applies to any company dissolved up to 20 years previously (s.651(4)).[73]

Restoration to register

538 An application may be made under section 653 within 20 years of the publication in the *Edinburgh Gazette* of the notice of dissolution under section 652 by the company or any member or creditor who "feels aggrieved" by the company having been struck off. "Creditor" includes "contingent or prospective creditor" or one whose claim is for damages or is otherwise illiquid.[74] "Member" includes the personal representatives of a deceased member.[75] On the other hand, a person who acquired shares in or acquires a debt of the company after dissolution is not qualified to apply under section 653.[76]

The court requires to be satisfied, under section 653, that the company was at the time of striking off in business or otherwise that it is just to restore it to the register.[77] This may be as a preliminary to winding-up proceedings,[78] no order for revesting of the property in the company being required.[79] No penalty for default can be made as a condition of granting an application under section 653,[80] but a penalty can in effect be imposed through an order in respect of expenses.[81] A debt incurred after the dissolution does not, however, entitle the creditor to petition for restoration under section 653.[82]

The court may attach such directions as it thinks fit to an order under sections 651 or 653. For example, it may cure retrospectively all defects including want of registration in a charge which a solvent company purported to grant in ignorance of its having been struck off.[83] A creditor who became such after the date of dissolution cannot, however, both have restoration and preserve the remedies against individuals which he had while the company remained struck off.[84] Opposition in name of the company to an application to restore a company to the register must be duly authorised by its directors or members.[85] The English court has, however, also held that the

---

[73] A company dissolved within the previous two years may be restored under the original provisions (s.651(5)).

[74] *Re Harvest Lane Motor Bodies Ltd.* [1969] 1 Ch. 457.

[75] *Re Bayswater Trading Co. Ltd.* [1970] 1 W.L.R. 343; 1 All E.R. 608.

[76] *Re New Timbiqui Gold Mines Ltd.* [1961] Ch. 319.

[77] See *Charles Dale Ltd.*, 1927 S.C. 130; *Beith Unionist Association*, 1950 S.C. 1. A remit to a reporter may be appropriate.

[78] *Re Cambridge Coffee Room Association* [1951] 2 T.L.R. 1155; *Beith Unionist Association*, *supra*.

[79] *Re C. W. Dixon Ltd.* [1947] Ch. 251.

[80] *Re Brown Bayley's Steel Works Ltd.* (1905) 21 T.L.R. 374; *Re Moses and Cohen Ltd.* [1957] 1 W.L.R. 1007.

[81] *Re Court Lodge Development Co. Ltd.* [1973] 1 W.L.R. 1097; 3 All E.R. 425.

[82] *Re A.G.A. Estates Ltd.* [1986] P.C.C. 358.

[83] *Re Boxco Ltd.* [1970] Ch. 442.

[84] *Re Lindsay Bowman Ltd.* [1969] 1 W.L.R. 1443; 3 All E.R. 601.

[85] *Re Regent Insulation Co. Ltd.*, *The Times*, November 5, 1981; [1981] C.L.Y. 250.

company cannot in fact oppose the application and a member whose shares are fully paid has no interest to do so.[86]

If the Crown has (after December 22, 1981) disposed of property vested in it as *bona vacantia* it must account to the company for the proceeds after the company has been restored to the register (s.655).

Power of court to cure defects in procedure

539 The court is given general powers to cure defects in winding-up procedure (Bankruptcy (Scotland) Act 1985, s.63, as applied by 1986 Rule 7.32). The liquidator and others can be relieved from the consequences of failure to comply with the Insolvency Act 1986 or the 1986 Rules. Any step in the liquidation which cannot otherwise be done may be authorised, and this power extends to acts not specifically dealt with in the Act or the Rules. The court can dispense with any required act, appoint a liquidator to a vacancy or in place of the existing liquidator and extend or waive any time limit. The order may be conditional, including conditions as to expenses. The court's decision must be recorded in the sederunt book.

VOLUNTARY WINDING UP

540 The majority of liquidations are voluntary, initiated by resolution of the members. The companies which may be wound up voluntarily are those formed and/or registered under the Companies Acts of Great Britain (1985 and earlier) (I.A., ss.73, 84 and 251; Companies Act 1985, Pt. XXVI). An unregistered company, as defined in the Insolvency Act, section 220 cannot be wound up voluntarily but may register under Part XXII of the Act and then wind up voluntarily (I.A., s.221(4)).[87] For the winding up of a European Economic Interest Group see paragraph 411A, *ante*.

Voluntary winding up may be a "members' voluntary" or a "creditors' voluntary" liquidation, depending on whether or not a "declaration of solvency" has been made under the Insolvency Act, s.89 (see below). The Insolvency Act 1986 deals with both forms, even where there is no question of "insolvency" in the financial sense. Chapters II and V of Part IV of the Act (ss.84–90 and 107–116) apply to both forms, Chapter III (ss.91–96) applies to a members' voluntary winding up and Chapter IV (ss.97–106) applies to a creditors' voluntary winding up.

In addition, a number of the remaining sections in Parts IV, VI, VII, XII, XIII, XV, XVII, XVIII and XIX of the Insolvency Act 1986 apply to voluntary winding up as well as to winding up by the court. These have already been noted above in that context. It may be assumed that

[86] *Re H. Clarkson (Overseas)* 3 B.C.C. 606.
[87] *Southall* v. *British Mutual Life Assurance Society* (1871) L.R. 6 Ch.App. 614. See para. 411, *ante*.

(unless otherwise indicated) the law and practice of voluntary winding up is the same as in winding up by the court. To avoid unnecessary repetition, the following apply to voluntary winding up as they do to winding up by the court, substituting (where relevant) the date of the resolution for the presentation of the petition as the date of commencement (see below):

—I.A., ss.74–83, defining "contributories" and their liability on list A or B (see paras. 459 to 465, *ante*);

—I.A., ss.163 and 188, requiring the liquidator to be designated by his official title and the company's stationery to show that it is in liquidation;

—I.A., s.164, penalising any attempt to influence the appointment of a liquidator by corrupt inducement;

—I.A., ss.175, 386, 387 and Sched. 6, defining "preferential debts" (see paras. 478 to 481 *ante*);

—I.A., s.185, on the "equalisation of diligence" (see paras. 499 and 500, *ante*)[88];

—I.A., s.186, on the power of the court to reduce contracts and substitute a liability for damages by or to the company (see para. 494, *ante*);

—I.A., s.187, allowing certain payments to employees and former employees (see para. 495, *ante*);

—I.A., s.189, regulating interest payable on debts due by the company (see para. 482, *ante*);

—I.A., s.191, as to the admissibility of books, etc., in evidence (along with 1986 Rule 7.33, the liquidator's sederunt book) and the Insolvency Practitioners Regulations 1990 (S.I. 1990 No. 439) Part IV (maintenance of records) (see para. 530, *ante*);

—I.A., s.192, providing for returns to the register in continuing liquidations (along with 1986 Rule 4.11, prescribing the six-monthly interval and form of return) (see para. 492, *ante*);

—I.A., s.193, dealing with unclaimed assets (along with 1986 Rule 4.68 and the Bankruptcy (Scotland) Act 1985, s.58, as there applied) (see para. 533, *ante*);

—I.A., ss.206–219 (together with the Company Directors Disqualification Act 1986), dealing with the misconduct of directors, etc. (see paras. 522 to 527, *ante*);

—I.A., ss.230–232 and 388–398, requiring liquidators to be "insolvency practitioners" and providing for their qualification, and saving the validity of their acts notwithstanding defects in their appointment or qualifications (see para. 440, *ante*);

—I.A., s.233, allowing the liquidator to obtain public utility supplies without payment of pre-liquidation accounts (see para. 518, *ante*);

---

[88] In a voluntary winding up I.A., s.185 takes effect from the commencement of winding up; in a winding up by the court it takes effect from the date of the order; see para. 599, *ante*.

—I.A., ss.242, 243, 244 and 245, invalidating "gratuitous alienations," "unfair preferences" "extortionate credit arrangements" and certain floating charges (together with the common law in this area) (see paras. 505 to 516, *ante*);

—sections 651–657 (of the Companies Act 1985), dealing with dissolution, striking off and restoration to the register (see paras. 535 to 538, *ante*).

These foregoing provisions are examined in detail in the part of this chapter dealing with winding up by the court.

The 1986 Rules Parts 5 (Creditors' Voluntary), 6 (Members' Voluntary) and 7 (General) as amended with effect from January 1, 1988 by the 1987 Amendments, which apply also to liquidations commenced before January 1, 1988, apply to voluntary liquidations and prescribe the appropriate forms. These Rules are based on Part 4, the Rules applying to winding up by the court. In creditors' voluntary liquidations Part 4 applies with modifications stated in Schedule 1 to the Rules. In members' voluntary liquidations only those Rules in Part 4 specified in Schedule 2, as modified therein, are applicable.

The resolution for voluntary winding up

541 Voluntary winding up is initiated by resolution of the company under the Insolvency Act, section 84, either:

1. a special resolution to wind up voluntarily, no reason being required (I.A., s.84(1)(*b*)); or
2. an extraordinary resolution that it cannot by reason of its liabilities continue its business and that it is advisable to wind up (I.A., s.84(1)(*c*)); or
3. an ordinary resolution passed in the event or at the time under which, in terms of its articles, the company is to be dissolved (I.A., s.84(1)(*a*)).

The proceedings resulting in the passing of a resolution to wind up should conform to the normal requirements for a valid resolution, *e.g.* as to prior authority of the directors[89] and the need to state that it is to be proposed as a special (or extraordinary) resolution,[90] and the necessity for a quorum to be present[91] all being duly registered members by authority of the board[92] but a valid resolution may be held to have been passed by the assent of all shareholders, even if the "meeting" was not properly constituted.[93] The "written resolution" procedure introduced by the Companies Act 1989 (inserting ss.381A

---

[89] *Haycroft Gold Reduction & Mining Co.* [1900] 2 Ch. 230; *State of Wyoming Syndicate* [1901] 2 Ch. 431.
[90] *Rennie* v. *Crichton's (Strichen) Ltd.*, 1927 S.L.T. 459.
[91] *Howling's Trs.* v. *Smith* (1905) 7 F. 390; 12 S.L.T. 628.
[92] *Re Zinotty Properties Ltd.* [1984] 3 All E.R. 754.
[93] *Re M. J. Shanley Contracting* [1980] C.L.Y. 268.

and 381B in the Companies Act 1985) may be used to pass a resolution for the commencement of voluntary winding up (s.381A(6)). It is, however, arguable that an extraordinary or special resolution cannot be "passed" by using a written resolution procedure contained in the articles.[94] A resolution having been passed, *ex facie* validly, shareholders and creditors must abide by it until it is shown to be invalid.[95] The minutes recording the resolution remain effective proof of its passing until shown otherwise, *e.g.* by declaratory action.[96] The fact that other, *ultra vires*, resolutions associated with the winding-up resolution were passed at the same time will not necessarily invalidate it.[97] When passed the resolution must be lodged with the registrar of companies within 15 days (I.A., s.84(3)). It must also be advertised in the *Edinburgh Gazette* within 14 days, (I.A., s.85), and failure to comply will necessitate a petition to the *nobile officium* for authority to insert the notice out of time.[98]

The Companies Act 1981, section 106 introduced a requirement (consolidated in s.588), now repealed, that, notwithstanding any power to foreshorten notice, at least seven days' notice of the company meeting had to be given. This was apparently in an attempt to overcome the mischief which might result if the members dispensed with notice and installed a liquidator of their own choice to realise the assets in a manner suitable to the members before the creditors could intervene.[99] It was not successful, because section 588(6) provided that the resolution remained valid even if less than seven days' notice had been given.[1] There is no similar requirement under the Insolvency Act, but creditors are better protected by the requirement that the liquidator must be an authorised insolvency practitioner (and hence subject to professional discipline), that the directors' powers if there is no liquidator are severely restricted[2] and that until the creditors' meeting takes place the powers of a liquidator appointed by the company are also very limited.[3]

Commencement of voluntary winding up

542 All voluntary liquidations commence on the date of the resolution

---

[94] *Re Barry Artist Ltd.* [1985] 1 W.L.R. 1305; see *Palmer*, paras. 7.715, *et seq.*

[95] *Lawson Seed and Nursery Co.* v. *Lawson & Son* (1886) 14 R. 154; *Howling's Trs.* v. *Smith, supra*; *Re Bailey Hay & Co. Ltd.* [1971] 3 All E.R. 693.

[96] *City of Glasgow Bank Liquidators* (1880) 7 R. 1196; *Grieve* v. *Kilmarnock Motor Co.*, 1923 S.C. 491; S.L.T. 308 (in which an action of declarator in the sheriff court was allowed to proceed).

[97] *Thomson* v. *Henderson's Transvaal Estates* [1908] Ch. 765.

[98] *Liquidator of Nairn Public Hall Co.*, 1946 S.C. 395; S.L.T. 326; *Liquidator of A. & J. McCredie & Co. Ltd.*, 1946 S.L.T. (Notes) 19.

[99] Nicknamed "Centrebinding" after *Re Centrebind Ltd.* [1967] 1 W.L.R. 377; [1966] 3 All E.R. 889.

[1] *E. V. Saxton & Sons Ltd.* v. *R. Miles (Confectioners) Ltd.* [1983] 1 W.L.R. 952.

[2] I.A., s.114; see para, 552 *post.*

[3] I.A., s.166; see para. 554, *post.*

(I.A., s.86). The company must cease to carry on its business "except so far as may be required for the beneficial winding up thereof," but its corporate existence and powers continue until dissolution (I.A., s.87). There can be no transfer of shares or alteration in the status of membership after winding up has commenced except with the sanction of the liquidator (I.A., s.88).

Members' voluntary winding up

Declaration of solvency in members' voluntary winding up

543 A winding up is a "members' voluntary winding up" if a declaration of solvency is made under the Insolvency Act, section 89. This is a statutory declaration by a majority of the directors to the effect that the company will be able to pay its debts in full within a period not exceeding 12 months after commencement of the winding up (I.A., s.89(1)). The declaration includes a statement of assets and liabilities, which need not be absolutely accurate provided that it is capable of being fairly described as such a statement (I.A., s.89(2)(*b*)).[4]

Under the Insolvency Act, section 89(2)(*a*) the declaration is to have no effect unless it is made within the five weeks immediately preceding the date of the resolution, or on that day but before the passing of the resolution. The absence of such a declaration results in the liquidation being a creditors' voluntary winding up, regardless of the financial position of the company (I.A., s.90).

Until the Companies Act 1981, section 105 the declaration of solvency had to be filed with the registrar of companies before the resolution was passed (otherwise the liquidation was automatically a creditors' voluntary winding up). The present law (I.A., s.89(3)) requires it to be filed within 15 days, but failure to do so has no effect on the nature of the liquidation.[5]

Criminal penalties attach to the making of a declaration of solvency without reasonable grounds. If the company is wound up as a members' voluntary winding up pursuant to the Insolvency Act, section 89, failure to pay or provide for the debts within the period specified in the declaration is prima facie evidence of an offence (I.A., s.89(5)). The effect of failure to pay within that period, or insolvency, on a members' voluntary winding up is considered below (para. 545, *post*).

Creditors' voluntary winding up

Resolution to wind up and first meeting of creditors

544 As has been noted, a creditors' voluntary winding up is one in which a

---

[4] *De Courcy* v. *Clement* [1971] Ch. 693.

[5] Special provisions apply to a company which made a declaration of solvency between April 7 and August 1, 1981, but failed to deliver it to the registrar before the resolution to wind up was passed (1981 Act, s.107; Companies (Consequential Provisions) Act 1985, s.24).

declaration of solvency has not been made (I.A., ss.89, 90), usually but not necessarily because of insolvency.

In a creditors' voluntary winding up the company must call a meeting of creditors to be held not later than 14 days after the meeting of the company at which the resolution to wind up is to be considered. The notice must be posted to the creditors not later than seven days before the day on which the company meeting is to be held, and must be advertised once in the *Edinburgh Gazette* and at least once in two newspapers circulating in the district of the company's principal place of business, or its places of business or (if it has no place of business in Great Britain) its registered office (I.A., s.98(1) and (3)).

If the company meeting is adjourned until after the creditors' meeting, any resolution by the creditors has effect only from the date the resolution of the company to wind up is passed (1986 Rule 7.8(7), added by the 1987 Amendments). The powers of a liquidator appointed by the members to act before the creditors' meeting have, however, been substantially limited (I.A., s.166, see para. 554, below).

The general provisions of the 1986 Rules (1986 Rules 7.1–7.27) as to the notice of meetings, voting, proxies and proceedings will apply to the meeting of creditors held under the Insolvency Act, section 98 (subject to the modifications required). Subject to disclosure and approval, the cost of convening this meeting may be treated as a liquidation expense (1986 Rule 4.14A, added by Sched. 1 to the Rules). Improper solicitation of votes or proxies may be penalised by refusal of expenses (1986 Rule 4.39, as applied by Sched. 1). The liquidator has power to require the attendance of any past and present officer, employee, etc., at the meeting, and may authorise payment of his expenses. Such personnel may be questioned, or the meeting adjourned to permit this (1986 Rule 4.14, applied by Sched. 1 to the Rules).

The notice of the meeting must (as well as the general requirements of the 1986 Rules) give the identity of an insolvency practitioner available to provide information to creditors, and an address in the locality of the company's principal place of business where a list of creditors may be inspected, free of charge (I.A., s.98(2)).

The directors are to make out a sworn statement of the affairs of the company in the form prescribed (Form 4.4 (Scot)) to be sent to the liquidator, when he is appointed, and laid before the first meeting of creditors. The statement is to be made up to a date not more than 14 days before the meeting and if the statement is not up to the date of the meeting, the directors must make a report on the up-to-date position to the meeting (1986 Rule 4.7(5) and (6), added by the 1987 Amendments). A copy of the statement must be given immediately to a liquidator who is nominated by a contributories' meeting if this is held before the meeting of creditors (1986 Rule 4.7(3A)). One of the directors is to preside over the meeting. There is power to meet the expenses of making up the statement from the assets of the company (I.A., s.99; 1986 Rules 4.7 and 4.9, as substituted in Sched. 1 to the Rules).

The purpose of the meeting is to consider the statement of affairs, to nominate a liquidator and to consider whether to establish a liquidation committee (I.A., ss.100, 101). The provisions of 1986 Rules 7.1 to 7.27 relating to the giving of notices, proxies and proceedings at meetings apply subject to the modifications required by section 98 in regard to notices (Rule 7.1; see Rule 7.3(7) (added by the 1987 Amendments)).

The liquidator must, within 28 days of a meeting held under the Insolvency Act, section 98 send to the creditors and contributories a copy of the statement of affairs and a report of the proceedings at the meeting (1986 Rule 4.10, as substituted in Sched. 1).

If the meeting of creditors under the Insolvency Act, section 98 is not duly convened, or if the directors fail to comply with the requirement to provide a sworn statement under the Insolvency Act, section 99, the members' nominee as liquidator must apply to the court for directions within seven days (I.A., s.166(5)).

The liquidator can require the company's present and former officers and other "personnel" as defined in the Insolvency Act, section 235(3)(*a*) to (*d*), to attend the first and any subsequent meeting of creditors (1986 Rule 4.14, applied by Sched. 1).

Insolvent members' voluntary winding up

545 If the liquidator in a members' voluntary winding up considers that the company will not be able to pay its debts in full (with interest) within the period stated in the declaration of solvency he must summon a meeting of creditors under the Insolvency Act, section 95 within 28 days (I.A., s.95(2)(*a*)). Notice must be sent to all creditors not less than seven days before the date of the meeting and it must also be advertised in the *Edinburgh Gazette* and at least two local newspapers. For this purpose the relevant locality is where the company had its principal place of business in Great Britain in the period of six months ending with the date the notices summoning the meeting of its members to resolve to wind up voluntarily were issued. If it had several places of business in Great Britain, circulation must be in two newspapers in each locality. If it has no place of business in Great Britain during that time the newspapers are to be those circulating in the locality of its registered office (I.A., s.95(2)(*b*) and (*c*), (5), (6) and (7)). The notice is to state that, during the period before the day of the meeting, information is to be freely available to creditors (I.A., s.95(2)(*d*)). The liquidator must make out a sworn statement of affairs of the company containing the information required by the Act and in the prescribed form (Form 4.4 (Scot)), lay it before the meeting and attend and preside over that meeting. The provisions of 1986 Rules 7.1 to 7.27, relating to the giving of notices, proxies and proceedings at meetings, apply subject to the modifications required by the

Insolvency Act, section 95 (1986 Rule 7.1; see Rule 7.3(7) (added by the 1987 Amendments) in regard to notices). The proceedings are to be recorded in the sederunt book, but there is no further requirement to advertise or make any return to the registrar of companies (unless another liquidator, or a liquidation committee, is appointed).

As from the day the meeting under the Insolvency Act, section 95 is held the winding up proceeds as if the declaration of solvency had not been made and as if the company meeting at the commencement of the winding up, together with the creditors' meeting under the Insolvency Act, section 95 were the initial meetings of a creditors' voluntary winding up held under the Insolvency Act, section 98. The liquidation then proceeds as a creditors' voluntary winding up (I.A., s.96). The creditors' meeting held under the Insolvency Act, section 95 may appoint another liquidator and a liquidation committee, as if it had been the meeting under the Insolvency Act, sections 98 to 101 (I.A., s.102). The liquidator must within 28 days of the meeting send to the creditors and contributories a copy of the statement of affairs and a report of the proceedings at the meeting (1986 Rule 4.10, as substituted in Sched. 1). Failure by the liquidator to comply with section 95 renders him liable to a fine (I.A., s.95(8)) but the validity of his acts as a continuing members' voluntary liquidator is not affected (I.A., s.232).

APPOINTMENT, REMOVAL, ETC., AND RELEASE OF VOLUNTARY LIQUIDATORS

Appointment

546 In a members' voluntary winding up the liquidator is appointed by the company in general meeting immediately the resolution to wind up has been passed (I.A., s.91(1)). No notice is required.[6] A vacancy is also filled by the company in general meeting, subject to any arrangement with creditors. Such a meeting may be convened by any contributory or continuing liquidator (I.A., s.92).

In a creditors' voluntary winding up the company and the creditors may nominate a liquidator at the relevant meetings under the Insolvency Act, sections 84 and 98 (or 95). The liquidator is to be the creditors' nominee, unless no person is nominated by them. If there are different nominees, however, any director, member or creditor may within seven days of the creditors' nomination apply to the court for another, or joint, appointment (I.A., s.100).[7] Vacancies are filled by the creditors unless the liquidator has been appointed by or on the direction of the court (when the court will fill the vacancy) (I.A., s.104). A creditors' meeting for this purpose may be convened by any creditor or surviving joint liquidator (1986 Rule 4.19(7), added to Sched. 1 by

---

[6] *Bethell* v. *Trench Tubeless Tyre Co. Ltd.* [1900] 1 Ch. 408.
[7] See *Karamelli and Barnett Ltd.* [1917] 1 Ch. 203.

the 1987 Amendments). The court can fill any vacancy, in addition to the foregoing powers of the company or creditors (I.A., s.108(1)).

Joint liquidators may be appointed. The resolution or court order making the appointment must declare whether any act is to be done or authorised by all or any one or more of those in office for the time being (I.A., s.232). The appointment should normally be framed so as to allow the remaining joint liquidator(s) to continue to act notwithstanding a vacancy. The acts of one joint liquidator may be presumed to have the consent of all, but one joint liquidator may be sued for negligence on his own account without having to call the others as co-defenders, even where that presumption is not challenged.[8]

The liquidator must be an "insolvency practitioner" duly qualified to act even in a (solvent) members' voluntary winding up (I.A., ss.230(3), 388–390). The liquidator must find caution, including a "certificate of specific penalty" in respect of the appointment.[9] The chairman of the company or creditors' meeting must be given a written statement by the liquidator that he is duly qualified and consents to act before certifying the appointment in the prescribed form (Form 4.8 (Scot)). The appointment is effective from the passing of the resolution appointing him (1986 Rule 11, as applied by Scheds. 1 and 2, and as amended by the 1987 Amendments). He is to be known as "the liquidator of (the company)" and not by his personal name (I.A., s.163). The liquidator's acts are valid notwithstanding any defects in his appointment, nomination or qualifications (I.A., s.232). It is an offence to attempt to influence the appointment by corrupt inducement (I.A., s.164) and such activity may deprive the liquidator of his right to remuneration (1986 Rule 4.39).

A voluntary liquidator (however appointed) must lodge a notice of his appointment with the registrar of companies within 14 days (Form 600) and within the same period publish a notice (Form 600a) in the *Edinburgh Gazette* (I.A., s.109).[10] He must also publish a notice in a local newspaper within 28 days (1986 Rule 4.19 as applied by Scheds. 1 and 2).

The remuneration of a members' voluntary liquidator is for agreement between him and the company.[11] The remuneration of a creditors' voluntary liquidator is determined by the liquidation committee (if any) which failing the court, under 1986 Rules 4.32 to 4.35 and the Bankruptcy (Scotland) Act 1985, section 53, as applied by the

---

[8] *Highland Engineering Ltd.* v. *Anderson*, 1979 S.L.T. 122.
[9] See para. 440, *ante*.
[10] Scheds. 1 and 2 disapply 1986 Rule 4.19(4)(*a*) which prescribes the form of notice of appointment of a liquidator by the court. The Forms 600 and 600a are to be found in the Companies (Forms) (Amendment) Regulations 1987 (S.I. 1987 No. 752).
[11] The reference to remuneration being fixed by the company in general meeting, which appeared in s.580, was repealed by the Insolvency Act 1985, Sched. 10. The former provision could give rise to prejudice to a liquidator who might have no recourse if the members arbitrarily withheld or abated his remuneration.

Rules. These provisions are discussed in paragraph 448, above, but the reference there to the creditors having the right to resolve upon the basis of remuneration at their first meeting (under I.A., s.138 and 1986 Rule 4.12) does not apply to a voluntary liquidation.

Removal of voluntary liquidators

547 A voluntary liquidator may be removed by the court (I.A., s.108(2)) or by a general meeting of members (in a members' voluntary winding up) or of creditors (in a creditors' voluntary winding up) (the Insolvency Act, s.171(1) and (2)). The procedure for holding the relevant meeting of creditors is set forth in the 1986 Rules (Rule 4.23, as applied by Schedule 1) and is similar to the equivalent procedure in a winding up by the court (see paras. 443 and 444, above). In a members' voluntary winding up the general rules for company meetings will apply. Where the court has appointed the voluntary liquidator, however, a meeting to consider his removal requires his consent or that of the court, or a requisition by half the creditors or members (as the case may be) (I.A., s.171(3); 1986 Rule 4.26 as applied by Scheds. 1 and 2). A certificate of removal of a creditors' voluntary liquidator (but not a members') must be filed with the registrar of companies (1986 Rule 4.24, as applied; Forms 4.10 (Scot) and 4.11 (Scot)).[12]

Vacation of office

548 If the liquidator dies his executors and partners must and any other person may intimate his death to the registrar and the liquidation committee (in a creditors' voluntary liquidation) or the directors (in a members' voluntary liquidation) (1986 Rule 4.36, as applied; Form 4.18 (Scot)).[13] Loss of qualification results in immediate vacation of office, also to be notified by the liquidator to the registrar (I.A., s.171(4); 1986 Rule 4.37; Form 4.19 (Scot)) but not, in terms of the Rules, to members or creditors.

Resignation

549 A liquidator may resign on grounds of health, cessation of practice, conflict of interest or personal circumstances inhibiting the discharge of his duties (I.A., s.171(5); 1986 Rule 4.28, as applied). He requires to convene a meeting of the company (members' voluntary) or creditors (creditors' voluntary) under 1986 Rule 4.28 (as applied), to which he

---

[12] Rule 4.24 is not among the rules applied to a members' voluntary winding up by Sched. 2 in the Rules. A resolution for the removal of a liquidator is not among the resolutions which have to be filed pursuant to s.380 (unless it is passed as a special or extraordinary resolution, which the Insolvency Act does not require). Any new liquidator appointed, however, requires to give notice of his appointment under I.A., s.109 (see para. 546, *ante*).

[13] *i.e.*, a single notification by one of such persons is required.

must submit an account of intromissions. In a members' voluntary winding up, his resignation is effected by notice to the registrar after the meeting (1986 Rule 4.28(5) in Sched. 2; Form 4.16 (Scot)) but in a creditors' voluntary winding up the consent of the creditors' meeting is required (1986 Rule 4.29, as applied) and if it is refused the liquidator may apply on Form 4.15 (Scot) to the court but still filing a return on Form 4.16 (Scot) with a copy of his application. If allowed to resign he will then file Form 4.16 (Scot) to disclose this fact (1986 Rule 4.30, as applied). A voluntary liquidator vacates office on completion of the final meetings and returns (I.A., s.171(6); Forms 4.17 (Scot) and 4.26 (Scot)).

Release

550 At the conclusion of the winding up, or when he demits office, a liquidator is released and discharged from all liability in relation to the winding up and his conduct as liquidator, except liability for misconduct under the Insolvency Act, section 212 (I.A., s.173(4)). Release is normally automatic and takes effect according to the circumstances of his demission of office (see I.A., s.173 and 1986 Rules 4.25–4.31 and 4.37 (as applied) for details).

The rules are complex, and follow the pattern established by the 1986 Rules for liquidators in a winding up by the court[14] with a number of modifications in Schedules 1 and 2. Automatic release takes effect upon the filing of the relevant return with the registrar on death, completion of the winding up or resignation of a members' voluntary liquidator. In a creditors' voluntary winding up, the creditors determine the date of release when accepting his resignation. If they refuse his resignation, but this is granted by the court, the court fixes the date of release. If the creditors refuse release either on resignation or at the final meeting, the liquidator must apply to the Accountant of Court for release, and the Accountant of Court is also responsible for releasing a liquidator who vacates office on ceasing to be an insolvency practitioner, or on a winding-up order, or who is removed by the court. If there is no quorum present at the meeting of creditors summoned to receive his resignation the meeting is deemed to have been held, a resolution is deemed to have been passed that the resignation be accepted and the creditors are deemed not to have resolved against his release. The liquidator's resignation and release take effect from the date for which the meeting is summoned (1986 Rule 4.29(6) and (7), as applied, added by the 1987 Amendments). In a members' voluntary liquidation, if no quorum is present at the meeting summoned to receive his resignation, the meeting is deemed to have been held (1986 Rule 4.28(7) as contained in Sched. 2, with 1987 Amendments).

Liquidation committee (creditors' voluntary winding up)

551 The creditors may appoint a liquidation committee at their first

---

[14] See para. 445, *ante*.

meeting (under I.A., s.98 or s.95) or subsequently. The committee will consist of up to five creditors, together with up to five nominees of the company (not necessarily directors or members), but the creditors can remove all or any of the company nominees. The court has power to override any such appointments (I.A., s.101(1)–(3)). The 1986 Rules 4.40 to 4.59 apply with modifications (in Sched. 1 to the Rules). There must be at least three members to permit the committee to function, two being a quorum (1986 Rules 4.41 and 4.47, as applied). The liquidator must certify its due constitution and notify the registrar of companies (1986 Rule 4.42; Form 4.22 (Scot)). The liquidator has a duty to report to the committee and convene its meetings (1986 Rules 4.44, 4.45 and 4.56). Other aspects of the committee's membership and proceedings and restrictions on its members' dealings with the company are similar to those of the liquidation committee in a winding up by the court, discussed in paragraphs 449, 450, 452, 453, above. Unless the contributories appoint the necessary members (two as a minimum), the committee will cease to exist when creditors have been paid in full (1986 Rule 4.59).

Apart from considering the liquidator's regular reports and accounts during the administration, the committee has specific functions in sanctioning the exercise of certain of his powers. These aspects are discussed below.

CONDUCT OF LIQUIDATION

General duties of the liquidator: directors' powers

552 The general duties of a voluntary liquidator are in principle the same as those in a compulsory liquidation, namely to prepare lists of contributories and creditors, realise assets, discharge liabilities and distribute any surplus among the members in accordance with their rights (I.A., ss.107 and 165(5)). On his appointment the powers of the directors cease, except so far as their continuance may be sanctioned, in a members' voluntary winding up by the company in general meeting (I.A., s.91(2))[15] and in a creditor's voluntary winding up by the liquidation committee or (if there is no committee) by the creditors (I.A., s.103). A voluntary liquidator in Scotland is in no sense "an officer of the court."[16] If there is no liquidator nominated by the company the directors' powers (in a creditors' voluntary winding up) are confined to the convening of the first meeting of creditors under the Insolvency Act, section 98 and providing it with the requisite statement of affairs under the Insolvency Act, section 99, disposing of

---

[15] The meeting of shareholders may be held at any time after commencement of winding up (*Re Fairbairn Engineering Co.* [1893] 3 Ch. 450).
[16] *Clyde Marine Insurance Co.* v. *Renwick*, 1924 S.C. 113, 125.

perishable goods and protecting the assets (I.A., s.114(2) and (3)). As noted above[17] the Insolvency Acts 1985 and 1986 introduced provisions, the effect of which was to restrict the powers of any liquidator appointed by the members until the creditors had had an opportunity to consider whether to replace him with their own nominee. It was recognised, however, that steps might have to be taken to safeguard certain assets in the meantime. Accordingly, power is given to both the members' appointee and the directors, in identical terms, to dispose of perishable goods and other goods the value of which is likely to diminish if they are not immediately disposed of and to do all such other things as may be necessary for the protection of the company's assets (I.A., ss.114(2) and (3) (directors) and 166(3) (liquidator)). The limits of these powers are not defined with any precision, nor does the Act indicate whether the directors have a continuing duty to exercise those powers if the liquidator does not, although this may be inferred from their general duty to act in the best interests of the company. The Act does not indicate how any conflict of view between the directors and the liquidator as to the nature of any such action should be resolved, presumably in the expectation that whoever takes the first step will not be challenged provided he has acted in good faith. In a members' voluntary winding up, the members can authorise the directors to continue to exercise their functions (I.A., s.91(2)). Otherwise, the directors require the sanction of the court (I.A., s.114(2)).

Contributories and claims; expenses

552A The provisions of the Insolvency Act, sections 94 to 83, defining a "contributory" and his liability, apply to a voluntary liquidation as to a winding up by the court.[18] In a voluntary liquidation, however, it is the liquidator and not the court who has power to settle the list of contributories and make calls (I.A., s.165(4)(a) and (b)).

As in a compulsory winding up a voluntary liquidator must exercise due diligence in investigating the existence of claims. He must reject all claims which have prescribed or are otherwise barred. In a creditors' voluntary winding up, the procedure for submission of claims, adjudication and evaluation thereof, and related matters, is the same as in a winding up by the court (1986 Rules 4.15–4.17, applied by Sched. 1). There is no formal procedure for dealing with claims in a members' voluntary winding up.[19]

The liquidator must satisfy all preferential debts, and then all other liabilities *pari passu* (I.A., s.107). The expenses of winding up must, however, be paid in priority (I.A., s.115). The definition of "preferential debts" (I.A., s.386 and Sched. 6) is the same as in a

---

[17] See para. 541, *ante.*
[18] See paras. 459 to 465, *ante.*
[19] The Bankrupcty (Scotland) Bill 1992 proposes to substitute "six months".

winding up by the court (see paras. 478 to 480, above). In a creditors' voluntary winding up, the order of priority of distribution of available funds and of expenses, and the requirement to effect distributions and submit accounts to the liquidation committee (if any) every 26 weeks[20] as in a winding up by the court also apply (1986 Rules 4.66 and 4.68, as applied by Sched. 1; see paras. 476, 477 and 492, above).

Powers of liquidator[21]

553 The liquidator is to take control of the assets with a view to realisation (1986 Rules 4.20 and 4.21, as applied by Scheds. 1 and 2).

A voluntary liquidator (in addition to settling the list of contributories and making calls under the I.A., s.165(4)), may exercise without any sanction the powers contained in the Insolvency Act, Schedule 4, Parts II and III (I.A., s.165(3)). These are:

(a) to institute or defend proceedings in the name of the company[22];
(b) to carry on its business so far as may be necessary for its beneficial winding up;
(c) to sell assets;
(d) to execute deeds and documents and to use the company's seal;
(e) to rank for dividends in sequestrations, etc.;
(f) to draw cheques, etc.;
(g) to borrow on the security of the assets;
(h) to confirm as executor-creditor on the estate of a deceased contributory and otherwise claim on his estate;
(i) to appoint an agent; and
(j) to do all such things as may be necessary for winding up the company's affairs and distributing its assets.

554 In a members' voluntary winding up the powers contained in Part I of the Insolvency Act, Schedule 4 require the sanction of an extraordinary resolution of the company. In a creditors' voluntary winding up they require the sanction of the court or the liquidation committee or (if there is no such committee) a meeting of creditors (I.A., s.165(2)). These are:

1. to pay any class of creditors in full;
2. to make compromises or arrangements; and
3. to compromise calls, debts, etc., and to accept security for payment or performance.

If a liquidator in a creditors' voluntary winding up disposes of

---

[20] *Pulsford* v. *Devenish* [1903] 2 Ch. 625.
[21] See further, paras. 485 to 489, *ante*.
[22] The appointment of a liquidator terminates any right which a shareholder may have to bring a "derivative action" in the name of the company (*Fargo Ltd.* v. *Godfroy and Others* [1986] 3 All E.R. 279).

property to a person "connected"[23] with the company and there is a liquidation committee, he must notify that committee of his action (I.A., s.165(6)). The court may set aside any improper transaction between a voluntary liquidator and an "associate"[24] and order payment of compensation (1986 Rule 4.11, applied by Scheds. 1 and 2; see para. 491, above).

As noted in para. 541 above, in a creditors' voluntary winding up there may be an interval (normally not more than 14 days) during which the members' nominee may be in office as liquidator before the creditors have met to consider a replacement and whether to appoint a liquidation committee. During this period the liquidator is accorded only limited powers of action. He is entitled to take action to obtain control of and protect the assets and to dispose of perishable goods which may lose value if not sold immediately. Any other step requires the sanction of the court, (I.A., s.166(2) and (3)). He must attend the creditors' meeting and report on any exercise of such powers (I.A., s.166(4)).

The liquidator in either form of voluntary winding up may apply to the court for the appointment of a "special manager" of the business or property of the company (I.A., s.177). The procedure and the rules applicable to him are as in a winding up by the court (1986 Rules 4.69–4.71, as applied by Scheds. 1 and 2; see paras. 488 and 489, above).

555   In addition to the foregoing, a number of other powers and facilities are available in a voluntary liquidation:

1. The liquidator may apply to the court for sanction of a scheme of arrangement under section 425 of the Act.[25]
2. Where a company is proposed to be, or is in course of being, wound up voluntarily, the liquidator may sell the whole or part of its business or property in consideration for shares, policies or other like interests of another company (I.A., s.110). In a members' voluntary winding up this requires the sanction of a special resolution; in a creditors' voluntary winding up it requires the sanction of the court or the liquidation committee (I.A., s.110(3)). A dissenting member may, within seven days, require the liquidator either to abstain from giving effect to the arrangement or buy his interest at a value to be fixed by arbitration (I.A., s.111) but subject to this an arrangement duly approved is binding on the selling company (I.A., s.110(5)). A special resolution approving a sale on these terms may be passed before the resolution to wind up but is invalid if there is a

---

[23] Defined in I.A., s.249 as a director or shadow director, or an "associate" of such a person or of the company; for "associate" see para. 517, *ante*.
[24] Defined in I.A., s.435; see para. 517, *ante*.
[25] See further *Palmer*, paras. 12.008 *et seq.*

      compulsory winding up within a year, unless it is specifically confirmed by the court (I.A., s.110(6)).[26]

3. The liquidator may summon general meetings of the company to obtain its sanction by special or ordinary resolution or for any other purpose (I.A., s.165(4)(c)).

4. The liquidator can apply to the court for an order sisting proceedings against the company and directing that they shall not continue except by leave of the court (I.A., s.113)). There is no automatic sisting of such proceedings as in a compulsory winding up under the Insolvency Act, section 130. The liquidator must show sufficient reason for denying the pursuer the right to proceed, *e.g.* that the claim is admitted and expense will be saved.[27]

5. The liquidator or any creditor or contributory may apply to the court to determine any question arising in the winding up or to exercise all or any of the powers of the court in a compulsory winding up (I.A., s.112).[28] This will enable the court to grant an order under a section which is not automatically applicable to a voluntary winding up, such as for restraint proceedings (I.A., s.130), a vesting order (I.A., s.145), a sist of the winding up (I.A., s.147), and the examination of books, officers and others (I.A., ss.155, 198, 236 and 237). The section is, however, not restricted to these examples and can be used in any appropriate circumstances. It cannot, however, be used to authorise *ultra vires* transactions,[29] nor should it be used to resolve questions more properly determined by an ordinary action, such as claims for damages.[30] It has been used to enable creditors to obtain access to information to assist them in pursuing a claim against the liquidator.[31] The court may order meetings of the contributories or creditors to ascertain their views under Insolvency Act, section 195. A liquidator who does a specific act after seeking and obtaining the sanction of the court cannot be liable in negligence.[32]

Carrying on business

556 As from the commencement of the winding up, the company must cease to carry on its business, "except so far as may be required for its beneficial winding up" but there is no change in the corporate state or powers of the company, notwithstanding any provision in its articles,

---

[26] See further *Palmer*, paras. 12.101 *et seq.*
[27] *Cook* v. *"X" Chair Patents Co. Ltd.* [1960] 1 W.L.R. 60; [1959] 3 All E.R. 906.
[28] A copy of such an order must be filed with the registrar under I.A., s.112(3).
[29] *Re Salisbury Railway and Market House Co. Ltd.* [1969] 1 Ch. 349.
[30] *Crawford* v. *McCulloch*, 1909 S.C. 1063; 1 S.L.T. 536; *Knoll Spinning Co.* v. *Brown*, 1977 S.L.T. (Notes) 62; S.C. 291.
[31] *Re Novitex Ltd.* [1992] 2 All E.R. 264 (C.A.); B.C.C. 101, (C.A.).
[32] *Highland Engineering Ltd.* v. *Anderson*, 1979 S.L.T. 122.

until it is dissolved (I.A., s.87). If the company or the liquidator has, in a members' voluntary winding up, sanctioned the continuance of the powers of the directors under the Insolvency Act, section 91(2) such powers must still be exercised for the purposes of winding up. The power to carry on the business is vested in the liquidator (I.A., Sched. 4, para. 5), which uses the same qualification as the Insolvency Act, section 87(1) except that (for no obvious reason) "necessary" is used instead of "required." The liquidator should exercise his power to carry on the business with this qualification and purpose in mind. It is not necessary that the motive for carrying on business be exclusively financial; for example, it may be in order to facilitate reconstruction.[33] It is sufficient if the liquidator *bona fide* and reasonably (in the circumstances in which he has to decide the matter) forms the opinion that the carrying on of the business is necessary for the beneficial winding up of the company.[34] If in doubt he should apply for court sanction under the Insolvency Act, section 112.

If he carries on the business the liquidator will have all the necessary powers, and will not be liable personally provided that he makes it clear that he is acting on behalf of the company and that it is in liquidation.[35] Debts incurred while carrying on the business rank in priority to all claims in the winding up.[36] In carrying on business the liquidator is acting on behalf of the company, and any employees whom he engages for the purposes are entitled to claim continuity of employment for the purpose of their entitlement to redundancy payments, etc.[37]

If there is no liquidation committee and the court has not ruled otherwise the liquidator can appoint himself the company's representative at meetings under section 375.[38]

Possession of books, etc.

557 The liquidator should take possession of all books, deeds, documents and assets of the company. He is entitled to require assistance from the directors and others, and to obtain a court order if necessary (I.A., ss.234–237; 1986 Rules 4.21–4.22).

Delinquent directors

558 In an "insolvent" liquidation the liquidator must submit reports on the directors to the Secretary of State under the Company Directors Disqualification Act 1986. He can seek recovery of losses caused by

---

[33] See *Willis* v. *Association of Universities of the British Commonwealth* [1965] 1 Q.B. 140.
[34] *Re Great Eastern Electric Co. Ltd.* [1941] Ch. 241.
[35] *Stead Hazel & Co.* v. *Cooper* [1933] 1 K.B. 840.
[36] *Re S. Davis & Co.* [1945] Ch. 402; 1986 Rule 4.67(1)(*a*).
[37] *Smith* v. *Lord Advocate*, 1979 S.L.T. 233. See also the Transfer of Undertakings (Protection of Employment) Regulations 1981 (S.I. 1981 No. 1794).
[38] *Hillman* v. *Crystal Bowl Amusements Ltd.* [1973] 1 W.L.R. 162; 1 All E.R. 379 (C.A.).

"fraudulent" or "wrongful" trading or breach of trust. See further paragraphs 522 to 526, above.

Sederunt book

559 The liquidator must maintain a sederunt book to record all proceedings, statements, etc., (1986 Rule 7.33).

These matters are discussed more fully above in the context of a winding up by the court.

Compulsory order

560 The existence of a voluntary winding up does not bar the right of a contributory or creditor to petition for a winding-up order (I.A., s.116).[39]

Continuing liquidations

561 Where a voluntary winding up continues for more than a year the liquidator must[40]:

(i) file with the registrar of companies within 30 days a statement of intromissions[41] then and every six months thereafter, including the final period (I.A., s.192; 1986 Rule 4.11, applied by Scheds. 1 & 2)[42];

(ii) call an annual meeting of members and lay before it a statement of his intromissions (I.A., ss.93 and 105);

(iii) in a creditors' voluntary winding up (including a members' voluntary which has become a creditors' voluntary by virtue of the Insolvency Act, ss.95 and 96) he must lay a statement of his intromissions before an annual meeting of creditors (I.A., s.105). He must also submit accounts, including proposed distributions, to the liquidation committee or (if there is no committee) the court every six months under 1986 Rule 4.68 (applying sections 52, 53 and 58 of the Bankruptcy (Scotland) Act 1985).[43]

Final meetings and dissolution

562 As soon as the affairs of the company have been fully wound up the liquidator must summon final meetings and submit his final statement. It is immaterial that matters of which the liquidator was unaware may still be outstanding and the emergence of such matters does not invalidate the final procedure.[44] In a members' voluntary winding up only a meeting of the company is required (I.A., s.94(1)).

---

[39] As to the considerations which will arise in deciding whether to allow such an application see para. 423, *ante*. See also *Re Zinotty Properties Ltd.* [1984] 3 All E.R. 754.
[40] See *Re Grantham Wholesale Fruit, Vegetable and Potato Merchants* [1972] 1 W.L.R. 559.
[41] Forms 4.5 (Scot) and 4.6 (Scot).
[42] The 1987 Amendments to Sched. 2 specify "26 weeks" in members' voluntary liquidations.
[43] See para. 492, *ante*.
[44] *Re Cornish Manures Ltd.* [1967] 1 W.L.R. 807; 2 All E.R. 875.

In a creditors' voluntary winding up, a meeting of creditors must also be held (I.A., s.106(1)).

The final meetings are convened by notice in the *Edinburgh Gazette* published at least one month before the date thereof (I.A., ss.94(2) and 106(2)). At least 28 days' notice must be given to every admitted creditor (including, apparently, any paid in full), who may question the liquidator at the meeting and vote against his release (1986 Rule 4.31, as applied by Sched. 1). The effect of refusal of release is considered in paragraph 550, above).

Within one week of the final meetings the liquidator must file a final return with the registrar, even where no quorum was present (I.A., ss.94(3)–(5) and 106(3)–(5); 1986 Rule 4.31(4); Form 4.17 (Scot)). Three months after registration of the final return the company is deemed dissolved subject to the power of the court to defer the date of dissolution (I.A., s.201). Official notification of the final return under section 711 is required.[45] The power of the court to order early dissolution if the company has insufficient assets (I.A., s.204 discussed in para. 535, above) does not apply in a voluntary winding up.

The powers of the court to declare a dissolution void under section 651 and to restore a company to the register under section 653 have been discussed earlier.[46]

The liquidator is obliged to hand over his books and other records to any succeeding insolvency practitioner. He may obtain directions for their disposal from the liquidation committee (if any) or from the creditors at or before the final meeting (in a creditors' voluntary winding up) or from the members by extraordinary resolution (in a members' voluntary winding up). If no such directions have been given within 12 months of dissolution, he may dispose of the company's books and records at his discretion but the sederunt book must be retained for at least 10 years (1986 Rules 7.33(5) to (7) and 7.34, added by the 1987 Amendments).

Compensation for loss of office

563 In a voluntary liquidation, the liquidator may pay compensation for loss of employment to persons employed or formerly employed by the company or any of its subsidiaries under section 711. He does not require the sanction of the liquidation committee (if any).[47]

Stamp duties

A creditors' voluntary winding up enjoys the same stamp duty reliefs as a compulsory liquidation (I.A., s.190).[48] There are no such general reliefs in a members' voluntary winding up.

---

[45] See paras. 2.1401 *et seq.*, *ante.*
[46] See paras. 536 to 538, *ante.*
[47] For the conditions for exercising such power see *ante*, para. 495.
[48] See para. 531, *ante.*

Striking off under section 652

564 As an alternative to members' voluntary liquidation, and to avoid the expense of this process, it is possible for any officer or the solicitor acting for a company to ask the registrar to initiate section 652 proceedings. This can be done simply by a letter stating that the company has neither assets nor liabilities, is not trading, and is not heritably vest in any property. The registrar will then write to the directors for confirmation that this step is desired. After further notification of intention to do so, he will publish a notice in the *Edinburgh Gazette* to the effect that (unless cause is shown to the contrary) the company will be struck off and dissolved three months thereafter.[49] A further notice is published stating that the company has been dissolved but without prejudice to any liability of its directors, managers or members and to the power of the court to wind it up.[50] Similar provisions apply to a company in liquidation.[51] The registrar may initiate section 652 proceedings, for example, if the company fails to lodge annual returns, etc. The effect of dissolution and the procedure for applying under section 653 to have the company restored to the register have already been considered.[52]

WINDING UP UNDER SUPERVISION

565 Chapter IV of Part XX (ss.606–610) dealt with (voluntary) winding up under the supervision of the court. Long in desuetude, these provisions were repealed by the Insolvency Acts 1985 and 1986.

POWER OF COURT TO CURE DEFECTS IN PROCEDURE

566 The 1986 Rules (Rule 7.32) allows the court to cure any defect in insolvency procedure (see para. 539, above).

---

[49] s.652(2) and (3).
[50] s.652(5). Such notice does not require to be "officially notified" under s.711: see *Palmer*, paras. 2.1401 *et seq.*
[51] s.652(4): see para. 535, *ante.*
[52] See paras. 536 to 538, *ante.*

STATUTORY APPENDIX

Bankruptcy (Scotland) Act 1985[1]

(1985 c. 66)

An Act to reform the law of Scotland relating to sequestration and personal insolvency; and for connected purposes.

[30th October 1985]

Further provisions relating to presentation of petitions

8.—... (5) The presentation of, or the concurring in, a petition for sequestration shall bar the effect of any enactment or rule of law relating to the limitation of actions in any part of the United Kingdom.

· · · · · ·

Submission of claims for voting purposes at statutory meeting

22.—... (5) If a creditor produces under this section a statement of claim, account, voucher or other evidence which is false—

(a) the creditor shall be guilty of an offence unless he shows that he neither knew nor had reason to believe that the statement of claim, account, voucher or other evidence was false;

(b) the debtor shall be guilty of an offence if he—

(i) knew or became aware that the statement of claim, account, voucher or other evidence was false; and

(ii) failed as soon as practicable after acquiring such knowledge to report it to the interim trustee or permanent trustee.

... (8) The submission of a claim under this section shall bar the effect of any enactment or rule of law relating to the limitation of actions in any part of the United Kingdom.

... (10) A person convicted of an offence under subsection (5) above shall be liable—

(a) on summary conviction to a fine not exceeding the statutory maximum or—

(i) to imprisonment for a term not exceeding three months; or

(ii) if he has previously been convicted of an offence inferring dishonest appropriation of property or an attempt at such appropriation, to imprisonment for a term not exceeding six months,

or (in the case of either sub-paragraph) to both such fine and such imprisonment; or

(b) on conviction on indictment to a fine or to imprisonment for a term not exceeding two years or to both.

· · · · · ·

---

[1] See the Financial Services Act 1986, s.45(2) and (3). Excluded by the Companies Act 1989, ss.159(2), 161(4) and 180(2).

Effect of sequestration on diligence

Effect of sequestration on diligence

37.—(1) The order of the court awarding sequestration shall as from the date of sequestration have the effect, in relation to diligence done (whether before or after the date of sequestration) in respect of any part of the debtor's estate, of—

(*a*) a decree of adjudication of the heritable estate of the debtor for payment of his debts which has been duly recorded in the register of inhibitions and adjudications on that date; and

(*b*) an arrestment in execution and decree of forthcoming, an arrestment in execution and warrant of sale, and a completed poinding,

in favour of the creditors according to their respective entitlements.

(2) No inhibition on the estate of the debtor which takes effect within the period of 60 days before the date of sequestration shall be effectual to create a preference for the inhibitor and any relevant right of challenge shall, at the date of sequestration, vest in the permanent trustee as shall any right of the inhibitor to receive payment for the discharge of the inhibition:

Provided that this subsection shall neither entitle the trustee to receive any payment made to the inhibitor before the date of sequestration nor affect the validity of anything done before that date in consideration of such payment.

(3) In subsection (2) above, "any relevant right of challenge" means any right to challenge a deed voluntarily granted by the debtor if it is a right which vested in the inhibitor by virtue of the inhibition.

(4) No arrestment or poinding of the estate of the debtor (including any estate vesting in the permanent trustee under section 32(6) of this Act) executed—

(*a*) within the period of 60 days before the date of sequestration and whether or not subsisting at that date; or

(*b*) on or after the date of sequestration,

shall be effectual to create a preference for the arrester or poinder; and the estate so arrested or poinded, or the proceeds of sale thereof, shall be handed over to the permanent trustee.

(5) An arrester or poinder whose arrestment or poinding is executed within the said period of 60 days shall be entitled to payment, out of the arrested or poinded estate or out of the proceeds of the sale thereof, of the expenses incurred—

(*a*) in obtaining the extract of the decree or other document on which the arrestment or poinding proceeded;

(*b*) in executing the arrestment or poinding; and

(*c*) in taking any further action in respect of the diligence.

[2] (5A) Nothing in subsection (4) or (5) above shall apply to an earnings arrestment, a current maintenance arrestment or a conjoined arrestment order.

(6) No poinding of the ground in respect of the estate of the debtor (including any estate vesting in the permanent trustee under section 32(6) of this Act) executed within the period of 60 days before the date of sequestration or on or after that date shall be effectual in a question with the permanent trustee, except for the interest on the debt of a secured creditor, being interest for the current half-yearly term and arrears of interest for one year immediately before the commencement of that term.

. . .

Administration of estate by permanent trustee

Taking possession of estate by permanent trustee

38.—. . . (2) The permanent trustee shall be entitled to have access to all documents relating to the assets or the business or financial affairs of the debtor sent by or on behalf of the debtor to a third party and in that third party's hands and to make copies of any such documents.

(3) If any person obstructs a permanent trustee who is exercising, or attempting to exercise, a power conferred by subsection (2) above, the sheriff, on the application of the permanent trustee, may order that person to cease so to obstruct the permanent trustee.

(4) The permanent trustee may require delivery to him of any title deed or other document of the debtor, notwithstanding that a right of lien is claimed over the title deed or document; but this subsection is without prejudice to any preference of the holder of the lien.

Management and realisation of estate

39.—[3] (1) As soon as may be after his confirmation in office, the permanent trustee shall consult with the commissioners or, if there are no commissioners, with the Accountant in Bankruptcy concerning the exercise of his functions under section 3(1)(*a*) of this Act; and, subject to subsection (6) below, the permanent trustee shall comply with any general or specific directions given to him, as the case may be—

(*a*) by the creditors;

(*b*) on the application under this subsection of the commissioners, by the court; or

(*c*) if there are no commissioners, by the Accountant in Bankruptcy,

as to the exercise by him of such functions.

---

[2] Inserted by the Debtors (Scotland) Act 1987, Sched. 6, para. 27. Amended (*prosp.*) by the Child Support Act 1991, Sched. 5, para. 6(3).

[3] See also ss.23(4), 24(5), 28(5) and Sched. 2, para. 7.

³ (2) The permanent trustee may, but if there are commissioners only with the consent of the commissioners, the creditors or the court, do any of the following things if he considers that its doing would be beneficial for the administration of the estate—

(*a*) carry on any business of the debtor;
(*b*) bring, defend or continue any legal proceedings relating to the estate of the debtor;
(*c*) create a security over any part of the estate;
(*d*) where any right, option or other power forms part of the debtor's estate, make payments or incur liabilities with a view to obtaining, for the benefit of the creditors, any property which is the subject of the right option or power.

(3) Any sale of the debtor's estate by the permanent trustee may be by either public sale or private bargain.

(4) The following rules shall apply to the sale of any part of the debtor's heritable estate over which a heritable security is held by a creditor or creditors if the rights of the secured creditor or creditors are preferable to those of the permanent trustee—

(*a*) the permanent trustee may sell that part only with the concurrence of every such creditor unless he obtains a sufficiently high price to discharge every such security;
(*b*) subject to paragraph (*c*) below, the following acts shall be precluded—
   (i) the taking of steps by a creditor to enforce his security over that part after the permanent trustee has intimated to the creditor that he intends to sell it;
   (ii) the commencement by the permanent trustee of the procedure for the sale of that part after a creditor has intimated to the permanent trustee that he intends to commence the procedure for its sale;
(*c*) where the permanent trustee or a creditor has given intimation under paragraph (*b*) above, but has unduly delayed in proceeding with the sale, then, if authorised by the court in the case of intimation under—
   (i) sub-paragraph (i) of that paragraph, any creditor to whom intimation has been given may enforce his security; or
   (ii) sub-paragraph (ii) of that paragraph, the permanent trustee may sell that part.

(5) The function of the permanent trustee under section 3(1)(*a*) of this Act to realise the debtor's estate shall include the function of selling, with or without recourse against the estate, debts owing to the estate.

(6) The permanent trustee may sell any perishable goods without complying with any directions given to him under subsection (1)(*a*) or (*c*) above if the permanent trustee considers that compliance with such directions would adversely affect the sale.

(7) The validity of the title of any purchaser shall not be challengeable on the ground that there has been a failure to comply with a requirement of this section.

(8) It shall be incompetent for the permanent trustee or an associate of his or for any commissioner, to purchase any of the debtor's estate in pursuance in this section.

. . . . . .

Contractual powers of permanent trustee

[4] **42.**—(1) Subject to subsections (2) and (3) below, the permanent trustee may adopt any contract entered into by the debtor before the date of sequestration where he considers that its adoption would be beneficial to the administration of the debtor's estate, except where the adoption is precluded by the express or implied terms of the contract, or may refuse to adopt any such contract.

(2) The permanent trustee shall, within 28 days from the receipt by him of a request in writing from any party to a contract entered into by the debtor or within such longer period of that receipt as the court on application by the permanent trustee may allow, adopt or refuse to adopt the contract.

(3) If the permanent trustee does not reply in writing to the request under subsection (2) above within the said period of 28 days or longer period, as the case may be, he shall be deemed to have refused to adopt the contract.

(4) The permanent trustee may enter into any contract where he considers that this would be beneficial for the administration of the debtor's estate.

Money received by permanent trustee

43.—(1) Subject to subsection (2) below, all money received by the permanent trustee in the exercise of his functions shall be deposited by him in the name of the debtor's estate in an appropriate bank or institution.

(2) The permanent trustee may at any time retain in his hands a sum not exceeding £200 or such other sum as may be prescribed.

Examination of debtor

Private examination

[5] **44.**—(1) The permanent trustee may request—

(a) the debtor to appear before him and to give information relating to his assets, his dealings with them or his conduct in relation to his business or financial affairs; or

---

[4] Excluded by the Companies Act 1989, s.164(2), subject to subs. (4).
[5] See also ss.23(4), 24(5), 28(5) and Sched. 2, para. 8.

(*b*) the debtor's spouse or any other person who the permanent trustee believes can give such information (in this Act such spouse or other person being referred to as a "relevant person"), to give that information,

and, if he considers it necessary, the permanent trustee may apply to the sheriff for an order to be made under subsection (2) below.

(2) Subject to section 46(2) of this Act, on application to him under subsection (1) above the sheriff may make an order requiring the debtor or a relevant person to attend for private examination before him on a date (being not earlier than eight days nor later than 16 days after the date of the order) and at a time specified in the order.

(3) A person who fails without reasonable excuse to comply with an order made under subsection (2) above shall be guilty of an offence and liable on summary conviction to a fine not exceeding level 5 on the standard scale or to imprisonment for a term not exceeding three months or to both.

(4) Where the debtor is an entity whose estate may be sequestrated by virtue of section 6(1) of this Act, the references in this section and in sections 45 to 47 of this Act to the debtor shall be construed, unless the context otherwise requires, as references to a person representing the entity.

Public examination

[6] **45.**—(1) Not less than eight weeks before the end of the first accounting period, the permanent trustee—

(*a*) may; or
(*b*) if requested to do so by the Accountant in Bankruptcy or the commissioners (if any) or one quarter in value of the creditors, shall,

apply to the sheriff for an order for the public examination before the sheriff of the debtor or of a relevant person relating to the debtor's assets, his dealings with them or his conduct in relation to his business or financial affairs:

Provided that, on cause shown, such application may be made by the permanent trustee at any time.

(2) Subject to section 46(2) of this Act, the sheriff, on an application under subsection (1) above, shall make an order requiring the debtor or relevant person to attend for examination before him in open court on a date (being not earlier than eight days nor later than 16 days after the date of the order) and at a time specified in the order.

(3) On the sheriff making an order under subsection (2) above, the permanent trustee shall—

---

[6] See also ss.23(4), 24(5), 28(5) and Sched. 2, para. 8.

(a) publish in the *Edinburgh Gazette* a notice in such form and containing such particulars as may be prescribed; and

(b) send a copy of the said notice—

    (i) to every creditor known to the permanent trustee; and

    (ii) where the order is in respect of a relevant person, to the debtor, and

inform the creditor and, where applicable, the debtor that he may participate in the examination.

(4) A person who fails without reasonable excuse to comply with an order made under subsection (2) above shall be guilty of an offence and liable on summary conviction to a fine not exceeding level 5 on the standard scale or to imprisonment for a term not exceeding three months or to both.

Provisions ancillary to sections 44 and 45

[7] **46.**—(1) If the debtor or relevant person is residing—

(a) in Scotland, the sheriff may, on the application of the permanent trustee, grant a warrant which may be executed by a messenger-at-arms or sheriff officer anywhere in Scotland; or

(b) in any other part of the United Kingdom, the Court of Session or the sheriff may, on the application of the permanent trustee, request any court having jurisdiction where the debtor or the relevant person, as the case may be, resides to take appropriate steps, which shall be enforceable by that court,

to apprehend the debtor or relevant person and have him taken to the place of the examination:

Provided that a warrant under paragraph (a) above shall not be granted nor a request under paragraph (b) above made unless the court is satisfied that it is necessary to do so to secure the attendance of the debtor or relevant person at the examination.

(2) If the debtor or a relevant person is for any good reason prevented from attending for examination, the sheriff may, without prejudice to subsection (3) below, grant a commission to take his examination (the commissioner being in this section and section 47 below referred to as an "examining commissioner").

---

[7] Amended (*prosp.*) by the Bankruptcy (Scotland) Act 1993, Sched. 1, para. 19:
"19.—(1) Section 46 (measures to secure the attendance of the debtor and others at private and public examinations) shall be amended as follows.

    (2) In subsection (1)—

      (a) in paragraph (a) at the end there shall be added the words 'to apprehend';

      (b) in paragraph (b) for the words from 'request' to the end of the paragraph there shall be substituted the words 'grant a warrant for the arrest of'; and

      (c) after paragraph (b)—

        (i) the words 'to apprehend' shall cease to have effect; and

        (ii) after the word 'and' there shall be inserted the word 'to'.

    (3) In the proviso to subsection (1) for the words from 'paragraph (a)' to 'made' there shall be substituted the words 'this subsection shall not be granted'."

(3) The sheriff or the examining commissioner may at any time adjourn the examination to such day as the sheriff or the examining commissioner may fix.

(4) The sheriff or the examining commissioner may order the debtor or a relevant person to produce for inspection any document in his custody or control relating to the debtor's assets, his dealings with them or his conduct in relation to his business or financial affairs, and to deliver the document or a copy thereof to the permanent trustee for further examination by him.

Conduct of examination

47.—(1) The examination, whether before the sheriff or an examining commissioner, shall be taken on oath.

(2) At the examination—

(*a*) the permanent trustee or a solicitor or counsel acting on his behalf and, in the case of public examination, any creditor may question the debtor or a relevant person; and

(*b*) the debtor may question a relevant person,

as to any matter relating to the debtor's assets, his dealings with them or his conduct in relation to his business or financial affairs.

(3) The debtor or a relevant person shall be required to answer any question relating to the debtor's assets, his dealings with them or his conduct in relation to his business or financial affairs and shall not be excused from answering any such question on the ground that the answer may incriminate or tend to incriminate him or on the ground of confidentiality:

Provided that—

(*a*) a statement made by the debtor or a relevant person in answer to such a question shall not be admissible in evidence in any subsequent criminal proceedings against the person making the statement, except where the proceedings are in respect of a charge of perjury relating to the statement;

(*b*) a person subject to examination shall not be required to disclose any information which he has received from a person who is not called for examination if the information is confidential between them.

[8] (4) The rules relating to the recording of evidence in ordinary causes specified in the First Schedule to the Sheriff Courts (Scotland) Act 1907 shall apply in relation to the recording of evidence at the examination before the sheriff or the examining commissioner.

(5) The debtor's deposition at the examination shall be subscribed by himself and by the sheriff (or, as the case may be, the examining commissioner) and shall be inserted in the sederunt book.

---

[8] As amended by S.I. 1986 No. 517.

(6) The permanent trustee shall insert a copy of the record of the examination in the sederunt book and send a copy of the record to the Accountant in Bankruptcy.

(7) A relevant person shall be entitled to fees or allowances in respect of his attendance at the examination as if he were a witness in an ordinary civil cause in the sheriff court:

Provided that, if the sheriff thinks that it is appropriate in all the circumstances, he may disallow or restrict the entitlement to such fees or allowances.

Submission and adjudication of claims

Submission of claims to permanent trustee

[9] **48.**—(1) Subject to subsection (2) below and subsections (8) and (9) of section 52 of this Act, a creditor in order to obtain an adjudication as to his entitlement—

(a) to vote at a meeting of creditors other than the statutory meeting; or

(b) (so far as funds are available), to a dividend out of the debtor's estate in respect of any accounting period,

shall submit a claim in accordance with this section to the permanent trustee respectively—

   (i) at or before the meeting; or

   (ii) not later than eight weeks before the end of the accounting period.

(2) A claim submitted by a creditor—

(a) under section 22 of this Act and accepted in whole or in part by the interim trustee for the purpose of voting at the statutory meeting; or

(b) under this section and accepted in whole or in part by the permanent trustee for the purpose of voting at a meeting or of drawing a dividend in respect of any accounting period,

shall be deemed to have been re-submitted for the purpose of obtaining an adjudication as to his entitlement both to vote at any subsequent meeting and (so far as funds are available) to a dividend in respect of an accounting period, or, as the case may be, any subsequent accounting period.

(3) Subsections (2) and (3) of section 22 of this Act shall apply for the purposes of this section but as if in the proviso to subsection (2) for the words "interim trustee" there were substituted the words "permanent trustee with the consent of the commissioners, if any", and for any other reference to the interim trustee there were substituted a reference to the permanent trustee.

---

[9] See the Criminal Justice (Scotland) Act 1987, s.33(2).

(4) A creditor who has submitted a claim under this section (or under section 22 of this Act, a statement of claim which has been deemed re-submitted as mentioned in subsection (2) above) may at any time submit a further claim under this section specifying a different amount for his claim:

Provided that a secured creditor shall not be entitled to produce a further claim specifying a different value for the security at any time after the permanent trustee requires the creditor to discharge, or convey or assign, the security under paragraph 5(2) of Schedule 1 to this Act.

(5) The permanent trustee, for the purpose of satisfying himself as to the validity or amount of a claim submitted by a creditor under this section, may require—

(*a*) the creditor to produce further evidence; or
(*b*) any other person who he believes can produce relevant evidence, to produce such evidence,

and, if the creditor or other person refuses or delays to do so, the permanent trustee may apply to the sheriff for an order requiring the creditor or other person to attend for his private examination before the sheriff.

(6) Sections 44(2) and (3) and 47(1) of this Act shall apply, subject to any necessary modifications, to the examination of the creditor or other person as they apply to the examination of a relevant person; and references in this subsection and subsection (5) above to a creditor in a case where the creditor is an entity mentioned in section 6(1) of this Act shall be construed, unless the context otherwise requires, as references to a person representing the entity.

(7) Subsections (5) to (10) of section 22 of this Act shall apply for the purposes of this section but as if—

(*a*) in subsection (5) the words "interim trustee or" were omitted;
(*b*) in subsection (7) for the words "interim" and "keep a record of it" there were substituted respectively the words "permanent" and "make an insertion relating thereto in the sederunt book".

(8) At any private examination under subsection (5) above, a solicitor or counsel may act on behalf of the permanent trustee or he may appear himself.

Adjudication of claims

49.—(1) At the commencement of every meeting of creditors (other than the statutory meeting), the permanent trustee shall, for the purposes of section 50 of this Act so far as it relates to voting at that meeting, accept or reject the claim of each creditor.

(2) Where funds are available for payment of a dividend out of the debtor's estate in respect of an accounting period, the permanent trustee for the purpose of determining who is entitled to such a dividend shall, not later than four weeks before the end of the period,

accept or reject every claim submitted or deemed to have been re-submitted to him under this Act; and shall at the same time make a decision on any matter requiring to be specified under paragraph (*a*) or (*b*) of subsection (5) below.

(3) If the amount of a claim is stated in foreign currency the permanent trustee in adjudicating on the claim under subsection (1) or (2) above shall convert the amount into sterling, in such manner as may be prescribed, at the rate of exchange prevailing at the close of business on the date of sequestration.

(4) Where the permanent trustee rejects a claim, he shall forthwith notify the creditor giving reasons for the rejection.

(5) Where the permanent trustee accepts or rejects a claim, he shall record in the sederunt book his decision on the claim specifying—

(*a*) the amount of the claim accepted by him,

(*b*) the category of debt, and the value of any security, as decided by him, and

(*c*) if he is rejecting the claim, his reasons therefor.

(6) The debtor or any creditor may, if dissatisfied with the acceptance or rejection of any claim (or, in relation to such acceptance or rejection, with a decision in respect of any matter requiring to be specified under subsection (5)(*a*) or (*b*) above), appeal therefrom to the sheriff—

(*a*) if the acceptance or rejection is under subsection (1) above, within two weeks of that acceptance or rejection;

(*b*) if the acceptance or rejection is under subsection (2) above, not later than two weeks before the end of the accounting period,

and the permanent trustee shall record the sheriff's decision in the sederunt book.

(7) Any reference in this section to the acceptance or rejection of a claim shall be construed as a reference to the acceptance or rejection of the claim in whole or in part.

Entitlement to vote and draw dividend

Entitlement to vote and draw dividend

50. A creditor who has had his claim accepted in whole or in part by the permanent trustee or on appeal under subsection (6) of section 49 of this Act shall be entitled—

(*a*) subject to sections 29(1)(*a*) and 30(1) and (4)(*b*) of this Act, in a case where the acceptance is under (or on appeal arising from) subsection (1) of the said section 49, to vote on any matter at the meeting of creditors for the purpose of voting at which the claim is accepted; and

(*b*) in a case where the acceptance is under (or on appeal arising from) subsection (2) of the said section 49, to payment out of the debtor's estate of a dividend in respect of the accounting period for the purposes of which the claim is accepted; but such entitlement to payment shall arise only in so far as that estate has funds available to make that payment, having regard to section 51 of this Act.

Distribution of debtor's estate

.   .   .   .   .

Estate to be distributed in respect of accounting periods

[10] **52.**—(1) Subject to subsection (6) below, the permanent trustee, until the funds of the estate are exhausted, shall make up accounts of his intromissions with the debtor's estate in respect of periods of 26 weeks, the first such period commencing with the date of sequestration.

(2) In this Act "accounting period" shall be construed in accordance with subsections (1) above and (6) below.

(3) Subject to the following provisions of this section, the permanent trustee shall, if the funds of the debtor's estate are sufficient and after making allowance for future contingencies, pay under section 53(7) of this Act a dividend out of the estate to the creditors in respect of each accounting period.

(4) The permanent trustee may pay—

(*a*) the debts mentioned in subsection (1)(*a*) to (*d*) of section 51 of this Act, other than his own remuneration, at any time;

---

[10] Amended (*prosp.*) by the Bankruptcy (Scotland) Act 1993, Sched. 1, para. 20 as follows: for subss. (1) and (2) substitute the following subsections—
"(1) The permanent trustee shall make up accounts of his intromissions with the debtor's estate in respect of each accounting period.
(2) In this Act 'accounting period' shall be construed as follows—
  (*a*) the first accounting period shall be the period of 6 months beginning with the date of sequestration; and
  (*b*) any subsequent accounting period shall be the period of 6 months beginning with the end of the last accounting period; except that—
    (i) in a case where the Accountant in Bankruptcy is not the permanent trustee, the permanent trustee and the commissioners or, if there are no commissioners, the Accountant in Bankruptcy agree; or
    (ii) in a case where the Accountant in Bankruptcy is the permanent trustee, he determines,
    that the accounting period shall be such other period beginning with the end of the last accounting period as may be agreed or, as the case may be determined, it shall be that other period.
(2A) An agreement or determination under subsection (2)(*b*)(i) or (ii) above—
  (*a*) may be made in respect of one or more than one accounting period;
  (*b*) may be made before the beginning of the accounting period in relation to which it has effect and, in any event, shall not have effect unless made before the day on which such accounting period would, but for the agreement or determination, have ended;
  (*c*) may provide for different accounting periods to be of different durations,
and shall be recorded in the sederunt book by the permanent trustee."

(b) the preferred debts at any time but only with the consent of the commissioners or, if there are no commissioners, of the Accountant in Bankruptcy.

(5) If the permanent trustee—

(a) is not ready to pay a dividend in respect of an accounting period; or

(b) considers it would be inappropriate to pay such a dividend because the expense of doing so would be disproportionate to the amount of the dividend,

he may, with the consent of the commissioners, or if there are no commissioners of the Accountant in Bankruptcy, postpone such payment to a date not later than the time for payment of a dividend in respect of the next accounting period.

[11] (6) Where the permanent trustee considers that it would be expedient to accelerate payment of a dividend other than a dividend in respect of the first accounting period, the accounting period shall be shortened so as to end on such date as the permanent trustee, with the consent of the commissioners (if any), may specify and the next accounting period shall run from the end of that shortened period; and the permanent trustee shall record in the sederunt book the date so specified.

(7) Where an appeal is taken under section 49(6)(b) of this Act against the acceptance or rejection of a creditor's claim, the permanent trustee shall, at the time of payment of dividends and until the appeal is determined, set aside an amount which would be sufficient, if the determination in the appeal were to provide for the claim being accepted in full, to pay a dividend in respect of that claim.

(8) Where a creditor—

(a) has failed to produce evidence in support of his claim earlier than eight weeks before the end of an accounting period on being required by the permanent trustee to do so under section 48(5) of this Act; and

(b) has given a reason for such failure which is acceptable to the permanent trustee,

the permanent trustee shall set aside, for such time as is reasonable to enable him to produce that evidence or any other evidence that will enable the permanent trustee to be satisfied under the said section 48(5), an amount which would be sufficient, if the claim were accepted in full, to pay a dividend in respect of that claim.

(9) Where a creditor submits a claim to the permanent trustee later than eight weeks before the end of an accounting period but more than eight weeks before the end of a subsequent accounting period in

---

[11] Repealed (*prosp.*) by the Bankruptcy (Scotland) Act 1993, Sched. 2.

respect of which, after making allowance for contingencies, funds are available for the payment of a dividend, the permanent trustee shall, if he accepts the claim in whole or in part, pay to the creditor—

(a) the same dividend or dividends as has or have already been paid to creditors of the same class in respect of any accounting period or periods; and

(b) whatever dividend may be payable to him in respect of the said subsequent accounting period:

Provided that paragraph (a) above shall be without prejudice to any dividend which has already been paid.

Procedure after end of accounting period

53.—[12] (1) Within two weeks after the end of an accounting period, the permanent trustee shall in respect of that period submit to the commissioners or, if there are no commissioners, to the Accountant in Bankruptcy—

(a) his accounts of his intromissions with the debtor's estate for audit and, where funds are available after making allowance for contingencies, a scheme of division of the divisible funds; and

(b) a claim for the outlays reasonably incurred by him and for his remuneration;

and, where the said documents are submitted to the commissioners, he shall send a copy of them to the Accountant in Bankruptcy.

[13] (2) All accounts in respect of legal services incurred by the permanent trustee shall, before payment thereof by him, be submitted for taxation to the auditor of the court before which the sequestration is pending:

Provided that the permanent trustee may be authorised by the Accountant in Bankruptcy to pay any such account without taxation.

(3) Within six weeks after the end of an accounting period—

[14] (a) the commissioners or, as the case may be, the Accountant in Bankruptcy shall—

---

[12] See also ss.23(4), 24(5), 28(5) and Sched. 2, para. 9 for further provision *re* procedure.

[13] Substituted (*prosp.*) by the Bankruptcy (Scotland) Act 1993, Sched. 1, para. 21 as follows:

"(2) Subject to subsection (2A) below, all accounts in respect of legal services incurred by the permanent trustee shall, before payment thereof by him, be submitted for taxation to the auditor of the court before which the sequestration is pending.

(2A) Where—

(a) any such account has been agreed between the permanent trustee and the person entitled to payment in respect of that account (in this subsection referred to as 'the payee');

(b) the permanent trustee is not an associate of the payee; and

(c) the commissioners have not determined that the account should be submitted for taxation,

the permanent trustee may pay such account without submitting it for taxation."

[14] Amended (*prosp.*) by the Bankruptcy (Scotland) Act 1993, Sched. 2 as follows: the word "shall" is repealed.

[15] (i) audit the accounts; and

[16] (ii) issue a determination fixing the amount of the outlays and the remuneration payable to the permanent trustee; and

(b) the permanent trustee shall make the audited accounts, scheme of division and the said determination available for inspection by the debtor and the creditors.

(4) The basis for fixing the amount of the remuneration payable to the permanent trustee may be a commission calculated by reference to the value of the debtor's estate which has been realised by the permanent trustee, but there shall in any event be taken into account—

(a) the work which, having regard to that value, was reasonably undertaken by him; and

(b) the extent of his responsibilities in administering the debtor's estate.

[17] (5) In fixing the amount of such remuneration in respect of the final accounting period, the commissioners or, as the case may be, the Accountant in Bankruptcy may take into account any adjustment which the commissioners or the Accountant in Bankruptcy may wish to make in the amount of the remuneration fixed in respect of any earlier accounting period.

[18] (6) Not later than eight weeks after the end of an accounting period, the permanent trustee, the debtor or any creditor may appeal against a determination issued under subsection (3)(a)(ii) above—

(a) where it is a determination of the commissioners, to the Accountant in Bankruptcy; and

(b) where it is a determination of the Accountant in Bankruptcy, to the sheriff;

and the determination of the Accountant in Bankruptcy under paragraph (a) above shall be appealable to the sheriff.

(7) On the expiry of the period within which an appeal may be taken under subsection (6) above or, if an appeal is so taken, on the final determination of the last such appeal, the permanent trustee shall pay to the creditors their dividends in accordance with the scheme of division.

(8) Any dividend—

(a) allocated to a creditor which is not cashed or uplifted; or

---

[15] Amended (*prosp.*) by the Bankruptcy (Scotland) Act 1993, Sched. 1, para. 21 as follows: before the word "audit" insert the word "may".

[16] Amended (*prosp.*) by the Bankruptcy (Scotland) Act 1993, Sched. 1, para. 21 as follows: before the word "issue" insert the word "shall".

[17] Amended (*prosp.*) by the Bankruptcy (Scotland) Act 1993, Sched. 1, para. 21 as follows: for the words "the final" substitute the word "any".

[18] Amended (*prosp.*) by the Bankruptcy (Scotland) Act 1993, Sched. 1, para. 21 as follows: at the end of the subsection add the words "; and the decision of the sheriff on such an appeal shall be final."

(b) dependent on a claim in respect of which an amount has been set aside under subsection (7) or (8) of section 52 of this Act,

shall be deposited by the permanent trustee in an appropriate bank or institution.

(9) If a creditor's claim is revalued, the permanent trustee may—

(a) in paying any dividend to that creditor, make such adjustment to it as he considers necessary to take account of that revaluation; or

(b) require the creditor to repay him the whole or part of a dividend already paid to him.

(10) The permanent trustee shall insert in the sederunt book the audited accounts, the scheme of division and the final determination in relation to the permanent trustee's outlays and remuneration.

. . . . . .

Discharge of permanent trustee

. . . . .

Unclaimed dividends

58.—[19] (1) Any person, producing evidence of his right, may apply to the Accountant in Bankruptcy to receive a dividend deposited under section 57(1)(a) of this Act, if the application is made not later than seven years after the date of such deposit.

(2) If the Accountant in Bankruptcy is satisfied of the applicant's right to the dividend, he shall authorise the appropriate bank or institution to pay to the applicant the amount of that dividend and of any interest which has accrued thereon.

[19] (3) The Accountant in Bankruptcy shall, at the expiry of seven years from the date of deposit of any unclaimed dividend or unapplied balance under section 57(1)(a) of this Act, hand over the deposit receipt or other voucher relating to such dividend or balance to the Secretary of State, who shall thereupon be entitled to payment of the amount due, principal and interest, from the bank or institution in which the deposit was made.

[20] *[Discharge of Accountant in Bankruptcy*

Discharge of Accountant in Bankruptcy

58A.—(1) This section applies where the Accountant in Bankruptcy has acted as the permanent trustee in any sequestration.

(2) After the Accountant in Bankruptcy has made a final division of the debtor's estate, he shall insert in the sederunt book—

---

[19] Amended (*prosp.*) by the Bankruptcy (Scotland) Act 1993, Sched. 1, para. 24 as follows: after the words "section 57(1)(a)" insert the words "or 58A(3)".
[20] Inserted (*prosp.*) by the Bankruptcy (Scotland) Act 1993, Sched. 1, para. 25.

(*a*) his final accounts of his intromissions (if any) with the debtor's estate;

(*b*) the scheme of division (if any); and

(*c*) a determination of his fees and outlays calculated in accordance with regulations made under section 69A of this Act.

(3) The Accountant in Bankruptcy shall deposit any unclaimed dividends and any unapplied balances in an appropriate bank or institution.

(4) The Accountant in Bankruptcy shall send to the debtor and to all creditors known to him—

(*a*) a copy of the determination mentioned in subsection (2)(*c*) above; and

(*b*) a notice in writing stating—

    (i) that the Accountant in Bankruptcy has commenced the procedure under this Act leading to discharge in respect of his actings as permanent trustee;

    (ii) that the sederunt book relating to the sequestration is available for inspection at such address as the Accountant in Bankruptcy may determine;

    (iii) that an appeal may be made to the sheriff under subsection (5) below; and

    (iv) the effect of subsection (7) below.

(5) The debtor and any creditor may appeal to the sheriff against—

(*a*) the determination of the Accountant in Bankruptcy mentioned in subsection (2)(*c*) above;

(*b*) the discharge of the Accountant in Bankruptcy in respect of his actings as permanent trustee; or

(*c*) both such determination and discharge.

(6) An appeal under subsection (5) above shall be made not more than 14 days after the issue of the notice mentioned in subsection (4)(*b*) above; and the decision of the sheriff on such an appeal shall be final.

(7) Where—

(*a*) the requirements of this section have been complied with; and

(*b*) no appeal to the sheriff is made under subsection (5) above or such an appeal is made but is refused as regards the discharge of the Accountant in Bankruptcy,

the Accountant in Bankruptcy shall be discharged from all liability (other than any liability arising from fraud) to the creditors or to the debtor in respect of any act or omission of the Accountant in Bankruptcy in exercising the functions of permanent trustee in the sequestration.

(8) Where the Accountant in Bankruptcy is discharged from all liability as mentioned in subsection (7) above, he shall make an entry in the sederunt book recording such discharge.

(9) Where the Accountant in Bankruptcy—

(*a*) has acted as both interim trustee and permanent trustee in a sequestration;

(*b*) has not been discharged under section 26A(7) of this Act,

references in this section to his acting as or exercising the functions of permanent trustee shall be construed as including references to his acting as or exercising the functions of interim trustee; and subsection (7) above shall have effect accordingly.]

· · · · ·

Miscellaneous and supplementary

Liabilities and rights of co-obligants

60.—(1) Where a creditor has an obligant (in this section referred to as the "co-obligant") bound to him along with the debtor for the whole or part of the debt, the co-obligant shall not be freed or discharged from his liability for the debt by reason of the discharge of the debt or by virtue of the creditor's voting or drawing a dividend or assenting to, or not opposing—

(*a*) the discharge of the debtor; or

(*b*) any composition.

(2) Where—

(*a*) a creditor has had a claim accepted in whole or in part; and

(*b*) a co-obligant holds a security over any part of the debtor's estate,

the co-obligant shall account to the permanent trustee so as to put the estate in the same position as if the co-obligant had paid the debt to the creditor and thereafter had had his claim accepted in whole or in part in the sequestration after deduction of the value of the security.

(3) Without prejudice to any right under any rule of law of a co-obligant who has paid the debt, the co-obligant may require and obtain at his own expense from the creditor an assignation of the debt on payment of the amount thereof, and thereafter may in respect of that debt submit a claim, and vote and draw a dividend, if otherwise legally entitled to do so.

(4) In this section a "co-obligant" includes a cautioner.

· · · · ·

Power to cure defects in procedure

63.—(1) The sheriff may, on the application of any person having an interest—

(*a*) if there has been a failure to comply with any requirement of this Act or any regulations made under it, make an order waiving any such failure and, so far as practicable, restoring any person prejudiced by the failure to the position he would have been in but for the failure;

(b) if for any reason anything required or authorised to be done in, or in connection with, the sequestration process cannot be done, make such order as may be necessary to enable that thing to be done.

(2) The sheriff, in an order under subsection (1) above, may impose such conditions, including conditions as to expenses, as he thinks fit and may—

(a) authorise or dispense with the performance of any act in the sequestration process;

(b) appoint as permanent trustee on the debtor's estate a person who would be eligible to be elected under section 24 of this Act, whether or not in place of an existing trustee;

(c) extend or waive any time limit specified in or under this Act.

(3) An application under subsection (1) above—

(a) may at any time be remitted by the sheriff to the Court of Session, of his own accord or on an application by any person having an interest;

(b) shall be so remitted, if the Court of Session so directs on an application by any such person,

if the sheriff or the Court of Session, as the case may be, considers that the remit is desirable because of the importance or complexity of the matters raised by the application.

(4) The permanent trustee shall record in the sederunt book the decision of the sheriff or the Court of Session under this section.

. . . . . .

Arbitration and compromise

65.—(1) The permanent trustee may (but if there are commissioners only with the consent of the commissioners, the creditors or the court)—

(a) refer to arbitration any claim or question of whatever nature which may arise in the course of the sequestration; or

(b) make a compromise with regard to any claim of whatever nature made against or on behalf of the sequestrated estate;

and the decree arbitral or compromise shall be binding on the creditors and the debtor.

(2) Where any claim or question is referred to arbitration under this section, the Accountant in Bankruptcy may vary any time limit in respect of which any procedure under this Act has to be carried out.

(3) The permanent trustee shall insert a copy of the decree arbitral, or record the compromise, in the sederunt book.

. . . . . .

Interpretation

73.—. . . (5) Any reference in this Act to any of the following acts by a creditor barring the effect of any enactment or rule of law relating to the limitation of actions in any part of the United Kingdom, namely—

(*a*) the presentation of a petition for sequestration;

(*b*) the concurrence in such a petition; and

(*c*) the submission of a claim,

shall be construed as a reference to that act having the same effect, for the purposes of any such enactment or rule of law, as an effective acknowledgment of the creditor's claim; and any reference in this Act to any such enactment shall not include a reference to an enactment which implements or gives effect to any international agreement or obligation.

Meaning of "associate"

[21] **74.**—(1) Subject to subsection (7) below, for the purposes of this Act any question whether a person is an associate of another person shall be determined in accordance with the following provisions of this section (any reference, whether in those provisions or in regulations under the said subsection (7), to a person being an associate of another person being taken to be a reference to their being associates of each other).

(2) A person is an associate of an individual if that person is the individual's husband or wife, or is a relative, or the husband or wife of a relative, of the individual or of the individual's husband or wife.

(3) A person is an associate of any person with whom he is in partnership, and of any person who is an associate of any person with whom he is in partnership; and a firm is an associate of any person who is a member of the firm.

(4) For the purposes of this section a person is a relative of an individual if he is that individual's brother, sister, uncle, aunt, nephew, niece, lineal ancestor or lineal descendant treating—

(*a*) any relationship of the half blood as a relationship of the whole blood and the stepchild or adopted child of any person as his child; and

(*b*) an illegitimate child as the legitimate child of his mother and reputed father,

and references in this section to a husband or wife include a former husband or wife and a reputed husband or wife.

(5) A person is an associate of any person whom he employs or by whom he is employed; and for the purposes of this subsection any

---

[21] As amended by S.I. 1985 No. 1925.

director or other officer of a company shall be treated as employed by that company.

(5A) A company is an associate of another company—

(a) if the same person has control of both, or a person has control of one and persons who are his associates, or he and persons who are his associates, have control of the other; or

(b) if a group of two or more persons has control of each company, and the groups either consist of the same persons or could be regarded as consisting of the same persons by treating (in one or more cases) a member of either group as replaced by a person of whom he is an associate.

(5B) A company is an associate of another person if that person has control of it or if that person and persons who are his associates together have control of it.

(5C) For the purposes of this section a person shall be taken to have control of a company if—

(a) the directors of the company or of another company which has control of it (or any of them) are accustomed to act in accordance with his directions or instructions; or

(b) he is entitled to exercise, or control the exercise of, one third or more of the voting power at any general meeting of the company or of another company which has control of it:

and where two or more persons together satisfy either of the above conditions, they shall be taken to have control of the company.

(6) In subsections (5), (5A), (5B) and (5C) above, "company" includes any body corporate (whether incorporated in Great Britain or elsewhere).

(7) The Secretary of State may by regulations—

(a) amend the foregoing provisions of this section so as to provide further categories of persons who, for the purposes of this Act, are to be associates of other persons; and

(b) provide that any or all of subsections (2) to (6) above (or any subsection added by virtue of paragraph (a) above) shall cease to apply, whether in whole or in part, or shall apply subject to such modifications as he may specify in the regulations;

and he may in the regulations make such incidental or transitional provision as he considers appropriate.

. . . . . .

SCHEDULES

Sections 5(5) and 22(9)   SCHEDULE 1

DETERMINATION OF AMOUNT OF CREDITOR'S CLAIM

Amount which may be claimed generally

1.—(1) Subject to the provisions of this Schedule, the amount in respect of which a creditor shall be entitled to claim shall be the accumulated sum of principal and any interest which is due on the debt as at the date of sequestration.

(2) If a debt does not depend on a contingency but would not be payable but for the sequestration until after the date of sequestration, the amount of the claim shall be calculated as if the debt were payable on the date of sequestration but subject to the deduction of interest at the rate specified in section 51(7) of this Act from the said date until the date for payment of the debt.

(3) In calculating the amount of his claim, a creditor shall deduct any discount (other than any discount for payment in cash) which is allowable by contract or course of dealing between the creditor and the debtor or by the usage of trade.

. . . . . .

Debts depending on contingency

3.—(1) Subject to sub-paragraph (2) below, the amount which a creditor shall be entitled to claim shall not include a debt in so far as its existence or amount depends upon a contingency.

(2) On an application by the creditor—

(*a*) to the permanent trustee; or
(*b*) if there is no permanent trustee, to the sheriff,

the permanent trustee or sheriff shall put a value on the debt in so far as it is contingent, and the amount in respect of which the creditor shall then be entitled to claim shall be that value but no more; and, where the contingent debt is an annuity, a cautioner may not then be sued for more than that value.

(3) Any interested person may appeal to the sheriff against a valuation under sub-paragraph (2) above by the permanent trustee, and the sheriff may affirm or vary that valuation.

. . . . . .

Secured debts

5.—(1) In calculating the amount of his claim, a secured creditor shall deduct the value of any security as estimated by him:

Provided that if he surrenders, or undertakes in writing to surrender, a security for the benefit of the debtor's estate, he shall not be required to make a deduction of the value of that security.

(2) The permanent trustee may, at any time after the expiry of 12 weeks from the date of sequestration, require a secured creditor at the expense of the debtor's estate to discharge the security or convey or assign it to the permanent trustee on payment to the creditor of the value specified by the creditor; and the amount in respect of which the creditor shall then be entitled to claim shall be any balance of his debt remaining after receipt of such payment.

(3) In calculating the amount of his claim, a creditor whose security has been realised shall deduct the amount (less the expenses of realisation) which he has received, or is entitled to receive, from the realisation.

. . . . . .

(1985 c. 6)

An Act to consolidate the greater part of the Companies Acts.

[11th March 1985]

. . . . . .

PART XVIII

FLOATING CHARGES AND RECEIVERS (SCOTLAND)

CHAPTER I

FLOATING CHARGES

Power of incorporated company to create floating charge

462.—(1) It is competent under the law of Scotland for an incorporated company (whether a company within the meaning of this Act or not), for the purpose of securing any debt or other obligation (including a cautionary obligation) incurred or to be incurred by, or binding upon, the company or any other person to create in favour of the creditor in the debt or obligation a charge, in this Part referred to as a floating charge, over all or any part of the property (including uncalled capital) which may from time to time be comprised in its property and undertaking.

(2) [Repealed by the Law Reform (Miscellaneous Provisions) (Scotland) Act 1990, Sched. 8, para. 33(6) and Sched. 9.]

(3) Execution in accordance with this section includes execution by an attorney authorised for such purpose by the company by writing under its common seal; and any such execution on behalf of the company binds the company.

(4) References in this Part to the instrument by which a floating charge was created are, in the case of a floating charge created by words in a bond or other written acknowledgment, references to the bond or, as the case may be, the other written acknowledgment.

[23] (5) Subject to this Act, a floating charge has effect in accordance with this Part and Part III of the Insolvency Act 1986 in relation to any heritable property in Scotland to which it relates, notwithstanding that the instrument creating it is not recorded in the Register of Sasines or,

---

[22] The extensive amendments to this Act by the Companies Act 1989 are being given effect as that Act is brought into force. See note to s.215 of the 1989 Act. For forms see S.I. 1985 No. 854, as amended by S.I. 1986 No. 2097, 1987 No. 752, 1988 No. 1359 and 1990 Nos. 572 and 1766.

[23] As amended by the Insolvency Act 1986, Sched. 13, Pt. I.

as appropriate, registered in accordance with the Land Registration (Scotland) Act 1979.

Effect of floating charge on winding up

[24] **463.**—[25] (1) On the commencement of the winding up of a company, a floating charge created by the company attaches to the property then comprised in the company's property and undertaking or, as the case may be, in part of that property and undertaking, but does so subject to the rights of any person who—

(a) has effectually executed diligence on the property or any part of it; or

(b) holds a fixed security over the property or any part of it ranking in priority to the floating charge; or

(c) holds over the property or any part of it another floating charge so ranking.

(2) The provisions of Part IV of the Insolvency Act (except section 185) have effect in relation to a floating charge, subject to subsection (1), as if the charge were a fixed security over the property to which it has attached in respect of the principal of the debt or obligation to which it relates and any interest due or to become due thereon.

(3) Nothing in this section derogates from the provisions of sections 53(7) and 54(6) of the Insolvency Act (attachment of floating charge on appointment of receiver), or prejudices the operation of sections 175 and 176 of that Act (payment of preferential debts in winding up).

(4) Interest accrues, in respect of a floating charge which after 16th November 1972 attaches to the property of the company, until payment of the sum due under the charge is made.

Ranking of floating charges

[26] **464.**—[27] (1) Subject to subsection (2), the instrument creating a floating charge over all or any part of the company's property under section 462 may contain—

(a) provisions prohibiting or restricting the creation of any fixed security or any other floating charge having priority over, or ranking *pari passu* with, the floating charge; or

---

[24] As amended by the Insolvency Act 1985, Sched. 6, para. 18 and the Insolvency Act 1986, Scheds. 12 and 13, Pt. I.

[25] Amended (*prosp.*) by the Companies Act 1989, s.140(1) as follows: For the words "On the commencement of the winding up of a company," there shall be substituted the words "Where a company goes into liquidation within the meaning of section 247(2) of the Insolvency Act 1986,".

[26] As amended by the Insolvency Act 1985, Sched. 6, para. 19 and the Insolvency Act 1986, Sched. 13, Pt. I.

[27] Amended (*prosp.*) by the Companies Act 1989, s.140(4), as follows: after subs. (1) insert the following: "(1A) Where an instrument creating a floating charge contains any such provision as is mentioned in subsection (1)(a), that provision shall be effective to confer priority on the floating charge over any fixed security or floating charge created after the date of the instrument.".

[28] (b) provisions regulating the order in which the floating charge shall rank with any other subsisting or future floating charges or fixed securities over that property or any part of it.

(2) Where all or any part of the property of a company is subject both to a floating charge and to a fixed security arising by operation of law, the fixed security has priority over the floating charge.

[29] (3) Where the order of ranking of the floating charge with any other subsisting or future floating charges or fixed securities over all or any part of the company's property is not regulated by provisions contained in the instrument creating the floating charge, the order of ranking is determined in accordance with the following provisions of this section.

(4) Subject to the provisions of this section—

(a) a fixed security, the right to which has been constituted as a real right before a floating charge has attached to all or any part of the property of the company, has priority of ranking over the floating charge;

(b) floating charges rank with one another according to the time of registration in accordance with Chapter II of Part XII;

(c) floating charges which have been received by the registrar for registration by the same postal delivery rank with one another equally.

[30] (5) Where the holder of a floating charge over all or any part of the company's property which has been registered in accordance with Chapter II of Part XII has received intimation in writing of the subsequent registration in accordance with that Chapter of another floating charge over the same property or any part thereof, the preference in ranking of the first-mentioned floating charge is restricted to security for—

(a) the holder's present advances;

(b) future advances which he may be required to make under the

---

[28] Amended (*prosp.*) by the Companies Act 1989, s.140(3) as follows: at the beginning insert the words "with the consent of the holder of any subsisting floating charge or fixed security which would be adversely affected,".

[29] Substituted (*prosp.*) by the Companies Act 1989, s.140(5) as follows: "(3) The order of ranking of the floating charge with any other subsisting or future floating charges or fixed securities over all or any part of the company's property is determined in accordance with the provisions of subsections (4) and (5) except where it is determined in accordance with any provision such as is mentioned in paragraph (a) or (b) of subsection (1).".

[30] Amended (*prosp.*) by the Companies Act 1989, s.140(6) as follows: at the end of the subsection add the following paragraph:

"; and

(e) (in the case of a floating charge to secure a contingent liability other than a liability arising under any further advances made from time to time) the maximum sum to which that contingent liability is capable of amounting whether or not it is contractually limited.".

instrument creating the floating charge or under any ancillary document;

(c) interest due or to become due on all such advances; and

(d) any expenses or outlays which may reasonably be incurred by the holder.

[31] (6) This section is subject to sections 175 and 176 of the Insolvency Act.

Continued effect of certain charges validated by Act of 1972

465.—(1) Any floating charge which—

(a) purported to subsist as a floating charge on 17th November 1972, and

(b) if it had been created on or after that date, would have been validly created by virtue of the Companies (Floating Charges and Receivers) (Scotland) Act 1972,

is deemed to have subsisted as a valid floating charge as from the date of its creation.

(2) Any provision which—

(a) is contained in an instrument creating a floating charge or in any ancillary document executed prior to, and still subsisting at, the commencement of that Act,

(b) relates to the ranking of charges, and

(c) if it had been made after the commencement of that Act, would have been a valid provision,

is deemed to have been a valid provision as from the date of its making.

Alteration of floating charges

466.—(1) The instrument creating a floating charge under section 462 or any ancillary document may be altered by the execution of an instrument of alteration by the company, the holder of the charge and the holder of any other charge (including a fixed security) which would be adversely affected by the alteration.

[32] (2) Without prejudice to any enactment or rule of law regarding the execution of documents, such an instrument of alteration is validly executed if it is executed—

(a) [Repealed by the Companies Act 1989, Sched. 17, para. 9 and Sched. 24.]

(b) where trustees for debenture-holders are acting under and in accordance with a trust deed, by those trustees; or

(c) where, in the case of a series of secured debentures, no such trustees are acting, by or on behalf of—

---

[31] Amended (*prosp.*) by the Companies Act 1989, s.140(7) as follows: after the words "subject to" insert the words "Part XII and to".

[32] As amended by the Companies Act 1989, Sched. 17, para. 9 and Sched. 24.

(i) a majority in nominal value of those present or represented by proxy and voting at a meeting of debenture-holders at which the holders of at least one-third in nominal value of the outstanding debentures of the series are present or so represented; or

(ii) where no such meeting is held, the holders of at least one-half in nominal value of the outstanding debentures of the series.

(*d*) [Repealed by the Companies Act 1989, Sched. 17, para. 9 and Sched. 24.]

(3) Section 464 applies to an instrument of alteration under this section as it applies to an instrument creating a floating charge.

[33] (4) Subject to the next subsection, section 410(2) and (3) and section 420 apply to an instrument of alteration under this section which—

(*a*) prohibits or restricts the creation of any fixed security or any other floating charge having priority over, or ranking *pari passu* with, the floating charge; or

(*b*) varies, or otherwise regulates the order of, the ranking of the floating charge in relation to fixed securities or to other floating charges; or

(*c*) releases property from the floating charge; or

(*d*) increases the amount secured by the floating charge.

[33] (5) Section 410(2) and (3) and section 420 apply to an instrument of alteration falling under subsection (4) of this section as if references in the said sections to a charge were references to an alteration to a floating charge, and as if in section 410(2) and (3)—

(*a*) references to the creation of a charge were references to the execution of such alteration; and

(*b*) for the words from the beginning of subsection (2) to the word "applies" there were substituted the words "Every alteration to a floating charge created by a company".

[34] (6) Any reference (however expressed) in any enactment, including this Act, to a floating charge is, for the purposes of this section and unless the context otherwise requires, to be construed as including a reference to the floating charge as altered by an instrument of alteration falling under subsection (4) of this section.

.   .   .   .   .   .

---

[33] Repealed (*prosp.*) by the Companies Act 1989, s.140(8) and Sched. 24.

[34] Amended (*prosp.*) by the Companies Act 1989, s.140(8) and Sched. 24 as follows: the words "falling under subsection (4) of this section" cease to have effect.

CHAPTER VI

MATTERS ARISING SUBSEQUENT TO WINDING UP

Power of court to declare dissolution of company void

[35] **651.**—(1) Where a company has been dissolved, the court may, on an application made for the purpose by the liquidator of the company or by any other person appearing to the court to be interested, make an order, on such terms as the court thinks fit, declaring the dissolution to have been void.

(2) Thereupon such proceedings may be taken as might have been taken if the company had not been dissolved.

(3) It is the duty of the person on whose application the order was made, within seven days after its making (or such further time as the court may allow), to deliver to the registrar of companies for registration an office copy of the order.

If the person fails to do so, he is liable to a fine and, for continued contravention, to a daily default fine.

(4) Subject to the following provisions, an application under this section may not be made after the end of the period of two years from the date of the dissolution of the company.

(5) An application for the purpose of bringing proceedings against the company—

(a) for damages in respect of personal injuries (including any sum claimed by virtue of section 1(2)(c) of the Law Reform (Miscellaneous Provisions) Act 1934 (funeral expenses)), or

(b) for damages under the Fatal Accidents Act 1976 or the Damages (Scotland) Act 1976,

may be made at any time; but no order shall be made on such an application if it appears to the court that the proceedings would fail by virtue of any enactment as to the time within which proceedings must be brought.

(6) Nothing in subsection (5) affects the power of the court on making an order under this section to direct that the period between the dissolution of the company and the making of the order shall not count for the purposes of any such enactment.

(7) In subsection (5)(a) "personal injuries" includes any disease and any impairment of a person's physical or mental condition.

Registrar may strike defunct company off register

652.—(1) If the registrar of companies has reasonable cause to believe that a company is not carrying on business or in operation, he may send to the company by post a letter inquiring whether the company is carrying on business or in operation.

---

[35] As amended by the Companies Act 1989, s.141(1)–(3). See *ibid.*, subss. (4)–(5).

(2) If the registrar does not within one month of sending the letter receive any answer to it, he shall within 14 days after the expiration of that month send to the company by post a registered letter referring to the first letter, and stating that no answer to it has been received, and that if an answer is not received to the second letter within one month from its date, a notice will be published in the *Gazette* with a view to striking the company's name off the register.

(3) If the registrar either receives an answer to the effect that the company is not carrying on business or in operation, or does not within one month after sending the second letter receive any answer, he may publish in the *Gazette*, and send to the company by post, a notice that at the expiration of three months from the date of that notice the name of the company mentioned in it will, unless cause is shown to the contrary, be struck off the register and the company will be dissolved.

(4) If, in a case where a company is being wound up, the registrar has reasonable cause to believe either that no liquidator is acting, or that the affairs of the company are fully wound up, and the returns required to be made by the liquidator have not been made for a period of six consecutive months, the registrar shall publish in the *Gazette* and send to the company or the liquidator (if any) a like notice as is provided in subsection (3).

(5) At the expiration of the time mentioned in the notice the registrar may, unless cause to the contrary is previously shown by the company, strike its name off the register, and shall publish notice of this in the *Gazette*; and on the publication of that notice in the *Gazette* the company is dissolved.

(6) However—

(a) the liability (if any) of every director, managing officer and member of the company continues and may be enforced as if the company had not been dissolved and

(b) nothing in subsection (5) affects the power of the court to wind up a company the name of which has been struck off the register.

(7) A notice to be sent to a liquidator under this section may be addressed to him at his last known place of business; and a letter or notice to be sent under this section to a company may be addressed to the company at its registered office or, if no office has been registered, to the care of some officer of the company.

If there is no officer of the company whose name and address are known to the registrar of companies, the letter or notice may be sent to each of the persons who subscribed the memorandum, addressed to him at the address mentioned in the memorandum.

Objection to striking off by person aggrieved

653.—(1) The following applies if a company or any member or creditor of it feels aggrieved by the company having been struck off the register.

(2) The court, on an application by the company or the member or creditor made before the expiration of 20 years from publication in the *Gazette* of notice under section 652, may, if satisfied that the company was at the time of the striking off carrying on business or in operation, or otherwise that it is just that the company be restored to the register, order the company's name to be restored.

(3) On an office copy of the order being delivered to the registrar of companies for registration the company is deemed to have continued in existence as if its name had not been struck off; and the court may by the order give such directions and make such provisions as seem just for placing the company and all other persons in the same position (as nearly as may be) as if the company's name had not been struck off.

Property of dissolved company to be *bona vacantia*

[36] **654.**—(1) When a company is dissolved, all property and rights whatsoever vested in or held on trust for the company immediately before its dissolution (including leasehold property, but not including property held by the company on trust for any other person) are deemed to be *bona vacantia* and—

   (a) accordingly belong to the Crown, or to the Duchy of Lancaster or to the Duke of Cornwall for the time being (as the case may be), and

   (b) vest and may be dealt with in the same manner as other *bona vacantia* accruing to the Crown, to the Duchy of Lancaster or to the Duke of Cornwall.

(2) Except as provided by the section next following, the above has effect subject and without prejudice to any order made by the court under section 651 or 653.

Effect on s.654 of company's revival after dissolution

[37] **655.**—(1) The person in whom any property or right is vested by section 654 may dispose of, or of an interest in, that property or right notwithstanding that an order may be made under section 651 or 653.

(2) Where such an order is made—

   (a) it does not affect the disposition (but without prejudice to the order so far as it relates to any other property or right previously vested in or held on trust for the company), and

   (b) the Crown or, as the case may be, the Duke of Cornwall shall pay to the company an amount equal to—

      (i) the amount of any consideration received for the property or right, or interest therein, or

---

[36] Applied (*mod.*) by the Building Societies Act 1986, Sched. 15, para. 57, with effect from 1st January 1988.

[37] Applied (*mod.*) by the Building Societies Act 1986, Sched. 15, para. 57, with effect from 1st January 1988.

(ii) the value of any such consideration at the time of the disposition,

or, if no consideration was received, an amount equal to the value of the property, right or interest disposed of, as at the date of the disposition.

(3) Where a liability accrues under subsection (2) in respect of any property or right which, before the order under section 651 or 653 was made, had accrued as *bona vacantia* to the Duchy of Lancaster, the Attorney-General of the Duchy shall represent Her Majesty in any proceedings arising in connection with that liability.

(4) Where a liability accrues under subsection (2) in respect of any property or right which, before the order under section 651 or 653 was made, had accrued as *bona vacantia* to the Duchy of Cornwall, such persons as the Duke of Cornwall (or other possessor for the time being of the Duchy) may appoint shall represent the Duke (or other possessor) in any proceedings arising out of that liability.

(5) This section applies in relation to the disposition of any property, right or interest on or after 22nd December 1981, whether the company concerned was dissolved before, on or after that day.

Crown disclaimer of property vesting as *bona vacantia*

[38] **656.**—(1) Where property vests in the Crown under section 654, the Crown's title to it under that section may be disclaimed by a notice signed by the Crown representative, that is to say the Treasury Solicitor, or, in relation to property in Scotland, the Queen's and Lord Treasurer's Remembrancer.

(2) The right to execute a notice of disclaimer under this section may be waived by or on behalf of the Crown either expressly or by taking possession or other act evincing that intention.

(3) A notice of disclaimer under this section is of no effect unless it is executed—

(a) within 12 months of the date on which the vesting of the property under section 654 came to the notice of the Crown representative, or

(b) if an application in writing is made to the Crown representative by any person interested in the property requiring him to decide whether he will or will not disclaim, within a period of three months after the receipt of the application or such further period as may be allowed by the court which would have had jurisdiction to wind up the company if it had not been dissolved.

(4) A statement in a notice of disclaimer of any property under this section that the vesting of it came to the notice of the Crown representatives on a specified date, or that no such application as

---

[38] Applied (*mod.*) by the Building Societies Act 1986, Sched. 15, para. 57, with effect from 1st January 1988.

above mentioned was received by him with respect to the property before a specified date, is sufficient evidence of the fact stated, until the contrary is proved.

(5) A notice of disclaimer under this section shall be delivered to the registrar of companies and retained and registered by him; and copies of it shall be published in the *Gazette* and sent to any persons who have given the Crown representative notice that they claim to be interested in the property.

(6) This section applies to property vested in the Duchy of Lancaster or the Duke of Cornwall under section 654 as if for references to the Crown and the Crown representative there were respectively substituted references to the Duchy of Lancaster and to the Solicitor to that Duchy, or to the Duke of Cornwall and to the Solicitor to the Duchy of Cornwall, as the case may be.

Effect of Crown disclaimer under s.656

[39] **657.**—(1) Where notice of disclaimer is executed under section 656 as respects any property, that property is deemed not to have vested in the Crown under section 654.

(2) As regards property in England and Wales, section 178(4) and sections 179 to 182 of the Insolvency Act shall apply as if the property had been disclaimed by the liquidator under the said section 91 immediately before the dissolution of the company.

(3) As regards property in Scotland, the following four subsections apply.

(4) The Crown's disclaimer operates to determine, as from the date of the disclaimer, the rights, interests and liabilities of the company, and the property of the company, in or in respect of the property disclaimed; but it does not (except so far as is necessary for the purpose of releasing the company and its property from liability) affect the rights or liabilities of any other person.

(5) The court may, on application by a person who either claims an interest in disclaimed property or is under a liability not discharged by this Act in respect of disclaimed property, and on hearing such persons as it thinks fit, make an order for the vesting of the property in or its delivery to any person entitled to it, or to whom it may seem just that the property should be delivered by way of compensation for such liability, or a trustee for him, and on such terms as the court thinks just.

(6) On such a vesting order being made, the property comprised in it vests accordingly in the person named in that behalf in the order, without conveyance or assignation for that purpose.

(7) Part II of Schedule 20 has effect for the protection of third parties where the property disclaimed is held under a lease.

· · · · · ·

---

[39] As amended by the Insolvency Act 1985, Sched. 6, para. 46 and the Insolvency Act 1986, Sched. 13, Pt. I. "Section 91" refers to the Insolvency Act 1985, now s.178 of the 1986 Act. Applied (*mod.*) by the Building Societies Act 1986, Sched. 15, para. 57 with effect from 1st January 1988.

Insolvency Act 1986[40, 41]

(1986 c. 45)

An Act to consolidate the enactments relating to company insolvency and winding up (including the winding up of companies that are not insolvent, and of unregistered companies); enactments relating to the insolvency and bankruptcy of individuals; and other enactments bearing on those two subject matters, including the functions and qualification of insolvency practitioners, the public administration of insolvency, the penalisation and redress of malpractice and wrongdoing, and the avoidance of certain transactions at an undervalue.

[25th July 1986]

THE FIRST GROUP OF PARTS

COMPANY INSOLVENCY; COMPANIES WINDING UP

PART I

COMPANY VOLUNTARY ARRANGEMENTS

The proposal

Those who may propose an arrangement

1.—(1) The directors of a company (other than one for which an administration order is in force, or which is being wound up) may make a proposal under this Part to the company and to its creditors for a composition in satisfaction of its debts or a scheme of arrangement of its affairs (from here on referred to, in either case, as a "voluntary arrangement").

(2) A proposal under this Part is one which provides for some person ("the nominee") to act in relation to the voluntary arrangement either as trustee or otherwise for the purpose of supervising its implementation; and the nominee must be a person who is qualified to act as an insolvency practitioner in relation to the company.

(3) Such a proposal may also be made—

(a) where an administration order is in force in relation to the company, by the administrator, and

---

[40] This Act replaces in all material respects the Insolvency Act 1985 formerly reprinted in *The Parliament House Book*.

[41] See also the Drug Trafficking Offences Act 1986, s.17, and the Criminal Justice Act 1988, s.86.

315

(*b*) where the company is being wound up, by the liquidator.

Procedure where nominee is not the liquidator or administrator

2.—(1) This section applies where the nominee under section 1 is not the liquidator or administrator of the company.

(2) The nominee shall, within 28 days (or such longer period as the court may allow) after he is given notice of the proposal for a voluntary arrangement, submit a report to the court stating—

(*a*) whether, in his opinion, meetings of the company and of its creditors should be summoned to consider the proposal, and

(*b*) if in his opinion such meetings should be summoned, the date on which, and time and place at which, he proposes the meetings should be held.

(3) For the purposes of enabling the nominee to prepare his report, the person intending to make the proposal shall submit to the nominee—

(*a*) a document setting out the terms of the proposed voluntary arrangement, and

(*b*) a statement of the company's affairs containing—

(i) such particulars of its creditors and of its debts and other liabilities and of its assets as may be prescribed, and

(ii) such other information as may be prescribed.

(4) The court may, on an application made by the person intending to make the proposal, in a case where the nominee has failed to submit the report required by this section, direct that the nominee be replaced as such by another person qualified to act as an insolvency practitioner in relation to the company.

Summoning of meetings

3.—(1) Where the nominee under section 1 is not the liquidator or administrator, and it has been reported to the court that such meetings as are mentioned in section 2(2) should be summoned, the person making the report shall (unless the court otherwise directs) summon those meetings for the time, date and place proposed in the report.

(2) Where the nominee is the liquidator or administrato⌐, he shall summon meetings of the company and of its creditors to consider the proposal for such a time, date and place as he thinks fit.

(3) The persons to be summoned to a creditors' meeting under this section are every creditor of the company of whose claim and address the person summoning the meeting is aware.

Consideration and implementation of proposal

Decisions of meetings

4.—(1) The meetings summoned under section 3 shall decide

whether to approve the proposed voluntary arrangement (with or without modifications).

(2) The modifications may include one conferring the functions proposed to be conferred on the nominee on another person qualified to act as an insolvency practitioner in relation to the company.

But they shall not include any modification by virtue of which the proposal ceases to be a proposal such as is mentioned in section 1.

(3) A meeting so summoned shall not approve any proposal or modification which affects the right of a secured creditor of the company to enforce his security, except with the concurrence of the creditor concerned.

(4) Subject as follows, a meeting so summoned shall not approve any proposal or modification under which—

(a) any preferential debt of the company is to be paid otherwise than in priority to such of its debts as are not preferential debts, or

(b) a preferential creditor of the company is to be paid an amount in respect of a preferential debt that bears to that debt a smaller proportion than is borne to another preferential debt by the amount that is to be paid in respect of that other debt.

However, the meeting may approve such a proposal or modification with the concurrence of the preferential creditor concerned.

(5) Subject as above, each of the meetings shall be conducted in accordance with the rules.

(6) After the conclusion of either meeting in accordance with the rules, the chairman of the meeting shall report the result of the meeting to the court, and, immediately after reporting to the court, shall give notice of the result of the meeting to such persons as may be prescribed.

(7) References in this section to preferential debts and preferential creditors are to be read in accordance with section 386 in Part XII of this Act.

Effect of approval

5.—(1) This section has effect where each of the meetings summoned under section 3 approves the proposed voluntary arrangement either with the same modifications or without modifications.

(2) The approved voluntary arrangement—

(a) takes effect as if made by the company at the creditors' meeting, and

(b) binds every person who in accordance with the rules had notice of, and was entitled to vote at, that meeting (whether or not he was present or represented at the meeting) as if he were a party to the voluntary arrangement.

(3) Subject as follows, if the company is being wound up or an

administration order is in force, the court may do one or both of the following, namely—

(a) by order stay or sist all proceedings in the winding up or discharge the administration order;

(b) give such directions with respect to the conduct of the winding up or the administration as it thinks appropriate for facilitating the implementation of the approved voluntary arrangement.

(4) The court shall not make an order under subsection (3)(a)—

(a) at any time before the end of the period of 28 days beginning with the first day on which each of the reports required by section 4(6) has been made to the court, or

(b) at any time when an application under the next section or an appeal in respect of such an application is pending, or at any time in the period within which such an appeal may be brought.

Challenge of decisions

6.—(1) Subject to this section, an application to the court may be made, by any of the persons specified below, on one or both of the following grounds, namely—

(a) that a voluntary arrangement approved at the meetings summoned under section 3 unfairly prejudices the interests of a creditor, member or contributory of the company;

(b) that there has been some material irregularity at or in relation to either of the meetings.

(2) The persons who may apply under this section are—

(a) a person entitled, in accordance with the rules, to vote at either of the meetings;

(b) the nominee or any person who has replaced him under section 2(4) or 4(2); and

(c) if the company is being wound up or an administration order is in force, the liquidator or administrator.

(3) An application under this section shall not be made after the end of the period of 28 days beginning with the first day on which each of the reports required by section 4(6) has been made to the court.

(4) Where on such an application the court is satisfied as to either of the grounds mentioned in subsection (1), it may do one or both of the following, namely—

(a) revoke or suspend the approvals given by the meetings or, in a case falling within subsection (1)(b), any approval given by the meeting in question;

(b) give a direction to any person for the summoning of further meetings to consider any revised proposal the person who made the original proposal may make or, in a case falling within subsection (1)(*b*), a further company or (as the case may be) creditors' meeting to reconsider the original proposal.

(5) Where at any time after giving a direction under subsection (4)(*b*) for the summoning of meetings to consider a revised proposal the court is satisfied that the person who made the original proposal does not intend to submit a revised proposal, the court shall revoke the direction and revoke or suspend any approval given at the previous meetings.

(6) In a case where the court, on an application under this section with respect to any meeting—

(*a*) gives a direction under subsection (4)(*b*), or
(*b*) revokes or suspends an approval under subsection (4)(*a*) or (5),

the court may give such supplemental directions as it thinks fit and, in particular, directions with respect to things done since the meeting under any voluntary arrangement approved by the meeting.

(7) Except in pursuance of the preceding provisions of this section, an approval given at a meeting summoned under section 3 is not invalidated by any irregularity at or in relation to the meeting.

Implementation of proposal

7.—(1) This section applies where a voluntary arrangement approved by the meetings summoned under section 3 has taken effect.

(2) The person who is for the time being carrying out in relation to the voluntary arrangement the functions conferred—

(*a*) by virtue of the approval on the nominee, or
(*b*) by virtue of section 2(4) or 4(2) on a person other than the nominee,

shall be known as the supervisor of the voluntary arrangement.

(3) If any of the company's creditors or any other person is dissatisfied by any act, omission or decision of the supervisor, he may apply to the court; and on the application the court may—

(*a*) confirm, reverse or modify any act or decision of the supervisor,
(*b*) give him directions, or
(*c*) make such other order as it thinks fit.

(4) The supervisor—

(*a*) may apply to the court for directions in relation to any particular matter arising under the voluntary arrangement, and
(*b*) is included among the persons who may apply to the court for the winding up of the company or for an administration order to be made in relation to it.

(5) The court may, whenever—

(*a*) it is expedient to appoint a person to carry out the functions of the supervisor, and (*b*) it is inexpedient, difficult or impracticable for an appointment to be made without the assistance of the court,

make an order appointing a person who is qualified to act as an insolvency practitioner in relation to the company, either in substitution for the existing supervisor or to fill a vacancy.

(6) The power conferred by subsection (5) is exercisable so as to increase the number of persons exercising the functions of supervisor or, where there is more than one person exercising those functions, so as to replace one or more of those persons.

Part II[42]

Administration Orders

Making etc. of administration order

Power of court to make order
[43] 8.—(1) Subject to this section, if the court—

(*a*) is satisfied that a company is or is likely to become unable to pay its debts (within the meaning given to that expression by section 123 of this Act), and

(*b*) considers that the making of an order under this section would be likely to achieve one or more of the purposes mentioned below,

the court may make an administration order in relation to the company.

(2) An administration order is an order directing that, during the period for which the order is in force, the affairs, business and property of the company shall be managed by a person ("the administrator") appointed for the purpose by the court.

(3) The purposes for whose achievement an administration order may be made are—

(*a*) the survival of the company, and the whole or any part of its undertaking, as a going concern;

(*b*) the approval of a voluntary arrangement under Part I;

(*c*) the sanctioning under section 425 of the Companies Act of a compromise or arrangement between the company and any such persons as are mentioned in that section; and

(*d*) a more advantageous realisation of the company's assets than would be effected on a winding up;

and the order shall specify the purpose or purposes for which it is made.

---

[42] See the Debtors (Scotland) Act 1987, s.93(4)(*c*).
[43] See the Banking Act 1987, ss.11(8) and 58(2).

(4) An administration order shall not be made in relation to a company after it has gone into liquidation, nor where it is—

(*a*) an insurance company within the meaning of the Insurance Companies Act 1982, or

[44] (*b*) an authorised institution or former authorised institution within the meaning of the Banking Act 1987.

Application for order

9.—(1) An application to the court for an administration order shall be by petition presented either by the company or the directors, or by a creditor or creditors (including any contingent or prospective creditor or creditors), or by all or any of those parties, together or separately.

(2) Where a petition is presented to the court—

(*a*) notice of the petition shall be given forthwith to any person who has appointed, or is or may be entitled to appoint, an administrative receiver of the company, and to such other persons as may be prescribed, and

(*b*) the petition shall not be withdrawn except with the leave of the court.

[45] (3) Where the court is satisfied that there is an administrative receiver of the company, the court shall dismiss the petition unless it is also satisfied either—

(*a*) that the person by whom or on whose behalf the receiver was appointed has consented to the making of the order, or

(*b*) that, if an administration order were made, any security by virtue of which the receiver was appointed would—

    (i) be liable to be released or discharged under sections 238 to 240 in Part VI (transactions at an undervalue and preferences),

    (ii) be avoided under section 245 in that Part (avoidance of floating charges), or

    (iii) be challengeable under section 242 (gratuitous alienations) or 243 (unfair preferences) in that Part, or under any rule of law in Scotland.

(4) Subject to subsection (3), on hearing a petition the court may dismiss it, or adjourn the hearing conditionally or unconditionally, or make an interim order or any other order that it thinks fit.

(5) Without prejudice to the generality of subsection (4), an interim order under that subsection may restrict the exercise of any powers of the directors or of the company (whether by reference to the consent of the court or of a person qualified to act as an insolvency practitioner in relation to the company, or otherwise).

---

[44] Substituted by the Banking Act 1987, Sched. 6, para. 25.
[45] Amended (*prosp.*) by the Companies Act 1989, Sched. 16, para. 3(2).

Effect of application

[46] **10.**—(1) During the period beginning with the presentation of a petition for an administration order and ending with the making of such an order or the dismissal of the petition—

(a) no resolution may be passed or order made for the winding up of the company;

(b) no steps may be taken to enforce any security over the company's property, or to repossess goods in the company's possession under any hire-purchase agreement, except with the leave of the court and subject to such terms as the court may impose; and

(c) no other proceedings and no execution or other legal process may be commenced or continued, and no distress may be levied, against the company or its property except with the leave of the court and subject to such terms as aforesaid.

(2) Nothing in subsection (1) requires the leave of the court—

(a) for the presentation of a petition for the winding up of the company,

(b) for the appointment of an administrative receiver of the company, or

(c) for the carrying out by such a receiver (whenever appointed) of any of his functions.

(3) Where—

(a) a petition for an administration order is presented at a time when there is an administrative receiver of the company, and

(b) the person by or on whose behalf the receiver was appointed has not consented to the making of the order,

the period mentioned in subsection (1) is deemed not to begin unless and until that person so consents.

(4) References in this section and the next to hire-purchase agreements include conditional sale agreements, chattel leasing agreements and retention of title agreements.

(5) In the application of this section and the next to Scotland, references to execution being commenced or continued include references to diligence being carried out or continued, and references to distress being levied shall be omitted.

Effect of order

11.—(1) On the making of an administration order—

(a) any petition for the winding up of the company shall be dismissed, and

---

[46] Amended (*prosp.*) by the Companies Act 1989, Sched. 24.

(*b*) any administrative receiver of the company shall vacate office.

(2) Where an administration order has been made, any receiver of part of the company's property shall vacate office on being required to do so by the administrator.

(3) During the period for which an administration order is in force—

(*a*) no resolution may be passed or order made for the winding up of the company;

(*b*) no administrative receiver of the company may be appointed;

(*c*) no other steps may be taken to enforce any security over the company's property, or to repossess goods in the company's possession under any hire-purchase agreement, except with the consent of the administrator or the leave of the court and subject (where the court gives leave) to such terms as the court may impose; and

(*d*) no other proceedings and no execution or other legal process may be commenced or continued, and no distress may be levied, against the company or its property except with the consent of the administrator or the leave of the court and subject (where the court gives leave) to such terms as aforesaid.

(4) Where at any time an administrative receiver of the company has vacated office under subsection (1)(*b*), or a receiver of part of the company's property has vacated office under subsection (2)—

(*a*) his remuneration and any expenses properly incurred by him, and

(*b*) any indemnity to which he is entitled out of the assets of the company,

shall be charged on and (subject to subsection (3) above) paid out of any property of the company which was in his custody or under his control at that time in priority to any security held by the person by or on whose behalf he was appointed.

(5) Neither an administrative receiver who vacates office under subsection (1)(*b*) nor a receiver who vacates office under subsection (2) is required on or after so vacating office to take any steps for the purpose of complying with any duty imposed on him by section 40 or 59 of this Act (duty to pay preferential creditors).

Notification of order

12.—(1) Every invoice, order for goods or business letter which, at a time when an administration order is in force in relation to a company, is issued by or on behalf of the company or the administrator, being a document on or in which the company's name appears, shall also contain the administrator's name and a statement that the affairs, business and property of the company are being managed by the administrator.

(2) If default is made in complying with this section, the company

and any of the following persons who without reasonable excuse authorises or permits the default, namely, the administrator and any officer of the company, is liable to a fine.

Administrators

Appointment of administrator

13.—(1) The administrator of a company shall be appointed either by the administration order or by an order under the next subsection.

(2) If a vacancy occurs by death, resignation or otherwise in the office of the administrator, the court may by order fill the vacancy.

(3) An application for an order under subsection (2) may be made—

(*a*) by any continuing administrator of the company; or

(*b*) where there is no such administrator, by a creditors' committee established under section 26 below; or

(*c*) where there is no such administrator and no such committee, by the company or the directors or by any creditor or creditors of the company.

General powers

14.—(1) The administrator of a company—

(*a*) may do all such things as may be necessary for the management of the affairs, business and property of the company, and

(*b*) without prejudice to the generality of paragraph (*a*), has the powers specified in Schedule 1 to this Act;

and in the application of that Schedule to the administrator of a company the words "he" and "him" refer to the administrator.

(2) The administrator also has power—

(*a*) to remove any director of the company and to appoint any person to be a director of it, whether to fill a vacancy or otherwise, and

(*b*) to call any meeting of the members or creditors of the company.

(3) The administrator may apply to the court for directions in relation to any particular matter arising in connection with the carrying out of his functions.

(4) Any power conferred on the company or its officers, whether by this Act or the Companies Act or by the memorandum or articles of association, which could be exercised in such a way as to interfere with the exercise by the administrator of his powers is not exercisable except with the consent of the administrator, which may be given either generally or in relation to particular cases.

(5) In exercising his powers the administrator is deemed to act as the company's agent.

(6) A person dealing with the administrator in good faith and for value is not concerned to inquire whether the administrator is acting within his powers.

Power to deal with charged property, etc.

15.—(1) The administrator of a company may dispose of or otherwise exercise his powers in relation to any property of the company which is subject to a security to which this subsection applies as if the property were not subject to the security.

(2) Where, on an application by the administrator, the court is satisfied that the disposal (with or without other assets) of—

(*a*) any property of the company subject to a security to which this subsection applies, or

(*b*) any goods in the possession of the company under a hire-purchase agreement,

would be likely to promote the purpose or one or more of the purposes specified in the administration order, the court may by order authorise the administrator to dispose of the property as if it were not subject to the security or to dispose of the goods as if all rights of the owner under the hire-purchase agreement were vested in the company.

(3) Subsection (1) applies to any security which, as created, was a floating charge; and subsection (2) applies to any other security.

(4) Where property is disposed of under subsection (1), the holder of the security has the same priority in respect of any property of the company directly or indirectly representing the property disposed of as he would have had in respect of the property subject to the security.

(5) It shall be a condition of an order under subsection (2) that—

(*a*) the net proceeds of the disposal, and

(*b*) where those proceeds are less than such amount as may be determined by the court to be the net amount which would be realised on a sale of the property or goods in the open market by a willing vendor, such sums as may be required to make good the deficiency,

shall be applied towards discharging the sums secured by the security or payable under the hire-purchase agreement.

(6) Where a condition imposed in pursuance of subsection (5) relates to two or more securities, that condition requires the net proceeds of the disposal and, where paragraph (*b*) of that subsection applies, the sums mentioned in that paragraph to be applied towards discharging the sums secured by those securities in the order of their priorities.

(7) An office copy of an order under subsection (2) shall, within 14 days after the making of the order, be sent by the administrator to the registrar of companies.

(8) If the administrator without reasonable excuse fails to comply with subsection (7), he is liable to a fine and, for continued contravention, to a daily default fine.

(9) References in this section to hire-purchase agreements include conditional sale agreements, chattel leasing agreements and retention of title agreements.

Operation of s.15 in Scotland

16.—(1) Where property is disposed of under section 15 in its application to Scotland, the administrator shall grant to the disponee an appropriate document of transfer or conveyance of the property, and—

(a) that document, or

(b) where any recording, intimation or registration of the document is a legal requirement for completion of title to the property, that recording, intimation or registration,

has the effect of disencumbering the property of or, as the case may be, freeing the property from the security.

(2) Where goods in the possession of the company under a hire-purchase agreement, conditional sale agreement, chattel leasing agreement or retention of title agreement are disposed of under section 15 in its application to Scotland, the disposal has the effect of extinguishing, as against the disponee, all rights of the owner of the goods under the agreement.

General duties

17.—(1) The administrator of a company shall, on his appointment, take into his custody or under his control all the property to which the company is or appears to be entitled.

(2) The administrator shall manage the affairs, business and property of the company—

(a) at any time before proposals have been approved (with or without modifications) under section 24 below, in accordance with any directions given by the court, and

(b) at any time after proposals have been so approved, in accordance with those proposals as from time to time revised, whether by him or a predecessor of his.

(3) The administrator shall summon a meeting of the company's creditors if—

(a) he is requested, in accordance with the rules, to do so by one-tenth, in value, of the company's creditors, or

(b) he is directed to do so by the court.

Discharge or variation of administration order

18.—(1) The administrator of a company may at any time apply to the court for the administration order to be discharged, or to be varied so as to specify an additional purpose.

(2) The administrator shall make an application under this section if—

(a) it appears to him that the purpose or each of the purposes specified in the order either has been achieved or is incapable of achievement, or (*b*) he is required to do so by a meeting of the company's creditors summoned for the purpose in accordance with the rules.

(3) On the hearing of an application under this section, the court may by order discharge or vary the administration order and make such consequential provision as it thinks fit, or adjourn the hearing conditionally or unconditionally, or make an interim order or any other order it thinks fit.

(4) Where the administration order is discharged or varied the administrator shall, within 14 days after the making of the order effecting the discharge or variation, send an office copy of that order to the registrar of companies.

(5) If the administrator without reasonable excuse fails to comply with subsection (4), he is liable to a fine and, for continued contravention, to a daily default fine.

Vacation of office

19.—(1) The administrator of a company may at any time be removed from office by order of the court and may, in the prescribed circumstances, resign his office by giving notice of his resignation to the court.

(2) The administrator shall vacate office if—

(*a*) he ceases to be qualified to act as an insolvency practitioner in relation to the company, or

(*b*) the administration order is discharged.

(3) Where at any time a person ceases to be administrator, the next two subsections apply.

(4) His remuneration and any expenses properly incurred by him shall be charged on and paid out of any property of the company which is in his custody or under his control at that time in priority to any security to which section 15(1) then applies.

(5) Any sums payable in respect of debts or liabilities incurred, while he was administrator, under contracts entered into or contracts of employment adopted by him or a predecessor of his in the carrying out of his or the predecessor's functions shall be charged on and paid out of any such property as is mentioned in subsection (4) in priority to any charge arising under that subsection.

For this purpose, the administrator is not to be taken to have adopted a contract of employment by reason of anything done or omitted to be done within 14 days after his appointment.

Release of administrator

20.—(1) A person who has ceased to be the administrator of a company has his release with effect from the following time, that is to say—

(*a*) in the case of a person who has died, the time at which notice is given to the court in accordance with the rules that he has ceased to hold office;

(*b*) in any other case, such time as the court may determine.

(2) Where a person has his release under this section, he is, with effect from the time specified above, discharged from all liability both in respect of acts or omissions of his in the administration and otherwise in relation to his conduct as administrator.

(3) However, nothing in this section prevents the exercise, in relation to a person who has had his release as above, of the court's powers under section 212 in Chapter X of Part IV (summary remedy against delinquent directors, liquidators, etc.).

Ascertainment and investigation of company's affairs

Information to be given by administrator

21.—(1) Where an administration order has been made, the administrator shall—

(*a*) forthwith send to the company and publish in the prescribed manner a notice of the order, and

(*b*) within 28 days after the making of the order, unless the court otherwise directs, send such a notice to all creditors of the company (so far as he is aware of their addresses).

(2) Where an administration order has been made, the administrator shall also, within 14 days after the making of the order, send an office copy of the order to the registrar of companies and to such other persons as may be prescribed.

(3) If the administrator without reasonable excuse fails to comply with this section, he is liable to a fine and, for continued contravention, to a daily default fine.

Statement of affairs to be submitted to administrator

22.—(1) Where an administration order has been made, the administrator shall forthwith require some or all of the persons mentioned below to make out and submit to him a statement in the prescribed form as to the affairs of the company.

(2) The statement shall be verified by affidavit by the persons required to submit it and shall show—

(*a*) particulars of the company's assets, debts and liabilities;
(*b*) the names and addresses of its creditors;
(*c*) the securities held by them respectively;
(*d*) the dates when the securities were respectively given; and
(*e*) such further or other information as may be prescribed.

(3) The persons referred to in subsection (1) are—

(*a*) those who are or have been officers of the company;
(*b*) those who have taken part in the company's formation at any time within one year before the date of the administration order;

(c) those who are in the company's employment or have been in its employment within that year, and are in the administrator's opinion capable of giving the information required;

(d) those who are or have been within that year officers of or in the employment of a company which is, or within that year was, an officer of the company.

In this subsection "employment" includes employment under a contract for services.

(4) Where any persons are required under this section to submit a statement of affairs to the administrator, they shall do so (subject to the next subsection) before the end of the period of 21 days beginning with the day after that on which the prescribed notice of the requirement is given to them by the administrator.

(5) The administrator, if he thinks fit, may—

(a) at any time release a person from an obligation imposed on him under subsection (1) or (2), or

(b) either when giving notice under subsection (4) or subsequently, extend the period so mentioned;

and where the administrator has refused to exercise a power conferred by this subsection, the court, if it thinks fit, may exercise it.

(6) If a person without reasonable excuse fails to comply with any obligation imposed under this section, he is liable to a fine and, for continued contravention, to a daily default fine.

Administrator's proposals

Statement of proposals

23.—(1) Where an administration order has been made, the administrator shall, within three months (or such longer period as the court may allow) after the making of the order—

(a) send to the registrar of companies and (so far as he is aware of their addresses) to all creditors a statement of his proposals for achieving the purpose or purposes specified in the order, and

(b) lay a copy of the statement before a meeting of the company's creditors summoned for the purpose on not less than 14 days' notice.

(2) The administrator shall also, within three months (or such longer period as the court may allow) after the making of the order, either—

(a) send a copy of the statement (so far as he is aware of their addresses) to all members of the company, or

(b) publish in the prescribed manner a notice stating an address to which members of the company should write for copies of the statement to be sent to them free of charge.

(3) If the administrator without reasonable excuse fails to comply

with this section, he is liable to a fine and, for continued contravention, to a daily default fine.

Consideration of proposals by creditors' meeting

24.—(1) A meeting of creditors summoned under section 23 shall decide whether to approve the administrator's proposals.

(2) The meeting may approve the proposals with modifications, but shall not do so unless the administrator consents to each modification.

(3) Subject as above, the meeting shall be conducted in accordance with the rules.

(4) After the conclusion of the meeting in accordance with the rules, the administrator shall report the result of the meeting to the court and shall give notice of that result to the registrar of companies and to such persons as may be prescribed.

(5) If a report is given to the court under subsection (4) that the meeting has declined to approve the administrator's proposals (with or without modifications), the court may by order discharge the administration order and make such consequential provision as it thinks fit, or adjourn the hearing conditionally or unconditionally, or make an interim order or any other order that it thinks fit.

(6) Where the administration order is discharged, the administrator shall, within 14 days after the making of the order effecting the discharge, send an office copy of that order to the registrar of companies.

(7) If the administrator without reasonable excuse fails to comply with subsection (6), he is liable to a fine and, for continued contravention, to a daily default fine.

Approval of substantial revisions

25.—(1) This section applies where—

(a) proposals have been approved (with or without modifications) under section 24, and

(b) the administrator proposes to make revisions of those proposals which appear to him substantial.

(2) The administrator shall—

(a) send to all creditors of the company (so far as he is aware of their addresses) a statement in the prescribed form of his proposed revisions, and

(b) lay a copy of the statement before a meeting of the company's creditors summoned for the purpose on not less than 14 days' notice;

and he shall not make the proposed revisions unless they are approved by the meeting.

(3) The administrator shall also either—

(a) send a copy of the statement (so far as he is aware of their addresses) to all members of the company, or

(b) publish in the prescribed manner a notice stating an address to which members of the company should write for copies of the statement to be sent to them free of charge.

(4) The meeting of creditors may approve the proposed revisions with modifications, but shall not do so unless the administrator consents to each modification.

(5) Subject as above, the meeting shall be conducted in accordance with the rules.

(6) After the conclusion of the meeting in accordance with the rules, the administrator shall give notice of the result of the meeting to the registrar of companies and to such persons as may be prescribed.

Miscellaneous

Creditors' committee

26.—(1) Where a meeting of creditors summoned under section 23 has approved the administrator's proposals (with or without modifications), the meeting may, if it thinks fit, establish a committee ("the creditors' committee") to exercise the functions conferred on it by or under this Act.

(2) If such a committee is established, the committee may, on giving not less than seven days' notice, require the administrator to attend before it at any reasonable time and furnish it with such information relating to the carrying out of his functions as it may reasonably require.

Protection of interests of creditors and members

27.—(1) At any time when an administration order is in force, a creditor or member of the company may apply to the court by petition for an order under this section on the ground—

(a) that the company's affairs, business and property are being or have been managed by the administrator in a manner which is unfairly prejudicial to the interests of its creditors or members generally, or of some part of its creditors or members (including at least himself), or

(b) that any actual or proposed act or omission of the administrator is or would be so prejudicial.

(2) On an application for an order under this section the court may, subject as follows, make such order as it thinks fit for giving relief in respect of the matters complained of, or adjourn the hearing conditionally or unconditionally, or make an interim order or any other order that it thinks fit.

(3) An order under this section shall not prejudice or prevent—

(a) the implementation of a voluntary arrangement approved under section 4 in Part I, or any compromise or arrangement sanctioned under section 425 of the Companies Act; or

(b) where the application for the order was made more than 28 days after the approval of any proposals or revised proposals under section 24 or 25, the implementation of those proposals or revised proposals.

(4) Subject as above, an order under this section may in particular—

(a) regulate the future management by the administrator of the company's affairs, business and property;

(b) require the administrator to refrain from doing or continuing an act complained of by the petitioner, or to do an act which the petitioner has complained he has omitted to do;

(c) require the summoning of a meeting of creditors or members for the purpose of considering such matters as the court may direct;

(d) discharge the administration order and make such consequential provision as the court thinks fit.

(5) Nothing in section 15 or 16 is to be taken as prejudicing applications to the court under this section.

(6) Where the administration order is discharged, the administrator shall, within 14 days after the making of the order effecting the discharge, send an office copy of that order to the registrar of companies; and if without reasonable excuse he fails to comply with this subsection, he is liable to a fine and, for continued contravention, to a daily default fine.

PART III

RECEIVERSHIP

. . . . . .

CHAPTER II

RECEIVERS (SCOTLAND)

Extent of this Chapter

50. This Chapter extends to Scotland only.

Power to appoint receiver

51.—(1) It is competent under the law of Scotland for the holder of a floating charge over all or any part of the property (including uncalled capital), which may from time to time be comprised in the property and undertaking of an incorporated company (whether a company within the meaning of the Companies Act or not) which the Court of Session has jurisdiction to wind up, to appoint a receiver of such part of the property of the company as is subject to the charge.

(2) It is competent under the law of Scotland for the court, on the application of the holder of such a floating charge, to appoint a receiver of such part of the property of the company as is subject to the charge.

(3) The following are disqualified from being appointed as receiver—

(*a*) a body corporate;
(*b*) an undischarged bankrupt; and
(*c*) a firm according to the law of Scotland.

(4) A body corporate or a firm according to the law of Scotland which acts as a receiver is liable to a fine.

(5) An undischarged bankrupt who so acts is liable to imprisonment or a fine, or both.

(6) In this section, "receiver" includes joint receivers.

Circumstances justifying appointment

52.—(1) A receiver may be appointed under section 51(1) by the holder of the floating charge on the occurrence of any event which, by the provisions of the instrument creating the charge, entitles the holder of the charge to make that appointment and, in so far as not otherwise provided for by the instrument, on the occurrence of any of the following events, namely—

(*a*) the expiry of a period of 21 days after the making of a demand for payment of the whole or any part of the principal sum secured by the charge, without payment having been made;
(*b*) the expiry of a period of two months during the whole of which interest due and payable under the charge has been in arrears;
(*c*) the making of an order or the passing of a resolution to wind up the company;
(*d*) the appointment of a receiver by virtue of any other floating charge created by the company.

(2) A receiver may be appointed by the court under section 51(2) on the occurrence of any event which, by the provisions of the instrument creating the floating charge, entitles the holder of the charge to make that appointment and, in so far as not otherwise provided for by the instrument, on the occurrence of any of the following events, namely—

(*a*) where the court, on the application of the holder of the charge, pronounces itself satisfied that the position of the holder of the charge is likely to be prejudiced if no such appointment is made;
(*b*) any of the events referred to in paragraphs (*a*) to (*c*) of subsection (1).

Mode of appointment by holder of charge

53.—(1) The appointment of a receiver by the holder of the floating charge under section 51(1) shall be by means of a validly executed instrument in writing ("the instrument of appointment"), a copy (certified in the prescribed manner to be a correct copy) whereof shall be delivered by or on behalf of the person making the appointment to the registrar of companies for registration within seven days of its execution and shall be accompanied by a notice in the prescribed form.

[47] (2) If any person without reasonable excuse makes default in complying with the requirements of subsection (1), he is liable to a fine and, for continued contravention, to a daily default fine.

(3) [Repealed by the Law Reform (Miscellaneous Provisions) (Scotland) Act 1990, Sched. 8, para. 35 and Sched. 9.]

(4) The instrument may be executed on behalf of the holder of the floating charge by virtue of which the receiver is to be appointed—

(a) by any person duly authorised in writing by the holder to execute the instrument, and

(b) in the case of an appointment of a receiver by the holders of a series of secured debentures, by any person authorised by resolution of the debenture-holders to execute the instrument.

(5) On receipt of the certified copy of the instrument of appointment in accordance with subsection (1), the registrar shall, on payment of the prescribed fee, enter the particulars of the appointment in the register of charges.

(6) The appointment of a person as a receiver by an instrument of appointment in accordance with subsection (1)—

(a) is of no effect unless it is accepted by that person before the end of the business day next following that on which the instrument of appointment is received by him or on his behalf, and

(b) subject to paragraph (a), is deemed to be made on the day on and at the time at which the instrument of appointment is so received, as evidenced by a written docquet by that person or on his behalf;

and this subsection applies to the appointment of joint receivers subject to such modifications as may be prescribed.

(7) On the appointment of a receiver under this section, the floating charge by virtue of which he was appointed attaches to the property then subject to the charge; and such attachment has effect as if the charge was a fixed security over the property to which it has attached.

Appointment by court

54.—(1) Application for the appointment of a receiver by the court under section 51(2) shall be by petition to the court, which shall be served on the company.

(2) On such an application, the court shall, if it thinks fit, issue an interlocutor making the appointment of the receiver.

[48] (3) A copy (certified by the clerk of the court to be a correct copy) of the court's interlocutor making the appointment shall be delivered by or on behalf of the petitioner to the registrar of companies for registration, accompanied by a notice in the prescribed form, within

---

[47] Amended (*prosp.*) by the Companies Act 1989, Sched. 16, para. 3(3).
[48] Amended (*prosp.*) by the Companies Act 1989, Sched. 16, para. 3(3).

seven days of the date of the interlocutor or such longer period as the court may allow.

If any person without reasonable excuse makes default in complying with the requirements of this subsection, he is liable to a fine and, for continued contravention, to a daily default fine.

(4) On receipt of the certified copy interlocutor in accordance with subsection (3), the registrar shall, on payment of the prescribed fee, enter the particulars of the appointment in the register of charges.

(5) The receiver is to be regarded as having been appointed on the date of his being appointed by the court.

(6) On the appointment of a receiver under this section, the floating charge by virtue of which he was appointed attaches to the property then subject to the charge; and such attachment has effect as if the charge were a fixed security over the property to which it has attached.

(7) In making rules of court for the purposes of this section, the Court of Session shall have regard to the need for special provision for cases which appear to the court to require to be dealt with as a matter of urgency.

Powers of receiver

55.—(1) Subject to the next subsection, a receiver has in relation to such part of the property of the company as is attached by the floating charge by virtue of which he was appointed, the powers, if any, given to him by the instrument creating that charge.

(2) In addition, the receiver has under this Chapter the powers as respects that property (in so far as these are not inconsistent with any provision contained in that instrument) which are specified in Schedule 2 to this Act.

(3) Subsections (1) and (2) apply—

(a) subject to the rights of any person who has effectually executed diligence on all or any part of the property of the company prior to the appointment of the receiver, and

(b) subject to the rights of any person who holds over all or any part of the property of the company a fixed security or floating charge having priority over, or ranking *pari passu* with, the floating charge by virtue of which the receiver was appointed.

(4) A person dealing with a receiver in good faith and for value is not concerned to inquire whether the receiver is acting within his powers.

Precedence among receivers

56.—(1) Where there are two or more floating charges subsisting over all or any part of the property of the company, a receiver may be appointed under this Chapter by virtue of each such charge; but a receiver appointed by, or on the application of, the holder of a floating charge having priority of ranking over any other floating charge by virtue of which a receiver has been appointed has the powers given to a receiver by section 55 and Schedule 2 to the exclusion of any other receiver.

(2) Where two or more floating charges rank with one another equally, and two or more receivers have been appointed by virtue of such charges, the receivers so appointed are deemed to have been appointed as joint receivers.

(3) Receivers appointed, or deemed to have been appointed, as joint receivers shall act jointly unless the instrument of appointment or respective instruments of appointment otherwise provide.

(4) Subject to subsection (5) below, the powers of a receiver appointed by, or on the application of, the holder of a floating charge are suspended by, and as from the date of, the appointment of a receiver by, or on the application of, the holder of a floating charge having priority of ranking over that charge to such extent as may be necessary to enable the receiver second mentioned to exercise his powers under section 55 and Schedule 2; and any powers so suspended take effect again when the floating charge having priority of ranking ceases to attach to the property then subject to the charge, whether such cessation is by virtue of section 62(6) or otherwise.

(5) The suspension of the powers of a receiver under subsection (4) does not have the effect of requiring him to release any part of the property (including any letters or documents) of the company from his control until he receives from the receiver superseding him a valid indemnity (subject to the limit of the value of such part of the property of the company as is subject to the charge by virtue of which he was appointed) in respect of any expenses, charges and liabilities he may have incurred in the performance of his functions as receiver.

(6) The suspension of the powers of a receiver under subsection (4) does not cause the floating charge by virtue of which he was appointed to cease to attach to the property to which it attached by virtue of section 53(7) or 54(6).

(7) Nothing in this section prevents the same receiver being appointed by virtue of two or more floating charges.

Agency and liability of receiver for contracts

57.—(1) A receiver is deemed to be the agent of the company in relation to such property of the company as is attached by the floating charge by virtue of which he was appointed.

(2) A receiver (including a receiver whose powers are subsequently suspended under section 56) is personally liable on any contract entered into by him in the performance of his functions, except in so far as the contract otherwise provides, and on any contract of employment adopted by him in the carrying out of those functions.

(3) A receiver who is personally liable by virtue of subsection (2) is entitled to be indemnified out of the property in respect of which he was appointed.

(4) Any contract entered into by or on behalf of the company prior to

the appointment of a receiver continues in force (subject to its terms) notwithstanding that appointment, but the receiver does not by virtue only of his appointment incur any personal liability on any such contract.

(5) For the purposes of subsection (2), a receiver is not to be taken to have adopted a contract of employment by reason of anything done or omitted to be done within 14 days after his appointment.

(6) This section does not limit any right to indemnity which the receiver would have apart from it, nor limit his liability on contracts entered into or adopted without authority, nor confer any right to indemnity in respect of that liability.

(7) Any contract entered into by a receiver in the performance of his functions continues in force (subject to its terms) although the powers of the receiver are subsequently suspended under section 56.

Remuneration of receiver

58.—(1) The remuneration to be paid to a receiver is to be determined by agreement between the receiver and the holder of the floating charge by virtue of which he was appointed.

(2) Where the remuneration to be paid to the receiver has not been determined under subsection (1), or where it has been so determined but is disputed by any of the persons mentioned in paragraphs (a) to (d) below, it may be fixed instead by the Auditor of the Court of Session on application made to him by—

(a) the receiver;
(b) the holder of any floating charge or fixed security over all or any part of the property of the company;
(c) the company; or
(d) the liquidator of the company.

(3) Where the receiver has been paid or has retained for his remuneration for any period before the remuneration has been fixed by the Auditor of the Court of Session under subsection (2) any amount in excess of the remuneration so fixed for that period, the receiver or his personal representatives shall account for the excess.

Priority of debts

59.—(1) Where a receiver is appointed and the company is not at the time of the appointment in course of being wound up, the debts which fall under subsection (2) of this section shall be paid out of any assets coming to the hands of the receiver in priority to any claim for principal or interest by the holder of the floating charge by virtue of which the receiver was appointed.

(2) Debts falling under this subsection are preferential debts (within the meaning given by section 386 in Part XII) which, by the end of a period of six months after advertisement by the receiver for claims in the *Edinburgh Gazette* and in a newspaper circulating in the district where the company carries on business either—

    (i) have been intimated to him, or

    (ii) have become known to him.

(3) Any payments made under this section shall be recouped as far as may be out of the assets of the company available for payment of ordinary creditors.

Distribution of moneys

60.—(1) Subject to the next section, and to the rights of any of the following categories of persons (which rights shall, except to the extent otherwise provided in any instrument, have the following order of priority), namely—

    (*a*) the holder of any fixed security which is over property subject to the floating charge and which ranks prior to, or *pari passu* with, the floating charge;

    (*b*) all persons who have effectually executed diligence on any part of the property of the company which is subject to the charge by virtue of which the receiver was appointed;

    (*c*) creditors in respect of all liabilities, charges and expenses incurred by or on behalf of the receiver;

    (*d*) the receiver in respect of his liabilities, expenses and remuneration, and any indemnity to which he is entitled out of the property of the company; and

    (*e*) the preferential creditors entitled to payment under section 59,

the receiver shall pay moneys received by him to the holder of the floating charge by virtue of which the receiver was appointed in or towards satisfaction of the debt secured by the floating charge.

(2) Any balance of moneys remaining after the provisions of subsection (1) and section 61 below have been satisfied shall be paid in accordance with their respective rights and interests to the following persons, as the case may require—

    (*a*) any other receiver;

    (*b*) the holder of a fixed security which is over property subject to the floating charge;

    (*c*) the company or its liquidator, as the case may be.

(3) Where any question arises as to the person entitled to a payment under this section, or where a receipt or a discharge of a security cannot be obtained in respect of any such payment, the receiver shall consign the amount of such payment in any joint stock bank of issue in Scotland in name of the Accountant of Court for behoof of the person or persons entitled thereto.

Disposal of interest in property

61.—(1) Where the receiver sells or disposes, or is desirous of selling or disposing, of any property or interest in property of the company which is subject to the floating charge by virtue of which the receiver was appointed and which is—

(*a*) subject to any security or interest of, or burden or encumbrance in favour of, a creditor the ranking of which is prior to, or *pari passu* with, or postponed to the floating charge, or

(*b*) property or an interest in property affected or attached by effectual diligence executed by any person,

and the receiver is unable to obtain the consent of such creditor or, as the case may be, such person to such a sale or disposal, the receiver may apply to the court for authority to sell or dispose of the property or interest in property free of such security, interest, burden, encumbrance or diligence.

(2) Subject to the next subsection, on such an application the court may, if it thinks fit, authorise the sale or disposal of the property or interest in question free of such security, interest, burden, encumbrance or diligence, and such authorisation may be on such terms or conditions as the court thinks fit.

(3) In the case of an application where a fixed security over the property or interest in question which ranks prior to the floating charge has not been met or provided for in full, the court shall not authorise the sale or disposal of the property or interest in question unless it is satisfied that the sale or disposal would be likely to provide a more advantageous realisation of the company's assets than would otherwise be effected.

(4) It shall be a condition of an authorisation to which subsection (3) applies that—

(*a*) the net proceeds of the disposal, and

(*b*) where those proceeds are less than such amount as may be determined by the court to be the net amount which would be realised on a sale of the property or interest in the open market by a willing seller, such sums as may be required to make good the deficiency,

shall be applied towards discharging the sums secured by the fixed security.

(5) Where a condition imposed in pursuance of subsection (4) relates to two or more such fixed securities, that condition shall require the net proceeds of the disposal and, where paragraph (*b*) of that subsection applies, the sums mentioned in that paragraph to be applied towards discharging the sums secured by those fixed securities in the order of their priorities.

(6) A copy of an authorisation under subsection (2) certified by the clerk of court shall, within 14 days of the granting of the authorisation, be sent by the receiver to the registrar of companies.

(7) If the receiver without reasonable excuse fails to comply with subsection (6), he is liable to a fine and, for continued contravention, to a daily default fine.

(8) Where any sale or disposal is effected in accordance with the

authorisation of the court under subsection (2), the receiver shall grant to the purchaser or disponee an appropriate document of transfer or conveyance of the property or interest in question, and that document has the effect, or, where recording, intimation or registration of that document is a legal requirement for completion of title to the property or interest, then that recording, intimation or registration (as the case may be) has the effect, of—

(a) disencumbering the property or interest of the security, interest, burden or encumbrance affecting it, and

(b) freeing the property or interest from the diligence executed upon it.

(9) Nothing in this section prejudices the right of any creditor of the company to rank for his debt in the winding up of the company.

Cessation of appointment of receiver

62.—(1) A receiver may be removed from office by the court under subsection (3) below and may resign his office by giving notice of his resignation in the prescribed manner to such persons as may be prescribed.

(2) A receiver shall vacate office if he ceases to be qualified to act as an insolvency practitioner in relation to the company.

(3) Subject to the next subsection, a receiver may, on application to the court by the holder of the floating charge by virtue of which he was appointed, be removed by the court on cause shown.

(4) Where at any time a receiver vacates office—

(a) his remuneration and any expenses properly incurred by him, and

(b) any indemnity to which he is entitled out of the property of the company,

shall be paid out of the property of the company which is subject to the floating charge and shall have priority as provided for in section 60 (1).

[49] (5) When a receiver ceases to act as such otherwise than by death he shall, and, when a receiver is removed by the court, the holder of the floating charge by virtue of which he was appointed shall, within 14 days of the cessation or removal (as the case may be) give the registrar of companies notice to that effect, and the registrar shall enter the notice in the register of charges.

If the receiver or the holder of the floating charge (as the case may require) makes default in complying with the requirements of this subsection, he is liable to a fine and, for continued contravention, to a daily default fine.

(6) If by the expiry of a period of one month following upon the removal of the receiver or his ceasing to act as such no other receiver

---

[49] Subs. (5) amended (*prosp.*) by the Companies Act 1989, Sched. 16, para. 3(3).

has been appointed, the floating charge by virtue of which the receiver was appointed—

    (*a*) thereupon ceases to attach to the property then subject to the charge, and

    (*b*) again subsists as a floating charge;

and for the purposes of calculating the period of one month under this subsection no account shall be taken of any period during which an administration order under Part II of this Act is in force.

Powers of court

    63.—(1) The court on the application of—

    (*a*) the holder of a floating charge by virtue of which a receiver was appointed, or

    (*b*) a receiver appointed under section 51,

may give directions to the receiver in respect of any matter arising in connection with the performance by him of his functions.

    (2) Where the appointment of a person as a receiver by the holder of a floating charge is discovered to be invalid (whether by virtue of the invalidity of the instrument or otherwise), the court may order the holder of the floating charge to indemnify the person appointed against any liability which arises solely by reason of the invalidity of the appointment.

Notification that receiver appointed

    64.—(1) Where a receiver has been appointed, every invoice, order for goods or business letter issued by or on behalf of the company or the receiver or the liquidator of the company, being a document on or in which the name of the company appears, shall contain a statement that a receiver has been appointed.

    (2) If default is made in complying with the requirements of this section, the company and any of the following persons who knowingly and wilfully authorises or permits the default, namely any officer of the company, any liquidator of the company and any receiver, is liable to a fine.

Information to be given by receiver

    65.—(1) Where a receiver is appointed, he shall—

    (*a*) forthwith send to the company and publish notice of his appointment, and

    (*b*) within 28 days after his appointment, unless the court otherwise directs, send such notice to all the creditors of the company (so far as he is aware of their addresses).

    (2) This section and the next do not apply in relation to the appointment of a receiver to act—

    (*a*) with an existing receiver, or

(*b*) in place of a receiver who has died or ceased to act,

except that, where they apply to a receiver who dies or ceases to act before they have been fully complied with, the references in this section and the next to the receiver include (subject to subsection (3) of this section) his successor and any continuing receiver.

(3) If the company is being wound up, this section and the next apply notwithstanding that the receiver and the liquidator are the same person, but with any necessary modifications arising from that fact.

(4) If a person without reasonable excuse fails to comply with this section, he is liable to a fine and, for continued contravention, to a daily default fine.

Company's statement of affairs

66.—(1) Where a receiver of a company is appointed, the receiver shall forthwith require some or all of the persons mentioned in subsection (3) below to make out and submit to him a statement in the prescribed form as to the affairs of the company.

(2) A statement submitted under this section shall be verified by affidavit by the persons required to submit it and shall show—

(*a*) particulars of the company's assets, debts and liabilities;
(*b*) the names and addresses of its creditors;
(*c*) the securities held by them respectively;
(*d*) the dates when the securities were respectively given; and
(*e*) such further or other information as may be prescribed.

(3) The persons referred to in subsection (1) are—

(*a*) those who are or have been officers of the company;
(*b*) those who have taken part in the company's formation at any time within one year before the date of the appointment of the receiver;
(*c*) those who are in the company's employment or have been in its employment within that year, and are in the receiver's opinion capable of giving the information required;
(*d*) those who are or have been within that year officers of or in the employment of a company which is, or within that year was, an officer of the company.

In this subsection "employment" includes employment under a contract for services.

(4) Where any persons are required under this section to submit a statement of affairs to the receiver they shall do so (subject to the next subsection) before the end of the period of 21 days beginning with the day after that on which the prescribed notice of the requirement is given to them by the receiver.

(5) The receiver, if he thinks fit, may—

(*a*) at any time release a person from an obligation imposed on him under subsection (1) or (2), or (*b*) either when giving the notice mentioned in subsection (4) or subsequently extend the period so mentioned,

and where the receiver has refused to exercise a power conferred by this subsection, the court, if it thinks fit, may exercise it.

(6) If a person without reasonable excuse fails to comply with any obligation imposed under this section, he is liable to a fine and, for continued contravention, to a daily default fine.

Report by receiver

67.—(1) Where a receiver is appointed under section 51, he shall within three months (or such longer period as the court may allow) after his appointment, send to the registrar of companies, to the holder of the floating charge by virtue of which he was appointed and to any trustees for secured creditors of the company and (so far as he is aware of their addresses) to all such creditors a report as to the following matters, namely—

(*a*) the events leading up to his appointment, so far as he is aware of them;

(*b*) the disposal or proposed disposal by him of any property of the company and the carrying on or proposed carrying on by him of any business of the company;

(*c*) the amounts of principal and interest payable to the holder of the floating charge by virtue of which he was appointed and the amounts payable to preferential creditors; and

(*d*) the amount (if any) likely to be available for the payment of other creditors.

(2) The receiver shall also, within three months (or such longer period as the court may allow) after his appointment, either—

(*a*) send a copy of the report (so far as he is aware of their addresses) to all unsecured creditors of the company, or

(*b*) publish in the prescribed manner a notice stating an address to which unsecured creditors of the company should write for copies of the report to be sent to them free of charge,

and (in either case), unless the court otherwise directs, lay a copy of the report before a meeting of the company's unsecured creditors summoned for the purpose on not less than 14 days' notice.

(3) The court shall not give a direction under subsection (2) unless—

(*a*) the report states the intention of the receiver to apply for the direction, and

(*b*) a copy of the report is sent to the persons mentioned in paragraph (*a*) of that subsection, or a notice is published as mentioned in paragraph (*b*) of that subsection, not less than 14 days before the hearing of the application.

(4) Where the company has gone or goes into liquidation, the receiver—

(*a*) shall, within seven days after his compliance with subsection (1) or, if later, the nomination or appointment of the liquidator, send a copy of the report to the liquidator, and

(*b*) where he does so within the time limited for compliance with subsection (2), is not required to comply with that subsection.

(5) A report under this section shall include a summary of the statement of affairs made out and submitted under section 66 and of his comments (if any) on it.

(6) Nothing in this section shall be taken as requiring any such report to include any information the disclosure of which would seriously prejudice the carrying out by the receiver of his functions.

(7) Section 65(2) applies for the purposes of this section also.

(8) If a person without reasonable excuse fails to comply with this section, he is liable to a fine and, for continued contravention, to a daily default fine.

(9) In this section "secured creditor", in relation to a company, means a creditor of the company who holds in respect of his debt a security over property of the company, and "unsecured creditor" shall be construed accordingly.

Committee of creditors

68.—(1) Where a meeting of creditors is summoned under section 67, the meeting may, if it thinks fit, establish a committee ("the creditors' committee") to exercise the functions conferred on it by or under this Act.

(2) If such a committee is established, the committee may on giving not less than seven days' notice require the receiver to attend before it at any reasonable time and furnish it with such information relating to the carrying out by him of his functions as it may reasonably require.

Enforcement of receiver's duty to make returns, etc.

69.—(1) If any receiver—

(*a*) having made default in filing, delivering or making any return, account or other document, or in giving any notice, which a receiver is by law required to file, deliver, make or give, fails to make good the default within 14 days after the service on him of a notice requiring him to do so; or

(*b*) has, after being required at any time by the liquidator of the company so to do, failed to render proper accounts of his receipts and payments and to vouch the same and to pay over to the liquidator the amount properly payable to him,

the court may, on an application made for the purpose, make an order directing the receiver to make good the default within such time as may be specified in the order.

(2) In the case of any such default as is mentioned in subsection (1)(*a*), an application for the purposes of this section may be made by any member or creditor of the company or by the registrar of companies; and, in the case of any such default as is mentioned in subsection (1)(*b*), the application shall be made by the liquidator; and, in either case, the order may provide that all expenses of and incidental to the application shall be borne by the receiver.

(3) Nothing in this section prejudices the operation of any enactments imposing penalties on receivers in respect of any such default as is mentioned in subsection (1).

Interpretation for Chapter II

70.—(1) In this Chapter, unless the contrary intention appears, the following expressions have the following meanings respectively assigned to them—

"company" means an incorporated company (whether or not a company within the meaning of the Companies Act) which the Court of Session has jurisdiction to wind up;

"fixed security", in relation to any property of a company, means any security, other than a floating charge or a charge having the nature of a floating charge, which on the winding up of the company in Scotland would be treated as an effective security over that property, and (without prejudice to that generality) includes a security over that property, being a heritable security within the meaning of the Conveyancing and Feudal Reform (Scotland) Act 1970;

"instrument of appointment" has the meaning given by section 53(1);

"prescribed" means prescribed by regulations made under this Chapter by the Secretary of State;

"receiver" means a receiver of such part of the property of the company as is subject to the floating charge by virtue of which he has been appointed under section 51;

"register of charges" means the register kept by the registrar of companies for the purposes of Chapter II of Part XII of the Companies Act;

"secured debenture" means a bond, debenture, debenture stock or other security which, either itself or by reference to any other instrument, creates a floating charge over all or any part of the property of the company, but does not include a security which creates no charge other than a fixed security; and

"series of secured debentures" means two or more secured debentures created as a series by the company in such a manner that the holders thereof are entitled *pari passu* to the benefit of the floating charge.

(2) Where a floating charge, secured debenture or series of secured debentures has been created by the company, then, except where the context otherwise requires, any reference in this Chapter to the holder of the floating charge shall—

(*a*) where the floating charge, secured debenture or series of secured debentures provides for a receiver to be appointed by any person or body, be construed as a reference to that person or body;

(*b*) where, in the case of a series of secured debentures, no such provision has been made therein but—

  (i) there are trustees acting for the debenture-holders under and in accordance with a trust deed, be construed as a reference to those trustees, and

 (ii) where no such trustees are acting, be construed as a reference to—

    (*aa*) a majority in nominal value of those present or represented by proxy and voting at a meeting of debenture-holders at which the holders of at least one-third in nominal value of the outstanding debentures of the series are present or so represented, or

    (*bb*) where no such meeting is held, the holders of at least one half in nominal value of the outstanding debentures of the series.

(3) Any reference in this Chapter to a floating charge, secured debenture, series of secured debentures or instrument creating a charge includes, except where the context otherwise requires, a reference to that floating charge, debenture, series of debentures or instrument as varied by any instrument.

(4) References in this Chapter to the instrument by which a floating charge was created are, in the case of a floating charge created by words in a bond or other written acknowledgment, references to the bond or, as the case may be, the other written acknowledgment.

Prescription of forms, etc.; regulations

71.—(1) The notice referred to in section 62(5), and the notice referred to in section 65(1)(*a*) shall be in such form as may be prescribed.

(2) Any power conferred by this Chapter on the Secretary of State to make regulations is exercisable by statutory instrument; and a statutory instrument made in the exercise of the power so conferred to prescribe a fee is subject to annulment in pursuance of a resolution of either House of Parliament.

CHAPTER III

RECEIVERS' POWERS IN GREAT BRITAIN AS A WHOLE

Cross-border operation of receivership provisions

72.—(1) A receiver appointed under the law of either part of Great Britain in respect of the whole or any part of any property or undertaking of a company and in consequence of the company having created a charge which, as created, was a floating charge may exercise his powers in the other part of Great Britain so far as their exercise is not inconsistent with the law applicable there.

(2) In subsection (1) "receiver" includes a manager and a person who is appointed both receiver and manager.

PART IV⁵⁰

WINDING UP OF COMPANIES REGISTERED UNDER THE COMPANIES ACTS

CHAPTER I

PRELIMINARY

Modes of winding up

Alternative modes of winding up

73.—(1) The winding up of a company, within the meaning given to that expression by section 735 of the Companies Act, may be either voluntary (Chapters II, III, IV and V in this Part) or by the court (Chapter VI).

(2) This Chapter, and Chapters VII to X, relate to winding up generally, except where otherwise stated.

Contributories

Liability as contributories of present and past members

74.—(1) When a company is wound up, every present and past member is liable to contribute to its assets to any amount sufficient for payment of its debts and liabilities, and the expenses of the winding up, and for the adjustment of the rights of the contributories among themselves.

(2) This is subject as follows—

(*a*) a past member is not liable to contribute if he has ceased to be a member for one year or more before the commencement of the winding up;

---

⁵⁰ Applied by the Building Societies Act 1986, Sched. 15, Pt. I, and applied (*mod.*) by *ibid.*, Pt. II. See the Criminal Justice (Scotland) Act 1987, s.35(4) and the Criminal Justice Act 1988, s.86(5).

(b) a past member is not liable to contribute in respect of any debt or liability of the company contracted after he ceased to be a member;

(c) a past member is not liable to contribute, unless it appears to the court that the existing members are unable to satisfy the contributions required to be made by them in pursuance of the Companies Act and this Act;

(d) in the case of a company limited by shares, no contribution is required from any member exceeding the amount (if any) unpaid on the shares in respect of which he is liable as a present or past member;

(e) nothing in the Companies Act or this Act invalidates any provision contained in a policy of insurance or other contract whereby the liability of individual members on the policy or contract is restricted, or whereby the funds of the company are alone made liable in respect of the policy or contract;

(f) a sum due to any member of the company (in his character of a member) by way of dividends, profits or otherwise is not deemed to be a debt of the company, payable to that member in a case of competition between himself and any other creditor not a member of the company, but any such sum may be taken into account for the purpose of the final adjustment of the rights of the contributories among themselves.

(3) In the case of a company limited by guarantee, no contribution is required from any member exceeding the amount undertaken to be contributed by him to the company's assets in the event of its being wound up; but if it is a company with a share capital, every member of it is liable (in addition to the amount so undertaken to be contributed to the assets), to contribute to the extent of any sums unpaid on shares held by him.

Directors, etc. with unlimited liability

75.—(1) In the winding up of a limited company, any director or manager (whether past or present) whose liability is under the Companies Act unlimited is liable, in addition to his liability (if any) to contribute as an ordinary member, to make a further contribution as if he were at the commencement of the winding up a member of an unlimited company.

(2) However—

(a) a past director or manager is not liable to make such further contribution if he has ceased to hold office for a year or more before the commencement of the winding up;

(b) a past director or manager is not liable to make such further contribution in respect of any debt or liability of the company contracted after he ceased to hold office;

(c) subject to the company's articles, a director or manager is not liable to make such further contribution unless the court deems it necessary to require that contribution in order to satisfy the company's debts and liabilities, and the expenses of the winding up.

Liability of past directors and shareholders

76.—(1) This section applies where a company is being wound up and—

(a) it has under Chapter VII of Part V of the Companies Act (redeemable shares; purchase by a company of its own shares) made a payment out of capital in respect of the redemption or purchase of any of its own shares (the payment being referred to below as "the relevant payment"), and

(b) the aggregate amount of the company's assets and the amounts paid by way of contribution to its assets (apart from this section) is not sufficient for payment of its debts and liabilities, and the expenses of the winding up.

(2) If the winding up commenced within one year of the date on which the relevant payment was made, then—

(a) the person from whom the shares were redeemed or purchased, and

(b) the directors who signed the statutory declaration made in accordance with section 173(3) of the Companies Act for purposes of the redemption or purchase (except a director who shows that he had reasonable grounds for forming the opinion set out in the declaration),

are, so as to enable that insufficiency to be met, liable to contribute to the following extent to the company's assets.

(3) A person from whom any of the shares were redeemed or purchased is liable to contribute an amount not exceeding so much of the relevant payment as was made by the company in respect of his shares; and the directors are jointly and severally liable with that person to contribute that amount.

(4) A person who has contributed any amount to the assets in pursuance of this section may apply to the court for an order directing any other person jointly and severally liable in respect of that amount to pay him such amount as the court thinks just and equitable.

(5) Sections 74 and 75 do not apply in relation to liability accruing by virtue of this section.

(6) This section is deemed included in Chapter VII of Part V of the Companies Act for the purposes of the Secretary of State's power to make regulations under section 179 of that Act.

Limited company formerly unlimited

77.—(1) This section applies in the case of a company being wound up which was at some former time registered as unlimited but has re-registered—

(a) as a public company under section 43 of the Companies Act (or the former corresponding provision, section 5 of the Companies Act 1980), or

(b) as a limited company under section 51 of the Companies Act (or the former corresponding provision, section 44 of the Companies Act 1967).

(2) Notwithstanding section 74(2)(a) above, a past member of the company who was a member of it at the time of re-registration, if the winding up commences within the period of three years beginning with the day on which the company was re-registered, is liable to contribute to the assets of the company in respect of debts and liabilities contracted before that time.

(3) If no persons who were members of the company at that time are existing members of it, a person who at that time was a present or past member is liable to contribute as above notwithstanding that the existing members have satisfied the contributions required to be made by them under the Companies Act and this Act.

This applies subject to section 74(2)(a) above and to subsection (2) of this section, but notwithstanding section 74(2)(c).

(4) Notwithstanding section 74(2)(d) and (3), there is no limit on the amount which a person who, at that time, was a past or present member of the company is liable to contribute as above.

Unlimited company formerly limited

78.—(1) This section applies in the case of a company being wound up which was at some former time registered as limited but has been re-registered as unlimited under section 49 of the Companies Act (or the former corresponding provision, section 43 of the Companies Act 1967).

(2) A person who, at the time when the application for the company to be re-registered was lodged, was a past member of the company and did not after that again become a member of it is not liable to contribute to the assets of the company more than he would have been liable to contribute had the company not been re-registered.

Meaning of "contributory"

79.—(1) In this Act and the Companies Act the expression "contributory" means every person liable to contribute to the assets of a company in the event of its being wound up, and for the purposes of all proceedings for determining, and all proceedings prior to the final determination of, the persons who are to be deemed contributories, includes any person alleged to be a contributory.

(2) The reference in subsection (1) to persons liable to contribute to the assets does not include a person so liable by virtue of a declaration by the court under section 213 (imputed responsibility for company's

fraudulent trading) or section 214 (wrongful trading) in Chapter X of this Part.

(3) A reference in a company's articles to a contributory does not (unless the context requires) include a person who is a contributory only by virtue of section 76.

This subsection is deemed included in Chapter VII of Part V of the Companies Act for the purposes of the Secretary of State's power to make regulations under section 179 of that Act.

Nature of contributory's liability

80. The liability of a contributory creates a debt (in England and Wales in the nature of a specialty) accruing due from him at the time when his liability commenced, but payable at the time when calls are made for enforcing the liability.

Contributories in case of death of a member

81.—(1) If a contributory dies either before or after he has been placed on the list of contributories, his personal representatives, and the heirs and legatees of heritage of his heritable estate in Scotland, are liable in a due course of administration to contribute to the assets of the company in discharge of his liability and are contributories accordingly.

(2) Where the personal representatives are placed on the list of contributories, the heirs or legatees of heritage need not be added, but they may be added as and when the court thinks fit.

(3) If in England and Wales the personal representatives make default in paying any money ordered to be paid by them, proceedings may be taken for administering the estate of the deceased contributory and for compelling payment out of it of the money due.

Effect of contributory's bankruptcy

82.—(1) The following applies if a contributory becomes bankrupt, either before or after he has been placed on the list of contributories.

(2) His trustee in bankruptcy represents him for all purposes of the winding up, and is a contributory accordingly.

(3) The trustee may be called on to admit to proof against the bankrupt's estate, or otherwise allow to be paid out of the bankrupt's assets in due course of law, any money due from the bankrupt in respect of his liability to contribute to the company's assets.

(4) There may be proved against the bankrupt's estate the estimated value of his liability to future calls as well as calls already made.

Companies registered under Companies Act, Part XXII, Chapter II

83.—(1) The following applies in the event of a company being wound up which has been registered under section 680 of the Companies Act (or previous corresponding provisions in the Companies Act 1948 or earlier Acts).

(2) Every person is a contributory, in respect of the company's debts and liabilities contracted before registration, who is liable—

(a) to pay, or contribute to the payment of, any debt or liability so contracted, or

(b) to pay, or contribute to the payment of, any sum for the adjustment of the rights of the members among themselves in respect of any such debt or liability, or

(c) to pay, or contribute to the amount of, the expenses of winding up the company, so far as relates to the debts or liabilities above-mentioned.

(3) Every contributory is liable to contribute to the assets of the company, in the course of the winding up, all sums due from him in respect of any such liability.

(4) In the event of the death, bankruptcy or insolvency of any contributory, provisions of this Act, with respect to the personal representatives, to the heirs and legatees of heritage of the heritable estate in Scotland of deceased contributories and to the trustees of bankrupt or insolvent contributories respectively, apply.

CHAPTER II

VOLUNTARY WINDING UP (INTRODUCTORY AND GENERAL)

Resolutions for, and commencement of, voluntary winding up

Circumstances in which company may be wound up voluntarily

84.—(1) A company may be wound up voluntarily—

(a) when the period (if any) fixed for the duration of the company by the articles expires, or the event (if any) occurs, on the occurrence of which the articles provide that the company is to be dissolved, and the company in general meeting has passed a resolution requiring it to be wound up voluntarily;

(b) if the company resolves by special resolution that it be wound up voluntarily;

(c) if the company resolves by extraordinary resolution to the effect that it cannot by reason of its liabilities continue its business, and that it is advisable to wind up.

(2) In this Act the expression "a resolution for voluntary winding up" means a resolution passed under any of the paragraphs of subsection (1).

(3) A resolution passed under paragraph (a) of subsection (1), as well as a special resolution under paragraph (b) and an extraordinary resolution under paragraph (c), is subject to section 380 of the Companies Act (copy of resolution to be forwarded to registrar of companies within 15 days).

Notice of resolution to wind up

85.—(1) When a company has passed a resolution for voluntary winding up, it shall, within 14 days after the passing of the resolution, give notice of the resolution by advertisement in the *Gazette*.

(2) If default is made in complying with this section, the company and every officer of it who is in default is liable to a fine and, for continued contravention, to a daily default fine.

For purposes of this subsection the liquidator is deemed an officer of the company.

Commencement of winding up

86. A voluntary winding up is deemed to commence at the time of the passing of the resolution for voluntary winding up.

Consequences of resolution to wind up

Effect on business and status of company

87.—(1) In case of a voluntary winding up, the company shall from the commencement of the winding up cease to carry on its business, except so far as may be required for its beneficial winding up.

(2) However, the corporate state and corporate powers of the company, notwithstanding anything to the contrary in its articles, continue until the company is dissolved.

Avoidance of share transfers, etc. after winding up resolution

88. Any transfer of shares, not being a transfer made to or with the sanction of the liquidator, and any alteration in the status of the company's members, made after the commencement of a voluntary winding up, is void.

Declaration of solvency

Statutory declaration of solvency

89.—(1) Where it is proposed to wind up a company voluntarily, the directors (or, in the case of a company having more than two directors, the majority of them) may at a directors' meeting make a statutory declaration to the effect that they have made a full inquiry into the company's affairs and that, having done so, they have formed the opinion that the company will be able to pay its debts in full, together with interest at the official rate (as defined in section 251), within such period, not exceeding 12 months from the commencement of the winding up, as may be specified in the declaration.

(2) Such a declaration by the directors has no effect for purposes of this Act unless—

(*a*) it is made within the five weeks immediately preceding the date of the passing of the resolution for winding up, or on that date but before the passing of the resolution, and

(*b*) it embodies a statement of the company's assets and liabilities as at the latest practicable date before the making of the declaration.

(3) The declaration shall be delivered to the registrar of companies

before the expiration of 15 days immediately following the date on which the resolution for winding up is passed.

(4) A director making a declaration under this section without having reasonable grounds for the opinion that the company will be able to pay its debts in full, together with interest at the official rate, within the period specified is liable to imprisonment or a fine, or both.

(5) If the company is wound up in pursuance of a resolution passed within five weeks after the making of the declaration, and its debts (together with interest at the official rate) are not paid or provided for in full within the period specified, it is to be presumed (unless the contrary is shown) that the director did not have reasonable grounds for his opinion.

(6) If a declaration required by subsection (3) to be delivered to the registrar is not so delivered within the time prescribed by that subsection, the company and every officer in default is liable to a fine and, for continued contravention, to a daily default fine.

Distinction between "members' " and "creditors' " voluntary winding up

90. A winding up in the case of which a directors' statutory declaration under section 89 has been made is a "members' voluntary winding up"; and a winding up in the case of which such a declaration has not been made is a "creditors' voluntary winding up".

CHAPTER III

MEMBERS' VOLUNTARY WINDING UP

Appointment of liquidator

91.—(1) In a members' voluntary winding up, the company in general meeting shall appoint one or more liquidators for the purpose of winding up the company's affairs and distributing its assets.

(2) On the appointment of a liquidator all the powers of the directors cease, except so far as the company in general meeting or the liquidator sanctions their continuance.

Power to fill vacancy in office of liquidator

92.—(1) If a vacancy occurs by death, resignation or otherwise in the office of liquidator appointed by the company, the company in general meeting may, subject to any arrangement with its creditors, fill the vacancy.

(2) For that purpose a general meeting may be convened by any contributory or, if there were more liquidators than one, by the continuing liquidators.

(3) The meeting shall be held in manner provided by this Act or by the articles, or in such manner as may, on application by any contributory or by the continuing liquidators, be determined by the court.

General company meeting at each year's end

93.—(1) Subject to sections 96 and 102, in the event of the winding up continuing for more than one year, the liquidator shall summon a general meeting of the company at the end of the first year from the commencement of the winding up, and of each succeeding year, or at the first convenient date within three months from the end of the year or such longer period as the Secretary of State may allow.

(2) The liquidator shall lay before the meeting an account of his acts and dealings, and of the conduct of the winding up, during the preceding year.

(3) If the liquidator fails to comply with this section, he is liable to a fine.

Final meeting prior to dissolution

94.—(1) As soon as the company's affairs are fully wound up, the liquidator shall make up an account of the winding up, showing how it has been conducted and the company's property has been disposed of, and thereupon shall call a general meeting of the company for the purpose of laying before it the account, and giving an explanation of it.

(2) The meeting shall be called by advertisement in the *Gazette*, specifying its time, place and object and published at least one month before the meeting.

(3) Within one week after the meeting, the liquidator shall send to the registrar of companies a copy of the account, and shall make a return to him of the holding of the meeting and of its date.

(4) If the copy is not sent or the return is not made in accordance with subsection (3), the liquidator is liable to a fine and, for continued contravention, to a daily default fine.

(5) If a quorum is not present at the meeting, the liquidator shall, in lieu of the return mentioned above, make a return that the meeting was duly summoned and that no quorum was present; and upon such a return being made, the provisions of subsection (3) as to the making of the return are deemed complied with.

(6) If the liquidator fails to call a general meeting of the company as required by subsection (1), he is liable to a fine.

Effect of company's insolvency

95.—(1) This section applies where the liquidator is of the opinion that the company will be unable to pay its debts in full (together with interest at the official rate) within the period stated in the directors' declaration under section 89.

(2) The liquidator shall—

(a) summon a meeting of creditors for a day not later than the 28th day after the day on which he formed that opinion;

(b) send notices of the creditors' meeting to the creditors by post not less than seven days before the day on which that meeting is to be held;

(c) cause notice of the creditors' meeting to be advertised once in the *Gazette* and once at least in two newspapers circulating in the relevant locality (that is to say the locality in which the company's principal place of business in Great Britain was situated during the relevant period); and

(d) during the period before the day on which the creditors' meeting is to be held, furnish creditors free of charge with such information concerning the affairs of the company as they may reasonably require;

and the notice of the creditors' meeting shall state the duty imposed by paragraph (d) above.

(3) The liquidator shall also—

(a) make out a statement in the prescribed form as to the affairs of the company;

(b) lay that statement before the creditors' meeting; and

(c) attend and preside at that meeting.

(4) The statement as to the affairs of the company shall be verified by affidavit by the liquidator and shall show—

(a) particulars of the company's assets, debts and liabilities;

(b) the names and addresses of the company's creditors;

(c) the securities held by them respectively;

(d) the dates when the securities were respectively given; and

(e) such further or other information as may be prescribed.

(5) Where the company's principal place of business in Great Britain was situated in different localities at different times during the relevant period, the duty imposed by subsection (2)(c) applies separately in relation to each of those localities.

(6) Where the company had no place of business in Great Britain during the relevant period, references in subsections (2)(c) and (5) to the company's principal place of business in Great Britain are replaced by references to its registered office.

(7) In this section "the relevant period" means the period of six months immediately preceding the day on which were sent the notices summoning the company meeting at which it was resolved that the company be wound up voluntarily.

(8) If the liquidator without reasonable excuse fails to comply with this section, he is liable to a fine.

Conversion to creditors' voluntary winding up

96. As from the day on which the creditors' meeting is held under section 95, this Act has effect as if—

(a) the directors' declaration under section 89 had not been made; and

(b) the creditors' meeting and the company meeting at which it was resolved that the company be wound up voluntarily were the meetings mentioned in section 98 in the next Chapter;

and accordingly the winding up becomes a creditors' voluntary winding up.

Chapter IV

Creditors' Voluntary Winding Up

Application of this Chapter

97.—(1) Subject as follows, this Chapter applies in relation to a creditors' voluntary winding up.

(2) Sections 98 and 99 do not apply where, under section 96 in Chapter III, a members' voluntary winding up has become a creditors' voluntary winding up.

Meeting of creditors

98.—(1) The company shall—

(*a*) cause a meeting of its creditors to be summoned for a day not later than the 14th day after the day on which there is to be held the company meeting at which the resolution for voluntary winding up is to be proposed;

(*b*) cause the notices of the creditors' meeting to be sent by post to the creditors not less than seven days before the day on which that meeting is to be held; and

(*c*) cause notice of the creditors' meeting to be advertised once in the *Gazette* and once at least in two newspapers circulating in the relevant locality (that is to say the locality in which the company's principal place of business in Great Britain was situated during the relevant period).

(2) The notice of the creditors' meeting shall state either—

(*a*) the name and address of a person qualified to act as an insolvency practitioner in relation to the company who, during the period before the day on which that meeting is to be held, will furnish creditors free of charge with such information concerning the company's affairs as they may reasonably require; or

(*b*) a place in the relevant locality where, on the two business days falling next before the day on which that meeting is to be held, a list of the names and addresses of the company's creditors will be available for inspection free of charge.

(3) Where the company's principal place of business in Great Britain was situated in different localities at different times during the relevant period, the duties imposed by subsections (1)(*c*) and (2)(*b*) above apply separately in relation to each of those localities.

(4) Where the company had no place of business in Great Britain

during the relevant period, references in subsections (1)(*c*) and (3) to the company's principal place of business in Great Britain are replaced by references to its registered office.

(5) In this section "the relevant period" means the period of six months immediately preceding the day on which were sent the notices summoning the company meeting at which it was resolved that the company be wound up voluntarily.

(6) If the company without reasonable excuse fails to comply with subsection (1) or (2), it is guilty of an offence and liable to a fine.

Directors to lay statement of affairs before creditors

99.—(1) The directors of the company shall—

(*a*) make out a statement in the prescribed form as to the affairs of the company;

(*b*) cause that statement to be laid before the creditors' meeting under section 98; and

(*c*) appoint one of their number to preside at that meeting;

and it is the duty of the director so appointed to attend the meeting and preside over it.

(2) The statement as to the affairs of the company shall be verified by affidavit by some or all of the directors and shall show—

(*a*) particulars of the company's assets, debts and liabilities;

(*b*) the names and addresses of the company's creditors;

(*c*) the securities held by them respectively;

(*d*) the dates when the securities were respectively given; and

(*e*) such further or other information as may be prescribed.

(3) If—

(*a*) the directors without reasonable excuse fail to comply with subsection (1) or (2); or

(*b*) any director without reasonable excuse fails to comply with subsection (1), so far as requiring him to attend and preside at the creditors' meeting,

the directors are or (as the case may be) the director is guilty of an offence and liable to a fine.

Appointment of liquidator

100.—(1) The creditors and the company at their respective meetings mentioned in section 98 may nominate a person to be liquidator for the purpose of winding up the company's affairs and distributing its assets.

(2) The liquidator shall be the person nominated by the creditors or, where no person has been so nominated, the person (if any) nominated by the company.

(3) In the case of different persons being nominated, any director, member or creditor of the company may, within seven days after the

date on which the nomination was made by the creditors, apply to the court for an order either—

(a) directing that the person nominated as liquidator by the company shall be liquidator instead of or jointly with the person nominated by the creditors, or

(b) appointing some other person to be liquidator instead of the person nominated by the creditors.

Appointment of liquidation committee

101.—(1) The creditors at the meeting to be held under section 98 or at any subsequent meeting may, if they think fit, appoint a committee ("the liquidation committee") of not more than five persons to exercise the functions conferred on it by or under this Act.

(2) If such a committee is appointed, the company may, either at the meeting at which the resolution for voluntary winding up is passed or at any time subsequently in general meeting, appoint such number of persons as they think fit to act as members of the committee, not exceeding five.

(3) However, the creditors may, if they think fit, resolve that all or any of the persons so appointed by the company ought not to be members of the liquidation committee; and if the creditors so resolve—

(a) the persons mentioned in the resolution are not then, unless the court otherwise directs, qualified to act as members of the committee; and

(b) on any application to the court under this provision the court may, if it thinks fit, appoint other persons to act as such members in place of the persons mentioned in the resolution.

(4) In Scotland, the liquidation committee has, in addition to the powers and duties conferred and imposed on it by this Act, such of the powers and duties of commissioners on a bankrupt estate as may be conferred and imposed on liquidation committees by the rules.

Creditors' meeting where winding up converted under s.96

102. Where, in the case of a winding up which was, under section 96 in Chapter III, converted to a creditors' voluntary winding up, a creditors' meeting is held in accordance with section 95, any appointment made or committee established by that meeting is deemed to have been made or established by a meeting held in accordance with section 98 in this Chapter.

Cesser of directors' powers

103. On the appointment of a liquidator, all the powers of the directors cease, except so far as the liquidation committee (or, if there is no such committee, the creditors) sanction their continuance.

Vacancy in office of liquidator

104. If a vacancy occurs, by death, resignation or otherwise, in the office of a liquidator (other than a liquidator appointed by, or by the direction of, the court), the creditors may fill the vacancy.

Meetings of company and creditors at each year's end

105.—(1) If the winding up continues for more than one year, the liquidator shall summon a general meeting of the company and a meeting of the creditors at the end of the first year from the commencement of the winding up, and of each succeeding year, or at the first convenient date within three months from the end of the year or such longer period as the Secretary of State may allow.

(2) The liquidator shall lay before each of the meetings an account of his acts and dealings and of the conduct of the winding up during the preceding year.

(3) If the liquidator fails to comply with this section, he is liable to a fine.

(4) Where under section 96 a members' voluntary winding up has become a creditors' voluntary winding up, and the creditors' meeting under section 95 is held three months or less before the end of the first year from the commencement of the winding up, the liquidator is not required by this section to summon a meeting of creditors at the end of that year.

Final meeting prior to dissolution

106.—(1) As soon as the company's affairs are fully wound up, the liquidator shall make up an account of the winding up, showing how it has been conducted and the company's property has been disposed of, and thereupon shall call a general meeting of the company and a meeting of the creditors for the purpose of laying the account before the meetings and giving an explanation of it.

(2) Each such meeting shall be called by advertisement in the *Gazette* specifying the time, place and object of the meeting, and published at least one month before it.

(3) Within one week after the date of the meetings (or, if they are not held on the same date, after the date of the later one) the liquidator shall send to the registrar of companies a copy of the account, and shall make a return to him of the holding of the meetings and of their dates.

(4) If the copy is not sent or the return is not made in accordance with subsection (3), the liquidator is liable to a fine and, for continued contravention, to a daily default fine.

(5) However, if a quorum is not present at either such meeting, the liquidator shall, in lieu of the return required by subsection (3), make a return that the meeting was duly summoned and that no quorum was present; and upon such return being made the provisions of that subsection as to the making of the return are, in respect of that meeting, deemed complied with.

(6) If the liquidator fails to call a general meeting of the company or a meeting of the creditors as required by this section, he is liable to a fine.

CHAPTER V

PROVISIONS APPLYING TO BOTH KINDS OF VOLUNTARY WINDING UP

Distribution of company's property
107. Subject to the provisions of this Act as to preferential payments, the company's property in a voluntary winding up shall on the winding up be applied in satisfaction of the company's liabilities *pari passu* and, subject to that application, shall (unless the articles otherwise provide) be distributed among the members according to their rights and interests in the company.

Appointment or removal of liquidator by the court
108.—(1) If from any cause whatever there is no liquidator acting, the court may appoint a liquidator.

(2) The court may, on cause shown, remove a liquidator and appoint another.

Notice by liquidator of his appointment
109.—(1) The liquidator shall, within 14 days after his appointment, publish in the *Gazette* and deliver to the registrar of companies for registration a notice of his appointment in the form prescribed by statutory instrument made by the Secretary of State.

(2) If the liquidator fails to comply with this section, he is liable to a fine and, for continued contravention, to a daily default fine.

Acceptance of shares, etc., as consideration for sale of company property
110.—(1) This section applies, in the case of a company proposed to be, or being, wound up voluntarily, where the whole or part of the company's business or property is proposed to be transferred or sold to another company ("the transferee company"), whether or not the latter is a company within the meaning of the Companies Act.

(2) With the requisite sanction, the liquidator of the company being, or proposed to be, wound up ("the transferor company") may receive, in compensation or part compensation for the transfer or sale, shares, policies or other like interests in the transferee company for distribution among the members of the transferor company.

(3) The sanction requisite under subsection (2) is—

(*a*) in the case of a members' voluntary winding up, that of a special resolution of the company, conferring either a general authority on the liquidator or an authority in respect of any particular arrangement, and

(*b*) in the case of a creditors' voluntary winding up, that of either the court or the liquidation committee.

(4) Alternatively to subsection (2), the liquidator may (with that sanction) enter into any other arrangement whereby the members of the transferor company may, in lieu of receiving cash, shares, policies

or other like interests (or in addition thereto), participate in the profits of, or receive any other benefit from, the transferee company.

(5) A sale or arrangement in pursuance of this section is binding on members of the transferor company.

(6) A special resolution is not invalid for purposes of this section by reason that it is passed before or concurrently with a resolution for voluntary winding up or for appointing liquidators; but, if an order is made within a year for winding up the company by the court, the special resolution is not valid unless sanctioned by the court.

Dissent from arrangement under s.110

111.—(1) This section applies in the case of a voluntary winding up where, for the purposes of section 110(2) or (4), there has been passed a special resolution of the transferor company providing the sanction requisite for the liquidator under that section.

(2) If a member of the transferor company who did not vote in favour of the special resolution expresses his dissent from it in writing, addressed to the liquidator and left at the company's registered office within seven days after the passing of the resolution, he may require the liquidator either to abstain from carrying the resolution into effect or to purchase his interest at a price to be determined by agreement or by arbitration under this section.

(3) If the liquidator elects to purchase the member's interest, the purchase money must be paid before the company is dissolved and be raised by the liquidator in such manner as may be determined by special resolution.

(4) For purposes of an arbitration under this section, the provisions of the Companies Clauses Consolidation Act 1845 or, in the case of a winding up in Scotland, the Companies Clauses Consolidation (Scotland) Act 1845 with respect to the settlement of disputes by arbitration are incorporated with this Act, and—

(*a*) in the construction of those provisions this Act is deemed the special Act and "the company" means the transferor company, and

(*b*) any appointment by the incorporated provisions directed to be made under the hand of the secretary or any two of the directors may be made in writing by the liquidator (or, if there is more than one liquidator, then any two or more of them).

Reference of questions to court

112.—(1) The liquidator or any contributory or creditor may apply to the court to determine any question arising in the winding up of a company, or to exercise, as respects the enforcing of calls or any other matter, all or any of the powers which the court might exercise if the company were being wound up by the court.

(2) The court, if satisfied that the determination of the question or the required exercise of power will be just and beneficial, may accede

wholly or partially to the application on such terms and conditions as it thinks fit, or may make such other order on the application as it thinks just.

(3) A copy of an order made by virtue of this section staying the proceedings in the winding up shall forthwith be forwarded by the company, or otherwise as may be prescribed, to the registrar of companies, who shall enter it in his records relating to the company.

Court's power to control proceedings (Scotland)

113. If the court, on the application of the liquidator in the winding up of a company registered in Scotland, so directs, no action or proceeding shall be proceeded with or commenced against the company except by leave of the court and subject to such terms as the court may impose.

No liquidator appointed or nominated by company

114.—(1) This section applies where, in the case of a voluntary winding up, no liquidator has been appointed or nominated by the company.

(2) The powers of the directors shall not be exercised, except with the sanction of the court or (in the case of a creditors' voluntary winding up) so far as may be necessary to secure compliance with sections 98 (creditors' meeting) and 99 (statement of affairs), during the period before the appointment or nomination of a liquidator of the company.

(3) Subsection (2) does not apply in relation to the powers of the directors—

(a) to dispose of perishable goods and other goods the value of which is likely to diminish if they are not immediately disposed of, and

(b) to do all such other things as may be necessary for the protection of the company's assets.

(4) If the directors of the company without reasonable excuse fail to comply with this section, they are liable to a fine.

Expenses of voluntary winding up

115. All expenses properly incurred in the winding up, including the remuneration of the liquidator, are payable out of the company's assets in priority to all other claims.

Saving for certain rights

116. The voluntary winding up of a company does not bar the right of any creditor or contributory to have it wound up by the court; but in the case of an application by a contributory the court must be satisfied that the rights of the contributories will be prejudiced by a voluntary winding up.

CHAPTER VI

WINDING UP BY THE COURT

. . . . . .

Jurisdiction (Scotland)

Court of Session and sheriff court jurisdiction

120.—(1) The Court of Session has jurisdiction to wind up any company registered in Scotland.

[51] (2) When the Court of Session is in vacation, the jurisdiction conferred on that court by this section may (subject to the provisions of this Part) be exercised by the judge acting as vacation judge.

(3) Where the amount of a company's share capital paid up or credited as paid up does not exceed £120,000, the sheriff court of the sheriffdom in which the company's registered office is situated has concurrent jurisdiction with the Court of Session to wind up the company; but—

(a) the Court of Session may, if it thinks expedient having regard to the amount of the company's assets to do so—
  (i) remit to a sheriff court any petition presented to the Court of Session for winding up such a company, or
  (ii) require such a petition presented to a sheriff court to be remitted to the Court of Session; and

(b) the Court of Session may require any such petition as above-mentioned presented to one sheriff court to be remitted to another sheriff court; and

(c) in a winding up in the sheriff court the sheriff may submit a stated case for the opinion of the Court of Session on any question of law arising in that winding up.

(4) For purposes of this section, the expression "registered office" means the place which has longest been the company's registered office during the six months immediately preceding the presentation of the petition for winding up.

(5) The money sum for the time being specified in subsection (3) is subject to increase or reduction by order under section 416 in Part XV.

Power to remit winding up to Lord Ordinary

121.—(1) The Court of Session may, by Act of Sederunt, make provision for the taking of proceedings in a winding up before one of the Lords Ordinary; and, where provision is so made, the Lord Ordinary has, for the purposes of the winding up, all the powers and jurisdiction of the court.

---

[51] As amended by the Court of Session Act 1988, Sched. 2.

(2) However, the Lord Ordinary may report to the Inner House any matter which may arise in the course of a winding up.

Grounds and effect of winding-up petition

Circumstances in which company may be wound up by the court

122.—(1) A company may be wound up by the court if—

(a) the company has by special resolution resolved that the company be wound up by the court,

(b) being a public company which was registered as such on its original incorporation, the company has not been issued with a certificate under section 117 of the Companies Act (public company share capital requirements) and more than a year has expired since it was so registered,

(c) it is an old public company, within the meaning of the Consequential Provisions Act,

(d) the company does not commence its business within a year from its incorporation or suspends its business for a whole year,

(e) the number of members is reduced below two,

(f) the company is unable to pay its debts,

(g) the court is of the opinion that it is just and equitable that the company should be wound up.

(2) In Scotland, a company which the Court of Session has jurisdiction to wind up may be wound up by the court if there is subsisting a floating charge over property comprised in the company's property and undertaking, and the court is satisfied that the security of the creditor entitled to the benefit of the floating charge is in jeopardy.

For this purpose a creditor's security is deemed to be in jeopardy if the court is satisfied that events have occurred or are about to occur which render it unreasonable in the creditor's interests that the company should retain power to dispose of the property which is subject to the floating charge.

Definition of inability to pay debts

123.—(1) A company is deemed unable to pay its debts—

(a) if a creditor (by assignment or otherwise) to whom the company is indebted in a sum exceeding £750 then due has served on the company, by leaving it at the company's registered office, a written demand (in the prescribed form) requiring the company to pay the sum so due and the company has for three weeks thereafter neglected to pay the sum or to secure or compound for it to the reasonable satisfaction of the creditor, or

(b) if, in England and Wales, execution or other process issued on a judgment, decree or order of any court in favour of a creditor of the company is returned unsatisfied in whole or in part, or

(c) if, in Scotland, the *induciae* of a charge for payment on an extract decree, or an extract registered bond, or an extract registered protest, have expired without payment being made, or

(d) if, in Northern Ireland, a certificate of unenforceability has been granted in respect of a judgment against the company, or

(e) if it is proved to the satisfaction of the court that the company is unable to pay its debts as they fall due.

(2) A company is also deemed unable to pay its debts if it is proved to the satisfaction of the court that the value of the company's assets is less than the amount of its liabilities, taking into account its contingent and prospective liabilities.

(3) The money sum for the time being specified in subsection (1)(*a*) is subject to increase or reduction by order under section 416 in Part XV.

Application for winding up

124.—(1) Subject to the provisions of this section, an application to the court for the winding up of a company shall be by petition presented either by the company, or the directors, or by any creditor or creditors (including any contingent or prospective creditor or creditors), contributory or contributories, or by all or any of those parties, together or separately.

(2) Except as mentioned below, a contributory is not entitled to present a winding-up petition unless either—

(a) the number of members is reduced below two, or

(b) the shares in respect of which he is a contributory, or some of them, either were originally allotted to him, or have been held by him, and registered in his name, for at least six months during the 18 months before the commencement of the winding up, or have devolved on him through the death of a former holder.

(3) A person who is liable under section 76 to contribute to a company's assets in the event of its being wound up may petition on either of the grounds set out in section 122(1)(*f*) and (*g*), and subsection (2) above does not then apply; but unless the person is a contributory otherwise than under section 76, he may not in his character as contributory petition on any other ground.

This subsection is deemed included in Chapter VII of Part V of the Companies Act (redeemable shares; purchase by a company of its own shares) for the purposes of the Secretary of State's power to make regulations under section 179 of that Act.

[52] (4) A winding-up petition may be presented by the Secretary of State—

(a) if the ground of the petition is that in section 122(1)(*b*) or (*c*), or

(b) in a case falling within section 124A below.

(5) Where a company is being wound up voluntarily in England and

---

[52] As amended by the Companies Act 1989, s.60(2).

Wales, a winding-up petition may be presented by the official receiver attached to the court as well as by any other person authorised in that behalf under the other provisions of this section; but the court shall not make a winding-up order on the petition unless it is satisfied that the voluntary winding up cannot be continued with due regard to the interests of the creditors or contributories.

Petition for winding up on grounds of public interest

[53] **124A.**—(1) Where it appears to the Secretary of State from—

(a) any report made or information obtained under Part XIV of the Companies Act 1985 (company investigations, etc.),

(b) any report made under section 94 or 177 of the Financial Services Act 1986 or any information obtained under section 105 of that Act,

(c) any information obtained under section 2 of the Criminal Justice Act 1987 or section 52 of the Criminal Justice (Scotland) Act 1987 (fraud investigations), or

(d) any information obtained under section 83 of the Companies Act 1989 (powers exercisable for purpose of assisting overseas regulatory authorities),

that it is expedient in the public interest that a company should be wound up, he may present a petition for it to be wound up if the court thinks it just and equitable for it to be so.

(2) This section does not apply if the company is already being wound up by the court.

Powers of court on hearing of petition

125.—(1) On hearing a winding-up petition the court may dismiss it, or adjourn the hearing conditionally or unconditionally, or make an interim order, or any other order that it thinks fit; but the court shall not refuse to make a winding-up order on the ground only that the company's assets have been mortgaged to an amount equal to or in excess of those assets, or that the company has no assets.

(2) If the petition is presented by members of the company as contributories on the ground that it is just and equitable that the company should be wound up, the court, if it is of opinion—

(a) that the petitioners are entitled to relief either by winding up the company or by some other means, and

(b) that in the absence of any other remedy it would be just and equitable that the company should be wound up,

shall make a winding-up order; but this does not apply if the court is also of the opinion both that some other remedy is available to the petitioners and that they are acting unreasonably in seeking to have the company wound up instead of pursuing that other remedy.

---

[53] Inserted by the Companies Act 1989, s.60(3).

Power to stay or restrain proceedings against company

126.—(1) At any time after the presentation of a winding-up petition, and before a winding-up order has been made, the company, or any creditor or contributory, may—

(*a*) where any action or proceeding against the company is pending in the High Court or Court of Appeal in England and Wales or Northern Ireland, apply to the court in which the action or proceeding is pending for a stay of proceedings therein, and

(*b*) where any other action or proceeding is pending against the company, apply to the court having jurisdiction to wind up the company to restrain further proceedings in the action or proceeding;

and the court to which application is so made may (as the case may be) stay, sist or restrain the proceedings accordingly on such terms as it thinks fit.

(2) In the case of a company registered under section 680 of the Companies Act (pre-1862 companies; companies formed under legislation other than the Companies Acts) or the previous corresponding legislation, where the application to stay, sist or restrain is by a creditor, this section extends to actions and proceedings against any contributory of the company.

Avoidance of property dispositions, etc.

127. In a winding up by the court, any disposition of the company's property, and any transfer of shares, or alteration in the status of the company's members, made after the commencement of the winding up is, unless the court otherwise orders, void.

Avoidance of attachments, etc.

128.—(1) Where a company registered in England and Wales is being wound up by the court, any attachment, sequestration, distress or execution put in force against the estate or effects of the company after the commencement of the winding up is void.

(2) This section, so far as relates to any estate or effects of the company situated in England and Wales, applies in the case of a company registered in Scotland as it applies in the case of a company registered in England and Wales.

Commencement of winding up

Commencement of winding up by the court

129.—(1) If, before the presentation of a petition for the winding up of a company by the court, a resolution has been passed by the company for voluntary winding up, the winding up of the company is deemed to have commenced at the time of the passing of the resolution; and unless the court, on proof of fraud or mistake, directs otherwise, all proceedings taken in the voluntary winding up are deemed to have been validly taken.

(2) In any other case, the winding up of a company by the court is deemed to commence at the time of the presentation of the petition for winding up.

Consequences of winding-up order

130.—(1) On the making of a winding-up order, a copy of the order must forthwith be forwarded by the company (or otherwise as may be prescribed) to the registrar of companies, who shall enter it in his records relating to the company.

(2) When a winding-up order has been made or a provisional liquidator has been appointed, no action or proceeding shall be proceeded with or commenced against the company or its property, except by leave of the court and subject to such terms as the court may impose.

(3) When an order has been made for winding up a company registered under section 680 of the Companies Act, no action or proceeding shall be commenced or proceeded with against the company or its property or any contributory of the company, in respect of any debt of the company, except by leave of the court, and subject to such terms as the court may impose.

(4) An order for winding up a company operates in favour of all the creditors and of all contributories of the company as if made on the joint petition of a creditor and of a contributory.

Investigation procedures

Company's statement of affairs

131.—(1) Where the court has made a winding-up order or appointed a provisional liquidator, the official receiver may require some or all of the persons mentioned in subsection (3) below to make out and submit to him a statement in the prescribed form as to the affairs of the company.

(2) The statement shall be verified by affidavit by the persons required to submit it and shall show—

(*a*) particulars of the company's assets, debts and liabilities;
(*b*) the names and addresses of the company's creditors;
(*c*) the securities held by them respectively;
(*d*) the dates when the securities were respectively given; and
(*e*) such further or other information as may be prescribed or as the official receiver may require.

(3) The persons referred to in subsection (1) are—

(*a*) those who are or have been officers of the company;
(*b*) those who have taken part in the formation of the company at any time within one year before the relevant date;
(*c*) those who are in the company's employment, or have been in its employment within that year, and are in the official receiver's opinion capable of giving the information required;

(*d*) those who are or have been within that year officers of, or in the employment of, a company which is, or within that year was, an officer of the company.

(4) Where any persons are required under this section to submit a statement of affairs to the official receiver, they shall do so (subject to the next subsection) before the end of the period of 21 days beginning with the day after that on which the prescribed notice of the requirement is given to them by the official receiver.

(5) The official receiver, if he thinks fit, may—

(*a*) at any time release a person from an obligation imposed on him under subsection (1) or (2) above; or

(*b*) either when giving the notice mentioned in subsection (4) or subsequently, extend the period so mentioned;

and where the official receiver has refused to exercise a power conferred by this subsection, the court, if it thinks fit, may exercise it.

(6) In this section—

"employment" includes employment under a contract for services; and

"the relevant date" means—

(*a*) in a case where a provisional liquidator is appointed, the date of his appointment; and

(*b*) in a case where no such appointment is made, the date of the winding-up order.

(7) If a person without reasonable excuse fails to comply with any obligation imposed under this section, he is liable to a fine and, for continued contravention, to a daily default fine.

(8) In the application of this section to Scotland references to the official receiver are to the liquidator or, in a case where a provisional liquidator is appointed, the provisional liquidator.

Investigation by official receiver

132.—(1) Where a winding-up order is made by the court in England and Wales, it is the duty of the official receiver to investigate—

(*a*) if the company has failed, the causes of the failure; and

(*b*) generally, the promotion, formation, business, dealings and affairs of the company,

and to make such report (if any) to the court as he thinks fit.

(2) The report is, in any proceedings, *prima facie* evidence of the facts stated in it.

Public examination of officers

133.—(1) Where a company is being wound up by the court, the official receiver or, in Scotland, the liquidator may at any time before the dissolution of the company apply to the court for the public examination of any person who—

(*a*) is or has been an officer of the company; or

(*b*) has acted as liquidator or administrator of the company or as receiver or manager or, in Scotland, receiver of its property; or

(*c*) not being a person falling within paragraph (*a*) or (*b*), is or has been concerned, or has taken part, in the promotion, formation or management of the company.

(2) Unless the court otherwise orders, the official receiver or, in Scotland, the liquidator shall make an application under subsection (1) if he is requested in accordance with the rules to do so by—

(*a*) one-half, in value, of the company's creditors; or

(*b*) three-quarters, in value, of the company's contributories.

(3) On an application under subsection (1), the court shall direct that a public examination of the person to whom the application relates shall be held on a day appointed by the court; and that person shall attend on that day and be publicly examined as to the promotion, formation or management of the company or as to the conduct of its business and affairs, or his conduct or dealings in relation to the company.

(4) The following may take part in the public examination of a person under this section and may question that person concerning the matters mentioned in subsection (3), namely—

(*a*) the official receiver;

(*b*) the liquidator of the company;

(*c*) any person who has been appointed as special manager of the company's property or business;

(*d*) any creditor of the company who has tendered a proof or, in Scotland, submitted a claim in the winding up;

(*e*) any contributory of the company.

Enforcement of s.133

134.—(1) If a person without reasonable excuse fails at any time to attend his public examination under section 133, he is guilty of a contempt of court and liable to be punished accordingly.

(2) In a case where a person without reasonable excuse fails at any time to attend his examination under section 133 or there are reasonable grounds for believing that a person has absconded, or is about to abscond, with a view to avoiding or delaying his examination under that section, the court may cause a warrant to be issued to a constable or prescribed officer of the court—

(*a*) for the arrest of that person; and

(*b*) for the seizure of any books, papers, records, money or goods in that person's possession.

(3) In such a case the court may authorise the person arrested under the warrant to be kept in custody, and anything seized under such a

warrant to be held, in accordance with the rules, until such time as the court may order.

Appointment of liquidator

Appointment and powers of provisional liquidator

135.—(1) Subject to the provisions of this section, the court may, at any time after the presentation of a winding-up petition, appoint a liquidator provisionally.

(2) In England and Wales, the appointment of a provisional liquidator may be made at any time before the making of a winding-up order; and either the official receiver or any other fit person may be appointed.

(3) In Scotland, such an appointment may be made at any time before the first appointment of liquidators.

(4) The provisional liquidator shall carry out such functions as the court may confer on him.

(5) When a liquidator is provisionally appointed by the court, his powers may be limited by the order appointing him.

Functions of official receiver in relation to office of liquidator

136.—(1) The following provisions of this section have effect, subject to section 140 below, on a winding-up order being made by the court in England and Wales.

(2) The official receiver, by virtue of his office, becomes the liquidator of the company and continues in office until another person becomes liquidator under the provisions of this Part.

(3) The official receiver is, by virtue of his office, the liquidator during any vacancy.

(4) At any time when he is the liquidator of the company, the official receiver may summon separate meetings of the company's creditors and contributories for the purpose of choosing a person to be liquidator of the company in place of the official receiver.

(5) It is the duty of the official receiver—

(a) as soon as practicable in the period of 12 weeks beginning with the day on which the winding-up order was made, to decide whether to exercise his power under subsection (4) to summon meetings, and

(b) if in pursuance of paragraph (a) he decides not to exercise that power, to give notice of his decision, before the end of that period, to the court and to the company's creditors and contributories, and

(c) (whether or not he has decided to exercise that power) to exercise his power to summon meetings under subsection (4) if he is at any time requested, in accordance with the rules, to do so by one quarter, in value, of the company's creditors;

and accordingly, where the duty imposed by paragraph (c) arises before the official receiver has performed a duty imposed by paragraph (*a*) or (*b*), he is not required to perform the latter duty.

(6) A notice given under subsection (5)(*b*) to the company's creditors shall contain an explanation of the creditors' power under subsection (5)(*c*) to require the official receiver to summon meetings of the company's creditors and contributories.

Appointment by Secretary of State

137.—(1) In a winding up by the court in England and Wales the official receiver may, at any time when he is the liquidator of the company, apply to the Secretary of State for the appointment of a person as liquidator in his place.

(2) If meetings are held in pursuance of a decision under section 136(5)(*a*), but no person is chosen to be liquidator as a result of those meetings, it is the duty of the official receiver to decide whether to refer the need for an appointment to the Secretary of State.

(3) On an application under subsection (1), or a reference made in pursuance of a decision under subsection (2), the Secretary of State shall either make an appointment or decline to make one.

(4) Where a liquidator has been appointed by the Secretary of State under subsection (3), the liquidator shall give notice of his appointment to the company's creditors or, if the court so allows, shall advertise his appointment in accordance with the directions of the court.

(5) In that notice or advertisement the liquidator shall—

(*a*) state whether he proposes to summon a general meeting of the company's creditors under section 141 below for the purpose of determining (together with any meeting of contributories) whether a liquidation committee should be established under that section, and

(*b*) if he does not propose to summon such a meeting, set out the power of the company's creditors under that section to require him to summon one.

Appointment of liquidator in Scotland

138.—(1) Where a winding-up order is made by the court in Scotland, a liquidator shall be appointed by the court at the time when the order is made.

(2) The liquidator so appointed (here referred to as "the interim liquidator") continues in office until another person becomes liquidator in his place under this section or the next.

(3) The interim liquidator shall (subject to the next subsection) as soon as practicable in the period of 28 days beginning with the day on which the winding-up order was made or such longer period as the court may allow, summon separate meetings of the company's creditors and contributories for the purpose of choosing a person (who

may be the person who is the interim liquidator) to be liquidator of the company in place of the interim liquidator.

(4) If it appears to the interim liquidator, in any case where a company is being wound up on grounds including its inability to pay its debts, that it would be inappropriate to summon under subsection (3) a meeting of the company's contributories, he may summon only a meeting of the company's creditors for the purpose mentioned in that subsection.

(5) If one or more meetings are held in pursuance of this section but no person is appointed or nominated by the meeting or meetings, the interim liquidator shall make a report to the court which shall appoint either the interim liquidator or some other person to be liquidator of the company.

(6) A person who becomes liquidator of the company in place of the interim liquidator shall, unless he is appointed by the court, forthwith notify the court of that fact.

Choice of liquidator at meetings of creditors and contributories

139.—(1) This section applies where a company is being wound up by the court and separate meetings of the company's creditors and contributories are summoned for the purpose of choosing a person to be liquidator of the company.

(2) The creditors and the contributories at their respective meetings may nominate a person to be liquidator.

(3) The liquidator shall be the person nominated by the creditors or, where no person has been so nominated, the person (if any) nominated by the contributories.

(4) In the case of different persons being nominated, any contributory or creditor may, within seven days after the date on which the nomination was made by the creditors, apply to the court for an order either—

(*a*) appointing the person nominated as liquidator by the contributories to be a liquidator instead of, or jointly with, the person nominated by the creditors; or

(*b*) appointing some other person to be liquidator instead of the person nominated by the creditors.

Appointment by the court following administration or voluntary arrangement

140.—(1) Where a winding-up order is made immediately upon the discharge of an administration order, the court may appoint as liquidator of the company the person who has ceased on the discharge of the administration order to be the administrator of the company.

(2) Where a winding-up order is made at a time when there is a supervisor of a voluntary arrangement approved in relation to the company under Part I, the court may appoint as liquidator of the company the person who is the supervisor at the time when the winding-up order is made.

(3) Where the court makes an appointment under this section, the official receiver does not become the liquidator as otherwise provided by section 136(2), and he has no duty under section 136(5)(*a*) or (*b*) in respect of the summoning of creditors' or contributories' meetings.

Liquidation committees

. . . . . .

Liquidation committee (Scotland)

142.—(1) Where a winding-up order has been made by the court in Scotland and separate meetings of creditors and contributories have been summoned for the purpose of choosing a person to be liquidator or, under section 138(4), only a meeting of creditors has been summoned for that purpose, those meetings or (as the case may be) that meeting may establish a committee ("the liquidation committee") to exercise the functions conferred on it by or under this Act.

(2) The liquidator may at any time, if he thinks fit, summon separate general meetings of the company's creditors and contributories for the purpose of determining whether such a committee should be established and, if it is so determined, of establishing it.

(3) The liquidator, if appointed by the court otherwise than under section 139(4)(*a*), is required to summon meetings under subsection (2) if he is requested, in accordance with the rules, to do so by one-tenth, in value, of the company's creditors.

(4) Where meetings are summoned under this section, or for the purpose of choosing a person to be liquidator, and either the meeting of creditors or the meeting of contributories decides that a liquidation committee should be established, but the other meeting does not so decide or decides that a committee should not be established, the committee shall be established in accordance with the rules, unless the court otherwise orders.

(5) Where in the case of any winding up there is for the time being no liquidation committee, the functions of such a committee are vested in the court except to the extent that the rules otherwise provide.

(6) In addition to the powers and duties conferred and imposed on it by this Act, a liquidation committee has such of the powers and duties of commissioners in a sequestration as may be conferred and imposed on such committees by the rules.

The liquidator's functions

General functions in winding up by the court

143.—(1) The functions of the liquidator of a company which is being wound up by the court are to secure that the assets of the company are got in, realised and distributed to the company's creditors and, if there is a surplus, to the persons entitled to it.

(2) It is the duty of the liquidator of a company which is being wound up by the court in England and Wales, if he is not the official receiver—

(*a*) to furnish the official receiver with such information,

(*b*) to produce to the official receiver, and permit inspection by the official receiver of, such books, papers and other records, and

(*c*) to give the official receiver such other assistance,

as the official receiver may reasonably require for the purposes of carrying out his functions in relation to the winding up.

Custody of company's property

144.—(1) When a winding-up order has been made, or where a provisional liquidator has been appointed, the liquidator or the provisional liquidator (as the case may be) shall take into his custody or under his control all the property and things in action to which the company is or appears to be entitled.

(2) In a winding up by the court in Scotland, if and so long as there is no liquidator, all the property of the company is deemed to be in the custody of the court.

Vesting of company property in liquidator

145.—(1) When a company is being wound up by the court, the court may on the application of the liquidator by order direct that all or any part of the property of whatsoever description belonging to the company or held by trustees on its behalf shall vest in the liquidator by his official name; and thereupon the property to which the order relates vests accordingly.

(2) The liquidator may, after giving such indemnity (if any) as the court may direct, bring or defend in his official name any action or other legal proceeding which relates to that property or which it is necessary to bring or defend for the purpose of effectually winding up the company and recovering its property.

Duty to summon final meeting

146.—(1) Subject to the next subsection, if it appears to the liquidator of a company which is being wound up by the court that the winding up of the company is for practical purposes complete and the liquidator is not the official receiver, the liquidator shall summon a final general meeting of the company's creditors which—

(*a*) shall receive the liquidator's report of the winding up, and

(*b*) shall determine whether the liquidator should have his release under section 174 in Chapter VII of this Part.

(2) The liquidator may, if he thinks fit, give the notice summoning the final general meeting at the same time as giving notice of any final distribution of the company's property but, if summoned for an earlier date, that meeting shall be adjourned (and, if necessary, further adjourned) until a date on which the liquidator is able to report to the

meeting that the winding up of the company is for practical purposes complete.

(3) In the carrying out of his functions in the winding up it is the duty of the liquidator to retain sufficient sums from the company's property to cover the expenses of summoning and holding the meeting required by this section.

General powers of court

Power to stay or sist winding up

147.—(1) The court may at any time after an order for winding up, on the application either of the liquidator or the official receiver or any creditor or contributory, and on proof to the satisfaction of the court that all proceedings in the winding up ought to be stayed or sisted, make an order staying or sisting the proceedings, either altogether or for a limited time, on such terms and conditions as the court thinks fit.

(2) The court may, before making an order, require the official receiver to furnish to it a report with respect to any facts or matters which are in his opinion relevant to the application.

(3) A copy of every order made under this section shall forthwith be forwarded by the company, or otherwise as may be prescribed, to the registrar of companies, who shall enter it in his records relating to the company.

Settlement of list of contributories and application of assets

148.—(1) As soon as may be after making a winding-up order, the court shall settle a list of contributories, with power to rectify the register of members in all cases where rectification is required in pursuance of the Companies Act or this Act, and shall cause the company's assets to be collected, and applied in discharge of its liabilities.

(2) If it appears to the court that it will not be necessary to make calls on or adjust the rights of contributories, the court may dispense with the settlement of a list of contributories.

(3) In settling the list, the court shall distinguish between persons who are contributories in their own right and persons who are contributories as being representatives of or liable for the debts of others.

Debts due from contributory to company

149.—(1) The court may, at any time after making a winding-up order, make an order on any contributory for the time being on the list of contributories to pay, in manner directed by the order, any money due from him (or from the estate of the person who he represents) to the company, exclusive of any money payable by him or the estate by virtue of any call in pursuance of the Companies Act or this Act.

(2) The court in making such an order may—

(*a*) in the case of an unlimited company, allow to the contributory by way of set-off any money due to him or the estate which he represents from the company on any independent dealing or contract with the company, but not any money due to him as a member of the company in respect of any dividend or profit, and

(b) in the case of a limited company, make to any director or manager whose liability is unlimited or to his estate the like allowance.

(3) In the case of any company, whether limited or unlimited, when all the creditors are paid in full (together with interest at the official rate), any money due on any account whatever to a contributory from the company may be allowed to him by way of set-off against any subsequent call.

Power to make calls

150.—(1) The court may, at any time after making a winding-up order, and either before or after it has ascertained the sufficiency of the company's assets, make calls on all or any of the contributories for the time being settled on the list of the contributories to the extent of their liability, for payment of any money which the court considers necessary to satisfy the company's debts and liabilities, and the expenses of winding up, and for the adjustment of the rights of the contributories among themselves, and make an order for payment of any calls so made.

(2) In making a call the court may take into consideration the probability that some of the contributories may partly or wholly fail to pay it.

Payment into bank of money due to company

151.—(1) The court may order any contributory, purchaser or other person from whom money is due to the company to pay the amount due into the Bank of England (or any branch of it) to the account of the liquidator instead of to the liquidator, and such an order may be enforced in the same manner as if it had directed payment to the liquidator.

(2) All money and securities paid or delivered into the Bank of England (or branch) in the event of a winding up by the court are subject in all respects to the orders of the court.

Order on contributory to be conclusive evidence

152.—(1) An order made by the court on a contributory is conclusive evidence that the money (if any) thereby appearing to be due or ordered to be paid is due, but subject to any right of appeal.

(2) All other pertinent matters stated in the order are to be taken as truly stated as against all persons and in all proceedings except proceedings in Scotland against the heritable estate of a deceased contributory; and in that case the order is only *prima facie* evidence for the purpose of charging his heritable estate, unless his heirs or legatees

of heritage were on the list of contributories at the time of the order being made.

Power to exclude creditors not proving in time

153. The court may fix a time or times within which creditors are to prove their debts or claims or to be excluded from the benefit of any distribution made before those debts are proved.

Adjustment of rights of contributories

154. The court shall adjust the rights of the contributories among themselves and distribute any surplus among the persons entitled to it.

Inspection of books by creditors, etc.

155.—(1) The court may, at any time after making a winding-up order, make such order for inspection of the company's books and papers by creditors and contributories as the court thinks just; and any books and papers in the company's possession may be inspected by creditors and contributories accordingly, but not further or otherwise.

(2) Nothing in this section excludes or restricts any statutory rights of a government department or person acting under the authority of a government department.

Payment of expenses of winding up

156. The court may, in the event of the assets being insufficient to satisfy the liabilities, make an order as to the payment out of the assets of the expenses incurred in the winding up in such order of priority as the court thinks just.

Attendance at company meetings (Scotland)

157. In the winding up by the court of a company registered in Scotland, the court has power to require the attendance of any officer of the company at any meeting of creditors or of contributories, or of a liquidation committee, for the purpose of giving information as to the trade, dealings, affairs or property of the company.

Power to arrest absconding contributory

158. The court, at any time either before or after making a winding-up order, on proof of probable cause for believing that a contributory is about to quit the United Kingdom or otherwise to abscond or to remove or conceal any of his property for the purpose of evading payment of calls, may cause the contributory to be arrested and his books and papers and moveable personal property to be seized and him and them to be kept safely until such time as the court may order.

Powers of court to be cumulative

159. Powers conferred by this Act and the Companies Act on the court are in addition to, and not in restriction of, any existing powers of instituting proceedings against a contributory or debtor of the company, or the estate of any contributory or debtor, for the recovery of any call or other sums.

. . . . . .

Enforcement of, and appeal from, orders

Orders for calls on contributories (Scotland)

161.—(1) In Scotland, where an order, interlocutor or decree has been made for winding up a company by the court, it is competent to the court, on production by the liquidators of a list certified by them of the names of the contributories liable in payment of any calls, and of the amount due by each contributory, and of the date when that amount became due, to pronounce forthwith a decree against those contributories for payment of the sums so certified to be due, with interest from that date until payment (at 5 per cent. per annum) in the same way and to the same effect as if they had severally consented to registration for execution, on a charge of six days, of a legal obligation to pay those calls and interest.

(2) The decree may be extracted immediately, and no suspension of it is competent, except on caution or consignation, unless with special leave of the court.

Appeals from orders in Scotland

162.—(1) Subject to the provisions of this section and to rules of court, an appeal from any order or decision made or given in the winding up of a company by the court in Scotland under this Act lies in the same manner and subject to the same conditions as an appeal from an order or decision of the court in cases within its ordinary jurisdiction.

[54] (2) In regard to orders or judgments pronounced by the judge acting as vacation judge—

(a) none of the orders specified in Part I of Schedule 3 to this Act are subject to review, reduction, suspension or stay of execution, and

(b) every other order or judgment (except as mentioned below) may be submitted to review by the Inner House by reclaiming motion enrolled within 14 days from the date of the order or judgment.

(3) However, an order being one of those specified in Part II of that Schedule shall, from the date of the order and notwithstanding that it has been submitted to review as above, be carried out and receive effect until the Inner House have disposed of the matter.

(4) In regard to orders or judgments pronounced in Scotland by a

[54] As amended by the Court of Session Act 1988, Sched. 2.

Lord Ordinary before whom proceedings in a winding up are being taken, any such order or judgment may be submitted to review by the Inner House by reclaiming motion enrolled within 14 days from its date; but should it not be so submitted to review during session, the provisions of this section in regard to orders or judgments pronounced by the judge acting as vacation judge apply.

(5) Nothing in this section affects provisions of the Companies Act or this Act in reference to decrees in Scotland for payment of calls in the winding up of companies, whether voluntary or by the court.

CHAPTER VII

LIQUIDATORS

Preliminary

Style and title of liquidators
163. The liquidator of a company shall be described—

(a) where a person other than the official receiver is liquidator, by the style of "the liquidator" of the particular company, or
(b) where the official receiver is liquidator, by the style of "the official receiver and liquidator" of the particular company;

and in neither case shall he be described by an individual name.

Corrupt inducement affecting appointment
164. A person who gives, or agrees or offers to give, to any member or creditor of a company any valuable consideration with a view to securing his own appointment or nomination, or to securing or preventing the appointment or nomination of some person other than himself, as the company's liquidator is liable to a fine.

Liquidator's powers and duties

Voluntary winding up
165.—(1) This section has effect where a company is being wound up voluntarily, but subject to section 166 below in the case of a creditors' voluntary winding up.

(2) The liquidator may—

(a) in the case of a members' voluntary winding up, with the sanction of an extraordinary resolution of the company, and
(b) in the case of a creditors' voluntary winding up, with the sanction of the court or the liquidation committee (or, if there is no such committee, a meeting of the company's creditors),

exercise any of the powers specified in Part I of Schedule 4 to this Act (payment of debts, compromise of claims, etc.).

(3) The liquidator may, without sanction, exercise either of the

powers specified in Part II of that Schedule (institution and defence of proceedings; carrying on the business of the company) and any of the general powers specified in Part III of that Schedule.

(4) The liquidator may—

(a) exercise the court's power of settling a list of contributories (which list is *prima facie* evidence of the liability of the persons named in it to be contributories),

(b) exercise the court's power of making calls,

(c) summon general meetings of the company for the purpose of obtaining its sanction by special or extraordinary resolution or for any other purpose he may think fit.

(5) The liquidator shall pay the company's debts and adjust the rights of the contributories among themselves.

(6) Where the liquidator in exercise of the powers conferred on him by this Act disposes of any property of the company to a person who is connected with the company (within the meaning of section 249 in Part VII), he shall, if there is for the time being a liquidation committee, give notice to the committee of that exercise of his powers.

Creditors' voluntary winding up

166.—(1) This section applies where, in the case of a creditors' voluntary winding up, a liquidator has been nominated by the company.

(2) The powers conferred on the liquidator by section 165 shall not be exercised, except with the sanction of the court, during the period before the holding of the creditors' meeting under section 98 in Chapter IV.

(3) Subsection (2) does not apply in relation to the power of the liquidator—

(a) to take into his custody or under his control all the property to which the company is or appears to be entitled;

(b) to dispose of perishable goods and other goods the value of which is likely to diminish if they are not immediately disposed of; and

(c) to do all such other things as may be necessary for the protection of the company's assets.

(4) The liquidator shall attend the creditors' meeting held under section 98 and shall report to the meeting on any exercise by him of his powers (whether or not under this section or under section 112 or 165).

(5) If default is made—

(a) by the company in complying with subsection (1) or (2) of section 98, or

(b) by the directors in complying with subsection (1) or (2) of section 99,

the liquidator shall, within seven days of the relevant day, apply to the court for directions as to the manner in which that default is to be remedied.

(6) "The relevant day" means the day on which the liquidator was nominated by the company or the day on which he first became aware of the default, whichever is the later.

(7) If the liquidator without reasonable excuse fails to comply with this section, he is liable to a fine.

Winding up by the court

167.—(1) Where a company is being wound up by the court, the liquidator may—

 (a) with the sanction of the court or the liquidation committee, exercise any of the powers specified in Parts I and II of Schedule 4 to this Act (payment of debts; compromise of claims, etc.; institution and defence of proceedings; carrying on of the business of the company), and
 (b) with or without that sanction, exercise any of the general powers specified in Part III of that Schedule.

(2) Where the liquidator (not being the official receiver), in exercise of the powers conferred on him by this Act—

 (a) disposes of any property of the company to a person who is connected with the company (within the meaning of section 249 in Part VII), or
 (b) employs a solicitor to assist him in the carrying out of his functions,

he shall, if there is for the time being a liquidation committee, give notice to the committee of that exercise of his powers.

(3) The exercise by the liquidator in a winding up by the court of the powers conferred by this section is subject to the control of the court, and any creditor or contributory may apply to the court with respect to any exercise or proposed exercise of any of those powers.

.   .   .   .   .   .

Supplementary powers (Scotland)

169.—(1) In the case of a winding up in Scotland, the court may provide by order that the liquidator may, where there is no liquidation committee, exercise any of the following powers, namely—

 (a) to bring or defend any action or other legal proceeding in the name and on behalf of the company, or
 (b) to carry on the business of the company so far as may be necessary for its beneficial winding up,

without the sanction or intervention of the court.

(2) In a winding up by the court in Scotland, the liquidator has (subject to the rules) the same powers as a trustee on a bankrupt estate.

Enforcement of liquidator's duty to make returns, etc.

170.—(1) If a liquidator who has made any default—

(*a*) in filing, delivering or making any return, account or other document, or

(*b*) in giving any notice which he is by law required to file, deliver, make or give,

fails to make good the default within 14 days after the service on him of a notice requiring him to do so, the court has the following powers.

(2) On an application made by any creditor or contributory of the company, or by the registrar of companies, the court may make an order directing the liquidator to make good the default within such time as may be specified in the order.

(3) The court's order may provide that all costs of and incidental to the application shall be borne by the liquidator.

(4) Nothing in this section prejudices the operation of any enactment imposing penalties on a liquidator in respect of any such default as is mentioned above.

Removal; vacation of office

Removal, etc. (voluntary winding up)

171.—(1) This section applies with respect to the removal from office and vacation of office of the liquidator of a company which is being wound up voluntarily.

(2) Subject to the next subsection, the liquidator may be removed from office only by an order of the court or—

(*a*) in the case of a members' voluntary winding up, by a general meeting of the company summoned specially for that purpose, or

(*b*) in the case of a creditors' voluntary winding up, by a general meeting of the company's creditors summoned specially for that purpose in accordance with the rules.

(3) Where the liquidator was appointed by the court under section 108 in Chapter V, a meeting such as is mentioned in subsection (2) above shall be summoned for the purpose of replacing him only if he thinks fit or the court so directs or the meeting is requested, in accordance with the rules—

(*a*) in the case of a members' voluntary winding up, by members representing not less than one-half of the total voting rights of all the members having at the date of the request a right to vote at the meeting, or

(*b*) in the case of a creditors' voluntary winding up, by not less than one-half, in value, of the company's creditors.

(4) A liquidator shall vacate office if he ceases to be a person who is

qualified to act as an insolvency practitioner in relation to the company.

(5) A liquidator may, in the prescribed circumstances, resign his office by giving notice of his resignation to the registrar of companies.

(6) Where—

(a) in the case of a members' voluntary winding up, a final meeting of the company has been held under section 94 in Chapter III, or

(b) in the case of a creditors' voluntary winding up, final meetings of the company and of the creditors have been held under section 106 in Chapter IV,

the liquidator whose report was considered at the meeting or meetings shall vacate office as soon as he has complied with subsection (3) of that section and has given notice to the registrar of companies that the meeting or meetings have been held and of the decisions (if any) of the meeting or meetings.

Removal, etc. (winding up by the court)

172.—(1) This section applies with respect to the removal from office and vacation of office of the liquidator of a company which is being wound up by the court, or of a provisional liquidator.

(2) Subject as follows, the liquidator may be removed from office only by an order of the court or by a general meeting of the company's creditors summoned specially for that purpose in accordance with the rules; and a provisional liquidator may be removed from office only by an order of the court.

(3) Where—

(a) the official receiver is liquidator otherwise than in succession under section 136(3) to a person who held office as a result of a nomination by a meeting of the company's creditors or contributories, or

(b) the liquidator was appointed by the court otherwise than under section 139(4)(a) or 140(1), or was appointed by the Secretary of State,

a general meeting of the company's creditors shall be summoned for the purpose of replacing him only if he thinks fit, or the court so directs, or the meeting is requested, in accordance with the rules, by not less than one-quarter, in value, of the creditors.

(4) If appointed by the Secretary of State, the liquidator may be removed from office by a direction of the Secretary of State.

(5) A liquidator or provisional liquidator, not being the official receiver, shall vacate office if he ceases to be a person who is qualified to act as an insolvency practitioner in relation to the company.

(6) A liquidator may, in the prescribed circumstances, resign his office by giving notice of his resignation to the court.

(7) Where an order is made under section 204 (early dissolution in Scotland) for the dissolution of the company, the liquidator shall

vacate office when the dissolution of the company takes effect in accordance with that section.

(8) Where a final meeting has been held under section 146 (liquidator's report on completion of winding up), the liquidator whose report was considered at the meeting shall vacate office as soon as he has given notice to the court and the registrar of companies that the meeting has been held and of the decisions (if any) of the meeting.

Release of liquidator

Release (voluntary winding up)

173.—(1) This section applies with respect to the release of the liquidator of a company which is being wound up voluntarily.

(2) A person who has ceased to be a liquidator shall have his release with effect from the following time, that is to say—

(*a*) in the case of a person who has been removed from office by a general meeting of the company or by a general meeting of the company's creditors that has not resolved against his release or who has died, the time at which notice is given to the registrar of companies in accordance with the rules that that person has ceased to hold office;

(*b*) in the case of a person who has been removed from office by a general meeting of the company's creditors that has resolved against his release, or by the court, or who has vacated office under section 171(4) above, such time as the Secretary of State may, on the application of that person, determine;

(*c*) in the case of a person who has resigned, such time as may be prescribed;

(*d*) in the case of a person who has vacated office under subsection (6)(*a*) of section 171, the time at which he vacated office;

(*e*) in the case of a person who has vacated office under subsection (6)(*b*) of that section—

(i) if the final meeting of the creditors referred to in that subsection has resolved against that person's release, such time as the Secretary of State may, on an application by that person, determine, and

(ii) if that meeting has not resolved against that person's release, the time at which he vacated office.

(3) In the application of subsection (2) to the winding up of a company registered in Scotland, the references to a determination by the Secretary of State as to the time from which a person who has ceased to be liquidator shall have his release are to be read as references to such a determination by the Accountant of Court.

(4) Where a liquidator has his release under subsection (2), he is, with effect from the time specified in that subsection, discharged from all liability both in respect of acts or omissions of his in the winding up and otherwise in relation to his conduct as liquidator.

But nothing in this section prevents the exercise, in relation to a person who has had his release under subsection (2), of the court's powers under section 212 of this Act (summary remedy against delinquent directors, liquidators, etc.).

Release (winding up by the court)

174.—(1) This section applies with respect to the release of the liquidator of a company which is being wound up by the court, or of a provisional liquidator.

(2) Where the official receiver has ceased to be liquidator and a person becomes liquidator in his stead, the official receiver has his release with effect from the following time, that is to say—

(*a*) in a case where that person was nominated by a general meeting of creditors or contributories, or was appointed by the Secretary of State, the time at which the official receiver gives notice to the court that he has been replaced;

(*b*) in a case where that person is appointed by the court, such time as the court may determine.

(3) If the official receiver while he is liquidator gives notice to the Secretary of State that the winding up is for practical purposes complete, he has his release with effect from such time as the Secretary of State may determine.

(4) A person other than the official receiver who has ceased to be a liquidator has his release with effect from the following time, that is to say—

(*a*) in the case of a person who has been removed from office by a general meeting of creditors that has not resolved against his release or who has died, the time at which notice is given to the court in accordance with the rules that that person has ceased to hold office;

(*b*) in the case of a person who has been removed from office by a general meeting of creditors that has resolved against his release, or by the court or the Secretary of State, or who has vacated office under section 172(5) or (7), such time as the Secretary of State may, on an application by that person, determine;

(*c*) in the case of a person who has resigned, such time as may be prescribed;

(*d*) in the case of a person who has vacated office under section 172(8)—

(i) if the final meeting referred to in that subsection has resolved against that person's release, such time as the Secretary of State may, on an application by that person, determine, and

(ii) if that meeting has not so resolved, the time at which that person vacated office.

(5) A person who has ceased to hold office as a provisional liquidator has his release with effect from such time as the court may, on an application by him, determine.

(6) Where the official receiver or a liquidator or provisional liquidator has his release under this section, he is, with effect from the time specified in the preceding provisions of this section, discharged from all liability both in respect of acts or omissions of his in the winding up and otherwise in relation to his conduct as liquidator or provisional liquidator.

But nothing in this section prevents the exercise, in relation to a person who has had his release under this section, of the court's powers under section 212 (summary remedy against delinquent directors, liquidators, etc.).

(7) In the application of this section to a case where the order for winding up has been made by the court in Scotland, the references to a determination by the Secretary of State as to the time from which a person who has ceased to be liquidator has his release are to such a determination by the Accountant of Court.

CHAPTER VIII

PROVISIONS OF GENERAL APPLICATION IN WINDING UP

Preferential debts

Preferential debts (general provision)

175.—(1) In a winding up the company's preferential debts (within the meaning given by section 386 in Part XII) shall be paid in priority to all other debts.

(2) Preferential debts—

(*a*) rank equally among themselves after the expenses of the winding up and shall be paid in full, unless the assets are insufficient to meet them, in which case they abate in equal proportions; and

(*b*) so far as the assets of the company available for payment of general creditors are insufficient to meet them, have priority over the claims of holders of debentures secured by, or holders of, any floating charge created by the company, and shall be paid accordingly out of any property comprised in or subject to that charge.

Preferential charge on goods distrained

176.—(1) This section applies where a company is being wound up by the court in England and Wales, and is without prejudice to section 128 (avoidance of attachments, etc.).

(2) Where any person (whether or not a landlord or person entitled to rent) has distrained upon the goods or effects of the company in the

period of three months ending with the date of the winding-up order, those goods or effects, or the proceeds of their sale, shall be charged for the benefit of the company with the preferential debts of the company to the extent that the company's property is for the time being insufficient for meeting them.

(3) Where by virtue of a charge under subsection (2) any person surrenders any goods or effects to a company or makes a payment to a company, that person ranks, in respect of the amount of the proceeds of sale of those goods or effects by the liquidator or (as the case may be) the amount of the payment, as a preferential creditor of the company, except as against so much of the company's property as is available for the payment of preferential creditors by virtue of the surrender or payment.

Special managers

Power to appoint special manager

177.—(1) Where a company has gone into liquidation or a provisional liquidator has been appointed, the court may, on an application under this section, appoint any person to be the special manager of the business or property of the company.

(2) The application may be made by the liquidator or provisional liquidator in any case where it appears to him that the nature of the business or property of the company, or the interests of the company's creditors or contributories or members generally, require the appointment of another person to manage the company's business or property.

(3) The special manager has such powers as may be entrusted to him by the court.

(4) The court's power to entrust powers to the special manager includes power to direct that any provision of this Act that has effect in relation to the provisional liquidator or liquidator of a company shall have the like effect in relation to the special manager for the purposes of the carrying out by him of any of the functions of the provisional liquidator or liquidator.

(5) The special manager shall—

(*a*) give such security or, in Scotland, caution as may be prescribed;

(*b*) prepare and keep such accounts as may be prescribed; and

(*c*) produce those accounts in accordance with the rules to the Secretary of State or to such other persons as may be prescribed.

Execution, attachment and the Scottish equivalents

.   .   .   .   .   .

Effect of diligence (Scotland)

185.—(1) In the winding up of a company registered in Scotland, the following provisions of the Bankruptcy (Scotland) Act 1985—

(*a*) subsections (1) to (6) of section 37 (effect of sequestration on diligence); and

(*b*) subsections (3), (4), (7) and (8) of section 39 (realisation of estate),

apply, so far as consistent with this Act, in like manner as they apply in the sequestration of a debtor's estate, with the substitutions specified below and with any other necessary modifications.

(2) The substitutions to be made in those sections of the Act of 1985 are as follows—

(*a*) for references to the debtor, substitute references to the company;

(*b*) for references to the sequestration, substitute references to the winding up;

(*c*) for references to the date of sequestration, substitute references to the commencement of the winding up of the company; and

(*d*) for references to the permanent trustee, substitute references to the liquidator.

(3) In this section, "the commencement of the winding up of the company" means, where it is being wound up by the court, the day on which the winding-up order is made.

(4) This section, so far as relating to any estate or effects of the company situated in Scotland, applies in the case of a company registered in England and Wales as in the case of one registered in Scotland.

Miscellaneous matters

Rescission of contracts by the court

186.—(1) The court may, on the application of a person who is, as against the liquidator, entitled to the benefit or subject to the burden of a contract made with the company, make an order rescinding the contract on such terms as to payment by or to either party of damages for the non-performance of the contract, or otherwise as the court thinks just.

(2) Any damages payable under the order to such a person may be proved by him as a debt in the winding up.

Power to make over assets to employees

187.—(1) On the winding up of a company (whether by the court or voluntarily), the liquidator may, subject to the following provisions of this section, make any payment which the company has, before the commencement of the winding up, decided to make under section 719 of the Companies Act (power to provide for employees or former employees on cessation or transfer of business).

(2) The power which a company may exercise by virtue only of that section may be exercised by the liquidator after the winding up has commenced if, after the company's liabilities have been fully satisfied and provision has been made for the expenses of the winding up, the exercise of that power has been sanctioned by such a resolution of the company as would be required of the company itself by section 719(3) before that commencement, if paragraph (*b*) of that subsection were omitted and any other requirement applicable to its exercise by the company had been met.

(3) Any payment which may be made by a company under this section (that is, a payment after the commencement of its winding up) may be made out of the company's assets which are available to the members on the winding up.

(4) On a winding up by the court, the exercise by the liquidator of his powers under this section is subject to the court's control, and any creditor or contributory may apply to the court with respect to any exercise or proposed exercise of the power.

(5) Subsections (1) and (2) above have effect notwithstanding anything in any rule of law or in section 107 of this Act (property of company after satisfaction of liabilities to be distributed among members).

Notification that company is in liquidation

188.—(1) When a company is being wound up, whether by the court or voluntarily, every invoice, order for goods or business letter issued by or on behalf of the company, or a liquidator of the company, or a receiver or manager of the company's property, being a document on or in which the name of the company appears, shall contain a statement that the company is being wound up.

(2) If default is made in complying with this section, the company and any of the following persons who knowingly and wilfully authorises or permits the default, namely, any officer of the company, any liquidator of the company and any receiver or manager, is liable to a fine.

Interest on debts

189.—(1) In a winding up interest is payable in accordance with this section on any debt proved in the winding up, including so much of any such debt as represents interest on the remainder.

(2) Any surplus remaining after the payment of the debts proved in a winding up shall, before being applied for any other purpose, be applied in paying interest on those debts in respect of the periods during which they have been outstanding since the company went into liquidation.

(3) All interest under this section ranks equally, whether or not the debts on which it is payable rank equally.

(4) The rate of interest payable under this section in respect of any debt ("the official rate" for the purposes of any provision of this Act in which that expression is used) is whichever is the greater of—

(a) the rate specified in section 17 of the Judgments Act 1838 on the day on which the company went into liquidation, and
(b) the rate applicable to that debt apart from the winding up.

(5) In the application of this section to Scotland—

(a) references to a debt proved in a winding up have effect as references to a claim accepted in a winding up, and
(b) the reference to section 17 of the Judgments Act 1838 has effect as a reference to the rules.

Documents exempt from stamp duty

190.—(1) In the case of a winding up by the court, or of a creditors' voluntary winding up, the following has effect as regards exemption from duties chargeable under the enactments relating to stamp duties.

(2) If the company is registered in England and Wales, the following documents are exempt from stamp duty—

(a) every assurance relating solely to freehold or leasehold property, or to any estate, right or interest in, any real or personal property, which forms part of the company's assets and which, after the execution of the assurance, either at law or in equity, is or remains part of those assets, and
(b) every writ, order, certificate, or other instrument or writing relating solely to the property of any company which is being wound up as mentioned in subsection (1), or to any proceeding under such a winding up.

"Assurance" here includes deed, conveyance, assignment and surrender.

(3) If the company is registered in Scotland, the following documents are exempt from stamp duty—

(a) every conveyance relating solely to property which forms part of the company's assets and which, after the execution of the conveyance, is or remains the company's property for the benefit of its creditors,
(b) any articles of roup or sale, submission and every other instrument and writing whatsoever relating solely to the company's property, and
(c) every deed or writing forming part of the proceedings in the winding up.

"Conveyance" here includes assignation, instrument, discharge, writing and deed.

Company's books to be evidence

191. Where a company is being wound up, all books and papers of the company and of the liquidators are, as between the contributories of the company, *prima facie* evidence of the truth of all matters purporting to be recorded in them.

Information as to pending liquidations

192.—(1) If the winding up of a company is not concluded within one year after its commencement, the liquidator shall, at such intervals as may be prescribed, until the winding up is concluded, send to the registrar of companies a statement in the prescribed form and containing the prescribed particulars with respect to the proceedings in, and position of, the liquidation.

(2) If a liquidator fails to comply with this section, he is liable to a fine and, for continued contravention, to a daily default fine.

Unclaimed dividends (Scotland)

193.—(1) The following applies where a company registered in Scotland has been wound up, and is about to be dissolved.

(2) The liquidator shall lodge in an appropriate bank or institution as defined in section 73(1) of the Bankruptcy (Scotland) Act 1985 (not being a bank or institution in or of which the liquidator is acting partner, manager, agent or cashier) in the name of the Accountant of Court the whole unclaimed dividends and unapplied or undistributable balances, and the deposit receipts shall be transmitted to the Accountant of Court.

(3) The provisions of section 58 of the Bankruptcy (Scotland) Act 1985 (so far as consistent with this Act and the Companies Act) apply with any necessary modifications to sums lodged in a bank or institution under this section as they apply to sums deposited under section 57 of the Act first mentioned.

Resolutions passed at adjourned meetings

194. Where a resolution is passed at an adjourned meeting of a company's creditors or contributories, the resolution is treated for all purposes as having been passed on the date on which it was in fact passed, and not as having been passed on any earlier date.

Meetings to ascertain wishes of creditors or contributories

195.—(1) The court may—

(a) as to all matters relating to the winding up of a company, have regard to the wishes of the creditors or contributories (as proved to it by any sufficient evidence), and

(b) if it thinks fit, for the purpose of ascertaining those wishes, direct meetings of the creditors or contributories to be called, held and conducted in such manner as the court directs, and appoint a person to act as chairman of any such meeting and report the result of it to the court.

(2) In the case of creditors, regard shall be had to the value of each creditor's debt.

(3) In the case of contributories, regard shall be had to the number of votes conferred on each contributory by the Companies Act or the articles.

Judicial notice of court documents

196. In all proceedings under this Part, all courts, judges and persons judicially acting, and all officers, judicial or ministerial, of any court, or employed in enforcing the process of any court shall take judicial notice—

- (a) of the signature of any officer of the High Court or of a county court in England and Wales, or of the Court of Session or a sheriff court in Scotland, or of the High Court in Northern Ireland, and also
- (b) of the official seal or stamp of the several offices of the High Court in England and Wales or Northern Ireland, or of the Court of Session, appended to or impressed on any document made, issued or signed under the provisions of this Act or the Companies Act, or any official copy of such a document.

Commission for receiving evidence

197.—(1) When a company is wound up in England and Wales or in Scotland, the court may refer the whole or any part of the examination of witnesses—

- (a) to a specified county court in England and Wales, or
- (b) to the sheriff principal for a specified sheriffdom in Scotland, or
- (c) to the High Court in Northern Ireland or a specified Northern Ireland County Court,

("specified" meaning specified in the order of the winding-up court).

(2) Any person exercising jurisdiction as a judge of the court to which the reference is made (or, in Scotland, the sheriff principal to whom it is made) shall then, by virtue of this section, be a commissioner for the purpose of taking the evidence of those witnesses.

(3) The judge or sheriff principal has in the matter referred the same power of summoning and examining witnesses, of requiring the production and delivery of documents, of punishing defaults by witnesses, and of allowing costs and expenses to witnesses, as the court which made the winding-up order.

These powers are in addition to any which the judge or sheriff principal might lawfully exercise apart from this section.

(4) The examination so taken shall be returned or reported to the court which made the order in such manner as that court requests.

(5) This section extends to Northern Ireland.

Court order for examination of persons in Scotland

198.—(1) The court may direct the examination in Scotland of any person for the time being in Scotland (whether a contributory of the company or not), in regard to the trade, dealings, affairs or property of any company in course of being wound up, or of any person being a contributory of the company, so far as the company may be interested by reason of his being a contributory.

(2) The order or commission to take the examination shall be directed to the sheriff principal of the sheriffdom in which the person to be examined is residing or happens to be for the time; and the sheriff principal shall summon the person to appear before him at a time and place to be specified in the summons for examination on oath as a witness or as a haver, and to produce any books or papers called for which are in his possession or power.

(3) The sheriff principal may take the examination either orally or on written interrogatories, and shall report the same in writing in the usual form to the court, and shall transmit with the report the books and papers produced, if the originals are required and specified by the order or commission, or otherwise copies or extracts authenticated by the sheriff.

(4) If a person so summoned fails to appear at the time and place specified, or refuses to be examined or to make the production required, the sheriff principal shall proceed against him as a witness or haver duly cited; and failing to appear or refusing to give evidence or make production may be proceeded against by the law of Scotland.

(5) The sheriff principal is entitled to such fees, and the witness is entitled to such allowances, as sheriffs principal when acting as commissioners under appointment from the Court of Session and as witnesses and havers are entitled to in the like cases according to the law and practice of Scotland.

(6) If any objection is stated to the sheriff principal by the witness, either on the ground of his incompetency as a witness, or as to the production required, or on any other ground, the sheriff principal may, if he thinks fit, report the objection to the court, and suspend the examination of the witness until it has been disposed of by the court.

Costs of application for leave to proceed (Scottish companies)

199. Where a petition or application for leave to proceed with an action or proceeding against a company which is being wound up in Scotland is unopposed and is granted by the court, the costs of the petition or application shall, unless the court otherwise directs, be added to the amount of the petitioner's or applicant's claim against the company.

Affidavits etc. in United Kingdom and overseas

200.—(1) An affidavit required to be sworn under or for the purposes of this Part may be sworn in the United Kingdom, or elsewhere in Her Majesty's dominions, before any court, judge or person lawfully authorised to take and receive affidavits, or before any of Her Majesty's consuls or vice-consuls in any place outside her dominions.

(2) All courts, judges, justices, commissioners and persons acting judicially shall take judicial notice of the seal or stamp or signature (as the case may be) of any such court, judge, person, consul or vice-consul attached, appended or subscribed to any such affidavit, or to any other document to be used for the purposes of this Part.

Chapter IX

Dissolution of Companies After Winding Up

Dissolution (voluntary winding up)

201.—(1) This section applies, in the case of a company wound up voluntarily, where the liquidator has sent to the registrar of companies his final account and return under section 94 (members' voluntary) or section 106 (creditors' voluntary).

(2) The registrar on receiving the account and return shall forthwith register them; and on the expiration of three months from the registration of the return the company is deemed to be dissolved.

(3) However, the court may, on the application of the liquidator or any other person who appears to the court to be interested, make an order deferring the date at which the dissolution of the company is to take effect for such time as the court thinks fit.

(4) It is the duty of the person on whose application an order of the court under this section is made within seven days after the making of the order to deliver to the registrar an office copy of the order for registration; and if that person fails to do so he is liable to a fine and, for continued contravention, to a daily default fine.

.   .   .   .   .   .

Early dissolution (Scotland)

204.—(1) This section applies where a winding-up order has been made by the court in Scotland.

(2) If after a meeting or meetings under section 138 (appointment of liquidator in Scotland) it appears to the liquidator that the realisable assets of the company are insufficient to cover the expenses of the winding up, he may apply to the court for an order that the company be dissolved.

(3) Where the liquidator makes that application, if the court is satisfied that the realisable assets of the company are insufficient to cover the expenses of the winding up and it appears to the court appropriate to do so, the court shall make an order that the company be dissolved in accordance with this section.

(4) A copy of the order shall within 14 days from its date be forwarded by the liquidator to the registrar of companies, who shall forthwith register it; and, at the end of the period of three months beginning with the day of the registration of the order, the company shall be dissolved.

(5) The court may, on an application by any person who appears to the court to have an interest, order that the date at which the dissolution of the company is to take effect shall be deferred for such period as the court thinks fit.

(6) It is the duty of the person on whose application an order is made under subsection (5), within seven days after the making of the order, to deliver to the registrar of companies such a copy of the order as is prescribed.

(7) If the liquidator without reasonable excuse fails to comply with the requirements of subsection (4), he is liable to a fine and, for continued contravention, to a daily default fine.

(8) If a person without reasonable excuse fails to deliver a copy as required by subsection (6), he is liable to a fine and, for continued contravention, to a daily default fine.

Dissolution otherwise than under ss.202–204

205.—(1) This section applies where the registrar of companies receives—

(a) a notice served for the purposes of section 172(8) (final meeting of creditors and vacation of office by liquidator), or

(b) a notice from the official receiver that the winding up of a company by the court is complete.

(2) The registrar shall, on receipt of the notice, forthwith register it; and, subject as follows, at the end of the period of three months beginning with the day of the registration of the notice, the company shall be dissolved.

(3) The Secretary of State may, on the application of the official receiver or any other person who appears to the Secretary of State to be interested, give a direction deferring the date at which the dissolution of the company is to take effect for such period as the Secretary of State thinks fit.

(4) An appeal to the court lies from any decision of the Secretary of State on an application for a direction under subsection (3).

(5) Subsection (3) does not apply in a case where the winding-up order was made by the court in Scotland, but in such a case the court may, on an application by any person appearing to the court to have an interest, order that the date at which the dissolution of the company is to take effect shall be deferred for such period as the court thinks fit.

(6) It is the duty of the person—

(a) on whose application a direction is given under subsection (3);

(b) in whose favour an appeal with respect to an application for such a direction is determined; or

(c) on whose application an order is made under subsection (5),

within seven days after the giving of the direction, the determination of the appeal or the making of the order, to deliver to the registrar for registration such a copy of the direction, determination or order as is prescribed.

(7) If a person without reasonable excuse fails to deliver a copy as required by subsection (6), he is liable to a fine and, for continued contravention, to a daily default fine.

CHAPTER X

MALPRACTICE BEFORE AND DURING LIQUIDATION; PENALISATION OF COMPANIES AND COMPANY OFFICERS; INVESTIGATIONS AND PROSECUTIONS

Offences of fraud, deception, etc.

Fraud, etc. in anticipation of winding up

206.—(1) When a company is ordered to be wound up by the court, or passes a resolution for voluntary winding up, any person, being a past or present officer of the company, is deemed to have committed an offence if, within the 12 months immediately preceding the commencement of the winding up, he has—

[55] (a) concealed any part of the company's property to the value of £500 or more, or concealed any debt due to or from the company, or

[55] (b) fraudulently removed any part of the company's property to the value of £500 or more, or

  (c) concealed, destroyed, mutilated or falsified any book or paper affecting or relating to the company's property or affairs, or

  (d) made any false entry in any book or paper affecting or relating to the company's property or affairs, or

  (e) fraudulently parted with, altered or made any omission in any document affecting or relating to the company's property or affairs, or

  (f) pawned, pledged or disposed of any property of the company which has been obtained on credit and has not been paid for (unless the pawning, pledging or disposal was in the ordinary way of the company's business).

(2) Such a person is deemed to have committed an offence if within the period above mentioned he has been privy to the doing by others of any of the things mentioned in paragraphs (c), (d) and (e) of subsection (1); and he commits an offence if, at any time after the commencement of the winding up, he does any of the things mentioned in paragraphs (a) to (f) of that subsection, or is privy to the doing by others of any of the things mentioned in paragraphs (c) to (e) of it.

(3) For purposes of this section, "officer" includes a shadow director.

(4) It is a defence—

---

[55] As amended by S.I. 1986 No. 1996.

(a) for a person charged under paragraph (*a*) or (*f*) of subsection (1) (or under subsection (2) in respect of the things mentioned in either of those two paragraphs) to prove that he had no intent to defraud, and

(b) for a person charged under paragraph (*c*) or (*d*) of subsection (1) (or under subsection (2) in respect of the things mentioned in either of those two paragraphs) to prove that he had no intent to conceal the state of affairs of the company or to defeat the law.

(5) Where a person pawns, pledges or disposes of any property in circumstances which amount to an offence under subsection (1)(*f*), every person who takes in pawn or pledge, or otherwise receives, the property knowing it to be pawned, pledged or disposed of in such circumstances, is guilty of an offence.

(6) A person guilty of an offence under this section is liable to imprisonment or a fine, or both.

(7) The money sums specified in paragraphs (*a*) and (*b*) of subsection (1) are subject to increase or reduction by order under section 416 in Part XV.

Transactions in fraud of creditors

207.—(1) When a company is ordered to be wound up by the court or passes a resolution for voluntary winding up, a person is deemed to have committed an offence if he, being at the time an officer of the company—

(a) has made or caused to be made any gift or transfer of, or charge on, or has caused or connived at the levying of any execution against, the company's property, or

(b) has concealed or removed any part of the company's property since, or within two months before, the date of any unsatisfied judgment or order for the payment of money obtained against the company.

(2) A person is not guilty of an offence under this section—

(a) by reason of conduct constituting an offence under subsection (1)(*a*) which occurred more than five years before the commencement of the winding up, or

(b) if he proves that, at the time of the conduct constituting the offence, he had no intent to defraud the company's creditors.

(3) A person guilty of an offence under this section is liable to imprisonment or a fine, or both.

Misconduct in course of winding up

208.—(1) When a company is being wound up, whether by the court or voluntarily, any person, being a past or present officer of the company, commits an offence if he—

(a) does not to the best of his knowledge and belief fully and truly discover to the liquidator all the company's property, and how and to whom and for what consideration and when the company disposed of any part of that property (except such part as has been disposed of in the ordinary way of the company's business), or

(b) does not deliver up to the liquidator (or as he directs) all such part of the company's property as is in his custody or under his control, and which he is required by law to deliver up, or

(c) does not deliver up to the liquidator (or as he directs) all books and papers in his custody or under his control belonging to the company and which he is required by law to deliver up, or

(d) knowing or believing that a false debt has been proved by any person in the winding up, fails to inform the liquidator as soon as practicable, or

(e) after the commencement of the winding up, prevents the production of any book or paper affecting or relating to the company's property or affairs.

(2) Such a person commits an offence if after the commencement of the winding up he attempts to account for any part of the company's property by fictitious losses or expenses; and he is deemed to have committed that offence if he has so attempted at any meeting of the company's creditors within the 12 months immediately preceding the commencement of the winding up.

(3) For purposes of this section, "officer" includes a shadow director.

(4) It is a defence—

(a) for a person charged under paragraph (a), (b) or (c) of subsection (1) to prove that he had no intent to defraud, and

(b) for a person charged under paragraph (e) of that subsection to prove that he had no intent to conceal the state of affairs of the company or to defeat the law.

(5) A person guilty of an offence under this section is liable to imprisonment or a fine, or both.

Falsification of company's books

209.—(1) When a company is being wound up, an officer or contributory of the company commits an offence if he destroys, mutilates, alters or falsifies any books, papers or securities, or makes or is privy to the making of any false or fraudulent entry in any register, book of account or document belonging to the company with intent to defraud or deceive any person.

(2) A person guilty of an offence under this section is liable to imprisonment or a fine, or both.

Material omissions from statement relating to company's affairs

210.—(1) When a company is being wound up, whether by the court or voluntarily, any person, being a past or present officer of the company, commits an offence if he makes any material omission in any statement relating to the company's affairs.

(2) When a company has been ordered to be wound up by the court, or has passed a resolution for voluntary winding up, any such person is deemed to have committed that offence if, prior to the winding up, he has made any material omission in any such statement.

(3) For purposes of this section, "officer" includes a shadow director.

(4) It is a defence for a person charged under this section to prove that he had no intent to defraud.

(5) A person guilty of an offence under this section is liable to imprisonment or a fine, or both.

False representations to creditors

211.—(1) When a company is being wound up, whether by the court or voluntarily, any person, being a past or present officer of the company—

(a) commits an offence if he makes any false representation or commits any other fraud for the purpose of obtaining the consent of the company's creditors or any of them to an agreement with reference to the company's affairs or to the winding up, and

(b) is deemed to have committed that offence if, prior to the winding up, he has made any false representation, or committed any other fraud, for that purpose.

(2) For purposes of this section, "officer" includes a shadow director.

(3) A person guilty of an offence under this section is liable to imprisonment or a fine, or both.

Penalisation of directors and officers

Summary remedy against delinquent directors, liquidators, etc.

212.—(1) This section applies if in the course of the winding up of a company it appears that a person who—

(a) is or has been an officer of the company,

(b) has acted as liquidator, administrator or administrative receiver of the company, or

(c) not being a person falling within paragraph (a) or (b), is or has been concerned, or has taken part, in the promotion, formation or management of the company,

has misapplied or retained, or become accountable for, any money or other property of the company, or been guilty of any misfeasance or breach of any fiduciary or other duty in relation to the company.

(2) The reference in subsection (1) to any misfeasance or breach of any fiduciary or other duty in relation to the company includes, in the case of a person who has acted as liquidator or administrator of the company, any misfeasance or breach of any fiduciary or other duty in

connection with the carrying out of his functions as liquidator or administrator of the company.

(3) The court may, on the application of the official receiver or the liquidator, or of any creditor or contributory, examine into the conduct of the person falling within subsection (1) and compel him—

(a) to repay, restore or account for the money or property or any part of it, with interest at such rate as the court thinks just, or

(b) to contribute such sum to the company's assets by way of compensation in respect of the misfeasance or breach of fiduciary or other duty as the court thinks just.

(4) The power to make an application under subsection (3) in relation to a person who has acted as liquidator or administrator of the company is not exercisable, except with the leave of the court, after that person has had his release.

(5) The power of a contributory to make an application under subsection (3) is not exercisable except with the leave of the court, but is exercisable notwithstanding that he will not benefit from any order the court may make on the application.

Fraudulent trading

213.—(1) If in the course of the winding up of a company it appears that any business of the company has been carried on with intent to defraud creditors of the company or creditors of any other person, or for any fraudulent purpose, the following has effect.

(2) The court, on the application of the liquidator may declare that any persons who were knowingly parties to the carrying on of the business in the manner above-mentioned are to be liable to make such contribution (if any) to the company's assets as the court thinks proper.

Wrongful trading

214.—(1) Subject to subsection (3) below, if in the course of the winding up of a company it appears that subsection (2) of this section applies in relation to a person who is or has been a director of the company, the court, on the application of the liquidator, may declare that that person is to be liable to make such contribution (if any) to the company's assets as the court thinks proper.

(2) This subsection applies in relation to a person if—

(a) the company has gone into insolvent liquidation,

(b) at some time before the commencement of the winding up of the company, that person knew or ought to have concluded that there was no reasonable prospect that the company would avoid going into insolvent liquidation, and

(c) that person was a director of the company at that time;

but the court shall not make a declaration under this section in any case where the time mentioned in paragraph (b) above was before 28th April 1986.

(3) The court shall not make a declaration under this section with respect to any person if it is satisfied that after the condition specified in subsection (2)(*b*) was first satisfied in relation to him that person took every step with a view to minimising the potential loss to the company's creditors as (assuming him to have known that there was no reasonable prospect that the company would avoid going into insolvent liquidation) he ought to have taken.

(4) For the purposes of subsections (2) and (3), the facts which a director of a company ought to know or ascertain, the conclusions which he ought to reach and the steps which he ought to take are those which would be known or ascertained, or reached or taken, by a reasonably diligent person having both—

(*a*) the general knowledge, skill and experience that may reasonably be expected of a person carrying out the same functions as are carried out by that director in relation to the company, and

(*b*) the general knowledge, skill and experience that that director has.

(5) The reference in subsection (4) to the functions carried out in relation to a company by a director of the company includes any functions which he does not carry out but which have been entrusted to him.

(6) For the purposes of this section a company goes into insolvent liquidation if it goes into liquidation at a time when its assets are insufficient for the payment of its debts and other liabilities and the expenses of the winding up.

(7) In this section "director" includes a shadow director.

(8) This section is without prejudice to section 213.

Proceedings under ss.213, 214

215.—(1) On the hearing of an application under section 213 or 214, the liquidator may himself give evidence or call witnesses.

(2) Where under either section the court makes a declaration, it may give such further directions as it thinks proper for giving effect to the declaration; and in particular, the court may—

(*a*) provide for the liability of any person under the declaration to be a charge on any debt or obligation due from the company to him, or on any mortgage or charge or any interest in a mortgage or charge on assets of the company held by or vested in him, or any person on his behalf, or any person claiming as assignee from or through the person liable or any person acting on his behalf, and

(*b*) from time to time make such further order as may be necessary for enforcing any charge imposed under this subsection.

(3) For the purposes of subsection (2), "assignee"—

(*a*) includes a person to whom or in whose favour, by the directions of the person made liable, the debt, obligation, mortgage or charge was created, issued or transferred or the interest created, but

(b) does not include an assignee for valuable consideration (not including consideration by way of marriage) given in good faith and without notice of any of the matters on the ground of which the declaration is made.

(4) Where the court makes a declaration under either section in relation to a person who is a creditor of the company, it may direct that the whole or any part of any debt owed by the company to that person and any interest thereon shall rank in priority after all other debts owed by the company and after any interest on those debts.

(5) Sections 213 and 214 have effect notwithstanding that the person concerned may be criminally liable in respect of matters on the ground of which the declaration under the section is to be made.

Restriction on re-use of company names

216.—(1) This section applies to a person where a company ("the liquidating company") has gone into insolvent liquidation on or after the appointed day and he was a director or shadow director of the company at any time in the period of 12 months ending with the day before it went into liquidation.

(2) For the purposes of this section, a name is a prohibited name in relation to such a person if—

(a) it is a name by which the liquidating company was known at any time in that period of 12 months, or

(b) it is a name which is so similar to a name falling within paragraph (a) as to suggest an association with that company.

(3) Except with leave of the court or in such circumstances as may be prescribed, a person to whom this section applies shall not at any time in the period of five years beginning with the day on which the liquidating company went into liquidation—

(a) be a director of any other company that is known by a prohibited name, or

(b) in any way, whether directly or indirectly, be concerned or take part in the promotion, formation or management of any such company, or

(c) in any way, whether directly or indirectly, be concerned or take part in the carrying on of a business carried on (otherwise than by a company) under a prohibited name.

(4) If a person acts in contravention of this section, he is liable to imprisonment or a fine, or both.

(5) In subsection (3) "the court" means any court having jurisdiction to wind up companies; and on an application for leave under that subsection, the Secretary of State or the official receiver may appear

and call the attention of the court to any matters which seem to him to be relevant.

(6) References in this section, in relation to any time, to a name by which a company is known are to the name of the company at that time or to any name under which the company carries on business at that time.

(7) For the purposes of this section a company goes into insolvent liquidation if it goes into liquidation at a time when its assets are insufficient for the payment of its debts and other liabilities and the expenses of the winding up.

(8) In this section "company" includes a company which may be wound up under Part V of this Act.

Personal liability for debts, following contravention of s.216

217.—(1) A person is personally responsible for all the relevant debts of a company if at any time—

(*a*) in contravention of section 216, he is involved in the management of the company, or

(*b*) as a person who is involved in the management of the company, he acts or is willing to act on instructions given (without the leave of the court) by a person whom he knows at that time to be in contravention in relation to the company of section 216.

(2) Where a person is personally responsible under this section for the relevant debts of a company, he is jointly and severally liable in respect of those debts with the company and any other person who, whether under this section or otherwise, is so liable.

(3) For the purposes of this section the relevant debts of a company are—

(*a*) in relation to a person who is personally responsible under paragraph (*a*) of subsection (1), such debts and other liabilities of the company as are incurred at a time when that person was involved in the management of the company, and

(*b*) in relation to a person who is personally responsible under paragraph (*b*) of that subsection, such debts and other liabilities of the company as are incurred at a time when that person was acting or was willing to act on instructions given as mentioned in that paragraph.

(4) For the purposes of this section, a person is involved in the management of a company if he is a director of the company or if he is concerned, whether directly or indirectly, or takes part, in the management of the company.

(5) For the purposes of this section a person who, as a person involved in the management of a company, has at any time acted on instructions given (without the leave of the court) by a person whom he knew at that time to be in contravention in relation to the company of section 216 is presumed, unless the contrary is shown, to have been

willing at any time thereafter to act on any instructions given by that person.

(6) In this section "company" includes a company which may be wound up under Part V.

Investigation and prosecution of malpractice

Prosecution of delinquent officers and members of company

218.—(1) If it appears to the court in the course of a winding up by the court that any past or present officer, or any member, of the company has been guilty of any offence in relation to the company for which he is criminally liable, the court may (either on the application of a person interested in the winding up or of its own motion) direct the liquidator to refer the matter to the prosecuting authority.

(2) "The prosecuting authority" means—

(*a*) in the case of a winding up in England and Wales, the Director of Public Prosecutions, and

(*b*) in the case of a winding up in Scotland, the Lord Advocate.

(3) If in the case of a winding up by the court in England and Wales it appears to the liquidator, not being the official receiver, that any past or present officer of the company, or any member of it, has been guilty of an offence in relation to the company for which he is criminally liable, the liquidator shall report the matter to the official receiver.

(4) If it appears to the liquidator in the course of a voluntary winding up that any past or present officer of the company, or any member of it, has been guilty of an offence in relation to the company for which he is criminally liable, he shall—

(*a*) forthwith report the matter to the prosecuting authority, and

(*b*) furnish to that authority such information and give to him such access to and facilities for inspecting and taking copies of documents (being information or documents in the possession or under the control of the liquidator and relating to the matter in question) as the authority requires.

[56] (5) Where a report is made to him under subsection (4), the prosecuting authority may, if he thinks fit, refer the matter to the Secretary of State for further enquiry; and the Secretary of State—

(*a*) shall thereupon investigate the matter reported to him and such other matters relating to the affairs of the company as appear to him to require investigation, and

(*b*) for the purpose of his investigation may exercise any of the powers which are exercisable by inspectors appointed under section 431 or 432 of the Companies Act to investigate a company's affairs.

---

[56] As amended by the Companies Act 1989, s.78.

(6) If it appears to the court in the course of a voluntary winding up that—

(a) any past or present officer of the company, or any member of it, has been guilty as above-mentioned, and
(b) no report with respect to the matter has been made by the liquidator to the prosecuting authority under subsection (4),

the court may (on the application of any person interested in the winding up or of its own motion) direct the liquidator to make such a report.

On a report being made accordingly, this section has effect as though the report had been made in pursuance of subsection (4).

Obligations arising under s.218

219.—(1) For the purpose of an investigation by the Secretary of State under section 218(5), any obligation imposed on a person by any provision of the Companies Act to produce documents or give information to, or otherwise to assist, inspectors appointed as mentioned in that subsection is to be regarded as an obligation similarly to assist the Secretary of State in his investigation.

(2) An answer given by a person to a question put to him in exercise of the powers conferred by section 218(5) may be used in evidence against him.

(3) Where criminal proceedings are instituted by the prosecuting authority or the Secretary of State following any report or reference under section 218, it is the duty of the liquidator and every officer and agent of the company past and present (other than the defendant or defender) to give to that authority or the Secretary of State (as the case may be) all assistance in connection with the prosecution which he is reasonably able to give.

For this purpose "agent" includes any banker or solicitor of the company and any person employed by the company as auditor, whether that person is or is not an officer of the company.

(4) If a person fails or neglects to give assistance in the manner required by subsection (3), the court may, on the application of the prosecuting authority or the Secretary of State (as the case may be) direct the person to comply with that subsection; and if the application is made with respect to a liquidator, the court may (unless it appears that the failure or neglect to comply was due to the liquidator not having in his hands sufficient assets of the company to enable him to do so) direct that the costs shall be borne by the liquidator personally.

PART V[57]

WINDING UP OF UNREGISTERED COMPANIES

Meaning of "unregistered company"

220.—(1) For the purposes of this Part, the expression "unregistered company" includes any trustee savings bank certified under the enactments relating to such banks, any association and any company, with the following exceptions—

(*a*) a railway company incorporated by Act of Parliament,
(*b*) a company registered in any part of the United Kingdom under the Joint Stock Companies Acts or under the legislation (past or present) relating to companies in Great Britain.

(2) On such day as the Treasury appoints by order under section 4(3) of the Trustee Savings Banks Act 1985, the words in subsection (1) from "any trustee" to "banks" cease to have effect and are hereby repealed.

Winding up of unregistered companies

221.—(1) Subject to the provisions of this Part, any unregistered company may be wound up under this Act; and all the provisions of this Act and the Companies Act about winding up apply to any unregistered company with the exceptions and additions mentioned in the following subsections.

(2) If an unregistered company has a principal place of business situated in Northern Ireland, it shall not be wound up under this Part unless it has a principal place of business situated in England and Wales or Scotland, or in both England and Wales and Scotland.

(3) For the purpose of determining a court's winding-up jurisdiction, an unregistered company is deemed—

(*a*) to be registered in England and Wales or Scotland, according as its principal place of business is situated in England and Wales or Scotland, or
(*b*) if it has a principal place of business situated in both countries, to be registered in both countries;

and the principal place of business situated in that part of Great Britain in which proceedings are being instituted is, for all purposes of the winding up, deemed to be the registered office of the company.

(4) No unregistered company shall be wound up under this Act voluntarily.

(5) The circumstances in which an unregistered company may be wound up are as follows—

(*a*) if the company is dissolved, or has ceased to carry on business,

---

[57] See the Criminal Justice (Scotland) Act 1987, s.35(4), and the Criminal Justice Act 1988, s.86(5).

or is carrying on business only for the purpose of winding up its affairs;

(b) if the company is unable to pay its debts;

(c) if the court is of opinion that it is just and equitable that the company should be wound up.

(6) A petition for winding up a trustee savings bank may be presented by the Trustee Savings Banks Central Board or by a commissioner appointed under section 35 of the Trustee Savings Banks Act 1981 as well as by any person authorised under Part IV of this Act to present a petition for the winding up of a company.

On such day as the Treasury appoints by order under section 4(3) of the Trustee Savings Banks Act 1985, this subsection ceases to have effect and is hereby repealed.

(7) In Scotland, an unregistered company which the Court of Session has jurisdiction to wind up may be wound up by the court if there is subsisting a floating charge over property comprised in the company's property and undertaking, and the court is satisfied that the security of the creditor entitled to the benefit of the floating charge is in jeopardy.

For this purpose a creditor's security is deemed to be in jeopardy if the court is satisfied that events have occurred or are about to occur which render it unreasonable in the creditor's interests that the company should retain power to dispose of the property which is subject to the floating charge.

Inability to pay debts: unpaid creditor for £750 or more

222.—(1) An unregistered company is deemed (for the purposes of section 221) unable to pay its debts if there is a creditor, by assignment or otherwise, to whom the company is indebted in a sum exceeding £750 then due and—

(a) the creditor has served on the company, by leaving at its principal place of business, or by delivering to the secretary or some director, manager or principal officer of the company, or by otherwise serving in such manner as the court may approve or direct, a written demand in the prescribed form requiring the company to pay the sum due, and

(b) the company has for three weeks after the service of the demand neglected to pay the sum or to secure or compound for it to the creditor's satisfaction.

(2) The money sum for the time being specified in subsection (1) is subject to increase or reduction by regulations under section 417 in Part XV; but no increase in the sum so specified affects any case in which the winding-up petition was presented before the coming into force of the increase.

Inability to pay debts: debt remaining unsatisfied after action brought

223. An unregistered company is deemed (for the purposes of

section 221) unable to pay its debts if an action or other proceeding has been instituted against any member for any debt or demand due, or claimed to be due, from the company, or from him in his character of member, and—

(a) notice in writing of the institution of the action or proceeding has been served on the company by leaving it at the company's principal place of business (or by delivering it to the secretary, or some director, manager or principal officer of the company, or by otherwise serving it in such manner as the court may approve or direct), and

(b) the company has not within three weeks after service of the notice paid, secured or compounded for the debt or demand, or procured the action or proceeding to be stayed or sisted, or indemnified the defendant or defender to his reasonable satisfaction against the action or proceeding, and against all costs, damages and expenses to be incurred by him because of it.

Inability to pay debts: other cases

224.—(1) An unregistered company is deemed (for purposes of section 221) unable to pay its debts—

(a) if in England and Wales execution or other process issued on a judgment, decree or order obtained in any court in favour of a creditor against the company, or any member of it as such, or any person authorised to be sued as nominal defendant on behalf of the company, is returned unsatisfied;

(b) if in Scotland the *induciae* of a charge for payment on an extract decree, or an extract registered bond, or an extract registered protest, have expired without payment being made;

(c) if in Northern Ireland a certificate of unenforceability has been granted in respect of any judgment, decree or order obtained as mentioned in paragraph (a);

(d) if it is otherwise proved to the satisfaction of the court that the company is unable to pay its debts as they fall due.

(2) An unregistered company is also deemed unable to pay its debts if it is proved to the satisfaction of the court that the value of the company's assets is less than the amount of its liabilities, taking into account its contingent and prospective liabilities.

Oversea company may be wound up though dissolved

225. Where a company incorporated outside Great Britain which has been carrying on business in Great Britain ceases to carry on business in Great Britain, it may be wound up as an unregistered company under this Act, notwithstanding that it has been dissolved or otherwise ceased to exist as a company under or by virtue of the laws of the country under which it was incorporated.

Contributories in winding up of unregistered company

226.—(1) In the event of an unregistered company being wound up, every person is deemed a contributory who is liable to pay or contribute to the payment of any debt or liability of the company, or to pay or contribute to the payment of any sum for the adjustment of the rights of members among themselves, or to pay or contribute to the payment of the expenses of winding up the company.

(2) Every contributory is liable to contribute to the company's assets all sums due from him in respect of any such liability as is mentioned above.

(3) In the case of an unregistered company engaged in or formed for working mines within the stannaries, a past member is not liable to contribute to the assets if he has ceased to be a member for two years or more either before the mine ceased to be worked or before the date of the winding-up order.

(4) In the event of the death, bankruptcy or insolvency of any contributory, the provisions of this Act with respect to the personal representatives, to the heirs and legatees of heritage of the heritable estate in Scotland of deceased contributories, and to the trustees of bankrupt or insolvent contributories, respectively apply.

Power of court to stay, sist or restrain proceedings

227. The provisions of this Part with respect to staying, sisting or restraining actions and proceedings against a company at any time after the presentation of a petition for winding up and before the making of a winding-up order extend, in the case of an unregistered company, where the application to stay, sist or restrain is presented by a creditor, to actions and proceedings against any contributory of the company.

Actions stayed on winding-up order

228. Where an order has been made for winding up an unregistered company, no action or proceeding shall be proceeded with or commenced against any contributory of the company in respect of any debt of the company, except by leave of the court, and subject to such terms as the court may impose.

Provisions of this Part to be cumulative

229.—(1) The provisions of this Part with respect to unregistered companies are in addition to and not in restriction of any provisions in Part IV with respect to winding up companies by the court; and the court or liquidator may exercise any powers or do any act in the case of unregistered companies which might be exercised or done by it or him in winding up companies formed and registered under the Companies Act.

(2) However, an unregistered company is not, except in the event of its being wound up, deemed to be a company under the Companies Act, and then only to the extent provided by this Part of this Act.

Part VI[58]

Miscellaneous Provisions Applying to Companies Which
are Insolvent or in Liquidation

Office-holders

Holders of office to be qualified insolvency practitioners

230.—(1) Where an administration order is made in relation to a company, the administrator must be a person who is qualified to act as an insolvency practitioner in relation to the company.

(2) Where an administrative receiver of a company is appointed, he must be a person who is so qualified.

(3) Where a company goes into liquidation, the liquidator must be a person who is so qualified.

(4) Where a provisional liquidator is appointed, he must be a person who is so qualified.

(5) Subsections (3) and (4) are without prejudice to any enactment under which the official receiver is to be, or may be, liquidator or provisional liquidator.

Appointment to office of two or more persons

231.—(1) This section applies if an appointment or nomination of any person to the office of administrator, administrative receiver, liquidator or provisional liquidator—

(*a*) relates to more than one person, or

(*b*) has the effect that the office is to be held by more than one person.

(2) The appointment or nomination shall declare whether any act required or authorised under any enactment to be done by the administrator, administrative receiver, liquidator or provisional liquidator is to be done by all or any one or more of the persons for the time being holding the office in question.

Validity of office-holder's acts

232. The acts of an individual as administrator, administrative receiver, liquidator or provisional liquidator of a company are valid notwithstanding any defect in his appointment, nomination or qualifications.

Management by administrators, liquidators, etc.

Supplies of gas, water, electricity, etc.

[59] **233.**—(1) This section applies in the case of a company where—

---

[58] Applied by the Building Societies Act 1986, Sched. 15, Pt. I, with effect from 1st January 1988.

[59] As amended by the Electricity Act 1989, Sched. 16, para. 35 and the Broadcasting Act 1990, Sched. 20, para. 43, with effect from 1st January 1991.

(*a*) an administration order is made in relation to the company, or

(*b*) an administrative receiver is appointed, or

(*c*) a voluntary arrangement under Part I, approved by meetings summoned under section 3, has taken effect, or

(*d*) the company goes into liquidation, or

(*e*) a provisional liquidator is appointed;

and "the office-holder" means the administrator, the administrative receiver, the supervisor of the voluntary arrangement, the liquidator or the provisional liquidator, as the case may be.

(2) If a request is made by or with the concurrence of the office-holder for the giving, after the effective date, of any of the supplies mentioned in the next subsection, the supplier—

(*a*) may make it a condition of the giving of the supply that the office-holder personally guarantees the payment of any charges in respect of the supply, but

(*b*) shall not make it a condition of the giving of the supply, or do anything which has the effect of making it a condition of the giving of the supply, that any outstanding charges in respect of a supply given to the company before the effective date are paid.

(3) The supplies referred to in subsection (2) are—

(*a*) a public supply of gas,

(*b*) a public supply of electricity,

(*c*) a supply of water by statutory water undertakers or, in Scotland, a water authority,

(*d*) a supply of telecommunication services by a public telecommunications operator.

(4) "The effective date" for the purposes of this section is whichever is applicable of the following dates—

(*a*) the date on which the administration order was made,

(*b*) the date on which the administrative receiver was appointed (or, if he was appointed in succession to another administrative receiver, the date on which the first of his predecessors was appointed),

(*c*) the date on which the voluntary arrangement was approved by the meetings summoned under section 3,

(*d*) the date on which the company went into liquidation,

(*e*) the date on which the provisional liquidator was appointed.

(5) The following applies to expressions used in subsection (3)—

(*a*) "public supply of gas" means a supply of gas by the British Gas Corporation or a public gas supplier within the meaning of Part I of the Gas Act 1986,

(*b*) "public supply of electricity" means a supply of electricity by a public electricity supplier within the meaning of Part I of the Electricity Act 1989,

(c) "water authority" means the same as in the Water (Scotland) Act 1980, and

(d) "telecommunication services" and "public telecommunications operator" mean the same as in the Telecommunications Act 1984, except that the former does not include local delivery services within the meaning of Part II of the Broadcasting Act 1990.

Getting in the company's property

234.—(1) This section applies in the case of a company where—

(a) an administration order is made in relation to the company, or

(b) an administrative receiver is appointed, or

(c) the company goes into liquidation, or

(d) a provisional liquidator is appointed;

and "the office-holder" means the administrator, the administrative receiver, the liquidator or the provisional liquidator, as the case may be.

(2) Where any person has in his possession or control any property, books, papers or records to which the company appears to be entitled, the court may require that person forthwith (or within such period as the court may direct) to pay, deliver, convey, surrender or transfer the property, books, papers or records to the office-holder.

(3) Where the office-holder—

(a) seizes or disposes of any property which is not property of the company, and

(b) at the time of seizure or disposal believes, and has reasonable grounds for believing, that he is entitled (whether in pursuance of an order of the court or otherwise) to seize or dispose of that property.

the next subsection has effect.

(4) In that case the office-holder—

(a) is not liable to any person in respect of any loss or damage resulting from the seizure or disposal except in so far as that loss or damage is caused by the office-holder's own negligence, and

(b) has a lien on the property, or the proceeds of its sale, for such expenses as were incurred in connection with the seizure or disposal.

Duty to co-operate with office-holder

235.—(1) This section applies as does section 234; and it also applies, in the case of a company in respect of which a winding-up order has been made by the court in England and Wales, as if references to the office-holder included the official receiver, whether or not he is the liquidator.

(2) Each of the persons mentioned in the next subsection shall—

(*a*) give to the office-holder such information concerning the company and its promotion, formation, business, dealings, affairs or property as the office-holder may at any time after the effective date reasonably require, and

(*b*) attend on the office-holder at such times as the latter may reasonably require.

(3) The persons referred to above are—

(*a*) those who are or have at any time been officers of the company,

(*b*) those who have taken part in the formation of the company at any time within one year before the effective date,

(*c*) those who are in the employment of the company, or have been in its employment (including employment under a contract for services) within that year, and are in the office-holder's opinion capable of giving information which he requires,

(*d*) those who are, or have within that year been, officers of, or in the employment (including employment under a contract for services) of, another company which is, or within that year was, an officer of the company in question, and

(*e*) in the case of a company being wound up by the court, any person who has acted as administrator, administrative receiver or liquidator of the company

(4) For the purposes of subsections (2) and (3), "the effective date" is whichever is applicable of the following dates—

(*a*) the date on which the administration order was made,

(*b*) the date on which the administrative receiver was appointed or, if he was appointed in succession to another administrative receiver, the date on which the first of his predecessors was appointed,

(*c*) the date on which the provisional liquidator was appointed, and

(*d*) the date on which the company went into liquidation.

(5) If a person without reasonable excuse fails to comply with any obligation imposed by this section, he is liable to a fine and, for continued contravention, to a daily default fine.

Inquiry into company's dealings, etc.

236.—(1) This section applies as does section 234; and it also applies in the case of a company in respect of which a winding-up order has been made by the court in England and Wales as if references to the office-holder included the official receiver, whether or not he is the liquidator.

(2) The court may, on the application of the office-holder, summon to appear before it—

(*a*) any officer of the company,

(*b*) any person known or suspected to have in his possession any property of the company or supposed to be indebted to the company, or

(c) any person whom the court thinks capable of giving information concerning the promotion, formation, business, dealings, affairs or property of the company.

(3) The court may require any such person as is mentioned in subsection (2)(*a*) to (*c*) to submit an affidavit to the court containing an account of his dealings with the company or to produce any books, papers or other records in his possession or under his control relating to the company or the matters mentioned in paragraph (*c*) of the subsection.

(4) The following applies in a case where—

(*a*) a person without reasonable excuse fails to appear before the court when he is summoned to do so under this section, or

(*b*) there are reasonable grounds for believing that a person has absconded, or is about to abscond, with a view to avoiding his appearance before the court under this section.

(5) The court may, for the purpose of bringing that person and anything in his possession before the court, cause a warrant to be issued to a constable or prescribed officer of the court—

(*a*) for the arrest of that person, and

(*b*) for the seizure of any books, papers, records, money or goods in that person's possession.

(6) The court may authorise a person arrested under such a warrant to be kept in custody, and anything seized under such a warrant to be held, in accordance with the rules, until that person is brought before the court under the warrant or until such other time as the court may order.

Court's enforcement powers under s.236

237.—(1) If it appears to the court, on consideration of any evidence obtained under section 236 or this section, that any person has in his possession any property of the company, the court may, on the application of the office-holder, order that person to deliver the whole or any part of the property to the office-holder at such time, in such manner and on such terms as the court thinks fit.

(2) If it appears to the court, on consideration of any evidence so obtained, that any person is indebted to the company, the court may, on the application of the office-holder, order that person to pay to the office-holder, at such time and in such manner as the court may direct, the whole or any part of the amount due, whether in full discharge of the debt or otherwise, as the court thinks fit.

(3) The court may, if it thinks fit, order that any person who if within the jurisdiction of the court would be liable to be summoned to appear before it under section 236 or this section shall be examined in any part

of the United Kingdom where he may for the time being be, or in a place outside the United Kingdom.

(4) Any person who appears or is brought before the court under section 236 or this section may be examined on oath, either orally or (except in Scotland) by interrogatories, concerning the company or the matters mentioned in section 236(2)(c).

Adjustment of prior transactions (administration and liquidation)

[60] **238.**—(1) This section applies in the case of a company where—

(a) an administration order is made in relation to the company, or
(b) the company goes into liquidation;

and "the office-holder" means the administrator or the liquidator, as the case may be.

· · · · · ·

Gratuitous alienations (Scotland)

242.—(1) Where this subsection applies and—

(a) the winding up of a company has commenced, an alienation by the company is challengeable by—
(i) any creditor who is a creditor by virtue of a debt incurred on or before the date of such commencement, or
(ii) the liquidator;
(b) an administration order is in force in relation to a company, and alienation by the company is challengeable by the administrator.

(2) Subsection (1) applies where—

(a) by the alienation, whether before or after 1st April 1986 (the coming into force of section 75 of the Bankruptcy (Scotland) Act 1985), any part of the company's property is transferred or any claim or right of the company is discharged or renounced, and
(b) the alienation takes place on a relevant day.

(3) For the purposes of subsection (2)(b), the day on which an alienation takes place is the day on which it becomes completely effectual; and in that subsection "relevant day" means, if the alienation has the effect of favouring—

(a) a person who is an associate (within the meaning of the Bankruptcy (Scotland) Act 1985) of the company, a day not earlier than five years before the date on which—
(i) the winding up of the company commences, or
(ii) as the case may be, the administration order is made; or

---

[60] Not applicable to Scotland; but see ss.244 and 245.

(*b*) any other person, a day not earlier than two years before that date.

(4) On a challenge being brought under subsection (1), the court shall grant decree of reduction or for such restoration of property to the company's assets or other redress as may be appropriate; but the court shall not grant such a decree if the person seeking to uphold the alienation establishes—

(*a*) that immediately, or at any other time, after the alienation the company's assets were greater than its liabilities, or
(*b*) that the alienation was made for adequate consideration, or
(*c*) that the alienation—
　　(i) was a birthday, Christmas or other conventional gift, or
　　(ii) was a gift made, for a charitable purpose, to a person who is not an associate of the company,
　　which, having regard to all the circumstances, it was reasonable for the company to make:

Provided that this subsection is without prejudice to any right or interest acquired in good faith and for value from or through the transferee in the alienation.

(5) In subsection (4) above, "charitable purpose" means any charitable, benevolent or philanthropic purpose, whether or not it is charitable within the meaning of any rule of law.

(6) For the purposes of the foregoing provisions of this section, an alienation in implementation of a prior obligation is deemed to be one for which there was no consideration or no adequate consideration to the extent that the prior obligation was undertaken for no consideration or no adequate consideration.

(7) A liquidator and an administrator have the same right as a creditor has under any rule of law to challenge an alienation of a company made for no consideration or no adequate consideration.

(8) This section applies to Scotland only.

Unfair preferences (Scotland)

243.—(1) Subject to subsection (2) below, subsection (4) below applies to a transaction entered into by a company, whether before or after 1st April 1986, which has the effect of creating a preference in favour of a creditor to the prejudice of the general body of creditors, being a preference created not earlier than six months before the commencement of the winding up of the company or the making of an administration order in relation to the company.

(2) Subsection (4) below does not apply to any of the following transactions—

(*a*) a transaction in the ordinary course of trade or business;
(*b*) a payment in cash for a debt which when it was paid had become payable, unless the transaction was collusive with the purpose of prejudicing the general body of creditors;

(c) a transaction whereby the parties to it undertake reciprocal obligations (whether the performance by the parties of their respective obligations occurs at the same time or at different times) unless the transaction was collusive as aforesaid;

(d) the granting of a mandate by a company authorising an arrestee to pay over the arrested funds or part thereof to the arrester where—

   (i) there has been a decree for payment or a warrant for summary diligence, and

   (ii) the decree or warrant has been preceded by an arrestment on the dependence of the action or followed by an arrestment in execution.

(3) For the purposes of subsection (1) above, the day on which a preference was created is the day on which the preference became completely effectual.

(4) A transaction to which this subsection applies is challengeable by—

(a) in the case of a winding up—

   (i) any creditor who is a creditor by virtue of a debt incurred on or before the date of commencement of the winding up, or

   (ii) the liquidator; and

(b) in the case of an administration order, the administrator.

(5) On a challenge being brought under subsection (4) above, the court, if satisfied that the transaction challenged is a transaction to which this section applies, shall grant decree of reduction or for such restoration of property to the company's assets or other redress as may be appropriate:

Provided that this subsection is without prejudice to any right or interest acquired in good faith and for value from or through the creditor in whose favour the preference was created.

(6) A liquidator and an administrator have the same right as a creditor has under any rule of law to challenge a preference created by a debtor.

(7) This section applies to Scotland only.

Extortionate credit transactions

244.—(1) This section applies as does section 238, and where the company is, or has been, a party to a transaction for, or involving, the provision of credit to the company.

(2) The court may, on the application of the office-holder, make an order with respect to the transaction if the transaction is or was extortionate and was entered into in the period of three years ending with the day on which the administration order was made or (as the case may be) the company went into liquidation.

(3) For the purposes of this section a transaction is extortionate if, having regard to the risk accepted by the person providing the credit—

(*a*) the terms of it are or were such as to require grossly exorbitant payments to be made (whether unconditionally or in certain contingencies) in respect of the provisions of the credit, or

(*b*) it otherwise grossly contravened ordinary principles of fair dealing;

and it shall be presumed, unless the contrary is proved, that a transaction with respect to which an application is made under this section is or, as the case may be, was extortionate.

(4) An order under this section with respect to any transaction may contain such one or more of the following as the court thinks fit, that is to say—

(*a*) provision setting aside the whole or part of any obligation created by the transaction,

(*b*) provision otherwise varying the terms of the transaction or varying the terms on which any security for the purposes of the transaction is held,

(*c*) provision requiring any person who is or was a party to the transaction to pay to the office-holder any sums paid to that person, by virtue of the transaction, by the company,

(*d*) provision requiring any person to surrender to the office-holder any property held by him as security for the purposes of the transaction,

(*e*) provision directing accounts to be taken between any persons.

(5) The powers conferred by this section are exercisable in relation to any transaction concurrently with any powers exercisable in relation to that transaction as a transaction at an undervalue or under section 242 (gratuitous alienations in Scotland).

Avoidance of certain floating charges

245.—(1) This section applies as does section 238, but applies to Scotland as well as to England and Wales.

(2) Subject as follows, a floating charge on the company's undertaking or property created at a relevant time is invalid except to the extent of the aggregate of—

(*a*) the value of so much of the consideration for the creation of the charge as consists of money paid, or goods or services supplied, to the company at the same time as, or after, the creation of the charge,

(*b*) the value of so much of that consideration as consists of the discharge or reduction, at the same time as, or after, the creation of the charge, of any debt of the company, and

(*c*) the amount of such interest (if any) as is payable on the amount falling within paragraph (*a*) or (*b*) in pursuance of any agreement under which the money was so paid, the goods or services were so supplied or the debt was so discharged or reduced.

(3) Subject to the next subsection, the time at which a floating charge is created by a company is a relevant time for the purposes of this section if the charge is created—

(*a*) in the case of a charge which is created in favour of a person who is connected with the company, at a time in the period of two years ending with the onset of insolvency,

(*b*) in the case of a charge which is created in favour of any other person, at a time in the period of 12 months ending with the onset of insolvency, or

(*c*) in either case, at a time between the presentation of a petition for the making of an administration order in relation to the company and the making of such an order on that petition.

(4) Where a company creates a floating charge at a time mentioned in subsection (3)(*b*) and the person in favour of whom the charge is created is not connected with the company, that time is not a relevant time for the purposes of this section unless the company—

(*a*) is at that time unable to pay its debts within the meaning of section 123 in Chapter VI of Part IV, or

(*b*) becomes unable to pay its debts within the meaning of that section in consequence of the transaction under which the charge is created.

(5) For the purposes of subsection (3), the onset of insolvency is—

(*a*) in a case where this section applies by reason of the making of an administration order, the date of the presentation of the petition on which the order was made, and

(*b*) in a case where this section applies by reason of a company going into liquidation, the date of the commencement of the winding up.

(6) For the purposes of subsection (2)(*a*) the value of any goods or services supplied by way of consideration for a floating charge is the amount in money which at the time they were supplied could reasonably have been expected to be obtained for supplying the goods or services in the ordinary course of business and on the same terms (apart from the consideration) as those on which they were supplied to the company.

.   .   .   .   .   .

Part VII[61]

Interpretation for First Group of Parts

"Insolvency" and "go into liquidation"

247.—(1) In this Group of Parts, except in so far as the context otherwise requires, "insolvency", in relation to a company, includes the approval of a voluntary arrangement under Part I, the making of an administration order or the appointment of an administrative receiver.

(2) For the purposes of any provision in this Group of Parts, a company goes into liquidation if it passes a resolution for voluntary winding up or an order for its winding up is made by the court at a time when it has not already gone into liquidation by passing such a resolution.

"Secured creditor", etc.

248. In this Group of Parts, except in so far as the context otherwise requires—

(*a*) "secured creditor", in relation to a company, means a creditor of the company who holds in respect of his debt a security over property of the company, and "unsecured creditor" is to be read accordingly; and

(*b*) "security" means—

(i) in relation to England and Wales, any mortgage, charge, lien or other security, and

(ii) in relation to Scotland, any security (whether heritable or moveable), any floating charge and any right of lien or preference and any right of retention (other than a right of compensation or set off).

"Connected" with a company

249. For the purposes of any provision in this Group of Parts, a person is connected with a company if—

(*a*) he is a director or shadow director of the company or an associate of such a director or shadow director, or

(*b*) he is an associate of the company;

and "associate" has the meaning given by section 435 in Part XVIII of this Act.

"Member" of a company

250. For the purposes of any provision in this Group of Parts, a person who is not a member of a company but to whom shares in the company have been transferred, or transmitted by operation of law, is

---

[61] Applied by the Building Societies Act 1986, Sched. 15, Pt. I, with effect from 1st January 1988.

to be regarded as a member of the company, and references to a member or members are to be read accordingly.

Expressions used generally

251. In this Group of Parts, except in so far as the context otherwise requires—

"administrative receiver" means—

(*a*) an administrative receiver as defined by section 29(2) in Chapter I of Part III, or

(*b*) a receiver appointed under section 51 in Chapter II of that Part in a case where the whole (or substantially the whole) of the company's property is attached by the floating charge;

"business day" means any day other than a Saturday, a Sunday, Christmas Day, Good Friday or a day which is a bank holiday in any part of Great Britain;

"chattel leasing agreement" means an agreement for the bailment or, in Scotland, the hiring of goods which is capable of subsisting for more than three months;

"contributory" has the meaning given by section 79;

"director" includes any person occupying the position of director, by whatever name called;

"floating charge" means a charge which, as created, was a floating charge and includes a floating charge within section 462 of the Companies Act (Scottish floating charges);

"office copy", in relation to Scotland, means a copy certified by the clerk of court;

"the official rate", in relation to interest, means the rate payable under section 189(4);

"prescribed" means prescribed by the rules;

"receiver", in the expression "receiver or manager", does not include a receiver appointed under section 51 in Chapter II of Part III;

"retention of title agreement" means an agreement for the sale of goods to a company, being an agreement—

(*a*) which does not constitute a charge on the goods, but

(*b*) under which, if the seller is not paid and the company is wound up, the seller will have priority over all other creditors of the company as respects the goods or any property representing the goods;

"the rules" means rules under section 411 in Part XV; and

"shadow director", in relation to a company, means a person in accordance with whose directions or instructions the directors of the company are accustomed to act (but so that a person is not deemed a shadow director by reason only that the directors act on advice given by him in a professional capacity);

and any expression for whose interpretation provision is made by Part XXVI of the Companies Act, other than an expression defined above in this section, is to be construed in accordance with that provision.

. . . . . .

THE THIRD GROUP OF PARTS
MISCELLANEOUS MATTERS BEARING ON BOTH COMPANY AND INDIVIDUAL
INSOLVENCY; GENERAL INTERPRETATION; FINAL PROVISIONS

PART XII[62]

PREFERENTIAL DEBTS IN COMPANY AND INDIVIDUAL INSOLVENCY

Categories of preferential debts

386.—[63] (1) A reference in this Act to the preferential debts of a company or an individual is to the debts listed in Schedule 6 to this Act (money owed to the Inland Revenue for income tax deducted at source; VAT, car tax, betting and gaming duties; social security and pension scheme contributions; remuneration etc. of employees; levies on coal and steel production); and references to preferential creditors are to be read accordingly.

(2) In that Schedule "the debtor" means the company or the individual concerned.

(3) Schedule 6 is to be read with Schedule 3 to the Social Security Pensions Act 1975 (occupational pension scheme contributions).

"The relevant date"

387.—(1) This section explains references in Schedule 6 to the relevant date (being the date which determines the existence and amount of a preferential debt).

(2) For the purposes of section 4 in Part I (meetings to consider company voluntary arrangement), the relevant date in relation to a company which is not being wound up is—

(a) where an administration order is in force in relation to the company, the date of the making of that order, and

(b) where no such order has been made, the date of the approval of the voluntary arrangement.

(3) In relation to a company which is being wound up, the following applies—

(a) if the winding up is by the court, and the winding-up order was made immediately upon the discharge of an administration order, the relevant date is the date of the making of the administration order;

---

[63] As amended by S.I. 1987 No. 2093.

(*b*) if the case does not fall within paragraph (*a*) and the company—
  (i) is being wound up by the court, and
  (ii) had not commenced to be wound up voluntarily before the date of the making of the winding-up order,
  the relevant date is the date of the appointment (or first appointment) of a provisional liquidator or, if no such appointment has been made, the date of the winding-up order;
(*c*) if the case does not fall within either paragraph (*a*) or (*b*), the relevant date is the date of the passing of the resolution for the winding up of the company.

(4) In relation to a company in receivership (where section 40 or, as the case may be, section 59 applies), the relevant date is—

(*a*) in England and Wales, the date of the appointment of the receiver by debenture-holders, and
(*b*) in Scotland, the date of the appointment of the receiver under section 53(6) or (as the case may be) 54(5).

(5) For the purposes of section 258 in Part VIII (individual voluntary arrangements), the relevant date is, in relation to a debtor who is not an undischarged bankrupt, the date of the interim order made under section 252 with respect to his proposal.

(6) In relation to a bankrupt, the following applies—

(*a*) where at the time the bankruptcy order was made there was an interim receiver appointed under section 286, the relevant date is the date on which the interim receiver was first appointed after the presentation of the bankruptcy petition;
(*b*) otherwise, the relevant date is the date of the making of the bankruptcy order.

PART XIII

INSOLVENCY PRACTITIONERS AND THEIR QUALIFICATION

Restrictions on unqualified persons acting as liquidator, trustee in bankruptcy, etc.

Meaning of "act as insolvency practitioner"

388.—(1) A person acts as an insolvency practitioner in relation to a company by acting—

(*a*) as its liquidator, provisional liquidator, administrator or administrative receiver, or
(*b*) as supervisor of a voluntary arrangement approved by it under Part I.

(2) A person acts as an insolvency practitioner in relation to an individual by acting—

(*a*) as his trustee in bankruptcy or interim receiver of his property or as permanent or interim trustee in the sequestration of his estate; or

(b) as trustee under a deed which is a deed of arrangement made for the benefit of his creditors or, in Scotland, a trust deed for his creditors; or

(c) as supervisor of a voluntary arrangement proposed by him and approved under Part VIII; or

(d) in the case of a deceased individual to the administration of whose estate this section applies by virtue of an order under section 421 (application of provisions of this Act to insolvent estates of deceased persons), as administrator of that estate.

(3) References in this section to an individual include, except in so far as the context otherwise requires, references to a partnership and to any debtor within the meaning of the Bankruptcy (Scotland) Act 1985.

(4) In this section—

"administrative receiver" has the meaning given by section 251 in Part VII;

"company" means a company within the meaning given by section 735(1) of the Companies Act or a company which may be wound up under Part V of this Act (unregistered companies); and

"interim trustee" and "permanent trustee" mean the same as in the Bankruptcy (Scotland) Act 1985.

[64] (5) Nothing in this section applies to anything done by the official receiver.

Acting without qualification an offence

389.—(1) A person who acts as an insolvency practitioner in relation to a company or an individual at a time when he is not qualified to do so is liable to imprisonment or a fine, or to both.

[65] (2) This section does not apply to the official receiver.

The requisite qualification, and the means of obtaining it

Persons not qualified to act as insolvency practitioners

[66] **390.**—(1) A person who is not an individual is not qualified to act as an insolvency practitioner.

(2) A person is not qualified to act as an insolvency practitioner at any time unless at that time—

---

[64] Substituted (*prosp.*) by the Bankruptcy (Scotland) Act 1993, s.11(1), as follows:
"(5) Nothing in this subsection applies to anything done by—
  (a) the official receiver; or
  (b) the Accountant in Bankruptcy (within the meaning of the Bankruptcy (Scotland) Act 1985)."

[65] Amended (*prosp.*) by the Bankruptcy (Scotland) Act 1993, s.11(2), as follows: at the end of the subsection, insert the words "or the Accountant in Bankruptcy (within the meaning of the Bankruptcy (Scotland) Act 1985)."

[66] For regulations see S.I. 1986 No. 1995, as amended by S.I. 1986 No. 2247.

(*a*) he is authorised so to act by virtue of membership of a professional body recognised under section 391 below, being permitted so to act by or under the rules of that body, or

(*b*) he holds an authorisation granted by a competent authority under section 393.

(3) A person is not qualified to act as an insolvency practitioner in relation to another person at any time unless—

(*a*) there is in force at that time security or, in Scotland, caution for the proper performance of his functions, and

(*b*) that security or caution meets the prescribed requirements with respect to his so acting in relation to that other person.

(4) A person is not qualified to act as an insolvency practitioner at any time if at that time—

(*a*) he has been adjudged bankrupt or sequestration of his estate has been awarded and (in either case) he has not been discharged,

(*b*) he is subject to a disqualification order made under the Company Directors Disqualification Act 1986, or

(*c*) he is a patient within the meaning of Part VII of the Mental Health Act 1983 or section 125(1) of the Mental Health (Scotland) Act 1984.

Recognised professional bodies

391.—(1) The Secretary of State may by order declare a body which appears to him to fall within subsection (2) below to be a recognised professional body for the purposes of this section.

(2) A body may be recognised if it regulates the practice of a profession and maintains and enforces rules for securing that such of its members as are permitted by or under the rules to act as insolvency practitioners—

(*a*) are fit and proper persons so to act, and

(*b*) meet acceptable requirements as to education and practical training and experience.

(3) References to members of a recognised professional body are to persons who, whether members of that body or not, are subject to its rules in the practice of the profession in question.

The reference in section 390(2) above to membership of a professional body recognised under this section is to be read accordingly.

(4) An order made under subsection (1) in relation to a professional body may be revoked by a further order if it appears to the Secretary of State that the body no longer falls within subsection (2).

(5) An order of the Secretary of State under this section has effect from such date as is specified in the order; and any such order revoking a previous order may make provision whereby members of the body in

question continue to be treated as authorised to act as insolvency practitioners for a specified period after the revocation takes effect.

Authorisation by competent authority

[67] **392.**—(1) Application may be made to a competent authority for authorisation to act as an insolvency practitioner.

(2) The competent authorities for this purpose are—

(a) in relation to a case of any description specified in directions given by the Secretary of State, the body or person so specified in relation to cases of that description, and

(b) in relation to a case not falling within paragraph (a), the Secretary of State.

(3) The application—

(a) shall be made in such manner as the competent authority may direct,

(b) shall contain or be accompanied by such information as that authority may reasonably require for the purpose of determining the application, and

(c) shall be accompanied by the prescribed fee;

and the authority may direct that notice of the making of the application shall be published in such manner as may be specified in the direction.

(4) At any time after receiving the application and before determining it the authority may require the applicant to furnish additional information.

(5) Directions and requirements given or imposed under subsection (3) or (4) may differ as between different applications.

(6) Any information to be furnished to the competent authority under this section shall, if it so requires, be in such form or verified in such manner as it may specify.

(7) An application may be withdrawn before it is granted or refused.

(8) Any sums received under this section by a competent authority other than the Secretary of State may be retained by the authority; and any sums so received by the Secretary of State shall be paid into the Consolidated Fund.

Grant, refusal and withdrawal of authorisation

[68] **393.**—(1) The competent authority may, on an application duly made in accordance with section 392 and after being furnished with all such information as it may require under that section, grant or refuse the application.

(2) The authority shall grant the application if it appears to it from the

---

[67] For regulations see S.I. 1986 No. 1995, as amended by S.I. 1986 No. 2247.
[68] For regulations see S.I. 1986 No. 1995, as amended by S.I. 1986 No. 2247.

information furnished by the applicant and having regard to such other information, if any, as it may have—

    (*a*) that the applicant is a fit and proper person to act as an insolvency practitioner, and

    (*b*) that the applicant meets the prescribed requirements with respect to education and practical training and experience.

(3) An authorisation granted under this section, if not previously withdrawn, continues in force for such period not exceeding the prescribed maximum as may be specified in the authorisation.

(4) An authorisation so granted may be withdrawn by the competent authority if it appears to it—

    (*a*) that the holder of the authorisation is no longer a fit and proper person to act as an insolvency practitioner, or

    (*b*) without prejudice to paragraph (*a*), that the holder—
        (i) has failed to comply with any provision of this Part or of any regulations made under this Part or Part XV, or
        (ii) in purported compliance with any such provision, has furnished the competent authority with false, inaccurate or misleading information.

(5) An authorisation granted under this section may be withdrawn by the competent authority at the request or with the consent of the holder of the authorisation.

Notices

394.—(1) Where a competent authority grants an authorisation under section 393, it shall give written notice of that fact to the applicant, specifying the date on which the authorisation takes effect.

(2) Where the authority proposes to refuse an application, or to withdraw an authorisation under section 393(4), it shall give the applicant or holder of the authorisation written notice of its intention to do so, setting out particulars of the grounds on which it proposes to act.

(3) In the case of a proposed withdrawal the notice shall state the date on which it is proposed that the withdrawal should take effect.

(4) A notice under subsection (2) shall give particulars of the rights exercisable under the next two sections by a person on whom the notice is served.

Right to make representations

395.—(1) A person on whom a notice is served under section 394(2) may within 14 days after the date of service make written representations to the competent authority.

(2) The competent authority shall have regard to any representations so made in determining whether to refuse the application or withdraw the authorisation, as the case may be.

Reference to Tribunal

396.—(1) The Insolvency Practitioners Tribunal ("the Tribunal") continues in being; and the provisions of Schedule 7 apply to it.

(2) Where a person is served with a notice under section 394(2), he may—

(a) at any time within 28 days after the date of service of the notice, or

(b) at any time after the making by him of representations under section 395 and before the end of the period of 28 days after the date of the service on him of a notice by the competent authority that the authority does not propose to alter its decision in consequence of the representations,

given written notice to the authority requiring the case to be referred to the Tribunal.

(3) Where a requirement is made under subsection (2), then, unless the competent authority—

(a) has decided or decides to grant the application or, as the case may be, not to withdraw the authorisation, and

(b) within seven days after the date of the making of the requirement, gives written notice of that decision to the person by whom the requirement was made,

it shall refer the case to the Tribunal.

Action of Tribunal on reference

397.—(1) On a reference under section 396 the Tribunal shall—

(a) investigate the case, and

(b) make a report to the competent authority stating what would in their opinion be the appropriate decision in the matter and the reasons for that opinion,

and it is the duty of the competent authority to decide the matter accordingly.

(2) The Tribunal shall send a copy of the report to the applicant or, as the case may be, the holder of the authorisation; and the competent authority shall serve him with a written notice of the decision made by it in accordance with the report.

(3) The competent authority may, if he thinks fit, publish the report of the Tribunal.

Refusal or withdrawal without reference to Tribunal

398. Where in the case of any proposed refusal or withdrawal of an authorisation either—

(a) the period mentioned in section 396(2)(a) has expired without the making of any requirement under that subsection or of any representations under section 395, or

(b) the competent authority has given a notice such as is mentioned in section 396(2)(*b*) and the period so mentioned has expired without the making of any such requirement,

the competent authority may give written notice of the refusal or withdrawal to the person concerned in accordance with the proposal in the notice given under section 394(2).

· · · · · ·

PART XV

SUBORDINATE LEGISLATION

General insolvency rules

Company insolvency rules

[69] **411.**—(1) Rules may be made—

(*a*) in relation to England and Wales, by the Lord Chancellor with the concurrence of the Secretary of State, or
(*b*) in relation to Scotland, by the Secretary of State,

for the purpose of giving effect to Parts I to VII of this Act.

(2) Without prejudice to the generality of subsection (1), or to any provision of those Parts by virtue of which rules under this section may be made with respect to any matter, rules under this section may contain—

(*a*) any such provision as is specified in Schedule 8 to this Act or corresponds to provision contained immediately before the coming into force of section 106 of the Insolvency Act 1985 in rules made, or having effect as if made, under section 663(1) or (2) of the Companies Act (old winding-up rules), and
(*b*) such incidental, supplemental and transitional provisions as may appear to the Lord Chancellor or, as the case may be, the Secretary of State necessary or expedient.

(3) In Schedule 8 to this Act "liquidator" includes a provisional liquidator; and references above in this section to Parts I to VII of this Act are to be read as including the Companies Act so far as relating to, and to matters connected with or arising out of, the insolvency or winding up of companies.

(4) Rules under this section shall be made by statutory instrument subject to annulment in pursuance of a resolution of either House of Parliament.

(5) Regulations made by the Secretary of State under a power conferred by rules under this section shall be made by statutory

---

[69] For regulations see S.I. 1986 No. 1925.

instrument and, after being made, shall be laid before each House of Parliament.

(6) Nothing in this section prejudices any power to make rules of court.

. . . . . .

Fees orders

Fees orders (company insolvency proceedings)

414.—(1) There shall be paid in respect of—

(*a*) proceedings under any of Parts I to VII of this Act, and

(*b*) the performance by the official receiver or the Secretary of State of functions under those Parts,

such fees as the competent authority may with the sanction of the Treasury by order direct.

(2) That authority is—

(*a*) in relation to England and Wales, the Lord Chancellor, and

(*b*) in relation to Scotland, the Secretary of State.

(3) The Treasury may by order direct by whom and in what manner the fees are to be collected and accounted for.

(4) The Lord Chancellor may, with the sanction of the Treasury, by order provide for sums to be deposited, by such persons, in such manner and in such circumstances as may be specified in the order, by way of security for fees payable by virtue of this section.

(5) An order under this section may contain such incidental, supplemental and transitional provisions as may appear to the Lord Chancellor, the Secretary of State or (as the case may be) the Treasury necessary or expedient.

(6) An order under this section shall be made by statutory instrument and, after being made, shall be laid before each House of Parliament.

(7) Fees payable by virtue of this section shall be paid into the Consolidated Fund.

(8) References in subsection (1) to Parts I to VII of this Act are to be read as including the Companies Act so far as relating to, and to matters connected with or arising out of, the insolvency or winding up of companies.

(9) Nothing in this section prejudices any power to make rules of court; and the application of this section to Scotland is without prejudice to section 2 of the Courts of Law Fees (Scotland) Act 1895.

. . . . . .

Specification, increase and reduction of money sums relevant in the operation of this Act

Monetary limits (companies winding up)

416.—(1) The Secretary of State may by order in a statutory instrument increase or reduce any of the money sums for the time being specified in the following provisions in the first Group of Parts—

section 117(2) (amount of company's share capital determining whether county court has jurisdiction to wind it up);

section 120(3) (the equivalent as respects sheriff court jurisdiction in Scotland);

section 123(1)(*a*) (minimum debt for service of demand on company by unpaid creditor);

section 184(3) (minimum value of judgment, affecting sheriff's duties on levying execution);

section 206(1)(*a*) and (*b*) (minimum value of company property concealed or fraudulently removed, affecting criminal liability of company's officer).

(2) An order under this section may contain such transitional provisions as may appear to the Secretary of State necessary or expedient.

(3) No order under this section increasing or reducing any of the money sums for the time being specified in section 117(2), 120(3) or 123(1)(*a*) shall be made unless a draft of the order has been laid before and approved by a resolution of each House of Parliament.

(4) A statutory instrument containing an order under this section, other than an order to which subsection (3) applies, is subject to annulment in pursuance of a resolution of either House of Parliament.

Money sum in s.222

417. The Secretary of State may by regulations in a statutory instrument increase or reduce the money sum for the time being specified in section 222(1) (minimum debt for service of demand on unregistered company by unpaid creditor); but such regulations shall not be made unless a draft of the statutory instrument containing them has been approved by resolution of each House of Parliament.

· · · · · ·

Insolvency practice

Regulations for purposes of Part XIII

[70] **419.**—(1) The Secretary of State may make regulations for the purpose of giving effect to Part XIII of this Act; and "prescribed" in that Part means prescribed by regulations made by the Secretary of State.

[70] See S.I. 1986 No. 1995.

(2) Without prejudice to the generality of subsection (1) or to any provision of that Part by virtue of which regulations may be made with respect to any matter, regulations under this section may contain—

(*a*) provision as to the matters to be taken into account in determining whether a person is a fit and proper person to act as an insolvency practitioner;

(*b*) provision prohibiting a person from so acting in prescribed cases, being cases in which a conflict of interest will or may arise;

(*c*) provision imposing requirements with respect to—

    (i) the preparation and keeping by a person who acts as an insolvency practitioner of prescribed books, accounts and other records, and

    (ii) the production of those books, accounts and records to prescribed persons;

(*d*) provision conferring power on prescribed persons—

    (i) to require any person who acts or has acted as an insolvency practitioner to answer any inquiry in relation to a case in which he is so acting or has so acted, and

    (ii) to apply to a court to examine such a person or any other person on oath concerning such a case;

(*e*) provision making non-compliance with any of the regulations a criminal offence; and

(*f*) such incidental, supplemental and transitional provisions as may appear to the Secretary of State necessary or expedient.

(3) Any power conferred by Part XIII or this Part to make regulations, rules or orders is exercisable by statutory instrument subject to annulment by resolution of either House of Parliament.

(4) Any rule or regulation under Part XIII or this Part may make different provision with respect to different cases or descriptions of cases, including different provision for different areas.

Other order-making powers

. . . . . .

Recognised banks, etc.

422.—[71] (1) The Secretary of State may, by order made with the concurrence of the Treasury and after consultation with the Bank of England, provide that such provisions in the first Group of Parts as may be specified in the order shall apply in relation to authorised institutions and former authorised institutions within the meaning of the Banking Act 1987 with such modifications as may be so specified.

(2) An order under this section may make different provision for different cases and may contain such incidental, supplemental and

---

[71] As amended by the Banking Act 1987, Sched. 6, para. 25.

transitional provisions as may appear to the Secretary of State necessary or expedient.

(3) An order under this section shall be made by statutory instrument subject to annulment in pursuance of a resolution of either House of Parliament.

· · · · · ·

Part XVII

Miscellaneous and General

Co-operation between courts exercising jurisdiction in relation to insolvency

426.—(1) An order made by a court in any part of the United Kingdom in the exercise of jurisdiction in relation to insolvency law shall be enforced in any other part of the United Kingdom as if it were made by a court exercising the corresponding jurisdiction in that other part.

(2) However, without prejudice to the following provisions of this section, nothing in subsection (1) requires a court in any part of the United Kingdom to enforce, in relation to property situated in that part, any order made by a court in any other part of the United Kingdom.

(3) The Secretary of State, with the concurrence in relation to property situated in England and Wales of the Lord Chancellor, may by order make provision for securing that a trustee or assignee under the insolvency law of any part of the United Kingdom has, with such modifications as may be specified in the order, the same rights in relation to any property situated in another part of the United Kingdom as he would have in the corresponding circumstances if he were a trustee or assignee under the insolvency law of that other part.

(4) The courts having jurisdiction in relation to insolvency law in any part of the United Kingdom shall assist the courts having the corresponding jurisdiction in any other part of the United Kingdom or any relevant country or territory.

(5) For the purposes of subsection (4) a request made to a court in any part of the United Kingdom by a court in any other part of the United Kingdom or in a relevant country or territory is authority for the court to which the request is made to apply, in relation to any matters specified in the request, the insolvency law which is applicable by either court in relation to comparable matters falling within its jurisdiction.

In exercising its discretion under this subsection, a court shall have regard in particular to the rules of private international law.

(6) Where a person who is a trustee or assignee under the insolvency law of any part of the United Kingdom claims property situated in any other part of the United Kingdom (whether by virtue of an order under subsection (3) or otherwise), the submission of that claim to the court

exercising jurisdiction in relation to insolvency law in that other part shall be treated in the same manner as a request made by a court for the purpose of subsection (4).

(7) Section 38 of the Criminal Law Act 1977 (execution of warrant of arrest throughout the United Kingdom) applies to a warrant which, in exercise of any jurisdiction in relation to insolvency law, is issued in any part of the United Kingdom for the arrest of a person as it applies to a warrant issued in that part of the United Kingdom for the arrest of a person charged with an offence.

(8) Without prejudice to any power to make rules of court, any power to make provision by subordinate legislation for the purpose of giving effect in relation to companies or individuals to the insolvency law of any part of the United Kingdom includes power to make provision for the purpose of giving effect in that part to any provision made by or under the preceding provisions of this section.

(9) An order under subsection (3) shall be made by statutory instrument subject to annulment in pursuance of a resolution of either House of Parliament.

(10) In this section "insolvency law" means—

(*a*) in relation to England and Wales, provision made by or under this Act or sections 6 to 10, 12, 15, 19(*c*) and 20 (with Schedule 1) of the Company Directors Disqualification Act 1986 and extending to England and Wales;

(*b*) in relation to Scotland, provision extending to Scotland and made by or under this Act, sections 6 to 10, 12, 15, 19(*c*) and 20 (with Schedule 1) of the Company Directors Disqualification Act 1986, Part XVIII of the Companies Act or the Bankruptcy (Scotland) Act 1985;

(*c*) in relation to Northern Ireland, provision made by or under the Bankruptcy Acts (Northern Ireland) 1857 to 1980, Part V, VI or IX of the Companies Act (Northern Ireland) 1960 or Part IV of the Companies (Northern Ireland) Order 1978;

(*d*) in relation to any relevant country or territory, so much of the law of that country or territory as corresponds to provisions falling within any of the foregoing paragraphs;

and references in this subsection to any enactment include, in relation to any time before the coming into force of that enactment the corresponding enactment in force at that time.

(11) In this section "relevant country or territory" means—

(*a*) any of the Channel Islands or the Isle of Man, or

[72] (*b*) any country or territory designated for the purposes of this section by the Secretary of State by order made by statutory instrument.

---

[72] See S.I. 1986 No. 2123.

Parliamentary disqualification

427.—(1) Where a court in England and Wales or Northern Ireland adjudges an individual bankrupt or a court in Scotland awards sequestration of an individual's estate, the individual is disqualified—

(a) for sitting or voting in the House of Lords,

(b) for being elected to, or sitting or voting in, the House of Commons, and

(c) for sitting or voting in a committee of either House.

(2) Where an individual is disqualified under this section, the disqualification ceases—

(a) except where the adjudication is annulled or the award recalled or reduced without the individual having been first discharged, on the discharge of the individual, and

(b) in the excepted case, on the annulment, recall or reduction, as the case may be.

(3) No writ of summons shall be issued to any lord of Parliament who is for the time being disqualified under this section for sitting and voting in the House of Lords.

(4) Where a member of the House of Commons who is disqualified under this section continues to be so disqualified until the end of the period of six months beginning with the day of the adjudication or award, his seat shall be vacated at the end of that period.

(5) A court which makes an adjudication or award such as is mentioned in subsection (1) in relation to any lord of Parliament or member of the House of Commons shall forthwith certify the adjudication or award to the Speaker of the House of Lords or, as the case may be, to the Speaker of the House of Commons.

(6) Where a court has certified an adjudication or award to the Speaker of the House of Commons under subsection (5), then immediately after it becomes apparent which of the following certificates is applicable, the court shall certify to the Speaker of the House of Commons—

(a) that the period of six months beginning with the day of the adjudication or award has expired without the adjudication or award having been annulled, recalled or reduced, or

(b) that the adjudication or award has been annulled, recalled or reduced before the end of that period.

(7) Subject to the preceding provisions of this section, so much of this Act and any other enactment (whenever passed) and of any subordinate legislation (whenever made) as—

(a) makes provision for or in connection with bankruptcy in one or more parts of the United Kingdom, or

(b) makes provision conferring a power of arrest in connection with the winding up or insolvency of companies in one or more parts of the United Kingdom,

applies in relation to persons having privilege of Parliament or peerage as it applies in relation to persons not having such privilege.

Exemptions from Restrictive Trade Practices Act

428.—(1) No restriction in respect of any of the matters specified in the next subsection shall, on or after the appointed day, be regarded as a restriction by virtue of which the Restrictive Trade Practices Act 1976 applies to any agreement (whenever made).

(2) Those matters are—

(*a*) the charges to be made, quoted or paid for insolvency services supplied, offered or obtained;

(*b*) the terms or conditions on or subject to which insolvency services are to be supplied or obtained;

(*c*) the extent (if any) to which, or the scale (if any) on which, insolvency services are to be made available, supplied or obtained;

(*d*) the form or manner in which insolvency services are to be made available, supplied or obtained;

(*e*) the persons or classes of persons for whom or from whom, or the areas or places in or from which, insolvency services are to be made available or supplied or are to be obtained.

(3) In this section "insolvency services" means the services of persons acting as insolvency practitioners or carrying out under the law of Northern Ireland functions corresponding to those mentioned in section 388(1) or (2) in Part XIII, in their capacity as such; and expressions which are also used in the Act of 1976 have the same meaning here as in that Act.

Disabilities on revocation of administration order against an individual

429.—. . . (3) A person to whom this section so applies shall not—

(*a*) either alone or jointly with another person, obtain credit to the extent of the amount prescribed for the purposes of section 360(1)(*a*) or more, or

(*b*) enter into any transaction in the course of or for the purposes of any business in which he is directly or indirectly engaged,

without disclosing to the person from whom he obtains the credit, or (as the case may be) with whom the transaction is entered into, the fact that this section applies to him.

(4) The reference in subsection (3) to a person obtaining credit includes—

(*a*) a case where goods are bailed or hired to him under a hire-purchase agreement or agreed to be sold to him under a conditional sale agreement, and (*b*) a case where he is paid in advance (whether in money or otherwise) for the supply of goods or services.

(5) A person who contravenes this section is guilty of an offence and liable to imprisonment or a fine, or both.

Provision introducing Schedule of punishments

430.—(1) Schedule 10 to this Act has effect with respect to the way in which offences under this Act are punishable on conviction.

(2) In relation to an offence under a provision of this Act specified in the first column of the Schedule (the general nature of the offence being described in the second column), the third column shows whether the offence is punishable on conviction on indictment, or on summary conviction, or either in the one way or the other.

(3) The fourth column of the Schedule shows, in relation to an offence, the maximum punishment by way of fine or imprisonment under this Act which may be imposed on a person convicted of the offence in the way specified in relation to it in the third column (that is to say, on indictment or summarily) a reference to a period of years or months being to a term of imprisonment of that duration.

(4) The fifth column shows (in relation to an offence for which there is an entry in that column) that a person convicted of the offence after continued contravention is liable to a daily default fine; that is to say, he is liable on a second or subsequent conviction of the offence to the fine specified in that column for each day on which the contravention is continued (instead of the penalty specified for the offence in the fourth column of the Schedule).

(5) For the purpose of any enactment in this Act whereby an officer of a company who is in default is liable to a fine or penalty, the expression "officer who is in default" means any officer of the company who knowingly and wilfully authorises or permits the default, refusal or contravention mentioned in the enactment.

Summary proceedings

431.—(1) Summary proceedings for any offence under any of Parts I to VII of this Act may (without prejudice to any jurisdiction exercisable apart from this subsection) be taken against a body corporate at any place at which the body has a place of business, and against any other person at any place at which he is for the time being.

(2) Notwithstanding anything in section 127(1) of the Magistrates' Courts Act 1980, an information relating to such an offence which is triable by a magistrates' court in England and Wales may be so tried if it is laid at any time within three years after the commission of the offence and within 12 months after the date on which evidence sufficient in the opinion of the Director of Public Prosecutions or the Secretary of State (as the case may be) to justify the proceedings comes to his knowledge.

(3) Summary proceedings in Scotland for such an offence shall not be

commenced after the expiration of three years from the commission of the offence.

Subject to this (and notwithstanding anything in section 331 of the Criminal Procedure (Scotland) Act 1975), such proceedings may (in Scotland) be commenced at any time within 12 months after the date on which evidence sufficient in the Lord Advocate's opinion to justify the proceedings came to his knowledge or, where such evidence was reported to him by the Secretary of State, within 12 months after the date on which it came to the knowledge of the latter; and subsection (3) of that section applies for the purpose of this subsection as it applies for the purpose of that section.

(4) For purposes of this section, a certificate of the Director of Public Prosecutions, the Lord Advocate or the Secretary of State (as the case may be) as to the date on which such evidence as is referred to above came to his knowledge is conclusive evidence.

Offences by bodies corporate

432.—(1) This section applies to offences under this Act other than those excepted by subsection (4).

(2) Where a body corporate is guilty of an offence to which this section applies and the offence is proved to have been committed with the consent or connivance of, or to be attributable to any neglect on the part of, any director, manager, secretary or other similar officer of the body corporate or any person who was purporting to act in any such capacity he, as well as the body corporate, is guilty of the offence and liable to be proceeded against and punished accordingly.

(3) Where the affairs of a body corporate are managed by its members, subsection (2) applies in relation to the acts and defaults of a member in connection with his functions of management as if he were a director of the body corporate.

(4) The offences excepted from this section are those under sections 30, 39, 51, 53, 54, 62, 64, 66, 85, 89, 164, 188, 201, 206, 207, 208, 209, 210 and 211.

Admissibility in evidence of statements of affairs, etc.

433. In any proceedings (whether or not under this Act)—

(a) a statement of affairs prepared for the purposes of any provision of this Act which is derived from the Insolvency Act 1985, and

(b) any other statement made in pursuance of a requirement imposed by or under any such provision or by or under rules made under this Act,

may be used in evidence against any person making or concurring in making the statement.

Crown application

434. For the avoidance of doubt it is hereby declared that provisions of this Act which derive from the Insolvency Act 1985 bind the Crown so far as affecting or relating to the following matters, namely—

(a) remedies against, or against the property of, companies or individuals;

(b) priorities of debts;

(c) transactions at an undervalue or preferences;

(d) voluntary arrangements approved under Part I or Part VIII, and

(e) discharge from bankruptcy.

Part XVIII

Interpretation

Meaning of "associate"

435.—(1) For the purposes of this Act any question whether a person is an associate of another person is to be determined in accordance with the following provisions of this section (any provision that a person is an associate of another person being taken to mean that they are associates of each other).

(2) A person is an associate of an individual if that person is the individual's husband or wife, or is a relative, or the husband or wife of a relative, of the individual or of the individual's husband or wife.

(3) A person is an associate of any person with whom he is in partnership, and of the husband or wife or a relative of any individual with whom he is in partnership; and a Scottish firm is an associate of any person who is a member of the firm.

(4) A person is an associate of any person whom he employs or by whom he is employed.

(5) A person in his capacity as trustee of a trust other than—

(a) a trust arising under any of the second Group of Parts or the Bankruptcy (Scotland) Act 1985, or

(b) a pension scheme or an employee's share scheme (within the meaning of the Companies Act),

is an associate of another person if the beneficiaries of the trust include, or the terms of the trust confer a power that may be exercised for the benefit of, that other person or an associate of that other person.

(6) A company is an associate of another company—

(a) if the same person has control of both, or a person has control of one and persons who are his associates, or he and persons who are his associates, have control of the other, or

(b) if a group of two or more persons has control of each company, and the groups either consist of the same persons or could be regarded as consisting of the same persons by treating (in one or more cases) a member of either group as replaced by a person of whom he is an associate.

(7) A company is an associate of another person if that person has

control of it or if that person and persons who are his associates together have control of it.

(8) For the purposes of this section a person is a relative of an individual if he is that individual's brother, sister, uncle, aunt, nephew, niece, lineal ancestor or lineal descendant, treating—

(a) any relationship of the half blood as a relationship of the whole blood and the stepchild or adopted child of any person as his child, and

(b) an illegitimate child as the legitimate child of his mother and reputed father;

and references in this section to a husband or wife include a former husband or wife and a reputed husband or wife.

(9) For the purposes of this section any director or other officer of a company is to be treated as employed by that company.

(10) For the purposes of this section a person is to be taken as having control of a company if—

(a) the directors of the company or of another company which has control of it (or any of them) are accustomed to act in accordance with his directions or instructions, or

(b) he is entitled to exercise, or control the exercise of, one-third or more of the voting power at any general meeting of the company or of another company which has control of it;

and where two or more persons together satisfy either of the above conditions, they are to be taken as having control of the company.

(11) In this section "company" includes any body corporate (whether incorporated in Great Britain or elsewhere); and references to directors and other officers of a company and to voting power at any general meeting of a company have effect with any necessary modifications.

Expressions used generally

436. In this Act, except in so far as the context otherwise requires (and subject to Parts VII and XI)—

"the appointed day" means the day on which this Act comes into force under section 443;

"associate" has the meaning given by section 435;

"business" includes a trade or profession;

"the Companies Act" means the Companies Act 1985;

"conditional sale agreement" and "hire-purchase agreement" have the same meanings as in the Consumer Credit Act 1974;

"modifications" includes additions, alterations and omissions and cognate expressions shall be construed accordingly;

"property" includes money, goods, things in action, land and every description of property wherever situated and also obligations and every description of interest, whether present or future or vested or contingent, arising out of, or incidental to, property;

"records" includes computer records and other non-documentary records;

"subordinate legislation" has the same meaning as in the Interpretation Act 1978; and

"transaction" includes a gift, agreement or arrangement, and references to entering into a transaction shall be construed accordingly.

PART XIX

FINAL PROVISIONS

Transitional provisions, and savings

437. The transitional provisions and savings set out in Schedule 11 to this Act shall have effect, the Schedule comprising the following Parts—

Part I: company insolvency and winding up (matters arising before appointed day, and continuance of proceedings in certain cases as before that day);

Part II: individual insolvency (matters so arising, and continuance of bankruptcy proceedings in certain cases as before that day);

Part III: transactions entered into before the appointed day and capable of being affected by orders of the court under Part XVI of this Act;

Part IV: insolvency practitioners acting as such before the appointed day; and

Part V: general transitional provisions and savings required consequentially on, and in connection with, the repeal and replacement by this Act and the Company Directors Disqualification Act 1986 of provisions of the Companies Act, the greater part of the Insolvency Act 1985 and other enactments.

Repeals

438. The enactments specified in the second column of Schedule 12 to this Act are repealed to the extent specified in the third column of that Schedule.

Amendment of enactments

439.—(1) The Companies Act is amended as shown in Parts I and II of Schedule 13 to this Act, being amendments consequential on this Act and the Company Directors Disqualification Act 1986.

(2) The enactments specified in the first column of Schedule 14 to this Act (being enactments which refer, or otherwise relate, to those which are repealed and replaced by this Act or the Company Directors

Disqualification Act 1986) are amended as shown in the second column of that Schedule.

(3) The Lord Chancellor may by order make such consequential modifications of any provision contained in any subordinate legislation made before the appointed day and such transitional provisions in connection with those modifications as appear to him necessary or expedient in respect of—

(a) any reference in that subordinate legislation to the Bankruptcy Act 1914;

(b) any reference in that subordinate legislation to any enactment repealed by Part III or IV of Schedule 10 to the Insolvency Act 1985; or

(c) any reference in that subordinate legislation to any matter provided for under the Act of 1914 or under any enactment so repealed.

(4) An order under this section shall be made by statutory instrument subject to annulment in pursuance of a resolution of either House of Parliament.

Extent (Scotland)

440.—(1) Subject to the next subsection, provisions of this Act contained in the first Group of Parts extend to Scotland except where otherwise stated.

(2) The following provisions of this Act do not extend to Scotland—

(a) in the first Group of Parts—
   section 43;
   sections 238 to 241; and
   section 246;

(b) the second Group of Parts;

(c) in the third Group of Parts—
   sections 399 to 402,
   sections 412, 413, 415, 418, 420 and 421,
   sections 423 to 425, and
   section 429(1) and (2); and

(d) in the Schedules—
   Parts II and III of Schedule 11; and
   Schedules 12 and 14 so far as they repeal or amend enactments which extend to England and Wales only.

. . . . . .

Commencement

443. This Act comes into force on the day appointed under section 236(2) of the Insolvency Act 1985 for the coming into force of Part III of that Act (individual insolvency and bankruptcy), immediately after that Part of that Act comes into force for England and Wales.

Citation

444. This Act may be cited as the Insolvency Act 1986.

SCHEDULES

SCHEDULE 1

POWERS OF ADMINISTRATOR OR ADMINISTRATIVE RECEIVER

1. Power to take possession of, collect and get in the property of the company and, for that purpose, to take such proceedings as may seem to him expedient.

2. Power to sell or otherwise dispose of the property of the company by public auction or private contract or, in Scotland, to sell, feu, hire out or otherwise dispose of the property of the company by public roup or private bargain.

3. Power to raise or borrow money and grant security therefor over the property of the company.

4. Power to appoint a solicitor or accountant or other professionally qualified person to assist him in the performance of his functions.

5. Power to bring or defend any action or other legal proceedings in the name and on behalf of the company.

6. Power to refer to arbitration any question affecting the company.

7. Power to effect and maintain insurances in respect of the business and property of the company.

8. Power to use the company's seal.

9. Power to do all acts and to execute in the name and on behalf of the company any deed, receipt or other document.

10. Power to draw, accept, make and endorse any bill of exchange or promissory note in the name and on behalf of the company.

11. Power to appoint any agent to do any business which he is unable to do himself or which can more conveniently be done by an agent and power to employ and dismiss employees.

12. Power to do all such things (including the carrying out of works) as may be necessary for the realisation of the property of the company.

13. Power to make any payment which is necessary or incidental to the performance of his functions.

14. Power to carry on the business of the company.

15. Power to establish subsidiaries of the company.

16. Power to transfer to subsidiaries of the company the whole or any part of the business and property of the company.

17. Power to grant or accept a surrender of a lease or tenancy of any of the property of the company, and to take a lease or tenancy of any property required or convenient for the business of the company.

18. Power to make any arrangement or compromise on behalf of the company.

19. Power to call up any uncalled capital of the company.

20. Power to rank and claim in the bankruptcy, insolvency, sequestration or liquidation of any person indebted to the company and to receive dividends, and to accede to trust deeds for the creditors of any such person.

21. Power to present or defend a petition for the winding up of the company.

22. Power to change the situation of the company's registered office.

23. Power to do all other things incidental to the exercise of the foregoing powers.

Section 55   SCHEDULE 2

POWERS OF A SCOTTISH RECEIVER (ADDITIONAL TO THOSE CONFERRED ON HIM BY THE INSTRUMENT OF CHARGE)

1. Power to take possession of, collect and get in the property from the company or a liquidator thereof or any other person, and for that purpose, to take such proceedings as may seem to him expedient.

2. Power to sell, feu, hire out or otherwise dispose of the property by public roup or private bargain and with or without advertisement.

3. Power to raise or borrow money and grant security therefor over the property.

4. Power to appoint a solicitor or accountant or other professionally qualified person to assist him in the performance of his functions.

5. Power to bring or defend any action or other legal proceedings in the name and on behalf of the company.

6. Power to refer to arbitration all questions affecting the company.

7. Power to effect and maintain insurances in respect of the business and property of the company.

8. Power to use the company's seal.

9. Power to do all acts and to execute in the name and on behalf of the company any deed, receipt or other document.

10. Power to draw, accept, make and endorse any bill of exchange or promissory note in the name and on behalf of the company.

11. Power to appoint any agent to do any business which he is unable to do himself or which can more conveniently be done by an agent, and power to employ and dismiss employees.

12. Power to do all such things (including the carrying out of works), as may be necessary for the realisation of the property.

13. Power to make any payment which is necessary or incidental to the performance of his functions.

14. Power to carry on the business of the company or any part of it.

15. Power to grant or accept a surrender of a lease or tenancy of any of the property, and to take a lease or tenancy of any property required or convenient for the business of the company.

16. Power to make any arrangement or compromise on behalf of the company.

17. Power to call up any uncalled capital of the company.

18. Power to establish subsidiaries of the company.

19. Power to transfer to subsidiaries of the company the business of the company or any part of it and any of the property.

20. Power to rank and claim in the bankruptcy, insolvency, sequestration or liquidation of any person or company indebted to the company and to receive dividends, and to accede to trust deeds for creditors of any such person.

21. Power to present or defend a petition for the winding up of the company.

22. Power to change the situation of the company's registered office.

23. Power to do all other things incidental to the exercise of the powers mentioned in section 55(1) of this Act or above in this Schedule.

Section 162 SCHEDULE 3

ORDERS IN COURSE OF WINDING UP PRONOUNCED IN VACATION (SCOTLAND)

PART I

ORDERS WHICH ARE TO BE FINAL

Orders under section 153, as to the time for proving debts and claims.

Orders under section 195 as to meetings for ascertaining wishes of creditors or contributories.

Orders under section 198, as to the examination of witnesses in regard to the property or affairs of a company.

PART II

ORDERS WHICH ARE TO TAKE EFFECT UNTIL MATTER DISPOSED OF BY INNER HOUSE

Orders under section 126(1), 130(2) or (3), 147, 227 or 228, restraining or permitting the commencement or the continuance of legal proceedings.

Orders under section 135(5), limiting the powers of provisional liquidators.

Orders under section 108, appointing a liquidator to fill a vacancy.

Orders under section 167 or 169, sanctioning the exercise of any powers by a liquidator, other than the powers specified in paragraphs 1, 2 and 3 of Schedule 4 to this Act.

Orders under section 158, as to the arrest and detention of an absconding contributory and his property.

Sections 165, 167 SCHEDULE 4

POWERS OF LIQUIDATOR IN A WINDING UP

PART I

POWERS EXERCISABLE WITH SANCTION

1. Power to pay any class of creditors in full.

2. Power to make any compromise or arrangement with creditors or persons claiming to be creditors, or having or alleging themselves to have any claim (present or future, certain or contingent, ascertained or sounding only in damages) against the company, or whereby the company may be rendered liable.

3. Power to compromise, on such terms as may be agreed—

    (*a*) all calls and liabilities to calls, all debts and liabilities capable of resulting in debts, and all claims (present or future, certain or contingent, ascertained or sounding only in damages) subsisting or supposed to subsist between the company and a contributory or alleged contributory or other debtor or person apprehending liability to the company, and

    (*b*) all questions in any way relating to or affecting the assets or the winding up of the company,

and take any security for the discharge of any such call, debt, liability or claim and give a complete discharge in respect of it.

Powers Exercisable without Sanction in Voluntary Winding Up, with Sanction in Winding Up by the Court

4. Power to bring or defend any action or other legal proceeding in the name and on behalf of the company.

5. Power to carry on the business of the company so far as may be necessary for its beneficial winding up.

Part III

Powers Exercisable Without Sanction in any Winding Up

6. Power to sell any of the company's property by public auction or private contract with power to transfer the whole of it to any person or to sell the same in parcels.

7. Power to do all acts and execute, in the name and on behalf of the company, all deeds, receipts and other documents and for that purpose to use, when necessary, the company's seal.

8. Power to prove, rank and claim in the bankruptcy, insolvency or sequestration of any contributory for any balance against his estate, and to receive dividends in the bankruptcy, insolvency or sequestration in respect of that balance, as a separate debt due from the bankrupt or insolvent, and rateably with the other separate creditors.

9. Power to draw, accept, make and indorse any bill of exchange or promissory note in the name and on behalf of the company, with the same effect with respect to the company's liability as if the bill or note had been drawn, accepted, made or indorsed by or on behalf of the company in the course of its business.

10. Power to raise on the security of the assets of the company any money requisite.

11. Power to take out in his official name letters of administration to any deceased contributory, and to do in his official name any other act necessary for obtaining payment of any money due from a contributory or his estate which cannot conveniently be done in the name of the company.
In all such cases the money due is deemed, for the purpose of enabling the liquidator to take out the letters of administration or recover the money, to be due to the liquidator himself.

12. Power to appoint an agent to do any business which the liquidator is unable to do himself.

13. Power to do all such other things as may be necessary for winding up the company's affairs and distributing its assets.

. . . .

Section 386   SCHEDULE 6

The Categories of Preferential Debts

Category 1: Debts due to Inland Revenue

1. Sums due at the relevant date from the debtor on account of deductions of income tax from emoluments paid during the period of 12 months next before that date.
The deductions here referred to are those which the debtor was liable to make under section 204 of the Income and Corporation Taxes Act 1970 (pay as you earn), less the amount of the repayments of income tax which the debtor was liable to make during that period.

2. Sums due at the relevant date from the debtor in respect of such deductions as are required to be made by the debtor for that period under section 69 of the Finance (No. 2) Act 1975 (sub-contractors in the construction industry).

Category 2: Debts due to Customs and Excise

3. Any value added tax which is referable to the period of six months next before the relevant date (which period is referred to below as "the six-month period").
For the purposes of this paragraph—

(*a*) where the whole of the prescribed accounting period to which any value added tax is attributable falls within the six-month period, the whole amount of that tax is referable to that period; and
(*b*) in any other case the amount of any value added tax which is referable to the six-month period is the proportion of the tax which is equal to such proportion (if any) of the accounting reference period in question as falls within the six-month period;

and in sub-paragraph (*a*) "prescribed" means prescribed by regulations under the Value Added Tax Act 1983.

4. The amount of any car tax which is due at the relevant date from the debtor and which became due within a period of 12 months next before that date.

5. Any amount which is due—

(*a*) by way of general betting duty or bingo duty, or
(*b*) under section 12(1) of the Betting and Gaming Duties Act 1981 (general betting duty and pool betting duty recoverable from agent collecting stakes), or
(*c*) under section 14 of, or Schedule 2 to, that Act (gaming licence duty),

from the debtor at the relevant date and which became due within the period of 12 months next before that date.

Category 3: Social security contributions

6. All sums which on the relevant date are due from the debtor on account of Class 1 or Class 2 contributions under the Social Security Act 1975 or the Social Security (Northern Ireland) Act 1975 and which became due from the debtor in the 12 months next before the relevant date.

7. All sums which on the relevant date have been assessed on and are due from the debtor on account of Class 4 contributions under either of those Acts of 1975, being sums which—

(*a*) are due to the Commissioners of Inland Revenue (rather than to the Secretary of State or a Northern Ireland department), and
(*b*) are assessed on the debtor up to 5th April next before the relevant date,

but not exceeding, in the whole, any one year's assessment.

Category 4: Contributions to occupational pension schemes, etc.

8. Any sum which is owed by the debtor and is a sum to which Schedule 3 to the Social Security Pensions Act 1975 applies (contributions to occupational pension schemes and state scheme premiums).

Category 5: Remuneration, etc., of employees

[73] 9. So much of any amount which—

---

[73] See S.I. 1986 No. 1996.

(*a*) is owed by the debtor to a person who is or has been an employee of the debtor, and

(*b*) is payable by way of remuneration in respect of the whole or any part of the period of four months next before the relevant date,

as does not exceed so much as may be prescribed by order made by the Secretary of State.

10. An amount owed by way of accrued holiday remuneration, in respect of any period of employment before the relevant date, to a person whose employment by the debtor has been terminated, whether before, on or after that date.

11. So much of any sum owed in respect of money advanced for the purpose as has been applied for the payment of a debt which, if it had not been paid, would have been a debt falling within paragraph 9 or 10.

[73] 12. So much of any amount which—

(*a*) is ordered (whether before or after the relevant date) to be paid by the debtor under the Reserve Forces (Safeguard of Employment) Act 1985, and

(*b*) is so ordered in respect of a default made by the debtor before that date in the discharge of his obligations under that Act,

as does not exceed such amount as may be prescribed by order made by the Secretary of State.

Interpretation for Category 5

13.—(1) For the purposes of paragraphs 9 to 12, a sum is payable by the debtor to a person by way of remuneration in respect of any period if—

(*a*) it is paid as wages or salary (whether payable for time or for piece work or earned wholly or partly by way of commission) in respect of services rendered to the debtor in that period, or

(*b*) it is an amount falling within the following sub-paragraph and is payable by the debtor in respect of that period.

(2) An amount falls within this sub-paragraph if it is—

(*a*) a guarantee payment under section 12(1) of the Employment Protection (Consolidation) Act 1978 (employee without work to do for a day or part of a day);

(*b*) remuneration on suspension on medical grounds under section 19 of that Act;

(*c*) any payment for time off under section 27(3) (trade union duties), 31(3) (looking for work, etc.) or 31A(4) (ante-natal care) of that Act; or

(*d*) remuneration under a protective award made by an industrial tribunal under section 101 of the Employment Protection Act 1975 (redundancy dismissal with compensation).

14.—(1) This paragraph relates to a case in which a person's employment has been terminated by or in consequence of his employer going into liquidation or being adjudged bankrupt or (his employer being a company not in liquidation) by or in consequence of—

(*a*) a receiver being appointed as mentioned in section 40 of this Act (debenture-holders secured by floating charge), or

(*b*) the appointment of a receiver under section 53(6) or 54(5) of this Act (Scottish company with property subject to floating charge), or

(*c*) the taking of possession by debenture-holders (so secured), as mentioned in section 196 of the Companies Act.

(2) For the purposes of paragraphs 9 to 12, holiday remuneration is deemed to have accrued to that person in respect of any period of employment if, by virtue of his contract of employment or of any enactment that remuneration would have accrued in respect of that period if his employment had continued until he became entitled to be allowed the holiday.

(3) The reference in sub-paragraph (2) to any enactment includes an order or direction made under an enactment.

15. Without prejudice to paragraphs 13 and 14—

(*a*) any remuneration payable by the debtor to a person in respect of a period of holiday or of absence from work through sickness or other good cause is deemed to be wages or (as the case may be) salary in respect of services rendered to the debtor in that period, and

(*b*) references here and in those paragraphs to remuneration in respect of a period of holiday include any sums which, if they had been paid, would have been treated for the purposes of the enactments relating to social security as earnings in respect of that period.

Category 6: Levies on coal and steel production

[74] 15A. Any sums due at the relevant date from the debtor in respect of—

(*a*) the levies on the production of coal and steel referred to in Articles 49 and 50 of the E.C.S.C. Treaty, or

(*b*) any surcharge for delay provided for in Article 50(3) of that Treaty and Article 6 of Decision 3/52 of the High Authority of the Coal and Steel Community.

Orders

16. An order under paragraph 9 or 12—

(*a*) may contain such transitional provisions as may appear to the Secretary of State necessary or expedient;

(*b*) shall be made by statutory instrument subject to annulment in pursuance of a resolution of either House of Parliament.

---

[74] Inserted by S.I. 1987 No. 1093, without affecting any declaration on payment of dividend before 1st January 1988: *ibid.*, reg. 3(2).

Act of Sederunt (Rules of Court, Consolidation and Amendment) 1965

(S.I. 1965 No. 321)

[10th November 1964]

The Lords of Council and Session, under and by virtue of the provisions of the Administration of Justice (Scotland) Act 1933 considering that the Rules of Court enacted by the Act of Sederunt of 1st July 1948 have been amended by subsequent Acts of Sederunt, and that it is desirable to make further amendments and to consolidate the Rules as so amended, do hereby enact and declare that the Rules attached hereto and embodied herein are approved as rules of the Court of Session in place of the Rules enacted and amended as aforesaid, and shall come into force on 4th May 1965.

And the Lords do further enact and declare as follows:—

[75] (1) The provisions of any Act of Parliament or Act of Sederunt relating to any of the matters regulated or prescribed by these Rules are hereby repealed, in so far as inconsistent with the provisions of these Rules, as from 15th June 1965.

[75] (2) Where any *induciae* or other period of time appointed or allowed by order of court or by pre-existing law and practice for taking any step of procedure is still current on 15th June 1965, such *induciae* or other period of time shall continue to be in force notwithstanding the provisions of these Rules.

[75] (3) If in any cause in dependence on 15th June 1965, it is shown to the Court that the enforcement in any particular of the provisions of these Rules would be productive of hardship or injustice to any of the parties, the Court may grant such relief as may be necessary to prevent such hardship or injustice.

[75] (4) From and after 15th June 1965, the Court may in its discretion relieve any party from the consequences of any failure to comply with the provisions of these Rules which is shown to be due to mistake, oversight or other cause, not being wilful non-observance of the same, on such terms and conditions as shall appear to be just; and in any such case the Court may make such order as may be just by way of extension of time, lodging or amendment of papers or otherwise so as to enable the cause to proceed as if such failure had not happened.

This Act may be cited as the Act of Sederunt (Rules of Court, consolidation and amendment) 1965.

. . . . . .

---

[75] As amended by S.I. 1965 No. 1090.

SECTION 3—COMPANIES[76]

Interpretation

202.—(1) In this Section—

"the Act of 1986" means the Insolvency Act 1986;

"registered office" means:—

(a) the place specified, in the statement of the company delivered to the registrar of companies under section 10 of the Companies Act 1985, as the intended place of its registered office on incorporation; or

(b) where notice has been given by the company to the registrar of companies under section 287 of the Companies Act 1985 of a change of registered office, the place specified in the last such notice;

"the insolvency judge" means the Lord Ordinary nominated by the Lord President to deal with proceedings under the Act of 1986 or any rules made under that Act or under the Company Directors Disqualification Act 1986, or a Lord Ordinary acting in his place;

"the Insolvency Rules" means the Insolvency (Scotland) Rules 1986.

(2) Unless the context otherwise requires, words and expressions used in this Section which are also used in the Act of 1986 or the Insolvency Rules have the same meaning as in that Act or those Rules.

PART I

COMPANY VOLUNTARY ARRANGEMENTS

Lodging of nominee's report (Part 1, Chapter 2 of the Insolvency Rules)

203.—(1) This rule applies where the company is not being wound up, is not in liquidation and an administration order is not in force in respect of it.

(2) A report of a nominee, sent to the court under section 2(2) of the Act of 1986, shall be accompanied by a covering letter, lodged in the Petition Department and marked by a clerk of court with the date on which it is received.

(3) The report shall be placed before the insolvency judge for consideration of any direction which he may make under section 3(1) of the Act of 1986.

(4) An application by a nominee to extend the time within which he

---

[76] Rules 202–218S substituted by S.I. 1986 No. 2298 in relation to proceedings commenced on or after 29th December 1986.

may lodge his report under section 2(2) of the Act of 1986 shall be made by letter addressed to the Deputy Principal Clerk, who shall cause it to be placed before the insolvency judge for determination.

(5) The letter of application under paragraph (4) and a copy of the reply by the court shall be placed by the clerk of court with the nominee's report when it is subsequently lodged.

(6) A person who states in writing that he is a creditor, member or director of the company may, by himself or his agent, on payment of the appropriate fee, inspect the nominee's report lodged under paragraph (2).

Lodging of nominee's report (Part 1, Chapter 4 of the Insolvency Rules)
204.—(1) This rule applies where the company is being wound up, is in liquidation or there is an administration order in force in respect of it.

(2) Where a report of a nominee is sent to the court under section 2(2) of the Act of 1986, it shall be lodged in the process of the petition to wind up the company or the petition for an administration order which is in force in respect of it, as the case may be.

(3) Where the nominee is not the liquidator or administrator, the report shall be placed before the insolvency judge for consideration of any direction which he may make under section 3(1) of the Act of 1986.

(4) An application by a nominee to extend the time within which he may lodge his report under section 2(2) of the Act of 1986 shall be made by letter addressed to the Deputy Principal Clerk who shall cause it to be placed before the insolvency judge for determination.

(5) The letter of application under paragraph (4) and a copy of the reply by the court shall be placed by the clerk of court in the process of the petition to wind up the company or the petition for an administration order which is in force in respect of it, as the case may be.

(6) A person who states in writing that he is a creditor, member or director of the company may, by himself or his agent, on payment of the appropriate fee, inspect the nominee's report lodged under paragraph (2).

Applications to replace nominee
205. An application under section 2(4) of the Act of 1986 to replace a nominee who has failed to lodge a report under section 2(2) of the Act of 1986, shall be made:—

(a) by petition where the company is not being wound up, is not in liquidation and an administration order is not in force in respect of it; or

(b) by note in the process of the petition to wind up the company or the petition for an administration order which is in force in respect of it, as the case may be,

and shall be intimated and served as the court shall direct.

Report of meetings to approve arrangement

206. The report of the result of a meeting to be sent to the court under section 4(6) of the Act of 1986 shall be sent to the Deputy Principal Clerk, who shall cause it to be lodged:—

(a) in a case to which rule 203 applies, with the nominee's report lodged under that rule; or

(b) in a case to which rule 204 applies, in the process of the petition to wind up the company or the petition for an administration order which is in force in respect of it, as the case may be.

Abstracts of supervisor's receipts and payments and notices of completion of arrangement

207. An abstract of receipts and payments prepared by a supervisor and sent to the court under rule 1.21(2) of the Insolvency Rules or a notice of completion of the arrangement (together with a copy of the supervisor's report) to be sent to the court under rule 1.23(3) of those rules shall be sent to the Deputy Principal Clerk, who shall cause it to be lodged—

(a) in a case to which rule 203 applies, with the nominee's report lodged under that rule; or

(b) in a case to which rule 204 applies, in the process of the petition to wind up the company or the petition for an administration order which is in force in respect of it, as the case may be.

Form of certain applications

208.—(1) This rule applies to applications under any of the following provisions of the Act of 1986 or the Insolvency Rules:—

(a) section 6 (to challenge a decision in relation to an arrangement);

(b) section 7(3) (to challenge actings of a supervisor);

(c) section 7(4)(a) (by supervisor for directions);

(d) section 7(5) (to appoint a supervisor);

(e) rule 1.21(5) (to dispense with sending abstracts or reports or to vary dates on which obligation to send abstracts or reports arises);

(f) rule 1.23(4) (by supervisor to extend period for sending notice of implementation of arrangement or report); and

(g) any other provision relating to company voluntary arrangements not specifically mentioned in this Part.

(2) An application shall be made—

(a) in a case to which rule 203 applies, by petition; or

(b) in a case to which rule 204 applies, by note in the process of the petition to wind up the company or the petition for an administration order which is in force in respect of it, as the case may be.

PART II

ADMINISTRATION ORDERS

Petitions for administration orders

209.—(1) A petition for an administration order under section 9 of the Act of 1986 shall be presented to the Outer House.

(2) Rules 191 to 198 shall apply to a petition presented under paragraph (1), subject to rule 210.

(3) A petition under paragraph (1) shall include averments in relation to:—

(*a*) the petitioner and the capacity in which he presents the petition, if other than the company;

(*b*) whether it is believed that the company is, or is likely to become, unable to pay its debts and the grounds of that belief;

(*c*) which of the purposes specified in section 8(3) of the Act of 1986 is expected to be achieved by the making of an administration order;

(*d*) the company's financial position, specifying (so far as known) assets and liabilities, including contingent and prospective liabilities;

(*e*) any security known or believed to be held by creditors of the company, whether in any case the security confers power on the holder to appoint a receiver, and whether a receiver has been appointed;

(*f*) so far as is known to the petitioner, whether any steps have been taken for the winding up of the company, giving details of them;

(*g*) other matters which, in the opinion of the petitioner, will assist the court in deciding whether to grant an administration order;

(*h*) whether a report has been prepared under the rule 2.1 of the Insolvency Rules (independent report on affairs of the company), and, if not, an explanation why not; and

(*i*) the person proposed to be appointed as administrator, giving his name and address and whether he is qualified to act as an insolvency practitioner in relation to the company.

(4) There shall be produced with the petition:—

(*a*) any document instructing the facts relied on, or otherwise founded on, by the petitioner; and

(*b*) where a report has been prepared under rule 2.1 of the Insolvency Rules, a copy of that report.

Notice of petition

210. Notice of the petition on the persons upon whom notice is to be given under rule 2.2 of the Insolvency Rules shall be in accordance with rule 195 of these rules unless the court otherwise directs.

Form of certain applications and appeals

211.—(1) An application or appeal under any of the following provisions of the Act of 1986 or the Insolvency Rules shall be made by note in the process of the petition for an administration order which is in force:—

(*a*) section 13(2) (application for appointment to fill a vacancy in office of administrator);

(*b*) section 14(3) (application by administrator for directions);

(*c*) section 15(2) (application by administrator for power to dispose of property subject to a security);

(*d*) section 18(1) (application by administrator for discharge or variation of administration order);

(*e*) section 19(1) (application for removal from office of administrator);

(*f*) section 22(5) (application for release from, or extension of time for, obligation to submit statement of affairs);

(*g*) section 27(1) (application for protection of interest of creditors and members);

(*h*) rule 2.6(2) (appeal against decision of administrator as to expenses of submitting statement of affairs);

(*i*) rule 2.16(3) (application by administrator for increase of remuneration); and

(*j*) any other application under a provision relating to administration orders not specifically mentioned in this Part.

(2) An application by an administrator to extend the period for sending an abstract of his receipts and payments under rule 2.17(2) of the Insolvency Rules shall be made by motion in the process of the petition.

[77] (3) Where a petition for an administration order has been presented or an administration order has been made, any person showing an interest who wishes to apply to the court for an order under section 175(2) of the Companies Act 1989 shall apply by note in the process of the petition for the administration order.

[77] (4) The court shall not make an order under section 175(2) of the Companies Act 1989 unless intimation has been made to such persons having an interest as the court considers necessary and any such person has had an opportunity to be heard.

Report of administrator's proposals

212.—(1) A report of the meeting to approve the administrator's proposals to be sent to the court under section 24(4) of the Act of 1986 shall be sent to the Deputy Principal Clerk, who shall cause it to be lodged in the process of the petition.

(2) Where the report lodged under paragraph (1) discloses that the

---

[77] Inserted by S.I. 1991 No. 1157, with effect from 27th May 1991.

meeting has declined to approve the administrator's proposals, the cause shall be put out "By Order" for determination by the insolvency judge of any order he may make under section 24(5) of the Act of 1986.

Abstracts of administrator's receipts and payments

213. An abstract of receipts and payments of an administrator to be sent to the court under rule 2.17(1) of the Insolvency Rules shall be sent to the Deputy Principal Clerk who shall cause it to be lodged in the process of the petition.

PART III

RECEIVERS

Applications to appoint a receiver

214.—(1) A petition under section 54(1) of the Act of 1986 to appoint a receiver shall be presented to the Outer House.

(2) Subject to rule 215, rules 191 to 198 apply to a petition presented under paragraph (1) of this rule.

(3) A petition under paragraph (1) shall include averments in relation to:—

(*a*) any floating charge and the property over which it is secured;

(*b*) so far as known to the petitioner, whether any petition for an administration order has been made in respect of the company, giving details of it;

(*c*) other matters which, in the opinion of the petitioners, will assist the court in deciding whether to appoint a receiver; and

(*d*) the person proposed to be appointed as receiver, giving his name and address and that he is qualified to act as a receiver.

(4) There shall be produced with the petition any document instructing the facts relied on, or otherwise founded on, by the petitioner.

Intimation, service and advertisement

215.—(1) Intimation, service and advertisement of the petition shall be made in accordance with rule 195 unless the court otherwise directs.

(2) Unless the court otherwise directs, there shall be included in the order for service, a requirement to serve:—

(*a*) upon the company; and

(*b*) where a petition for an administration order has been presented, on that petitioner and any respondent to that petition.

(3) Subject to paragraph (5), service of a petition on the company shall be effected at its registered office:—

(*a*) by registered or recorded delivery post addressed to the company; or

(*b*) by messenger-at-arms:—

(i) leaving the citation in the hands of a person who, after due inquiry, he has reasonable grounds for believing to be a director, other officer or responsible employee of the company or authorised to accept service on behalf of the company; or

(ii) if there is no such person as is mentioned in head (i) present, depositing it in the registered office in such a way that it is likely to come to the attention of such a person attending at that office.

(4) Where service is effected in accordance with paragraph (3)(*b*)(ii), the messenger-at-arms thereafter shall send a copy of the petition and citation by ordinary first class post to the registered office of the company.

(5) Where service cannot be effected at the registered office of the company or the company has no registered office:—

(*a*) service may be effected at the last known principal place of business of the company in Scotland or at some place in Scotland at which the company carries on business, by leaving the citation in the hands of such a person as is mentioned in paragraph (3)(*b*)(i) or by depositing it as specified in paragraph (3)(*b*)(ii); and

(*b*) where the citation is deposited as is specified in paragraph (3)(*b*)(ii), the messenger-at-arms thereafter shall send a copy of the petition and citation by ordinary first class post to such place mentioned in sub-paragraph (*a*) of this paragraph in which the citation was deposited.

(6) Unless the court otherwise directs, the petition shall be advertised forthwith:—

(*a*) once in the *Edinburgh Gazette*; and

(*b*) once in one or more newspapers as the court shall direct for ensuring that it comes to the notice of creditors of the company.

(7) An advertisement under paragraph (6) shall state:—

(*a*) the name and address of the petitioner;

(*b*) the name and address of the solicitor for the petitioner;

(*c*) the date on which the petition was presented;

(*d*) the precise order sought;

(*e*) the *induciae*; and

(*f*) that any person who intends to appear in the petition must lodge answers to the petition within the *induciae*.

(8) The *induciae* within which answers may be lodged and after which further consideration of the petition may proceed shall be eight days after such intimation, service and advertisement as the court may have ordered.

Form of certain applications where receiver appointed

216.—(1) An application under any of the following sections of the Act of 1986 shall be made by petition or, where the receiver was appointed by the court, by note in the process of the petition for appointment of the receiver:—

(*a*) section 61(1) (by receiver for authority to dispose of interest in property);

(*b*) section 62 (for removal or resignation of receiver);

(*c*) section 63(1) (by receiver for directions);

(*d*) section 69(1) (to enforce receiver to make returns, etc.); and

(*e*) any other section relating to receivers not specifically mentioned in this Part.

(2) An application under any of the following provisions of the Act of 1986 or the Insolvency Rules shall be made by motion in the process of the petition:—

(*a*) section 67(1) or (2) (by receiver to extend time for sending report); and

(*b*) rule 3.9(2) (by receiver to extend time for sending abstract of receipts and payments).

PART IV

WINDING UP BY THE COURT OF COMPANIES REGISTERED UNDER THE COMPANIES ACTS AND OF UNREGISTERED COMPANIES

Petitions to wind up a company

217.—(1) A petition to wind up a company by the court under the Act of 1986 shall be presented to the Outer House.

(2) Rules 191 to 198 apply to a petition under paragraph (1), subject to the following provisions of this Part.

(3) A petition under paragraph (1) shall include:—

(*a*) particulars of the petitioner, if other than the company;

(*b*) in respect of the company:—

(i) its registered name;

(ii) the address of its registered office, and any change of that address within the last six months so far as known to the petitioner;

(iii) a statement of its nature and objects, the amount of its capital (nominal and issued) and indicating what part is called up, paid up or credited as paid, and the amount of the assets of the company so far as known to the petitioner;

(*c*) a narrative of the facts on which the petitioner relies and any particulars required to instruct the title of the petitioner to present the petition;

(*d*) the name and address of the person to be appointed as interim liquidator and a statement that he is qualified to act as an insolvency practitioner in relation to the company; and

(*e*) a prayer setting out the orders applied for, including any intimation, service and advertisement and any appointment of an interim liquidator.

(4) There shall be lodged with the petition any document:—

(*a*) instructing the title of the petitioner; and

(*b*) instructing the facts relied on, or otherwise founded on, by the petitioner.

Intimation, service and advertisement

218.—(1) Subject to the following provisions of this rule, intimation, service and advertisement shall be in accordance with rule 195 unless the court:—

(*a*) summarily dismisses the petition; or

(*b*) otherwise directs.

(2) Unless the court otherwise directs, there shall be included in the order for service, a requirement:—

(*a*) to intimate on the walls of the court;

(*b*) where the petitioner is other than the company, to serve upon the company;

(*c*) where the company is being wound up voluntarily and a liquidator has been appointed, to serve upon the liquidator;

(*d*) where a receiver has been appointed for the company, to serve upon the receiver;

(*e*) where the company is:—

(i) a recognised bank or licensed institution within the meaning of the Banking Act 1979; or

(ii) an institution to which sections 16 and 18 of that Act apply as if it were licensed,

and the petitioner is not the Bank of England, to serve upon the Bank of England.

(3) Subject to paragraph (5), service of a petition on the company shall be effected at its registered office:—

(*a*) by registered or recorded delivery post addressed to the company; or

(*b*) by messenger-at-arms:—

(i) leaving the citation in the hands of a person who, after due inquiry, he has reasonable grounds for believing to be a director, other officer or responsible employee of the company or authorised to accept service on behalf of the company; or

(ii) if there is no such person as is mentioned in head (i) present, depositing it in the registered office in such a way that it is likely to come to the attention of such a person attending at that office.

(4) Where service is effected in accordance with paragraph (3)(*b*)(ii), the messenger-at-arms thereafter shall send a copy of the petition and citation by ordinary first class post to the registered office of the company.

(5) Where service cannot be effected at the registered office or the company has no registered office:—

(*a*) service may be executed at the last known principal place of business of the company in Scotland or at some place in Scotland at which the company carries on business by leaving the citation in the hands of such a person as is mentioned in paragraph (3)(*b*)(i) or by depositing it as specified in paragraph (3)(*b*)(ii); and

(*b*) where the citation is deposited as is specified in paragraph (3)(*b*)(ii), the messenger-at-arms thereafter shall send a copy of the petition and the citation by ordinary first class post to such place mentioned in sub-paragraph (*a*) of this paragraph in which the citation was deposited.

(6) Unless the court otherwise directs, the petition shall be advertised forthwith:—

(*a*) once in the *Edinburgh Gazette*; and

(*b*) once in one or more newspapers as the court shall direct for ensuring that it comes to the notice of creditors of the company.

(7) An advertisement under paragraph (6) shall state:—

(*a*) the name and address of the petitioner and, where the petitioner is the company, its registered office;

(*b*) the name and address of the solicitor for the petitioner;

(*c*) the date on which the petition was presented;

(*d*) the precise order sought;

(*e*) where a provisional liquidator has been appointed by the court, his name, address and the date of his appointment;

(*f*) the *induciae*; and

(*g*) that any person who intends to appear in the petition must lodge answers to the petition within the *induciae*.

(8) The *induciae* within which answers may be lodged and after which further consideration of the petition may proceed shall be eight days after such intimation, service and advertisement as the court may have ordered.

Lodging of caveats

218A.—(1) A company, debenture holder, holder of a floating charge, receiver, shareholder of a company or other person claiming an interest, apprehensive that a petition to wind up that company may be presented and wishing to be heard by the court before an order for intimation, service and advertisement is pronounced, may lodge a caveat in the Petition Department.

(2) [Revoked by S.I. 1990 No. 2118.]

(3) Where a caveat has been lodged and has not expired, no order may be pronounced without the person lodging the caveat having been given an opportunity to be heard by the court.

Remits

218B.—(1) An application by virtue of section 120(3)(*a*)(i) of the Act of 1986 to remit a petition to a sheriff court shall be made by note in the process of the petition.

(2) An application by virtue of section 120(3)(*a*)(ii) of the Act of 1986 to remit a petition from a sheriff court to the Court of Session, or section 120(3)(*b*) of that Act to remit a petition from one sheriff court to another, shall be made by petition.

(3) A note under paragraph (1) or a petition under paragraph (2) shall include a statement of the grounds on which the remit is sought.

Substitution of creditor or contributory for petitioner

218C.—(1) This rule applies where a petitioner:—

(*a*) is subsequently found not entitled to present the petition;
(*b*) fails to make intimation, service and advertisement as directed by the court;
(*c*) consents to withdraw the petition or to allow it to be dismissed or refused;
(*d*) fails to appear when the petition is called for hearing; or
(*e*) appears, but does not move for an order in terms of the prayer of the petition.

(2) The court may, on such terms as it considers just, sist as petitioner in room of the original petitioner any creditor or contributory who, in the opinion of the court, is entitled to present a petition.

(3) An application by a creditor or contributory to be sisted under paragraph (2):—

(*a*) may be at any time before the petition is dismissed or refused; and
(*b*) shall be made by note in the process of the petition, and if necessary the court may continue the cause for a specified period to allow a note to be presented.

Advertisement of appointment of liquidator

218D. Where a liquidator is appointed by the court, the court may order that the liquidator shall advertise his appointment once in one or more newspapers as the court shall direct for ensuring that it comes to the notice of creditors of the company.

Provisional liquidators

218E.—(1) An application to appoint a provisional liquidator under section 135 of the Act of 1986 may be made:—

(*a*) by the petitioner, in the prayer of the petition or subsequently by note in the process of the petition; or

(*b*) by a creditor or contributory of the company, the company, the Secretary of State or a person entitled under any enactment to present a petition to wind up the company, in a note in the process of the petition.

(2) The petition or note, as the case may be, shall include averments in relation to:—

(*a*) the grounds on which it is proposed that a provisional liquidator should be appointed;

(*b*) the name and address of the person to be appointed as provisional liquidator and that he is qualified to act as an insolvency practitioner in relation to the company; and

(*c*) whether, to the knowledge of the applicant, there is a receiver for the company or a liquidator has been appointed for the voluntary winding up of the company.

(3) Where the court is satisfied that sufficient grounds exist for the appointment of a provisional liquidator, it shall, on making the appointment, specify the functions to be carried out by him in relation to the affairs of the company.

(4) The applicant shall send a certified copy of the interlocutor appointing a provisional liquidator forthwith to the person appointed.

(5) On receiving a certified copy of his appointment on an application by note, the provisional liquidator shall intimate his appointment forthwith:—

(*a*) once in the *Edinburgh Gazette*; and

(*b*) once in one or more newspapers as the court shall direct for ensuring that it comes to the notice of the creditors of the company.

(6) An application for discharge of a provisional liquidator shall be by note in the process of the petition.

Applications and appeals in relation to a statement of affairs

218F.—(1) An application under section 131(5) of the Act of 1986 for:—

(*a*) release from an obligation imposed under section 131(1) or (2) of the Act of 1986; or

(*b*) an extension of time for the submission of a statement of affairs,

shall be made by note in the process of the petition.

(2) A note under paragraph (1) shall be served on the liquidator or provisional liquidator, as the case may be.

(3) The liquidator or provisional liquidator may lodge answers to the note or lodge a report of any matters which he considers should be drawn to the attention of the court.

(4) Where the liquidator or provisional liquidator lodges a report under paragraph (3), he shall send a copy of it to the noter forthwith.

(5) Where the liquidator or provisional liquidator does not appear, a certified copy of the interlocutor pronounced by the court disposing of the note shall be sent by the noter forthwith to him.

(6) An appeal under rule 4.9(6) of the Insolvency Rules against a refusal by the liquidator of an allowance towards the expenses of preparing a statement of affairs shall be made by note in the process of the petition.

Appeals against adjudication of claims

218G.—(1) An appeal under section 49(6) of the Bankruptcy (Scotland) Act 1985 as applied by rule 4.16 of the Insolvency Rules, by a creditor or contributory of the company against a decision of the liquidator shall be made by note in the process of the petition.

(2) A note under paragraph (1) shall be served on the liquidator.

(3) On receipt of the note served on him under this rule, the liquidator forthwith shall send or deliver to the court the claim in question and a copy of his adjudication for lodging in process.

(4) After the note has been disposed of, the court shall return the claim and the adjudication to the liquidator together with a copy of the interlocutor.

Appointment of liquidator by the court

218H.—(1) An application to appoint a liquidator under section 139(4) of the Act of 1986 shall be made by note in the process of the petition.

(2) Where the court appoints a liquidator under section 138(5) of the Act of 1986, it shall send a certified copy of the interlocutor pronounced by the court to the liquidator forthwith.

Removal of liquidator

218J. An application by a creditor of the company for removal of a liquidator or provisional liquidator from office under section 172 of the Act of 1986 or for an order under section 171(3) of that Act directing a liquidator to summon a meeting of creditors for the purpose of removing him shall be made by note in the process of the petition.

Applications in relation to remuneration of liquidator

218K.—(1) An application by a liquidator under rule 4.34 of the Insolvency Rules shall be made by note in the process of the petition.

(2) An application by a creditor of the company under rule 4.35 of the Insolvency Rules shall be made by note in the process of the petition.

(3) A note under paragraph (2) shall be served on the liquidator.

Application to appoint a special manager

218L.—(1) An application under section 177 of the Act of 1986 by a liquidator or provisional liquidator for the appointment of a special manager shall be made by note in the process of the petition.

(2) The cautioner, for the caution to be found by the special manager within such time as the court shall direct, may be:—

(*a*) a private person, if approved by the court; or

(*b*) a guarantee company, chosen from a list of such companies prepared for this purpose annually by the Accountant of Court and approved by the Lord President.

(3) A bond of caution certified by the noter under rule 4.70(4) of the Insolvency Rules shall be delivered to the Petition Department by the noter, marked as received by a clerk of court and transmitted forthwith by him to the Accountant of Court.

(4) On receipt of the bond of caution, there shall be issued forthwith to the person appointed to be special manager a certified copy of the interlocutor appointing him.

(5) An application by a special manager to extend the time within which to find caution shall be made by motion.

Other applications

[78] **218M.** An application under the Act of 1986 or rules made under that Act, or under Part VII of the Companies Act 1989, in relation to a winding up by the court not specifically mentioned in this Part shall be made by note in the process of the petition.

PART V

DISQUALIFICATION OF COMPANY DIRECTORS

Applications for disqualification orders

218N.—(1) This rule applies to the following applications:—

(*a*) applications under the following provisions of the Company Directors Disqualification Act 1986:—
   (i) section 3(2) (for disqualification for persistent breaches of companies legislation);
   (ii) section 6(1) (to disqualify unfit directors of insolvent companies);
   (iii) section 8 (for disqualification of unfit director after investigation of company);
   (iv) section 11(1) (for leave by undischarged bankrupt to be concerned in a company);

(*b*) an application for leave under that Act; and

(*c*) an application by the Secretary of State under rule 4(2) of the

---

[78] As amended by S.I. 1991 No. 1157, with effect from 27th May 1991.

Insolvent Companies (Reports on Conduct of Directors) (No. 2) (Scotland) Rules 1986 (for direction to comply with requirement to furnish information, etc.).

(2) An application to which this rule applies shall be made by petition presented to the Outer House and shall be dealt with by the insolvency judge.

[79] (3) Rules 191 to 198 and 218 (except paragraphs (6) and (8)) shall apply to a petition under this rule; and the petition shall be intimated to the Secretary of State for Trade and Industry unless presented by him.

PART VI

GENERAL PROVISIONS

Application
218P. This Part applies to Parts I to IV of this Section.

Applications by note and appeals
218Q.—(1) An application by note, or an appeal, to the court shall be intimated, served and, if necessary, advertised as the court shall direct.

(2) A petition, application by note, appeal or motion, to the court shall be dealt with by the insolvency judge.

Affidavits
218R. The court may accept as evidence an affidavit lodged in support of a petition or note.

Notices, reports and other documents sent to the court
218S. Where, under the Act of 1986 or rules made under that Act:—

(*a*) notice of a fact is to be given to the court;
(*b*) a report is to be made, or sent, to the court; or
(*c*) some other document is to be sent to the court,

it shall be sent or delivered to the Deputy Principal Clerk, who shall cause it to be lodged in the appropriate process.

---

[79] Substituted by S.I. 1990 No. 705.

Sheriff Court Company Insolvency Rules 1986

(S.I. 1986 No. 2297)

[19th December 1986]

The Lords of Council and Session, under and by virtue of the powers conferred on them by section 32 of the Sheriff Courts (Scotland) Act 1971, and of all other powers enabling them in that behalf, after consultation with the Sheriff Court Rules Council, do hereby enact and declare:—

Citation and commencement

1.—(1) This Act of Sederunt may be cited as the Act of Sederunt (Sheriff Court Company Insolvency Rules) 1986 and shall come into operation on 29th December 1986.

(2) This Act of Sederunt shall be inserted in the Books of Sederunt.

Revocation and transitional provision

2.—(1) The Act of Sederunt (Sheriff Court Liquidations) 1930 is hereby revoked.

(2) Notwithstanding paragraph (1), the Act of Sederunt (Sheriff Court Liquidations) 1930 shall continue to have effect in relation to proceedings commenced before the coming into operation of this Act of Sederunt.

Interpretation

3.—(1) In these rules—

"the Act of 1986" means the Insolvency Act 1986;
"the Insolvency Rules" means the Insolvency (Scotland) Rules 1986;
"registered office" means—
(*a*) the place specified, in the statement of the company delivered to the registrar of companies under section 10 of the Companies Act 1985, as the intended place of its registered office on incorporation; or
(*b*) where notice has been given by the company to the registrar of companies under section 287 of the Companies Act 1985 of a change of registered office, the place specified in the last such notice;
"sheriff clerk" has the meaning assigned to it in section 3(*f*) of the Sheriff Courts (Scotland) Act 1907.

(2) Unless the context otherwise requires, words and expressions used in these rules which are also used in the Act of 1986 or the Insolvency Rules have the same meaning as in that Act or those Rules.

469

Part I

Company Voluntary Arrangements

Lodging of nominee's report (Part 1, Chapter 2 of the Insolvency Rules)

4.—(1) This rule applies where the company is not being wound up, is not in liquidation and an administration order is not in force in respect of it.

(2) A report of a nominee, sent to the court under section 2(2) of the Act of 1986, shall be accompanied by a covering letter, lodged in the offices of the court and marked by the sheriff clerk with the date on which it is received.

(3) The report shall be placed before the sheriff for consideration of any direction which he may make under section 3(1) of the Act of 1986.

(4) An application by a nominee to extend the time within which he may lodge his report under section 2(2) of the Act of 1986 shall be made by letter addressed to the sheriff clerk, who shall place the matter before the sheriff for determination.

(5) The letter of application under paragraph (4) and a copy of the reply by the court shall be placed by the sheriff clerk with the nominee's report when it is subsequently lodged.

(6) A person who states in writing that he is a creditor, member or director of the company may, by himself or his agent, on payment of the appropriate fee, inspect the nominee's report lodged under paragraph (2).

Lodging of nominee's report (Part 1, Chapter 4 of the Insolvency Rules)

5.—(1) This rule applies where the company is being wound up, is in liquidation or there is an administration order in force in respect of it.

(2) Where a report of a nominee is sent to the court under section 2(2) of the Act of 1986, it shall be lodged in the process of the petition to wind up the company or the petition for an administration order which is in force in respect of it, as the case may be.

(3) Where the nominee is not the liquidator or administrator, the report shall be placed before the sheriff for consideration of any direction which he may make under section 3(1) of the Act of 1986.

(4) An application by a nominee to extend the time within which he may lodge his report under section 2(2) of the Act of 1986 shall be made by letter addressed to the sheriff clerk, who shall place the matter before the sheriff for determination.

(5) The letter of application under paragraph (4) and a copy of the reply by the court shall be placed by the sheriff clerk in the process of the petition to wind up the company or the petition for an administration order which is in force in respect of it, as the case may be.

(6) A person who states in writing that he is a creditor, member or director of the company may, by himself or his agent, on payment of the appropriate fee, inspect the nominee's report lodged under paragraph (2).

Applications to replace nominee

6. An application under section 2(4) of the Act of 1986 to replace a nominee who has failed to lodge a report under section 2(2) of the Act of 1986, shall be made—

(*a*) by petition where the company is not being wound up, is not in liquidation and an administration order is not in force in respect of it; or

(*b*) by note in the process of the petition to wind up the company or the petition for an administration order which is in force in respect of it, as the case may be,

and shall be intimated and served as the court shall direct.

Report of meetings to approve arrangement

7. The report of the result of a meeting to be sent to the court under section 4(6) of the Act of 1986 shall be sent to the sheriff clerk who shall cause it to be lodged—

(*a*) in a case to which rule 4 applies, with the nominee's report lodged under that rule; or

(*b*) in a case to which rule 5 applies, in the process of the petition to wind up the company or the petition for an administration order which is in force in respect of it, as the case may be.

Abstracts of supervisor's receipts and payments and notices of completion of arrangement

8. An abstract of receipts and payments prepared by a supervisor to be sent to the court under rule 1.21(2) of the Insolvency Rules or a notice of completion of the arrangement (together with a copy of the supervisor's report) to be sent to the court under rule 1.23(3) of those Rules shall be sent to the sheriff clerk, who shall cause it to be lodged—

(*a*) in a case to which rule 4 applies, with the nominee's report lodged under that rule; or

(*b*) in a case to which rule 5 applies, in the process of the petition to wind up the company or the petition for an administration order which is in force in respect of it, as the case may be.

Form of certain applications

9.—(1) This rule applies to applications under any of the following provisions of the Act of 1986 and the Insolvency Rules:—

(*a*) section 6 (to challenge a decision in relation to an arrangement);

(*b*) section 7(3) (to challenge actings of a supervisor);

(*c*) section 7(4)(*a*) (by supervisor for directions);

(*d*) section 7(5) (to appoint a supervisor);

(*e*) rule 1.21(5) (to dispense with sending abstracts or reports or to vary dates on which obligation to send abstracts or reports arises);

(*f*) rule 1.23(4) (by supervisor to extend period for sending notice of implementation of arrangement); and (*g*) any other provision relating to company voluntary arrangements not specifically mentioned in this Part.

(2) An application shall be made—

(*a*) in a case to which rule 4 applies, by petition; or
(*b*) in a case to which rule 5 applies, by note in the process of the petition to wind up the company or the petition for an administration order which is in force in respect of it, as the case may be.

PART II

ADMINISTRATION ORDERS

Petitions for administration orders

10.—(1) A petition for an administration order shall include averments in relation to—

(*a*) the petitioner and the capacity in which he presents the petition, if other than the company;
(*b*) whether it is believed that the company is, or is likely to become, unable to pay its debts and the grounds of that belief;
(*c*) which of the purposes specified in section 8(3) of the Act of 1986 is expected to be achieved by the making of an administration order;
(*d*) the company's financial position, specifying (so far as known) assets and liabilities, including contingent and prospective liabilities;
(*e*) any security known or believed to be held by creditors of the company, whether in any case the security confers power on the holder to appoint a receiver, and whether a receiver has been appointed;
(*f*) so far as known to the petitioner, whether any steps have been taken for the winding up of the company, giving details of them;
(*g*) other matters which, in the opinion of the petitioner, will assist the court in deciding whether to grant an administration order;
(*h*) whether a report has been prepared under rule 2.1 of the Insolvency Rules (independent report on affairs of the company), and, if not, an explanation why not; and
(*i*) the person proposed to be appointed as administrator, giving his name and address and that he is qualified to act as an insolvency practitioner in relation to the company.

(2) There shall be produced with the petition—

(*a*) any document instructing the facts relied on, or otherwise founded on, by the petitioner; and
(*b*) where a report has been prepared under rule 2.1 of the Insolvency Rules, a copy of that report.

Notice of petition

11. Notice of the petition on the persons to whom notice is to be given under rule 2.2 of the Insolvency Rules shall be made in such manner as the court shall direct.

Form of certain applications and appeals where administration order in force

12.—(1) An application or appeal under any of the following provisions of the Act of 1986 or the Insolvency Rules shall be made by note in the process of the petition for an administration order which is in force:—

(a) section 13(2) (application for appointment to fill a vacancy in office of administrator);

(b) section 14(3) (application by administrator for directions);

(c) section 15(2) (application by administrator for power to dispose of property subject to a security);

(d) section 18(1) (application by administrator for discharge or variation of administration order);

(e) section 19(1) (application for removal from office of administrator);

(f) section 22(5) (application for release from, or extension of time for, obligation to submit statement of affairs);

(g) section 27(1) (application for protection of interest of creditors and members);

(h) rule 2.6(2) (appeal against decision of administrator as to expenses of submitting statement of affairs);

(i) rule 2.16(3) (application by administrator for increase of remuneration); and

(j) any other application under a provision relating to administration orders not specifically mentioned in this Part.

(2) An application by an administrator to extend the period for sending an abstract of his receipts and payments under rule 2.17(2) of the Insolvency Rules shall be made by motion in the process of the petition.

Report of administrator's proposals

13.—(1) A report of the meeting to approve the administrator's proposals to be sent to the court under section 24(4) of the Act of 1986 shall be sent to the sheriff clerk, who shall cause it to be lodged in the process of the petition.

(2) Where the report lodged under paragraph (1) discloses that the meeting has declined to approve the administrator's proposals, the court shall appoint a special diet for determination by the sheriff of any order he may make under section 24(5) of the Act of 1986.

Abstracts of administrator's receipts and payments

14. An abstract of receipts and payments of an administrator to be sent to the court under rule 2.17(1) of the Insolvency Rules shall be sent to the sheriff clerk, who shall cause it to be lodged in the process of the petition.

PART III

RECEIVERS

Petitions to appoint receivers

15.—(1) A petition to appoint a receiver for a company shall include averments in relation to—

(*a*) any floating charge and the property over which it is secured;

(*b*) so far as known to the petitioner whether any petition for an administration order has been made in respect of the company, giving details of it;

(*c*) other matters which, in the opinion of the petitioner, will assist the court in deciding whether to appoint a receiver; and

(*d*) the person proposed to be appointed as receiver, giving his name and address and that he is qualified to act as a receiver.

(2) There shall be produced with the petition any document instructing the facts relied on, or otherwise founded on, by the petitioner.

Intimation, service and advertisement

16.—(1) Intimation, service and advertisement of the petition shall be made in accordance with the following provisions of this rule unless the court otherwise directs.

(2) There shall be included in the order for service, a requirement to serve—

(*a*) upon the company; and

(*b*) where a petition for an administration order has been presented, on that petitioner and any respondent to that petition.

(3) Subject to paragraph (5), service of a petition on the company shall be effected at its registered office—

(*a*) by registered or recorded delivery post addressed to the company; or

(*b*) by sheriff officer—

(i) leaving the citation in the hands of a person who, after due inquiry, he has reasonable grounds for believing to be a director, other officer or responsible employee of the company or authorised to accept service on behalf of the company; or

(ii) if there is no such person as is mentioned in head (i) present, depositing it in the registered office in such a way that it is likely to come to the attention of such a person attending at that office.

(4) Where service is effected in accordance with paragraph (3)(*b*)(ii), the sheriff officer thereafter shall send a copy of the petition and citation by ordinary first class post to the registered office of the company.

(5) Where service cannot be effected at the registered office of the company or the company has no registered office—

(*a*) service may be effected at the last known principal place of business of the company in Scotland or at some place in Scotland at which the company carries on business, by leaving the citation in the hands of such a person as is mentioned in paragraph (3)(*b*)(i) or by depositing it as specified in paragraph (3)(*b*)(ii); and

(*b*) where the citation is deposited as is specified in paragraph (3)(*b*)(ii), the sheriff officer thereafter shall send a copy of the petition and citation by ordinary first class post to such place mentioned in sub-paragraph (*a*) of this paragraph in which the citation was deposited.

(6) The petition shall be advertised forthwith—

(*a*) once in the *Edinburgh Gazette*; and

(*b*) once in one or more newspapers as the court shall direct for ensuring that it comes to the notice of the creditors of the company.

(7) The advertisement under paragraph (6) shall state—

(*a*) the name and address of the petitioner;

(*b*) the name and address of the solicitor for the petitioner;

(*c*) the date on which the petition was presented;

(*d*) the precise order sought;

(*e*) the period of notice; and

(*f*) that any person who intends to appear in the petition must lodge answers to the petition within the period of notice.

(8) The period of notice within which answers to the petition may be lodged and after which further consideration of the petition may proceed shall be eight days after such intimation, service and advertisement as the court may have ordered.

Form of certain applications where receiver appointed

17.—(1) An application under any of the following sections of the Act of 1986 shall be made by petition or, where the receiver was appointed by the court, by note in the process of the petition for appointment of a receiver:—

(*a*) section 61(1) (by receiver for authority to dispose of interest in property);

(*b*) section 62 (for removal or resignation of receiver);

(*c*) section 63(1) (by receiver for directions);

(*d*) section 69(1) (to enforce receiver to make returns, etc.); and (*e*) any other section relating to receivers not specifically mentioned in this Part.

(2) An application under any of the following provisions of the Act of 1986 or the Insolvency Rules shall be made by motion in the process of the petition:—

(*a*) section 67(1) or (2) (by receiver to extend time for sending report); and
(*b*) rule 3.9(2) (by receiver to extend time for sending abstract of receipts and payments).

PART IV

WINDING UP BY THE COURT OF COMPANIES REGISTERED UNDER THE COMPANIES ACTS AND OF UNREGISTERED COMPANIES

Petitions to wind up a company

18.—(1) A petition to wind up a company under the Act of 1986 shall include—

(*a*) particulars of the petitioner, if other than the company;
(*b*) in respect of the company—
   (i) the registered name;
   (ii) the address of the registered office and any change of that address within the last six months so far as known to the petitioner;
   (iii) a statement of the nature and objects, the amount of its capital (nominal and issued) and indicating what part is called up, paid up or credited as paid, and the amount of the assets of the company so far as known to the petitioner;
(*c*) a narrative of the facts on which the petitioner relies and any particulars required to instruct the title of the petitioner to present the petition;
(*d*) the name and address of the person to be appointed as interim liquidator and a statement that he is qualified to act as an insolvency practitioner in relation to the company; and
(*e*) a crave setting out the orders applied for, including any intimation, service and advertisement and any appointment of an interim liquidator.

(2) There shall be lodged with the petition any document—

(*a*) instructing the title of the petitioner; and
(*b*) instructing the facts relied on, or otherwise founded on, by the petitioner.

Intimation, service and advertisement

19.—(1) Intimation, service and advertisement shall be in accordance with the following provisions of this rule unless the court—

(a) summarily dismisses the petition; or

(b) otherwise directs.

(2) There shall be included in the order for intimation and service, a requirement—

(a) to intimate on the walls of the court;

(b) where the petitioner is other than the company, to serve upon the company;

(c) where the company is being wound up voluntarily and a liquidator has been appointed, to serve upon the liquidator;

(d) where a receiver has been appointed for the company, to serve upon the receiver;

(e) where the company is—

(i) a recognised bank or licensed institution within the meaning of the Banking Act 1979; or

(ii) an institution to which sections 16 and 18 of that Act apply as if it were licensed,

and the petitioner is not the Bank of England, to serve upon the Bank of England.

(3) Subject to paragraph (5), service of a petition on the company shall be executed at its registered office—

(a) by registered or recorded delivery post addressed to the company; or

(b) by sheriff officer—

(i) leaving the citation in the hands of a person who, after due inquiry, he has reasonable grounds for believing to be a director, other officer or responsible employee of the company or authorised to accept service on behalf of the company; or

(ii) if there is no such person as is mentioned in head (i) present, depositing it in the registered office in such a way that it is likely to come to the attention of such a person attending at that office.

(4) Where service is effected in accordance with paragraph (3)(b)(ii), the sheriff officer thereafter shall send a copy of the petition and citation by ordinary first class post to the registered office of the company.

(5) Where service cannot be effected at the registered office or the company has no registered office—

(a) service may be effected at the last known principal place of business of the company in Scotland or at some place in Scotland at which the company carries on business, by leaving the citation in the hands of such a person as is mentioned in paragraph (3)(b)(i) or by depositing it as specified in paragraph (3)(b)(ii); and

(b) where the citation is deposited as is specified in paragraph

(3)(*b*)(ii), the sheriff officer thereafter shall send a copy of the petition and the citation by ordinary first class post to such place mentioned in sub-paragraph (*a*) of this paragraph in which the citation was deposited.

(6) The petition shall be advertised forthwith—

(*a*) once in the *Edinburgh Gazette*; and
(*b*) once in one or more newspapers as the court shall direct for ensuring that it comes to the notice of the creditors of the company.

(7) The advertisement under paragraph (6) shall state—

(*a*) the name and address of the petitioner and, where the petitioner is the company, the registered office;
(*b*) the name and address of the solicitor for the petitioner;
(*c*) the date on which the petition was presented;
(*d*) the precise order sought;
(*e*) where a provisional liquidator has been appointed, his name, address and the date of his appointment;
(*f*) the period of notice; and
(*g*) that any person who intends to appear in the petition must lodge answers to the petition within the period of notice.

(8) The period of notice within which answers to the petition may be lodged and after which further consideration of the petition may proceed shall be eight days after such intimation, service and advertisement as the court may have ordered.

Lodging of caveats

20.—(1) A company, debenture holder, holder of a floating charge, receiver, shareholder of a company or other person claiming an interest, apprehensive that a petition to wind up that company may be presented and wishing to be heard by the court before an order for intimation, service and advertisement is pronounced, may lodge a caveat with the sheriff clerk.

(2) A caveat shall endure for 12 months on the expiry of which a new caveat may be lodged.

(3) Where a caveat has been lodged and has not expired, no order may be pronounced without the person lodging the caveat having been given an opportunity to be heard by the court.

Substitution of creditor or contributory for petitioner

21.—(1) This rule applies where a petitioner—

(*a*) is subsequently found not entitled to present the petition;
(*b*) fails to make intimation, service and advertisement as directed by the court;
(*c*) consents to withdraw the petition or to allow it to be dismissed or refused;

(*d*) fails to appear when the petition is called for hearing; or

(*e*) appears, but does not move for an order in terms of the prayer of the petition.

(2) The court may, on such terms as it considers just, sist as petitioner in room of the original petitioner any creditor or contributory who, in the opinion of the court, is entitled to present a petition.

(3) An application by a creditor or contributory to be sisted under paragraph (2)—

(*a*) may be made at any time before the petition is dismissed or refused; and

(*b*) shall be made by note in the process of the petition, and if necessary the court may continue the cause for a specified period to allow a note to be presented.

Advertisement of appointment of liquidator

22. Where a liquidator is appointed by the court, the court may order that the liquidator shall advertise his appointment once in one or more newspapers as the court shall direct for ensuring that it comes to the notice of creditors of the company.

Provisional liquidators

23.—(1) An application to appoint a provisional liquidator under section 135 of the Act of 1986 may be made—

(*a*) by the petitioner, in the crave of the petition or subsequently by note in the process of the petition; or

(*b*) by a creditor or contributory of the company, the company, Secretary of State or a person entitled under any enactment to present a petition to wind up the company, in a note in the process of the petition.

(2) The petition or note, as the case may be, shall include averments in relation to—

(*a*) the grounds on which it is proposed that a provisional liquidator should be appointed;

(*b*) the name and address of the person to be appointed as provisional liquidator and that he is qualified to act as an insolvency practitioner in relation to the company; and

(*c*) whether, to the knowledge of the applicant, there is a receiver for the company or a liquidator has been appointed for the voluntary winding up of the company.

(3) Where the court is satisfied that sufficient grounds exist for the appointment of a provisional liquidator, it shall, on making the appointment, specify the functions to be carried out by him in relation to the affairs of the company.

(4) The applicant shall send a certified copy of the interlocutor appointing a provisional liquidator forthwith to the person appointed.

(5) On receiving a certified copy of his appointment on an application by note, the provisional liquidator shall intimate his appointment forthwith—

(a) once in the *Edinburgh Gazette*; and

(b) once in one or more newspapers as the court shall direct for ensuring that it comes to the notice of creditors of the company.

(6) An application for discharge of a provisional liquidator shall be by note in the process of the petition.

Applications and appeals in relation to a statement of affairs

24.—(1) An application under section 131(5) of the Act of 1986 for—

(a) release from an obligation imposed under section 131(1) or (2) of the Act of 1986; or

(b) an extension of time for the submission of a statement of affairs,

shall be made by note in the process of the petition.

(2) A note under paragraph (1) shall be served on the liquidator or provisional liquidator, as the case may be.

(3) The liquidator or provisional liquidator may lodge answers to the note or lodge a report of any matters which he considers should be drawn to the attention of the court.

(4) Where the liquidator or provisional liquidator lodges a report under paragraph (3), he shall send a copy of it to the noter forthwith.

(5) Where the liquidator or provisional liquidator does not appear, a certified copy of the interlocutor pronounced by the court disposing of the note shall be sent by the noter forthwith to him.

(6) An appeal under rule 4.9(6) of the Insolvency Rules against a refusal by the liquidator of an allowance towards the expense of preparing a statement of affairs shall be made by note in the process of the petition.

Appeals against adjudication of claims

25.—(1) An appeal under section 49(6) of the Bankruptcy (Scotland) Act 1985, as applied by rule 4.16 of the Insolvency Rules, by a creditor or contributory of the company against a decision of the liquidator shall be made by note in the process of the petition.

(2) A note under paragraph (1) shall be served on the liquidator.

(3) On receipt of the note served on him under this rule, the liquidator forthwith shall send to the court the claim in question and a copy of his adjudication for lodging in process.

(4) After the note has been disposed of, the court shall return the claim and the adjudication to the liquidator together with a copy of the interlocutor.

Appointment of liquidator by the court

26.—(1) An application to appoint a liquidator under section 139(4) of the Act of 1986 shall be made by note in the process of the petition.

(2) Where the court appoints a liquidator under section 138(5) of the Act of 1986, the sheriff clerk shall send a certified copy of the interlocutor pronounced by the court to the liquidator forthwith.

Removal of liquidator

27. An application by a creditor of the company for removal of a liquidator or provisional liquidator from office under section 172 of the Act of 1986 or for an order under section 171(3) of the Act of 1986 directing a liquidator to summon a meeting of creditors for the purpose of removing him shall be made by note in the process of the petition.

Applications in relation to remuneration of liquidator

28.—(1) An application by a liquidator under rule 4.34 of the Insolvency Rules shall be made by note in the process of the petition.

(2) An application by a creditor of the company under rule 4.35 of the Insolvency Rules shall be made by note in the process of the petition.

(3) A note under paragraph (2) shall be served on the liquidator.

Application to appoint a special manager

29.—(1) An application under section 177 of the Act of 1986 by a liquidator or provisional liquidator for the appointment of a special manager shall be made by note in the process of the petition.

(2) The cautioner, for the caution to be found by the special manager within such time as the court shall direct, may be—

(a) a private person, if approved by the court; or

(b) a guarantee company, chosen from a list of such companies prepared for this purpose annually by the accountant of court and approved by the Lord President of the Court of Session.

(3) A bond of caution certified by the noter under rule 4.70(4) of the Insolvency Rules shall be delivered to the sheriff clerk by the noter, marked as received by him and transmitted forthwith by him to the accountant of court.

(4) On receipt of the bond of caution, the sheriff clerk shall issue forthwith to the person appointed to be special manager a certified copy of the interlocutor appointing him.

(5) An application by a special manager to extend the time within which to find caution shall be made by motion.

Other applications

30. An application under the Act of 1986 or rules made under that Act in relation to a winding up by the court not specifically mentioned in this Part shall be made by note in the process of the petition.

PART V

GENERAL PROVISIONS

Application

31. This Part applies to Parts I to IV of these rules.

Intimation, service and advertisement of notes and appeals

32. An application by note, or an appeal, to the court under these rules shall be intimated, served and, if necessary, advertised as the court shall direct.

Affidavits

33. The court may accept as evidence an affidavit lodged in support of a petition or note.

Notices, reports and other documents sent to the court

34. Where, under the Act of 1986 or rules made under that Act—

(*a*) notice of a fact is to be given to the court;

(*b*) a report is to be made, or sent, to the court; or

(*c*) some other document is to be sent to the court;

it shall be sent or delivered to the sheriff clerk of the court, who shall cause it to be lodged in the appropriate process.

Failure to comply with rules

35.—(1) The court may, in its discretion, relieve a party from the consequences of any failure to comply with the provisions of a rule shown to be due to mistake, oversight or other cause, which is not wilful non-observance of the rule, on such terms and conditions as the court considers just.

(2) Where the court relieves a party from the consequences of failure to comply with a rule under paragraph 1, the court may pronounce such interlocutor as may be just so as to enable the cause to proceed as if the failure to comply with the rule had not occurred.

PART VI

APPEALS

Appeals to the sheriff principal or Court of Session

36.—(1) Where an appeal to the sheriff principal or the Court of Session is competent, it shall be taken by note of appeal which shall—

(*a*) be written by the appellant or his solicitor on—

    (i) the interlocutor sheet or other written record containing the interlocutor appealed against; or

    (ii) a separate document lodged with the sheriff clerk;

(*b*) be as nearly as may be in the following terms:— "The (*petitioner, noter, respondent or other party*) appeals to the Sheriff Principal [*or* Court of Session]"; and

(*c*) be signed by the appellant or his solicitor and bear the date on which it is signed.

(2) Such an appeal shall be marked within 14 days of the date of the interlocutor appealed against.

(3) Where the appeal is to the Court of Session, the note of appeal shall specify the name and address of the solicitor in Edinburgh who will be acting for the appellant.

(4) On an appeal being taken, the sheriff clerk shall within four days—

(a) transmit the process—
   (i) where the appeal is to sheriff principal, to him; or
   (ii) where the appeal is to the Court of Session, to the deputy principal clerk of session; and

(b) send written notice of the appeal to any other party to the cause and certify in the interlocutor sheet, or other written record containing the interlocutor appealed against, that he has done so.

(5) Failure of the sheriff clerk to give notice under paragraph 4(b) shall not invalidate the appeal.

THE INSOLVENCY (SCOTLAND) RULES 1986[79a]

(1986 No. 1915 (S.139))

Made	–	–	–	*10th November* 1986
Laid before Parliament			*26th November* 1986
Coming into Operation			*29th December* 1986

The Secretary of State, in exercise of the powers conferred on him by section 411 of the Insolvency Act 1986 and of all other powers enabling him in that behalf, hereby makes the following Rules:—

INTRODUCTORY PROVISIONS

Citation and commencement

0.1. These Rules may be cited as the Insolvency (Scotland) Rules 1986 and shall come into operation on 29th December 1986.

Interpretation

0.2.—[80] (1) In these Rules

"the Act" means the Insolvency Act 1986;
"the Companies Act" means the Companies Act 1985;
"the Banking Act" means the Banking Act 1987;
"the Bankruptcy Act" means the Bankruptcy (Scotland) Act 1985;
"the Rules" means the Insolvency (Scotland) Rules 1986;

[79a] These Rules set out the detailed procedure for the conduct of insolvency proceedings under the Insolvency Act 1986 ("the Act") relating to companies registered in Scotland and other companies which the Scottish courts have jurisdiction to wind up and otherwise give effect to the Act in relation to Scotland.
   Part 1 of the Rules sets out the procedure relating to company voluntary arrangements under Part 1 of the Act.
   Part 2 of the Rules sets out the procedure relating to the administration procedure in Part II of the Act (Administration Orders).
   Part 3 of the Rules sets out the procedure relating to the administration procedure relating to receivers in Chapter II of Part III of the Act (Receivers (Scotland)). In addition, the Receivers (Scotland) Regulations 1986 (S.I. 1986 No. 1917) prescribe matters which expressly fall to be prescribed in terms of that Chapter.
   Parts 4–6 of the Rules set out the procedure relating to winding up of companies in Part IV of the Act. Part 4 of the Rules deals with winding up by the court. Parts 5 and 6 of, and Schedules 1 and 2 to, the Rules apply the provisions of Part 4, with modifications, to creditors' voluntary winding up and members' voluntary winding up respectively. Part 7 of the Rules contains provisions of general application to insolvency proceedings. They include provisions relating to meetings (Chapter 1), proxies and company representation (Chapter 2) and miscellaneous matters (Chapter 3). In particular, Schedule 5 contains the forms which are to be used for the purposes of the provisions of the Act or the Rules which are referred to in those forms.
   The Rules come into force on 29th December 1986 when the Act comes into force and will apply to insolvency proceedings which are commenced on or after that day.
[80] Added by S.I. 1987 No. 1921.

"accounting period" in relation to the winding up of a company, shall be construed in accordance with section 52(1) and (6) of the Bankruptcy Act as applied by Rule 4.68;

"business day" means any day other than a Saturday, a Sunday, Christmas Day, Good Friday or a day which is a bank holiday in any part of Great Britain;

"company" means a company which the courts in Scotland have jurisdiction to wind up;

"insolvency proceedings" means any proceedings under the first group of Parts in the Act or under these Rules;

"proxy-holder" shall be construed in accordance with Rule 7.14;

"receiver" means a receiver appointed under section 51 (Receivers (Scotland)); and

"responsible insolvency practitioner" means, in relation to any insolvency proceedings, the person acting as supervisor of a voluntary arrangement under Part 1 of the Act, or as administrator, receiver, liquidator or provisional liquidator.

(2) In these Rules, unless the context otherwise requires, any reference—

(a) to a section is a reference to a section of the Act;
(b) to a Rule is a reference to a Rule of the Rules;
(c) to a Part or a Schedule is a reference to a Part of, or Schedule to, the Rules;
(d) to a Chapter is a reference to a Chapter of the Part in which that reference is made.

Application

0.3. These Rules apply—

(a) to receivers appointed, and
(b) to all other insolvency proceedings which are commenced, on or after the date on which the Rules come into operation.

PART I

COMPANY VOLUNTARY ARRANGEMENTS

CHAPTER 1

PRELIMINARY

Scope of this Part; interpretation

1.1.—(1) The Rules in this Part apply where, pursuant to Part I of the Act, it is intended to make and there is made a proposal to a company and to its creditors for a voluntary arrangement, that is to say, a composition in satisfaction of its debts or a scheme of arrangement of its affairs.

(2) In this Part—

(a) Chapter 2 applies where the proposal for a voluntary arrangement is made by the directors of the company, and neither is the company in liquidation nor is an administration order under Part II of the Act in force in relation to it;

(b) Chapter 3 applies where the company is in liquidation or an administration order is in force and the proposal is made by the liquidator or (as the case may be) the administrator, he in either case being the nominee for the purposes of the proposal;

(c) Chapter 4 applies in the same case as Chapter 3, but where the nominee is an insolvency practitioner other than the liquidator or administrator; and

(d) Chapters 5 and 6 apply in all of the three cases mentioned in sub-paragraphs (a) to (c) above.

(3) In Chapters 3, 4 and 5 the liquidator or the administrator is referred to as the "responsible insolvency practitioner".

CHAPTER 2

PROPOSAL BY DIRECTORS

Preparation of proposal

1.2. The directors shall prepare for the intended nominee a proposal on which (with or without amendments to be made under Rule 1.3 below) to make his report to the court under section 2.

Contents of proposal

1.3.—(1) The directors' proposal shall provide a short explanation why, in their opinion, a voluntary arrangement under Part I of the Act is desirable, and give reasons why the company's creditors may be expected to concur with such an arrangement.

(2) The following matters shall be stated, or otherwise dealt with, in the directors' proposal—

(a) the following matters, so far as within the directors' immediate knowledge—
  (i) the company's assets, with an estimate of their respective values;
  (ii) the extent (if any) to which the assets are subject to any security in favour of any creditors;
  (iii) the extent (if any) to which particular assets of the company are to be excluded from the voluntary arrangement;

(b) particulars of any property other than assets of the company itself, which is proposed to be included in the arrangement, the source of such property and the terms on which it is to be made available for inclusion;

(c) the nature and amount of the company's liabilities (so far as within the directors' immediate knowledge), the manner in which they are proposed to be met, modified, postponed or otherwise dealt with by means of the arrangement, and (in particular)—

    (i) how it is proposed to deal with preferential creditors (defined in section 386) and creditors who are, or claim to be, secured;

    (ii) how persons connected with the company (being creditors) are proposed to be treated under the arrangement; and

    (iii) whether there are, to the directors' knowledge, any circumstances giving rise to the possibility, in the event that the company should go into liquidation, of claims under—

section 242 (gratuitous alienations),

section 243 (unfair preferences),

section 244 (extortionate credit transactions), or

section 245 (floating charges invalid);

and, where any such circumstances are present, whether, and if so how, it is proposed under the voluntary arrangement to make provision for wholly or partly indemnifying the company in respect of such claims;

(d) whether any, and if so what, cautionary obligations (including guarantees) have been given of the company's debts by other persons, specifying which (if any) of the cautioners are persons connected with the company;

(e) the proposed duration of the voluntary arrangement;

(f) the proposed dates of distributions to creditors, with estimates of their amounts;

(g) the amount proposed to be paid to the nominee (as such) by way of remuneration and expenses;

(h) the manner in which it is proposed that the supervisor of the arrangement should be remunerated and his expenses defrayed;

(i) whether, for the purposes of the arrangement, any cautionary obligations (including guarantees) are to be offered by directors, or other persons, and whether (if so) any security is to be given or sought;

(j) the manner in which funds held for the purposes of the arrangement are to be banked, invested or otherwise dealt with pending distribution to creditors;

(k) the manner in which funds held for the purpose of payment to creditors, and not so paid on the termination of the arrangement, are to be dealt with;

(l) the manner in which the business of the company is being and is proposed to be conducted during the course of the arrangement;

(m) details of any further credit facilities which it is intended to arrange for the company and how the debts so arising are to be paid;

(*n*) the functions which are to be undertaken by the supervisor of the arrangement;

(*o*) the name, address and qualification of the person proposed as supervisor of the voluntary arrangement, and confirmation that he is (so far as the directors are aware) qualified to act as an insolvency practitioner in relation to the company.

(3) With the agreement in writing of the nominee, the directors' proposal may be amended at any time up to delivery of the former's report to the court under section 2(2).

Notice to intended nominee

1.4.—(1) The directors shall give to the intended nominee written notice of their proposal.

(2) The notice, accompanied by a copy of the proposal, shall be delivered either to the nominee himself, or to a person authorised to take delivery of documents on his behalf.

(3) If the intended nominee agrees to act, he shall cause a copy of the notice to be endorsed to the effect that it has been received by him on a specified date; and the period of 28 days referred to in section 2(2) then runs from that date.

(4) The copy of the notice so endorsed shall be returned by the nominee forthwith to the directors at an address specified by them in the notice for that purpose.

Statement of affairs

1.5.—(1) The directors shall, within seven days after their proposal is delivered to the nominee, or within such longer time as he may allow, deliver to him a statement of the company's affairs.

(2) The statement shall comprise the following particulars (supplementing or amplifying, so far as is necessary for clarifying the state of the company's affairs, those already given in the directors' proposal):—

(*a*) a list of the company's assets, divided into such categories as are appropriate for easy identification, with estimated values assigned to each category;

(*b*) in the case of any property on which a claim against the company is wholly or partly secured, particulars of the claim and its amount and of how and when the security was created;

(*c*) the names and addresses of the company's preferential creditors (defined in section 386), with the amounts of their respective claims;

(*d*) the names and addresses of the company's unsecured creditors, with the amounts of their respective claims;

(*e*) particulars of any debts owed by or to the company to or by persons connected with it;

(*f*) the names and addresses of the company's members and details of their respective shareholdings; and

(g) such other particulars (if any) as the nominee may in writing require to be furnished for the purposes of making his report to the court on the directors' proposal.

(3) The statement of affairs shall be made up to a date not earlier than two weeks before the date of the notice given by the directors to the nominee under Rule 1.4. However the nominee may allow an extension of that period to the nearest practicable date (not earlier than two months before the date of the notice under Rule 1.4); and if he does so, he shall give his reasons in his report to the court on the directors' proposal.

(4) The statement shall be certified as correct, to the best of their knowledge and belief, by two or more directors of the company or by the company secretary and at least one director (other than the secretary himself).

Additional disclosure for assistance of nominee

1.6.—(1) If it appears to the nominee that he cannot properly prepare his report on the basis of information in the directors' proposal and statement of affairs, he may call on the directors to provide him with—

(a) further and better particulars as to the circumstances in which, and the reasons why, the company is insolvent or (as the case may be) threatened with insolvency;

(b) particulars of any previous proposals which have been made in respect of the company under Part I of the Act;

(c) any further information with respect to the company's affairs which the nominee thinks necessary for the purposes of his report.

(2) The nominee may call on the directors to inform him, with respect to any person who is, or at any time in the two years preceding the notice under Rule 1.4 has been, a director or officer of the company, whether and in what circumstances (in those two years or previously) that person—

(a) has been concerned in the affairs of any other company (whether or not incorporated in Scotland) which has become insolvent, or

(b) has had his estate sequestrated, granted a trust deed for his creditors, been adjudged bankrupt or compounded or entered into an arrangement with his creditors.

(3) For the purpose of enabling the nominee to consider their proposal and prepare his report on it, the directors must give him access to the company's accounts and records.

Nominee's report on the proposal

1.7.—(1) With his report to the court under section 2 the nominee shall lodge—

(a) a copy of the directors' proposal (with amendments, if any, authorised under Rule 1.3(3));

(*b*) a copy or summary of the company's statement of affairs.

(2) If the nominee makes known his opinion that meetings of the company and its creditors should be summoned under section 3, his report shall have annexed to it his comments on the proposal. If his opinion is otherwise, he shall give his reasons for that opinion.

(3) The nominee shall send a copy of his report and of his comments (if any) to the company. Any director, member or creditor of the company is entitled, at all reasonable times on any business day, to inspect the report and comments.

Replacement of nominee

1.8. Where any person intends to apply to the court under section 2(4) for the nominee to be replaced he shall give to the nominee at least seven days' notice of his application.

Summoning of meetings under section 3

1.9.—(1) If in his report the nominee states that in his opinion meetings of the company and its creditors should be summoned to consider the directors' proposal, the date on which the meetings are to be held shall be not less than 14, nor more than 28 days from the date on which he lodged his report in court under section 2.

(2) The notice summoning the meeting shall specify the court in which the nominee's report under section 2 has been lodged and with each notice there shall be sent—

(*a*) a copy of the directors' proposal;

(*b*) a copy of the statement of affairs or, if the nominee thinks fit, a summary of it (the summary to include a list of creditors and the amount of their debts); and

(*c*) the nominee's comments on the proposal.

CHAPTER 3

PROPOSAL BY ADMINISTRATOR OR LIQUIDATOR WHERE HE IS THE NOMINEE

Preparation of proposal

1.10. The responsible insolvency practitioner's proposal shall specify—

[81](*a*) all such matters as under Rule 1.3 in Chapter 2 of the directors of the company would be required to include in a proposal by them, with, in addition, where the company is subject to an administration order, the names and addresses of the company's preferential creditors (defined in section 386), with the amounts of their respective claims; and

(*b*) such other matters (if any) as the insolvency practitioner

---

[81] As amended by S.I. 1987 No. 1921.

considers appropriate for ensuring that members and creditors of the company are enabled to reach an informed decision on the proposal.

Summoning of meetings under section 3

1.11.—(1) The responsible insolvency practitioner shall give at least 14 days' notice of the meetings of the company and of its creditors under section 3(2).

(2) With each notice summoning the meeting, there shall be sent—

(*a*) a copy of the responsible insolvency practitioner's proposal; and

(*b*) a copy of the company's statement of affairs or, if he thinks fit, a summary of it (the summary to include a list of the creditors and the amount of their debts).

CHAPTER 4

PROPOSAL BY ADMINISTRATOR OR LIQUIDATOR WHERE ANOTHER INSOLVENCY PRACTITIONER IS THE NOMINEE

Preparation of proposal and notice to nominee

1.12.—(1) The responsible insolvency practitioner shall give notice to the intended nominee, and prepare his proposal for a voluntary arrangement, in the same manner as is required of the directors in the case of a proposal by them, under Chapter 2.

(2) Rule 1.2 applies to the responsible insolvency practitioner as it applies to the directors; and Rule 1.4 applies as regards the action to be taken by the nominee.

[82](3) The content of the proposal shall be as required by Rule 1.10.

(4) Rule 1.6 applies, in respect of the information to be provided to the nominee, reading references to the directors as referring to the responsible insolvency practitioner.

(5) With the proposal the responsible insolvency practitioner shall provide a copy of the company's statement of affairs.

(6) Rules 1.7 to 1.9 apply as regards a proposal under this Chapter as they apply to a proposal under Chapter 2.

CHAPTER 5

MEETINGS

General

1.13. The provisions of Chapter 1 of Part 7 (Meetings) shall apply with regard to the meetings of the company and of the creditors which are summoned under section 3, subject to Rules 1.9, 1.11 and 1.12(6) and the provisions in this Chapter.

---

[82] As amended by S.I. 1987 No. 1921.

Summoning of meetings

1.14.—(1) In fixing the date, time and place for the creditors' meeting and the company meeting, the person summoning the meetings ("the convener") shall have regard primarily to the convenience of the creditors.

(2) The meetings shall be held on the same day and in the same place, but the creditors' meeting shall be fixed for a time in advance of the company meeting.

Attendance by company officers

1.15.—(1) At least 14 days' notice to attend the meetings shall be given by the convener to—

(a) all directors of the company, and

(b) any persons in whose case the convener thinks that their presence is required as being officers of the company or as having been directors or officers of it at any time in the two years immediately preceding the date of the notice.

(2) The chairman may, if he thinks fit, exclude any present or former director or officer from attendance at a meeting, either completely or for any part of it; and this applies whether or not a notice under this Rule has been sent to the person excluded.

Adjournments

1.16.—(1) On the day on which the meetings are held, they may from time to time be adjourned; and, if the chairman thinks fit for the purpose of obtaining the simultaneous agreement of the meetings to the proposal (with the same modifications, if any), the meetings may be held together.

(2) If on the day the requisite majority for the approval of the voluntary arrangement (with the same modifications, if any) has not been obtained from both creditors and members of the company, the chairman may, and shall, if it is so resolved, adjourn the meetings for not more than 14 days.

(3) If there are subsequently further adjournments, the final adjournment shall not be to a day later than 14 days after the date on which the meetings were originally held.

(4) There shall be no adjournment of either meeting unless the other is also adjourned to the same business day.

(5) In the case of a proposal by the directors, if the meetings are adjourned under paragraph (2), notice of the fact shall be given by the nominee forthwith to the court.

(6) If following any final adjournment of the meetings the proposal (with the same modifications, if any) is not agreed by both meetings, it is deemed rejected.

Report of meetings

1.17.—(1) A report of the meetings shall be prepared by the person who was chairman of them.

(2) The report shall—

(a) state whether the proposal for a voluntary arrangement was approved or rejected and, if approved, with what (if any) modifications;

(b) set out the resolutions which were taken at each meeting, and the decision on each one;

(c) list the creditors and members of the company (with their respective values) who were present or represented at the meeting, and how they voted on each resolution; and

(d) include such further information (if any) as the chairman thinks it appropriate to make known to the court.

(3) A copy of the chairman's report shall, within four days of the meetings being held, be lodged in court.

(4) In respect of each of the meetings the persons to whom notice of the result of the meetings is to be sent under section 4(6) are all those who were sent notice of the meeting. The notice shall be sent immediately after a copy of the chairman's report is lodged in court under paragraph (3).

(5) If the voluntary arrangement has been approved by the meetings *Form 1.1. (Scot)* (whether or not in the form proposed) the chairman shall forthwith send a copy of the report to the registrar of companies.

CHAPTER 6

IMPLEMENTATION OF THE VOLUNTARY ARRANGEMENT

Resolutions to follow approval

1.18.—(1) If the voluntary arrangement is approved (with or without modifications) by the two meetings, a resolution may be taken by the creditors, where two or more insolvency practitioners are appointed to act as supervisor, on the question whether acts to be done in connection with the arrangement may be done by one of them or are to be done by both or all.

(2) A resolution under paragraph (1) may be passed in anticipation of the approval of the voluntary arrangement by the company meeting if such meeting has not at that time been concluded.

(3) If at either meeting a resolution is moved for the appointment of some person other than the nominee to be supervisor of the arrangement, there must be produced to the chairman, at or before the meeting—

(a) that person's written consent to act (unless the person is present and then and there signifies this consent), and

(b) his written confirmation that he is qualified to act as an insolvency practitioner in relation to the company.

Hand-over of property, etc. to supervisor

1.19.—(1) After the approval of the voluntary arrangement, the directors or, where—

(a) the company is in liquidation or is subject to an administration order, and

(b) a person other than the responsible insolvency practitioner is appointed as supervisor of the voluntary arrangement,

the responsible insolvency practitioner, shall forthwith do all that is required for putting the supervisor into possession of the assets included in the arrangement.

(2) Where paragraph (1)(a) and (b) applies, the supervisor shall, on taking possession of the assets, discharge any balance due to the responsible insolvency practitioner by way of remuneration or on account of—

(a) fees, costs, charges and expenses properly incurred and payable under the Act or the Rules, and

(b) any advances made in respect of the company, together with interest on such advances at the official rate (within the meaning of Rule 4.66(2)(b)) ruling at the date on which the company went into liquidation or (as the case may be) became subject to the administration order.

(3) Alternatively, the supervisor shall, before taking possession, give the responsible insolvency practitioner a written undertaking to discharge any such balance out of the first realisation of assets.

(4) The sums due to the responsible insolvency practitioner as above shall be paid out of the assets included in the arrangement in priority to all other sums payable out of those assets, subject only to the deduction from realisations by the supervisor of the proper costs and expenses of such realisations.

(5) The supervisor shall from time to time out of the realisation of assets discharge all cautionary obligations (including guarantees) properly given by the responsible insolvency practitioner for the benefit of the company and shall pay all the responsible insolvency practitioner's expenses.

Revocation or suspension of the arrangement

1.20.—(1) This Rule applies where the court makes an order of revocation or suspension under section 6.

(2) The person who applied for the order shall serve copies of it—

(a) on the supervisor of the voluntary arrangement, and

(b) on the directors of the company or the administrator or liquidator (according to who made the proposal for the arrangement).

Service on the directors may be effected by service of a single copy of the order on the company at its registered office.

(3) If the order includes a direction given by the court, under section 6(4)(b), for any further meetings to be summoned notice shall also be given by the person who applied for the order to whoever is, in accordance with the direction, required to summon the meetings.

(4) The directors or (as the case may be) the administrator or liquidator shall—

(*a*) forthwith after receiving a copy of the court's order, give notice of it to all persons who were sent notice of the creditors' and the company meetings or who, not having been sent that notice, appear to be affected by the order; and

(*b*) within seven days of their receiving a copy of the order (or within such longer period as the court may allow), give notice to the court whether it is intended to make a revised proposal to the company and its creditors, or to invite reconsideration of the original proposal.

(5) The person on whose application the order of revocation or suspension was made shall, within seven days after the making of the order, deliver a copy of the order to the registrar of companies. *Form 1.2. (Scot)*

Supervisor's accounts and reports
1.21.—(1) Where the voluntary arrangement authorises or requires the supervisor—

(*a*) to carry on the business of the company, or to trade on its behalf or in its name, or

(*b*) to realise assets of the company, or

(*c*) otherwise to administer or dispose of any of its funds,

he shall keep accounts and records of his acts and dealings in and in connection with the arrangement, including in particular records of all receipts and payments of money.

(2) The supervisor shall, not less often than once in every 12 months beginning with the date of his appointment, prepare an abstract of such receipts and payments and send copies of it, accompanied by his comments on the progress and efficacy of the arrangement, to—

(*a*) the court, *Form 1.3. (Scot)*

(*b*) the registrar of companies,

(*c*) the company,

(*d*) all those of the company's creditors who are bound by the arrangement,

(*e*) subject to paragraph (5) below, the members of the company who are so bound, and

(*f*) where the company is not in liquidation, the company's auditors for the time being.

If in any period of 12 months he has made no payments and had no receipts, he shall at the end of that period send a statement to that effect to all those specified in sub-paragraphs (*a*) to (*f*) above.

(3) An abstract provided under paragraph (2) shall relate to a period beginning with the date of the supervisor's appointment or (as the case may be) the day following the end of the last period for which an abstract was prepared under this Rule; and copies of the abstract shall

be sent out, as required by paragraph (2), within the two months following the end of the period to which the abstract relates.

(4) If the supervisor is not authorised as mentioned in paragraph (1), he shall, not less often than once in every 12 months beginning with the date of his appointment, send to all those specified in paragraphs 2(*a*) to (*f*) a report on the progress and efficacy of the voluntary arrangement.

(5) The court may, on application by the supervisor,—

(*a*) dispense with the sending under this Rule of abstracts or reports to members of the company, either altogether or on the basis that the availability of the abstract or report to members on request is to be advertised by the supervisor in a specified manner;

(*b*) vary the dates on which the obligation to send abstracts or reports arises.

Fees, costs, charges and expenses

1.22. The fees, costs, charges and expenses that may be incurred for any of the purposes of a voluntary arrangement are—

(*a*) any disbursements made by the nominee prior to the approval of the arrangement, and any remuneration for his services as is agreed between himself and the company (or, as the case may be, the administrator or liquidator);

(*b*) any fees, costs, charges or expenses which—
(i) are sanctioned by the terms of the arrangement, or
(ii) would be payable, or correspond to those which would be payable, in an administration or winding up.

Completion of the arrangement

1.23.—(1) Not more than 28 days after the final completion of the voluntary arrangement, the supervisor shall send to all creditors and members of the company who are bound by it a notice that the voluntary arrangement has been fully implemented.

(2) With the notice there shall be sent to each creditor and member a copy of a report by the supervisor, summarising all receipts and payments made by him in pursuance of the arrangement, and explaining any difference in the actual implementation of it as compared with the proposal approved by the creditors' and company meetings.

Form 1.4. (Scot) (3) The supervisor shall, within the 28 days mentioned above, send to the registrar of companies and to the court a copy of the notice to creditors and members under paragraph (1), together with a copy of the report under paragraph (2).

(4) The court may, on application by the supervisor, extend the period of 28 days under paragraphs (1) or (3).

False representations, etc.

1.24.—(1) A person being a past or present officer of a company commits an offence if he make any false representation or commits any other fraud for the purpose of obtaining the approval of the company's members or creditors to a proposal for a voluntary arrangement under Part I of the Act.

(2) For this purpose "officer" includes a shadow director.

(3) A person guilty of an offence under this Rule is liable to imprisonment or a fine, or both.

PART 2

ADMINSTRATION PROCEDURE

CHAPTER 1

APPLICATION FOR, AND MAKING OF, THE ORDER

Independent report on company's affairs

2.1.—(1) Where it is proposed to apply to the court by way of petition for an administration order to be made under section 8 in relation to a company, there may be prepared in support of the petition a report by an independent person to the effect that the appointment of an administrator for the company is expedient.

(2) The report may be by the person proposed as administrator, or by any other person having adequate knowledge of the company's affairs, not being a director, secretary, manager, member or employee of the company.

(3) The report shall specify which of the purposes specified in section 8(3) may, in the opinion of the person preparing it, be achieved for the company by the making of an administration order in relation to it.

Notice of petition

2.2.—[83] (1) Under section 9(2)(*a*), notice of the petition shall forthwith be given by the petitioner to any person who has appointed, *Form 2.1 (Scot)* or is or may be entitled to appoint, an administrative receiver, and to the following persons:—

(*a*) an administrative receiver, if appointed;
(*b*) if a petition for the winding up of the company has been presented but no order for winding up has yet been made, the petitioner under that petition;
(*c*) a provisional liquidator, if appointed;
(*d*) the person proposed in the petition to be the administrator;
(*e*) the registrar of companies;
(*f*) the Keeper of the Register of Inhibitions and Adjudications for recording in that register; and
(*g*) the company, if the petition for the making of an administration

---

[83] As amended by S.I. 1987 No. 1921.

order is presented by the directors or by a creditor or creditors of the company.

(2) Notice of the petition shall also be given to the persons upon whom the court orders that the petition be served.

Notice and advertisement of administration order

2.3.—(1) If the court makes an administration order, it shall forthwith give notice of the order to the person appointed as administrator.

(2) Under section 21(1)(*a*) the administrator shall forthwith after the order is made advertise the making of the order once in the *Edinburgh Gazette* and once in a newspaper circulating in the area where the company has its principal place of business or in such newspaper as he thinks most appropriate for ensuring that the order comes to the notice of the company's creditors.

Form 2.2 (Scot) (3) Under section 21(2), the administrator shall send a notice with a copy of the court's order certified by the clerk of court to the registrar of companies, and in addition shall send a copy of the order to the following persons:—

[84](*a*) any person who has appointed, or is or may be entitled to appoint, an administrative receiver;

(*b*) an administrative receiver, if appointed;

(*c*) a petitioner in a petition for the winding up of the company, if that petition is pending;

(*d*) any provisional liquidator of the company, if appointed; and

(*e*) the Keeper of the Register of Inhibitions and Adjudications for recording in that register.

(4) If the court dismisses the petition under section 9(4) or discharges the administration order under section 18(3) or 24(5), the petitioner or, as the case may be, the administrator shall—

Form 2.3 (Scot)
Form 2.4 (Scot) (*a*) forthwith send a copy of the court's order dismissing the petition or effecting the discharge to the Keeper of the Register of Inhibitions and Adjudications for recording in that register; and

Form 2.3 (Scot)
Form 2.4 (Scot) (*b*) within 14 days after the date of making of the order, send a notice with a copy, certified by the clerk of court, of the court's order dismissing the petition or effecting the discharge to the register of companies.

(5) Paragraph (4) is without prejudice to any order of the court as to the persons by and to whom, and how, notice of any order made by the court under section 9(4), 18 or 24 is to be given and to section 18(4) or 24(6) (notice by administrator of court's order discharging administration order).

---

[84] Substituted by S.I. 1987 No. 1921.

CHAPTER 2

STATEMENT OF AFFAIRS AND PROPOSALS TO CREDITORS

Notice requiring statement of affairs

2.4.—(1) This Rule and Rules 2.5 and 2.6 apply where the administrator decides to require a statement as to the affairs of the company to be made out and submitted to him in accordance with section 22.

(2) The administrator shall send to each of the persons upon whom he decides to make such a requirement under section 22, a notice in the form required by Rule 7.30 and Schedule 5 requiring him to make out *Form 2.5 (Scot)* and submit a statement of affairs.

(3) Any person to whom a notice is sent under this Rule is referred to in this Chapter as "a deponent".

Form of the statement of affairs *Form 2.6 (Scot)*

2.5.—(1) The statement of affairs shall be in the form required by Rule 7.30 and Schedule 5.

(2) The Administrator shall insert any statement of affairs submitted to him in the sederunt book.

Expenses of statement of affairs

2.6.—(1) A deponent who makes up and submits to the administrator a statement of affairs shall be allowed and be paid by the administrator out of his receipts, any expenses incurred by the deponent in so doing which the administrator considers to be reasonable.

(2) Any decision by the administrator under this Rule is subject to appeal to the court.

(3) Nothing in this Rule relieves a deponent from any obligation to make up and submit a statement of affairs, or to provide information to the administrator.

Statement to be annexed to proposals

2.7.—(1) There shall be annexed to the administrator's proposals, when sent to the registrar of companies under section 23 and laid *Form 2.7 (Scot)* before the creditors' meeting to be summoned under that section, a statement by him showing—

(a) details relating to his appointment as administrator, the purposes for which an administration order was applied for and made, and any subsequent variation of those purposes;

(b) the names of the directors and secretary of the company;

(c) an account of the circumstances giving rise to the application for an administration order;

(d) if a statement of affairs has been submitted, a copy or summary of it with the administrator's comments, if any;

(e) if no statement of affairs has been submitted, details of the financial position of the company at the latest practicable date (which must, unless the court otherwise orders, be a date not earlier than that of the administration order);

[85](*f*) the manner in which the affairs and business of the company—

    (i) have, since the date of the administrator's appointment, been managed and financed, and

    (ii) will, if the administrator's proposals are approved, continue to be managed and financed; and

  (*g*) such other information (if any) as the administrator thinks necessary to enable creditors to decide whether or not to vote for the adoption of the proposals.

[86] (2) Where the administrator intends to apply to the court under section 18 for the administration order to be discharged at a time before he has sent a statement of his proposals to creditors, in accordance with section 23(1), he shall, at least 10 days before he makes such an application, send to all creditors of the company of whom he is aware, a report containing the information required by paragraph (1)(*a*) to (*f*)(i) of this Rule.

Notices of proposals to members

2.8. Any notice required to be published by the administrator—

(*a*) under section 23(2)(*b*) (notice of address for members of the company to write for a copy of the administrator's statement of proposals), and

(*b*) under section 25(3)(*b*) (notice of address for members of the company to write for a copy of the administrator's statement of proposed revisions to the proposals),

shall be inserted once in the *Edinburgh Gazette* and once in the newspaper in which the administrator's appointment was advertised.

Chapter 3

Meetings and Notices

General

2.9. The provisions of Chapter 1 of Part 7 (Meetings) shall apply with regard to meetings of the company's creditors or members which are summoned by the administrator, subject to the provisions in this Chapter.

Meeting to consider administrator's proposals

2.10.—(1) The administrator shall give at least 14 days' notice to attend the meeting of the creditors under section 23(1) to any directors

---

[85] Substituted by S.I. 1987 No. 1921.
[86] Inserted by S.I. 1987 No. 1921.

or officers of the company (including persons who have been directors or officers in the past) whose presence at the meeting is, in the administrator's opinion, required.

(2) If at the meeting there is not the requisite majority for approval of the administrator's proposals (with modifications, if any), the chairman may, and shall if a resolution is passed to that effect, adjourn the meeting for not more than 14 days.

Retention of title creditors

2.11. For the purpose of entitlement to vote at a creditors' meeting in administration proceedings, a seller of goods to the company under a retention of title agreement shall deduct from his claim the value, as estimated by him, of any rights arising under that agreement in respect of goods in the possession of the company.

Hire-purchase, conditional sale and hiring agreements

2.12.—(1) Subject as follows, an owner of goods under a hire-purchase agreement or under an agreement for the hire of goods for more than three months, or a seller of goods under a conditional sale agreement, is entitled to vote in respect of the amount of the debt due and payable to him by the company as at the date of the administration order.

(2) In calculating the amount of any debt for this purpose, no account shall be taken of any amount attributable to the exercise of any right under the relevant agreement, so far as the right has become exercisable solely by virtue of the presentation of the petition for an administration order or any matter arising in consequence of that or of the making of the order.

[87] *Report and notice of meetings*

2.13. Any report or notice by the administrator of the result of creditors' meetings held under section 23(1) or 25(2) shall have annexed to it details of the proposals which were considered by the meeting in question and of any revisions and modifications to the proposals which were also considered.

Notices to creditors

2.14.—(1) Within 14 days after the conclusion of a meeting of creditors to consider the administrator's proposals or proposed revisions under section 23(1) or 25(2), the administrator shall send notice of the result of the meeting (including, where appropriate, details of the proposals as approved) to every creditor to whom notice of the meeting was sent and to any other creditor of whom the administrator has become aware since the notice was sent.

(2) Within 14 days after the end of every period of six months beginning with the date of approval of the administrator's proposals or

[87] Substituted by S.I. 1987 No. 1921.

proposed revisions, the administrator shall send to all creditors of the company a report on the progress of the administration.

(3) On vacating office, the administrator shall send to creditors a report on the administration up to that time. This does not apply where the administration is immediately followed by the company going into liquidation, nor where the administrator is removed from office by the court or ceases to be qualified to act as an insolvency practitioner.

CHAPTER 4

THE CREDITORS' COMMITTEE

Application of provisions in Part 3 (Receivers)

2.15.—(1) Chapter 3 of Part 3 (The creditors' committee) shall apply *Form 4.20 (Scot)* with regard to the creditors' committee in the administration as it *Form 4.22 (Scot)* applies to the creditors' committee in receivership, subject to the modifications specified below and to any other necessary modifications.

(2) For any reference in the said Chapter 3, or in any provision of Chapter 7 of Part 4 as applied by Rule 3.6, to the receiver, receivership or the creditors' committee in receivership, there shall be substituted a reference to the administrator, the administration and the creditors' committee in the administration.

(3) In Rule 3.4(1) and 3.7(1), for the reference to section 68 or 68(2), there shall be substituted a reference to section 26 or 26(2).

(4) For Rule 3.5 there shall be substituted the following Rule:—

> *"Functions of the Committee*
>
> **3.5.** The creditors' committee shall assist the administrator in discharging his functions and shall act in relation to him in such manner as may be agreed from time to time.".

CHAPTER 5

THE ADMINISTRATOR

Remuneration

2.16.—(1) The administrator's remuneration shall be determined from time to time by the creditors' committee or, if there is no creditors' committee, by the court, and shall be paid out of the assets as an expense of the administration.

(2) The basis for determining the amount of the remuneration payable to the administrator may be a commission calculated by reference to the value of the company's property with which he has to deal, but there shall in any event be taken into account—

(*a*) the work which, having regard to that value, was reasonably undertaken by him; and

(*b*) the extent of his responsibilities in administering the company's assets.

(3) Rules 4.32 to 4.34 of Chapter 6 of Part 4 shall apply to an administration as they apply to a liquidation but as if for any reference to the liquidator or the liquidation committee there was substituted a reference to the administrator or the creditors' committee.

Abstract of receipts and payments

2.17.—(1) The administrator shall—

(a) within two months after the end of six months from the date of *Form 2.9 (Scot)* his appointment, and of every subsequent period of six months, and

(b) within two months after he ceases to act as administrator,

send to the court, and to the registrar of companies, and to each member of the creditors' committee, the requisite accounts of the receipts and payments of the company.

(2) The court may, on the administrator's application, extend the period of two months mentioned in paragraph (1).

(3) The accounts are to be in the form of an abstract showing— *Form 2.9 (Scot)*

(a) receipts and payments during the relevant period of six months, or

(b) where the administrator has ceased to act, receipts and payments during the period from the end of the last six month period to the time when he so ceased (alternatively, if there has been no previous abstract, receipts and payments in the period since his appointment as administrator).

(4) If the administrator makes default in complying with this Rule, he is liable to a fine and, for continued contravention, to a daily default fine.

Resignation from office

2.18.—(1) The administrator may give notice of his resignation on *Form 2.13 (Scot)* grounds of ill health or because—

(a) he intends ceasing to be in practice as an insolvency practitioner, or

(b) there is some conflict of interest or change of personal circumstances, which precludes or makes impracticable the further discharge by him of the duties of administrator.

(2) The administrator may, with the leave of the court, give notice of his resignation on grounds other than those specified in paragraph (1).

(3) The administrator must give to the persons specified below at least seven days' notice of his intention to resign, or to apply for the court's leave to do so—

(a) if there is a continuing administrator of the company, to him;

(b) if there is no such administrator, to the creditors' committee; and

(c) if there is no such administrator and no creditors' committee, to the company and its creditors.

Administrator deceased

2.19.—(1) Subject to the following paragraph, where the administrator has died, it is the duty of his executors or, where the deceased administrator was a partner in a firm, of a partner of that firm to give notice of that fact to the court, specifying the date of the death. This does not apply if notice has been given under the following paragraph.

(2) Notice of the death may also be given by any person producing to the court a copy of the death certificate.

Order filling vacancy

[88] **2.20.** Where the court makes an order filling a vacancy in the office of administrator, the same provisions apply in respect of giving notice of, and advertising, the appointment as in the case of the administration order.

CHAPTER 6

VAT BAD DEBT RELIEF

Application of provisions in Part 3 (Receivers)

2.21. Chapter 5 of Part 3 (VAT bad debt relief) shall apply to an administrator as it applies to an administrative receiver, subject to the modification that, for any reference to the administrative receiver, there shall be substituted a reference to the administrator.

PART 3

RECEIVERS

CHAPTER 1

APPOINTMENT

Acceptance of appointment

3.1.—(1) Where a person has been appointed a receiver by the holder of a floating charge under section 53, his acceptance (which need not be in writing) of that appointment for the purposes of paragraph (*a*) of section 53(6) shall be intimated by him to the holder of the floating charge or his agent within the period specified in that paragraph and he shall, as soon as possible after his acceptance, endorse a written docquet to that effect on the instrument of appointment.

(2) The written docquet evidencing receipt of the instrument of appointment, which is required by section 53(6)(*b*), shall also be endorsed on the instrument of appointment.

---

[88] As amended by S.I. 1987 No. 1921.

(3) The receiver shall, as soon as possible after his acceptance of the appointment, deliver a copy of the endorsed instrument of appointment to the holder of the floating charge or his agent.

(4) This Rule shall apply in the case of the appointment of joint receivers as it applies to the appointment of a receiver, except that, where the docquet of acceptance required by paragraph (1) is endorsed by each of the joint receivers, or two or more of them, on the same instrument of appointment, it is the joint receiver who last endorses his docquet of acceptance who is required to send a copy of the instrument of appointment to the holder of the floating charge or his agent under paragraph (3).

CHAPTER 2

STATEMENT OF AFFAIRS

Notice requiring statement of affairs
3.2.—(1) Where the receiver decides to require from any person or persons a statement as to the affairs of the company to be made out and submitted to him in accordance with section 66, he shall send to each of those persons a notice in the form required by Rule 7.30 and Schedule 5 requiring him to make out and submit a statement of affairs in the form prescribed by the Receivers (Scotland) Regulations 1986.

(2) Any person to whom a notice is sent under this Rule is referred to in this Chapter as "a deponent".

(3) The receiver shall insert any statement of affairs submitted to him in the sederunt book.

Expenses of statement of affairs
3.3.—(1) A deponent who makes up and submits to the receiver a statement of affairs shall be allowed and be paid by the receiver, as an expense of the receivership, any expenses incurred by the deponent in so doing which the receiver considers to be reasonable.

(2) Any decision by the receiver under this Rule is subject to appeal to the court.

(3) Nothing in this Rule relieves a deponent from any obligation to make up and submit a statement of affairs, or to provide information to the receiver.

CHAPTER 3

THE CREDITORS' COMMITTEE

Constitution of committee
3.4.—(1) Where it is resolved by the creditors' meeting to establish a creditors' committee under section 68, the committee shall consist of at least three and not more than five creditors of the company elected at the meeting.

(2) Any creditor of the company who has lodged a claim is eligible to be a member of the committee, so long as his claim has not been rejected for the purpose of his entitlement to vote.

(3) A body corporate or a partnership may be a member of the committee, but it cannot act as such otherwise than by a representative appointed under Rule 7.20, as applied by Rule 3.6.

Functions of the committee

3.5. In addition to the functions conferred on it by the Act, the creditors' committee shall represent to the receiver the views of the unsecured creditors and shall act in relation to him in such manner as may be agreed from time to time.

Application of provisions relating to liquidation committee

3.6.—(1) Chapter 7 of Part 4 (The liquidation committee) shall apply with regard to the creditors' committee in the receivership and its *Form 4.20 (Scot)* members as it applies to the liquidation committee and the creditor *Form 4.22 (Scot)* members thereof, subject to the modifications specified below and to any other necessary modifications.

(2) For any reference in the said Chapter 7 to—

(*a*) the liquidator or the liquidation committee, there shall be substituted a reference to the receiver or to the creditors' committee;

(*b*) to the creditor member, there shall be substituted a reference to a creditor,

and any reference to a contributory member shall be disregarded.

(3) In Rule 4.42(3) and 4.52(2), for the reference to Rule 4.41(1), there shall be substituted a reference to Rule 3.4(1).

(4) In Rule 4.57,

(*a*) for the reference to an expense of the liquidation, there shall be substituted a reference to an expense of the receivership;

(*b*) at the end of that Rule there shall be inserted the following:— "This does not apply to any meeting of the committee held within three months of a previous meeting, unless the meeting in question is summoned at the instance of the receiver.".

(5) The following Rules shall not apply, namely—
Rules 4.40, 4.41, 4.43 to 4.44, 4.53, 4.56, 4.58 and 4.59.

Information from receiver

3.7.—(1) Where the committee resolves to require the attendance of the receiver under section 68(2), the notice to him shall be in writing signed by the majority of the members of the committee for the time being or their representatives.

(2) The meeting at which the receiver's attendance is required shall be fixed by the committee for a business day, and shall be held at such time and place as he determines.

(3) Where the receiver so attends, the members of the committee may elect any one of their number to be chairman of the meeting, in place of the receiver or any nominee of his.

Members' dealings with the company

3.8.—(1) Membership of the committee does not prevent a person from dealing with the company while the receiver is acting, provided that any transactions in the course of such dealings are entered into on normal commercial terms.

(2) The court may, on the application of any person interested, set aside a transaction which appears to it to be contrary to the requirements of this Rule, and may give such consequential directions as it thinks fit for compensating the company for any loss which it may have incurred in consequence of the transaction.

CHAPTER 4

MISCELLANEOUS

Abstract of receipts and payments

3.9.—(1) The receiver shall—

(a) within two months after the end of 12 months from the date of his appointment, and of every subsequent period of 12 months, and

(b) within two months after he ceases to act as receiver,

send the requisite accounts of his receipts and payments as receiver to—

    (i) the registrar of companies,

    (ii) the holder of the floating charge by virtue of which he was appointed,

    (iii) the members of the creditors' committee (if any),

    (iv) the company or, if it is in liquidation, the liquidator.

(2) The court may, on the receiver's application, extend the period of two months referred to in paragraph (1).

(3) The accounts are to be in the form of an abstract showing—

(a) receipts and payments during the relevant period of 12 months, or

(b) where the receiver has ceased to act, receipts and payments during the period from the end of the last 12-month period to the time when he so ceased (alternatively, if there has been no previous abstract, receipts and payments in the period since his appointment as receiver).

(4) This Rule is without prejudice to the receiver's duty to render proper accounts required otherwise than as above.

(5) If the receiver makes default in complying with this Rule, he is liable to a fine and, for continued contravention, to a daily default fine.

Receiver deceased

3.10. If the receiver dies, the holder of the floating charge by virtue of which he was appointed shall, forthwith on his becoming aware of the death, give notice of it to—

(*a*) the registrar of companies,
(*b*) the members of the creditors' committee (if any),
(*c*) the company or, if it is in liquidation, the liquidator,
(*d*) the holder of any other floating charge and any receiver appointed by him.

Vacation of office

3.11. The receiver, on vacating office on completion of the receivership or in consequence of his ceasing to be qualified as an insolvency practitioner, shall, in addition to giving notice to the registrar of companies under section 62(5), give notice of his vacating office, within 14 days thereof, to—

(*a*) the holder of the floating charge by virtue of which he was appointed,
(*b*) the members of the creditors' committee (if any),
(*c*) the company or, if it is in liquidation, the liquidator,
(*d*) the holder of any other floating charge and any receiver appointed by him.

CHAPTER 5

VAT BAD DEBT RELIEF

Issue of certificate of insolvency

3.12.—(1) In accordance with this Rule, it is the duty of the administrative receiver to issue a certificate in the terms of paragraph (*b*) of section 22(3) of the Value Added Tax Act 1983 (which specifies the circumstances in which a company is deemed insolvent for the purposes of that section) forthwith upon his forming the opinion described in that paragraph.

(2) There shall in the certificate be specified—

(*a*) the name of the company and its registered number;
(*b*) the name of the administrative receiver and the date of his appointment; and
(*c*) the date on which the certificate is issued.

(3) The certificate shall be entitled "CERTIFICATE OF INSOLVENCY FOR THE PURPOSES OF SECTION 22(3)(*b*) OF THE VALUE ADDED TAX ACT 1983".

Notice to creditors

3.13.—(1) Notice of the issue of the certificate shall be given by the administrative receiver within three months of his appointment or within two months of issuing the certificate, whichever is the later, to all of the company's unsecured creditors of whose address he is then aware and who have, to his knowledge, made supplies to the company, with a charge to value added tax, at any time before his appointment.

(2) Thereafter, he shall give the notice to any such creditor of whose address and supplies to the company he becomes aware.

(3) He is not under obligation to provide any creditor with a copy of the certificate.

Preservation of certificate with company's records

3.14.—(1) The certificate shall be retained with the company's accounting records, and section 222 of the Companies Act (where and for how long records are to be kept) shall apply to the certificate as it applies to those records.

(2) It is the duty of the administrative receiver, on vacating office, to bring this Rule to the attention of the directors or (as the case may be) any successor of his as receiver.

PART 4

WINDING UP BY THE COURT

CHAPTER 1

PROVISIONAL LIQUIDATOR

Appointment of provisional liquidator

4.1.—(1) An application to the court for the appointment of a provisional liquidator under section 135 may be made by the petitioner in the winding up, or by a creditor of the company, or by a contributory, or by the company itself, or by any person who under any enactment would be entitled to present a petition for the winding up of the company.

[89] (2) The court shall be satisfied that a person has caution for the proper performance of his functions as provisional liquidator if a statement is lodged in court or it is averred in the winding up petition that the person to be appointed is an insolvency practitioner, duly qualified under the Act to act as liquidator, and that he consents so to act.

Order of appointment

4.2.—(1) The provisional liquidator shall forthwith after the order appointing him is made, give notice of his appointment to—   *Form 4.9 (Scot)*

(*a*) the registrar of companies;

---

[89] Inserted by S.I. 1987 No. 1921.

(b) the company; and

(c) any receiver of the whole or any part of the property of the company.

(2) The provisional liquidator shall advertise his appointment in accordance with any directions of the court.

Caution

4.3. The cost of providing the caution required by the provisional liquidator under the Act shall unless the court otherwise directs be—

(a) if a winding up order is not made, reimbursed to him out of the property of the company, and the court may make an order against the company accordingly, and

(b) if a winding up order is made, reimbursed to him as an expense of the liquidation.

Failure to find or to maintain caution

4.4.—(1) If the provisional liquidator fails to find or to maintain his caution, the court may remove him and make such order as it thinks fit as to expenses.

(2) If an order is made under this Rule removing the provisional liquidator, or discharging the order appointing him, the court shall give directions as to whether any, and if so what, steps should be taken for the appointment of another person in his place.

Remuneration

4.5.—(1) The remuneration of the provisional liquidator shall be fixed by the court from time to time.

(2) Section 53(4) of the Bankruptcy Act shall apply to determine the basis for fixing the amount of the remuneration of the provisional liquidator, subject to the modifications specified in Rule 4.16(2) and to any other necessary modifications.

[90] (3) Without prejudice to any order of the court as to expenses, the provisional liquidator's remuneration shall be paid to him, and the amount of any expenses incurred by him (including the remuneration and expenses of any special manager appointed under section 177) reimbursed—

(a) if a winding up order is not made, out of the property of the company;

(b) if a winding up order is made, as an expense of the liquidation.

[91] (4) Unless the court otherwise directs, in a case falling within paragraph (3)(a) above, the provisional liquidator may retain out of the company's property such sums or property as are or may be required for meeting his remuneration and expenses.

---

[90] As amended by S.I. 1987 No. 1921.
[91] Inserted by S.I. 1987 No. 1921.

Termination of appointment

4.6.—(1) The appointment of the provisional liquidator may be terminated by the court on his application, or on that of any of the persons entitled to make application for his appointment under Rule 4.1.

[92] (2) If the provisional liquidator's appointment terminates, in consequence of the dismissal of the winding up petition or otherwise, the court may give such directions as it thinks fit with respect to—

(*a*) the accounts of his administration;

(*b*) the expenses properly incurred by the provisional liquidator; or

(*c*) any other matters which it thinks appropriate.

CHAPTER 2

STATEMENT OF AFFAIRS

Notice requiring statement of affairs

4.7.—(1) This Chapter applies where the liquidator or, in a case where a provisional liquidator is appointed, the provisional liquidator decides to require a statement as to the affairs of the company to be made out and submitted to him in accordance with section 131.

(2) In this Chapter the expression "liquidator" includes "provisional liquidator".

(3) The liquidator shall send to each of the persons upon whom he decides to make such a requirement under section 131, a notice in the form required by Rule 7.30 and Schedule 5 requiring him to make out *Form 4.3 (Scot)* and submit a statement of affairs.

(4) Any person to whom a notice is sent under this Rule is referred to in this Chapter as "a deponent".

Form of the statement of affairs

4.8.—(1) The statement of affairs shall be in the form required by *Form 4.4 (Scot)* Rule 7.30 and Schedule 5.

(2) The liquidator shall insert any statement of affairs submitted to him in the sederunt book.

Expenses of statement of affairs

4.9.—(1) At the request of any deponent, made on the grounds that he cannot himself prepare a proper statement of affairs, the liquidator may authorise an allowance towards expenses to be incurred by the deponent in employing some person or persons to be approved by the liquidator to assist the deponent in preparing it.

(2) Any such request by the deponent shall be accompanied by an estimate of the expenses involved.

(3) An authorisation given by the liquidator under this Rule shall be

---

[92] As amended by S.I. 1987 No. 1921.

subject to such conditions (if any) as he thinks fit to impose with respect to the manner in which any person may obtain access to relevant books and papers.

(4) Nothing in this Rule relieves a deponent from any obligation to make up and submit a statement of affairs, or to provide information to the liquidator.

(5) Any allowance by the liquidator under this Rule shall be an expense of the liquidation.

(6) The liquidator shall intimate to the deponent whether he grants or refuses his request for an allowance under this Rule and where such request is refused the deponent affected by the refusal may appeal to the court not later than 14 days from the date intimation of such refusal is made to him.

CHAPTER 3

INFORMATION

Information to creditors and contributories

4.10.—(1) The liquidator shall report to the creditors and, except where he considers it would be inappropriate to do so, the contributories with respect to the proceedings in the winding up within six weeks after the end of each accounting period or he may submit such a report to a meeting of creditors or of contributories held within such period.

(2) Any reference in this Rule to creditors is to persons known to the liquidator to be creditors of the company.

(3) Where a statement of affairs has been submitted to him, the liquidator may send out to creditors and contributories with the next convenient report to be made under paragraph (1) a summary of the statement and such observations (if any) as he thinks fit to make with respect to it.

[93] (4) Any person appointed as liquidator of a company under section 140(1) who, following such appointment becomes aware of creditors of the company of whom he was not aware when he was acting as the administrator of the company, shall send to such creditors a copy of any statement or report which was sent by him to creditors under Rule 2.7, with a note to the effect that it is being sent under this Rule.

Information to registrar of companies

[94] **4.11.** The statement which section 192 requires the liquidator to *Form 4.5 (Scot)* send to the registrar of companies if the winding up is not concluded within one year from its commencement, shall be sent not more than

---

[93] Added by S.I. 1987 No. 1921.
[94] As amended by S.I. 1987 No. 1921.

30 days after the expiration of that year and thereafter at not more than *Form 4.6 (Scot)* 30 days after the end of each accounting period which ends after that year until the winding up is concluded in the form required by Rule 7.30 and Schedule 5 and shall contain the particulars specified therein.

CHAPTER 4

MEETINGS OF CREDITORS AND CONTRIBUTORIES

First meetings in the liquidation

4.12.—[95] (1) This Rule applies where under section 138(3) or (4) the interim liquidator summons meetings of the creditors and the contributories of the company or, as the case may be, a meeting of the creditors for the purpose of choosing a person to be liquidator of the company in place of the interim liquidator.

(2) Meetings summoned by the interim liquidator under that section are known respectively as "the first meeting of creditors" and "the first meeting of contributories", and jointly as "the first meetings in the liquidation".

[96] (2A) Any meetings of creditors or contributories under section 138(3) or (4) shall be summoned for a date not later than 42 days after the date of the winding up order or such longer period as the court may allow.

(3) Subject as follows, no resolutions shall be taken at the first meeting of creditors other than the following:—

(a) a resolution to appoint one or more named insolvency practitioners to be liquidator or, as the case may be, joint liquidators and, in the case of joint liquidators, whether any act required or authorised to be done by the liquidator is to be done by both or all of them, or by any one or more;

(b) a resolution to establish a liquidation committee under section 142(1);

(c) unless a liquidation committee is to be established, a resolution specifying the terms on which the liquidator is to be remunerated, or to defer consideration of that matter;

(d) a resolution to adjourn the meeting for not more than three weeks;

(e) any other resolution which the chairman considers it right to allow for special reason.

(4) This rule also applies with respect to the first meeting of contributories except that that meeting shall not pass any resolution to the effect of paragraph (3)(c).

Other meetings

4.13.—(1) The liquidator shall summon a meeting of the creditors in each year during which the liquidation is in force.

---

[95] As amended by S.I. 1987 No. 1921.
[96] Inserted by S.I. 1987 No. 1921.

(2) Subject to the above provision, the liquidator may summon a meeting of the creditors or of the contributories at any time for the purpose of ascertaining their wishes in all matters relating to the liquidation.

Attendance at meetings of company's personnel

4.14.—(1) This Rule applies to meetings of creditors and to meetings of contributories.

(2) Whenever a meeting is summoned, the liquidator may, if he thinks fit, give at least 21 days' notice to any one or more of the company's personnel that he is or they are required to be present at the meeting or be in attendance.

(3) In this Rule, "the company's personnel" means the persons referred to in paragraphs (*a*) to (*d*) of section 235(3) (present and past officers, employees, etc.).

(4) The liquidator may authorise payment to any person whose attendance is requested at a meeting under this Rule of his reasonable expenses incurred in travelling to the meeting and any payment so authorised shall be an expense of the liquidation.

(5) In the case of any meeting, any of the company's personnel may, if he has given reasonable notice of his wish to be present, be admitted to take part; but this is at the discretion of the chairman of the meeting, whose decision as to what (if any) intervention may be made by any of them is final.

(6) If it is desired to put questions to any of the company's personnel who are not present, the meeting may be adjourned with a view to obtaining his attendance.

(7) Where one of the company's personnel is present at a meeting, only such questions may be put to him as the chairman may in his discretion allow.

CHAPTER 5

CLAIMS IN LIQUIDATION

Submission of claims

4.15.—(1) A creditor, in order to obtain an adjudication as to his entitlement—

(*a*) to vote at any meeting of the creditors in the liquidation; or
(*b*) to a dividend (so far as funds are available) out of the assets of the company in respect of any accounting period,

shall submit his claim to the liquidator—

(*a*) at or before the meeting; or, as the case may be,
(*b*) not later than eight weeks before the end of the accounting period.

(2) A creditor shall submit his claim by producing to the liquidator—

(*a*) a statement of claim in the form required by Rule 7.30 and *Form 4.7 (Scot)* Schedule 5; and

(*b*) an account or voucher (according to the nature of the debt claimed) which constitutes *prima facie* evidence of the debt,

but the liquidator may dispense with any requirement of this paragraph in respect of any debt or any class of debt.

(3) A claim submitted by a creditor, which has been accepted in whole or in part by the liquidator for the purpose of voting at a meeting or of drawing a dividend in respect of any accounting period, shall be deemed to have been resubmitted for the purpose of obtaining an adjudication as to his entitlement both to vote at any subsequent meeting and (so far as funds are available) to a dividend in respect of an accounting period or, as the case may be, any subsequent accounting period.

(4) A creditor, who has submitted a claim, may at any time submit a further claim specifying a different amount for his claim:

Provided that a secured creditor shall not be entitled to produce a further claim specifying a different value for the security at any time after the liquidator has required the creditor to discharge, or convey or assign, the security under paragraph 5(2) of Schedule 1 to the Bankruptcy Act, as applied by the following Rule.

(5) Votes are calculated according to the amount of a creditor's debt as at the date of the commencement of the winding up within the meaning of section 129, deducting any amount paid in respect of that debt after that date.

(6) In this Rule and in Rule 4.16, including the provisions of the Bankruptcy Act applied by that Rule, any reference to the liquidator includes a reference to the chairman of the meeting.

Application of the Bankruptcy Act

4.16.—(1) Subject to the provisions in this Chapter, the following provisions of the Bankruptcy Act shall apply in relation to a liquidation of a company in like manner as they apply in a sequestration of a debtor's estate, subject to the modifications specified in paragraph (2) and to any other necessary modifications:—

(*a*) section 22(5) and (10) (criminal offence in relation to producing false claims or evidence);

(*b*) section 48(5), (6) and (8), together with sections 44(2) and (3) and 47(1) as applied by those sections (further evidence in relation to claims);

(*c*) section 49 (adjudication of claim);

(*d*) section 50 (entitlement to vote and draw dividend);

(*e*) section 60 (liabilities and rights of co-obligants); and

(*f*) Schedule 1 except paragraphs 2, 4 and 6 (determination of amount of creditor's claim).

(2) For any reference in the provisions of the Bankruptcy Act, as

applied by these Rules, to any expression in column 1 below, there shall be substituted a reference to the expression in column 2 opposite thereto—

Column 1	*Column 2*
Interim trustee	Liquidator
Permanent trustee	Liquidator
Sequestration	Liquidation
Date of sequestration	Date of commencement of winding up within the meaning of section 129
Debtor	[97] The company or, in the application of section 49(6) of the Bankruptcy Act, any member or contributory of the company
[97] Debtor's estate	Company's assets
Accountant in Bankruptcy	The court
Commissioners	Liquidation committee
Sheriff	The court
Preferred debts	Preferential debts within the meaning of section 386

Claims in foreign currency

4.17.—(1) A creditor may state the amount of his claim in currency other than sterling where—

    (*a*) his claim is constituted by decree or other order made by a court ordering the company to pay the creditor a sum expressed in a currency other than sterling, or

    (*b*) where it is not so constituted, his claim arises from a contract or bill of exchange in terms of which payment is or may be required to be made by the company to the creditor in a currency other than sterling.

(2) Where a claim is stated in currency other than sterling for the purpose of the preceding paragraph, it shall be converted into sterling at the rate of exchange for that other currency at the mean of the buying and selling spot rates prevailing in the London market at the close of business on the date of commencement of winding up.

CHAPTER 6

THE LIQUIDATOR

SECTION A: APPOINTMENT AND FUNCTIONS OF LIQUIDATOR

Appointment of liquidator by the court

4.18.—(1) This Rule applies where a liquidator is appointed by the court under section 138(1) (appointment of interim liquidator), 138(5) (no person appointed or nominated by the meetings of creditors and contributories), 139(4) (different persons nominated by creditors and

---

[97] As amended by S.I. 1987 No. 1921.

contributories) or 140(1) or (2) (liquidation following administration or voluntary arrangement).

(2) The court shall not make the appointment unless and until there is lodged in court a statement to the effect that the person to be appointed is an insolvency practitioner, duly qualified under the Act to be the liquidator, and that he consents so to act.

(3) Thereafter, the court shall send a copy of the order to the liquidator, whose appointment takes effect from the date of the order.

(4) The liquidator shall—

(a) within seven days of his appointment, give notice of it to the registrar of companies; and *Form 4.9 (Scot)*

(b) within 28 days of his appointment, give notice of it to the creditors and contributories or, if the court so permits, he shall advertise his appointment in accordance with the directions of the court.

[98] (5) In any notice or advertisement to be given by him under this Rule, the liquidator shall state whether a liquidation committee has been established by a meeting of creditors or contributories, and, if this is not the case, he shall—

(a) state whether he intends to summon meetings of creditors and contributories for the purpose of establishing a liquidation committee or whether he proposes to summon only a meeting of creditors for that purpose; and

(b) if he does not propose to summon any meeting, set out the powers of the creditors under section 142(3) to require him to summon such a meeting.

Appointment by creditors or contributories

4.19.—(1) This Rule applies where a person is nominated for appointment as liquidator under section 139(2) either by a meeting of creditors or by a meeting of contributories.

(2) Subject to section 139(4) the interim liquidator, as chairman of the meeting, or, where the interim liquidator is nominated as liquidator, *Form 4.8 (Scot)* the chairman of the meeting, shall certify the appointment of a person as liquidator by the meeting but not until and unless the person to be appointed has provided him with a written statement to the effect that he is an insolvency practitioner, duly qualified under the Act to be the liquidator and that he consents so to act.

[99] (3) The appointment of the liquidator takes effect upon the passing of the resolution for his appointment and the date of his appointment shall be stated in the certificate.

---

[98] As amended by S.I. 1987 No. 1921.
[99] As amended by S.I. 1987 No. 1921.

(4) The liquidator shall—

(*a*) within seven days of his appointment, give notice of his appointment to the court and to the registrar of companies; and

(*b*) within 28 days of his appointment, give notice of it in a newspaper circulating in the area where the company has its principal place of business, or in such newspaper as he thinks most appropriate for ensuring that it comes to the notice of the company's creditors and contributories.

(5) The provisions of Rule 4.18(5) shall apply to any notice given by the liquidator under this Rule.

[99] (6) Paragraphs (4) and (5) need not be complied with in the case of a liquidator appointed by a meeting of contributories and replaced by another liquidator appointed on the same day by a creditors' meeting.

Authentication of liquidator's appointment

4.20. A copy certified by the clerk of court of any order of court appointing the liquidator or, as the case may be, a copy, certified by the chairman of the meeting which appointed the liquidator, of the certificate of the liquidator's appointment under Rule 4.19(2), shall be sufficient evidence for all purposes and in any proceedings that he has been appointed to exercise the powers and perform the duties of liquidator in the winding up of the company.

Hand-over of assets to liquidator

4.21.—(1) This Rule applies where a person appointed as liquidator ("the succeeding liquidator") succeeds a previous liquidator ("the former liquidator") as the liquidator.

(2) When the succeeding liquidator's appointment takes effect, the former liquidator shall forthwith do all that is required for putting the succeeding liquidator into possession of the assets.

(3) The former liquidator shall give to the succeeding liquidator all such information, relating to the affairs of the company and the course of the winding up, as the succeeding liquidator considers to be reasonably required for the effective discharge by him of his duties as such and shall hand over all books, accounts, statements of affairs, statements of claim and other records and documents in his possession relating to the affairs of the company and its winding up.

Taking possession and realisation of the company's assets

[1] **4.22.**—(1) The liquidator shall—

(*a*) as soon as may be after his appointment take possession of the whole assets of the company and any property, books, papers or records in the possession or control of the company or to which the company appears to be entitled; and

---

[1] Substituted by S.I. 1987 No. 1921.

(*b*) make up and maintain an inventory and valuation of the assets which he shall retain in the sederunt book.

(2) The liquidator shall be entitled to have access to all documents or records relating to the assets or the property or the business or financial affairs of the company sent by or on behalf of the company to a third party and in that third party's hands and to make copies of any such documents or records.

(3) If any person obstructs a liquidator who is exercising, or attempting to exercise, a power conferred by sub-section (2) above, the court, on the application of the liquidator, may order that person to cease so to obstruct the liquidator.

(4) The liquidator may require delivery to him of any title deed or other document or record of the company, notwithstanding that a right of lien is claimed over the title deed or document or record, but this paragraph is without prejudice to any preference of the holder of the lien.

(5) Section 39(4) and (7) of the Bankruptcy Act shall apply in relation to a liquidation of a company as it applies in relation to a sequestration of a debtor's estate, subject to the modifications specified in Rule 4.16(2) and to any other necessary modifications.

SECTION B: REMOVAL AND RESIGNATION; VACATION OF OFFICE

Summoning of meeting for removal of liquidator
4.23.—(1) Subject to section 172(3) and without prejudice to any other method of summoning the meeting, a meeting of creditors for the removal of the liquidator in accordance with section 172(2) shall be summoned by the liquidator if requested to do so by not less than one quarter in value of the creditors.

(2) Where a meeting of creditors is summoned especially for the purpose of removing the liquidator in accordance with section 172(2), the notice summoning it shall draw attention to section 174(4)(*a*) or (*b*) with respect to the liquidator's release.

(3) At the meeting, a person other than the liquidator or his nominee may be elected to act as chairman; but if the liquidator or his nominee is chairman and a resolution has been proposed for the liquidator's removal, the chairman shall not adjourn the meeting without the consent of at least one-half (in value) of the creditors present (in person or by proxy) and entitled to vote.

(4) Where a meeting is to be held or is proposed to be summoned under this Rule, the court may, on the application of any creditor, give directions as to the mode of summoning it, the sending out and return of forms of proxy, the conduct of the meeting, and any other matter which appears to the court to require regulation or control under this Rule.

Procedure on liquidator's removal

4.24.—[2] (1) Where the creditors have resolved that the liquidator be removed, the chairman of the creditors' meeting shall forthwith—

Form 4.10 (Scot)
Form 4.11 (Scot)

    (*a*) if, at the meeting, another liquidator was not appointed, send a certificate of the liquidator's removal to the court and a copy of the certificate to the registrar of companies, and

Form 4.10 (Scot)
Form 4.11 (Scot)

    (*b*) otherwise, deliver the certificate to the new liquidator, who shall forthwith send a copy of the certificate to the court and to the registrar of companies.

(2) The liquidator's removal is effective as from such date as the meeting of the creditors shall determine, and this shall be stated in the certificate of removal.

Release of liquidator on removal

4.25.—(1) Where the liquidator has been removed by a creditors' meeting which has not resolved against his release, the date on which

Form 4.10 (Scot)
Form 4.11 (Scot)

he has his release in terms of section 174(4)(*a*) shall be stated in the certificate of removal before a copy of it is sent to the court and to the registrar of companies under Rule 4.24(1).

Form 4.12 (Scot)

(2) Where the liquidator is removed by a creditors' meeting which has resolved against his release, or is removed by the court, he must apply to the Accountant of Court for his release.

(3) When the Accountant of Court releases the former liquidator, he shall—

Form 4.13 (Scot)
Form 4.14 (Scot)

    (*a*) issue a certificate of release to the new liquidator who shall send a copy of it to the court and to the registrar of companies, and

    (*b*) send a copy of the certificate to the former liquidator,

and in this case release of the former liquidator is effective from the date of the certificate.

Removal of liquidator by the court

4.26.—(1) This Rule applies where application is made to the court for the removal of the liquidator, or for an order directing the liquidator to summon a meeting of creditors for the purpose of removing him.

(2) The court may require the applicant to make a deposit or give caution for the expenses to be incurred by the liquidator on the application.

(3) The applicant shall, at least 14 days before the hearing, send to the liquidator a notice stating its date, time and place and accompanied by a copy of the application, and of any evidence which he intends to adduce in support of it.

(4) Subject to any contrary order of the court, the expenses of the application are not payable as an expense of the liquidation.

---

[2] As amended by S.I. 1987 No. 1921.

(5) Where the court removes the liquidator—

(a) it shall send two copies of the order of removal to him;

(b) the order may include such provision as the court thinks fit with respect to matters arising in connection with the removal; and

(c) if the court appoints a new liquidator, Rule 4.18 applies,

and the liquidator, on receipt of the two court orders under sub-paragraph (a), shall send one copy of the order to the registrar of companies, together with a notice of his ceasing to act as a liquidator. *Form 4.11 (Scot)*

Advertisement of removal

4.27. Where a new liquidator is appointed in place of the one removed, Rules 4.19 to 4.21 shall apply to the appointment of the new liquidator except that the notice to be given by the new liquidator under Rule 4.19(4) shall also state— *Form 4.9 (Scot)*

(a) that his predecessor as liquidator has been removed; and

(b) whether his predecessor has been released.

Resignation of liquidator

4.28.—(1) Before resigning his office under section 172(6) the liquidator shall call a meeting of creditors for the purpose of receiving his resignation.

(2) The notice summoning the meeting shall draw attention to section 174(4)(c) and Rule 4.29(4) with respect of the liquidator's release and shall also be accompanied by an account of the liquidator's administration of the winding up, including a summary of his receipts and payments.

(3) Subject to paragraph (4), the liquidator may only proceed under this Rule on the grounds of ill health or because—

(a) he intends ceasing to be in practice as an insolvency practitioner; or

(b) there has been some conflict of interest or change of personal circumstances which precludes or makes impracticable the further discharge by him of the duties of the liquidator.

(4) Where two or more persons are acting as liquidator jointly, any one of them may resign (without prejudice to the continuation in office of the other or others) on the grounds that, in his opinion and that of the other or others, it is no longer expedient that there should continue to be the present number of joint liquidators.

Action following acceptance of liquidator's resignation

4.29.—(1) This Rule applies where a meeting is summoned to receive the liquidator's resignation.

(2) If the liquidator's resignation is accepted, it is effective as from such date as the meeting of the creditors may determine and that date shall be stated in the notice given by the liquidator under paragraph (3).

Form 4.15 (Scot)
Form 4.16 (Scot)
(3) The liquidator, whose resignation is accepted, shall forthwith after the meeting give notice of his resignation to the court as required by section 172(6) and shall send a copy of it to the registrar of companies.

(4) The meeting of the creditors may grant the liquidator his release from such date as they may determine. If the meeting resolves against the liquidator having his release, Rule 4.25(2) and (3) shall apply.

(5) Where the creditors have resolved to appoint a new liquidator in place of the one who has resigned, Rules 4.19 to 4.21 shall apply to the appointment of the new liquidator, except that the notice to be given by the new liquidator under Rule 4.19(4) shall also state that his predecessor as liquidator has resigned and whether he has been *Form 4.9 (Scot)* released.

³ (6) If there is no quorum present at the meeting summoned to receive the liquidator's resignation, the meeting is deemed to have been held, a resolution is deemed to have been passed that the liquidator's resignation be accepted, and the creditors are deemed not to have resolved against the liquidator having his release.

³ (7) Where paragraph (6) applies—

(*a*) the liquidator's resignation is effective as from the date for which the meeting was summoned and that date shall be stated in the notice given by the liquidator under paragraph (3), and

(*b*) the liquidator is deemed to have been released as from that date.

Leave to resign granted by the court

4.30.—(1) If, at a creditors' meeting summoned to receive the liquidator's resignation, it is resolved that it be not accepted, the court may, on the liquidator's application, make an order giving him leave to resign.

(2) The court's order under this Rule may include such provision as it thinks fit with respect to matters arising in connection with the resignation including the notices to be given to the creditors and the *Form 4.16 (Scot)* registrar of companies and shall determine the date from which the liquidator's release is effective.

SECTION C: RELEASE ON COMPLETION OF WINDING UP

Final meeting

4.31.—(1) The liquidator shall give at least 28 days' notice of the final meeting of creditors to be held under section 146. The notice shall be sent to all creditors whose claims in the liquidation have been accepted.

(2) The liquidator's report laid before the meeting shall contain an account of his administration of the winding up, including a summary of his receipts and payments.

(3) At the final meeting, the creditors may question the liquidator

---

³ Added by S.I. 1987 No. 1921.

with respect to any matter contained in his report, and may resolve against the liquidator having his release.

(4) The liquidator shall within seven days of the meeting give notice to the court and to the registrar of companies under section 172(8) that the final meeting has been held and the notice shall state whether or not he has been released, and be accompanied by a copy of the report *Form 4.17 (Scot)* laid before the meeting.

(5) If there is no quorum present at the final meeting, the liquidator shall report to the court that a final meeting was summoned in accordance with the Rules, but that there was no quorum present; and the final meeting is then deemed to have been held and the creditors not to have resolved against the liquidator being released.

[4] (6) If the creditors at the final meeting have not resolved against the liquidator having his release, he is released in terms of section 174(4)(d)(ii) when he vacates office under section 172(8). If they have so resolved he shall apply for his release to the Accountant of Court, and Rules 4.25(2) and (3) shall apply accordingly subject to the modifications that in Rule 4.25(3) sub-paragraph (a) shall apply with the word "new" replaced by the word "former" and sub-paragraph (b) shall not apply.

SECTION D: OUTLAYS AND REMUNERATION

Determination of amount of outlays and remuneration

4.32.—(1) Subject to the provisions of Rules 4.33 to 4.35, claims by the liquidator for the outlays reasonably incurred by him and for his remuneration shall be made in accordance with section 53 of the Bankruptcy Act as applied by Rule 4.68 and as further modified by paragraphs (2) and (3) below.

(2) After section 53(1) of the Bankruptcy Act, there shall be inserted the following subsection:—

"(1A) The liquidator may, at any time before the end of an accounting period, submit to the liquidation committee (if any) an interim claim in respect of that period for the outlays reasonably incurred by him and for his remuneration and the liquidation committee may make an interim determination in relation to the amount of the outlays and remuneration payable to the liquidator and, where they do so, they shall take into account that interim determination when making their determination under subsection (3)(a)(ii).".

(3) In section 53(6) of the Bankruptcy Act, for the reference to "subsection (3)(a)(ii)" there shall be substituted a reference to "subsection (1A) or (3)(a)(ii)".

Recourse of liquidator to meeting of creditors

4.33. If the liquidator's remuneration has been fixed by the

---

[4] As amended by S.I. 1987 No. 1921.

liquidation committee and he considers the amount to be insufficient, he may request that it be increased by resolution of the creditors.

Recourse to the court

4.34.—(1) If the liquidator considers that the remuneration fixed for him by the liquidation committee, or by resolution of the creditors, is insufficient, he may apply to the court for an order increasing its amount or rate.

(2) The liquidator shall give at least 14 days' notice of his application to the members of the liquidation committee; and the committee may nominate one or more members to appear or be represented, and to be heard, on the application.

(3) If there is no liquidation committee, the liquidator's notice of his application shall be sent to such one or more of the company's creditors as the court may direct, which creditors may nominate one or more of their number to appear or be represented.

⁵ (4) The court may, if it appears to be a proper case, order the expenses of the liquidator's application, including the expenses of any member of the liquidation committee appearing or being represented on it, or any creditor so appearing or being represented, to be paid as an expense of the liquidation.

Creditors' claim that remuneration is excessive

4.35.—(1) If the liquidator's remuneration has been fixed by the liquidation committee or by the creditors, any creditor or creditors of the company representing in value at least 25 per cent of the creditors may apply to the court for an order that the liquidator's remuneration be reduced, on the grounds that it is, in all the circumstances, excessive.

(2) If the court considers the application to be well-founded, it shall make an order fixing the remuneration at a reduced amount or rate.

(3) Unless the court orders otherwise, the expenses of the application shall be paid by the applicant, and are not payable as an expense of the liquidation.

SECTION E: SUPPLEMENTARY PROVISIONS

Liquidator deceased

Form 4.18 (Scot) **4.36.**—(1) Subject to the following paragraph, where the liquidator has died, it is the duty of his executors or, where the deceased liquidator was a partner in a firm, of a partner in that firm to give notice of that fact to the court and to the registrar of companies, specifying the date of death. This does not apply if notice has been given under the following paragraph.

Form 4.19 (Scot) (2) Notice of the death may also be given by any person producing to the court and to the registrar of companies a copy of the death certificate.

Loss of qualification as insolvency practitioner

4.37.—(1) This Rule applies where the liquidator vacates office on

---

⁵ As amended by S.I. 1987 No. 1921.

ceasing to be qualified to act as an insolvency practitioner in relation to the company.

(2) He shall forthwith give notice of his doing so to the court and to *Form 4.19 (Scot)* the registrar of companies.

(3) Rule 4.25(2) and (3) apply as regards the liquidator obtaining his release, as if he had been removed by the court.

Power of court to set aside certain transactions

4.38.—(1) If in the course of the liquidation the liquidator enters into any transaction with a person who is an associate of his, the court may, on the application of any person interested, set the transaction aside and order the liquidator to compensate the company for any loss suffered in consequence of it.

(2) This does not apply if either—

(*a*) the transaction was entered into with the prior consent of the court, or

(*b*) it is shown to the court's satisfaction that the transaction was for value, and that it was entered into by the liquidator without knowing, or having any reason to suppose, that the person concerned was an associate.

(3) Nothing in this Rule is to be taken as prejudicing the operation of any rule of law with respect to a trustee's dealings with trust property, or the fiduciary obligations of any person.

Rule against solicitation

4.39.—(1) Where the court is satisfied that any improper solicitation has been used by or on behalf of the liquidator in obtaining proxies or procuring his appointment, it may order that no remuneration be allowed as an expense of the liquidation to any person by whom, or on whose behalf, the solicitation was exercised.

(2) An order of the court under this Rule overrides any resolution of the liquidation committee or the creditors, or any other provision of the Rules relating to the liquidator's remuneration.

CHAPTER 7

THE LIQUIDATION COMMITTEE

Preliminary

4.40. For the purposes of this Chapter—

(*a*) an "insolvent winding up" takes place where a company is being wound up on grounds which include its inability to pay its debts, and

(*b*) a "solvent winding up" takes place where a company is being wound up on grounds which do not include that one.

Membership of committee

4.41.—(1) Subject to Rule 4.43 below, the liquidation committee shall consist as follows:—

(*a*) in the case of any winding up, of at least three and not more than five creditors of the company, elected by the meeting of creditors held under section 138 or 142 of the Act, and also

[6](*b*) in the case of a solvent winding up where the contributories' meeting held under either of those sections so decides, of up to three contributories, elected by that meeting.

(2) Any creditor of the company (other than one whose debt is fully secured and who has not agreed to surrender his security to the liquidator) is eligible to be a member of the committee, so long as—

(*a*) he has lodged a claim of his debt in the liquidation, and

(*b*) his claim has neither been wholly rejected for voting purposes, nor wholly rejected for the purposes of his entitlement so far as funds are available to a dividend.

(3) No person can be a member as both a creditor and a contributory.

(4) A body corporate or a partnership may be a member of the committee, but it cannot act as such otherwise than by a member's representative appointed under Rule 4.48 below.

(5) In this Chapter, members of the committee elected or appointed by a creditors' meeting are called "creditor members", and those elected or appointed by a contributories' meeting are called "contributory members".

[6] (6) Where the Deposit Protection Board exercises the right (under section 58 of the Banking Act) to be a member of the committee, the Board is to be regarded as an additional creditor member.

Formalities of establishment

4.42.—(1) The liquidation committee shall not come into being, and

Form 4.20 (Scot) accordingly cannot act, until the liquidator has issued a certificate of its due constitution.

(2) If the chairman of the meeting which resolves to establish the committee is not the liquidator, he shall forthwith give notice of the resolution to the liquidator (or, as the case may be, the person appointed as liquidator by the same meeting), and inform him of the names and addresses of the persons elected to be members of the committee.

[7] (3) No person may act as a member of the committee unless and

Form 4.20 (Scot) until he has agreed to do so and, unless the relevant proxy or authorisation contains a statement to the contrary, such agreement may be given on behalf of the member by his proxy-holder or any representative under section 375 of the Companies Act who is present at the meeting at which the committee is established; and the liquidator's certificate of the committee's due constitution shall not be issued until at least the minimum number of persons in accordance

[6] As amended by S.I. 1987 No. 1921.
[7] As amended by S.I. 1987 No. 1921.

with Rule 4.41 who are to be members of it have agreed to act, but shall be issued forthwith thereafter.

(4) As and when the others (if any) agree to act, the liquidator shall issue an amended certificate. *Form 4.20 (Scot)*

(5) The certificate (and any amended certificate) shall be sent by the liquidator to the registrar of companies. *Form 4.22 (Scot)*

(6) If after the first establishment of the committee there is any change in its membership, the liquidator shall report the change to the registrar of companies. *Form 4.22 (Scot)*

Committee established by contributories

4.43.—(1) The following applies where the creditors' meeting under section 138 or 142 of the Act does not decide that a liquidation committee should be established or decides that a liquidation committee should not be established.

(2) A meeting of contributories under section 138 or 142 may appoint one of their number to make application to the court for an order to the liquidator that a further creditors' meeting be summoned for the purpose of establishing a liquidation committee; and—

(a) the court may, if it thinks that there are special circumstances to justify it, make that order, and
(b) the creditors' meeting summoned by the liquidator in compliance with the order is deemed to have been summoned under section 142.

(3) If the creditors' meeting so summoned does not establish a liquidation committee, a meeting of contributories may do so.

[8] (4) The committee shall then consist of at least three, and not more than five, contributories elected by that meeting; and Rule 4.42 shall apply to such a committee with the substitution of the reference to Rule 4.41 in paragraph (3) of that Rule by a reference to this paragraph.

Obligations of liquidator to committee

4.44.—(1) Subject as follows, it is the duty of the liquidator to report to the members of the liquidation committee all such matters as appear to him to be, or as they have indicated to him as being, of concern to them with respect to the winding up.

(2) In the case of matters so indicated to him by the committee, the liquidator need not comply with any request for information where it appears to him that—

(a) the request is frivolous or unreasonable, or
(b) the cost of complying would be excessive, having regard to the relative importance of the information, or
(c) there are not sufficient assets to enable him to comply.

(3) Where the committee has come into being more than 28 days after

---

[8] As amended by S.I. 1987 No. 1921.

the appointment of the liquidator, he shall report to them, in summary form, what actions he has taken since his appointment, and shall answer all such questions as they may put to him regarding his conduct of the winding up hitherto.

(4) A person who becomes a member of the committee at any time after its first establishment is not entitled to require a report to him by the liquidator, otherwise than in summary form, of any matters previously arising.

(5) Nothing in this Rule disentitles the committee, or any member of it, from having access to the liquidator's cash book and sederunt book, or from seeking an explanation of any matter within the committee's responsibility.

Meetings of the committee

4.45.—(1) Subject as follows, meetings of the liquidation committee shall be held when and where determined by the liquidator.

(2) The liquidator shall call a first meeting of the committee to take place within three months of his appointment or of the committee's establishment (whichever is the later); and thereafter he shall call a meeting—

- (a) if so requested by a creditor member of the committee or his representative (the meeting then to be held within 21 days of the request being received by the liquidator), and
- (b) for a specified date, if the committee has previously resolved that a meeting be held on that date.

(3) The liquidator shall give seven days' written notice of the time and place of any meeting to every member of the committee (or his representative, if designated for that purpose), unless in any case the requirement of the notice has been waived by or on behalf of any member. Waiver may be signified either at or before the meeting.

The chairman at meetings

4.46.—(1) The chairman at any meeting of the liquidation committee shall be the liquidator, or a person nominated by him to act.

(2) A person so nominated must be either—

- (a) a person who is qualified to act as an insolvency practitioner in relation to the company, or
- (b) an employee of the liquidator or his firm who is experienced in insolvency matters.

Quorum

4.47. A meeting of the committee is duly constituted if due notice of it has been given to all the members, and at least two creditor members or, in the case of a committee of contributories, two contributory members are present or represented.

Committee members' representatives

4.48.—(1) A member of the liquidation committee may, in relation to the business of the committee, be represented by another person duly authorised by him for that purpose.

[9] (2) A person acting as a committee-member's representative must hold a mandate entitling him so to act (either generally or specially) and signed by or on behalf of the committee-member, and for this purpose any proxy or authorisation under section 375 of the Companies Act in relation to any meeting of creditors (or, as the case may be, members or contributories) of the company shall, unless it contains a statement to the contrary, be treated as such a mandate to act generally signed by or on behalf of the committee-member.

(3) The chairman at any meeting of the committee may call on a person claiming to act as a committee-member's representative to produce his mandate and may exclude him if it appears that his mandate is deficient.

(4) No member may be represented by a body corporate or by a partnership, or by an undischarged bankrupt.

(5) No person shall—

(a) on the same committee, act at one and the same time as representative of more than one committee-member, or

(b) act both as a member of the committee and as representative of another member.

(6) Where a member's representative signs any document on the member's behalf, the fact that he so signs must be stated below his signature.

Resignation

4.49. A member of the liquidation committee may resign by notice in writing delivered to the liquidator.

Termination of membership

4.50. Membership of the liquidation committee of any person is automatically terminated if—

(a) his estate is sequestrated or he becomes bankrupt or grants a trust deed for the benefit of or makes a composition with his creditors, or

(b) at three consecutive meetings of the committee he is neither present nor represented (unless at the third of those meetings it is resolved that this Rule is not to apply in his case), or

(c) that creditor being a creditor member, he ceases to be, or is found never to have been a creditor.

Removal

4.51. A creditor member of the committee may be removed by resolution at a meeting of creditors; and a contributory member may be removed by a resolution of a meeting of contributories.

---

[9] As amended by S.I. 1987 No. 1921.

Vacancy (creditor members)

4.52.—(1) The following applies if there is a vacancy among the creditor members of the committee.

(2) The vacancy need not be filled if the liquidator and a majority of the remaining creditor members so agree, provided that the total number of members does not fall below the minimum required by Rule 4.41(1).

(3) The liquidator may appoint any creditor, who is qualified under the Rules to be a member of the committee, to fill the vacancy, if a majority of the other creditor members agrees to the appointment, and the creditor concerned consents to act.

(4) Alternatively, a meeting of creditors may resolve that a creditor be appointed (with his consent) to fill the vacancy. In this case, at least 14 days' notice must have been given of the resolution to make such an appointment (whether or not of a person named in the notice).

(5) Where the vacancy is filled by an appointment made by a creditors' meeting at which the liquidator is not present, the chairman of the meeting shall report to the liquidator the appointment which has been made.

Vacancy (contributory members)

4.53.—(1) The following applies if there is a vacancy among the contributory members of the committee.

[10] (2) The vacancy need not be filled if the liquidator and a majority of the remaining contributory members so agree, provided that, in the case of a committee of contributory members only, the total number of members does not fall below the minimum required by Rule 4.43(4) or, as the case may be, 4.59(4).

(3) The liquidator may appoint any contributory member (being qualified under the Rules to be a member of the committee) to fill the vacancy, if a majority of the other contributory members agree to the appointment, and the contributory concerned consents to act.

(4) Alternatively, a meeting of contributories may resolve that a contributory be appointed (with his consent) to fill the vacancy. In this case, at least 14 days' notice must have been given of the resolution to make such an appointment (whether or not of a person named in the notice).

(5) Where the vacancy is filled by an appointment made by a contributories' meeting at which the liquidator is not present, the chairman of the meeting shall report to the liquidator the appointment which has been made.

Voting rights and resolutions

4.54.—(1) At any meeting of the committee, each member of it (whether present himself, or by his representative) has one vote; and a

[10] As amended by S.I. 1987 No. 1921.

resolution is passed when a majority of the creditor members present or represented have voted in favour of it.

(2) Subject to the next paragraph, the votes of contributory members do not count towards the number required for passing a resolution, but the way in which they vote on any resolution shall be recorded.

(3) Paragraph (2) does not apply where, by virtue of Rule 4.43(4) or 4.59, the only members of the committee are contributories. In that case the committee is to be treated for voting purposes as if all its members were creditors.

(4) Every resolution passed shall be recorded in writing, either separately or as part of the minutes of the meeting. The record shall be signed by the chairman and kept as part of the sederunt book.

Resolutions by post

4.55.—(1) In accordance with this Rule, the liquidator may seek to obtain the agreement of members of the liquidation committee to a resolution by sending to every member (or his representative designated for the purpose) a copy of proposed resolution.

[11] (2) Where the liquidator makes use of the procedure allowed by this Rule, he shall send out to members of the committee or their representatives (as the case may be) a copy of any proposed resolution on which a decision is sought, which shall be set out in such a way that agreement with or dissent from each separate resolution may be indicated by the recipient on the copy so sent.

(3) Any creditor member of the committee may, within seven business days from the date of the liquidator sending out a resolution, require him to summon a meeting of the committee to consider the matters raised by the resolution.

(4) In the absence of such a request, the resolution is deemed to have been passed by the committee if and when the liquidator is notified in writing by a majority of the creditor members that they concur with it.

(5) A copy of every resolution passed under this Rule, and a note that the committee's concurrence was obtained, shall be kept in the sederunt book.

Liquidator's reports

4.56.—(1) The liquidator shall, as and when directed by the liquidation committee (but not more often than once in any period of two months), send a written report to every member of the committee setting out the position generally as regards the progress of the winding up and matters arising in connection with it, to which the liquidator considers the committee's attention should be drawn.

(2) In the absence of such directions by the committee, the liquidator shall send such a report not less often than once in every period of six months.

---

[11] As amended by S.I. 1987 No. 1921.

(3) The obligations of the liquidator under this Rule are without prejudice to those imposed by Rule 4.44.

Expenses of members, etc.

4.57.—(1) The liquidator shall defray any reasonable travelling expenses directly incurred by members of the liquidation committee or their representatives in respect of their attendance at the committee's meetings, or otherwise on the committee's business, as an expense of the liquidation.

(2) Paragraph (1) does not apply to any meeting of the committee held within three months of a previous meeting.

Dealings by committee-members and others

4.58.—(1) This Rule applies to—

(*a*) any member of the liquidation committee;
(*b*) any committee-member's representative;
(*c*) any person who is an associate of a member of the committee or of a committee-member's representative; and
(*d*) any person who has been a member of the committee at any time in the last 12 months.

(2) Subject as follows, a person to whom this rule applies shall not enter into any transaction whereby he—

(*a*) receives out of the company's assets any payment for services given or goods supplied in connection with the liquidation, or
(*b*) obtains any profit from the liquidation, or
(*c*) acquires any part of the company's assets.

(3) Such a transaction may be entered into by a person to whom this Rule applies—

(*a*) with the prior leave of the court, or
(*b*) it he does so as a matter of urgency, or by way of performance of a contract in force before the date on which the company went into liquidation, and obtains the court's leave for the transaction, having applied for it without undue delay, or
(*c*) with the prior sanction of the liquidation committee, where it is satisfied (after full disclosure of the circumstances) that the transaction will be on normal commercial terms.

(4) Where in the committee a resolution is proposed that sanction be accorded for a transaction to be entered into which, without that sanction or the leave of the court, would be in contravention of this Rule, no member of the committee, and no representative of a member, shall vote if he is to participate directly or indirectly in the transaction.

(5) The court may, on the application of any person interested,—

(*a*) set aside a transaction on the ground that it has been entered into in contravention of this Rule, and (*b*) make with respect to it such other order as it thinks fit, including (subject to the following paragraph) an order requiring a person to whom this Rule applies to account for any profit obtained from the transaction and compensate the company's assets for any resultant loss.

(6) In the case of a person to whom this Rule applies as an associate of a member of the committee or of a committee-member's representative, the court shall not make any order under paragraph (5), if satisfied that he entered into the relevant transaction without having any reason to suppose that in doing so he would contravene this Rule.

(7) The expenses of an application to the court for leave under this Rule are not payable as an expense of the liquidation, unless the court so orders.

Composition of committee when creditors paid in full

4.59.—(1) This Rule applies if the liquidator issues a certificate that the creditors have been paid in full, with interest in accordance with *Form 4.23 (Scot)* section 189.

(2) The liquidator shall forthwith send a copy of the certificate to the *Form 4.24 (Scot)* registrar of companies.

(3) The creditor members of the liquidation committee shall cease to be members of the committee.

(4) The committee continues in being unless and until abolished by decision of a meeting of contributories, and (subject to the next paragraph) so long as it consists of at least two contributory members.

(5) The committee does not cease to exist on account of the number of contributory members falling below two, unless and until 28 days have elapsed since the issue of the liquidator's certificate under paragraph (1), but at any time when the committee consists of less than two contributory members, it is suspended and cannot act.

(6) Contributories may be co-opted by the liquidator, or appointed by a contributories' meeting, to be members of the committee; but the maximum number of members is five.

(7) The foregoing Rules in this Chapter continue to apply to the liquidation committee (with any necessary modifications) as if all the members of the committee were creditor members.

[12] *Formal defects*

4.59A. The acts of the liquidation committee established for any winding up are valid notwithstanding any defect in the appointment, election or qualification of any member of the committee or any committee-member's representative or in the formalities of its establishment.

---

[12] Inserted by S.I. 1987 No. 1921.

Chapter 8

The Liquidation Committee where Winding Up Follows Immediately on Administration

Preliminary

4.60.—(1) The Rules in this Chapter apply where—

(*a*) the winding up order has been made immediately upon the discharge of an administration order under Part II of the Act, and

(*b*) the court makes an order under section 140(1) appointing as liquidator the person who was previously the administrator.

(2) In this Chapter the expressions "insolvent winding up", "solvent winding up", "creditor member", and "contributory member" each have the same meaning as in Chapter 7.

Continuation of creditors' committee

4.61.—(1) If under section 26 a creditors' committee has been established for the purposes of the administration, then (subject as follows in this Chapter) that committee continues in being as the liquidation committee for the purposes of the winding up, and—

(*a*) it is deemed to be a committee established as such under section 142, and

(*b*) no action shall be taken under subsections (1) to (4) of that section to establish any other.

(2) This Rule does not apply if, at the time when the court's order under section 140(1) is made, the committee under section 26 consists of less than three members; and a creditor who was, immediately before the date of that order, a member of such a committee ceases to be a member on the making of the order if his debt is fully secured (and he has not agreed to surrender his security to the liquidator).

Membership of committee

4.62.—(1) Subject as follows, the liquidation committee shall consist of at least three, and not more than five, creditors of the company, elected by the creditors' meeting held under section 26 or (in order to make up numbers or fill vacancies) by a creditors' meeting summoned by the liquidator after the company goes into liquidation.

(2) In the case of a solvent winding up, the liquidator shall, on not less than 21 days' notice, summon a meeting of contributories, in order to elect (if it so wishes) contributory members of the liquidation committee, up to three in number.

Liquidator's certificate

4.63.—(1) The liquidator shall issue a certificate of the liquidation committee's continuance specifying the persons who are, or are to be, members of it.

(2) It shall be stated in the certificate whether or not the liquidator has summoned a meeting of contributories under Rule 4.62(2), and whether (if so) the meeting has elected contributories to be members of the committee.

(3) Pending the issue of the liquidator's certificate, the committee is suspended and cannot act.

(4) No person may act, or continue to act, as a member of the committee unless and until he has agreed to do so; and the liquidator's certificate shall not be issued until at least the minimum number of persons required under Rule 4.62 to form a committee elected, whether under Rule 4.62 above or under section 26, have signified their agreement.

(5) As and when the others signify their agreement, the liquidator *Form 4.21 (Scot)* shall issue an amended certificate.

(6) The liquidator's certificate (or, as the case may be, the amended *Form 4.22 (Scot)* certificate) shall be sent by him to the registrar of companies.

(7) If subsequently there is any change in the committee's *Form 4.22 (Scot)* membership, the liquidator shall report the change to the registrar of companies.

Obligations of liquidator to committee

4.64.—(1) As soon as may be after the issue of the liquidator's certificate under Rule 4.63, the liquidator shall report to the liquidation committee what actions he has taken since the date on which the company went into liquidation.

(2) A person who becomes a member of the committee after that date is not entitled to require a report to him by the liquidator, otherwise than in a summary form, of any matters previously arising.

(3) Nothing in this Rule disentitles the committee, or any member of it, from having access to the sederunt book (whether relating to the period when he was administrator, or to any subsequent period), or from seeking an explanation of any matter within the committee's responsibility.

Application of Chapter 7

[13] **4.65.** Except as provided elsewhere in this Chapter, Rules 4.44 to 4.59A of Chapter 7 shall apply to a liquidation committee established under this Chapter from the date of issue of the certificate under Rule *Form 4.21 (Scot)* 4.63 as if it had been established under section 142.

CHAPTER 9

DISTRIBUTION OF COMPANY'S ASSETS BY LIQUIDATOR

Order of priority in distribution

4.66.—(1) The funds of the company's assets shall be distributed by

[13] As amended by S.I. 1987 No. 1921.

the liquidator to meet the following expenses and debts in the order in which they are mentioned—

    (*a*) the expenses of the liquidation;

[14](*aa*) Where the court makes a winding up in relation to a company and, at the time when the petition for winding up was first presented to the court, there was in force in relation to the company a voluntary arrangement under Part I of the Act, any expenses properly incurred as expenses of the administration of that arrangement;

    (*b*) any preferential debts within the meaning of section 386 (excluding any interest which has been accrued thereon to the date of commencement of the winding up within the meaning of section 129);

    (*c*) ordinary debt, that is to say a debt which is neither a secured debt nor a debt mentioned in any other sub-paragraph of this paragraph;

    (*d*) interest at the official rate on—
        (i) the preferential debts, and
        (ii) the ordinary debts,
    between the said date of commencement of the winding up and the date of payment of the debt; and

    (*e*) any postponed debt.

(2) In the above paragraph—

    (*a*) "postponed debt" means a creditor's right to any alienation which has been reduced or restored to the company's assets under section 242 or to the proceeds of sale of such an alienation; and

    (*b*) "official rate" shall be construed in accordance with subsection (4) of section 189 and, for the purposes of paragraph (*a*) of that subsection, as applied to Scotland by subsection (5), the rate specified in the Rules shall be 15 per centum per annum.

(3) The expenses of the liquidation mentioned in sub-paragraph (*a*) of paragraph (1) are payable in the order of priority mentioned in Rule 4.67.

(4) Subject to the provisions of section 175, any debt falling within any of sub-paragraphs (*b*) to (*e*) of paragraph (1) shall have the same priority as any other debt falling within the same sub-paragraph and, where the funds of the company's assets are inadequate to enable the debts mentioned in this sub-paragraph to be paid in full, they shall abate in equal proportions.

(5) Any surplus remaining, after all expenses and debts mentioned in paragraph (1) have been paid in full, shall (unless the articles of the

[14] Inserted by S.I. 1987 No. 1921.

company otherwise provide) be distributed among the members according to their rights and interests in the company.

(6) Nothing in this Rule shall affect—

(a) the right of a secured creditor which is preferable to the rights of the liquidator; or

[15](b) any preference of the holder of a lien over a title deed or other document which has been delivered to the liquidator in accordance with a requirement under Rule 4.22(4).

Order of priority of expenses of liquidation

4.67.—(1) Subject to section 156 and paragraph (2), the expenses of the liquidation are payable out of the assets in the following order of priority—

(a) any outlays properly chargeable or incurred by the provisional liquidator or liquidator in carrying out his functions in the liquidation, except those outlays specifically mentioned in the following sub-paragraphs;

(b) the cost, or proportionate cost, of any caution provided by a provisional liquidator, liquidator or special manager in accordance with the Act or the Rules;

(c) the remuneration of the provisional liquidator (if any);

(d) the expenses of the petitioner in the liquidation, and of any person appearing in the petition whose expenses are allowed by the court;

(e) the remuneration of the special manager (if any);

(f) any allowance made by the liquidator under Rule 4.9(1) (expenses of statement of affairs);

(g) the remuneration or emoluments of any person who has been employed by the liquidator to perform any services for the company, as required or authorised by or under the Act or the Rules;

(h) the remuneration of the liquidator determined in accordance with Rule 4.32;

[16](i) the amount of any corporation tax on chargeable gains accruing on the realisation of any asset of the company (without regard to whether the realisation is effected by the liquidator, a secured creditor or otherwise).

(2) In any winding up by the court which follows immediately on a voluntary winding up (whether members' voluntary or creditors' voluntary), such outlays and remuneration of the voluntary liquidator as the court may allow, shall have the same priority as the outlays mentioned in sub-paragraph (a) of paragraph (1).

(3) Nothing in this Rule applies to or affects the power of any court,

---

[15] As amended by S.I. 1987 No. 1921.
[16] As amended by S.I. 1987 No. 1921.

in proceedings by or against the company, to order expenses to be paid by the company, or the liquidator; nor does it affect the rights of any person to whom such expenses are ordered to be paid.

Application of the Bankruptcy Act

4.68.—(1) Sections 52, 53 and 58 of the Bankruptcy Act shall apply in relation to the liquidation of a company as they apply in relation to a sequestration of a debtor's estate, subject to the modifications specified in Rules 4.16(2) and 4.32(2) and (3) and the following paragraph and to any other necessary modifications.

(2) In section 52, the following modifications shall be made:—

(*a*) in subsection (4)(*a*) for the reference to "the debts mentioned in subsection 1(*a*) to (*d*)", there shall be substituted a reference to the expenses of the winding up mentioned in Rule 4.67(1)(*a*);

(*b*) in subsection (5), the words "with the consent of the commissioners or if there are no commissioners of the Accountant in Bankruptcy" should be deleted; and

(*c*) in subsection (7) and (8) for the references to section 48(5) and 49(6)(*b*) there should be substituted a reference to those sections as applied by Rule 4.16(1).

CHAPTER 10

SPECIAL MANAGER

Appointment and remuneration

4.69.—(1) This Chapter applies to an application under section 177 by the liquidator or, where one has been appointed, by the provisional liquidator for the appointment of a person to be special manager (references in this Chapter to the liquidator shall be read as including the provisional liquidator).

(2) An application shall be supported by a report setting out the reasons for the appointment. The report shall include the applicant's estimate of the value of the assets in respect of which the special manager is to be appointed.

(3) The order of the court appointing the special manager shall specify the duration of his appointment, which may be for a period of time or until the occurrence of a specified event. Alternatively the order may specify that the duration of the appointment is to be subject to a further order of the court.

(4) The appointment of a special manager may be renewed by order of the court.

(5) The special manager's remuneration shall be fixed from time to time by the court.

(6) The acts of the special manager are valid notwithstanding any defect in his appointment or qualifications.

Caution

4.70.—(1) The appointment of the special manager does not take effect until the person appointed has found (or, being allowed by the court to do so, has undertaken to find) caution to the person who applies for him to be appointed.

(2) It is not necessary that caution be found for each separate company liquidation; but it may be found either specially for a particular liquidation, or generally for any liquidation in relation to which the special manager may be employed as such.

(3) The amount of the caution shall be not less than the value of the assets in respect of which he is appointed, as estimated by the applicant in his report under Rule 4.69.

(4) When the special manager has found caution to the person applying for his appointment, that person shall certify the adequacy of the security and notify the court accordingly.

(5) The cost of finding caution shall be paid in the first instance by the special manager; but—

(a) where a winding up order is not made, he is entitled to be reimbursed out of the property of the company, and the court may make an order on the company accordingly, and

(b) where a winding up order has been or is subsequently made, he is entitled to be reimbursed as an expense of the liquidation.

Failure to find or to maintain caution

4.71.—(1) If the special manager fails to find the required caution within the time stated for that purpose by the order appointing him, or any extension of that time that may be allowed, the liquidator shall report the failure to the court, which may thereupon discharge the order appointing the special manager.

(2) If the special manager fails to maintain his caution the liquidator shall report his failure to the court, which may thereupon remove the special manager and make such order as it thinks fit as to expenses.

(3) If an order is made under this Rule removing the special manager, or recalling the order appointing him, the court shall give directions as to whether any, and if so what, steps should be taken to appoint another special manager in his place.

Accounting

4.72.—(1) The special manager shall produce accounts containing details of his receipts and payments for the approval of the liquidator.

(2) The accounts shall be in respect of three-month periods for the duration of the special manager's appointment (or for a lesser period if his appointment terminates less than three months from its date, or from the date to which the last accounts were made up).

(3) When the accounts have been approved, the special manager's receipts and payments shall be added to those of the liquidator.

Termination of appointment

4.73.—(1) The special manager's appointment terminates if the winding up petition is dismissed or, if a provisional liquidator having been appointed, he is discharged without a winding up order having been made.

(2) If the liquidator is of opinion that the employment of the special manager is no longer necessary or profitable for the company, he shall apply to the court for directions, and the court may order the special manager's appointment to be terminated.

(3) The liquidator shall make the same application if a resolution of the creditors is passed, requesting that the appointment be terminated.

CHAPTER 11

PUBLIC EXAMINATION OF COMPANY OFFICERS AND OTHERS

Notice of order for public examination

4.74. Where the court orders the public examination of any person under section 133(1), then, unless the court otherwise directs, the liquidator shall give at least 14 days' notice of the time and place of the examination to the persons specified in paragraphs (*c*) to (*e*) of section 133(4) and the liquidator may, if he thinks fit, cause notice of the order to be given, by public advertisement in one or more newspapers circulating in the area of the principal place of business of the company, at least 14 days before the date fixed for the examination but there shall be no such advertisement before at least seven days have elapsed from the date when the person to be examined was served with the order.

Order on request by creditors or contributories

4.75.—(1) A request to the liquidator by a creditor or creditors or contributory or contributories under section 133(2) shall be made in writing and be accompanied by—

(*a*) a list of the creditors (if any) concurring with the request and the amounts of their respective claims in the liquidation, or (as the case may be) of the contributories (if any) so concurring, with their respective values, and

(*b*) from each creditor or contributory concurring, written confirmation of his concurrence.

(2) The request must specify the name of the proposed examinee, the relationship which he has, or has had, to the company and the reasons why his examination is requested.

(3) Before an application to the court is made on the request, the requisitionists shall deposit with the liquidator such sum as the latter may determine to be appropriate by way of caution for the expenses of the hearing of a public examination, if ordered.

(4) Subject as follows, the liquidator shall, within 28 days of receiving the request, make the application to the court required by section 133(2).

(5) If the liquidator is of opinion that the request is an unreasonable one in the circumstances, he may apply to the court for an order relieving him from the obligation to make the application otherwise required by that subsection.

(6) If the court so orders, and the application for the order was made *ex parte*, notice of the order shall be given forthwith by the liquidator to the requisitionists. If the application for an order is dismissed, the liquidator's application under section 133(2) shall be made forthwith on conclusion of the hearing of the application first mentioned.

(7) Where a public examination of the examinee has been ordered by the court on a creditors' or contributories' requisition under this Rule the court may order that the expenses of the examination are to be paid, as to a specified proportion, out of the caution under paragraph (3), instead of out of the assets.

CHAPTER 12

MISCELLANEOUS

Limitation
4.76. The provisions of section 8(5) and 22(8), as read with section 73(5), of the Bankruptcy (Scotland) Act 1985 (presentation of petition or submission of claim to bar effect of limitation of actions) shall apply in relation to the liquidation as they apply in relation to a sequestration, subject to the modifications specified in Rule 4.16(2) and to any other necessary modifications.

Dissolution after winding up
4.77. Where the court makes an order under section 204(5) or 205(5), the person on whose application the order was made shall deliver to *Form 4.28 (Scot)* the registrar of companies a copy of the order.

CHAPTER 13

COMPANY WITH PROHIBITED NAME

Preliminary
4.78. The Rules in this Chapter—

(a) relate to the leave required under section 216 (restriction on re-use of name of company in insolvent liquidation) for a person to act as mentioned in section 216(3) in relation to a company with a prohibited name,

(b) prescribe the cases excepted from that provision, that is to say, those in which a person to whom the section applies may so act without that leave, and

[17](*c*) apply to all windings up to which section 216 applies, whether or not the winding up commenced before or after the coming into force of the Insolvency (Scotland) Amendment Rules 1987.

Application for leave under section 216(3)

4.79. When considering an application for leave under section 216, the court may call on the liquidator, or any former liquidator, of the liquidating company for a report of the circumstances in which that company became insolvent, and the extent (if any) of the applicant's apparent responsibility for its doing so.

First excepted case

4.80.—(1) Where a company ("the successor company") acquires the whole, or substantially the whole, of the business of an insolvent company, under arrangements made by an insolvency practitioner acting as its liquidator, administrator or receiver, or as supervisor of a voluntary arrangement under Part I of the Act, the successor company may for the purposes of section 216 give notice under this Rule to the insolvent company's creditors.

(2) To be effective, the notice must be given within 28 days from the completion of the arrangements to all creditors of the insolvent company of whose addresses the successor is aware in that period; and it must specify—

(*a*) the name and registered number of the insolvent company and the circumstances in which its business has been acquired by the successor company,

(*b*) the name which the successor company has assumed, or proposes to assume for the purpose of carrying on the business, if that name is or will be a prohibited name under section 216, and

(*c*) any change of name which it has made, or proposes to make, for that purpose under section 28 of the Companies Act.

(3) The notice may name a person to whom section 216 may apply as having been a director or shadow director of the insolvent company, and give particulars as to the nature and duration of that directorship, with a view to his being a director of the successor company or being otherwise associated with its management.

(4) If the successor company has effectively given notice under this Rule to the insolvent company's creditors, a person who is so named in the notice may act in relation to the successor company in any of the ways mentioned in section 216(3), notwithstanding that he has not the leave of the court under that section.

[18] *Second excepted case*

4.81.—(1) Where a person to whom section 216 applies as having

---

[17] Inserted by S.I. 1987 No. 1921.
[18] Substituted by S.I. 1987 No. 1921.

been a director or shadow director of the liquidating company applies for leave of the court under that section not later than seven days from the date on which the company went into liquidation, he may, during the period specified in paragraph (2) below, act in any of the ways mentioned in section 216(3), notwithstanding that he has not the leave of the court under that section.

(2) The period referred to in paragraph (1) begins with the day on which the company goes into liquidation and ends either on the day falling six weeks after that date or on the day on which the court disposes of the application for leave under section 216, whichever of those days occurs first.

Third excepted case

4.82. The court's leave under section 216(3) is not required where the company there referred to, though known by a prohibited name within the meaning of the section,—

(a) has been known by that name for the whole of the period of 12 months ending with the day before the liquidating company went into liquidation, and

(b) has not at any time in those 12 months been dormant within the meaning of section 252(5) of the Companies Act.

PART 5

CREDITORS' VOLUNTARY WINDING UP

Application of Part 4

5. The provisions of Part 4 shall apply in a creditors' voluntary winding up of a company as they apply in a winding up by the court subject to the modifications specified in Schedule 1 and to any other necessary modifications.

PART 6

MEMBERS' VOLUNTARY WINDING UP

Application of Part 4

6. The provisions of Part 4, which are specified in Schedule 2, shall apply in relation to a members' voluntary winding up of a company as they apply in a winding up by the court, subject to the modifications specified in Schedule 2 and to any other necessary modifications.

PART 7

PROVISIONS OF GENERAL APPLICATION

CHAPTER 1

MEETINGS

Scope of Chapter 1

7.1.—(1) This Chapter applies to any meetings held in insolvency proceedings other than meetings of a creditors' committee in administration or receivership, or of a liquidation committee.

(2) The Rules in this Chapter shall apply to any such meeting subject to any contrary provision in the Act or in the Rules, or to any direction of the court.

Summoning of meetings

7.2.—(1) In fixing the date, time and place for a meeting, the person summoning the meeting ("the convenor") shall have regard to the convenience of the persons who are to attend.

(2) Meetings shall in all cases be summoned for commencement between 10.00 and 16.00 hours on a business day, unless the court otherwise directs.

Notice of meeting

7.3.—(1) The convenor shall give not less than 21 days' notice of the date, time and place of the meeting to every person known to him as being entitled to attend the meeting.

(2) In paragraph (1), for the reference to 21 days, there shall be substituted a reference to 14 days in the following cases:—

(a) any meeting of the company or of its creditors summoned under section 3 (to consider directors' proposal for voluntary arrangement);

(b) a meeting of the creditors under section 23(1)(b) or 25(2)(b) (to consider administrator's proposals or proposed revisions);

(c) a meeting of creditors under section 67(2) (meeting of unsecured creditors in receivership); and

[19](d) a meeting of creditors or contributories under section 138(3) or (4).

(3) The convenor may also publish notice of the date, time and place of the meeting in a newspaper circulating in the area of the principal place of business of the company or in such other newspaper as he thinks most appropriate for ensuring that it comes to the notice of the persons who are entitled to attend the meeting. In the case of a creditors' meeting summoned by the administrator under section 23(1)(b), the administrator shall publish such a notice.

[19] (3A) Any notice under this paragraph shall be published not less than 21 days or, in cases to which paragraph (2) above applies, 14 days before the meeting.

(4) Any notice under this Rule shall state—

(a) the purpose of the meeting;

(b) the persons who are entitled to attend and vote at the meeting;

(c) the effects of Rule 7.9 or, as the case may be, 7.10 (Entitlement to Vote) and of the relevant provisions of Rule 7.12 (Resolutions);

---

[19] Inserted by S.I. 1987 No. 1921.

(*d*) in the case of a meeting of creditors or contributories, that proxies may be lodged at or before the meeting and the place where they may be lodged; and

(*e*) in the case of a meeting of creditors, that claims may be lodged by those who have not already done so at or before the meeting and the place where they may be lodged.

Where a meeting of creditors is summoned specially for the purpose of removing the liquidator in accordance with section 171(2) or 172(2), or of receiving his resignation under Rule 4.28, the notice summoning it shall also include the information required by Rule 4.23(2) or, as the case may be, 4.28(2).

(5) With the notice given under paragraph (1), the convenor shall also send out a proxy form.

(6) In the case of any meeting of creditors or contributories, the court may order that notice of the meeting be given by public advertisement in such form as may be specified in the order and not by individual notice to the persons concerned. In considering whether to make such an order, the court shall have regard to the cost of the public advertisement, to the amount of the assets available and to the extent of the interest of creditors or contributories or any particular class of either.

[19] (7) The provisions of this Rule shall not apply to a meeting of creditors summoned under section 95 or 98 but any notice advertised in accordance with section 95(2)(*c*) or 98(1)(*c*) shall give not less than seven days' notice of the meeting.

Additional notices in certain cases

7.4.—[20] (1) This Rule applies where a company goes, or proposes to go, into liquidation and it is an authorised institution or a former authorised institution within the meaning of the Banking Act.

(2) Notice of any meeting of the company at which it is intended to propose a resolution for its voluntary winding up shall be given by the directors to the Bank of England ("the Bank") and to the Deposit Protection Board ("the Board") as such notice is given to members of the company.

(3) Where a creditors' meeting is summoned by the liquidator under section 95 or 98, the same notice of meeting must be given to the Bank and Board as is given to the creditors under this Chapter.

(4) Where the company is being wound up by the court, notice of the first meetings of creditors and contributories within the meaning of Rule 4.12 shall be given to the Bank and the Board by the liquidator.

(5) Where in any winding up a meeting of creditors or contributories is summoned for the purpose of—

(*a*) receiving the liquidator's resignation, or

---

[20] Substituted by S.I. 1987 No. 1921.

(*b*) removing the liquidator, or

(*c*) appointing a new liquidator,

the person summoning the meeting and giving notice of it shall also give notice to the Bank and the Board.

(6) The Board is entitled to be represented at any meeting of which it is required by this Rule to be given notice; and Schedule 3 has effect with respect to the voting rights of the Board at such a meeting.

Chairman of meetings

7.5.—[21] (1) The chairman at any meeting of creditors in insolvency proceedings, other than at a meeting of creditors under section 98, shall be the responsible insolvency practitioner, or except at a meeting of creditors summoned under section 95, a person nominated by him in writing.

(2) A person nominated under this Rule must be either—

(*a*) a person who is qualified to act as an insolvency practitioner in relation to the company, or

(*b*) an employee of the administrator, receiver or liquidator, as the case may be, or his firm who is experienced in insolvency matters.

(3) This Rule also applies to meetings of contributories in a liquidation.

(4) At the first meeting of creditors or contributories in a winding up by the court, the interim liquidator shall be the chairman except that, where a resolution is proposed to appoint the interim liquidator to be the liquidator, another person may be elected to act as chairman for the purpose of choosing the liquidator.

(5) This Rule is subject to Rule 4.23(3) (meeting for removal of liquidator).

Meetings requisitioned

7.6.—[22] (1) Subject to paragraph (8), this Rule applies to any request by a creditor or creditors—

(*a*) to—
    (i) an administrator under section 17(3), or
    (ii) a liquidator under section 171(3) or 172(3),

for a meeting of creditors; or

(*b*) to a liquidator under section 142(3) for separate meetings of creditors and contributories,

or for any other meeting under any other provision of the Act or the Rules.

---

[21] As amended by S.I. 1987 No. 1921.
[22] Substituted by S.I. 1987 No. 1921.

(2) Any such request shall be accompanied by—

(a) a list of any creditors concurring with the request, showing the amounts of the respective claims against the company of the creditor making the request and the concurring creditors;

(b) from each creditor concurring, written confirmation of his concurrence; and

(c) a statement of the purpose of the proposed meeting.

(3) If the administrator or, as the case may be, the liquidator considers the request to be properly made in accordance with the Act or the Rules, he shall summon a meeting of the creditors to be held on a date not more than 35 days from the date of his receipt of the request.

[23] (4) Expenses of summoning and holding a meeting under this Rule shall be paid by the creditor or creditors making the request, who shall deposit with the administrator or, as the case may be, the liquidator caution for their payment.

(5) The sum to be deposited shall be such as the administrator or, as the case may be, the liquidator may determine and he shall not act without the deposit having been made.

(6) The meeting may resolve that the expenses of summoning and holding it are to be payable out of the assets of the company as an expense of the administration or, as the case may be, the liquidation.

(7) To the extent that any caution deposited under this Rule is not required for the payment of expenses of summoning and holding the meeting, it shall be repaid to the person or persons who made it.

(8) This Rule applies to requests by a contributory or contributories for a meeting of contributories, with the modification that, for the reference in paragraph (2) to the creditors' respective claims, there shall be substituted a reference to the contributories' respective values (being the amounts for which they may vote at any meeting).

(9) This Rule is without prejudice to the powers of the court under Rule 4.67(2) (voluntary winding up succeeded by winding up by the court).

Quorum

7.7.—(1) Subject to the next paragraph, a quorum is—

(a) in the case of a creditors' meeting, at least one creditor entitled to vote;

(b) in the case of a meeting of contributories, at least two contributories so entitled, or all the contributories, if their number does not exceed two.

(2) For the purposes of this Rule, the reference to the creditor or contributories necessary to constitute a quorum is not confined to those persons present or duly represented under section 375 of the

---

[23] As amended by S.I. 1987 No. 1921.

Companies Act but includes those represented by proxy by any person (including the chairman).

[24] (3) Where at any meeting of creditors or contributories—

(a) the provisions of this Rule as to a quorum being present are satisfied by the attendance of—
(i) the chairman alone, or
(ii) one other person in addition to the chairman, and
(b) the chairman is aware, by virtue of claims and proxies received or otherwise, that one or more additional persons would, if attending, be entitled to vote,

the meeting shall not commence until at least the expiry of 15 minutes after the time appointed for its commencement.

Adjournment

7.8.—(1) This Rule applies to meetings of creditors and to meetings of contributories.

(2) If, within a period of 30 minutes from the time appointed for the commencement of a meeting, a quorum is not present, then, unless the chairman otherwise decides, the meeting shall be adjourned to the same time and place in the following week or, if that is not a business day, to the business day immediately following.

(3) In the course of any meeting, the chairman may, in his discretion, and shall, if the meeting so resolves, adjourn it to such date, time and place as seems to him to be appropriate in the circumstances.

(4) Paragraph (3) is subject to Rule 4.23(3) where the liquidator or his nominee is chairman and a resolution has been proposed for the liquidator's removal.

[25] (5) An adjournment under paragraph (2) or (3) shall not be for a period of more than 21 days and notice of the adjourned meeting may be given by the chairman.

(6) Where a meeting is adjourned, any proxies given for the original meeting may be used at the adjourned meeting.

[26] (7) Where a company meeting at which a resolution for voluntary winding up is to be proposed is adjourned without that resolution having been passed, any resolution passed at a meeting under section 98 held before the holding of the adjourned company meeting only has effect on and from the passing by the company of a resolution for winding up.

Entitlement to vote (creditors)

7.9.—(1) This Rule applies to a creditors' meeting in any insolvency proceedings.

(2) A creditor is entitled to vote at any meeting if he has submitted his

---

[24] Inserted by S.I. 1987 No. 1921.
[25] As amended by S.I. 1987 No. 1921.
[26] Inserted by S.I. 1987 No. 1921.

claim to the responsible insolvency practitioner and his claim has been accepted in whole or in part.

(3) Chapter 5 of Part 4 (claims in liquidation) shall apply for the purpose of determining a creditor's entitlement to vote at any creditors' meeting in any insolvency proceedings as it applies for the purpose of determining a creditor's entitlement to vote at a meeting of creditors in a liquidation, subject to the modifications specified in the following paragraphs and to any other necessary modification.

(4) For any reference in the said Chapter 5, or in any provision of the Bankruptcy Act as applied by Rule 4.16(1), to—

(a) the liquidator, there shall be substituted a reference to the supervisor, administrator or receiver, as the case may be;

(b) the liquidation, there shall be substituted a reference to the voluntary arrangement, administration or receivership as the case may be;

(c) the date of commencement of winding up, there shall be substituted a reference—

(i) in the case of a meeting in a voluntary arrangement, to the date of the meeting or, where the company is being wound up or is subject to an administration order, the date of its going into liquidation or, as the case may be, of the administration order; and

(ii) in the case of a meeting in the administration or receivership, to the date of the administration order or, as the case may be, the date of appointment of the receiver;

(5) In the application to meetings of creditors other than in liquidation proceedings of Schedule 1 to the Bankruptcy Act, paragraph 5(2) and (3) (secured creditors) shall not apply.

(6) This Rule is subject to Rule 7.4(6) and Schedule 3.

Entitlement to vote (members and contributories)

7.10.—(1) Members of a company or contributories at their meetings shall vote according to their rights attaching to their shares respectively in accordance with the articles of association.

(2) In the case of a meeting of members of the company in a voluntary arrangement, where no voting rights attach to a member's share, he is nevertheless entitled to vote either for or against the proposal or any modification of it.

(3) Reference in this Rule to a person's share include any other interests which he may have as a member of the company.

Chairman of meeting as proxy holder

7.11.—(1) Where the chairman at a meeting of creditors or contributories holds a proxy which requires him to vote for a particular resolution and no other person proposes that resolution—

(a) he shall propose it himself, unless he considers that there is good reason for not doing so, and

(b) if he does not propose it, he shall forthwith after the meeting notify the person who granted him the proxy of the reason why he did not do so.

(2) At any meeting in a voluntary arrangement, the chairman shall not, by virtue of any proxy held by him, vote to increase or reduce the amount of the remuneration or expenses of the nominee or the supervisor of the proposed arrangement, unless the proxy specifically directs him to vote in that way.

Resolutions

7.12.—(1) Subject to any contrary provision in the Act or the Rules, at any meeting of creditors, contributories or members of a company, a resolution is passed when a majority in value of those voting, in person or by proxy, have voted in favour of it.

(2) In a voluntary arrangement, at a creditors' meeting for any resolution to pass approving any proposal or modification, there must be at least three quarters in value of the creditors present or represented and voting, in person or by proxy, in favour of the resolution.

(3) In a liquidation, in the case of a resolution for the appointment of a liquidator—

(a) if, on any vote, there are two nominees for appointment, the person for whom a majority in value has voted shall be appointed;

(b) if there are three or more nominees, and one of them has a clear majority over both or all the others together, that one is appointed; and

(c) in any other case, the chairman of the meeting shall continue to take votes (disregarding at each vote any nominee who has withdrawn and, if no nominee has withdrawn, the nominee who obtained the least support last time), until a clear majority is obtained for any one nominee.

The chairman may, at any time, put to the meeting a resolution for the joint appointment of any two or more nominees.

[27] (4) Where a resolution is proposed which affects a person in respect of his remuneration or conduct as a responsible insolvency practitioner, the vote of that person, or of his firm or of any partner or employee of his shall not be reckoned in the majority required for passing the resolution. This paragraph applies with respect to a vote given by a person (whether personally or on his behalf by a proxy-holder), either as creditor or contributory or member or as proxy-holder for a creditor, contributory, or member.

Report of meeting

7.13.—(1) The chairman at any meeting shall cause a report to be made of the proceedings at the meeting which shall be signed by him.

---

[27] As amended by S.I. 1987 No. 1921.

(2) The report of the meeting shall include—

(*a*) a list of all the creditors or, as the case may be, contributories who attended the meeting, either in person or by proxy;

(*b*) a copy of every resolution passed; and

(*c*) if the meeting established a creditors' committee or a liquidation committee, as the case may be, a list of the names and addresses of those elected to be members of the committee.

(3) The chairman shall keep a copy of the report of the meeting as part of the sederunt book in the insolvency proceedings.

CHAPTER 2

PROXIES AND COMPANY REPRESENTATION

Definition of "proxy"

7.14.—(1) For the purposes of the Rules, a person ("the principal") may authorise another person ("the proxy-holder") to attend, speak and vote as his representative at meetings of creditors or contributories or of the company in insolvency proceedings, and any such authority is referred to as a proxy.

(2) A proxy may be given either generally for all meetings in insolvency proceedings or specifically for any meeting or class of meetings.

(3) Only one proxy may be given by the principal for any one meeting; and it may only be given to one person, being an individual aged 18 or over. The principal may nevertheless nominate one or more other such persons to be proxy-holder in the alternative in the order in which they are named in the proxy.

[28] (4) Without prejudice to the generality of paragraph (3), a proxy for a particular meeting may be given to whoever is to be the chairman of the meeting and any person to whom such a proxy is given cannot decline to be a proxy-holder in relation to that proxy.

(5) A proxy may require the holder to vote on behalf of the principal on matters arising for determination at any meeting, or to abstain, either as directed or in accordance with the holder's own discretion; and it may authorise or require the holder to propose, in the principal's name, a resolution to be voted on by the meeting.

Form of proxy

7.15.—(1) With every notice summoning a meeting of creditors or contributories or of the company in insolvency proceedings there shall be sent out forms of proxy.

(2) A form of proxy shall not be sent out with the name or description of any person inserted in it.

---

[28] As amended by S.I. 1987 No. 1921.

(3) A proxy shall be in the form sent out with the notice summoning the meeting or in a form substantially to the same effect.

(4) A form of proxy shall be filled out and signed by the principal, or by some person acting under his authority and, where it is signed by someone other than the principal, the nature of his authority shall be stated on the form.

Use of proxy at meeting

7.16.—(1) A proxy given for a particular meeting may be used at any adjournment of that meeting.

(2) A proxy may be lodged at or before the meeting at which it is to be used.

(3) Where the responsible insolvency practitioner holds proxies to be used by him as chairman of the meeting, and some other person acts as chairman, the other person may use the insolvency practitioner's proxies as if he were himself proxy-holder.

[29] (4) Where a proxy directs a proxy-holder to vote for or against a resolution for the nomination or appointment of a person to be the responsible insolvency practitioner, the proxy-holder may, unless the proxy states otherwise, vote for or against (as he thinks fit) any resolution for the nomination or appointment of that person jointly with another or others.

[29] (5) A proxy-holder may propose any resolution which, if proposed by another, would be a resolution in favour of which he would be entitled to vote by virtue of the proxy.

[29] (6) Where a proxy gives specific directions as to voting, this does not, unless the proxy states otherwise, preclude the proxy-holder from voting at his discretion on resolutions put to the meeting which are not dealt with in the proxy.

Retention of proxies

7.17.—(1) Proxies used for voting at any meeting shall be retained by the chairman of the meeting.

(2) The chairman shall deliver the proxies forthwith after the meeting to the responsible insolvency practitioner (where he was not the chairman).

(3) The responsible insolvency practitioner shall retain all proxies in the sederunt book.

Right of inspection

7.18.—(1) The responsible insolvency practitioner shall, so long as proxies lodged with him are in his hands, allow them to be inspected at all reasonable times on any business day, by—

(a) the creditors, in the case of proxies used at a meeting of creditors,

---

[29] Inserted by S.I. 1987 No. 1921.

(*b*) a company's members or contributories, in the case of proxies used at a meeting of the company or of its contributories.

(2) The reference in paragraph (1) to creditors is—

(*a*) in the case of a company in liquidation, those creditors whose claims have been accepted in whole or in part, and

(*b*) in any other case, persons who have submitted in writing a claim to be creditors of the company concerned,

but in neither case does it include a person whose claim has been wholly rejected for purposes of voting, dividend or otherwise.

(3) The right of inspection given by this Rule is also exercisable, in the case of an insolvent company, by its directors.

[30] (4) Any person attending a meeting in insolvency proceedings is entitled, immediately before or in the course of the meeting, to inspect proxies and associated documents (including claims)—

(*a*) to be used in connection with that meeting, or

(*b*) sent or given to the chairman of that meeting or to any other person by a creditor, member or contributory for the purpose of that meeting, whether or not they are to be used at it.

Proxy-holder with financial interest

7.19.—(1) A proxy-holder shall not vote in favour of any resolution which would directly or indirectly place him, or any associate of his, in a position to receive any remuneration out of the insolvent estate, unless the proxy specifically directs him to vote in that way.

[31] (1A) Where a proxy-holder has signed the proxy as being authorised to do so by his principal and the proxy specifically directs him to vote in the way mentioned in paragraph (1), he shall nevertheless not vote in that way unless he produces to the chairman of the meeting written authorisation from his principal sufficient to show that the proxy-holder was entitled so to sign the proxy.

[32] (2) This Rule applies also to any person acting as chairman of a meeting and using proxies in that capacity in accordance with Rule 7.16(3); and in the application of this rule to any such person, the proxy holder is deemed an associate of his.

Representation of corporations

7.20.—(1) Where a person is authorised under section 375 of the Companies Act to represent a corporation at a meeting of creditors or contributories, he shall produce to the chairman of the meeting a copy of the resolution from which he derives his authority.

(2) The copy resolution must be executed in accordance with the provisions of section 36(3) of the Companies Act, or certified by the secretary or a director of the corporation to be a true copy.

---

[30] As amended by S.I. 1987 No. 1921.
[31] Inserted by S.I. 1987 No. 1921.
[32] As amended by S.I. 1987 No. 1921.

[33] (3) Nothing in this Rule requires the authority of a person to sign a proxy on behalf of a principal which is a corporation to be in the form of a resolution of that corporation.

CHAPTER 3

MISCELLANEOUS

Giving of notices, etc.

7.21.—(1) All notices required or authorised by or under the Act or the Rules to be given, sent or delivered must be in writing, unless it is otherwise provided, or the court allows the notice to be sent or given in some other way.

[34] (2) Any reference in the Act or the Rules to giving, sending or delivering a notice or any such document means, without prejudice to any other way and unless it is otherwise provided, that the notice or document may be sent by post, and that, subject to Rule 7.22, any form of post may be used. Personal service of the notice or document is permissible in all cases.

(3) Where under the Act or the Rules a notice or other document is required or authorised to be given, sent or delivered by a person ("the sender") to another ("the recipient"), it may be given, sent or delivered by any person duly authorised by the sender to do so to any person duly authorised by the recipient to receive or accept it.

(4) Where two or more persons are acting jointly as the responsible insolvency practitioner in any proceedings, the giving, sending or delivering of a notice or document to one of them is to be treated as the giving, sending or delivering of a notice or document to each or all.

Sending by post

7.22.—(1) For a document to be properly sent by post, it must be contained in an envelope addressed to the person to whom it is to be sent, and pre-paid for either first or second class post.

[35] (1A) Any document to be sent by post may be sent to the last known address of the person to whom the document is to be sent.

(2) Where first class post is used, the document is to be deemed to be received on the second business day after the date of posting, unless the contrary is shown.

(3) Where second class post is used, the document is to be deemed to be received on the fourth business day after the date of posting, unless the contrary is shown.

Certificate of giving notice, etc.

7.23.—(1) Where in any proceedings a notice or document is

---

[33] Inserted by S.I. 1987 No. 1921.
[34] As amended by S.I. 1987 No. 1921.
[35] Inserted by S.I. 1987 No. 1921.

required to be given, sent or delivered by the responsible insolvency practitioner, the date of giving, sending or delivery of it may be proved by means of a certificate signed by him or on his behalf by his solicitor, or a partner or an employee of either of them, that the notice or document was duly given, posted or otherwise sent, or delivered on the date stated in the certificate.

(2) In the case of a notice or document to be given, sent or delivered by a person other than the responsible insolvency practitioner, the date of giving, sending or delivery of it may be proved by means of a certificate by that person that he gave, posted or otherwise sent or delivered the notice or document on the date stated in the certificate, or that he instructed another person (naming him) to do so.

(3) A certificate under this Rule may be endorsed on a copy of the notice to which it relates.

(4) A certificate purporting to be signed by or on behalf of the responsible insolvency practitioner, or by the person mentioned in paragraph (2), shall be deemed, unless the contrary is shown, to be sufficient evidence of the matters stated therein.

Validity of proceedings

7.24. Where in accordance with the Act or the Rules a meeting of creditors or other persons is summoned by notice, the meeting is presumed to have been duly summoned and held, notwithstanding that not all those to whom the notice is to be given have received it.

Evidence of proceedings at meetings

7.25. A report of proceedings at a meeting of the company or of the company's creditors or contributories in any insolvency proceedings, which is signed by a person describing himself as the chairman of that meeting, shall be deemed, unless the contrary is shown, to be sufficient evidence of the matters contained in that report.

Right to list of creditors and copy documents

7.26.—(1) Paragraph (2) applies to—

(*a*) proceedings under Part II of the Act (company administration), and

(*b*) proceedings in a creditors' voluntary winding up, or a winding up by the court.

(2) Subject to Rule 7.27, in any such proceedings, a creditor who has the right to inspect documents also has the right to require the responsible insolvency practitioner to furnish him with a list of the company's creditors and the amounts of their respective debts.

[36] (2A) Where the responsible insolvency practitioner is requested by a creditor, member, contributory or by a member of a liquidation

---

[36] Inserted by S.I. 1987 No. 1921.

committee or of a creditors' committee to supply a copy of any document, he is entitled to require payment of the appropriate fee in respect of the supply of that copy.

(3) Subject to Rule 7.27, where a person has the right to inspect documents, the right includes that of taking copies of those documents, on payment of the appropriate fee.

(4) In this Rule, the appropriate fee means 15 pence per A4 or A5 page and 30 pence per A3 page.

Confidentiality of documents

7.27.—(1) Where, in any insolvency proceedings, the responsible insolvency practitioner considers, in the case of a document forming part of the records of those proceedings,—

(*a*) that it should be treated as confidential, or

(*b*) that it is of such a nature that its disclosure would be calculated to be injurious to the interests of the company's creditors or, in the case of the winding up of a company, its members or the contributories in its winding up,

he may decline to allow it to be inspected by a person who would otherwise be entitled to inspect it.

(2) The persons who may be refused the right to inspect documents under this Rule by the responsible insolvency practitioner include the members of a creditors' committee in administration or in receivership, or of a liquidation committee.

(3) Where under this Rule the responsible insolvency practitioner refuses inspection of a document, the person who made that request may apply to the court for an order to overrule the refusal and the court may either overrule it altogether, or sustain it, either unconditionally or subject to such conditions, if any, as it thinks fit to impose.

[37] (4) Nothing in this Rule entitles the responsible insolvency practitioner to decline to allow inspection of any claim or proxy.

Insolvency practitioner's caution

7.28.—(1) Wherever under the Rules any person has to appoint, or certify the appointment of, an insolvency practitioner to any office, he is under a duty to satisfy himself that the person appointed or to be appointed has caution for the proper performance of his functions.

(2) it is the duty—

(*a*) of the creditors' committee in administration or in receivership,

(*b*) of the liquidation committee in companies winding up, and

(*c*) of any committee of creditors established for the purposes of a voluntary arrangement under Part I of the Act,

to review from time to time the adequacy of the responsible insolvency practitioner's caution.

---

[37] Inserted by S.I. 1987 No. 1921.

(3) In any insolvency proceedings the cost of the responsible insolvency practitioner's caution shall be paid as an expense of the proceedings.

Punishment of offences

7.29.—(1) Schedule 4 has effect with respect to the way in which contraventions of the Rules are punishable on conviction.

(2) In that Schedule—

(a) the first column specifies the provision of the Rules which creates an offence;

(b) in relation to each such offence, the second column describes the general nature of the offence;

(c) the third column indicates its mode of trial, that is to say whether the offence is punishable on conviction on indictment, or on summary conviction, or either in the one way or the other;

(d) the fourth column shows the maximum punishment by way of fine or imprisonment which may be imposed on a person convicted of the offence in the mode of trial specified in relation to it in the third column (that is to say, on indictment or summarily), a reference to a period of years or months being to a maximum term of imprisonment of that duration; and

(e) the fifth column shows (in relation to an offence for which there is an entry in that column) that a person convicted of the offence after continued contravention is liable to a daily default fine; that is to say, he is liable on a second or subsequent conviction of the offence to the fine specified in that column for each day on which the contravention is continued (instead of the penalty specified for the offence in the fourth column of that Schedule).

(3) Section 431 (summary proceedings), as it applies to Scotland, has effect in relation to offences under the Rules as to offences under the Act.

Forms for use in insolvency proceedings

7.30. The forms contained in Schedule 5, with such variations as circumstances require, are the forms to be used for the purposes of the provisions of the Act or the Rules which are referred to in those forms.

Fees, expenses, etc.

7.31. All fees, costs, charges and other expenses incurred in the course of insolvency proceedings are to be regarded as expenses of those proceedings.

Power of court to cure defects in procedure

7.32.—(1) Section 63 of the Bankruptcy Act (power of court to cure defects in procedure) shall apply in relation to any insolvency proceedings as it applies in relation to sequestration, subject to the modifications specified in paragraph (2) and to any other necessary modifications.

(2) For any reference in the said section 63 to any expression in column 1 below, there shall be substituted a reference to the expression in column 2 opposite thereto:—

Column 1	Column 2
This Act or any regulations made under it	The Act or the Rules
Permanent trustee	Responsible insolvency practitioner
Sequestration process	Insolvency proceedings
Debtor	Company
Sheriff	The court
Person who would be eligible to be elected under section 24 of this Act	Person who would be eligible to act as a responsible insolvency practitioner

Sederunt book

7.33.—(1) The responsible insolvency practitioner shall maintain a sederunt book during his term of office for the purpose of providing an accurate record of the administration of each insolvency proceedings.

(2) Without prejudice to the generality of the above paragraph, there shall be inserted in the sederunt book a copy of anything required to be recorded in it by any provision of the Act or of the Rules.

(3) The responsible insolvency practitioner shall make the sederunt book available for inspection at all reasonable hours by any interested person.

(4) Any entry in the sederunt book shall be sufficient evidence of the facts stated therein, except where it is founded on by the responsible insolvency practitioner in his own interest.

[38] (5) Without prejudice to paragraph (3), the responsible insolvency practitioner shall retain, or shall make arrangements for retention of, the sederunt book for a period of ten years from the relevant date.

[38] (6) Where the sederunt book is maintained in non-documentary form it shall be capable of reproduction in legible form.

[38] (7) In this Rule "the relevant date" has the following meanings:—

(*a*) in the case of a company voluntary arrangement under Part I of the Act, the date of final completion of the voluntary arrangement;

(*b*) in the case of an administration order under Part II of the Act, the date on which the administration order is discharged;

(*c*) in the case of a receivership under Part III of the Act, the date on which the receiver resigns and the receivership terminates without a further receiver being appointed; and

(*d*) in the case of a winding-up, the date of dissolution of the company.

[39] *Disposal of company's books, papers and other records*

7.34.—(1) Where a company has been the subject of insolvency

---

[38] Inserted by S.I. 1987 No. 1921.
[39] Inserted by S.I. 1987 No. 1921.

proceedings ("the original proceedings") which have terminated and other insolvency proceedings ("the subsequent proceedings") have commenced in relation to that company, the responsible insolvency practitioner appointed in relation to the original proceedings, shall, before the expiry of the later of—

(a) the period of 30 days following a request to him to do so by the responsible insolvency practitioner appointed in relation to the subsequent proceedings, or

(b) the period of six months after the relevant date (within the meaning of Rule 7.33),

deliver to the responsible insolvency practitioner appointed in relation to the subsequent proceedings the books, papers and other records of the company.

(2) In the case of insolvency proceedings, other than winding up, where—

(a) the original proceedings have terminated, and

(b) no subsequent proceedings have commenced within the period of six months after the relevant date in relation to the original proceedings,

the responsible insolvency practitioner appointed in relation to the original proceedings may dispose of the books, papers and records of the company after the expiry of the period of six months referred to in sub-paragraph (b), but only in accordance with directions given by—

(i) the creditors' committee (if any) appointed in the original proceedings,

(ii) the members of the company by extraordinary resolution, or

(iii) the court.

(3) Where a company is being wound up the liquidator shall dispose of the books, papers and records of the company either in accordance with—

(a) in the case of a winding up by the court, directions of the liquidation committee, or, if there is no such committee, directions of the court;

(b) in the case of a members' voluntary winding up, directions of the members by extraordinary resolution; and

(c) in the case of a creditors' voluntary winding up, directions of the liquidation committee, or, if there is no such committee, of the creditors given at or before the final meeting under section 106,

or, if, by the date which is 12 months after the dissolution of the company, no such directions have been given, he may do so after that date in such a way as he deems appropriate.

SCHEDULE 1 **Rule 5**

MODIFICATIONS OF PART 4 IN RELATION TO CREDITORS' VOLUNTARY
WINDING UP

1. The following paragraphs describe the modifications to be made to the provisions of Part 4 in their application by Rule 5 to a creditors' voluntary winding up of a company.

General
2. Any reference, in any provision in Part 4, which is applied to a creditors' voluntary winding up, to any other Rule is a reference to that Rule as so applied.

Chapter 1 (Provisional liquidator)
3. This Chapter shall not apply.

Chapter 2 (Statement of affairs)

Rules 4.7 and 4.8

4. For these Rules, there shall be substituted the following:—

"**4.7.**—(1) This Rule applies with respect to the statement of affairs made out by the liquidator under section 95(3) (or as the case may be) by the directors under section 99(1).
(2) The statement of affairs shall be in the form required by Rule 7.30 and Schedule 5.
(3) Where the statement of affairs is made out by the directors under section 99(1), it shall be sent by them to the liquidator, when appointed.
[40] (3A) Where a liquidator is nominated by the company at a general meeting held on a day prior to that on which the creditors' meeting summoned under section 98 is held, the directors shall forthwith after his nomination or the making of the statement of affairs, whichever is the later, deliver to him a copy of the statement of affairs.
(4) The liquidator shall insert a copy of the statement of affairs made out under this Rule in the sederunt book.".
[40] (5) The statement of affairs under section 99(1) shall be made up to the nearest practicable date before the date of the meeting of creditors under section 98 or to a date not more than 14 days before that on which the resolution for voluntary winding up is passed by the company, whichever is the later.
[40] (6) At any meeting held under section 98 where the statement of affairs laid before the meeting does not state the company's affairs as at the date of the meeting, the directors of the company shall cause to be made to the meeting, either by the director presiding at the meeting or by another person with knowledge of the relevant matters, a report (written or oral) on any material transactions relating to the company occurring between the date of the making of the statement of affairs and that of the meeting and any such report shall be recorded in the report of the meeting kept under Rule 7.13.

Rule 4.9

5. For this Rule, there shall be substituted—

"Expenses of statement of affairs
4.9.—(1) Payment may be made as an expense of the liquidation, either before or after the commencement of the winding up, of any reasonable and necessary expenses of preparing the statement of affairs under section 99.
(2) Where such a payment is made before the commencement of the winding up, the director presiding at the creditors' meeting held under section 98 shall inform the meeting of the amount of the payment and the identity of the person to whom it was made.

[40] Inserted by S.I. 1987 No. 1921.

(3) The liquidator appointed under section 100 may make such a payment (subject to the next paragraph); but if there is a liquidation committee, he must give the committee at least seven days' notice of his intention to make it.

(4) Such a payment shall not be made by the liquidator to himself, or to any associate of his, otherwise than with the approval of the liquidation committee, the creditors, or the court.

(5) This Rule is without prejudice to the powers of the court under Rule 4.67(2) (voluntary winding up succeeded by winding up by the court).".

Chapter 3 (Information)

Rule 4.10

6. For this Rule, there shall be substituted the following:—

"Information to creditors and contributories
   4.10. The liquidator shall, within 28 days of a meeting held under section 95 or 98, send to creditors and contributories of the company—
   (*a*) a copy or summary of the statement of affairs, and
   (*b*) a report of the proceedings at the meeting.".

Chapter 4 (Meetings of creditors and contributories)

Rule 4.12

7. This Rule shall not apply.

Rule 4.14

8. After this Rule, there shall be inserted the following:—

"Expenses of meeting under section 98
   4.14A.—(1) Payment may be made out of the company's assets as an expense of the liquidation, either before or after the commencement of the winding up, of any reasonable and necessary expenses incurred in connection with the summoning, advertisement and holding of a creditors' meeting under section 98.
   (2) Where any such payments are made before the commencement of the winding up, the director presiding at the creditors' meeting shall inform the meeting of their amount and the identity of the persons to whom they were made.
   (3) The liquidator appointed under section 100 may make such a payment (subject to the next paragraph); but if there is a liquidation committee, he must give the committee at least seven days' notice of his intention to make the payment.
   (4) Such a payment shall not be made by the liquidator to himself, or to any associate of his, otherwise than with the approval of the liquidation committee, the creditors, or the court.
   (5) This Rule is without prejudice to the powers of the court under Rule 4.67(2) (voluntary winding up succeeded by winding up by the court).".

Rule 4.15

9. (1) In paragraph (5), for the reference to section 129, there shall be substituted a reference to section 86.
   [41] (2) In paragraph (6) these shall be inserted at the end of the following:—
   "and to the director who presides over any meeting of creditors as provided by section 99(1)".

Rule 4.16

10. In paragraph (2), for the reference to section 129, there shall be substituted a reference to section 86.

---

[41] Inserted by S.I. 1987 No. 1921.

Chapter 6 (The liquidator)

Rule 4.18

    11.—(1) For paragraph (1), there shall be substituted the following:—

    "(1) This Rule applies where the liquidator is appointed by the court under section 100(3) or 108.".

    (2) Paragraphs 4(*a*) and 5 shall be deleted.

Rule 4.19

    12.—(1) For paragraphs (1) to (3) there shall be substituted the following:—

    "(1) This Rule applies where a person is nominated for appointment as liquidator under section 100(1) either by a meeting of the creditors or by a meeting of the company.

    [42] (2) Subject as follows, the chairman of the meeting shall certify the appointment, but not unless and until the person to be appointed has provided him with a written statement to the effect that he is an insolvency practitioner, duly qualified under the Act to be the liquidator and that he consents so to act. The liquidator's appointment takes effect on the passing of the resolution for his appointment.

    (3) The chairman shall forthwith send the certificate to the liquidator, who shall keep it in the sederunt book.".

    (2) Paragraphs (4)(*a*) and (5) shall not apply.

    (3) In paragraph (6), for the reference to paragraphs (4) and (5), there shall be substituted a reference to paragraphs (3) and (4).

    [43] (4) After paragraph 6 there shall be inserted the following paragraph:—

    "(7) Where a vacancy in the office of liquidator occurs in the manner mentioned in section 104, a meeting of creditors to fill the vacancy may be convened by any creditor or, if there were more liquidators than one, by any continuing liquidator".

Rule 4.23

    13.—(1) In paragraph (1), for the references to section 172(2) and (3), there shall be substituted a reference to section 171(2) and (3).

    (2) In paragraph (2), for the references to section 172(2) and 174(4)(*a*) or (*b*), there shall be substituted a reference to section 171(2) and 173(2)(*a*) or (*b*).

Rule 4.24

    14. In this Rule the references to the court shall be deleted.

Rule 4.25

    15. In paragraph (1), for the reference to section 174(4)(*a*), there shall be substituted a reference to section 173(2)(*a*), and the reference to the court shall be deleted.

Rule 4.28

    16.—(1) In paragraph (1), for the reference to section 172(6), there shall be substituted a reference to section 171(5).

    (2) In paragraph (2), for the reference to section 174(4)(*c*), there shall be substituted a reference to section 173(2)(*c*).

Rule 4.29

    17. In this Rule for paragraph (3) there shall be substituted the following:—

---

[42] As amended by S.I. 1987 No. 1921.
[43] Inserted by S.I. 1987 No. 1921.

"(3) The liquidator, whose resignation is accepted, shall forthwith after the meeting give notice of his resignation to the registrar of companies as required by section 171(5).".

Rule 4.31

18. For this Rule, substitute the following:—

"Final Meeting
4.31.—(1) The liquidator shall give at least 28 days' notice of the final meeting of creditors to be held under section 106. The notice shall be sent to all creditors whose claims in the liquidation have been accepted.

(2) At the final meeting, the creditors may question the liquidator with respect to any matter contained in the account required under that section and may resolve against the liquidator having his release.

(3) The liquidator shall, within seven days of the meeting, give notice to the registrar of companies under section 171(6) that the final meeting has been held. The notice shall state whether or not he has been released.

[44] (4) If the creditors at the final meeting have not resolved against the liquidator having his release, he is released in terms of section 173(2)(*e*)(ii) when he vacates office under section 171(6). If they have so resolved, he must obtain his release from the Accountant of Court and Rule 4.25(2) and (3) shall apply accordingly subject to the modifications that in Rule 4.25(3) sub-paragraph (*a*) shall apply with the word "new" replaced by the word "former" and sub-paragraph (*b*) shall not apply."

Rule 4.36

19. For the reference to the court there shall be substituted a reference to the liquidation committee (if any) or a member of that committee.

Rule 4.37

20.—(1) In paragraph (2), the reference to the court shall be omitted.
(2) At the end of this Rule, there shall be inserted the following:—

"Vacation of office on making of winding up order
4.37A. Where the liquidator vacates office in consequence of the court making a winding up order against the company, Rule 4.25(2) and (3) apply as regards the liquidator obtaining his release, as if he had been removed by the court.".

Chapter 7 (The liquidation committee)

Rule 4.40

21. This Rule shall not apply.

Rule 4.41

22. For paragraph (1) there shall be substituted the following:—

"(1) The committee must have at least three members before it can be established.".

Rule 4.43

23. This Rule shall not apply.

Rule 4.47

24. For this Rule, there shall be substituted the following:—

[44] As amended by S.I. 1987 No. 1921.

"Quorum

4.47. A meeting of the committee is duly constituted if due notice of it has been given to all the members and at least two members are present or represented.".

Rule 4.53

25. After paragraph (4) there shall be inserted the following:—

"(4A) Where the contributories make an appointment under paragraph (4), the creditor members of the committee may, if they think fit, resolve that the person appointed ought not to be a member of the committee; and—
(a) that person is not then, unless the court otherwise directs, qualified to act as a member of the committee, and
(b) on any application to the court for a direction under this paragraph the court may, if it thinks fit, appoint another person (being a contributory) to fill the vacancy on the committee.".

Rule 4.54

26. Paragraphs (2) and (3) shall not apply.

Rule 4.55

27. In paragraphs (3) and (4), the word "creditor" shall be omitted.

Chapter 8 (The liquidation committee where winding up follows immediately on administration)
28. This Chapter shall not apply.

Chapter 9 (Distribution of company's assets by liquidator)

Rule 4.66

29.—(1) At the beginning of paragraph (1), insert the following:—

"Subject to the provision of section 107,".

(2) In paragraph (1)(*b*), for the reference to section 129, there shall be substituted a reference to section 86.

Chapter 10 (Special manager)

Rule 4.70

30. For paragraph (5), there shall be substituted the following:—

"(5) The cost of finding caution shall be paid in the first instance by the special manager; but he is entitled to be reimbursed out of the assets as an expense of the liquidation.".

Rule 4.71

31. Paragraph (1) shall not apply.

Chapter 11 (Public examination of company officers and others)
32. This Chapter shall not apply.

Chapter 12 (Miscellaneous)

Rule 4.77

33. This Rule shall not apply.

SCHEDULE 2 **Rule 6**

Application of Part 4 in Relation to Members' Voluntary Winding Up

1. The following paragraphs describe the provisions of Part 4 which, subject to the modifications set out in those paragraphs and any other necessary modifications, apply to a members' voluntary winding up.

General

2. Any reference in any provision of Part 4, which is applied to a members' voluntary winding up, to any other Rule is a reference to that Rule as so applied.

Chapter 3 (Information)

Rule 4.11

[45] **3.** This Rule shall apply subject to the modifications that for the words "accounting period" where they occur, there shall be substituted the words "period of twenty six weeks".

Chapter 6 (The liquidator)

Rule 4.18

4.—(1) This Rule shall apply subject to the following modifications.
(2) For paragraph (1), there shall be substituted the following:—

"(1) This Rule applies where the liquidator is appointed by the court under section 108.".

(3) Paragraphs 4 and 5 shall be deleted.

Rule 4.19

5.—(1) This Rule shall apply subject to the following modifications.
[46] (2) For paragraphs (1) to (3) there shall be substituted the following:—

"(1) This Rule applies where the liquidator is appointed by a meeting of the company.
(2) Subject as follows, the chairman of the meeting shall certify the appointment, but not unless and until the person to be appointed has provided him with a written statement to the effect that he is an insolvency practitioner, duly qualified under the Act to be the liquidator and that he consents so to act. The liquidator's appointment takes effect on the passing of the resolution for his appointment.
(3) The chairman shall forthwith send the certificate to the liquidator, who shall keep it in the sederunt book.".

(3) Paragraphs 4(*a*), (5) and (6) shall be deleted.

Rules 4.20 to 4.22

6. These Rules shall apply.

Rule 4.26

7. This Rule shall apply except that in paragraph (1) for the reference to "creditors" there shall be substituted the words "the company".

Rule 4.27

8. This Rule shall apply.

Rule 4.28

9.—(1) This Rule shall apply subject to the following modifications.

---

[45] As amended by S.I. 1987 No. 1921.
[46] As amended by S.I. 1987 No. 1921.

(2) In paragraph (1)—

(*a*) for the reference to section 172(6), there shall be substituted a reference to section 171(5), and

(*b*) for the reference to a meeting of creditors, there shall be substituted a reference to a meeting of the company.

(3) In paragraph (2)—

(*a*) for reference to section 174(4)(*c*) there shall be substituted a reference to section 173(2)(*c*), and

(*b*) for the reference to Rule 4.29(4), there shall be substituted a reference to Rule 4.28A.

(4) After paragraph (4) there shall be inserted the following paragraphs:—

"(5) The notice of the liquidator's resignation required by section 171(5) shall be given by him to the registrar of companies forthwith after the meeting.
(6) Where a new liquidator is appointed in place of the one who has resigned, the former shall, in giving notice of his appointment, state that his predecessor has resigned and whether he has been released.
[47] (7) If there is no quorum present at the meeting summoned to receive the liquidator's resignation the meeting is deemed to have been held.".

(5) After this Rule, there shall be inserted the following Rule:—

"Release of resigning or removed liquidator
    4.28A.—(1) Where the liquidator resigns, he has his release from the date on which he gives notice of his resignation to the registrar of companies.
    (2) Where the liquidator is removed by a meeting of the company, he shall forthwith give notice to the registrar of companies of his ceasing to act.
    (3) Where the liquidator is removed by the court, he must apply to the Accountant of Court for his release.
    (4) Where the Accountant of Court gives the release, he shall certify it accordingly, and send the certificate to the registrar of companies.
    (5) A copy of the certificate shall be sent by the Accountant of Court to the former liquidator, whose release is effective from the date of the certificate.".

Rule 4.36

10. This Rule shall apply, except that for any reference to the court, there shall be substituted a reference to the directors of the company or any one of them.

Rule 4.37

11.—(1) This Rule shall apply subject to the following modifications.
(2) In paragraph (2), the reference to the court shall be omitted.
(3) For paragraph (3), there shall be substituted the following:—

"(3) Rule 4.28A applies as regards the liquidator obtaining his release, as if he had been removed by the court.".

(4) At the end of this Rule, there shall be inserted the following:—

"Vacation of office on making of winding up order
    4.37A. Where the liquidator vacates office in consequence of the court making a winding up order against the company, Rule 4.28A applies as regards the liquidator obtaining his release, as if he had been removed by the court.".

Rule 4.38

12. This Rule shall apply.

Rule 4.39

13. This Rule shall apply.

[47] Inserted by S.I. 1987 No. 1921.

Chapter 10 (Special manager)

14.—(1) This Chapter shall apply subject to the following modifications.

(2) In Rule 4.70 for paragraph (5), there shall be substituted the following:—

"(5) The cost of finding caution shall be paid in the first instance by the special manager; but he is entitled to be reimbursed out of the assets as an expense of the liquidation.".

(3) In Rule 4.71, paragraph (1) shall not apply.

SCHEDULE 3   **Rule 7.4(6)**

DEPOSIT PROTECTION BOARD'S VOTING RIGHTS

1. This Schedule applies where Rule 7.4 does.

2. In relation to any meeting at which the Deposit Protection Board is under Rule 7.4 entitled to be represented, the Board may submit in the liquidation, instead of a claim, a written statement of voting rights ("the statement").

3. The statement shall contain details of:—

(a) the names of creditors of the company in respect of whom an obligation of the Board has arisen or may reasonably be expected to arise as a result of the liquidation or proposed liquidation;

(b) the amount of the obligation so arising; and

(c) the total amount of all such obligations specified in the statement.

4. The Board's statement shall, for the purpose of voting at a meeting (but for no other purpose), be treated in all respects as if it were a claim.

5. Any voting rights which a creditor might otherwise exercise at a meeting in respect of a claim against the company are reduced by a sum equal to the amount of that claim in relation to which the Board, by virtue of its having submitted a statement, is entitled to exercise voting rights at that meeting.

6. The Board may from time to time submit a further statement, and, if it does so, that statement supersedes any statement previously submitted.

SCHEDULE 4   **Rule 7.29**

PUNISHMENT OF OFFENCES UNDER THE RULES

Note: In the fourth and fifth columns of this Schedule, "the statutory maximum" means the prescribed sum under section 289B(6) of the Criminal Procedure (Scotland) Act 1975 (c.21).

Rule creating Daily default offence fine (where applicable)	*General nature*	*Mode of of offence*		*Punishment prosecution*
In Part 1, Rule 1.24	False representation or fraud for purpose of obtaining members' or creditors' to proposal for voluntary arrangement	1. On indictment 2. Summary	7 years or a fine, or both 6 months or the statutory maximum, or both	

Rule creating Daily default offence fine (where applicable)	General nature	Mode of of offence		Punishment prosecution
In Part 2, Rule 2.17(4)	Administrator failing to send notification as to progress of administration	Summary	One-fifth of the statutory maximum	One-fiftieth of the statutory maximum
In Part 3, Rule 3.9(5)	Receiver failing to send notification as to progress of receivership	Summary	One-fifth of the statutory maximum	One-fiftieth of the statutory maximum

SCHEDULE 5   **Rule 7.30**

INDEX OF FORMS

.   .   .   .   .   .

Part 4:   *Winding up*
Form 4.1 (Scot)   Statutory demand.

.   .   .   .   .   .

Form 4.7 (Scot)   Statement of claim by creditor.

.   .   .   .   .   .

Form 4.25 (Scot)   Declaration of solvency.

.   .   .   .   .   .

Form 4.29 (Scot)   Proxy.

. . . . . .

The Insolvency Act 1986   **Form 4.1 (Scot)**

The following form was substituted by S.I. 1987 No. 1921:

Statutory Demand for Payment of Debt

Pursuant to Section 123(1)(a) or Section 222(1)(a) of the Insolvency Act 1986

Warning

● This is an important document. This demand must be dealt with within 21 days of its service upon the company or a winding up order could be made in respect of the company

● Please read the demand and the notes carefully

● There are additional notes on the two following pages

Demand

To _____

Address _____

_____

This demand is served by the creditor:

Name _____

Address _____

_____

The creditor claims that the company owes

the sum of | £ _____ |

Full particulars of the debt/s claimed to be owed by the company are set out on page 2 of this Demand.

The creditor demands that the company pays the above sum or secures or compounds for it to the creditor's satisfaction

Signature _____

Name _____
　　　　　(BLOCK LETTERS)

Position with or relationship to creditor _____
_____ duly authorised

Address _____

_____

Tel. No. _____

Ref. _____

N.B. The person making this demand must complete the whole of this page and Parts A and B on page 3.

Notes for Creditors

● This demand can only be used by the creditor to demand a sum exceeding £750.

● If the creditor is entitled to the debt by way of assignation, details of the original creditor and any intermediate assignees should be given in Part B on page 3.

● If the amount of debt includes interest, details should be given including the grounds upon which interest is charged. The amount of interest must be shown separately.

● Any other charge payable from time to time may be claimed. The amount or rate of the charge must be identified and the grounds on which it is claimed must be stated.

● In either case the amount claimed must be limited to that which has accrued and is due at the date of the demand.

● If the signatory of the demand is a solicitor or other agent of the creditor the name of his/her firm should be given.

Particulars of Debts. (These particulars must include (a) the date or dates when the debt/s was/were incurred, (b) the grounds of claim and (c) the amount due as at the date of this demand.)

Notes for Creditor

Please make sure that you have read the notes on page 1 before completing this page.

Note:

If the space is insufficient continue on reverse of page 3 and clearly indicate on this page that you are doing so.

Part A

The person or persons to whom any communication regarding this demand should be addressed is/are

Name _____
(BLOCK LETTERS)

Address _____

_____

Tel. No. _____

Reference _____

Part B

For completion if the creditor is entitled to the debt by way of assignation

	Name	Date(s) of Assignation
Original creditor		
Assignees		

How to comply with a statutory demand

If the company wishes to avoid a winding-up petition being presented it must pay the sum shown on page 1 and of which particulars are set out on page 2 of this Demand within the period of 21 days of its service upon the company.

Alternatively, the company may attempt to reach a settlement with the creditor. To do this the company should:

inform the person (or one of them, if more than one) named in Part A above immediately that it is willing and able to offer security for the debt to the creditor's satisfaction; or

inform the person (or one of them) named in Part A immediately that it is willing and able to compound for the debt to the creditor's satisfaction.

If the company disputes the demand in whole or in part it should:

contact the person (or one of them) named in Part A immediately.

REMEMBER! The company has only 21 days from the date of service on it of this document before the creditor may present a winding-up petition

· · · · · ·

Rule 4.15   **The Insolvency Act 1986**   Form 4.7 (Scot)

The following form was substituted by S.I. 1987 No. 1921:

Statement of Claim by Creditor

Pursuant to Rule 4.15(2)(a) of the Insolvency (Scotland) Rules 1986

WARNING

It is a criminal offence

● for a creditor to produce a statement of claim, account, voucher or other evidence which is false, unless he shows that he neither knew nor had reason to believe that it was false; or

● for a director or other officer of the company who knows or becomes aware that it is false to fail to report it to the liquidator within one month of acquiring such knowledge.

On conviction either the creditor or such director or other officer of the company may be liable to a fine and/or imprisonment.

Notes

(a) Insert name of company

(a) _____

(b) Insert name and address of creditor

(b) _____

(c) Insert name and address, if applicable, of authorised person acting on behalf of the creditor

(c) _____

(d) Insert total amount as at the due date (see note (e) below) claimed in respect of all the debts, the particulars of which are set out overleaf.

I submit a claim of *(d)* £_____ in the liquidation of the above company and certify that the particulars of the debt or debts making up that claim, which are set out overleaf, are true, complete and accurate, to the best of my knowledge and belief.

(e) The due date in the case of a company

(i) which is subject to a voluntary arrangement is the date of a creditors' meeting in the voluntary arrangement;
(ii) which is in administration is the date of the administration order;
(iii) which is in receivership is the date of appointment of the receiver; and
(iv) which is in liquidation is the commencement of the winding up.

The date of commencement of the winding up is

(i) in a voluntary winding up the date of the resolution by the company for winding up (section 86 or 98); and
(ii) in a winding up by the court, the date of the presentation of the petition for winding up unless it is preceded by a resolution for voluntary winding up (section 129).

Signed_____
Creditor/person acting on behalf of creditor

Date _____

Rule 4.15

PARTICULARS OF EACH DEBT

Form 4.7 (Scot)
(contd)

Notes

*A separate set of particulars should be
made out in respect of each debt.*

1. *Describe briefly the debt, giving details of
   its nature, the date when it was incurred
   and when payment became due.*

   *Attach any documentary evidence of the
   debt, if available.*

1. **Particulars of debt**

2. *Insert total amount of the debt, showing
   separately the amount of principal and
   any interest which is due on the debt as
   at the due date (see note (e)). Interest
   may only be claimed if the creditor is
   entitled to it. Show separately the V.A.T.
   on the debt and indicate whether the
   V.A.T. is being claimed back from H.M.
   Customs and Excise.*

2. **Amount of debt**

3. *Insert the nature and amount of any
   preference under Schedule 6 to the Act
   claimed in respect of the debt.*

3. **Preference claimed for debt**

4. *Specify and give details of the nature of
   any security held in respect of the debt
   including—*

   *(a) the subjects covered and the date
   when it was given;*

   (b) the value of the security.

   *Security is defined in section 248(b) of
   the Insolvency Act 1986 as meaning "any
   security (whether heritable or moveable),
   any floating charge and any right of lien
   or preference and any right of retention
   (other than a right of compensation or
   set off)". For claims in administration
   procedure security also includes a
   retention of title agreement, hire
   purchase agreement, agreement for the
   hire of goods for more than three
   months and a conditional sale agreement
   (see Rules 2.11 and 2.12).*

4. **Security for debt**

*In liquidation only the creditor should state
whether he is surrendering or undertakes to
surrender his security; the liquidator may at
any time after 12 weeks from the date of
commencement of the winding up (note (e))
require a creditor to discharge a security or
to convey or assign it to him on payment of
the value specified by the creditor.*

5. *In calculating the total amount of his
   claim in a liquidation, a creditor shall
   deduct the value of any security as
   estimated by him unless he surrenders it
   (see note 4). This may apply in
   administration (see Rule 2.11).*

5. **Total amount of the debt**

· · · · · ·

Section 89(3)

The Insolvency Act 1986

Declaration of Solvency

Form 4.25 (Scot)

S89(3)

Pursuant to section 89(3) of the Insolvency Act 1986

To the Registrar of Companies

For official use

Company number

Name of Company

(a) Insert name of company

(a)

(b) Insert full name(s) and address(es)

I/We (b)

attach a declaration of solvency embodying a statement of assets and liabilities.

Signed _____ Date _____

Presentor's name, address and reference (if any)

For Official use

Liquidation Section | Post Room

Section 89(3)   **The Insolvency Act 1986**   Form 4.25 (Scot)
(contd.)

Declaration of Solvency
Embodying a Statement of
Assets and Liabilities

Company Number _____

Insert name of the
company

Name of Company_____
_____

Presented by _____

Declaration of Solvency

(a) Insert name(s)
and address(es)

We (a) _____
_____
_____
_____

(b) Delete as
applicable

being (b) [all the]/[the majority of the] directors of (c) _____
_____

(c) Insert name of
company

do solemnly and sincerely declare that we have made a full
enquiry into the affairs of this company, and that, having done so,
we have formed the opinion that this company will be able to pay

(d) Insert a period of
months not
exceeding 12

its debts in full together with interest at the official rate within a
period of (d) _____ months, from the commencement of the
winding-up.

We append a statement of the company's assets and liabilities as

(e) Insert date

at (e) _____ being the latest practicable date before the
making of this declaration.

We make this solemn declaration, conscientiously believing it to
be true, and by virtue of the provisions of the Statutory
Declarations Act 1835.

Declared at _____ the _____ day

of _____

before me,

_____
_____
_____
_____

_____
Notary Public, Justice of the Peace or
Commissioner for Oaths

Signature(s) of person(s) making declaration

Section 89(3)

Form 4.25 (Scot)
(contd.)

Statement as at _____ showing assets at estimated realisable values
and liabilities expected to rank:

ASSETS AND LIABILITIES	Estimated to realise or to rank for payment to nearest £
ASSETS	£
Balance at Bank	
Cash in Hand	
Marketable Securities	
Bills Receivable	
Trade Debtors	
Loans and Advances	
Unpaid Calls	
Stock in Trade	
Work in Progress	
Heritable Property	
Leasehold Property	
Plant and Machinery	
Furniture, Fittings, Utensils, etc	
Patents, Trade Marks, etc	
Investments other than Marketable Securities	
Other Property, viz	
Estimated Realisable Value of Assets ... ... £	
LIABILITIES	£
Secured on specific assets, viz	
Secured by a Floating Charge(s)	
Estimated Expenses of Liquidation and other expenses including interest accruing until payment of debts in full	
Unsecured Creditors (amounts estimated to rank for payment)	
£ £	
Trade Accounts	
Bills payable	
Accrued Expenses	
Other Liabilities	
Contingent Liabilities	
Estimated Surplus after paying Debts in full £	

Remarks:

. . . . . .

Rule 7.15   **The Insolvency Act 1986**   Form 4.29 (Scot)

The following form was substituted by S.I. 1987 No. 1921:

Proxy

Pursuant to Rules 7.14 and 7.15 of the Insolvency (Scotland) Rules 1986

(a) Insert name of the company

(a) _____

(b) Insert nature of Insolvency proceedings

(b) _____

Name of Creditor/Member _____

Address _____

_____

_____ (hereinafter called "the principal").

(c) Insert the name and address of the proxy-holder and of any alternatives. A proxy-holder must be an individual aged over 18.

Name of proxy-holder (c) 1. _____

Address _____

_____

whom failing 2. _____

_____

_____

whom failing 3. _____

_____

_____

I appoint the above person to be the principal's proxy-holder at

*Delete as appropriate

*[all meetings in the above Insolvency proceedings relating to the above company]

*[the meeting of *creditors/members of the above Company to be held on _____ or at any adjournment of that meeting].

Voting Instructions

The proxy-holder is authorised to vote or abstain from voting in the name, and on behalf, of the principal in respect of any matter*/s, including resolution*/s, arising for determination at said meeting*/s and any adjournment*/s thereof and to propose any resolution*/s in the name of the principal, either

    (i) in accordance with instructions given below or,

    (ii) if no instructions are given, in accordance with his/her own discretion.

<table>
<tr>
<td>(d) Complete only if you wish to instruct the proxy-holder to vote for a specific person as liquidator</td>
<td>(d) 1. To *propose/support a resolution for the appointment of _____

of_____

whom failing _____

as liquidator of the company.</td>
</tr>
<tr>
<td>(e) Delete if the proxy-holder is only to vote as directed in (1).</td>
<td>(e) [in the event of a person named in paragraph (1) withdrawing or being eliminated from any vote the proxy-holder may vote or abstain in any further ballot at *his/her discretion.]</td>
</tr>
<tr>
<td>(f) Set forth any voting instructions for the proxy-holder. If more room is required attach a separate sheet</td>
<td>2. (f) _____</td>
</tr>
</table>

Signed _____ Date _____

Namè in BLOCK LETTERS _____

Position of signatory in relation to the *creditor/or member or other authority for signing.

_____

Notes for the Principal and Proxy-holder

1. The chairman of the meeting who may be nominated as proxy-holder, will be the insolvency practitioner who is presently *liquidator/receiver/administrator/ nominee under the voluntary arrangement or a director of the company.

2. All proxies must be in this form or a form substantially to the same effect with such variations as circumstances may require. (Rules 7.15(3) and 7.30).

3. To be valid the proxy must be lodged at or before the meeting at which it is to be used. (Rule 7.16(2)).

4. Where the chairman is nominated as proxy-holder he cannot decline the nomination. (Rule 7.14(4)).

5. The proxy-holder may vote for or against a resolution for the appointment of a named person to be liquidator jointly with another person, unless the proxy states otherwise. (Rule 7.16(4)).

6. The proxy-holder may propose any resolution in favour of which he could vote by virtue of this proxy. (Rule 7.16(5)).

7. The proxy-holder may vote at his discretion on any resolutions not dealt with in the proxy, unless the proxy states otherwise. (Rule 7.16(6)).

8. The proxy-holder may not vote in favour of any resolution which places him, or any associate of his, in a position to receive remuneration out of the insolvent estate unless the proxy specifically directs him so to vote. (Rule 7.19(1)).

9. Unless the proxy contains a statement to the contrary the proxy-holder has a mandate to act as representative of the principal on the creditors' or liquidation committee. (Rule 4.48).

• • • • • •

THE INSOLVENT COMPANIES (REPORTS ON CONDUCT OF DIRECTORS) (NO. 2) (SCOTLAND) RULES 1986

(1986 No. 1916 (S.140))

Made – – –	*10th November 1986*
Laid before Parliament	*26th November 1986*
Coming into Operation	*29th December 1986*

The Secretary of State, in exercise of the powers conferred on him by section 106 of the Insolvency Act 1985 and section 411 of the Insolvency Act 1986 as read with section 21(2) of the Company Directors' Disqualification Act 1986, and of all other powers enabling him in that behalf, hereby makes the following Rules:—

Citation, commencement and interpretation

1.—(1) These Rules may be cited as the Insolvent Companies (Reports on Conduct of Directors) (No. 2) (Scotland) Rules 1986.

(2) These Rules shall come into operation on 29th December 1986.

(3) In these Rules—

"the Act" means the Company Directors Disqualification Act 1986,

"commencement date" means the date on which these Rules come into operation, and

"a company" means a company which the courts in Scotland have jurisdiction to wind up.

Reports required under section 7(3) of the Act

2.—(1) This Rule applies to any report made to the Secretary of State under section 7(3) of the Act by—

(a) the liquidator of a company which is being wound up by an order of the court made on or after the commencement date;

(b) the liquidator of a company which passes a resolution for voluntary winding up on or after that date;

(c) a receiver of a company, appointed under section 51 of the Insolvency Act 1986 (power to appoint receivers under the law of Scotland) on or after that date, who is an administrative receiver; or

(d) an administrator of a company in relation to which an administration order is made on or after that date.

(2) Such a report shall be made in the Form D1 (Scot), D2 (Scot) or D5 (Scot) set out in the Schedule hereto, as the case may be, and in the manner and to the extent required by the applicable form.

Return of office-holder

3.—(1) This Rule applies where it appears to a liquidator of a

579

company as mentioned in Rule 2(1)(*a*) or (*b*), to an administrative receiver as mentioned in Rule 2(1)(*c*) or to an administrator as mentioned in Rule 2(1)(*d*) (each of whom is referred to hereinafter as "the officer-holder") that the company has at any time become insolvent within the meaning of section 6(2) of the Act.

(2) Subject as follows, there may be furnished to the Secretary of State by an office-holder, at any time during the period of six months from the relevant date, a return with respect to every person who—

(*a*) was, on the relevant date, a director or shadow director of the company, or

(*b*) had been a director or shadow director of the company at any time in the three years immediately preceding that date.

(3) The return shall be made in the Form D3 (Scot) D4 (Scot) or D6 (Scot) set out in the Schedule hereto, as the case may be, and in the manner and to the extent required by the applicable form.

(4) For the purposes of this Rule, "the relevant date" means—

(*a*) in the case of a company in liquidation (except in the case mentioned in paragraph (4)(*b*) below), the date on which the company goes into liquidation within the meaning of section 247(2) of the Insolvency Act 1986,

(*b*) in the case of a company in members' voluntary winding up, the date on which the liquidator forms the opinion that, at the time when the company went into liquidation, its assets were insufficient for the payment of its debts and other liabilities and the expenses of winding up,

(*c*) in the case of the administrative receiver, the date of his appointment,

(*d*) in the case of the administrator, the date of the administration order made in relation to the company,

and for purposes of sub-paragraph (*c*) above the only appointment of an administrative receiver to be taken into account in determining the relevant date shall be that appointment which is not that of a successor in office to an administrative receiver who has vacated office either by death or pursuant to section 62 of the Insolvency Act 1986.

(5) It shall be the duty of the responsible office-holder to furnish a return complying with the provisions of paragraphs (3) and (4) of this Rule to the Secretary of State not later than the expiry of the period of six months from the relevant date, where no return has been so furnished by a day one week before the expiry of that period; and for the purposes of this paragraph the responsible office-holder shall be the person in office in relation to the company on the day specified above or, where no person is in office on that day, the office-holder who vacated office nearest to that day.

(6) A return need not be provided under this Rule if the office-holder has, since the relevant date, made reports to the Secretary of State

under section 7(3) of the Act with respect to all the persons falling within paragraph (2) and (apart from this paragraph) required to be the subject of return.

(7) If a responsible office-holder without reasonable excuse fails to comply with the duty imposed by paragraph (5) of this Rule, he is liable on summary conviction to a fine not exceeding £400 and, for continued contravention, to a daily default fine not exceeding £40.

Enforcement of section 7(4)

4.—(1) This Rule applies where, under section 7(4) of the Act (power to call on liquidators, former liquidators and others to provide information), the Secretary of State requires a person—

(*a*) to furnish him with information with respect to a person's conduct as director or shadow director of a company, and

(*b*) to produce and permit inspection of relevant books, papers and other records.

(2) On the application of the Secretary of State, the court may make an order directing compliance within such period as may be specified.

(3) The court's order may provide that all expenses of and incidental to the application shall be borne by the person to whom the order is directed.

Revocation and transitional provisions

5.—(1) The Insolvent Companies (Reports on Conduct of Directors) (Scotland) Rules 1986 ("the former Rules") are hereby revoked.

(2) Notwithstanding paragraph (1), the provisions of Rules 2 and 3 of the former Rules shall continue to apply and have effect in relation to—

(*a*) any report to which the provisions of Rule 2 of those Rules applies, and

(*b*) any interim return required to be made by Rule 3 of those Rules.

SCHEDULE   **Rules 2(2) and 3(3)**

FORMS

Form	Title
D1 (Scot)	Companies in Liquidation: Report on Conduct of Directors under Section 7(3) of the Company Directors' Disqualification Act 1986.
D2 (Scot)	Report on Conduct of Directors by an Administrative Receiver under Section 7(3) of the Company Directors' Disqualification Act 1986.
D3 (Scot)	Companies in Liquidation: Return of Directors under Rule 3 of the Insolvent Companies (Reports on Conduct of Directors) (No. 2) (Scotland) Rules 1986.
D4 (Scot)	Return of Directors by an Administrative Receiver under Rule 3 of the Insolvent Companies (Reports on Conduct of Directors) (No. 2) (Scotland) Rules 1986.
D5 (Scot)	Report on Conduct of Directors by an Administrator

Form	*Title*
	under Section 7(3) of the Company Directors' Disqualification Act 1986.
D6 (Scot)	Return of Directors by an Administrator under Rule 3 of the Insolvent Companies (Reports on Conduct of Directors) (No. 2) (Scotland) Rules 1986.

THE RECEIVERS (SCOTLAND) REGULATIONS 1986

(S.I. 1986 No. 1917 (S.141))

Made – – –	*10th November 1986*
Coming into Operation	*29th December 1986*

The Secretary of State, in Exercise of the powers conferred upon him by sections 53(1) and (6), 54(3), 62(1) and (5), 65(1)(a), 66(1), 67(1), 67(2)(b), 70(1) and 71 of the Insolvency Act 1986 and all other powers enabling him in that behalf hereby makes the following regulations:—

Citation and commencement

1. These regulations may be cited as the Receivers (Scotland) Regulations 1986 and shall come into operation on 29th December 1986.

Interpretation

2. In these regulations, "the Act" means the Insolvency Act 1986.

Forms

3. The forms set out in the Schedule to these regulations, with such variations as circumstances require, are the forms prescribed for the purposes of the provisions of the Act which are referred to in those forms.

Instrument of appointment

4. The certified copy instrument of appointment of a receiver which is required to be submitted to the registrar of companies by or on behalf of the person making the appointment under section 53(1) of the Act shall be certified to be a correct copy by or on behalf of that person.

Joint receivers

5. Where two or more persons are appointed joint receivers by the holder of a floating charge under section 53 of the Act, subsection (6) of that section shall apply subject to the following modifications:—

(a) the appointment of any of the joint receivers shall be of no effect unless the appointment is accepted by all of them in accordance with paragraph (a) of that subsection and Rule 3.1 of the Insolvency (Scotland) Rules 1986; and

(b) their appointment as joint receivers shall be deemed to be made on the day on and at the time at which the instrument of appointment is received by the last of them, as evidenced by the written docquet required by paragraph (b) of that subsection.

Resignation

6. For the purposes of section 62(1) of the Act, a receiver, who wishes to resign his office, shall give at least seven days' notice of his resignation to—

(*a*) the holder of the floating charge by virtue of which he was appointed;

(*b*) the holder of any other floating charge and any receiver appointed by him;

(*c*) the members of any committee of creditors established under section 68 of the Act; and

(*d*) the company, or if it is then in liquidation, its liquidator,

and the notice shall specify the date on which the resignation takes effect.

Report to creditors

7. Where the receiver determines to publish a notice under paragraph (*b*) of section 67(2) of the Act, the notice shall be published in a newspaper circulating in the area where the company has its principal place of business or in such other newspaper as he thinks most appropriate for ensuring that it comes to the notice of the unsecured creditors of the company.

SCHEDULE   **Regulation 3**

FORMS

Form 1 (Scot)	Notice of appointment of a receiver by the holder of a floating charge.
Form 2 (Scot)	Notice of appointment of a receiver by the court.
Form 3 (Scot)	Notice of the receiver ceasing to act or of his removal.
Form 4 (Scot)	Notice of appointment of receiver.
Form 5 (Scot)	Statement of affairs.

INDEX